Longman Annotated English Poets

GENERAL EDITORS: F. W. BATESON AND JOHN BARNARD

THE POEMS OF

SHELLEY

EDITED BY

GEOFFREY
MATTHEWS

AND

KELVIN
EVEREST

– Volume I –
1804–1817

LONGMAN
London and New York

Longman Group UK Limited,
Longman House, Burnt Mill, Harlow,
Essex CM20 2JE, England
and Associated Companies throughout the world.

Published in the United States by Longman Inc., New York

First published 1989

British Library Cataloguing in Publication Data
Shelley, Percy Bysshe, *1792–1822*
 The poems of Shelley. —(Longman annotated
English poets).
 Vol. 1: 1809–1817
 I. Title II. Matthews, Geoffrey
 III. Everest, Kelvin
 821'.7

ISBN 0-582-48448-0

Library of Congress Cataloging-in-Publication Data
Shelley, Percy Bysshe, 1792–1822
 [Poems]
 The poems of Shelley / edited by Geoffrey Matthews and Kelvin
Everest.
  p. cm.—(Longman annotated English poets)
 Includes index.
 Contents: v. 1. 1809–1817.
 ISBN 0–582–48448–0 (v. 1)
 I. Matthews, Geoffrey, 1920– . II. Everest, Kelvin.
 III. Title. IV. Series.
 PR5402 1989   89–8056
 821'.7—dc20   CIP

Set in Linotron 202 Bembo Roman 10/10

Produced by Longman Singapore Publishers (Pte) Ltd.
Printed in Great Britain by Biddles Ltd, King's Lynn

Contents

POEMS

Note by the General Editor

Longman Annotated English Poets was launched in 1965 with the publication of Kenneth Allott's edition of *The Poems of Matthew Arnold*. F. W. Bateson wrote that the 'new series is the first designed to provide university students and readers, and the general reader with complete and fully annotated editions of the major English poets'. That remains the aim of the series, and Bateson's original vision of its policy remains essentially the same. Its 'concern is primarily with the *meaning* of the extant texts in their various contexts'.

Bateson formulated the rationale of the series as follows:

'Our ideal of comprehension, for the reader, combined with comprehensiveness, for the poet, has three logical consequences:

1. Since an essential clue to an author's intentions at any point is provided on the one hand, by what he has already written, and, on the other hand, by what he will write later, an editor will print the poems as far as possible in the order in which they were composed.

2. A poet writing in a living language, such as English, requires elucidation of a different kind from that suitable to the poetry of a dead language such as Sanskrit, Latin or Old English; with minor exceptions vocabulary and syntax can be taken for granted, but sources, allusions, implications and stylistic devices need to be spelled out.

3. Since the reader in any English-speaking country will tend to pronounce an English poet of the past (any rate to Chaucer) as if he were a contemporary, whatever impedes the reader's sympathetic response that is implicit in that fact—whether of spelling, punctuation or the use of initial capitals—must be regarded as undesirable. A modern pronunciation demands a modern presentation, except occasionally for rhymes (e.g. *bind–wind*) or obsolete archaisms (*eremite*, hermit).

Some exceptions have had to be admitted to the principles summarized above, but they have been few and unimportant.'

These broad principles still govern the series. Its primary purpose is to provide an annotated text giving the reader any necessary contextual information. However, flexibility in the detailed application has proved necessary in the light of experience and the needs of a particular case (and each poet is by definition, a particular case).

First, proper glossing of a poet's vocabulary has proved essential and not something which can be taken for granted. Second, modernization has presented difficulties, which have been resolved pragmatically, trying to reach a balance between sensitivity to the text in question and attention to the needs of a modern reader. Thus, to modernize Browning's text has a double redundancy: Victorian conventions are very close to modern conventions, and Browning had firm ideas on punctuation. Equally, to impose modern pointing on the ambiguities of Herbert or Marvell, or onto the rhetorical punctuation of Dryden, would create a misleading clarity. Third, in the very early days of the series Bateson hoped that editors would be able in many cases to annotate a *textus receptus*. That has not always been possible, and where no accepted text exists or where the text is controversial, editors have been obliged to go back to the originals and create their own text. The series has taken, and will continue to take, the opportunity of not only providing thorough annotations not available elsewhere, but also of making important scholarly textual contributions where necessary. A case in point is the edition of *The Poems of Tennyson* by Christopher Ricks, the Second Edition of which (1987) takes into account a full collation of the Trinity College Manuscripts, not previously available for an edition of this kind. Yet the series' primary purpose remains annotation and editions do not attempt a comprehensive recording of textual variants.

The requirements of a particular author take precedence over 'principle'. It would make little sense to print Herbert's *Temple* in the order of composition even if it could be established. Where Ricks rightly decided that Tennyson's reader needs to be given the circumstances of composition, the attitude to Tennyson and his circle, allusions, and important variants, a necessary consequence was the exclusion of twentieth-century critical responses. Milton, however, is a very different case. John Carey and Alastair Fowler, looking to the needs of their readers, undertook synopses of the main lines of the critical debate over Milton's poetry. Finally, chronological ordering will almost always have a greater or lesser degree of speculation or arbitrariness. The evidence is usually partial, and is confused further by the fact that poets do not always write one poem at a time and frequently revise at a later period than that of composition.

JOHN BARNARD
University of Leeds
December 1987

Introduction

This edition of Shelley's poetry is not based on any single previous edition. Each poem has been newly edited on the basis of close examination of the earliest printed authorities and, wherever relevant and practicable, of the manuscripts. This work has been made possible by the availability, since 1946, of virtually the whole of the extensive manuscript collection once kept at Boscombe Manor, where it had been assembled by Sir Percy Florence Shelley (only surviving offspring of the poet's marriage to Mary Wollstonecraft Godwin), and by his wife Jane, Lady Shelley, who was an enthusiastic admirer of Shelley's work. These fundamental materials, now accessible to scholarship in the Bodleian Library, have been richly supplemented by a number of other fine manuscript collections, in the Houghton Library (Harvard), the Huntington Library, and the Carl H. Pforzheimer Collection in particular, which are all now available. The basic records and documents have been further enriched by recent scholarly editions of the letters and journals of Mary Shelley, and by a wealth of meticulous research on Shelley's life and text which has developed in England and America since the war, especially over the past twenty years.

In accordance with the principles of the series in which this edition appears, the arrangement of the poetry is chronological. Each poem is preceded by a headnote giving full particulars of composition, publication, sources (including biographical context), influences (including Shelley's intellectual and literary development), and where appropriate, some account of past and present critical commentary. The text which follows is accompanied by full explanatory and textual annotation, including all substantive variants from authoritative witnesses and a selection of punctuational and other 'accidental' variants where these are significant.

The chronological arrangement inevitably involves uncertainty and approximation in many instances. Shelley often worked on several poems at the same time. He often left a poem unfinished and then returned to it after weeks or months or, in a few cases, even years. Many of his poems, particularly fragments and incomplete items of verse, are all but impossible to date exactly. Some poems were finished by Shelley and then subsequently extended; in these cases (most notably *Prometheus Unbound*) the poem is placed at the point of its first completion. Within these limitations every poem is assigned a definite or most plausible date and, where the circumstances require it, the headnote offers full discussion of the issues and evidence. The only previous complete edition of the poems with full annotation, C. D. Locock's edition published in 1911, is limited by its many omissions and by the very incomplete access Locock had to manuscript materials. No edition has before attempted a strict chronological arrangement, although several have presented the poetry in partly chronological order, for example A. H. Koszul's Everyman edition of 1907, and the two volumes, published in 1972 and 1975, of Neville Rogers's Oxford English Texts edition. Most editions, including the major nineteenth-century editions of Rossetti, Forman, and Woodberry, have employed an arrangement of poems deriving from Mary Shelley's four-volume *Poetical Works* of 1839. Major longer works are printed first, in a loosely chronological order, and are followed by shorter poems grouped by their year of composition, with fragments and variously unfinished items placed after completed poems. The juvenilia, including *Queen Mab*, are placed at the end of the edition together with Shelley's translations although *Queen Mab* is placed first by Rossetti and Woodberry, who also both collect into one grouping Shelley's verse fragments.

Some recent selections of Shelley's poetry have however ordered the poems chronologically, including G. M. Matthews's New Oxford English Series selection of 1964, Timothy Webb's Everyman selection of 1977 (both these selections have good notes and careful texts, but both are severely limited by space), and the influential and textually important selection edited by Donald H. Reiman and Sharon B. Powers for Norton Critical Editions, also published in 1977. There is now general agreement that Shelley's poetry is best read in its chronological development, and that very little is lost by an abandonment of Mary Shelley's arrangement. Something definitely *is* lost, on the other hand, by obscuring Shelley's arrangement of poems within volumes published in his own lifetime. In order to enable the reader to reconstruct the original arrangement of Shelley's own collections, their contents, keyed to the numbering of the present edition, are given in appendices to the relevant volumes of this edition. The most important collections of verse in this respect are *Alastor* . . . *and Other Poems* (1816), *Rosalind and Helen* . . . *with Other Poems* (1819), and *Prometheus Unbound* . . . *with Other Poems* (1820).

In order to clarify the purposes of the present edition it is necessary to provide some brief context for its principles and methods. This context is provided by the broad development of Shelley's text since his short working career as a writer was ended by his accidental death by drowning in 1822, twenty-seven days short of his thirtieth birthday.

The History of the Text

Shelley's text falls into two basic categories; poems published in his lifetime, and poems published after his death. Poems published in Shelley's lifetime may be divided into those which the poet himself saw through the press without serious external interference in his own judgement, and those poems the printing of which he did not so supervise. The first group includes the earliest collections, and then notably *Queen Mab*, the *Alastor* volume, *The Cenci*, and *Adonais*. In these cases the first edition is taken as copy text, and this text is disturbed as little as possible. The second group includes *Laon and Cythna*, often known as *The Revolt of Islam*, the title of its revised re-issue (because of legal objections by the publisher), and (because of his exile in Italy) those collections and poems published in England in Shelley's absence, notably *Rosalind and Helen*, *Epipsychidion*, *Hellas*, *Swellfoot the Tyrant*, and, notoriously, *Prometheus Unbound*. In the case of these poems copy text is determined by a consideration of all significant factors known to bear on the circumstances of composition and publication, and the solution to the problems involved naturally varies considerably between different cases. Broadly speaking, the criterion has been to arrive at that copy text which, given what the author's intentions may be supposed to have been, requires the least editorial disturbance. But this criterion nevertheless frequently involves editorial emendation which is sometimes quite extensive, particularly where there are complex relations between printed and manuscript sources (as for example in the case of *Prometheus Unbound*), or where resort is made to a manuscript source which is not in a highly finished state. Other kinds of textual witness which have been considered significant in dealing with particular problems include: manuscript press copies made under Shelley's supervision; Shelley's corrections to proofs, where these are known to exist; Shelley's corrections to printed texts (including errata lists), or to copies of his poems made by his wife or by friends and acquaintances; comments about the text of his poems made by Shelley to friends, by letter or in reported conversation. The problems presented by Shelley's own manuscripts are

discussed separately below. At all times the endeavour has been to
make clear the reasons for the choice of a copy text, and to display
without ambiguity the editorial changes made to this copy text, and
their reasons.

There are about four hundred and fifty poems in the present edition, including all fragments and apocrypha. Of these, some seventy
or so had been published at the time of Shelley's death. This relatively
small number of course includes most (although by no means all) of
the longer poems written by Shelley. It is nevertheless true that a very
significant proportion of Shelley's poetic output has been published
since his death. Indeed, since the publication in 1904 of Thomas
Hutchinson's still widely current Oxford Standard Authors edition,
about one hundred and fifty items in the present edition have appeared
in print for the first time. The evolution and growth of Shelley's
canon has been extremely complicated, and has always been difficult
to disentangle from the related histories of Shelley's critical and personal reputation, and of the discipline of textual criticism itself. Shelley's first editor was his widow. Mary Shelley spent the months
following her husband's sudden death in deep grief, but she soon
fought free of it by devoting her energies, and her considerable
literary abilities, to compiling Shelley's poetic remains. She labor-
iously and skilfully transcribed and edited a large number of manuscript poems, mostly taken from working notebooks which were
then, as they are now, in many places extraordinarily difficult to read.
These poems she published, together with various poems published
by Shelley which had become scarce, as *Posthumous Poems*. The
volume appeared in June 1824, and included more than sixty new
poems (the largest collection of previously unpublished poems by
Shelley). By August it had been suppressed with about three hundred
copies sold (of the printing of five hundred). The poet's father, Sir
Timothy, outraged by this posthumous visitation of his infamous and
publicly reviled eldest son, insisted that the book be withdrawn from
sale, on the threat of suspending financial aid to Mary and her one
surviving son, Percy.[1] This prohibition caused Mary to delay preparing a full edition of her husband's poems until 1835, by when
she had received offers for the project from Edward Moxon.[2] Sir
Timothy not only long outlived his famous son, but, exasperatingly,
he almost outlived Mary too, finally dying in 1844 at the age of
ninety-two. Mary was thus prevented from producing a biography,
but she was cleverly to circumvent the prohibition by her discursive
Notes to the edition of 1839. The 1824 *Posthumous Poems* formed
the basis for all subsequent texts of all the new poems it contained,

broadly speaking up until the nineteen-fifties. The majority of the manuscripts gathered by Mary in the preparation of the volume remained in private hands until after the Second World War, although, as we shall see, various versions of parts of them gradually entered the public domain, and were in varying ways taken up into successive editions.

Mary Shelley's efforts in the volume of 1824 were truly remarkable. In the face of appalling difficulties, and under the most distressing personal circumstances, she produced a large number of readable texts out of what must have at first seemed irredeemable chaos. But her work has its limitations. Her anxiety to do full justice to the mind and heart of her dead husband–particularly as their last months together appear to have been less than perfectly happy–led her into some exaggeration and mistake in her notes to the poems. Inexperience, lack of practice, and the want of any established methodology and techniques for the analysis of manuscript materials, inevitably left a good deal of error in her transcriptions. This was compounded by an understandable desire to supplement and modify the material in order at least to produce the appearance of as much presentable poetry as possible. So Shelley's grammar, punctuation, diction, rhymes, indentations, and stanza orders were altered and supplemented with freedom.

Mary Shelley's work on the text of her husband's poetry was consolidated and established in authoritative form in her four-volume *Poetical Works* of 1839. It has been conclusively demonstrated that this edition, which has until recent years provided the starting-point for all subsequent complete editions, was in fact printed from marked-up copies of two unauthorized editions of Shelley's poetry which had appeared between 1824 and 1839.[3] One of these, the *Poetical Works of Coleridge, Shelley, and Keats*, published in Paris by Galignani in 1829 had the encouragement and indeed the direct assistance of Mary Shelley, who provided a list of errata to the *Prometheus* volume of 1820 compiled by Shelley himself. The other unauthorized edition used in the preparation of the 1839 *Poetical Works* was John Ascham's pirated two-volume *Works*, published in 1834. Mary Shelley presumably used the editions of 1829 and 1834 because she wished to hold on to her own copies of Shelley's first editions. She probably also assumed that Galignani's edition already included the corrections from the errata list which she had previously supplied. Whatever the reasons, it is certain that the edition of 1839, which was to be so very influential, compounded the limitations inherent in the text of 1824 with the introduction of errors of various kinds deriving from the pirated

editions used as printer's copy, even as Mary at the same time introduced changes from errata lists and from her own study of the text in
the years since 1824.

The *Poetical Works* of 1839 were quickly re-issued, with some
changes (chiefly, the restoration of some passages dropped from
Queen Mab, and the addition of *Swellfoot the Tyrant* and *Peter Bell the
Third*), in a one-volume edition dated 1840 on the title-page but
actually published before the end of 1839. Other developments had
taken place in Shelley's text since the *Posthumous Poems* of 1824. The
growth in a readership for Shelley in this period was reflected in a
number of pirated editions; apart from Ascham's, already mentioned,
there were editions in 1826 (by William Benbow), 1830 (by Stephen
Hunt), and 1836 (by Charles Daly). None of these is here regarded as
possessing any textual significance. There were, though, further publications before 1839 of real significance, including the appearance in
two versions, one in 1829, the other in 1831, of *The Wandering Jew*.
There was also the belated appearance of *The Mask of Anarchy*, which
Leigh Hunt finally published with a Preface in 1832, after waiting for
thirteen years for the political situation in England to catch up with the
sentiments of Shelley's poem.

The edition of 1839 added some forty further items to Shelley's
canon. After its appearance it was reprinted in various forms a number
of times in the middle years of the century. The next important
contributions to knowledge of Shelley's poetic text came with the
appearance in 1858 of Thomas Jefferson Hogg's *Life of Shelley*, and
then in 1862 of Richard Garnett's *Relics of Shelley*. Hogg's biography
published for the first time a number of early poems, mostly from
manuscripts in Hogg's possession. Garnett's edition presented some
of the results of his work on the collection of Shelley manuscripts
which had passed to Sir Percy and Lady Jane Shelley at Boscombe
Manor on the death of Mary Shelley in 1851. Garnett was able to add
twenty-five more items to those originally produced by Mary Shelley
in her work on the manuscript notebooks, though his work, like that
of his predecessor, was inevitably vitiated by a lack of time and
resources. The *Relics* does however mark the first significant attempt
to supplement the received text by a close examination of the manuscript collection which stayed in the Shelley family throughout the
nineteenth century.

Garnett's friend and frequent collaborator in Shelley scholarship,
William Michael Rossetti, also had limited access in the eighteen-
sixties to the manuscripts at Boscombe Manor, and, by various
means, to parts of certain other manuscript sources such as the Esdaile

notebook. This enabled him to produce in 1870 a two-volume edition of the *Poetical Works*, which marked the first major advance in Shelley's text since 1839. His edition contained just under thirty new items of varying importance, together with, for example, a greatly enlarged and improved text of *Charles the First*. Rossetti's approach to several aspects of Shelley's poetry marks the beginning of a trend in the emendation of the text which was often dominant in the assumptions of subsequent editors. It had become clear to discerning readers and admirers by the eighteen-sixties that many of Shelley's poems were textually corrupt. Swinburne, for example, writing in 1869, considered that many obscurities in Shelley's poems derived from misguided tinkerings with his punctuation, and from still more damaging attempts to 'correct' grammatical constructions which were in themselves merely difficult or characteristically idiosyncratic. Swinburne's proposed solution was to return where possible to the earliest editions, and to modify punctuation and other accidentals by criteria carefully derived from Shelley's own known practices.[4] But this advice was not heeded by Rossetti. Sharing the conviction that the received text was extensively corrupt, and strengthened in confidence by his own powerful literary background and practised judgement, Rossetti chose to emend the punctuation, grammar and diction in his text on a very large scale, working from the assumption that 'Shelley was essentially a careless writer'.[5] For these emendations the primary criteria were Rossetti's sharp ear for metre, a common-sense approach to the question of Shelley's paraphrasable meaning, and a supreme trust in the reliability of his own literary judgement. The result was a text with very drastically revised punctuation and a large number of wholly conjectural substantive emendations. The effects of this were certainly not all bad. Rossetti focused attention, much more sharply than had previously been the case, on very detailed problems of grammar, sense, and metre, in their inter-relations. He also turned out, later (when the relevant manuscripts had become available and had been correctly read), to have been perfectly right in a number of speculative conjectural readings. Nevertheless, the overall result was further to burden the text with accretions of the kind which had been accumulating steadily since 1824. Some contemporary scholarly reaction to Rossetti's edition recognized the dangers of his assumptions. Mathilde Blind in the *Westminster Review* corrected some of Rossetti's readings from her own work on the Boscombe manuscripts,[6] and Rossetti adopted these corrections, and generally moderated the extent of his revisions to punctuation, in a revised three-volume edition which appeared in 1878.

In the meantime, H. Buxton Forman's four-volume Library Edition of the *Poetical Works*, the first truly scholarly edition of Shelley's poetry, had appeared in 1876–7. Forman's edition included some new material, notably the second part of Shelley's revised version of *Queen Mab, The Daemon of the World*. The edition was characterized by Forman's very wide bibliographical knowledge, by a scrupulous conservatism of approach, and by exceptionally high standards of accuracy. Forman also displayed a respect for Shelley's own stylistic and presentational preferences as a writer, which led him to return where possible to early editions, and generally to modify accidentals only with great circumspection and explicit reason. His edition formed a helpful counterweight to Rossetti's, and it has enjoyed justified respect from all subsequent editors. It was re-issued in 1880 together with Forman's edition of the prose, and there were further editions in 1882 (in two volumes, adding Mary Shelley's Notes) and in Shelley's centenary year of 1892 (in five volumes, the 'Aldine' edition).

Forman's work is limited primarily by the sheer extent of relevant material which was inaccessible to him, and by the number of errors which he inadvertently introduced or, more frequently, perpetuated. These limitations also affected the long-term authority of two further late nineteenth-century editions of the complete poems. Edward Dowden's one-volume collection published in 1891 was able to add some material from the Esdaile notebook, to which Dowden had for the first time been allowed effective access for the purposes of his biography of Shelley (published in 1886). But Dowden's work on the text is otherwise not original and broadly dependent on Forman. George Woodberry's four-volume 'Centenary' edition, published in America in 1892 and in England the following year, was a good deal more interesting. Woodberry was able to use materials from manuscripts in the possession of the great American collector C. W. Frederickson. He was also able to consult the fair-copy notebooks at Harvard which had originally been obtained from Claire Clairmont by Captain Edward Silsbee. But Woodberry too suffered in his efforts from the unavailability of a vast amount of manuscript material. He also made a number of mistakes and omissions in his contents and his collations. The Woodberry text followed Rossetti in rather free emendation of punctuation, indeed with some direct influence from Rossetti, but otherwise he too, like Dowden, essentially based his own text on Forman's.

In the nineties, and then around the turn of the century, Shelley's surviving hologaph manuscripts began at last to make a really signi-

ficant impact on the study of his text. Sir Percy Florence Shelley died
in 1889, and in 1893 part of the Boscombe collection of Shelley
manuscripts passed to the Bodleian Library. They were studied in
detail by a number of scholars, including J. Zupitza and J. Schick,[7] and
also, most importantly, C. D. Locock. His *Examination of the Shelley
Manuscripts in the Bodleian Library*, published in 1903, made clear the
extent of the superior readings and generally illuminating materials
that could be provided by Shelley's manuscripts. The *Examination*
appeared in time for Thomas Hutchinson to make use of its readings
in his one-volume 1904 edition, which in the following year became
the Oxford Standard Authors edition which has continued to provide
the basic working text of Shelley's complete poems up to the present
day. Apart from the material from Locock's *Examination* the Hutchinson edition in fact contributed virtually nothing new to the canon.
Its text closely followed Forman's, but with the addition of numerous
small alterations to the layout, punctuation, orthography, and indentation of the verse. Its textual apparatus was unsystematic and oddly
distributed, and no real attempt was made at sustained commentary
on the text, of the kind provided for example by both Forman and
Woodberry. But it did on the other hand provide a convenient comprehensive collection of all of Shelley's poetry that had come into
print up to the beginning of the twentieth century, in a compact and,
on the whole, carefully printed form.[8] But its text furthered the long
process by which Shelley's actual writings and early printed poems
had become very seriously overlaid by the successive modifications of
editors who for the most part built on, rather than cleared away, the
effects of their predecessors' labours.

C. D. Locock followed his work on the Bodley manuscripts with a
two-volume edition of the *Poems* in 1911. This was by no means
complete, and it was based on an eclectic text supplemented by
Locock's work on the limited range of manuscript sources which
were then available. But it was fully and carefully annotated throughout, and Locock's intelligently skilful and informed handling of detailed problems is still of immense value to students of Shelley's
poetry from every point of view. His was the last full-scale edition of
the complete poems to be published, and in many ways it has remained the most useful for the reader.

The process by which Shelley's text became encrusted with layers
of editorial interference was carried yet further by two later twentieth-
century editions which call for brief notice. In the late twenties (1926–
30) Roger Ingpen and Walter Peck edited Shelley's *Complete Works* in
ten volumes (the 'Julian' edition), the first four volumes of which

contained the poetry. In the absence of any alternative edition, this has provided the standard library edition of Shelley's works in verse and prose up to the present day, but it has many marked disadvantages. The text is extraordinarily eclectic, founded on no clearly enunciated or easily discernible principles, and waywardly unpredictable and inconsistent in editorial practices and, even more strikingly, in its commentaries. In fairness to the editors, the Julian edition was produced quickly and under difficult personal circumstances which caused much of the work to fall exclusively upon Ingpen. But it too has played its part in the history of increasing error and confusion in the transmission of Shelley's text, even though it appeared after some significant manuscripts had become fully accessible and could greatly have aided clarification and correction in many instances.

In 1972 appeared the first volume of Neville Rogers's Oxford English Texts edition, which was planned in a four-volume format. An inadequate but interesting account of the three Huntington Library notebooks had been published by Forman in 1911.[9] Woodberry had provided a photofacsimile of the Harvard fair-copy notebook in 1929.[10] The manuscripts still in the possession of the Shelley family had provided materials for a privately printed selection of *Verse and Prose from the Manuscripts of Shelley*, edited by Sir John Shelley-Rolls and Roger Ingpen and published in 1934. This volume was not a very coherent or particularly useful account of the manuscripts on which it drew, but these manuscripts themselves became available in 1946 when they were presented to the Bodleian Library. With these resources, and with the all but complete availability of all other known Shelley manuscripts by the mid-sixties, the materials for a thoroughgoing overhaul and reappraisal of the text of Shelley's poetry were now to hand. The Esdaile notebook had entered the public domain in 1962. The Pforzheimer Library, while maintaining a strict policy of closed access to items in its collection before their publication as diplomatic texts in the *Shelley and his Circle* series, had begun to publish its volumes. The development of scholarship on Shelley's text, over almost a century and a half, amounted to a rich and diverse body of commentary and careful reflection, of great value in the task of establishing a consistent text by a return to its basis in the original editions and the large body of manuscript materials.

But Rogers chose instead to base his edition on Hutchinson's Oxford Standard Authors volume, which was nothing more than a reworking of Forman's text, supplemented by Hutchinson in various unsatisfactory ways. Rogers regarded Shelley's poetry as though it were a Classical text, of the kind which, in the permanent absence of any sources close to the author, was to be elaborated and improved by the cumulative labours of generations of scholarship. Shelley's own holograph manuscripts were regarded as virtually the least authoritative of witnesses, even though they are very frequently the sole source of a poem's text:

> Out of the two accidental facts of Shelley's residence in Italy and the posthumous publication of much of his poetry has grown the bibliographical myth of a text corrupted by an incompetent publisher during his lifetime and by editors after his death, and needing to be 'corrected' by 'accurate' reproductions of his manuscripts. The truth, as shown by history, is the exact opposite—his editors have provided correction of the error of which his manuscripts are usually the source. It is the task of a new editor to continue their labour.[11]

This explicit inversion of the kind of editorial procedure required by the existence of manuscript material, and by the history of the text, led Rogers into numerous difficulties and illogicalities, which were seriously compounded by a pervasive lack of accuracy, frequent factual error, and a markedly distortive bias in critical commentary. The Oxford English Texts edition was withdrawn by its publishers in 1983.[12]

The improved situation in terms of scholarly resources has however been met in a thoroughly constructive way by other Shelley editors over the past thirty years or so. Many excellent scholars have engaged powerfully in the difficult task of understanding the vast amount of manuscript material which is now known, and of returning to the original sources of Mary Shelley's work for her 1824 *Posthumous Poems*, to examine its accuracy, and to correct and supplement it where possible. Especially valuable contributions have been made in this area by Peter Butter, Kenneth Neill Cameron, Judith Chernaik, Stuart Curran, Paul Dawson, Irving Massey, Donald H. Reiman, and Timothy Webb, amongst others. Their work has proved invaluable in the preparation of the present edition.

The Manuscripts

It was Shelley's practice, from at least as early as 1814, to compose his poetry in bound notebooks. He is known also to have used loose sheets sometimes, but these have naturally tended not to survive in great number. A substantial number of the notebooks were left in Mary Shelley's possession after the death of her husband, most of them containing material written over a relatively short and easily datable period, but some containing material from various periods separated by years. Most of these notebooks contain poetry, in many different stages of composition. This collection of manuscripts in Mary Shelley's possession also included various other important materials such as letters, and copies by herself or by her husband of individual poems and other writings.

Twenty-five notebooks and other manuscripts owned by Mary Shelley passed after her death to Sir Percy and Lady Shelley. Four of these were subsequently given to Richard Garnett, three of which were eventually bought by W. K. Bixby and then finally by their present owner, the Huntington Library. The fourth found its way to the Library of Congress. A fifth notebook was given by Lady Shelley to Stopford Brooke, and has become a part of the Pforzheimer Collection now deposited in the New York Public Library. The remaining twenty notebooks are all now in the Bodleian Library. Six of them, including the three notebooks containing a copy of *Prometheus Unbound*, were deposited in 1893; the other fourteen were presented to the library in 1946. A further, final portion of the manuscript collection descended from Mary had passed to the Abinger family at the time of the first Bodley presentation. This material, consisting of a wide range of papers connected with the Shelley circle (but no manuscripts of poetry by Shelley) was itself finally deposited in the Bodleian Library. A quite large number of other manuscript materials which are of importance to Shelley's text is dispersed, mostly in libraries in Britain and the United States. Some of these were given away by Shelley himself, or by Mary after her husband's death, and others were passed on by friends of Shelley such as the Gisbornes, Elizabeth Hitchener, Leigh Hunt, Thomas Jefferson Hogg, Thomas Medwin, Sophia Stacey, and Edward Trelawny. The important notebook containing fair copies by Shelley and by Mary of a number of poems, which is now in the Houghton Library, Harvard, was acquired by Captain Edward Silsbee, in competition with H. B. Forman, from Claire Clairmont's niece Paola Clairmont in 1879.[13] Still other manuscripts were held by Shelley's publishers the Ollier brothers, or have a provenance entirely outside the circles of Shelley's known friends and associates. Every effort has been made to establish the relation of such manuscripts to the appearance and subsequent textual history of Shelley's printed poems, and full details of these relations are given in the headnotes to the relevant poems.[14]

A special case is provided by the so-called Esdaile notebook. This notebook was left in Harriet Shelley's possession after her separation from Shelley in 1814. After her suicide in 1816 the notebook passed eventually to her daughter Ianthe (Shelley's son by Harriet, Charles Bysshe, died in 1826), who left it in the ownership of the Esdaile family into which she married in 1837. It was finally sold by the Esdaile family heirs in 1962, when it was purchased by the Pforzheimer Library. The then editor of the *Shelley and his Circle* series, Kenneth Neill Cameron, published the poems from the notebook in 1964 in a text described as a 'minimal clean-up type',[15] that is, with relatively light and very careful emendation to the punctuation of the poems. Neville Rogers, who had enjoyed access to the notebook before its sale, published his own edition of the Esdaile poems in 1966. This volume is edited according to Rogers's methods already characterized. Rogers printed the poems again, very slightly modified, in the first volume of his Oxford English Texts edition in 1972. The contents of the notebook were also published, in a diplomatic text by Cameron, in the fourth volume of *Shelley and his Circle* (1970), and in the Garland *Manuscripts of the Younger British Romantics* series edited with an introduction and facsimile by Donald H. Reiman (1987). The present editor has not been able to establish precisely what access G. M. Matthews had to the Esdaile notebook, but he possessed a full transcript which slightly differs in substantives from the *Shelley and his Circle* text. Matthews also possessed a copy of Dowden's transcript of part of the notebook, which was used in the preparation of his 1886 biography and in his 1891 edition of the poems.[16] But it appears that Matthews also had access to the notebook itself, perhaps through a microfilm made in the early nineteen-fifties and owned by Neville Rogers. The Esdaile notebook is now deposited in the New York Public Library. It contains fifty-eight poems, five of which are in Harriet Shelley's hand. The others are in Shelley's hand. The present edition differs from previous editions in assigning all fifty-eight of the poems to Shelley. The poems are here published for the first time in a proposed chronological order, and fully integrated with the other known poems of Shelley's early period. The poems are numbered and arranged in the Esdaile notebook as if for publication (the fact that Shelley also supplies cumulative and final line-counts bears out this impression). This arrangement has been followed in all previous printings; to aid the reader, an appendix to this volume lists the poems in the order and with the numbering of the Esdaile notebook, and keyed to their numbering in the present edition.[17]

The last Shelley manuscript of major importance to come to light was discovered in 1976 in the vaults of the Pall Mall branch of Barclay's Bank. This manuscript, a notebook, was found together with Byron manuscripts and a number of other papers in a trunk deposited by Byron's friend Scrope Berdmore Davis before he fled the country to escape his creditors in 1820. It was presumably left with Byron when the Shelleys returned to England from Switzerland in August 1816. Byron must have given the notebook to Davis, who was staying with him at the time, for Davis to return either to Shelley or to a publisher on his arrival back in England.[18] It contains two previously unknown sonnets by Shelley (in Mary's hand), and neat copies of the two important poems written by Shelley during his stay in Switzerland in the company of Byron, 'Hymn to Intellectual Beauty' (in Mary's hand) and 'Mont Blanc' (in Shelley's hand). These contents are of great textual interest, and their significance is discussed in full in the headnotes to the relevant poems.

Shelley appears to have drafted his poems at first very rapidly, indoors or out, stationary, or in a boat or carriage. The first drafts can be extraordinarily chaotic, with much cancellation, correction, interlineation, and over-writing, in pencil or ink or both (one over the other). They are typically jumbled together with notes on reading, titles of and quotations from books, prescriptions, calculations, and numerous large and small-scale sketches, of trees, mountains, buildings, boats, faces, even insects. Quite often a notebook will be used from both ends, with one faintly legible draft travelling one way and being met and overtaken by a different draft, made at a different time, coming–upside-down–the other way. Shelley's rough drafts, where they were not simply left for later revision or abandoned altogether, provided the basis for more carefully finished intermediate or fair copies, which might themselves form a starting-point for very neatly written copy, for the press or for presentation to a friend. Shelley sometimes also made safe-keeping copies of poems transcribed for the press. Shelley's handwriting varies in legibility depending on which of these possible conditions a given poem is in. It also alters over the years. It can be exceedingly difficult to read, but patience and experience can often yield an at least likely reading in the end, particularly as Shelley's drafts are invariably mindful of metrical considerations and frequently use rhyme and distinct indentation patterns. There is thus a great mass of material, frequently crammed tightly together, in a range of conditions from wholly illegible tangle to perfectly and beautifully written finished poem. There is abundant material, in the notebooks and in other manuscripts of various kinds, in a sufficiently finished state to provide a model for what Shelley's own preferences were in punctuation, spelling, capitalization, indentation, and so forth. There is too, of course, the model provided by these presentational forms as they appear in the works which Shelley himself saw through the press. The present edition assumes that when a poem has been retrieved from its unfinished draft state, then insofar as it absolutely requires editorial emendation in order to be intelligible, it should be emended as little as possible, and as far as possible in accordance with what Shelley's own practices are understood to have been.

The Present Edition

Each poem in the present edition has been newly edited. For poems published in Shelley's lifetime, and under his supervision, the first edition provides copy text. In such cases, substantive variants from important early printings, and from manuscript sources where these are known to exist, are given in full in the notes. Variants of punctuation, capitalization and general layout are given when they are of critical or textual usefulness and interest. Sometimes this involves nothing more than an indication that accents or pointing have been added in specific lines. Sometimes, where circumstances require, there is full collation of early sources.

For poems published in Shelley's lifetime but not in a printing reliably supervised by him, the first edition usually provides copy text, but it is collated with the manuscripts where appropriate, and with other early printed sources. Where, in these instances, manuscripts or editions other than the first provide a preferred reading, reasons and sources are explained in the notes. For poems which derive from manuscript sources only, the text is taken from the manuscript, collated with the first published version or versions. For poems published posthumously which have no surviving or known manuscript source, the first published version is taken as copy text. Substantive variants between copy text and the other sources described are noted, but accidentals are noted only when a difficulty of meaning or form presents itself. There has been no attempt at comprehensive collation of all the major editions, but particular readings and commentaries on points of detail are very frequently given and discussed in the notes, and occasionally such readings are adopted. The editors have leant most heavily in this respect on the work of Rossetti, Forman, and especially Locock. Poems of acknowledged importance, or which present particular difficulties, are provided with fuller collations and more extensive textual commentary, in the headnote and notes. All of Shelley's notes and Prefaces to his own poems are included in full, and are annotated where necessary. Mary

Shelley's notes to the poems have not been included, but naturally their information and judgements are very extensively drawn on in the editorial commentary.

Shelley's spelling, capitalization, and punctuation are very difficult matters to rationalize and make consistent, and have provided the subjects of much debate. Shelley's spellings fairly often deviate from what are now accepted norms, and their preservation has been argued for on the legitimate grounds that he clearly had conscious and fairly consistent preferences. But these preferences are all but impossible to explain at the semantic level, and their prosodic significance is usually impossible to assess with any confidence. English orthography was in a period of crucial change in the early nineteenth century, and many of Shelley's orthographic choices were made between alternatives which were then equally live and customary forms. Nevertheless, in those cases where Shelley's choice was for forms which subsequently fell into disuse, the effect now of retaining them is to give an air of archaic quaintness to Shelley's diction where none seems to have been intended. There is a danger that a mock-Spenserian effect in the manner of James Thomson, of the kind deployed by Byron in Canto One of *Childe Harold's Pilgrimage*, may in these cases inadvertently be produced. Shelley's spellings have therefore been modernized throughout in the present edition, except when a clear prosodic effect is lost by so doing, or when an archaism seems intended. These editorial choices are inevitably matters of personal judgement in the end, and readers will doubtless disagree about some detailed results of this policy. But modernization makes for a more accessible text overall, with very small damage to Shelley's apparent intentions.[19] Participle forms in *ed* have been modernized throughout; there is no consistency in this respect in Shelley's manuscripts or early printed texts, and the editors have discovered no prosodic weight at all in substituting such forms as *cracked* for *crackt*, *clipped* for *clipt*, and so on. Certain spellings have however proved difficult to standardize in a consistent way. The forms *past* and *passed* are exceptional cases, where it can sometimes be difficult to decide which form is grammatically correct. But in the interests of consistency an effort has been made to find the best modern usage in each occurrence. Various words sometimes hyphenated by Shelley or his printers, such as *sun-light* and *sun-rise*, are here printed without a hyphen. The alternative forms *sat* and *sate* do appear to indicate differences of sound, and they have both been preserved, as have the forms *lightning* and *lightening*, which mark different metrical numbers. A particular difficulty is presented by the forms *O* and *Oh*. Shelley, and his printers, use both forms, although on balance Shelley's preference was perhaps for *O*. But this form looks odd in a number of contexts, even while looking right in many others. The careful reader will therefore find a wide variety of instances in which both forms are used within single poems; mechanical consistency seems impossible of attainment in this case, and editorial interference has been kept to a minimum. The use of an apostrophe to mark unsounded vowels in participle endings, e.g. *form'd*, has also been modernized. The abbreviated forms *tho'* and *thro'*, and all ampersands, have been expanded wherever they occur in the text of the poems.

It has been still more difficult to arrive at a consistent and practicable policy in the matter of capitalization. Here the changes that were taking place in early nineteenth-century usage, among writers and printers, were more subtle and in some ways more important than the changes in spelling. Romantic writing increasingly blurs the personificatory and abstracting force of capitalization, by using capitals to mark names of things which are at once abstractions and physical realities. This tendency has deep intellectual roots and implications, and it is definitely at work in Shelley's poetry. But it is a tendency unfortunately mingled with inconsistency and some casualness in his deployment of capitals, particularly in the manuscripts, which on occasion makes it extremely difficult to decide on the most preferable printed form. The general policy has been to preserve Shelley's manuscript capitals except where they are manifestly unnecessary, and to record variant capitals where a poem is well known and often studied, or sufficiently difficult in itself or in its text to make the recording of such details worthwhile for the reader.

English practices in punctuation too were altering in the late eighteenth and early nineteenth centuries. The development here was from a rhetorical to a syntactic system of pointing, and Shelley's pointing of his own verse heavily bears the marks of this difficult transition. Shelley's punctuation has been much tampered-with by editors. The present edition respects Shelley's own punctuation, and emends the pointing of finished poems as little as possible. An exception is formed by the case of purely rhetorical pointing which now has a confusing effect to the modern ear and eye, for instance in the use of a comma solely to mark an internal rhyme. Every effort has been made to offer explanation of grammatical forms where the sense is difficult, particularly in cases where past editors have considered emendation essential. Shelley's grammar is left as it stands, including instances where there is a definite hiatus in the text. Characteristic structures and idiosyncrasies are identified and glossed, for example: the use of a singular verb governed by a plural subject, especially where the plural subject consists of a series of noun sub-clauses or phrases; the use of absolute participial constructions; very long syntactic structures dispersed through complex metrical and stanzaic forms. Shelley's punctuation, like Jane Austen's, uses the dash a very great deal, on its own, and also combined with the colon, semi-colon, comma, full-stop, and suspension points. Different usages in different contexts have a clear metrical weight, and such forms are always preserved. Shelley's punctuation in his manuscripts is frequently very slight (as it is also in the manuscripts of many other poets, as for example Keats, and Yeats). Pointing can be careful and minutely detailed where the local sense requires it, but sometimes even very neat final copies are almost or completely unpunctuated. Line-endings in particular are normally not punctuated, or are very lightly punctuated. Pointing has been added where absolutely necessary, in whichever ways presented themselves as least intrusive and least disturbing to the text, and most in key with Shelley's known practices. Editorial punctuation of this kind is indicated in the relevant headnote, or, where it is very extensive, in the notes.

In the case of poems from the Esdaile notebook, all substantive variants are noted, but only those punctuational and other accidental variants are noted which involve a disputed or doubtful grammatical structure producing real disagreement over the sense of a given passage. The Esdaile notebook is itself very sparsely punctuated, and almost all pointing in the present edition is editorial.

Many of Shelley's poems are untitled in their manuscript source, and a considerable number of these have become known by the title assigned to them by the editor of their first published form. Where such a title has become widely recognized it is generally preserved, with an indication of its origin. Otherwise, poems left untitled by Shelley are usually titled in the present edition by their first line.

Shelley's stanza-forms and patterns of rhyme have frequently been typographically accentuated by the editorial introduction of indentation, sometimes distinctly fussy-looking and intrusive in character. The present edition restricts itself to patterns of indentation originating in early editions or manuscript sources, but there are instances where indentation has been supplied in the interests of internal consistency.

Shelley seems never to have used accents to mark syllables which require to be sounded within the metrical scheme. Such accents have here been supplied.

Words or passages of poetry enclosed within square brackets in the present text and notes are cancelled by Shelley in the manuscript. Space enclosed within square brackets indicates space left in the manuscript, or space created by irreparable damage, for example by a burn, or a tear, or a blot. A question-mark within space in square brackets indicates the presence of illegible words. A question-mark before words within square brackets indicates a doubtful reading.

Where a variant reading recorded in the notes is to be found in most or all major editions, the abbreviation *eds* is preferred to a comprehensive listing of all authorities.

The Genesis of the Present Edition

The present edition bears the names of two editors, but it has not been produced by a collaboration. G. M. Matthews began serious work on the edition in the mid-sixties, and worked steadily at it for some twenty years, up to his sudden and untimely death in 1984.[21] During this time he succeeded in establishing a canon and its chronology, and assembled a large amount of materials for dating and annotation, a substantial number of transcriptions of Shelley manuscripts (particularly those in the Bodleian Library, the Huntington Library, and the Houghton Library, Harvard), and an exceptionally fine and comprehensive collection of books by and about Shelley. This collection is now owned by Reading University Library.[21] Matthews also succeeded in preparing to a state of virtual completeness the headnotes, texts, and notes for about one hundred and thirty of the four hundred poems he placed in the canon. After some discussion, and a period of close examination of the papers left by Matthews, the present editor formally undertook to complete the edition early in 1985.

This edition is therefore predominantly Matthews's work, in its conception, materials, editorial principles, and, in this first volume, in the bulk of its execution. The present editor has supplemented, modified, brought up to date and extended Matthews's work where revision has been necessary. Five distinct kinds of work have fallen to the present editor in the production of this first volume: revising and polishing work mainly completed by Matthews; filling in more significant gaps, such as headnotes, or notes, or texts, where one or two of these were found to be lacking for particular poems; the preparation of headnote, text, and notes, for poems not begun by Matthews; establishing the presentational and editorial consistency of the whole edition; and performing the various tasks involved in the preparation of a final typescript.

Poems which Matthews had completed, in headnote, text, and

notes, have been finished and polished in detail, and made consistent with the edition as a whole. This has involved the checking and completion of incomplete references and explanatory notes, checking the text and confirming its collation, modernizing and correcting inconsistencies throughout, and bringing the material up to date where appropriate. Except for this revision, the first ninety-one items are Matthews's work, with the exception of five poems which required more extensive attention from the present editor (Nos 3, 33, 44, 79, and 83), and the addition of a number of explanatory and source notes. Poem No. 92 is *Queen Mab*, and from that point on the proportion of material finished by Matthews slowly decreases, although it remains dominant. The text and headnote for *Queen Mab*, and for Shelley's notes to *Queen Mab*, are the work of the present editor; the notes to the poem and to Shelley's notes are by Matthews. Nos 93–113 are by Matthews, but supplemented with new material to a more considerable extent than is true for earlier poems. No. 114, *Alastor*, has a text and headnote by the present editor, with notes by Matthews. Nos 115, 116, 118–23, 126–30, and 134–40, are by Matthews, but all supplemented to some extent. The remaining poems, Nos 117 ('Verses . . . on . . . a Celandine'), 124 ('Mont Blanc'), 125, 131 ('To the [Lord Chancellor]'), 132, 133, and 141, are the work of the present editor, as are the chronological arrangement of poems 124–41, the Chronological Table, the Abbreviations, the indexes, the appendices, and the Introduction.

Notes

1. For Sir Timothy Shelley's response to *Posthumous Poems* see *S in Eng* 576–86.
2. See *Mary L* ii 221.
3. *Taylor* 34–6.
4. A. C. Swinburne, 'Notes on the Text of Shelley's Poems', *The Fortnightly Review* (May 1869) 539–61; reprinted with slight modifications in his *Essays and Studies* (1875) 184–237.
5. *Rossetti 1870* I xi.
6. Mathilde Blind, 'Shelley', *Westminster Review* n. s. xxxviii (1870) 75–97.
7. Julius Zupitza and Joseph Schick, 'Zu Shelley's Prometheus Unbound', *Archiv für das Studium der neueren Sprachen und Litteraturen* cii (1899) 297–316; ciii (1899) 91–106, 209–34.
8. A 'New Edition' of Hutchinson's Oxford Standard Authors text was published in 1970, corrected by G. M. Matthews. This edition has been widely used by scholars since its appearance, but it is in no sense a newly edited text; see Matthews's 'Note on the Second Edition', printed on page xi of the corrected 1970 edition.
9. *Notebooks of Percy Bysshe Shelley. From the Originals in the Library of W. K. Bixby*, ed. H. B. Forman, 3 vols (Boston 1911).

10. *The Shelley Notebook in the Harvard College Library. Reproduced with Notes and a Postscript* by G. E. Woodberry (Cambridge, Mass. 1929).
11. *1972* xxii.
12. See Donald H. Reiman's review of *1972* in *JEGP* lxxiii (1974) 250–60, reprinted in his *Romantic Texts and Contexts* (Columbia, Missouri 1987) 41–54; and Judith Chernaik's review of *1975* in *MLR* lxxiii (1978) 166–9.
13. See *SC* ii 910–13.
14. For further details of the provenance of Shelley's manuscripts, see *SC* ii 892–910.
15. *Esd Nbk* 31.
16. Dowden's transcript is in two volumes, the second of which is now in the library of Trinity College, Dublin, Dowden Papers R.4.38. The first volume is now in the Pforzheimer collection.
17. For further information on the Esdaile notebook, and discussion of the problems it presents, see *Esd Nbk* 3–33; *Esd Poems* xix–xxxiii; *SC* iv 911–21; and *MYR* 1 xiii–xxvi.
18. For full details of the discovery, see the *Guardian* 21 December 1976, 11; Judith Chernaik and Timothy Burnett, 'The Byron and Shelley Notebooks in the Scrope Davies Find', *RES* xxix (1978) 36–49; T. A. J. Burnett, *The Rise and Fall of a Regency Dandy*, 1981; and the headnotes to poems Nos 120, 121, 123, and 124.
19. Relatively common words modernized in this edition include the following (and many cognate forms): *aether, antient, centinel, chrystal, desart, extatic, favorite, fervor, gulph, honors, inchantment, ingulph, mimickry, phantasy, pityless, pullies, reliques, scull, shew* (for *show*), *stedfast, teints* (for *tints*), *tyger, vallies*.
20. See Kelvin Everest, 'G. M. Matthews (1920–1984)', *KSMB* xxxvi (1985), xiii–xvi.
21. The Matthews collection in Reading University Library is freely available for the use of researchers, by appointment with the Librarian.

Acknowledgements

Many people have been generous with their assistance in the preparation of this volume. I must first acknowledge, in circumstances which are still saddening, the numerous friends and scholars whom Geoffrey Matthews would have wished to thank. Daphne Matthews has been a marvellous source of support and encouragement, and has frequently gone out of her way to help me through the difficulties involved in picking up the threads of her husband's work. Jamie Matthews also provided much valuable assistance, particularly with Shelley's readings in, and translations from Greek texts. I would like to dedicate this volume to Daphne, Lucinda and David Matthews, and to the memory of Jamie.

My own thanks are due, for good advice, encouragement, and information, to Carlene Adamson, Marilyn Butler, Peter Butter, Judith Chernaik, Duncan Cloud, Nora Crook, Michael Erkelenz, Tony Fitton-Brown, Paul Foot, Neil Fraistat, Elaine Hawkins, Desmond King-Hele, Jerome J. McGann, Ken Phillipps, David Pirie, Donald H. Reiman, Michael Rossington, Rick Rylance, and Carol Smith. Conversations with Jon Stone greatly helped the development of my critical understanding of Shelley's poetry. Deborah Cartmell carried out her tasks as research assistant with fortifying zest and intelligence. I owe a special debt to Roger Fallon for his fiercely unremitting and perspicacious efforts to improve the consistency and accuracy of the editorial commentary. My General Editor, John Barnard, has been an exacting reader, whose informed and constructive comments I have found very helpful. Faith Everest has been a supportive and tactfully critical reader. I am pleased also to acknowledge the assistance, in general forbearance and various detailed particulars, of Lucy and Sophie Everest.

An edition of this kind is impossible without adequate research funding. I have enjoyed strong support from the Research Board of Leicester University, and also from my colleagues in the English Department at Leicester; for lively and thoughtful interest I am thankful in particular to Sandy Cunningham, Bill Myers, and Martin Stannard. The Fellows of St John's College, Oxford, elected me to a

Visiting Scholarship to pursue research on Shelley, and provided a stimulating intellectual environment to complement their exceptional hospitality; I wish to thank especially Stephen Harrison, John Kelly, John Pitcher, D. A. Russell, Bob Welch, and the late Edwin Ardener, for their detailed comments and suggestions on my work in progress. The Leverhulme Trust awarded me a Research Fellowship at a crucial time in the preparation of this first volume. The staff of various libraries have provided numerous invaluable services and advice: the Bodleian Library, and especially Dr Bruce Barker-Benfield and the staff in Duke Humphrey's Library; the British Library; Leicester University Library; Reading University Library, where David Knott has been unfailingly helpful; the National Library of Scotland; the National Library of Wales; and the Marciana Library in Venice.

I am also grateful to the following for granting permission to reproduce poems from manuscript material in their possession: Barclays Bank PLC (Nos 120, 121, 123 & 124); The Bodleian Library (Nos 27, 102, 103, 118, 119, 122, 125, 126, 127, 128, 129, 132, 133, 134, 135, 136, 137, 139 & 141); the British Library (Nos 40, 74, 75 & 100); the Houghton Library, Harvard (Nos 117, 123, 131 & 140); the Huntington Library, San Marino, California (No. 99); the *Keats–Shelley Memorial Bulletin* (No. 57); the New York Public Library, Berg Collection (No. 56); the Carl and Lily Pforzheimer Foundation Inc. (Nos 1, 2, 4, 7, 14, 17, 18, 20, 29, 38, 39, 41, 42, 43, 44, 45, 46, 47, 48, 49, 50, 51, 52, 53, 54, 55, 58, 59, 61, 62, 63, 64, 65, 66, 67, 68, 69, 70, 71, 72, 73, 77, 78, 79, 80, 81, 82, 84, 85, 86, 87, 88, 89, 90, 92, 94, 95, 96, 97, 104 & 115); The Pierpont Morgan Library, New York (No. 16); and the Public Record Office (No. 83).

Chronological Table of Shelley's Life and Publications

1792 Born at Field Place, near Horsham, Sussex, 4 August, eldest son of Timothy Shelley, landowner and Whig M.P. (Baronet, 1806).

1802–4 At Syon House Academy, Isleworth, near London.

1804–10 At Eton, where he is bullied. Develops scientific as well as literary interests.

1808 Begins correspondence with Harriet Grove, his cousin; relationship ended in 1810 by religious prejudices of her family.

1810 Publishes two Gothic novels, *Zastrozzi* (spring) and *St Irvyne* (December). Publishes *Original Poetry by Victor and Cazire* (September), written with his sister Elizabeth. At University College, Oxford (from October); meets Thomas Jefferson Hogg. Publishes *Posthumous Fragments of Margaret Nicholson* (November).

1811 Meets Harriet Westbrook (January). Expelled in his second term at Oxford (25 March) for refusing to answer questions about a sceptical pamphlet written with Hogg, *The Necessity of Atheism* (published February). Hogg also expelled. Elopes with Harriet Westbrook, and marries her in Edinburgh, 29 August. Quarrels with Hogg over his attempted seduction of Harriet. Meets Southey in the Lake District.

1812 Campaigns for political reform in Ireland (February–March); publishes two pamphlets, *Address to the Irish People* and *Proposals for an Association . . . of Philanthropists* (February). Prints *Declaration of Rights*. Adopts vegetarianism (March). Returns to Wales, 6 April, then moves to Devon where he is kept under surveillance by Government agents; writes *Letter to Lord Ellenborough*; his servant is imprisoned for distributing the *Declaration* and S.'s *The Devil's Walk* (August). To Tremadoc, North Wales, where he is involved in further political activity, and where, from September, he works on *Queen Mab*. Meets William Godwin (October) and Thomas Love Peacock (November). Copies out the 'Esdaile Notebook' (November–December).

1813   Flees from Tremadoc (27 February) after mysterious incident
        at Tanyrallt in which S. is apparently attacked at night. Visits
        Dublin and Killarney (March), then returns to London (April).
        Publishes *A Vindication of Natural Diet*, one of the notes to
        Queen Mab. *Queen Mab* privately published in May. Ianthe
        Shelley born, 23 June. Moves to Bracknell in Berkshire (July).
        Writes *A Refutation of Deism* (published 1814).

1814   Visiting Godwin in London (May–June); growing estrange-
        ment from Harriet. Elopes with Mary Godwin, daughter of
        William Godwin and Mary Wollstonecraft, 27 July. They
        travel to Switzerland accompanied by Mary's step-sister Claire
        Clairmont (daughter of Godwin's second wife by her previous
        husband). Returns to England 13 September. Problems with
        debt and ill-health. Charles Shelley born to Harriet, 30
        November. S.'s review of Hogg's *Memoirs of Prince Alexy
        Haimatoff* published (December).

1815   Mary's first child born, 22 February (dies two weeks later). S.'s
        grandfather Sir Bysshe Shelley dies 5 January; by June S. is
        receiving annual income of £1000 (of which £200 is made over
        to Harriet). Gives large sums of money to Godwin. Moves to
        cottage at Bishopsgate, Windsor Park (August). River excur-
        sion up the Thames with Mary Godwin and Peacock (August–
        September); writes *Alastor*.

1816   William Shelley born to Mary, 24 January. *Alastor . . . and
        Other Poems* published (February). Visit to Switzerland with
        Mary and Claire (25 May–29 August); meets Byron; writes
        'Hymn to Intellectual Beauty' (June) and 'Mont Blanc' (July).
        Returns to England, 8 September. Suicide of Mary's half-sister
        Fanny Imlay (daughter of Mary Wollstonecraft by her lover
        Gilbert Imlay), 9 October. Suicide of Harriet Shelley, by
        drowning in the Serpentine, 9 November (discovered, 10 De-
        cember). Meets Keats, Horace Smith, through friendship with
        Leigh Hunt (December). Receives news of Harriet's suicide,
        15 December. Marries Mary Godwin, 30 December.

1817   Allegra, Claire Clairmont's daughter by Byron, born at Bath,
        12 January. Meetings with Keats (February). Writes *A Proposal
        for Putting Reform to the Vote* (published in March). Lord Eldon,
        Lord Chancellor, denies S. custody of his two children by
        Harriet, 27 March. Moves to Marlow (March); close
        friendship with Peacock. Writes *Laon and Cythna* (April–
        September). Starts *Rosalind and Helen* (September). Clara Shel-
        ley born, 2 September. *History of a Six Weeks' Tour*, by S. and

Mary, published anonymously (winter). Writes *An Addres* to the People on the Death of Princess Charlotte (November; published until *c.* 1843). *Laon and Cythna* published and s₁ pressed (December). Writes 'Ozymandias' (December).

1818 *Laon and Cythna* re-issued in a revised version as *The Revolt of Islam* (January). Leaves England for Italy, 13 March. Sends Allegra to Byron, 28 April. Meets Maria and John Gisborne, with Maria's son Henry Reveley, at Livorno (May). Moves to Bagni di Lucca, 11 June; finishes *Rosalind and Helen*, translates Plato's *Symposium*, writes 'On Love', 'Discourse on the Manners of the Ancient Greeks'. Travels to Venice with Claire to meet Byron (August). Stays at the Villa I Capuccini in Este, near Venice. Mary follows with William and Clara (early September). Clara Shelley dies at Venice, aged 1, 24 September. At Este, begins *Julian and Maddalo*, 'Lines Written Among the Euganean Hills', writes Act I of *Prometheus Unbound* (August–October). Travels to Rome, visiting Ferrara and Bologna *en route*; in Rome, 20–27 November. Goes on to Naples, 1 December. Visits volcanic scenery around Naples, writes 'Stanzas Written in Dejection . . . near Naples' (December).

1819 Visits Pompeii and Paestum (February). Returns to Rome, arriving 5 March. Writes *Prometheus Unbound* Acts II and III (March–April). Finishes *Julian and Maddalo* (May). *Rosalind and Helen . . . with Other Poems* published (spring). William Shelley dies aged 3½, 7 June. Moves to Livorno (arrives 17 June). *The Cenci* completed at Villa Valsovano, Livorno, 8 August. Receives news of the Peterloo massacre, 5 September; writes *The Mask of Anarchy* (not published until 1832) and other political poems (September). Moves to Florence, 2 October. Writes 'Ode to the West Wind', *Peter Bell the Third* (October–November); letter to *The Examiner* on the trial of Richard Carlile (not published until 1880); 'On Life', and *A Philosophical View of Reform* (November–December; not published until 1920). Completes a fourth act of *Prometheus Unbound* (August–December). Percy Florence Shelley born, 12 November. Meets Sophia Stacey (November). Writes 'England in 1819' (December).

1820 Moves to Pisa, 29 January. *The Cenci* published (spring). Writes 'The Sensitive-Plant'. Moves to Livorno, 15 June. Writes *Letter to Maria Gisborne*, 'To a Sky-Lark', 'Ode to Liberty'. Moves to Casa Prinni in the Baths of San Giuliano, near Pisa (August). Writes *The Witch of Atlas, Swellfoot the Tyrant*, 'Ode to Naples'. *Prometheus Unbound . . . with Other Poems* published (September). Returns to Pisa, 31 October. Friendship with Emilia Viviani (from December). *Swellfoot the Tyrant* published and suppressed (December).

1821   Edward and Jane Williams arrive in Pisa (January). Writes *Epipsychidion* (January–February). Writes *A Defence of Poetry* (February–March; not published until 1840). Receives news of Keats's death, 23 February in Rome, on 11 April. *Epipsychidion* published (May). Writes *Adonais* (May–June; published in July). Travels to Ravenna to meet Byron (August). Writes *Hellas* (October). Byron moves to Pisa, 1 November.

1822   Writing *Charles the First*. Edward Trelawny arrives in Pisa, 14 January. Writes lyrical poems to Jane Williams. translations from Goethe, Calderón. *Hellas* published (February). Death of Allegra Byron in a convent, 19 April. Moves with his family and Edward and Jane Williams to Casa Magni at San Terenzo on the Bay of Spezzia, near Lerici, 30 April. Takes delivery of his boat, the *Don Juan*, at Lerici, 12 May. Writing *The Triumph of Life* (May–June). Sails to Livorno with Williams to meet Leigh Hunt, 1 July. Drowns with Williams on return voyage, 8 July. Cremated on the beach between La Spezia and Livorno, in the presence of Trelawny, Byron, and Hunt, 15 August (his ashes are interred in the Protestant Cemetery in Rome in 1823).

Abbreviations

Poems by Shelley

Alastor = *Alastor: or, the Spirit of Solitude*
Daemon = *The Daemon of the World*
L&C = *Laon and Cythna; or, The Revolution of the Golden City: A Vision of the Nineteenth Century*
PU = *Prometheus Unbound*
Q Mab = *Queen Mab*
R&H = *Rosalind and Helen. A Modern Eclogue*
RofI = *The Revolt of Islam* .
TL = *The Triumph of Life*
WJ = *The Wandering Jew*

Manuscript Sources

CHPL = The Carl H. Pforzheimer Library.
Esd = The Esdaile Notebook, Carl H. Pforzheimer Library SC 372: 1810–14 (fair copies).
SDMS = The Scrope Davis Notebook, BL Loan 70/8: 15 May–29 August 1816 (fair copies).
Nbk 1 = Bod. MS Shelley adds. e. 16: June 1816 through July 1817.
Nbk 2 = Bod. MS Shelley adds. e. 19: early April 1817.
Nbk 3 = Bod. MS Shelley adds. e. 10: May through September 1817.
Nbk 4 = Bod. MS Shelley adds. e. 14: October 1817.
Nbk 5 = Bod. MS Shelley e. 4: November 1817 through June 1818.
Nbk 6 = Bod. MS Shelley adds. e. 11: July 1818 through April 1819.
Nbk 7 = Bod. MS Shelley e. 1: April–May 1819.
Nbk 8 = Bod. MS Shelley e. 2: April–May 1819.
Nbk 9 = Bod. MS Shelley e. 3: April–May 1819.
Nbk 10 = HM 2177 (Huntington Library): May through September 1819.
Nbk 11 = Bod. MS Shelley adds. e. 12: various dates, mainly August 1819 through March 1820.
Harvard Nbk = Harvard MS Eng. 258.2: September 1819 through July 1820 (fair copies).
Nbk 12 = HM 2176 (Huntington Library): October 1819 through mid-January 1820.

Nbk 13 = Bod. MS Shelley adds. e. 15: late October 1819.

Nbk 14 = Bod. MS Shelley adds. e. 6: April through mid-August 1820.

Nbk 15 = Bod. MS Shelley adds. e. 9: mid-June through July 1820, and mid-November 1820 through mid-January 1821.

Nbk 16 = Bod. MS Shelley d. 1: mid-August 1820 through January 1821.

Nbk 17 = Bod. MS Shelley adds. e. 8: December 1820 through March 1821.

Nbk 18 = Bod. MS Shelley adds. e. 18: April 1821, and February through April 1822.

Nbk 19 = Bod. MS Shelley adds. e. 17: May 1821 through January 1822.

Nbk 20 = Bod. MS Shelley adds. e. 20: June 1821.

Nbk 21 = Bod. MS Shelley adds. e. 7: October through December 1821.

Nbk 22 = HM 2111 (Huntington Library): December 1821 through April 1822.

Box 1 = Bod. MS Shelley adds. c. 4: various dates.

Box 2 = Bod. MS Shelley adds. c. 5: various dates.

The following abbreviations designate MS collections, now dispersed, originally in the possession of H. B. Forman, C. W. Frederickson, the Gisbornes, Elizabeth Hitchener, T. J. Hogg, Leigh Hunt, Charles Madocks, Thomas Medwin, Charles Ollier, Sophia Stacey, E. J. Trelawny: *Forman MSS, Frederickson MSS, Gisborne MSS, Hitch. MSS, Hogg MSS, Hunt MSS, Madocks MSS, Medwin MSS, Ollier MSS, Stacey MSS, Trelawny MSS.*

Printed Sources

1816 = Percy Bysshe Shelley, *Alastor: or, the Spirit of Solitude, and Other Poems,* 1816.

1817 = [Anon.], *History of a Six Weeks' Tour through a Part of France, Switzerland, Germany and Holland,* 1817 [by Shelley and Mary Shelley].

1819 = Percy Bysshe Shelley, *Rosalind and Helen: A Modern Eclogue; with Other Poems,* 1819.

1820 = Percy Bysshe Shelley, *Prometheus Unbound: A Lyrical Drama in Four Acts, with Other Poems,* 1820.

1824 = Percy Bysshe Shelley, *Posthumous Poems,* 1824 [edited by Mary Shelley; edition suppressed].

1829 = *Poetical Works of Coleridge, Shelley, and Keats* (the Galignani edition), Paris 1829.

1839 = *Poetical Works*, ed. Mary Shelley, 4 vols., 1839.

1840 = *Poetical Works*, ed. Mary Shelley, 1840 [a revised one-volume edition of *1839*, dated '1840' on the title-page but actually published November 1839].

1907 = *Poetical Works*, ed. A. H. Koszul, 2 vols., 1907 (the 'Everyman' edition).

1951 = *Selected Poetry, Prose and Letters*, ed. A. S. B. Glover (the 'Nonesuch' edition), 1951.

1972 = *Complete Poetical Works*, ed. Neville Rogers [4 vols., only two published], vol. 1, 1802–13, Oxford 1972.

1975 = *Complete Poetical Works*, ed. Neville Rogers [4 vols., only two published], vol. 2, 1814–17, Oxford 1975.

Baker = Carlos Baker, *Shelley's Major Poetry: The Fabric of a Vision*, Princeton 1948.

BSM = *The Bodleian Shelley Manuscripts* (D. H. Reiman, general editor): vol. 1, *The Triumph of Life: Shelley's Rough Draft . . . and Drafts of Other Poems and Fragments* [bound with] *Peter Bell the Third: Mary Shelley's Press-Copy Transcript*, transcribed and ed. D. H. Reiman, 1986; vol. 2, *Bodleian MS Shelley adds. d. 7*, transcribed and ed. Irving Massey, 1987; vol. 3, *Bodleian MS Shelley e. 4*, transcribed and ed. Paul Dawson, 1987; vol. 4, *Bodleian MS Shelley d. 1*, transcribed and ed. E. B. Murray (in two parts), 1988.

Butter (1954) = Peter Butter, *Shelley's Idols of the Cave*, Edinburgh 1954.

Butter (1970) = *Shelley: Alastor, Prometheus Unbound, Adonais, and other poems*, ed. Peter Butter, 1970.

Byron L&J = *Byron's Letters and Journals*, ed. Leslie Marchand, 12 vols., 1973–82.

Byron PW = Lord Byron, *Complete Poetical Works*, ed. Jerome Mc-Gann, 5 vols., Oxford 1980–86.

Cameron (1951) = Kenneth Neill Cameron, *The Young Shelley: Genesis of a Radical* (New York 1950), 1951.

Cameron (1974) = Kenneth Neill Cameron, *Shelley: The Golden Years*, Cambridge, Mass. 1974.

Chernaik = Judith Chernaik, *The Lyrics of Shelley*, 1970.

Claire Jnl = *Journals of Claire Clairmont*, ed. Marion Kingston Stocking, Cambridge, Mass. 1968.

Concordance = *A Lexical Concordance to the Poetical Works of Shelley*, compiled by F. S. Ellis, 1892 [based on *Forman 1882*].

Curran (1970) = Stuart Curran, *Shelley's 'Cenci': Scorpions Ringed with Fire*, Princeton 1970.

Curran (1975) = Stuart Curran, *Shelley's Annus Mirabilis,* San Marino, California 1975.

Dowden 1891 = *Poetical Works,* ed. Edward Dowden, 1891.

Dowden Life = Edward Dowden, *Life of Percy Bysshe Shelley,* 2 vols., 1886.

Enquirer = William Godwin, *The Enquirer, Reflections on Education, Manners, and Literature, in a Series of Essays,* 1797.

Esd Nbk = *The Esdaile Notebook: A Volume of Early Poems,* ed. K. N. Cameron (New York 1964), slightly revised, 1964.

Esd Poems = *The Esdaile Poems,* ed. Neville Rogers, Oxford 1966.

Forman 1876–7 = *Poetical Works,* ed. Harry Buxton Forman, 4 vols., 1876–77.

Forman 1880 = *Works of Percy Bysshe Shelley in Verse and Prose,* ed. Harry Buxton Forman, 8 vols., 1880.

Forman 1882 = *Poetical Works,* ed. Harry Buxton Forman, 2 vols., 1882.

Forman 1892 = *Poetical Works,* ed. Harry Buxton Forman, 5 vols. (the 'Aldine' edition), 1892.

Gisborne Jnl = *Maria Gisborne and Edward E. Williams, Shelley's Friends: Their Journals and Letters,* ed. F. L. Jones, Norman, Oklahoma 1951.

GM = G. M. Matthews.

GM = *Gentleman's Magazine*

Grabo (1930) = C. H. Grabo, *A Newton Among Poets: Shelley's Use of Science in Prometheus Unbound,* Chapel Hill 1930.

Grabo (1935) = C. H. Grabo, *Prometheus Unbound: An Interpretation,* Chapel Hill 1935.

Harvard Nbk (Woodberry) = *The Shelley Notebook in the Harvard College Library. Reproduced with Notes and a Postscript* by G. E. Woodberry, Cambridge, Mass. 1929 (= *Harvard Nbk*).

Hogg = Thomas Jefferson Hogg, *Life of Shelley,* 2 vols. [two further volumes announced on title page but never published], 1858.

Holmes = Richard Holmes, *Shelley: The Pursuit,* 1974.

Hughes = A. M. D. Hughes, *The Nascent Mind of Shelley,* Oxford 1947.

Hunt Autobiography = *The Autobiography of Leigh Hunt; with Reminiscences of Friends and Contemporaries,* 3 vols., 1850.

Hunt Correspondence = *The Correspondence of Leigh Hunt,* ed. [Thornton Hunt], 2 vols., 1862.

Huntington Nbks = *Notebooks of Percy Bysshe Shelley. From the Originals in the Library of W. K. Bixby,* ed. Harry Buxton Forman, 3 vols., Boston 1911 (= *Nbk 10, Nbk 12,* and *Nbk 22*).

Hutchinson = *Complete Poetical Works,* ed. Thomas Hutchinson, Oxford 1904.

Julian = *Complete Works*, ed. R. Ingpen and W. E. Peck, 10 vols., 1926–30 (the 'Julian' edition).

KSJ = *Keats–Shelley Journal*.

KSMB = *Keats–Shelley Memorial Bulletin*.

L = *Letters of Percy Bysshe Shelley*, ed. F. L. Jones, 2 vols., Oxford 1964.

L about S = Edward Dowden, Richard Garnett, and William Michael Rossetti, *Letters about Shelley*, ed. R. S. Garnett, 1917.

Locock Ex = C. D. Locock, *An Examination of the Shelley Manuscripts in the Bodleian Library*, Oxford 1903.

Locock 1911 = *Poems*, ed. C. D. Locock, 2 vols., 1911.

Mac-Carthy = Denis Florence Mac-Carthy, *Shelley's Early Life*, 1872.

Mary Jnl = *The Journals of Mary Shelley*, ed. Paula R. Feldman and Diana Scott-Kilvert, 2 vols., Oxford 1987.

Mary Jnl (Jones) = *Mary Shelley's Journal*, ed. F. L. Jones, Norman, Oklahoma 1944.

Mary L = *Letters of Mary Wollstonecraft Shelley*, ed. Betty T. Bennett, 3 vols., vol. 1, 'A part of the Elect', 1980; vol. 2, 'Treading in unknown paths', 1983; vol. 3, 'What years I have spent!', 1988.

Massey = I. Massey, *Posthumous Poems of Shelley*, Montreal 1969.

Medwin = Thomas Medwin, *Life of Percy Bysshe Shelley*, 2 vols., 1847.

Medwin (1913) = Thomas Medwin, *Life of Percy Bysshe Shelley* (2 vols., 1847), ed. Harry Buxton Forman, 1913.

MYR = *The Manuscripts of the Younger British Romantics: Shelley* (D. H. Reiman, general editor): vol. 1, *The Esdaile Notebook*, ed. D. H. Reiman, 1985; vol. 2, *The Mask of Anarchy*, ed. D. H. Reiman, 1985; vol. 3, *Hellas: A Lyrical Drama*, ed. D. H. Reiman, 1985.

New SL = *New Shelley Letters*, ed. W. S. Scott, 1948.

Notopoulos = James A. Notopoulos, *The Platonism of Shelley: A Study of the Poetic Mind*, Durham, N.C. 1949.

Paine Writings = *Writings of Thomas Paine*, ed. M. D. Conway, 4 vols., New York 1894–96.

Peacock Works = *The Works of Thomas Love Peacock*, ed. H. F. B. Brett-Smith and C. E. Jones, 10 vols., 1924–34.

Peck = Walter Edwin Peck, *Shelley, His Life and Work*, 2 vols., Boston 1927.

PFMN = Percy Bysshe Shelley, *Posthumous Fragments of Margaret Nicholson*, Oxford 1810.

Political Justice = William Godwin, *Enquiry Concerning Political Justice* (1793) 3rd edition 1797, ed. F. E. L. Priestley, 3 vols., Toronto 1946.

Prose = *Shelley's Prose; or, The Trumpet of a Prophecy*, ed. David Lee Clark (Albuquerque 1954), corrected edition Albuquerque 1966.

Recollections = E. J. Trelawny, *Recollections of the Last Days of Shelley and Byron*, 1858.

Records = E. J. Trelawny, *Records of Shelley, Byron and the Author*, 2 vols., 1878.

Reiman (1969) = D. H. Reiman, *Percy Bysshe Shelley*, New York 1969.

Reiman (1977) = *Shelley's Poetry and Prose*, ed. D. H. Reiman and Sharon B. Powers, 1977.

Relics = *Relics of Shelley*, ed. R. Garnett, 1862.

Robinson = Charles H. Robinson, *Shelley and Byron: The Snake and Eagle Wreathed in Fight*, 1976.

Rogers = Neville Rogers, *Shelley at Work: A Critical Inquiry* (Oxford 1956), revised edition Oxford 1968.

Rossetti 1870 = *Poetical Works*, ed. W. M. Rossetti, 2 vols., 1870.

Rossetti 1878 = *Poetical Works*, ed. W. M. Rossetti, 3 vols., 1878.

Ruins = Constantin-François Chasseboeuf, Comte de Volney, *Les Ruines, ou Méditations sur les Revolutions des Empires* (Paris 1791) [there were many English editions; references are to chapters, and quotations are from the English translation of 1796].

S in Eng = R. Ingpen, *Shelley in England: New Facts and Letters from the Shelley–Whitton Papers*, 1917.

S Memorials = *Shelley Memorials*, ed. Lady Jane Shelley [and R. Garnett], 1859.

SC = *Shelley and his Circle 1773–1822* (an edition of the manuscripts of Shelley and others in The Carl H. Pforzheimer Library), ed. K. N. Cameron (vols. 1–4, Cambridge, Mass. 1961–1970), D. H. Reiman (vols. 5–8, Cambridge, Mass. 1973–1986). SC followed by a number = the Pforzheimer's classification of a manuscript in its collection.

Shepherd 1871–5 = *Poetical Works*, ed. R. H. Shepherd, 4 vols., 1871–75.

St Irvyne = Percy Bysshe Shelley, *St Irvyne or The Rosicrucian*, 1811.

Système de la Nature = Baron D'Holbach, *Système de la Nature* (Paris 1770; attributed to Mirabaud), 1774 edition.

Taylor = C. H. Taylor, *The Early Collected Editions of Shelley's Poems*, New Haven 1958.

TL (Reiman) = D. H. Reiman, *Shelley's 'The Triumph of Life': A Critical Study based on a Text Newly Edited from the Bodleian MS*, Urbana 1965.

TL (GM) = 'The Triumph of Life: a New Text', ed. G. M. Matthews, *Studia Neophilologica*, xxxii (1960).

Unextinguished Hearth = *The Unextinguished Hearth: Shelley and His Contemporary Critics*, ed. Newman Ivey White, Durham, N.C. 1938.

V&C = *Original Poetry by Victor and Cazire*, Worthing 1810 [by Shelley and his sister Elizabeth].

V&C (1898) = *Original Poetry by Victor and Cazire* (Worthing 1810), ed. Richard Garnett, 1898.

V&P = *Verse and Prose from the Manuscripts of Shelley*, ed. J. C. E. Shelley-Rolls and R. Ingpen, 1934.

Wasserman = Earl R. Wasserman, *Shelley: A Critical Reading*, Baltimore 1971.

White = Newman Ivey White, *Shelley*, 2 vols., New York 1940.

Woodberry 1893 = *Complete Poetical Works*, ed. G. E. Woodberry, 4 vols. (Boston 1892), 1893.

Zillman Text = *Shelley's Prometheus Unbound: The Text and the Drafts*, ed. L. J. Zillman, 1968.

Zillman Variorum = *Shelley's Prometheus Unbound: A Variorum Edition*, ed. L. J. Zillman, Seattle 1959.

THE POEMS

1 'A Cat in distress'

S.'s first recorded poem; date of composition 1802–05, probably about 1804 (for arguments that the poem dates from 1811 see Nora Crook, 'Shelley's earliest poem?', N&Q ccxxxii (1987) 486–90). S.'s sister Hellen called it 'a very early effusion of Bysshe's, with a cat painted on the top of the sheet . . . but there is no promise of future excellence in the lines, the versification is defective' ⁓ Hogg i 14). She added that it 'evidently had a story, but it must have been before I can remember. It is in Elizabeth's hand-writing, copied probably later than the composition of the lines [the watermark is 1809], though the hand-writing is unformed' (i 21). The phrase 'hold their jaw' (line 30), mentioned by Hellen S. as 'classical at boys' schools and . . . a favourite one of Bysshe's' (ibid.), could date from S.'s entry to Sion House Academy in 1802, but rather suggests Eton in 1804–05. At Christmas 1804 S. was 12, Elizabeth S. 10, and Hellen S. 5. A note added in another hand to Elizabeth's original watercolour sketch and transcript in CHPL, 'Percy Bysshe Shelley written at 10 years of age to his Sister at School' (SC iv 816), has no likely authority. Nothing is known of the tabby cat; and S.'s MS is lost.

Text from SC 346 (quoted by permission of the Carl H. Pforzheimer Library). Published in Hogg i 21. The transcript is unpunctuated; Hogg's text was from Hellen S.'s copy of Elizabeth's copy, so its variants may be Hellen's.

1.

A Cat in distress
Nothing more or less,
Good folks I must faithfully tell ye,
As I am a sinner
5   It wants for some dinner
To stuff out its own little belly.

2.

You mightn't easily guess
All the modes of distress
Which torture the tenants of earth,
10   And the various evils

¶ 1.2. or] nor Hogg.
5. wants] waits Hogg.
7. mightn't] would not Hogg.
7–12. Peck comments (Peck i 8) 'Here is expressed that sympathy with suffering humanity . . . which . . . is heard as an undertone in almost all of his poetry'. But all the 'evils' enumerated (except 'food') are those of traditional comic drama.

Which like many devils
Attend the poor dogs from their birth.

3.
Some a living require,
And others desire
15   An old fellow out of the way,
And which is the best
I leave to be guessed
For I cannot pretend to say.

4.
One wants society,
20   T'other variety,
Others a tranquil life,
Some want food,
Others as good
Only require a wife.

5.
25   But this poor little Cat
Only wanted a Rat
To stuff out its own little maw,
And 'twere as good
Had some people such food
30   To make them hold their jaw.

2 Written in Very Early Youth

'Very early youth', unless intentionally misleading, must indicate 15–16 years of age, possibly April–May 1808. An Eton friend recalled of S. that 'Another of his favourite rambles was Stoke Park, and the picturesque churchyard, where Gray is said to have written his Elegy, of which he was very fond', and that 'his speculations were then . . . of the world beyond the grave' (*Hogg* i 43). Lines 1 and 7 suggest late spring; see also note on lines 3–4 below. Apart from its debts to Gray's *Elegy* the content is guesswork, but perhaps concerns S.'s cousin

11. *like many*] like so many *Hogg*. A pencilled *so* has been added in the transcript, apparently in Elizabeth S.'s hand, but whether the correction is textual or stylistic is uncertain.
12. *dogs*] souls *Hogg*.
13. *a living*] an ecclesiastical benefice.
20. *T'other*] Another *Hogg*.
24. *Only require*] Only want *Hogg*.
28. *'twere*] it were *Hogg*.
29. *Had some people*] *Some* people had *Hogg*.

Harriet Grove, whom he had first met probably at Easter 1805 and whose response may not have suited his boyish ardour before her presumed visit to Field Place in August 1808, after which they corresponded. See F. L. Jones's Introduction to the Diary of Harriet G., *SC* i 475–506, and K. N. Cameron's commentary on 'To St Irvyne', *Esd Nbk* 305–9.

Text from *Esd* f. 80^r–80^v (*Esd* No. 48: quoted by permission of the Carl H. Pforzheimer Library).

Published in *Esd Nbk* 147; *Esd Poems* 95; *SC* iv 1038–9 (transcript of *Esd*).

I'll lay me down by the church-yard tree
And resign me to my destiny;
I'll bathe my brow with the poison dew
That falls from yonder deadly yew,
5   And if it steal my soul away
To bid it wake in realms of day,
Spring's sweetest flowers shall never be
So dear to gratitude and me!

Earthborn glory cannot breathe
10   Within the damp recess of death;
Avarice, Envy, Lust, Revenge,
Suffer there a fearful change;
All that grandeur ever gave
Moulders in the silent grave;
15   Oh! that I slept near yonder yew,
That this tired frame might moulder too!

Yet Pleasure's folly is not mine,
No votarist I at Glory's shrine;
The sacred gift for which I sigh
20   Is not to live to feel alone,
I only ask to calmly die

¶ *2.3–4*. Traditionally associated with death (cp. Parnell, 'A Night-Piece on Death' 53–4: 'yon black and funeral yew, / That bathes the charnel-house with dew'; Erasmus Darwin, *Temple of Nature* ii (1803) 189–90: 'O'er gaping tombs where shed umbrageous Yews / On mouldering bones their cold unwholesome dews'), the yew in literature acquired further sinister powers after 1783 from the legendary Upas, 'The baleful tree of Java, / Whose death-distilling boughs dropt poisonous dew' (Coleridge, *The Fall of Robespierre* (Cambridge 1794) III 1–2. Act III was written by Southey).

9–14. This stanza draws heavily on Gray's *Elegy*, esp. 33–6.

18. shrine] shine *Esd*.

19–20. Unpunctuated in *Esd*. S. probably means 'The gift I seek is that of no longer existing merely to experience emotions in solitude'. Cameron (*Esd Nbk* 147) punctuates line 20: 'Is not to live, to feel, alone;'; Rogers (*Esd Poems* 95): 'Is not to live, to feel alone;'; but no pointing avoids ambiguities.

That the tomb might melt this heart of stone
To love beyond the grave.

3 Sadak the Wanderer.
A Fragment

Date of composition unknown; first identified as S.'s by Davidson Cook (see
TLS below) from the ascription in a file of MSS contributed to *The Keepsake*
for 1828. Garnett knew of this ascription (*L about S* 36), but there is no evidence
that he or any other editor actually saw the MS, which was bought by J. Dykes
Campbell at the Dawson Turner sale, and had been abstracted from the file by
1936. Although in the absence of the MS S.'s authorship cannot be certainly
authenticated, forgery or misattribution is unlikely at a date as early as
November 1827, when the *Keepsake* material was sent to press, and the internal
evidence favours S.'s claim. S.'s interest in volcanoes, etc., dates from at least
as early as 1805 (Sir John Rennie, *Autobiography* (1875) 2); in 1810 at Oxford S.
'perused with more than ordinary eagerness . . . the translations of the
marvellous tales of oriental fancy' (*Hogg* i 108), but Hogg shows no knowledge
of this poem, whose provenance must lie outside the S. circle. Just possibly it
was the poem on 'an excellent subject' promised to J. T. Tisdall on 7 April 1809
(*L* i 4). The happy ending foreseen after separation might then reflect S.'s
hopeful situation in relation to Harriet Grove in spring 1809. The episode is
taken from Tale VII, 'Sadak and Kalasrade', of the popular *The Tales of the
Genii; or the Delightful Lessons of Horam . . . translated from the Persian by Sir
Charles Morell* [i.e. written by Rev. J. Ridley] (1764). There was an edition in
1805. Sadak's wife, Kalasrade, is abducted to Sultan Amurath's harem. She
feigns willingness to submit to his desires if he will procure for her the Waters
of Oblivion, to enable her to forget her husband, from a volcanic island
'fortified by inaccessible precipices' in the Pacific. Amurath sends Sadak
himself, who survives fearful hardships to bring a goblet of the Water back to
Amurath, who drinks it himself in order to forget his perfidy, and dies. Some
favourite Shelleyan themes are introduced in this Tale: Adiram's overshadow-
ing pinions ('Hymn to Intellectual Beauty' (Text B) 1–12; *Mask of Anarchy*
110–17), and the fountain in the cave; Sadak foreshadows Ahasuerus (*WJ*; *Q
Mab* vii 49–275; *Hellas* 738–861), as Amurath foreshadows the tyrant Othman
in *L&C*; and the quest within the volcano suggests Asia's visit to Demogorgon
in *PU* II.

Text from *The Keepsake*.
Published in *The Keepsake* (1828) 117–19; *TLS* 16 May 1936, 424.

22. *this heart of stone*] Presumably Harriet Grove's, i.e. 'That this hard-hearted
mistress of mine might be induced to love me when I am dead'. Cp. 'Lines
Written among the Euganean Hills' 24–44; 'Stanzas Written in Dejection at
Naples' 37–45.

He through storm and cloud has gone,
To the mountain's topmost stone;
He has climbed to tear the food
From the eagle's screaming brood;
5   By the turbid jungle tide,
For his meal the wolf has died;
He has braved the tiger's lair,
In his bleeding prey to share.
Hark! the wounded panther's yell,
10   Flying from the torn gazelle!
By the food, wild, weary, wan,
Stands a thing that once was man!

Look upon that withered brow,
See the glance that burns below!
15   See the lank and scattered hair!
See the limb, swart, withered, bare!
See the feet, that leave their mark
On the soil in bloodstains dark!
Who thus o'er the world doth roam,
20   With the desert for his home?
Hath he wandered with the brand
Of the robber in his hand?
Hath his soul been steeped in crime
That hath smote him in his prime?
25   Stainless as the newborn child,
Strays this wanderer through the wild;
Day by day, and year by year,
Must the pilgrim wander there;
Through the mountain's rocky pile,
30   Through the ocean, through the isle,
Through the sunshine, through the snow,
Still in weariness, and woe;
Pacing still the world's huge round,
Till the mystic Fount is found,

¶ 3. 3–10. These animal sources of food are S.'s invention; in the original story Sadak merely gnawed his own sandals.

17–18. Not in the original tale, but featured in several tales known to S., e.g. Jane Porter, *Thaddeus of Warsaw* (1803; 2nd edn 1804) i 37: '. . . they obliged the king to keep up with them on foot: he literally marked his path with his blood'; also Charlotte Dacre, *Zofloya* (1806) ch. xxix: '[Lilla's] delicate feet . . . left their blood red traces at every step'; Southey, *Thalaba* (1805) ii 18; Scott, 'The Maid of Toro' (1806) 15.

27–34. Cp. 'Lines Written among the Euganean Hills' 5–33: 'Day and night, and night and day, / Drifting on his dreary way' etc.

35   Till the waters of the Spring
      Round the roofs their splendours fling,
      Round the pearl-embroidered path
      Where the tyrant, Amurath,
      Leaves the harem for the throne:—
40   Then shall all his woe be done.

      Onward, Sadak, to thy prize!
      But what night has hid the skies?
      Like a dying star the sun
      Struggles on through cloud-wreaths dun;
45   From yon mountain's shattered brow
      Bursts the lava's burning flow:
      Warrior! wilt thou dare the tomb
      In the red volcano's womb?

      In he plunges: spire on spire
50   Round him shoots the living fire;
      Rivers round his footstep pour,
      Where the wave is molten ore;
      Like the metal in the mould
      Springs the cataract of gold;
55   O'er the warrior's scorching head
      Sweeps the arch of burning lead;
      O'er the warrior's dazzled glance
      Eddying flames of silver dance;
      By a thousand fountains fed
60   Roars the iron torrent red;
      Still, beneath a mighty hand,
      Treads he o'er the fiery land.
      O'er his head thy purple wing,
      Angel spirit of the Spring!
65   Through the flood, and through the field,
      Long has been the warrior's shield.

---

36. *the roofs*] Those of Amurath's palace.

37. *path*] path, *Keepsake.*

45. *shattered*] shelter'd *Keepsake.* A presumed misreading of S.'s orthography.

48. *womb?*] womb! *Keepsake.*

49–60. Sadak's unsequential plunge into the crater, with its torrents of molten metals, is again S.'s invention. See note to lines 71–4 below.

61. *beneath a mighty hand*] That of the Genius Adiram, Mahomet's servant and Sadak's protector.

63–4. S. apparently identifies Adiram with the tutelary virgin who guards the Fountain of the Waters of Oblivion; neither of these is winged in the Tale, though there is a 'bird of Adiram' which comforts the persecuted Kalasrade.

Never fell the shepherd's tread
Softer on the blossomed mead,
Than, thou man of anguish! thine,
70 Guided through this burning mine.

Hanging now upon the ledge,
That the precipice doth edge,
Warrior! take the fearful leap,
Though 'twere as the ocean deep:
75 Through the realm of death and night
Shall that pinion scatter light,
Till the Fount before thee lies.
Onward, warrior, to the prize!
Till thy woes are all repaid:
80 Thine, all thine, young Kalasrade!

4 To the Moonbeam

Probably written on or immediately after 23 September 1809, the date which forms the only heading in *Esd*. There was a full moon, with showers, on 24 September (see lines 8–10). The personal correspondence between S. and Harriet Grove had virtually ceased early in September 1809, when Harriet first visited William Helyar, her future husband, although contacts between the two families were kept up through S.'s mother and elder sister. Cameron notes (*Esd Nbk* 241) that the 'verse form anticipates that of some of the Choruses of *Prometheus Unbound*–for instance, on the colonization of the planets' (IV 135–58). The present text is the revised version sent to Hogg on 17 May 1811 (*Hogg* i 377–8), with the comment 'Here is raphsody [*sic*]–now I think that after this you ought to send me poetry' (*L* i 91).
Text from SC 160 (quoted by permission of the Carl H. Pforzheimer Library). Published in *Hogg* i 377–8; *SC* ii 790–1 (rev. version); *Esd Nbk* 113–14; *Esd Poems* 67–8 (first version); *SC* iv 1003–4 (transcript of *Esd* f. 55ʳ–55ᵛ, *Esd* No. 36).

Moonbeam, leave the shadowy vale
To bathe this burning brow:
Moonbeam, why art thou so pale

71–4. In the Tale, the final hazard confronting Sadak is a lake under the volcano which he has to swim in order to reach the cave containing the Spring.
¶ 4. *Title. To the Moonbeam*] September 23. 1809 *Esd*.
1. *vale*] dale *Esd*.
2. *To bathe*] To cool *Esd*.

As thou walkest o'er the dewy dale
5   Where humble wild flowers grow?
            Is it to mimic me?
            But that can never be,
            For thine orb is bright
            And the clouds are light
10   That at intervals shadow the star-studded night.

Now all is deathy still on Earth:
      Nature's tired frame reposes;
And ere the golden morning's birth
      Its radiant hues discloses
15   Flies forth her balmy breath,
            But mine is the midnight of death,
            And Nature's morn
            To my bosom forlorn
Brings but a gloomier night, implants a deadlier thorn.

20   Wretch! suppress the glare of madness
            Struggling in thine haggard eye,
For the keenest throb of sadness,
            Pale despair's most sickening sigh,
            Is but to mimic me,
25   And this must ever be
            When the twilight of care
            And the night of despair
Seem in my breast but joys to the pangs that wake there.

4–5.   As thou glidest along the midnight vale
                            Where dewy flowrets glow *Esd*

7. *But*] Ah *Esd*.

8. *thine orb*] thy path *Esd*.

11. *deathy*] An acceptable form for 'deathly' in S.'s day.

13–15. 'Before sunrise, Nature breathes afresh (in the awakening wind of dawn)'.

14. *radiant hues discloses*] radiant gates uncloses *Esd*.

15. *her balmy breath*] *Esd*; the letter to Hogg has 'its balmy breath', presumably a dittography from the previous line.

25. *And this must ever be*] But that can never be *Esd*.

26. *twilight*] darkness *Esd*.

27. *night*] death *Esd*.

28. *that wake there*] that rankle there *Esd*. The verb is blotted in the letter and looks like 'walk'. *Hogg* (i 378) prints 'wake', which conforms with the imagery of night and morning.

5 Song.
Translated from the German

Dated 'October, 1809' in *V&C* (1810). S. could not read German in 1809 (*Hogg* i 52–3), and his subtitle exploits the fashion for German translations initiated by M. G. Lewis and others in *Tales of Terror* (Kelso 1799) and *Tales of Wonder* (1801).
Text from *V&C* 27–8.
Published in *V&C*; *V&C (1898)* 27–8.

Ah! grasp the dire dagger and couch the fell spear,
If vengeance and death to thy bosom be dear,
The dastard shall perish, death's torment shall prove,
For fate and revenge are decreed from above.

5   Ah! where is the hero whose nerves strung by youth
Will defend the firm cause of justice and truth;
With insatiate desire whose bosom shall swell
To give up the oppressor to judgment and Hell–

For him shall the fair one twine chaplets of bays,
10   To him shall each warrior give merited praise,
And triumphant returned from the clangour of arms
He shall find his reward in his loved maiden's charms.

In ecstatic confusion the warrior shall sip
The kisses that glow on his love's dewy lip,
15   And mutual, eternal, embraces shall prove
The rewards of the brave are the transports of love.

6 The Irishman's Song

Dated 'October, 1809' in *V&C*. Written in a metre used several times by Thomas Moore in his earliest *Irish Melodies* (1808), whose influence is strong; but the note of vigorous resistance is original. R. Garnett noted of the poems in *V&C (1898)* that 'The most remarkable is 'The Irishman's Song,' which shows that Shelley's Irish sympathies were of very early date. They were in all probability derived from the conversations on Catholic Emancipation which he must have been accustomed to hear at his father's' (xxiv).
Text from *V&C* 29–30.
Published in *V&C*; *V&C (1898)* 29–30.

The stars may dissolve, and the fountain of light
May sink into ne'er ending chaos and night,
Our mansions must fall, and earth vanish away,
But thy courage O Erin! may never decay.

5   See! the wide wasting ruin extends all around,
Our ancestors' dwellings lie sunk on the ground,
Our foes ride in triumph throughout our domains,
And our mightiest heroes lie stretched on the plains.

Ah! dead is the harp which was wont to give pleasure,
10   Ah! sunk is our sweet country's rapturous measure,
But the war note is waked, and the clangour of spears,
The dread yell of Sloghan yet sounds in our ears.

Ah! where are the heroes! triumphant in death,
Convulsed they recline on the blood-sprinkled heath,
15   As the yelling ghosts ride on the blast that sweeps by,
And 'my countrymen! vengeance!' incessantly cry.

¶ *6.1–4*. 'Thy sun is but rising, when others are set: / And though slavery's cloud o'er thy morning hath hung, / The full noon of freedom shall beam round thee yet' (Moore, *Irish Melodies* Pt. 1, 'Erin, O Erin!' 8–10). 'Star after star decays, / Every bright name that shed / Light o'er the land is fled' (ibid., 'How oft has the benshee cried' 10–12).

9. 'No more to chiefs and ladies bright / The harp of Tara swells' (ibid., 'The harp that once through Tara's halls' 9–10).

12. The dread yell of Sloghan] Cp. 'the slogan's deadly yell' (Scott, *Lay of the Last Minstrel* I vii 12). Scott's poem (1805), which furnishes the epigraph for *V&C*, had recently revived this 16th-century word *slogan* (from Gaelic *sleoghan*, 'war cry') in a Scottish context.

13. where are the heroes!] Derives ultimately from the Bards' Songs in Ossian's notes to 'Croma', published with *Fingal, an Ancient Epic Poem* (1762): 'Where are our chiefs of old? Where are our Kings of mighty name? The fields of their battles are silent. Scarce their mossy tombs remain'. See also 'Henry and Louisa' 1 and note, and cp. Byron, 'The Death of Calmar and Orla', *Hours of Idleness* (1807): 'Past is the race of heroes! But their fame rises on the harp', etc. The 'ubi sunt' formula was of course an ancient commonplace.

13–14. 'Forget not our wounded companions, who stood / In the day of distress by our side; / While the moss of the valley grew red with their blood, / They stirr'd not, but conquer'd and died' (Moore, ibid., 'War Song' 17–20).

15. As] Or *V&C*. Presumably a printer's misreading. *yelling ghosts*] 'It was long thought, in the North of Scotland, that storms were raised by the ghosts of the deceased' (James McPherson, *Fingal* (2nd edn 1762) 123, note to 'Conlath and Cuthona: a Poem'). See also 'Despair' 9; *WJ* ii 482–92 and notes.

7 Henry and Louisa

Dated '1809' in heading of *Esd* and probably written after the initial break with
Harriet Grove in September; Charles Henry and Louisa were the names of
Harriet's younger brother and sister (the latter died on 19 June 1810). But the
anti-religious theme which emerges very abruptly at the end of Part One only
to submerge again in Part Two seems adventitious to what is essentially an
attack on accepted military ideals, and may well have been inserted in 1811 or
later. S.'s retrospective note shows that he had become critical of this first
ambitious narrative poem. Cameron (*Esd Nbk* 265–6) notes that 'Henry and
Louisa' would fit either of two British campaigns in the Napoleonic Wars, the
capture of Alexandria from the French in 1801 or the reverse at Rosetta against
the Turks in 1807, preferring the latter on grounds of topicality and because the
religious issue is then more meaningful. But 'the Tyrant of the World' (72)
must be Napoleon, and the naval contenders in 171–4 seem both to be from the
'Boreal' north. The night battle of Alexandria, though hailed as a great victory,
cost 1500 casualties (*Annual Register* (1803) 948–56). The influence of James
Montgomery's poem 'The Battle of Alexandria', published in *The Wanderer in
Switzerland, and Other Poems* (1806), is also clear. Apparently S. was not
concerned to depict a specific battle, and may be conflating the two campaigns.
The names 'Afric' and 'Britannia' may derive from Montgomery's fierce
attack on slavery in his poem *The West Indies* (1809). The motif of a woman
finding her dying lover on the battlefield was a commonplace: see e.g. Camp-
bell's popular ballad 'The Wounded Hussar' (1797) in which the war-casualty
is also named 'Henry' as he is too in Scott's 'Maid of Toro' (1806) and in Janetta
Phillipps's *Poems* (Oxford 1811) 24. Cp. also Joseph Cottle, *Malvern Hills and
other Poems* (3rd edn 1802) 83–90; Thomas Penrose, *Poems* (1781), 'The Field of
Battle'; and 'The Triumph of Death' in *Old Ballads, Historical and Narrative*, ed.
Thomas Evans (1810) iv 176–84. King-Hele (*The Essential Writings of Erasmus
Darwin* (1968) 172) cites Darwin's *Loves of the Plants* iii 263–308, where 'Eliza'
(a similar-sounding name to 'Louisa') seeks her dead husband after the Battle of
Minden (1759). In Montgomery's 'Battle of Alexandria' a distracted war-
widow bids 'her orphan child / Seek his sire among the slain'. But S.'s poem, as
its epigraph asserts, serves a new motive of moral choice between 'Love' and
'Glory'.

Text from *Esd* ff. 66ʳ–75ᵛ (*Esd* No. 46: quoted by permission of the Carl H.
Pforzheimer Library).
Published in *Esd Nbk* 131–43; *Esd Poems* 79–99; *SC* iv 1022–35 (transcript of
Esd).

¶ 7. *Title*. 'The stanza of this Poem is radically that of Spencer altho I suffered
myself at the time of writing it to be led into occasional deviations. These
defects I do not alter now, being unwilling to offer any outrage to the living
portraiture of my own mind; bad as it may be pronounced' (S.'s note, added
presumably early 1813). Alternate lines are generally indented in *Esd*, but
because of irregularities the stanzas are printed here as in the *Faerie Queene*.

A POEM IN TWO PARTS

She died for love – and he for glory

PART THE FIRST: THE PARTING.

Scene: England

I

Where are the Heroes? sunk in death they lie.
  What toiled they for? titles and wealth and fame.
  But the wide Heaven is now their canopy,
  And legal murderers their loftiest name.
5   Enshrined on brass their glory and their shame
  What though torn Peace and martyred Freedom see?
  What though to most remote posterity
  Their names, their selfishness, for aye enscrolled
  A shuddering world's blood–boltered eyes behold,
10   Mocking mankind's unbettered misery;
  Can this perfection give, can valour prove
One wish for others' bliss, one throb of love? . . .

II

Yet dar'st thou boast thyself superior. Thou!
  Vile worm! whom lovely woman deigns to bless,

Epigraph. died] dies SC.

Stanza i. 'Animosity, battles, treachery, cruelty, and *murders*! The successful perpetrators of these horrid crimes are celebrated, both by their own *historians*, and by unthinking *pedagogues*, under the grand appellation of HEROES! What was the Renowned *Alexander*? A great Hero? And what is a *great Hero*? An unrelenting *butcher* of his own *species*! Such was ALEXANDER, such was CAESAR, and such were all *the similar vagabonds*, thieves, and *murderers* of antiquity. These men, however, are exhibited by our *teachers*, as glorious examples of human *virtues*' (William Smellie, *The Philosophy of Natural History* (1790) i 447).

1. See note to 'The Irishman's Song' 13. S.'s direct source may be Kirke White, 'Time' (published 1807) 134–9:

        Where are the heroes of the ages past?
        Where the brave chieftains, where the mighty ones
        Who flourished in the infancy of days?
        All to the grave gone down. On their fallen fame
        Exultant, mocking at the pride of man,
        Sits grim Forgetfulness.

9. blood-boltered eyes] eyes covered with blood–clotted hair, like Banquo's in *Macbeth* (IV i 123).

13. dar'st] darest *Esd. superior. Thou!*] superior thou, *Esd Poems.*

15 And meanly selfish, bask in glory's glow,
    Rending the soul-spun ties of tenderness
    Where all desires rise for thine happiness?
    Canst thou boast thus and hope to be forgiven?
    Oh! when thou startedst from her last caress,
20 From purest love by vulgar Glory driven,
Couldst thou have e'er deserved, if thou resignedst,
                                    Heaven?

                    III
                    IV
                    V
        ★   ★   ★   ★   ★

    And shadowed by affection's purple wing
    Bid thee forget how Time's fast footstep sped:
Would die in peace when thou wert mingled with the
                                    dead.

                    VI
25 Had Glory's fire consumed each tender tie
    That links to love the Heaven-aspiring soul?
    Could not that voice quivering in agony,
    That struggling pale resolve that dared control
    Passion's wild flood when wildest it did roll,
30 Could not impassioned tenderness that burst
    Cold prudery's bondage, owning all it felt, –
    Could not these, warrior, quench thy battle-thirst,
    Nought this availed thine iron-bound breast to melt,
To make thy footsteps pause where love and freedom
                                    dwelt?

                    VII
35 Yes! every soul-nerve vibrated . . . a space
    Enchained in speechless awe the warrior stood.
    Superior reason, virtue, manner, grace
    Claimed for a space their rights . . . in varying mood
    Before her lovely eyes in thought he stood,
40 Whilst Glory's train flashed on his mental eye
    Which wandered wildly where the fight's red flood,

---

15. 'And [who], meanly selfish, bask[est] in . . .'
Stanzas iii, iv, v. Blanks left in Esd under iii, iv, and for the first six lines of v;
evidently S. had lost one sheet of his copy text. He allowed in his line-count for
28 missing lines.
22. purple] Lat. purpureus, 'bright', 'beautiful'.
26. soul?] soul Esd; soul, Esd Nbk (i.e. 'even if Glory's fire had consumed . . . yet
could not that voice', etc).

The crash of Death, the storm of Victory,
Roll round the hopes of love that only breathe to die.

VIII

Then she exclaimed, as love-nerved sense returned,
45   'Go . . . mingle in thy country's battle-tide . . .
Forget that love's pale torch hath ever burned.
Until thou meet'st me clothed in Victor-pride
May guardian spirits keep thee . . . far and wide
O'er the red regions of the day-scorched zone
50   For glory seek . . . but here thou wilt abide,
Here—in this breast—thou wilt abide alone,
I will thine empire be. My heart shall be thy throne.'

IX

When Princes at fair Reason's bidding bend,
Resigning power for Virtue's fadeless meed,
55   Or spirits of Heaven to man submission lend,
The debt of gratitude is great indeed:
In vain the heart its thankfulness to prove
Aye might attempt to do the debt away;
Yet what is this compared to Woman's love,
60   Dear Woman's love, the dawn of Virtue's day,
The bliss-inspiring beam, the soul-illuming ray?

X

Then Henry spoke, as he checked the rising tear,
'That I have loved thee and must love for ever
Heaven is a witness—Heaven to whom are dear
65   The hearts that earthly chances cannot sever,
Where bloom the flowers that cease to blossom
                                        never.
Religion sanctifies the cause, I go
To execute its vengeance; Heaven will give
To me (so whispers hope) to quell the foe.

---

44. *as love-nerved sense returned,*] as love nerved sense returned *Esd*; as, love-nerved, sense returned *Esd Nbk*.

50–1. abide / Here in this breast—thou wilt abide alone *Esd*; abide / Here—in this breast. Thou wilt abide alone *Esd Nbk*; abide / Here in this breast thou wilt abide alone,– *Esd Poems*.

57–8. 'The heart might well ever vainly try to discount the obligation to prove its gratitude'. S.'s fondness for inversions in his early poems derives from Gray: cp. *Elegy in a Country Churchyard* 77–80.

70   Heaven gives the good to conquer and to live,
    And thou shalt next to God his votive heart receive.

XI

    'Say, is not he the Tyrant of the World,
    And are not we the injured and the brave?
    Unmoved shall we behold his flag unfurled
75   Flouting with impious wing Religion's grave,
    Triumphant gleaming o'er the passive wave,
    Nor raise an arm, nor one short pleasure yield
    The boon of immortality to save?
    Hope is our tempered lance, faith is our shield;
80   Conquest or death for these wait on the gory field.

XII

    'Even at that hour when hostile myriads clash
    And terrible death shakes his resistless dart,
    Mingling wild wailings with the battle crash,
    Then thou and Heaven shall share this votive heart;
85   When from pale dissolution's grasp I start
    (If Heaven so wills), even then will I be thine,
    Nor can the whelming tomb have power to part
    From all it loves a heart that loves like mine,
    From thee—round whom its hopes, its joys, its fears
                       entwine.'

XIII

90   A sicklier tint crept o'er Louisa's cheek . . .
    'But thou art dearer far to me than all
    That fancy's visions feign, or tongue can speak.
    Yes! may I die, and be that death eternal,
    When other thoughts but thee my soul enthral.
95   The joys of Heaven I prize thee far above;
    Thee, dearest, will my Soul its Saviour call.
    My faith is thine . . . my faith-gained heaven thy love,
    My Hell, when cruel fates thee from these arms remove.

XIV

    'Farewell' . . . she spoke. The warrior's war-steeled
                          breast
100   Quivering in feeling's agonized excess
    Scarce drew its breath, to sickliness oppressed
    By mingled self-reproach and tenderness;

70–1. i.e. 'Heaven gives it to the good [man] to conquer, and thou, after God,
shalt receive [the good man's] heart'.
72. *the Tyrant of the World*] Napoleon Bonaparte.

He dared not speak, but rushed from her caress.
The sunny glades; the little birds of spring
105   Twittering from every garlanded recess
Returning verdure's joy that seemed to sing,
Whilst woe with stern hand smote his every mental
                                            string;

XV

The fragrant dew-mists from the ivied thorn
Whose form o'ershadowed love's most blissful
                                            bower,
110   Where oft would fly the tranquil time of morn,
Or swifter urge its flight dear evening's hour
When purple twilight in the East would lower
And the amorous starbeam kiss the loveliest form
That ever bruised a pleasure-fainting flower,
115   Whose emanative eyebeam thrilling warm
Around her sacred presence shed a rapturing charm;–

XVI

Each object so beloved, each varied tone
Of heavenly feeling that can never die,
Each little throb his heart had ever known
120   Impetuous rushed on fainting memory;
Yet not alone for parted ecstasy
To which he now must bid a long adieu

---

103. caress.] caress *Esd*; caress, *Esd Poems*. Apparently suggested by Thomas Penrose, 'The Field of Battle' 29–32:

> She heard, and clasp'd him to her breast,
>   Yet scarce could urge th' inglorious stay;
> His manly heart the charm confess'd–
>   Then broke the charm,–and rush'd away.

104–120. The syntactic structure is clear, though elements in it are much elaborated: 'The glades; the birds . . .; the dew-mists . . .–each object and feeling rushed on his memory'.

104–6. 'the twittering birds that seemed to celebrate the joy of returning spring'.

107. mental string] i.e. nerve.

108. ivied thorn] Ivied Thorn *Esd*. The capitalization may indicate some local sentimental significance.

112–16. '. . . and the starlight would kiss the loveliest girl ever to tread on gratified flowers–a girl whose shining eyes radiated charm round her presence'. The first occurrence of a characteristic image in S.; see e.g. *PU* II v 16–71, and 'To Jane. The Recollection' 41–52.

121. parted] i.e. departed, lost.

Started the bitter tear or burst the sigh,
For all the pangs that, spite concealment, grew
125   O'er his Louisa's peace, a deeper soul-pang drew.

XVII

The balmy breath of soul-reviving dawn
That kissed the bosom of the waveless lake,
Scented with spring flowers o'er the level lawn,
Struck on his sense, to woe scarce yet awake;
130   He felt its still reproach, the upland brake
Rustled beneath his war steed's eager prance.
Hastening to Egypt's shore his way to take
But swifter hastening to dispel the trance
Of grief, he hurried on, smothering the last sad glance.

XVIII

135   Sweet flower! in dereliction's solitude
That scatterest perfume to the unheeding gale,
And in the grove's unconscious quietude
Murmurest (thyself scarce conscious) thy sad tale,
Sure it is subject for the Poet's wail,
140   Though faint, that one so worthy to be prized
The fairest flower of the loveliest vale
To withering Glory should be sacrificed,
That hides his hateful form in Virtue's garb disguised.

XIX

Religion! hated cause of all the woe
145   That makes the world this wilderness. Thou spring
Whence terror, pride, revenge and perfidy flow,
The curses which thy pampered minions bring
On thee shall Virtue's votary fear to fling?
And thou, dear Love! thy tender ties to sever,
150   To drown in shouts thy bliss-fraught murmuring,
Ceaseless shall selfish Prejudice endeavour?
Shall she succeed?—oh no, while I live, never, never.

---

124. For all] GM *conj*; In all *Esd, SC, Esd Nbk*; No, all *Esd Poems*.
126. An echo of Gray's *Elegy* 17: 'The breezy call of incense-breathing morn'.
135–6. Cp. Gray's *Elegy* 55–6: 'Full many a flower is born to blush unseen /
And waste its sweetness on the desert air'.
137–8 unconscious . . . conscious] Virtually a pun: *unconscious* = 'indifferent',
'unsympathetic'; *conscious* = 'self-aware'. For some 19th-century usages of
conscious see C. S. Lewis, *Studies in Words* (Cambridge 1960) 181–90.
152. while] GM; whilst *Esd, SC, Esd Nbk, Esd Poems*.

XX

For by the wrongs that flaming sleep
  Within this bosom's agony,
155 That dry the source whence others weep,
  I swear that thou shalt die.

PART THE SECOND: THE MEETING.

Scene: Egypt

I

'Tis night . . . No planet's brilliance dares to light
  The dim and battle-blushing scenery;
  Friends mixed with foes urge unremitting fight
160 Beneath War's suffocating canopy,
  And as sulphureous meteors fire the sky
  Fast flash the deathful thunderbolts of War,
  Whilst groans unite in frightful harmony,
  And wakened vultures shrieking from afar
165 Scent their half-murdered prey amid the battle's jar.

II

Now had the Genius of the South, sublime
  On mighty Atlas' tempest-cinctured throne,

153. *sleep*] GM *conj*; deep *Esd, SC, Esd Nbk, Esd Poems.*
155. *dry*] day *SC.*
Sub-title. Scene: *Egypt*] GM.
166–175. Syntactically confusing and perhaps confused: MS has no pointing or apostrophes except a comma after *South*. The general concept seems to invite the construction: 'If the Genius of the South had looked now . . . [he would have seen . . .]' but the last two singular main verbs cannot be attached either to *Genius* or *wings*. The following makes reasonable sense: 'Now the Genius . . . had surveyed Africa and deeply bewailed her slavery; and his beloved nations are lamenting the northern fleets that have invaded the southern world, which hears the sound of sea-warfare, sees hostile armies confronting each other, and—consigned to ruin as Egypt is—relays her every least outcry'.
166. *the Genius of the South*] Cameron (*Esd Nbk* 269) refers to Southey's poem 'To the Genius of Africa' (1795) which begins:

> O thou, who from the mountains height
> Rollest thy clouds with all their weight
> Of waters to old Nile's majestic tide . . .
> Hear, Genius, hear thy children's cry . . .
> And thou hast heard! and o'er their blood-fed plains
> Sent thine avenging hurricanes
> And bade thy storms with whirlwind roar
> Dash their proud navies on the shore . . .

167. *Atlas*] A mountain-range in Morocco. Its highest summit is Jebel Toubkal (13,500 ft).

Looked over Afric's desolated clime,
Deep wept at slavery's everlasting moan:
170 And his most dear beloved nations groan
The Boreal whirlwind's shadowy wings that sweep
The veinèd bosom of the southern world
That hears contending thunders on the deep,
Sees hostile flags on Egypt's strand unfurled,
175 Brings Egypt's faintest groan, to waste and ruin hurled.

III

Is this then all that sweeps the midnight sand?
Tells the wild blast no tales of deeper woe?
Does war alone pollute the unhappy land?
No–the low fluttering and the hectic glow
180 Of hope, whose sickly flowret scarce can blow
Chilled by the ice-blast of intense despair,
Anguish that dries the big tear ere it flow,
And maniac love, that sits by the beacon's glare
With eyes on nothing fixed, dim like a mist-clothed star.

IV

185 No fear save one could daunt her. –Ocean's wave
Bearing Britannia's hired assassins on
To victory's shame or an unhonoured grave

169. *Deep wept*] In MS, *Deep* is added a half-line above *wept*. Presumably 'had looked over and wept deeply at' was intended; just possibly *Deep-wept* qualifies *clime* ('exhausted by weeping'). *slavery's everlasting moan*] Although British ships were discouraged from carrying slaves after 1807, slavery itself continued in the British Empire for more than another quarter of a century.

170. *nations groan*] nation's groan. *Esd Nbk*; nation's groan *Esd Poems*. The singular *nation's* implies, without reason given, that Egypt was the Genius's favourite nation. *groan* is transitive, with *wings* as object (see *OED groan* 7a); all the African nations bewail the naval assault.

171. *The Boreal whirlwind's shadowy wings*] 'The dire sails of belligerents from the north'. The wind becomes literal in 176–7.

172. *veinèd*] varied *Esd Poems*. *southern*] GM *conj*; northern *Esd, SC, Esd Nbk, Esd Poems*. See 176, 'midnight sand'. The *veinèd bosom of the southern world* is the fertile Delta of Lower Egypt with its branching waterways.

173. *contending thunders on the deep*] A British squadron had forced the Dardenelles in February 1807, before being ejected by the shore batteries. But the reference may be to the Battle of the Nile on 1 August 1798

184. *dim like a mist-clothed star.*] The first use of a characteristic image; cp. 'The Zucca' 24: 'Veiled art thou like a storm-extinguished star'. Perhaps suggested by *Ecclesiasticus* i 6: 'He was as the morning star in the midst of a cloud'.

Beheld Louisa mid an host alone:
The womanly dress that veiled her fair form's gone,
190   Gone is the timid wandering of her eye;
Pale firmness nerved her anguished heart to stone;
The sense of shame, the flush of modesty
By stern resolve were quenched or only glowed to die.

V

'Where is my love!–my Henry–is he dead?'
195   Half drowned in smothered anguish wildly burst
From her parched lips–'Is my adored one dead?
Knows none my Henry? War! thou source accursed
In whose red flood I see these sands immersed,
Hast thou quite whelmed compassion's tearful spring
200   Where thy fierce tide rolls to slake Glory's thirst?
Perhaps thou, warrior, some kind word dost bring
From my poor Henry's lips when Death its shade did
fling?'

VI

A tear of pity dimmed the warrior's gaze.
'I know him not, sweet maiden, yet the fight
205   That casts on Britain's fame a brighter blaze
Should spare all yours, if ought I guess aright.
But ah! by yonder flash of sulphurous light
The dear-loved work of battle has begun.
Fame calls her votaries.' He fled. The night
210   Had far advanced before the fray was done;
Scarce sunk the roar of war before the rising Sun.

VII

But sight of wilder grief where slept the dead
Was witnessed by the morn's returning glow
When frantic o'er the waste Louisa sped
215   To drink her dying lover's latest vow:
Sighed mid her locks the sea-gales as they blew
Bearing along faint shrieks of dying men,

189. *form's gone*] form is gone *Esd*. An unmetrical line unless the elision was intended.

198. *flood*] GM, *Esd Poems*; blood *Esd, SC, Esd Nbk*.

199. *whelmed*] Replaces *dried* in *Esd*.

Stanzas viii–xii. S.'s description owes much to Campbell's description of Henry in 'The Wounded Hussar': 'From his bosom that heaved the last torrent was streaming, / And pale was his visage deep mark'd with a scar! / And dim was that eye, once expressively beaming, / That melted in love and that kindled in war!' (9–12).

As if they sympathized with her deep woe;
Silent she paused a space, and then again
220 New nerved by fear and hope sprang wild across the
                                                    plain.

VIII

See where she stops again! . . . a ruin's shade
Darkens his fading lineaments, his cheek
On which remorseful pain is deep portrayed
Glares death-convulsed and ghastly. Utterings break,
225 Shuddering, unformed – his tongue essays to speak.
Thus low he lies! poor Henry! where is now
Thy dear, deserted love? Is there no friend
To bathe with tears that anguish-burning brow,
None comfort in this fearful hour to lend
230 When to remorseful grief thy parting spirits bend?

IX

Yes! pain had steeped each dying limb in flame,
When mad with mingled hope and pale dismay
Fleet as the wild deer his Louisa came
Nerved by distraction. – A pale tremulous ray
235 Flashed on her eyes from the expiring day;
Life for a space rushed to his fainting breast.
The breathing form of love-enlivened clay
In motionless rapture pale Louisa pressed,
And stung by maddening hope in tears her bliss
                                                    expressed.

X

240 Yet was the transport wavering . . . the dew
Of bodily pain that bathed his pallid brow,
The pangs that through his anguished members flew,
Though half subdued by Love's returning glow,
Doubt mixed with lingering hope must needs
                                                    bestow.
245 Then she exclaimed – 'Love, I have sought thee far,
Whence our own Albion's milder sea gales blow
To this stern scene of fame-aspiring war;
Through waves of danger past thou wert my polar star.

227. *deserted*] devoted *Esd Poems*.
233. Suggested by Erasmus Darwin's Eliza, 'so wings the wounded Deer her
headlong flight' (*Loves of the Plants* iii 263).
237. *love-enlivened*] love-entwined *Esd Nbk*.
240–4. Inverted syntax: 'the dew of pain . . . the pangs . . . necessarily mingled
doubt with her hope'.
246. *Albion's*] Albion *SC*.

XI

'Live then, dear source of life! and let the ray
250   Which lights thy kindling eyebeam softly speak
That thou hast loved when I was far away:–
Yet thou art pale. Death's hectic lights thy cheek.
Oh! if one moment fate the chain should break
Which binds thy soul unchangeably to mine!
255   Another moment's pause . . . fate dare not wreak–
Another moment . . . I am ever thine!
Love, turn those eyes on me! ah, death has dimmed their
                    shine.'

XII

Ceased her voice. The accents mild
In frightful stillness died away,
260   More sweet than Memnon's plainings wild
That float upon the morning ray.
Died every sound . . . save when
At distance o'er the plain
Britannia's legions swiftly sweeping,
265   Glory's ensanguined harvest reaping,
Mowed down the field of men,
And the silent ruins crumbling nigh
With echoes low prolonged the cry
Of mingled defeat and victory.

252. *art*] are *Esd.*

254. *binds*] bind *Esd.*

255. Another moments pause fate dare not wreak *Esd*; Another moment's pain fate dare not wreak *Esd Nbk, Esd Poems*. MS *pause* could be read as *pain*, but makes dubious sense. Louisa's seem to be 'unconnected exclamations of agony' like those of *Julian and Maddalo* 390–7.

259. *away,*] away. *Esd Nbk*; away; *Esd Poems*. A heavy stop after *away* makes *Died every sound* more sweet than Memnon's plainings, whereas that quality clearly belongs to Louisa's *accents mild. Esd* has no pointing between *The accents* and *sound*.

260. *Memnon's plainings wild*] The famous statue supposedly of a legendary Ethiopian king Memnon which Strabo described (*Geography* XVII i 46) as emitting music when touched by the rays of the rising sun. This statue's ruins at Luxor in Egypt provided Akenside (*Pleasures of the Imagination* i 109–15) and others with a symbol related to that of the Aeolian Harp. S. was indebted to Montgomery's 'Battle of Alexandria', which has a headnote on Memnon and opens: 'Harp of Memnon! sweetly strung / To the music of the spheres, / While the hero's dirge is sung, / Breathe enchantment to our ears'; and to Bowles's 'Battle of the Nile' (1802) 148–50: 'the sounds that in the morning ray / Trembled and died away / From Memnon's statue'. See also 'A Retrospect of Times of Old' (No. 86) line 26 and note.

XIII

270 More low, more faint, yet far more dread
    Arose the expiring warrior's groan;
Stretched on the sand, his bloody bed,
In agonized death was Henry laid,
    But he did not fall alone . . .
275 Why then that anguished sigh
Which seems to tear the vital tie
Fiercer than death, more fell
Than tyranny, contempt, or hate?
    Why does that breast with horror swell
280 Which ought to triumph over fate?
    Why? Ask the pallid, griefworn mien
Of poor Louisa, let it speak:
But her firm heart would sooner break
    Than doubt the soul where love had been.

XIV

285 Now, now he dies! his parting breath
    The sulphurous gust of battle bears;
The shriek, the groan, the gasp of death
    Unmoved Louisa hears,
And a smile of triumph lights her eye
290 With more than mortal radiancy.–
Sacred to Love a deed is done!–
Gleams through battle-clouds the Sun,
Gleams it on all that's good and fair
Stretched on the Earth to moulder there.
295   Shall Virtue perish? No;
        Superior to Religion's tie,
        Emancipate from misery,
    Despising self, their souls can know
    All the delight love can bestow
300 When Glory's phantom fades away
Before Affection's purer ray,
When tyrants cease to wield the rod
And slaves to tremble at their nod.

270–1. Cp. 'Battle of Alexandria' 89–92: 'None but solemn, tender tones, /
Tremble from thy [Memnon's] plaintive wires; / Hark!–the wounded warrior
groans! / Hush thy warbling!–he expires.'
271–2. *groan; . . . bed,*] *Esd* has no stop after *groan* and a semi-colon after *bed*.
291. *a deed is done*] Louisa commits suicide.
293–4. Cp. *Adonais* 24–5: 'he is gone, where all things wise and fair / Descend'.

XV

There near the stunted palms that shroud
305   The spot from which their spirits fled
Shall pause the human hounds of blood
    And own a secret dread;
There shall the victor's steel-clad brow,
Though flushed by conquest's crimson glow,
310   Be changed with inward fear;
There stern and steady by long command
The pomp-fed despot's sceptred hand
    Shall shake as if death were near,
Whilst the lone captive in his train
315   Feels comfort as he shakes his chain.

8 Revenge

Dated 'December, 1809' in *V&C*, and reflecting S.'s recent preoccupation with frustrated love and with 'Gothic' literature. S. wrote to Tisdall: 'to dissipate the stagnation of my spirits I . . . read Novels & Romances all day, till in the Evening I fancy myself a Character–' (10 January [1809]; this letter is misdated 1808 in *L* i 2). The 'plot' is similar to one in S.'s novel *Zastrozzi* (published March 1810 but probably completed by September 1809), where Zastrozzi hounds his half-brother Verezzi to suicide because V.'s father had seduced Z.'s mother. Both stories derive from *Zofloya, or the Moor* (1806) by 'Rosa Matilda' (Charlotte Dacre), which had 'enraptured' S. (*Medwin* i 30). In *Zofloya*, Leonardo, brother of the depraved Victoria, finally avenges the earlier seduction of his mother by Count Ardolph, a German. Most of S.'s 'Gothic' names at this period are from romances and ballads, and those in 'Revenge' are all supplied or suggested by M. G. Lewis's *The Monk* (1796). Thus it is on the road to *Strasbourg* that Don Raymond saves the Baroness Lindenberg from bandits and so meets her beautiful niece *Agnes*, who is later incarcerated in the burial vault of a convent and rescued when almost dead herself. S.'s *Adolphus* conflates Don Raymond's assumed name *Alphonso* d'Alvarada with the Baroness's name, Donna *Rodolpha*. *Conrad* is the porter of Lindenberg Castle. For parallels with *The Monk*, see H. Richter, *Englische Studien* xxvi (1899) 138–44. The metre of 'Revenge' is that of 'The Wanderer of the Wold' in the anonymous verse collection *Tales of Terror* (Kelso 1799), another strong influence on the early S. 'The Wanderer' itself tells a tale of brotherly jealousy and murder. A theme common to nearly all these sources is the supernatural climax in which a gigantic figure, Satan himself or his representative, bears off

304. *There*] Then *Esd Nbk.*
309. An echo of Gray's 'Bard' 3: 'Tho' fann'd by Conquest's crimson wing'. Cp. 'A Translation of the Marseillaise' 54.
311. *steady*] Replaces *bronzed* in *Esd.*

his victim to hell or to destruction. In 'Revenge' the victim is apparently innocent; in Lewis's 'Alonzo the Brave and Fair Imogine', first published in *The Monk* ch. ix and reprinted in *Tales of Wonder* (1801), Imogine vows to Alonzo that if proved unfaithful 'Your ghost at the marriage may sit by my side, / May tax me with perjury, claim me as bride, / And bear me away to the grave'. Alonzo duly returns as a gigantic skeleton and exacts fulfilment of her vow. 'Revenge' imitates Lewis's economy, and even the sub-burlesque effect of his slick versification, with fair success.

Text from *V&C* 45–9.   Published in *V&C*; *V&C (1898)* 45–9.

> 'Ah! quit me not yet, for the wind whistles shrill,
> Its blast wanders mournfully over the hill,
> The thunder's wild voice rattles madly above,
> You will not then, cannot then, leave me, my love.'–
>
> 5 'I must, dearest Agnes, the night is far gone–
> I must wander this evening to Strasbourg alone,
> I must seek the drear tomb of my ancestors' bones,
> And must dig their remains from beneath the cold
>   stones.
>
> 'For the spirit of Conrad there meets me this night,
> 10 And we quit not the tomb till dawn of the light,
> And Conrad's been dead just a month and a day!
> So farewell, dearest Agnes, for I must away;–
>
> 'He bid me bring with me what most I held dear,
> Or a month from that time should I lie on my bier,
> 15 And I'd sooner resign this false fluttering breath
> Than my Agnes should dread either danger or death,
>
> 'And I love you to madness, my Agnes,–I love,
> My constant affection this night will I prove,
> This night will I go to the sepulchre's jaw,
> 20 Alone will I glut its all-conquering maw.'–
>
> 'No! no, loved Adolphus, thy Agnes will share
> In the tomb all the dangers that wait for you there;
> I fear not the spirit,–I fear not the grave,
> My dearest Adolphus I'd perish to save–
>
> 25 'Nay, seek not to say that thy love shall not go,
> But spare me those ages of horror and woe,

¶ *8.7–8*. Cp. 'The Pilgrim of Valencia' 34, in *Tales of Terror*: 'My parents sleep near in yon dark vaulted tomb!'. In 'Wanderer of the Wold' Sir Edric buries his brother's bones under a pile of stones and haunts the scene of the murder.

17. Agnes,–I love,] GM; Agnes I love *V&C*; Agnes; my love, *conj.*

26. those ages] i.e. spent in waiting alone for A.'s return.

For I swear to thee here that I'll perish ere day
If you go unattended by Agnes away.' –

The night it was bleak; the fierce storm raged around,
30   The lightning's blue fire-light flashed on the ground;
Strange forms seemed to flit, – and howl tidings of fate,
As Agnes advanced to the sepulchre gate. –

The youth struck the portal, – the echoing sound
Was fearfully rolled midst the tombstones around,
35   The blue lightning gleamed o'er the dark chapel spire,
And tinged were the storm clouds with sulphurous fire.

Still they gazed on the tombstone where Conrad
reclined,
Yet they shrank at the cold chilling blast of the wind,
When a strange silver brilliance pervaded the scene,
40   And a figure advanced – tall in form – fierce in mien.

A mantle encircled his shadowy form,
As light as a gossamer borne on the storm,
Celestial terror sat throned in his gaze,
Like the midnight pestiferous meteor's blaze. –

SPIRIT
45   'Thy father, Adolphus! was false, false as hell,
And Conrad has cause to remember it well;
He ruined my Mother, despised me his son, –
I quitted the world ere my vengeance was done.

'I was nearly expiring – 'twas close of the day, –
50   A demon advanced to the bed where I lay,
He gave me the power from whence I was hurled
To return to revenge, to return to the world. –

30, 35. Supernatural light was conventionally blue in Gothic romance; there are 'blue lightnings' in 'Wanderer of the Wold' 52, and in 'Alonzo' 45 'The lights in the chamber burned blue!'. Cp. *Richard III* V iii 180: 'The lights burn blue. It is now dead midnight. / Cold fearful drops stand on my trembling flesh'. The association of blue with evil has a classical ancestry: see note to *PU* I 170.

37. Still] 'Ever' (the normal meaning of *still* at this date).

42. gossamer] i.e. a fine cobweb.

43. Intended to recall Satan (*PL* iv 988–9): 'His stature reachd the Skie, and on his Crest / Sat horror plum'd'.

44. midnight pestiferous meteor] The *ignis fatuus*. Any phenomenon above the earth's surface was a 'meteor'.

51–2. 'the power to return from hell to revenge myself on earth'.

'Now, Adolphus, I'll seize thy best loved in my arms,
I'll drag her to Hades all blooming in charms,
55   On the black whirlwind's thundering pinion I'll ride,
And fierce yelling fiends shall exult o'er thy bride.' –

He spoke, and extending his ghastly arms wide,
Majestic advanced with a swift noiseless stride;
He clasped the fair Agnes – he raised her on high,
60   And cleaving the roof sped his way to the sky. –

All was now silent, – and over the tomb,
Thicker, deeper, was swiftly extended a gloom;
Adolphus in horror sank down on the stone,
And his fleeting soul fled with a harrowing groan.

9 Song

Dated 'December, 1809' in *V&C*; perhaps written about 12–13 December,
when severe storms at night were recorded all over the country (*GM* lxxx
(January 1810) 2). The storm setting, however, may derive from the Introduction to Canto iv of Scott's *Marmion* (1808) 31–97. Imitated in metre and tone
from Fitz-Eustace's song in *Marmion* III x–xi ('Where shall the lover rest');
although printed in quatrains, S.'s poem like Scott's falls naturally into
octaves. S. had read *Marmion* by summer 1809, because an epigraph from the
poem is used to head ch. xvi of *Zastrozzi*. Scott's song contrasts the sad but
calm death of the true lover with the destruction and dishonour of the false (it is
aimed at the guilty Marmion); whereas in S.'s, a similar dramatic comment on
his relationship with Harriet Grove, it is the girl who is false and who is
abandoned in death by all but her forgiving lover.
Text from *V&C* 31–2.
Published in *V&C*; *V&C (1898)* 31–2.

Fierce roars the midnight storm
    O'er the wild mountain,
Dark clouds the night deform,
    Swift rolls the fountain –

5   See! o'er yon rocky height
        Dim mists are flying –

59–60. In *The Monk* ch. xii Satan rescued the evil Ambrosio from the dungeon
of the Inquisition: '. . . the daemon grasped one of A.'s arms . . . and sprang
with him into the air. The rood opened as they soared upwards . . .' In 'Alonzo'
68 the skeleton 'sank with is prey through the wide-yawning ground'.

See by the moon's pale light,
   Poor Laura's dying!

Shame and remorse shall howl
10   By her false pillow –
   Fiercer than storms that roll
   O'er the white billow;

No hand her eyes to close,
   When life is flying,
15   But she will find repose,
   For Laura's dying!

Then will I seek my love,
   Then will I cheer her,
   Then my esteem will prove,
20   When no friend is near her.

On her grave I will lie,
   When life is parted,
On her grave I will die
   For the false hearted.

10 Ghasta; or the Avenging Demon!!!

Dated 'January, 1810' in *V&C*, but may date from the previous autumn. In his
'Memoir' of S. (*Athenaeum* 21 July 1832, 472) Medwin called it 'the first of his

¶ *9.8. Laura*] The name was possibly suggested by that of Laurina di Cornari in
Zofloya, who at 'scarcely fifteen' undertook 'a marriage contracted without the
concurrence . . . of respective friends, resolved on in the delirium of passion,
concluded in the madness of youth!' (ch. i) but nevertheless successful, until
her seduction by Count Arnulph. She is forgiven on her deathbed by her son
Leonardo.

21–4. A reversal of the sentiments in *Marmion* III xi 10–17:

           Her wing shall the eagle flap
             O'er the false-hearted;
           His warm blood the wolf shall lap,
             Ere life be parted.
           Shame and dishonour sit
             By his grave ever;
           Blessing shall hallow it,
             Never, O never!

¶ *10. Title. Tales of Wonder* has several poems with similar double titles, e.g.
'Grim, King of the Ghosts; or, the Dance of Death'. It was also a convention in
the titles of prose romances.

effusions, a very German-like fragment [quotes stanza 1] . . . I think he was
then about fifteen', but in *Medwin (1913)* 44–5 this was amended to 'one of his
earliest effusions' (now dated autumn 1809) and the quoted stanza was correctly referred to Chatterton ('then one of his great favourites'). Most probably
Medwin knew nothing of this poem except from *V&C*. 'Ghasta' may have
been the germ of *WJ* (written September 1809–February 1810); both poems
derive largely from M. G. Lewis's *The Monk* (1796). In recounting the episode
of the Bleeding Nun in *The Monk* (ch. iv), Raymond describes to Lorenzo how
he arranged for Agnes to elope with him from Lindenberg Castle by dressing
up as the local ghost, 'a female of more than human stature, clothed in the habit
of some religious order . . . stained with the blood, which trickled from a
wound upon her bosom.' The plan fails because the actual Bleeding Nun takes
Agnes's place and extorts a pledge of fidelity:

> Agnes! Agnes! thou art mine!
> Agnes! Agnes! I am thine!
> In my veins while blood shall roll,
> Thou art mine! I am thine!
> Thine my body! thine my soul!
>
> (Cp. 'Ghasta' 73–6; 93–6)

She is finally exorcised by a stranger of mysterious origin and powers, to
whom she confesses that she was a nun, Beatrice, who had escaped from her
convent in order to live with Baron Lindenberg, but deserted him for his
brother Otto. She killed the Baron for Otto's sake, but Otto killed her for his
own sake. Her ghost then haunted Otto to death, and is prepared to serve
Raymond (her distant relation) likewise, unless her corpse is found and buried.
This is done; but the stranger, now identified as the Wandering Jew, decamps
before he can be further questioned. S.'s poem is often very close verbally to
this episode, and some of the more striking parallels are noted below. The
haunting is also closely imitated. S.'s ghost is 'Theresa', a name perhaps
borrowed from 'The Troubadour' in *Tales of Terror*, where Theresa, now
become a nun, is the forlorn sister of a minstrel who has died of unrequited
love. The chief differences are in motivation, in the figure of Ghasta, and in the
treatment of the Wandering Jew. Lewis's Stranger is sad but courteous and
benevolent; before vanishing he tells Raymond 'to think that I have been of use
to you, is some consolation . . . May the ghost of your relation enjoy that rest in
the tomb which the Almighty's vengeance has denied me for ever!' His
exorcism is performed with Bible, crucifix, and a goblet of Christ's blood,
which confers power to overrule Beatrice's supernatural taskmasters, and she
will rest after a century's suffering despite her crimes. S.'s Stranger, on the
other hand, is an ambiguous and treacherous figure, addressed as 'Mightiest
power of the sky' (170) but operating with a sorcerer's wand, who extracts
information and then delivers Theresa back to the vengeance of Hell and
dooms the mortal witness to death. Yet no guilt seems involved beyond
Theresa's sexual weakness (81–4) and Rodolph's betrayal, whereas Beatrice
had been guilty of adultery and murder. Thus S.'s poem highlights the

merciless vindictiveness of Heaven and Heaven's instruments, even implying an alliance between Heaven and Hell. The linking figure of Ghasta seems entirely S.'s invention, as does the refrain 'Mortal! Mortal! thou must die'. Text from *V&C* 50–62.
Published in *V&C*; *V&C (1898)* 50–62.

Hark! the owlet flaps her wing
    In the pathless dell beneath,
Hark! night ravens loudly sing
    Tidings of despair and death:–

5   'Horror covers all the sky,
        Clouds of darkness blot the moon,
    Prepare! for mortal thou must die,
        Prepare to yield thy soul up soon.'–

    Fierce the tempest raves around,
10   Fierce the volleyed lightnings fly,
    Crashing thunder shakes the ground,
        Fire and tumult fill the sky.–

    Hark! the tolling village bell
        Tells the hour of midnight come,
15   Now can blast the powers of Hell,
        Fiend-like Goblins now can roam.–

    See! his crest all stained with rain,
        A warrior hastening speeds his way;
    He starts, looks round him, starts again,
20   And sighs for the approach of day.

    See! his frantic steed he reins,
        See! he lifts his hands on high,
    Implores a respite to his pains
        From the powers of the sky.–

1–4. Medwin first noted (*Medwin (1913)* 44–5) that these lines are borrowed from the minstrel's song in Chatterton's *Aella* (1777) cvi:
        Harke! the ravenne flappes hys wynge,
        In the briered delle belowe;
        Harke! the dethe-owle loude dothe synge,
        To the nyghte-mares as heie goe;
9–12. During Raymond's flight with the phantom in *The Monk* ch. iv, 'thick clouds obscured the sky: the winds howled around us, the lightning flashed, and the thunder roared tremendously'. After his carriage overturns, the injured Raymond is carried to an inn, where he meets the Wandering Jew.
21. Cp. *Monk* iv: 'the horses refused to answer the rein, and continued to rush on with astonishing swiftness'.

25   He seeks an Inn, for faint from toil
        Fatigue had bent his lofty form,
    To rest his wearied limbs awhile,
        Fatigued with wandering and the storm.

★   ★   ★   ★   ★

    Slow the door is opened wide—
30   With trackless tread a stranger came,
    His form majestic, slow his stride;
        He sat, nor spake,—nor told his name.—

    Terror blanched the warrior's cheek,
        Cold sweat from his forehead ran,
35   In vain his tongue essayed to speak,—
        At last the stranger thus began:

    'Mortal! thou that saw'st the sprite,
        Tell me what I wish to know,
    Or come with me before 'tis light
40   Where cypress trees and mandrakes grow.

    'Fierce the avenging Demon's ire,
        Fiercer than the wintry blast,
    Fiercer than the lightning's fire
        When the hour of twilight's past.'—

45   The warrior raised his sunken eye,
        It met the stranger's sullen scowl;
    'Mortal! Mortal! thou must die'
        In burning letters chilled his soul.—

WARRIOR

    'Stranger! whosoe'er you are,
50   I feel impelled my tale to tell—
    Horrors, stranger, shalt thou hear,
        Horrors drear as those of Hell.

    'O'er my Castle silence reigned,
        Late the night and drear the hour,

---

28. After this line *V&C* has a double row of asterisks, elsewhere with S. commonly a sign of omission.

31. Cp. *Monk* iv: 'He was a man of majestic presence . . . his step was slow'.

38. In *Monk* iv the Stranger says he already knows of Raymond's affliction, but why the phantom walks 'she must herself explain: it lies not in my knowledge'.

40. *mandrakes*] A poisonous plant with forked roots resembling a human form; it was fabled to shriek when plucked.

55   When on the terrace I observed
  A fleeting shadowy mist to lower. –

 'Light the cloud as summer fog,
  Which transient shuns the morning beam;
 Fleeting as the cloud on bog
60 That hangs, or on the mountain stream. –

 'Horror seized my shuddering brain,
  Horror dimmed my starting eye,
 In vain I tried to speak, – in vain
  My limbs essayed the spot to fly. –

65 'At last the thin and shadowy form
  With noiseless, trackless footsteps came, –
 Its light robe floated on the storm,
  Its head was bound with lambent flame.

 'In chilling voice drear as the breeze
70 Which sweeps along th'autumnal ground,
 Which wanders through the leafless trees,
  Or the mandrake's groan which floats around:

 ' "Thou art mine and I am thine,
  Till the sinking of the world,
75 I am thine and thou art mine,
  Till in ruin death is hurled –

 ' "Strong the power and dire the fate
  Which drags me from the depths of Hell,
 Breaks the tomb's eternal gate
80 Where fiendish shapes and dead men yell;

 ' "Haply I might ne'er have shrank
  From flames that rack the guilty dead,
 Haply I might ne'er have sank
  On pleasure's flowry, thorny bed –

85 ' " – But stay! no more I dare disclose
  Of the tale I wish to tell,
 On Earth relentless were my woes,
  But fiercer are my pangs in Hell –

 ' "Now I claim thee as my love,
90 Lay aside all chilling fear,

55. *observed*] Unrhymed. Possibly a printer's misreading of *discerned*.
59–60. on bog, / that hangs or on *V&C*. The text punctuation is from *1907*.
63–4. Cp. *Monk* iv: 'I would have called for aid, but the sound expired ere it could pass my lips. My nerves were bound up in impotence, and I remained in the same attitude inanimate as a statue'.

My affection will I prove
 Where sheeted ghosts and spectres are!

 ' "For thou art mine and I am thine,
  Till the dreaded judgment day,
95 I am thine and thou art mine—
  Night is past—I must away."

 'Still I gazed, and still the form
  Pressed upon my aching sight,
Still I braved the howling storm,
100 When the ghost dissolved in night.—

 'Restless, sleepless fled the night,
  Sleepless as a sick man's bed
When he sighs for morning light,
  When he turns his aching head,—

105 'Slow and painful passed the day,
  Melancholy seized my brain,
Lingering fled the hours away,
  Lingering to a wretch in pain.—

 'At last came night, ah! horrid hour,
110 Ah! chilling time that wakes the dead,
When demons ride the clouds that lower,
  —The phantom sat upon my bed.

 'In hollow voice, low as the sound
  Which in some charnel makes it moan,
115 And floats along the burying ground,
  The phantom claimed me as her own.

 'Her chilling finger on my head
  With coldest touch congealed my soul—
Cold as the finger of the dead,
120 Or damps which round a tombstone roll.—

 'Months are passed in lingering round,
  Every night the spectre comes;
With thrilling step it shakes the ground,
  With thrilling step it round me roams.—

125 'Stranger! I have told to thee
  All the tale I have to tell—

114. i.e. 'which in some charnel makes the charnel moan'.
115. *And floats*] GM; *What floats V&C.* Possibly the emendation should be
Which floats.
121. *in lingering round*] 'in a slow circuit'. In *Monk* iv, likewise, 'several months
elapsed' bringing nightly visits from the phantom.

Stranger! canst thou tell to me
   How to scape the powers of Hell?' –

STRANGER

'Warrior! I can ease thy woes,
   Wilt thou, wilt thou, come with me –
130   Warrior! I can all disclose,
   Follow, follow, follow me.'

Yet the tempest's duskiest wing
   Its mantle stretches o'er the sky,
135   Yet the midnight ravens sing:
   'Mortal! Mortal! thou must die.'

At last they saw a river clear
   That crossed the heathy path they trod,
The Stranger's look was wild and drear,
140   The firm Earth shook beneath his nod –

He raised a wand above his head,
   He traced a circle on the plain,
In a wild verse he called the dead,
   The dead with silent footsteps came.

145   A burning brilliance on his head
   Flaming filled the stormy air,
In a wild verse he called the dead,
   The dead in motley crowd were there. –

'Ghasta! Ghasta! come along,
150   Bring thy fiendish crowd with thee,
Quickly raise th'avenging Song,
   Ghasta! Ghasta! come to me.'

Horrid shapes in mantles grey
   Flit athwart the stormy night,
155   'Ghasta! Ghasta! come away,
   Come away before 'tis light.'

See! the sheeted Ghost they bring,
   Yelling dreadful o'er the heath,
Hark! the deadly verse they sing,
160   Tidings of despair and death!

---

137. *a river clear*] The Stranger needs running water for protection against the
demons he raises. Hogg relates that while at school S. tried once to raise a ghost
at midnight, standing astride one 'of the many beautiful clear streams near
Eton' (*Hogg* i 34).

The yelling Ghost before him stands,
　　See! she rolls her eyes around,
Now she lifts her bony hands,
　　Now her footsteps shake the ground.

STRANGER
165　'Phantom of Theresa, say
　　Why to earth again you came,
Quickly speak, I must away!
　　Or you must bleach for aye in flame.'–

PHANTOM
'Mighty one, I know thee now,
170　　Mightiest power of the sky,
Know thee by thy flaming brow,
　　Know thee by thy sparkling eye.

'That fire is scorching! Oh! I came,
　　From the caverned depth of Hell,
175　My fleeting false Rodolph to claim,
　　Mighty one! I know thee well.'–

STRANGER
'Ghasta! seize yon wandering sprite,
　　Drag her to the depth beneath,
Take her swift, before 'tis light,
180　　Take her to the cells of death!

'Thou that heardst the trackless dead
　　In the mouldering tomb must lie,
Mortal! look upon my head,
　　Mortal! Mortal! thou must die.'

185　Of glowing flame a cross was there
　　Which threw a light around his form,

---

167. I must away] The Wandering Jew says in *Monk* iv: 'Fate obliges me to be constantly in movement; I am not permitted to pass more than a fortnight in the same place'.
169–72. Raymond in *Monk* iv says: 'I raised [my eyes] and beheld a burning cross impressed upon his brow'; the Stranger explains 'God has set his seal upon me, and all his creatures respect this fatal mark'.
173. That fire is scorching!] Cp. *Monk* iv: 'Now let me depart. Those flames are scorching!'
175. Rodolph] A masculine version of 'Rodolpha', the Baroness Lindenberg of *The Monk.*

Whilst his lank and raven hair
    Floated wild upon the storm. –

The Warrior upward turned his eyes,
190   Gazed upon the cross of fire,
There sat horror and surprise,
    There sat God's eternal ire. –

A shivering through the Warrior flew,
    Colder than the nightly blast,
195   Colder than the evening dew
    When the hour of twilight's past. –

Thunder shakes th'expansive sky,
    Shakes the bosom of the heath,
    'Mortal! Mortal! thou must die' –
200   The warrior sank convulsed in death.

11 The Wandering Jew; or the Victim of the Eternal Avenger

Composed between *c*. 1 September 1809 (i.e. after completing *Zastrozzi*) and 5 March 1810, when Harriet Grove was lent a MS copy (*SC* ii 571), possibly transcribed by Elizabeth S. The Preface was probably written, and part of the poem may have been revised, in summer 1810. The bewildering textual history of *WJ* is investigated by M. Eimer, *Anglia* xxxviii (1914) 433–76, A. E. and F. J. Glasheen, *MLR* xxxviii (January 1943) 12–17, and in *Cameron (1951)* 306–13. Medwin made various self-contradictory claims in an attempt to implicate himself with the authorship (see his 'Memoir of S.', *Athenaeum* 21 July 1832, 472–3; *Medwin (1913)* 40–2), but there is no other reason to suppose that he had any part whatever in the genesis of the poem. S. submitted the poem, probably just after leaving Eton (30 July 1810), to Messrs. Ballantyne in Edinburgh, publishers of Scott's recent *Lady of the Lake*, who declined it (without returning it) on 24 September as unsuited to the 'bigoted narrow spirit' of certain northerners who had attacked even Scott 'for having promulgated atheistical doctrines in the Lady of the Lake' (*L* i 17). On 28 September S. offered it to Stockdale, and when the copy sent to Scotland was not returned, promised him 'a Mss copy which I possess' (*L* i 21). On 2 December S. wrote to Stockdale: 'Will you, if you have got two copies of the Wandering Jew send one of them to me, as I have thought of some corrections which I wish to make' (*L* i 23–4). Two copies of the poem certainly existed, therefore;

187. *raven hair*] Perhaps suggested by Lenore's 'Rabenhaar' in Gottfried August Bürger's ballad *Lenore* (1774) 30, which had greatly impressed S. (*Medwin (1913) 45*), but in translation.

but these must then have been identical, or S. would have specified the one he required. Stockdale, however, declared in 1826 'that, after all, the poem of the Wandering Jew never reached my hands, nor have I either seen or heard of it, from that time' (*Stockdale's Budget*, 27 December 1826, 19). Nevertheless, two differing versions of the poem were eventually published. In 1829 Henry Glassford Bell, editor of the *Edinburgh Literary Journal* (*ELJ*), acquired the MS notebook submitted to James Ballantyne (*Memoirs and Portraits of One Hundred Glasgow Men*, anon. (Glasgow 1886) i 30), and announced for publication 'a poem in four cantos, by the late poet Shelley, and entirely written in his own hand' (*ELJ* No. xxxii, 20 June 1829, 41). It appeared, as long extracts linked by synopses, in three issues of *ELJ* (see below), the final extract ('An Incantation Scene') printed as a separate poem. Later the MS notebook was lent 'to a gentleman who was writing an essay on the genius of Shelley [possibly the anonymous essay printed in *Tait's Edinburgh Magazine*, Nos. vii and ix, October and December 1832, 92–103 and 331–42; see especially note to 97], with permission to make a few extracts. That person copied the whole poem, and transmitted it to Fraser' (*ELJ* 9 July 1831). The editor of *Fraser's Magazine for Town and Country*, having consulted Mrs S. (*Fraser's* July 1831, on verso of Table of Contents), printed the poem 'for the first time, in a complete state' (*Fraser's* III, June 1831, 536), i.e. as a continuous whole but (as the Glasheens have shown) severely abridged editorially. Mrs S. confirms that the text (presumably *Fraser's*) 'was considerably altered before it was printed' (Note on *Q Mab*, *1839* i 102). Thus *ELJ* gives extracts only, but printed verbatim from S.'s MS, while *Fraser* gives a drastically condensed version of the whole poem from a transcript of the same MS. The text below therefore follows *ELJ*, supplementing only when this is wanting from *Fraser*. Since *Fraser* derives from a transcript, its punctuation is in general emended silently. And since both texts are based on the same MS, no advantage is gained by distinguishing them typographically, as Dobell (who assumed that *Fraser* derived from a later, revised text) attempted to do in his 'Shelley Society' edition (1887); but the indentation of *ELJ* is preserved, and the two texts are distinguished in the notes. Revision of S.'s MS after 1810 seems unlikely. Although Bell reported (doubtless from the younger Ballantyne) that the poem 'was brought by the poet to Edinburgh' (*ELJ* No. xxxii, 20 June 1829, 41), it had in fact been sent earlier by post. S. did visit Edinburgh before the end of August and *c*. 1 September 1811, and perhaps called on Ballantyne, but he cannot well have left a revised copy of the poem then. The Preface is dated 'January, 1811'– explicable as an anticipation if written the previous summer or autumn, but hardly as a back-dating of six months (the date may rather have prompted Ballantyne's error). Moreover a poem rejected in 1810 for atheistical tendencies could not have been made acceptable in 1811 by a slighting prefatorial reference to 'the personal reign of J—— C——'. The dedication to Burdett argues no deeper political commitment than the partisanship widely aroused by Burdett's defiance of the House of Commons in April 1810 (see note). That 'the preface bears internal marks of having been written after the poem' (*ELJ* No. xxxiii, 27 June 1829, 43) reflects only S.'s normal habit. The heading to ch.

viii of *St Irvyne* (written April–October 1810) is a quotation from *WJ* 94, 102–10, and that of ch.x is from *WJ* 781, 783–91 (noted below), but the variants need not presuppose a revised text: S. may simply have changed the words as he copied them from the poem.

WJ is S.'s first ambitious poem, and (with No. 10 and perhaps No. 3) his first treatment of a figure which continued to haunt his imagination with varying emphases (cp. esp. *Q Mab* vii 49–275; 'The Wandering Jew's Soliloquy'; 'The Assassins', chs. iii–iv; *Alastor* 675–681; *Hellas* 638–862). 'He appears . . . on each occasion . . . as the bearer of the curse and prophet of the blessedness of man' (*Hughes* 37).

The Jew of tradition, known either as Cartaphilus or Ahasuerus, doomed by an offended God to the torture of unresting existence, shades into a Cain-figure on the one hand (an exile carrying the brand of guilt on his forehead: lines 609–705), and into the figures of Satan and Prometheus (lines 800–14) on the other (hero or anti-hero defying the vengeance of seemingly omnipotent power), and appealed powerfully in various forms to the European imagination during the revolutionary period (see James Rieger, *The Mutiny Within* (New York 1967) 51–77). Here the Jew is on the whole the traditional prototype of the eternal sufferer, bearing his punishment nobly and stoically, with little or no stress on divine malice (the alternative title, or subtitle, may have been added at the same time as the Preface). For S.'s other presentations, see W. H. Marshall, '*Queen Mab*: The Inconsistency of Ahasuerus', *MLN* lxxiv (May 1959) 397–400. S. probably first met the legend in ch. iv of M. G. Lewis's *The Monk* (1794), where the ghost of Beatrice de las Cisternas is exorcized by a majestic stranger whose black velvet fillet conceals a burning cross. S.'s plot involving the rescue of Rosa from investiture as a nun also derives from *The Monk*. But S. must already have seen the translation of C. F. D. Schubart's 'Der ewige Jude. Eine lyrische Rhapsodie' (1802), which in the notes to *Q Mab* he claimed (without identifying it) to have 'picked up, dirty and torn, in Lincoln's Inn Fields' (see page 395). What S. evidently 'picked up' was a copy of *La Belle Assemblée, or Bell's Court & Fashionable Magazine* VI No. xli (January 1809) 19–20, which carried a translation (by Peter Will) of Schubart's poem that S. undoubtedly knew in full because Hogg later printed the conclusion of it (which S. had suppressed) from S.'s papers (*Hogg* i 194–6; *SC* ii 650–1). S. must also have known Schubart's name, which could not have been torn away without mutilating a part of the text which he transcribed. In his notes to *Q Mab* S. prints part of this translation accurately; here he seems deliberately to have reworded it in order to disguise his indebtedness: his reference to 'the *style* of the German author' (S. knew no German in 1810) reveals this. No source other than Schubart for this prose note is known (or likely). A literal translation of 'Der ewige Jude' appears in *Fraser* IV (September 1831) 172–3.

The principal stylistic influences on this very sensational and repetitive poem are Scott, and especially Gray, whose habits of inversion are sometimes followed to extremes. Only the more significant echoes are noticed in the notes; and minor variants in punctuation between *ELJ* and *Fraser* are not recorded.

Southey's *Curse of Kehama*, soon to be a favourite poem, could not have influenced *WJ* as it was not published until 21 December 1810; but S. seems to have read Richard Cumberland's *Calvary; or, the Death of Christ* (1792; 7th edn 1810) and to have admired the spectacular Crucifixion episode, which is very similar to his own (see notes). Satan, expelled from earth by Christ, returns to Calvary with full accompaniments:

> And now the prostrate fiend
> Rear'd his terrific head with lightnings scorch'd
> And furrowed deep with scars of livid hue (vii 378–80)

Like the Wandering Jew's, his curse is an immortality of suffering, 'The whirlwind's blast / Had shatter'd his proud form; now scorch'd by fires, / Now driv'n to regions of perpetual frost' (vii 365–7); and he asks for Death 'that oblivious sleep for which I sigh' (vii 396), but the Almighty is relentless:

> Ask not repose of me,
> Tormented fiend: There is no grave for sin,
> No sleep for SATAN (vii 486–8)

Some specifi '' ·'· are recorded in the notes; and a general influence seems unmistakable.

Text from *ELJ*, supplemented by *Fraser*.

Published in *ELJ*, Nos. xxxiii (27 June) 43–5, xxxiv (4 July) 56–60, lix (26 December 1829) 425–6; *Fraser's Magazine for Town and Country* III, Nos. xvii (June) 529–36 (Introduction), xviii (July 1831) 666–77 (text); ed. B. Dobell (1887, based on *Fraser*); R. H. Shepherd, *Poetical Works of P. B. Shelley* (1888) i 35–79.

To Sir Francis Burdett, bart. M.P., in consideration of the active virtues by which both his public and private life is so eminently distinguished, the following poem is inscribed by the Author.

Preface

The subject of the following Poem is an imaginary personage, noted for the various and contradictory traditions which have prevailed concerning him–The Wandering Jew. Many sage monkish writers

¶ *11. Dedication.* Sir Francis Burdett (1770–1844), MP for Westminster from 1807, had introduced Reform proposals into the Commons on 15 June 1809 and was committed to the Tower on 9 April 1810 in connection with his protest over the Walcheren expedition. His infidelities gave his opponents an opening for attack, but S. disbelieved 'the story of his keeping *five* mistresses in Tottenham Court Road' (*L* i 245). His children helped him resist arrest, and he was said to have been translating Magna Carta with them when finally taken. His son Robert (b. 1796) was at Eton with S.

have supported the authenticity of this fact, the reality of his existence. But as the quoting them would have led me to annotations perfectly uninteresting, although very fashionable, I decline presenting to the public any thing but the bare poem, which they will agree with me not to be of sufficient consequence to authorise deep antiquarian researches on its subject. I might, indeed, have introduced, by anticipating future events, the no less grand, although equally groundless, superstitions of the battle of Armageddon, the personal reign of J————C————, &c.; but I preferred, improbable as the following tale may appear, retaining the old method of describing past events: it is certainly more consistent with reason, more interesting, even in works of imagination. With respect to the omission of elucidatory notes, I have followed the well-known maxim of 'Do unto others as thou wouldest they should do unto thee.'

January, 1811.

'If I will that he tarry till I come, what is that to thee? Follow thou me.'

St. John xxi. 22.

CANTO I

'Me miserable, which way shall I fly?
Infinite wrath and infinite despair—
Which way I fly is hell—myself am hell;
And in this lowest deep a lower deep,
To which the hell I suffer seems a heaven.'

Paradise Lost. [iv 73–8]

The brilliant orb of parting day
Diffused a rich and a mellow ray

Preface 3–4. The chief 'monkish writers' were Chrysostomus Dudulaeus, *Ahasver* (Leyden 1602; many edns), and Roger Wendover, *Chronica, sive Flores Historiarum* (*c.* 1235), then ascribed to Matthew Paris, to which S. could have found a reference in Percy's *Reliques of Ancient English Poetry* (1765) II, Bk iii, no. 3. (See *Roger of Wendover's Flowers of History*, transl. J. A. Giles (1849) ii 512–14).
Epigraph from St John. Omitted ELJ.
Canto I. 1. Echoes various lines, including Gray's *Elegy* 1; T. Warton's 'The Suicide. An Ode', 76–7: 'Sudden the half-sunk orb of day / More radiant shot its parting ray'; and Scott's *Lady of the Lake* (published early May 1810) I xi 1. Cp. *St Irvyne* ch. iv: 'the yellow beams of the sun, as his orb shed the parting glory on the verge of the horizon . . .'
2. *and a mellow*] and mellow *Fraser.*

Above the mountain's brow;
It tinged the hills with lustrous light,
5   It tinged the promontory's height
    Still sparkling with the snow;
And, as aslant it threw its beam,
Tipped with gold the mountain stream
    That laved the vale below.
10 Long hung the eye of glory there,
    And lingered as if loth to leave
A scene so lovely and so fair,
    'Twere there even luxury to grieve;
So soft the clime, so balm the air,
15   So pure and genial were the skies,
    In sooth 'twas almost Paradise, –
For ne'er did the sun's splendour close
On such a picture of repose; –
All, all was tranquil, all was still,
20 Save when the music of the rill,
    Or a distant waterfall,
At intervals broke on the ear,
Which Echo's self was pleased to hear,
    And ceased her babbling call.
25 With every charm the landscape glowed
Which partial Nature's hand bestowed;
Nor could the mimic hand of art
Such beauties or such hues impart.

Light clouds, in fleeting livery gay,
30 Hung painted in grotesque array
    Upon the western sky;
Forgetful of the approaching dawn,
The peasants danced upon the lawn,
    For the vintage time was nigh;
35 How jocund to the tabor's sound,
The smooth turf trembling as they bound,
In every measure light and free,
The very soul of harmony!
    Grace in each attitude, they move,
40   They thrill to amorous ecstasy,

---

13. 'Twere luxury even, there to grieve. *Fraser.*
14–18. Omitted Fraser.
20. when] Fraser; *where ELJ* (a probable misreading of S's hand).
23. pleased] charmed *Fraser.*
25–8. Omitted Fraser.
36. O'er the smooth, trembling turf they bound *Fraser.*

Light as the dew-drops of the morn
That hang upon the blossomed thorn,
    Subdued by the pow'r of resistless Love.

Ah! days of innocence, of joy,
45   Of rapture that knows no alloy,
Haste on, – ye roseate hours,
Free from the world's tumultuous cares,
From pale distrust, from hopes and fears,
Baneful concomitants of time, –
50   'Tis yours, beneath this favoured clime,
Your pathway strewn with flowers,
Upborne on pleasure's downy wing,
To quaff a long unfading spring,
And beat with light and careless step the ground;
55 The fairest flowers too soon grow sere,
Too soon shall tempests blast the year,
And sin's eternal winter reign around.

But see, what forms are those,
Scarce seen by glimpse of dim twilight,
60 Wandering o'er the mountain's height?
They swiftly haste to the vale below:
One wraps his mantle around his brow,
As if to hide his woes;
And as his steed impetuous flies,
65 What strange fire flashes from his eyes!
The far off city's murmuring sound
Was borne on the breeze which floated around;
Noble Padua's lofty spire
Scarce glowed with the sunbeam's latest fire,
70 Yet dashed the travellers on–
Ere night o'er the earth was spread,
Full many a mile they must have sped,
Ere their destined course was run.
Welcome was the moonbeam's ray,
75 Which slept upon the towers so grey.
But, hark! a convent's vesper bell–
It seemed to be a very spell–
The stranger checked his courser's rein,
And listened to the mournful sound:
80 Listened–and paused–and paused again:
A thrill of pity and of pain

44–57. *Omitted Fraser.*
58–59. *Omitted ELJ.*
64. *his steed*] S. seems to be the first to represent the Wandering Jew on
horseback.

Through his inmost soul had passed,
While gushed the tear-drops silently and fast.

A crowd was at the convent gate,
85   The gate was opened wide;
No longer on his steed he sate,
But mingled with the tide.
He felt a solemn awe and dread,
As ɪ⌐ the chapel enterèd;
90   Dim was the light from the pale moon beaming,
     As it fell on the saint-ciphered panes,
   Or, from the western window streaming,
     Tinged the pillars with varied stains.
   To the eye of enthusiasm strange forms were gliding,
95   In each dusky recess of the aisle,
   And indefined shades in succession were striding
     O'er the coigns of the pillared pile;–
   The pillars to the vaulted roof
     In airy lightness rose;
100 Now they mount to the rich Gothic ceiling aloof,
     And exquisite tracery disclose.

The altar illumined now darts its bright rays,
The train passed in brilliant array;
On the shrine Saint Pietro's rich ornaments blaze,
105 And rival the brilliance of day.
Hark!–now the loud organ swells full on the ear–
So sweetly mellow, chaste, and clear;
Melting, kindling, raising, firing,
Delighting now, and now inspiring,
110 Peal upon peal the music floats–

90–3. The ultimate source of Romantic imagery of light falling through Gothic
windows is Milton, *Il Penseroso* 155–60, but S.'s immediate sources seem to be
T. Warton, 'The Pleasures of Melancholy' (1747) 30–1: 'Where through some
western window the pale moon / Pours her long-levell'd rule of streaming
light', and Scott's *Lay of the Last Minstrel* (1805) II xi. See also Southey, *Joan of
Arc* (1796) iii 267–74. *saint-ciphered panes*] 'storied windows' depicting the lives
of saints.
97. *coigns*] '"Buttress nor coigne of 'vantage"–*Macbeth* [I vi 7]' (S.'s note).
pillared] gothic *Fraser*.
98–9. Cp. *Lay of the Last Minstrel* II ix 3–4: 'The darken'd roof rose high aloof /
On pillars lofty and light and small'.
102–49. *Omitted ELJ.*
108. Possibly recalling Pope's 'Dying Christian to his Soul' 3: 'Trembling,
hoping, ling'ring, flying' (an imitation of the Emperor Hadrian's address to his
dying soul).

Now they list still as death to the dying notes;
Whilst the soft voices of the choir,
Exalt the soul from base desire;
Till it mounts on unearthly pinions free,
115   Dissolved in heavenly ecstasy.

Now a dead stillness reigned around,
Uninterrupted by a sound;
Save when in deadened response ran
The last faint echoes down the aisle,
120   Reverberated through the pile,
As within the pale the holy man,
With voice devout and saintly look,
Slow chaunted from the sacred book,
Or pious prayers were duly said,
125   For spirits of departed dead.
With beads and crucifix and hood,
Close by his side the abbess stood;
Now her dark penetrating eyes
Were raised in suppliance to heaven,
130   And now her bosom heaved with sighs,
As if to human weakness given.
Her stern, severe, yet beauteous brow
Frowned on all who stood below;
And the fire which flashed from her steady gaze,
135   As it turned on the listening crowd its rays,
Superior virtue told, –
Virtue as pure as heaven's own dew,
But which, untainted, never knew
To pardon weaker mould.
140   The heart though chaste and cold as snow –
'Twere faulty to be virtuous so.

Not a whisper now breathed in the pillared aisle –
The stranger advanced to the altar high –
Convulsive was heard a smothered sigh!
145   Lo! four fair nuns to the altar draw near,
With solemn footstep, as the while
A fainting novice they bear –
The roses from her cheek are fled,
But there the lily reigns instead;
150   Light as a sylph's, her form confessed,

136–51. The prioress of St Clare in *The Monk* ch. i (like Ambrosio himself) is
similarly cold-hearted to the erring Agnes from excessive virtue.
150–61. *Omitted Fraser.*

Beneath the drapery of her vest,
   A perfect grace and symmetry;
Her eyes, with rapture formed to move,
To melt with tenderness and love,
155   Or beam with sensibility,
To Heaven were raised in pious prayer,
   A silent eloquence of woe;
Now hung the pearly tear-drop there,
Sate on her cheek a fixed despair;
160   And now she beat her bosom bare,
   As pure as driven snow.
Nine graceful Novices around
Fresh roses strewed upon the ground,
   In purest white arrayed;
165   Three spotless vestal virgins shed
Sabaean incense o'er the head
   Of the devoted maid.

They dragged her to the altar's pale,
The traveller leant against the rail,
170   And gazed with eager eye, –
His cheek was flushed with sudden glow,
On his brow sate a darker shade of woe,
As a transient expression fled by.

The sympathetic feeling flew
175   Through every breast, from man to man,
Confused and open clamours ran,
Louder and louder still they grew;
When the abbess waved her hand,
A stern resolve was in her eye,
180   And every wild tumultuous cry
Was stilled at her command.

The abbess made the well known sign–
The novice reached the fatal shrine,
And mercy implored from the power divine;
185   At length she shrieked aloud,
She dashed from the supporting nun,
Ere the fatal rite was done,
And plunged amid the crowd.

151. vest] vesture, garment.
165. Three] Nine Fraser.
166. Sabaean] Sabean ELJ (S.'s spelling is that of Paradise Lost iv 162 and of Thalaba XI viii 12). Saba, or Sheba, now in the Yemen, was famous for frankincense. Cp. Virgil, Aen. i 416–17: Sabaeo ture calent arae.
168–419. Omitted ELJ.

Confusion reigned throughout the throng,
190 Still the novice fled along,
Impelled by frantic fear,
When the maddened traveller's eager grasp
In firmest yet in wildest clasp
Arrested her career.
195 As fainting from terror she sank on the ground,
Her loosened locks floated her fine form around;
The zone which confined her shadowy vest
No longer her throbbing bosom pressed,
Its animation dead;
200 No more her feverish pulse beat high,
Expression dwelt not in her eye,
Her wildered senses fled.

        *   *   *   *   *

Hark! hark! the demon of the storm!
I see his vast expanding form
205 Blend with the strange and sulphurous glare
Of comets through the turbid air.
Yes, 'twas his voice, I heard its roar,
The wild waves lashed the caverned shore
In angry murmurs hoarse and loud,
210 Higher and higher still they rise;
Red lightnings gleam from every cloud
And paint wild shapes upon the skies;
The echoing thunder rolls around,
Convulsed with earthquake rocks the ground.

215 The traveller yet undaunted stood,
He heeded not the roaring flood;
Yet Rosa slept, her bosom bare,
Her cheek was deadly pale,
The ringlets of her auburn hair
220 Streamed in a lengthened trail,
And motionless her seraph form;
Unheard, unheeded raved the storm.
Whilst, borne on the wing of the gale,
The harrowing shriek of the white sea mew
225 As o'er the midnight surge she flew;
The howlings of the squally blast
As o'er the beetling cliffs it passed;
Mingled with the peals on high,
That, swelling louder, echoed by,
230 Assailed the traveller's ear.
He heeded not the maddened storm
As it pelted against his lofty form,

He felt no awe, no fear.
In contrast, like the courser pale
235 That stalks along Death's pitchy vale
With silent, with gigantic tread,
Trampling the dying and the dead.

Rising from her death-like trance,
Fair Rosa met the stranger's glance;
240 She started from his chilling gaze,
Wild was it as the tempest's blaze,
It shot a lurid gleam of light,
A secret spell of sudden dread,
A mystic, strange, and harrowing fear,
245 As when the spirits of the dead
Dressed in ideal shapes appear,
And hideous glance on human sight–
Scarce could Rosa's frame sustain
The chill that pressed upon her brain.

250 Anon, that transient spell was o'er,
Dark clouds deform his brow no more,
But rapid fled away;
Sweet fascination dwelt around,
Mixed with a soft, a silver sound,
255 As soothing to the ravished ear
As what enthusiast lovers hear;
Which seems to steal along the sky,
When mountain mists are seen to fly,
Before the approach of day.
260 He seized on wondering Rosa's hand,
And, 'Ah!' cried he, 'be this the band
Shall join us, till this earthly frame
Sinks convulsed in bickering flame–

---

234. '"Behold a pale horse, and his name that sate upon him was Death, and Hell followed with him."–*Revelation*, vi. 8' (S.'s note).
261–3. The *ELJ* editor noted (*ELJ* 27 June 1829, 44): 'in illustration of something said by Paulo [in Canto i], Shelley quotes, in the margin, the following line from Aeschylus . . . "Ἐμοῦ Θανόντος γαῖα μιχθήτω πυρί"' ('When I am dead, let earth be consumed by fire': Nauck, *Tragicorum Graecorum Fragmenta* (Lipsiae 1856) Adesp. 430. Nero was supposed to have quoted this when Rome was burning). S. also echoes Gray's 'Descent of Odin' 93–4: 'Till wrap'd in flames, in ruin hurl'd, / Sinks the fabric of the world', which he recalls again in lines 298–9, 310–11, 862–3, 870–1. Another account of the *dies irae* that influenced S. was Scott, *Lay of the Last Minstrel* VI xxi. The conflagration of the world was a Stoic doctrine (e.g. Seneca, *Dialogues* VI xxvi 6).

When around the demons yell,
265 And drag the sinful wretch to hell,
Then, Rosa, will we part—
Then fate, and only fate's decree,
Shall tear thy lovely soul from me,
And rend thee from my heart.
270 Long has Paulo soug. ˙ in vain
A friend to share his gr. ˢ;—
Never will he seek again,
For the wretch has found re. ˙ef,
Till the Prince of Darkness bursts his chain,
275 Till death and desolation reign—
Rosa, wilt thou then be mine?
Ever, fairest, I am thine!'

He ceased, and on the howling blast,
Which wildly round the mountain passed,
280 Died his accents low;
Yet fiercely howled the midnight storm,
As Paulo bent his awful form,
And leaned his lofty brow.

ROSA
'Stranger, mystic stranger, rise;
285 Whence do these tumults fill the skies?
Who conveyed me, say, this night,
To this wild and cloud-capped height?
Who art thou? and why am I
Beneath Heaven's pitiless canopy?
290 For the wild winds roar around my head;
Lightnings redden the wave;—
Was it the power of the mighty dead,
Who live beneath the grave?
Or did the Abbess drag me here,
295 To make yon swelling surge my bier?'

PAULO
'Ah, lovely Rosa! cease thy fear,
It was thy friend who bore thee here—
I, thy friend, till this fabric of earth
Sinks in the chaos that gave it birth;
300 Till the meteor-bolt of the God above
Shall tear its victim from his love,—
That love which must unbroken last,
Till the hour of envious fate is passed;

277. *Ever, fairest,*] Ever fairest, *Fraser.*
301. i.e. 'shall tear Paulo from Rosa'.

Till the mighty basements of the sky
305 In bickering hell-flames heated fly:
E'en then will I sit on some rocky height,
Whilst around lower clouds of eternal night,
E'en then will I loved Rosa save
From the yawning abyss of the grave. –
310 Or, into the gulf impetuous hurled,
If sinks with its latest tenants the world,
Then will our souls in union fly
Throughout the wide and boundles sky:
Then, free from th'ills that envious fate
315 Has heaped upon our mortal state,
We'll taste etherial pleasure;
Such as none but thou canst give, –
Such as none but I receive,
And rapture without measure.'

320 As thus he spoke, a sudden blaze
Of pleasure mingled in his gaze:
Illumined by the dazzling light,
He glows with radiant lustre bright;
His features with new glory shine,
325 And sparkle as with beams divine.
'Strange, awful being,' Rosa said,
'Whence is this superhuman dread,
That harrows up my inmost frame?
Whence does this unknown tingling flame
330 Consume and penetrate my soul?
By turns with fear and love possessed,
Tumultuous thoughts swell high my breast;
A thousand wild emotions roll,
And mingle their resistless tide;
335 O'er these some magic arts preside;
As by the influence of a charm,
Lulled into rest my griefs subside,
And safe in thy protecting arm,
I feel no power can do me harm:
340 But the storm raves wildly o'er the sea,
Bear me away! I confide in thee!'

CANTO II

'I could a tale unfold, whose slightest word
Would harrow up thy soul, freeze thy young blood,
Make thy two eyes, like stars, start from their spheres;
Thy knotted and combined locks to part,

> *And each particular hair to stand on end,*
> *Like quills upon the fretful porcupine.'*
>
> *Hamlet* [i v 15–20]

  The horrors of the nightly blast,
  The lowering tempest clouds were past,
  Had sunk beneath the main;
345 Light baseless mists were all that fled
  Above the weary traveller's head,
  As he left the spacious plain.

  Fled were the vapours of the night,
  Faint streaks of rosy tinted light
350 Were painted on the matin grey;
  And as the sun began to rise,
  To pour his animating ray,
  Glowed with his fire the eastern skies,
  The distant rocks–the far-off bay,
355 The ocean's sweet and lovely blue,
  The mountain's variegated breast,
  Blushing with tender tints of dawn,
  Or with fantastic shadows dressed.
  The waving wood, the opening lawn,
360 Rose to existence, waked anew,
  In colours exquisite of hue,
  Their mingled charms Victorio viewed,
  And lost in admiration stood.

  From yesternight how changed the scene,
365 When howled the blast o'er the dark cliffs' side,
  And mingled with the maddened roar
  Of the wild surge that lashed the shore.
  To-day–scarce heard the whispering breeze,
  And still and motionless the seas
370 Scarce heard the murmuring of their tide;
  All, all is peaceful and serene,
  Serenely on Victorio's breast
  It breathed a soft and tranquil rest,
  Which bade each wild emotion cease,
375 And hushed the passions into peace.

Canto II. 342. nightly] *Julian*; mighty *Dobell*. Cp. 'Ghasta' 194.
348–64. The first of S.'s addresses to the morning sun, culminating in *TL* 1–32.
362. C. Small (*Ariel Like a Harpy* (1972) 101) notes that '"Victory" is a word that occurs with striking frequency in [S.'s] poetry', citing 'Fitzvictor', *Victor & Cazire*, 'Victoria' (in *St Irvyne*), 'Victorio'.
369–70. An absolute construction: 'The seas being still, their murmur was scarcely heard'.

Along the winding Po he went,
His footsteps to the spot were bent
Where Paulo dwelt, his wandered friend,
For thither did his wishes tend.
380 Noble Victorio's race was proud,
From Cosmo's blood he came;
To him a wild untutored crowd
Of vassals in allegiance bowed,
Illustrious was his name;
385 Yet vassals and wealth he scorned, to go
Unnoticed with a man of woe:
Gay hope and expectation sate
Throned in his eager eye,
And ere he reached the castle gate,
390 The sun had mounted high.

Wild was the spot where the castle stood,
Its towers embosomed deep in wood,
Gigantic cliffs, with craggy steeps,
Reared their proud heads on high,
395 Their bases were washed by the foaming deeps,
Their summits were hid in the sky;
From the valley below they excluded the day,
That valley ne'er cheered by the sunbeam's ray;
Nought broke on the silence drear,
400 Save the hungry vultures darting by,
Or eagles yelling fearfully,
As they bore to the rocks their prey,
Or when the fell wolf ravening prowled,
Or the gaunt wild boar fiercely howled
405 His hideous screams on the night's dull ear.

Borne on pleasure's downy wing,
Downy as the breath of spring,
Not thus fled Paulo's hours away,
Though brightened by the cheerful day:
410 Friendship or wine, or softer love,
The sparkling eye, the foaming bowl,
Could with no lasting rapture move,
Nor still the tumults of his soul.
And yet there was in Rosa's kiss
415 A momentary thrill of bliss;
Oft the dark clouds of grief would fly,
Beneath the beam of sympathy;

381. *Cosmo's blood*] Doubtless that of Cosimo dei Medici, who ruled Florence in the 14th century. S. may have derived the name from Gr. κόσμος, 'order'.

And love and converse sweet bestow,
A transient requiem from woe. –

420 Strange business, and of import vast,
On things which long ago were past,
　　Drew Paulo oft from home;
Then would a darker, deeper shade,
By sorrow traced, his brow o'erspread
425 　　And o'er his features roam.
Oft as they spent the midnight hour,
　　And heard the wintry wild winds rave
　　Midst the roar and spray of the dashing wave,
Was Paulo's dark brow seen to lour.
430 Then, as the lamp's uncertain blaze
Shed o'er the hall its partial rays,
And shadows strange were seen to fall,
And glide upon the dusky wall,
Would Paulo start with sudden fear.
435 Why then unbidden gushed the tear,
As he muttered strange words to the ear? –
Why frequent heaved the smothered sigh? –
Why did he gaze on vacancy,
As if some strange form was near?
440 Then would the fillet of his brow
Fierce as a fiery furnace glow,
As it burned with red and lambent flame;
Then would cold shuddering seize his frame,
As gasping he laboured for breath.
445 The strange light of his gorgon eye,
As, frenzied and rolling dreadfully,
　　It glared with terrific gleam,
Would chill like the spectre gaze of death,
　　As, conjured by feverish dream,

---

419. *requiem*] 'rest' (a recognized meaning, from Lat. *requies*).
443–51. These lines (preceded by line 435) appear thus as the epigraph to ch. viii
of *St Irvyne*:

> Then would cold shudderings seize his brain,
> 　　As gasping he labour'd for breath;
> The strange gaze of his meteor eye,
> Which, frenzied, and rolling dreadfully,
> 　　Glar'd with hideous gleam,
> Would chill like the spectre gaze of Death,
> 　　As, conjur'd by feverish dream, 　·
> He seems o'er the sick man's couch to stand,
> 　　And shakes the fell lance in his skeleton hand.

450 He seems o'er the sick man's couch to stand,
And shakes the dread lance in his skeleton hand.

But when the paroxysm was o'er,
And clouds deformed his brow no more,
Would Rosa soothe his tumults dire,
455   Would bid him calm his grief,
Would quench reflection's rising fire,
    And give his soul relief.
As on his form with pitying eye,
    The ministering angel hung,
460 And wiped the drops of agony,
    The music of her siren tongue
Lulled forcibly his griefs to rest.
Like fleeting visions of the dead,
Or midnight dreams, his sorrows fled:
465 Waked to new life, through all his soul
A soft delicious languor stole,
And lapped in heavenly ecstasy
    · He sank and fainted on her breast.

'Twas on an eve, the leaf was sere,
470 Howled the blast round the castle drear,
The boding night-bird's hideous cry
Was mingled with the warning sky;
Heard was the distant torrent's dash,
Seen was the lightning's dark red flash,
475   As it gleamed on the stormy cloud;
Heard was the troubled ocean's roar,
As its wild waves lashed the rocky shore;
    The thunder muttered loud,
As wilder still the lightnings flew;
480 Wilder as the tempest blew,
More wildly strange their converse grew.

They talked of the ghosts of the mighty dead,
If, when the spark of life were fled,
    They visited this world of woe?
485 Or, were it but a fantasy,
Deceptive to the feverish eye,
When strange forms flashed upon the sight,
And stalked along at the dead of night?
    Or if, in the realms above,

482. *ghosts of the mighty dead*] See 'Ghosts of the Dead!' 1–2 and note; 'Despair'
7–9 and note, 19. Here S. may be echoing James Montgomery's 'Ode to the
Volunteers of Britain on the Prospect of Invasion' (published 1806) 37–8:
'Ghosts of the mighty dead, / Your children's hearts inspire' etc.

490 They still, for mortals left below,
Retained the same affection's glow,
   In friendship or in love?—
Debating thus, a pensive train,
   Thought upon thought began to rise;
495 Her thrilling wild harp Rosa took;
What sounds in softest murmurs broke
   From the seraphic strings!
Celestials borne on odorous wings
   Caught the dulcet melodies,
500 The life-blood ebbed in every vein,
As Paulo listened to the strain.

SONG.

'What sounds are those that float upon the air,
   As if to bid the fading day farewell,—
What form is that so shadowy, yet so fair,
505 Which glides along the rough and pathless dell?

'Nightly those sounds swell full upon the breeze,
   Which seems to sigh as if in sympathy;
They hang amid yon cliff-embosomed trees,
   Or float in dying cadence through the sky.

510 'Now rests that form upon the moonbeam pale,
   In piteous strains of woe its vesper sings;
Now—now it traverses the silent vale,
   Borne on transparent ether's viewless wings.

'Oft will it rest beside yon Abbey's tower,
515   Which lifts its ivy-mantled mass so high;
Rears its dark head to meet the storms that lour,
   And braves the trackless tempests of the sky.

'That form, the embodied spirit of a maid,
   Forced by a perjured lover to the grave;
520 A desperate fate the maddened girl obeyed,
   And from the dark cliff plunged into the wave.

'There the deep murmurs of the restless surge,
   The mournful shriekings of the white sea-mew,
The warring waves, the wild winds, sang her dirge,
525   And o'er her bones the dark red coral grew.

'Yet though that form be sunk beneath the main,
   Still rests her spirit where it vows were given;

510. i.e. 'Now the pale moonbeam rests upon that form' (with three inversions).

Still fondly visits each loved spot again,
        And pours its sorrows on the ear of Heaven.

530 'That spectre wanders through the Abbey dale,
        And suffers pangs which such a fate must share;
    Early her soul sank in death's darkened vale,
        And ere long all of us must meet her there.'

    She ceased, and on the listening ear
535 Her pensive accents died;
    So sad they were, so softly clear,
    It seemed as if some angel's sigh
    Had breathed the plaintive symphony;
    So ravishingly sweet their close,
540 The tones awakened Paulo's woes;
    Oppressive recollections rose,
    And poured their bitter tide.

    Absorbed awhile in grief he stood;
    At length he seemed as one inspired,
545 His burning fillet blazed with blood—
    A lambent flame his features fired.
    'The hour is come, the fated hour;
    Whence is this new, this unfelt power?—
    Yes, I've a secret to unfold,
550 And such a tale as ne'er was told,
    A dreadful, dreadful mystery!
    Scenes, at whose retrospect e'en now,
    Cold drops of anguish on my brow,
    The icy chill of death I feel:
555 Wrap, Rosa, bride, thy breast in steel,
    Thy soul with nerves of iron brace,
    As to your eyes I darkly trace
    My sad, my cruel destiny.

    'Victorio, lend your ears, arise,
560 Let us seek the battling skies,

534–76. *Omitted ELJ.*
537–8. According to Medwin (*Medwin (1913)* 40) these were pronounced by
Campbell, to whom S. had sent the MS, to be 'the only two good lines in it'.
Campbell, an admirer of Smollett, no doubt recognized the echo from *The
Adventures of Ferdinand Count Fathom* (1752) ch. xxxiv, in which the music of an
Aeolian harp 'gradually decayed upon the ear, until it died away in distant
sound, as if a flight of angels had raised the song in their ascent to heaven'. Cp.
Ann Radcliffe, *Mysteries of Udolpho* (1794) I ix: 'music yet came to her ear in
strains such as angels might breathe'.

With o'er our heads the thunder crashing,
And at our feet the wild waves dashing;
As tempest, clouds, and billows roll,
In gloomy concert with my soul.
565   Rosa, follow me—
For my soul is joined to thine,
And thy being's linked to mine—
Rosa, list to me.'

CANTO III

'His form had not yet lost
All its original brightness, nor appeared
Less than archangel ruined, and the excess
Of glory obscured; but his face
Deep scars of thunder had intrenched, and care
Sate on his faded cheek.'

Paradise Lost [i 591–4, 600–2]

PAULO

' 'Tis sixteen hundred years ago,
570   Since I came from Israel's land;
Sixteen hundred years of woe!—
With deep and furrowing hand,
God's mark is painted on my head;
Must there remain until the dead
575   Hear the last trump, and leave the tomb,
And earth spouts fire from her riven womb.

'How can I paint that dreadful day,
That time of terror and dismay,
When, for our sins, a Saviour died,
580   And the meek Lamb was crucified!
'Twas on that day, as borne along

561. *With*] Wild *Dobell.*
566–7. An echo of the refrain in *The Monk* ch. iv: 'Thou art mine! I am thine!'
Canto III. 577–799. Medwin (*Medwin (1913)* 40) pronounced the crucifixion
scene 'altogether a plagiarism from a volume of Cambridge Prize Poems', but
the influence of Thomas Zouch's *The Crucifixion* (1765), which must be the
poem meant, is imperceptible. However, Medwin may typically have confused Zouch's poem with Richard Cumberland's *Calvary; or, the Death of
Christ* (1792; 7th edn 1810) where the resemblances are much greater (see
headnote).
581. As dread that day, when borne along *Fraser.*
581–90. *as borne . . . I return again*] This episode derives from Roger of
Wendover's *Chronica, sive Flores Historiarum* (1640; then attrib. to Matthew
Paris), trans. J. A. Giles as *Flowers of History* (1849) ii 513: '. . . when therefore

To slaughter by the insulting throng,
Infuriate for Deicide,
I mocked our Saviour, and I cried,
585 "Go! go!" "Ah! I will go," said he,
"Where scenes of endless bliss invite,
To the blessed regions of the light;
I go—but thou shalt here remain,
    Nor see thy dying day
590 Till I return again."
E'en now, by horror traced, I see
His perforated feet and hands;
The maddened crowd around him stands,
Pierces his side the ruffian spear,
595 Big rolls the bitter anguished tear;
Hark that deep groan! He dies, he dies!
And breathes, in death's last agonies,
Forgiveness to his enemies!
Then was the noonday glory clouded,
600 The sun in pitchy darkness shrouded;
Then were strange forms through the darkness
                                    gleaming,
And the red orb of night on Jerusalem beaming,
Which faintly, with ensanguined light,
Dispersed the thickening shades of night;
605 Convulsed, all nature shook with fear,
As if the very end was near;
    Earth to her centre tremblèd;

the Jews were dragging Jesus forth, and had reached the door, Cartaphilus . . .
impiously struck him on his back with his hand, and said in mockery, "Go
quicker, Jesus, go quicker, why do you loiter?" And Jesus looking back on him
with a severe countenance said to him "I am going, and you will wait till I
return"'. The anecdote is re-told in Q *Mab* vii 176–83.
585. said he,] *Fraser*; he said *ELJ* (a rhyme is needed for *see* (591); perhaps a
printer's error).
589–90. Fraser condenses these lines into '*Thou diest not till I come again*' – (589).
599–600. Cp. *Calvary* (vi 662–4): 'Now darkness fell / On all the region round;
the shrouded sun / From the impen'tent earth withdrew his light'.
606–9. Fraser condenses these lines into:
            Earth trembled as if the end was near.
            Rent was the Temple's veil in twain–
            The graves gave up their dead again.
Cp *Calvary* (vi 683–5):
            The temple's sacred veil was rent in twain
            From top to bottom 'midst th'attesting shocks
            Of earthquake and the rending up of graves

Rent in twain was the temple's veil,
    The graves gave up their dead;
610 Whilst ghosts and spirits, ghastly pale,
    Glared hideous on the sight,
Seen through the dark and lurid air,
    As fiends arrayed in light
Threw on the scene a frightful glare,
615 And, howling, shrieked with hideous yell–
They shrieked in joy, for a Saviour fell!
'Twas then I felt the Almighty's ire;
    Then full on my remembrance came
Those words despised, alas! too late!
620 The horrors of my endless fate
    Flashed on my soul and shook my frame;
    They scorched my breast as with a flame
Of unextinguishable fire;
    An exquisitely torturing pain
625 Of frenzying anguish fired my brain.
By keen remorse and anguish driven,
I called for vengeance down from Heaven.
But, ah! the all-wasting hand of Time
Might never wear away my crime!
630 I scarce could draw my fluttering breath–
Was it the appalling grasp of death?
I lay entranced, and deemed he shed
His dews of poppy o'er my head;
But though the kindly warmth was dead,
635 The self-inflicted torturing pangs
    Of conscience lent their scorpion fangs,
Still life prolonging, after life was fled.

'Methought, what glories met my sight,
    As burst a sudden blaze of light,
640 Illumining the azure skies,
    I saw the blessed Saviour rise.

610–16. *Omitted Fraser. Cp. Calvary* (vii 441–6):
                  Now a troop
      Of shrowded ghosts upon a signal given
      By their terrific Monarch start to sight,
      Each with a torch funereal in his grasp,
      That o'er the hall diffus'd a dying light,
      Than darkness' self more horrible:
616. *fell!*] Vb. not adj. (in contrast with *Q Mab* 163–83).
618–25. *Fraser condenses into:*
      Those words flashed on my soul, my frame,
      Scorched breast and brain as with a flame
      Of unextinguished fire!
626–727. *Omitted ELJ.*

But how unlike to him who bled!
Where then his thorn-encircled head?
Where the big drops of agony
645 Which dimmed the lustre of his eye?
Or deathlike hue that overspread
The features of that heavenly face?
Gone now was every mortal trace;
His eyes with radiant lustre beamed—
650 His form confessed celestial grace,
And with a blaze of glory streamed.
Innumerable hosts around,
Their brows with wreaths immortal crowned,
With amaranthine chaplets bound,
655 As on their wings the cross they bore,
Deep dyed in the Redeemer's gore,
Attune their golden harps, and sing
Loud hallelujahs to their King.

'But, in an instant, from my sight,
660 Fled were the visions of delight.
Darkness had spread her raven pall;
Dank, lurid duskness covered all.
All was as silent as the dead;
I felt a petrifying dread,
665 Which harrowed up my frame;
When suddenly a lurid stream
Of dark red light, with hideous gleam,
Shot like a meteor through the night,
And painted Hell upon the skies—
670 The Hell from whence it came.
What clouds of sulphur seemed to rise!
What sounds were borne upon the air!
The breathings of intense despair—
The piteous shrieks—the wails of woe—
675 The screams of torment and of pain—

661–76. Cp. *Calvary* (vii 254–64):
> At farthest end
> Of that Obscure a pillary cloud arose
> Of sulph'rous smoke, that from hell's crater steam'd;
> Whence here and there by intermittent gleams
> Blue flashing fires burst forth, that sparkling blaz'd
> Up to the iron roof, whose echoing vault
> Resounded ever with the dolorous groans
> Of the sad crew beneath: Thence might be heard
> The wailing suicide's remorseful plaint;—
> The murd'rer's yelling scream, and the loud cry
> Of tyrants in that fiery furnace hurl'd

662. *duskness covered*] darkness cover'd *Dobell*.

The red–hot rack–the clanking chain!
I gazed upon the gulf below,
Till, fainting from excess of fear,
My tottering knees refused to bear
680   My odious weight. I sink–I sink!
Already had I reached the brink.
The fiery waves disparted wide,
To plunge me in their sulphurous tide;
When, racked by agonizing pain,
685   I started into life again.

'Yet still the impression left behind
Was deeply graven on my mind,
In characters whose inward trace
No change or time could e'er deface;
690   A burning cross illumed my brow,
I hid it with a fillet grey,
But could not hide the wasting woe
That wore my wildered soul away,
And ate my heart with living fire.
695   I knew it was the avenger's sway,
I felt it was the avenger's ire!

'A burden on the face of earth,
I cursed the mother who gave me birth;
I cursed myself–my native land.
700   Polluted by repeated crimes,
I sought in distant foreign climes
If change of country could bestow
A transient respite from my woe.
Vain from myself the attempt to fly,
705   Sole cause of my own misery.

'Since when, in deathlike trance I lay,
Passed, slowly passed, the years away
That poured a bitter stream on me,
When once I fondly longed to see
710   Jerusalem, alas! my native place.
Jerusalem, alas! no more in name,
No portion of her former fame
Had left behind a single trace.
Her pomp–her splendour–was no more.
715   Her towers no longer seem to rise,
To lift their proud heads to the skies.
Fane and monumental bust,
Long levelled even with the dust.

690–1. The burning cross derives from *The Monk* ch. iv, where 'a band of black velvet' hides the 'burning cross impressed upon his brow'.

The holy pavements were stained with gore.
720 The place where the sacred temple stood
Was crimson-dyed with Jewish blood.
Long since, my parents had been dead,
All my posterity had bled.
Beneath the dark Crusader's spear,
725 No friend was left my path to cheer,
To shed a few lasting setting rays
Of sunshine on my evening days!

'Racked by the tortures of the mind,
    How have I longed to plunge beneath
730   The mansions of repelling death!
And strove that resting place to find
    Where earthly sorrows cease.
Oft, when the tempest-fiends engaged,
And the warring winds tumultuous raged,
735   Confounding skies with seas,
Then would I rush to the towering height
    Of the gigantic Teneriffe,
    Or some precipitous cliff,
All in the dead of the silent night.

740 'I have cast myself from the mountain's height,
Above was day—below was night;
The substantial clouds that lowered beneath
    Bore my detested form;
They whirled it above the volcanic breath,
745   And the meteors of the storm;
The torrents of electric flame
Scorched to a cinder my fated frame.
Hark to the thunder's awful crash—
    Hark to the midnight lightning's hiss!
750 At length was heard a sullen dash,
Which made the hollow rocks around
Rebellow to the awful sound;

728. *Omitted Fraser.*
731. *Omitted Fraser.*
733-5. *Omitted Fraser.*
736. *Then would I rush*] Oft have I rushed *Fraser.*
739-40.   All in the dead of the stormy night,
                And flung me to the seas. *Fraser (without break)*
740-1. *Omitted Fraser.*
746-7. *Omitted Fraser* (perhaps rightly, as they reappear, better integrated, in 767, 772).
751-2. Cp. Gray, 'Progress of Poesy' 12: 'The rocks, and nodding groves rebellow to the roar'.

The yawning ocean opening wide
        Received me in its vast abyss,
755   And whelmed me in its foaming tide.
        Though my astounded senses fled,
        Yet did the spark of life remain;
        Then the wild surges of the main
        Dashed and left me on the rocky shore.
760   Oh! would that I had waked no more!
        Vain wish! I lived again to feel
        Torments more fierce than those of hell!
        A tide of keener pain to roll,
        And the bruises to enter my inmost soul!

765   'I cast myself in Etna's womb,
        If haply I might meet my doom

756–60. For these lines *Fraser* gives:
              My astounded senses fled!
              Oh—would that I had waked no more,
              But the wild surge swept my corpse ashore—
              I was not with the dead!

761–4. *Omitted Fraser.*

765. '"I cast myself from the overhanging summit of the gigantic Teneriffe
into the wide weltering ocean. The clouds which hung upon its base below,
bore up my odious weight; the foaming billows, swoln by the fury of the
northern blast, opened to receive me, and, burying in a vast abyss, at length
dashed my almost inanimate frame against the crags. The bruises entered into
my soul, but I awoke to life and all its torments. I precipitated myself into the
crater of Vesuvius, the bickering flames and melted lava vomited me up again
and though I felt the tortures of the damned, though the sulphureous bitumen
scorched the blood within my veins, parched up my flesh, and burnt it to a
cinder, still did I live to drag the galling chain of existence on. Repeatedly have
I exposed myself to the tempestuous battling of the elements; the clouds which
burst upon my head in crash terrific and exterminating, and the flaming
thunderbolt hurled headlong on me its victim, stunned but not destroyed me.
The lightning, in bickering coruscation, blasted me; and like the scathed oak,
which remains a monument of faded grandeur, and outlives the other
monarchs of the forest, doomed me to live for ever. Nine times did this dagger
enter into my heart—the ensanguined tide of existence followed the repeated
plunge; at each stroke, unutterable anguish seized my frame, and every limb
was convulsed by the pangs of approaching dissolution. The wounds still
closed, and still I breathe the hated breath of life." I have endeavoured to
deviate as little as possible from the extreme sublimity of idea which the *style* of
the German author, of which this is a translation, so forcibly impresses.' (S.'s
note.) The vocabulary indicates S. as the author of this 'translation', while the
content clearly derives mainly from Schubart's poem 'Der Ewige Jude',
although disguised (Vesuvius for Etna, etc.). The reference to 'the German
author' shows that S. knew its source all along. For comparison and details see

In torrents of electric flame;
Thrice happy had I found a grave
Mid fierce combustion's tumults dire,
770 Mid oceans of volcanic fire,
Which whirled me in their sulphurous wave,
    And scorched to a cinder my hated frame,
Parched up the blood within my veins,
And racked my breast with damning pains;
775 Then hurled me from the mountain's entrails dread.
With what unutterable woe
Even now I feel this bosom glow –
I burn – I melt with fervent heat –
Again life's pulses wildly beat –
780 What endless throbbing pangs I live to feel!
The elements respect their Maker's seal, –
That seal deep printed on my fated head.

'Still like the scathèd pine-tree's height,
Braving the tempests of the night
785   Have I 'scaped the bickering fire.
Like the scathed pine which a monument stands
Of faded grandeur, which the brands
    Of the tempest-shaken air
Have riven on the desolate heath,
790 Yet it stands majestic even in death,
    And rears its wild form there.
Thus have I 'scaped the ocean's roar,
The red-hot bolt from God's right hand,
The flaming midnight meteor brand,
795   And Etna's flames of bickering fire.
Thus am I doomed by fate to stand,
    A monument of the Eternal's ire;
Nor can this being pass away,
Till time shall be no more.

800 'I pierce with intellectual eye
Into each hidden mystery;

S.'s note to Q *Mab* vii 67, and editorial note. *scathed oak*] *conj.*; scattered oak
ELJ, Fraser.
781, 783–91. These lines were used as epigraph to ch. x in *St Irvyne*, unaltered
except that *scath'd* shows the corresponding word in line 786 to be unaccented.
786–9. Like the scathed pine . . . desolate heath] S.'s model was Satan's host in
Paradise Lost (i 612–15): 'As when Heaven's Fire / Hath scath'd the Forrest
Oaks, or Mountain Pines, / With singed top their stately growth though bare /
Stands on the blasted Heath'.
800–39. Omitted ELJ.

I penetrate the fertile womb
Of nature; I produce to light
The secrets of the teeming earth,
805   And give air's unseen embryos birth:
The past, the present, and to come,
Float in review before my sight:
To me is known the magic spell
To summon e'en the Prince of Hell;
810   Awed by the Cross upon my head,
His fiends would obey my mandates dread,
To twilight change the blaze of noon,
And stain with spots of blood the moon,
But that an interposing hand
815   Restrains my potent arts, my else supreme command.'

He raised his passion-quivering hand,
He loosed the grey encircling band,
A burning cross was there;
Its colour was like to recent blood,
820   Deep marked upon his brow it stood,
And spread a lambent glare.
Dimmer grew the taper's blaze,
Dazzled by the brighter rays,
Whilst Paulo spoke—'twas dead of night—
825   Fair Rosa shuddered with affright;
Victorio, fearless, had braved death
Upon the blood-besprinkled heath;
Had heard, unmoved, the cannon's roar,
Echoing along the Volga's shore,
830   When the thunder of battle was swelling,
When the birds for their dead prey were yelling,
When the ensigns of slaughter were streaming,
And falchions and bayonets were gleaming,
And almost felt death's chilling hand,
835   Stretched on ensanguined Volga's strand;
And, careless, scorned for life to cry.
Yet now he turned aside his eye,
Scarce could his death-like terror bear,
And owned now what it was to fear.

840   'Once a funeral met my aching sight,
It blasted my eyes at the dead of night,

---

813. *moon,*] moon. *Fraser*; moon— *Dobell*.
829. *the Volga's shore*] Perhaps Victorio had fought on the Volga in the peasant
war of 1773–5. *shore,*] shore. *Fraser, Dobell*.

When the sightless fiends of the tempest rave,
And hell-birds howl o'er the storm-blackened wave.
Nought was seen, save at fits, but the meteor's glare,
845 And the lightnings of God painting hell on the air;
Nought was heard save the thunder's wild voice in the
                                                    sky,
And strange birds who, shrieking, fled dismally by.
'Twas then from my head my drenched hair that I tore,
And bid my vain dagger's point drink my life's gore;
850 'Twas then I fell on the ensanguined earth,
And cursed the mother who gave me birth!
My maddened brain could bear no more—
Hark! the chilling whirlwind's roar;
The spirits of the tombless dead
855 Flit around my fated head, –
Howl horror and destruction round,
As they quaff my blood that stains the ground,
And shriek amid their deadly stave, –
'Never shalt thou find the grave!
860 Ever shall thy fated soul
In life's protracted torments roll,
Till, in latest ruin hurled,
And fate's destruction, sinks the world!
Till the dead arise from the yawning ground,
865   To meet their Maker's last decree,
Till angels of vengeance flit around,
  And loud yelling demons seize on thee!'

'Ah! would were come that fated hour,
When the clouds of Chaos around shall lower;
870 When this globe calcined by the fury of God
Shall sink beneath his wrathful nod!'

As thus he spake, a wilder gaze
Of fiend-like horror lit his eye
With a most unearthly blaze,
875 As if some phantom-form passed by.
At last he stilled the maddening wail
Of grief, and thus pursued his tale:–

'Oft I invoke the fiends of hell,
And summon each in dire array–

868–917. *Omitted ELJ.*
878–91. The Jew's manipulation of the Powers of Darkness is not traditional
but derives from *The Monk* ch. iv, in which the spectre is subdued by a
combination of Christian exorcism and black art. 'Ghasta' uses the same
formula. S. himself dabbled in magic art at this time (see *White* i 40–1).

880   I know they dare not disobey
       My stern, my powerful spell.
       —Once on a night, when not a breeze
       Ruffled the surface of the seas,
       The elements were lulled to rest,
885   And all was calm, save my sad breast,
       On Death resolved—intent,
       I marked a circle round my form;
       About me sacred relics spread,
       The relics of magicians dead,
890   And potent incantations read—
       I waited their event.

       'All at once grew dark the night,
       Mists of swarthiness hung o'er the pale moonlight.
       Strange yells were heard, the boding cry
895   Of the night raven that flitted by,
       Whilst the silver wingèd mew
       Startled with screams o'er the dark wave flew.
       'Twas then I seized a magic wand,
       The wand by an enchanter given,
900   And deep dyed in his heart's red blood.
       The crashing thunder pealed aloud;
       I saw the portentous meteor's glare,
       And the lightning's gleam o'er the lurid air;
       I raised the wand in my trembling hand,
905   And pointed Hell's mark at the zenith of Heaven.

       'A superhuman sound
       Broke faintly on the listening ear,
       Like to a silver harp the notes,
       And yet they were more soft and clear.
910   I wildly strained my eyes around—
       Again the unknown music floats.
       Still stood Hell's mark above my head—
       In wildest accents I summoned the dead—
       And through the insubstantial night,
915   It diffused a strange and fiendish light;
       Spread its rays to the charnel-house air,
       And marked mystic forms on the dark vapours there.
       The winds had ceased—a thick dark smoke
       From beneath the pavement broke;
920   Around ambrosial perfumes breathe
       A fragrance, grateful to the sense,
       And bliss, past utterance, dispense.

914. *insubstantial*] unsubstantial *Dobell*.

The heavy mists encircling, wreathe,
Disperse, and gradually unfold
925   A youthful female form;–she rode
  Upon a rosy-tinted cloud;
Bright streamed her flowing locks of gold;
She shone with radiant lustre bright,
And blazed with strange and dazzling light;
930 A diamond coronet decked her brow,
Bloomed on her cheek a vermeil glow;
  The terrors of her fiery eye
  Poured forth insufferable day,
And shed a wildly lurid ray.
935 A smile upon her features played,
  But there, too, sate portrayed
The inventive malice of a soul
Where wild demoniac passions roll;
Despair and torment on her brow
940 Had marked a melancholy woe
  In dark and deepened shade.
Under those hypocritic smiles,
Deceitful as the serpent's wiles,
  Her hate and malice were concealed;
945 Whilst on her guilt-confessing face,
Conscience, the strongly printed trace
  Of agony betrayed,
And all the fallen angel stood revealed.
She held a poniard in her hand,
950 The point was tinged by the lightning's brand;
In her left a scroll she bore,
Crimsoned deep with human gore;
And, as above my head she stood,
Bade me smear it with my blood.
955   She said, that then it was my doom
That every earthly pang should cease;
The evening of my mortal woe
  Would close beneath the yawning tomb;
And, lulled into the arms of death,
960 I should resign my labouring breath;
And in the sightless realms below
Enjoy an endless reign of peace.

---

923. The heavy mists encircling wreath *ELJ, Fraser.*
932. Indented in *ELJ,* but no rhyme is provided for *eye.*
946–7. An inversion, i e 'the marks of agony indicated conscience'.
955. then] *ELJ, Fraser;* when *Dobell.* The witch is offering immediate death in return for the Jew's soul.

She ceased—oh, God, I thank thy grace,
Which bade me spurn the deadly scroll;
965   Uncertain for a while I stood—
The dagger's point was in my blood.
    Even now I bleed!—I bleed!
When suddenly what horrors flew,
Quick as the lightnings through my frame;
970   Flashed on my mind the infernal deed,
The deed which would condemn my soul
To torments of eternal flame.
Drops colder than the cavern dew
Quick coursed each other down my face,
975   I laboured for my breath;
At length I cried, 'Avaunt! thou fiend of Hell,
    Avaunt! thou minister of death!'
I cast the volume on the ground,
Loud shrieked the fiend with piercing yell,
980   And more than mortal laughter pealed around.
The scattered fragments of the storm
Floated along the Demon's form,
Dilating till it touched the sky;
The clouds that rolled athwart his eye,
985   Revealed by its terrific ray,
Brilliant as the noontide day,
    Gleamed with a lurid fire;
Red lightnings darted around his head,
Thunders hoarse as the groans of the dead
990   Pronounced their Maker's ire;
A whirlwind rushed impetuous by,
Chaos of horror filled the sky;
I sunk convulsed with awe and dread.
When I waked the storm was fled,
995   But sounds unholy met my ear,
And fiends of hell were flitting near.

'Here let me pause—here end my tale,
My mental powers begin to fail;
At this short retrospect I faint:
1000   Scarce beats my pulse—I lose my breath,
I sicken even unto death.
Oh! hard would be the task to paint
And gift with life past scenes again;
To knit a long and linkless chain,
1005   Or strive minutely to relate
The varied horrors of my fate.

997–1023. *Omitted ELJ.*

Rosa! I could a tale disclose,
So full of horror—full of woes,
Such as might blast a demon's ear,
1010   Such as a fiend might shrink to hear—
But, no.'—

Here ceased the tale. Convulsed with fear,
The tale yet lived in Rosa's ear—
She felt a strange mysterious dread,
1015   A chilling awe as of the dead;
Gleamed on her sight the demon's form.
Heard she the fury of the storm?
The cries and hideous yells of death?
Tottered the ground her feet beneath?
1020   Was it the fiend before her stood?
Saw she the poniard drop with blood?
All seemed to her distempered eye
A true and sad reality.

★   ★   ★   ★   ★

CANTO IV

Οὗτοι, γυναῖκας, ἀλλὰ Γοργόνας λέγω·
οὐδ' αὖτε Γοργείοισιν εἰκάσω τύποις·
—— μέλαιναι δ'ἐς τὸ πᾶν βδελύκτροποι·
ῥέγκουσι, δ'οὐ πλαστοῖσι φυσιάμσιν·
εκ δ'ὀμμάτων λείβουσι δυσφιλῆ βίαν.
Aeschylus. Eumenides, v. 48.

'—— *What are ye*
So withered and so wild in your attire,
That look not like th'inhabitants of earth,
And yet are on't?—Live you, or are you aught
That man may question?'
Macbeth [I iii 39—43]

Ah! why does man, whom God has sent
1025   As the Creation's ornament,
Who stands amid his works confessed
The first—the noblest—and the best;
Whose vast—whose comprehensive eye
Is bounded only by the sky,

Canto IV. Epigraph. 'Not women, rather Gorgons I call them; yet I cannot
compare them to the shapes of Gorgons either (two lines omitted)—black,
utterly abominable. They blow with undisguised snortings; from their eyes
they pour out hateful power' (*The Furies*, lines 48–9, 52–4).

1030 O'erlook the charms which Nature yields,
      The garniture of woods and fields,
      The sun's all vivifying light,
      The glory of the moon by night,
      And to himself alone a foe,
1035 Forget from whom these blessings flow?
      And is there not in friendship's eye,
      Beaming with tender sympathy,
      An antidote to every woe,
      And cannot woman's love bestow
1040 An heav'nly paradise below?
      Such joys as these to man are given,
      And yet you dare to rail at Heaven,
      Vainly oppose the Almighty Cause,
      Transgress His universal laws,
1045 Forfeit the pleasures that await
      The virtuous in this mortal state,
      Question the goodness of the Power on high,
      In misery live, despairing die.
      What then is man, how few his days,
1050 And heightened by what transient rays,
      Made up of plans of happiness,
      Of visionary schemes of bliss,
      The varying passions of his mind
      Inconstant, varying as the wind,
1055 Now hushed to apathetic rest,
      Now tempested with storms his breast,
      Now with the fluctuating tide
      Sunk low in meanness, swoln with pride,
      Thoughtless, or overwhelmed with care,
1060 Hoping, or tortured by despair!

      The sun had sunk beneath the hill,
      Soft fell the dew, the scene was still;
      All nature hailed the evening's close.
      Far more did lovely Rosa bless
1065 The twilight of her happiness.
      Even Paulo blessed the tranquil hour
      As in the aromatic bower,
      Or wandering through the olive grove,
      He told his plaintive tale of love;
1070 But welcome to Victorio's soul
      Did the dark clouds of evening roll!

1051–2. *Omitted Fraser.*
1061–1108. *Omitted ELJ.*

But, ah! what means his hurried pace,
Those gestures strange, that varying face;
Now pale with mingled rage and ire,
1075   Now burning with intense desire;
That brow where brood the imps of care,
That fixed expression of despair,
That haste, that labouring for breath—
His soul is madly bent on death.
1080   A dark resolve is in his eye,
Victorio raves—I hear him cry,
'Rosa is Paulo's eternally.'

But whence is that soul-harrowing moan,
Deep drawn and half suppressed—
1085   A low and melancholy tone,
That rose upon the wind?
Victorio wildly gazed around,
He cast his eyes upon the ground,
He raised them to the spangled air,
1090   But all was still—was quiet there.
Hence, hence, this superstitious fear;
'Twas but the fever of his mind
That conjured the ideal sound
To his distempered ear.

1095   With rapid step, with frantic haste,
He scoured the long and dreary waste;
And now the gloomy cypress spread
Its darkened umbrage o'er his head;
The stately pines above him high,
1100   Lifted their tall heads to the sky;
Whilst o'er his form, the poisonous yew
And melancholy nightshade threw
Their baleful deadly dew.
At intervals the moon shone clear;
1105   Yet, passing o'er her disc, a cloud
Would now her silver beauty shroud.
The autumnal leaf was parched and sere;
It rustled like a step to fear.
The precipice's battled height
1110   Was dimly seen through the mists of night,
    As Victorio moved along.
At length he reached its summit dread,
The night-wind whistled round his head,
    A wild funereal song.
1115   A dying cadence swept around
    Upon the waste of air,

It scarcely might be called a sound,
  For stillness yet was there,
Save when the roar of the waters below
1120 Was wafted by fits to the mountain's brow.
Here for a while Victorio stood
Suspended o'er the yawning flood,
And gazed upon the gulf beneath.
No apprehension paled his cheek,
1125 No sighs from his torn bosom break,
  No terror dimmed his eye.
'Welcome, thrice welcome, friendly death,'
In desperate harrowing tone he cried,
'Receive me, ocean, to your breast,
1130 Hush this ungovernable tide,
  This troubled sea to rest.
Thus do I bury all my grief—
This plunge shall give my soul relief,
  This plunge into eternity!'
1135 I see him now about to spring
  Into the watery grave:
Hark! the death angel flaps his wing
  O'er the blackened wave.
Hark! the night-raven shrieks on high
1140 To the breeze which passes on;
Clouds o'ershade the moonlight sky—
  The deadly work is almost done—
When a soft and silver sound,
  Softer than the fairy song,
1145 Which floats at midnight hour along
The daisy-spangled ground,
  Was borne upon the wind's soft swell.
  Victorio started—'twas the knell
Of some departed soul;
1150 Now on the pinion of the blast,
  Which o'er the craggy mountain passed,
The lengthened murmurs roll—
  Till lost in ether, dies away
  The plaintive, melancholy lay.
1155 'Tis said congenial sounds have power
To dissipate the mists that lower

1122. o'er] Fraser, on ELJ.
1137–40. Apparently the source of the unascribed epigraph to ch. ii of St Irvyne:
'The fiends of fate are heard to rave, / And the death-angel flaps his broad wing
o'er the wave'. See 'Ghasta' 1–6 and note.

Upon the wretch's brow–
To still the maddening passions' war–
To calm the mind's impetuous jar–
1160   To turn the tide of woe.
Victorio shuddered with affright,
Swam o'er his eyes thick mists of night;
Even now he was about to sink
Into the ocean's yawning womb,
1165 But that the branches of an oak,
Which, riven by the lightning's stroke,
O'erhung the precipice's brink,
Preserved him from the billowy tomb;
Quick throbbed his pulse with feverish heat,
1170 He wildly started on his feet,
And rushed from the mountain's height.

The moon was down, but through the air
Wild meteors spread a transient glare;
Borne on the wing of the swelling gale,
1175 Above the dark and woody dale,
Thick clouds obscured the sky.
All was now wrapped in silence drear,
Not a whisper broke on the listening ear,
Not a murmur floated by.

1180 In thought's perplexing labyrinth lost
The trackless heath he swiftly crossed.
Ah! why did terror blanch his cheek?
Why did his tongue attempt to speak,
And fail in the essay?
1185 Through the dark midnight mists, an eye,
Flashing with crimson brilliancy,
Poured on his face its ray.
What sighs pollute the midnight air?
What mean those breathings of despair?
1190 Thus asked a voice, whose hollow tone
Might seem but one funereal moan.
Victorio groaned, with faltering breath,
'I burn with love, I pant for death!'

Suddenly a meteor's glare
1195 With brilliant flash illumed the air;

1163–8. Cp. the doomed Lilla in Charlotte Dacre's *Zofloya* (1806) ch. xxix,
who 'caught frantic, for safety, at the scathed branches of a blasted oak, that,
bowed by repeated storms, hung almost perpendicularly over the yawning
depth beneath'.
1172–1293. *Omitted ELJ.*

Bursting through clouds of sulphurous smoke,
As on a Witch's form it broke;
Of herculean bulk her frame
Seemed blasted by the lightning's flame;
1200 Her eyes that flared with lurid light,
Were now with bloodshot lustre filled.
They blazed like comets through the night,
And now thick rheumy gore distilled;
Black as the raven's plume, her locks
1205 Loose streamed upon the pointed rocks,
Wild floated on the hollow gale,
Or swept the ground in matted trail;
Vile loathsome weeds, whose pitchy fold
Were blackened by the fire of Hell,
1210 Her shapeless limbs of giant mould
Scarce served to hide—as she the while
'Grinned horribly a ghastly smile'
And shrieked with demon yell.

Terror unmanned Victorio's mind,
1215 His limbs, like lime leaves in the wind,
Shook, and his brain in wild dismay
Swam—vainly he strove to turn away.
'Follow me to the mansions of rest,'
The weird female cried;
1220 The life-blood rushed through Victorio's breast
In full and swelling tide.
Attractive as the eagle's gaze,
And bright as the meridian blaze,
Led by a sanguine stream of light,
1225 He followed through the shades of night—
Before him his conductress fled,
As swift as the ghosts of the dead,
When on some dreadful errand they fly,
In a thunderblast sweeping the sky.

1230 They reached a rock whose beetling height
Was dimly seen through the clouds of night;

1197–1213, 1327–40. According to Medwin (*Medwin (1913)* 39) the portrait of
the Witch was 'almost versified from a passage in our *Nightmare*', a romance
written by S. and Medwin in alternate chapters in winter 1809. The romance (if
it ever existed) is lost.
1204–6. An echo of Gray's *Bard* 19–20: '(Loose his beard and hoary hair /
Streamed, like a meteor, to the troubled air)'.
1212. Misquoting Milton's *PL* ii 845–6: 'Death / Grinned horrible a ghastly
smile'.

Illumined by the meteor's blaze,
Its wild crags caught the reddened rays,
And their refracted brilliance threw
1235 Around a solitary yew,
Which stretched its blasted form on high,
Braving the tempests of the sky.
As glared the flame—a caverned cell,
More pitchy than the shades of hell,
1240 Lay open to Victorio's view.
Lost for an instant was his guide;
He rushed into the mountain's side.
At length with deep and harrowing yell
She bade him quickly speed,
1245 For that ere again had risen the moon
'Twas fated that there must be done
A strange—a deadly deed.

Swift as the wind Victorio sped;
Beneath him lay the mangled dead;
1250 Around dank putrefaction's power
Had caused a dim blue mist to lower.
Yet an unfixed, a wandering light
Dispersed the thickening shades of night;
Yet the weird female's features dire
1255 Gleamed through the lurid yellow air
With a deadly livid fire,
Whose wild, inconstant, dazzling light
Dispelled the tenfold shades of night,
Whilst her hideous fiendlike eye
1260 Fixed on her victim with horrid stare,
Flamed with more kindled radiancy;
More frightful far than that of Death,
When exulting he stalks o'er the battle heath;
Or of the dread prophetic form
1265 Who rides the curled clouds in the storm,
And borne upon the tempest's wings,
Death, despair, and horror brings.
Strange voices then and shrieks of death
Were borne along the trackless heath;
1270 Tottered the ground his steps beneath;
Rustled the blast o'er the dark cliff's side,
And their works unhallowed spirits plied,
As they shed their baneful breath.

1265. Ariel in *The Tempest* (I ii 191–2) came 'to ride / On the curled clouds'.

Yet Victorio hastened on—
1275   Soon the dire deed will be done.
'Mortal,' the female cried, 'this night
Shall dissipate thy woe;
And, ere return of morning light,
The clouds that shade thy brow
1280   Like fleeting summer mists shall fly
Before the sun that mounts on high.
I know the wishes of thy heart—
A soothing balm I could impart:
Rosa is Paulo's—can be thine,
1285   For the secret power is mine.'

VICTORIO

'Give me that secret power—Oh! give
To me fair Rosa—I will live
To bow to thy command.
Rosa but mine—and I will fly
1290   E'en to the regions of the sky,
Will traverse every land.'

WITCH

'Calm then those transports and attend,
Mortal, to one who is thy friend—
The charm begins.'
                              —An ancient book
1295   Of mystic characters she took;
Her loose locks floated on the air,
Her eyes were fixed in lifeless stare;
She traced a circle on the floor,
Around, dark chilling vapours lower;
1300   A golden cross on the pavement she threw;
'Twas tinged by a flame of lambent blue,
From which bright scintillations flew;—
By it she cursed her Saviour's soul!—
Then savage laughter round did roll,
1305   A hollow, wild, and frightful sound,
In air above, and under ground.

1299. *dark*] dank *Fraser.*
1301. *by*] with *Fraser.*
1304. Around strange fiendish laughs did roll, *Fraser.*
1306. At fits was heard to float around. *Fraser* (possibly a line omitted from *ELJ*).

She uttered then, in accents dread,
Some maddening rhyme that wakes the dead,
And forces every shivering fiend
1310   To her their demon-forms to bend.
At length a wild and piercing shriek,
As the dark mists disperse and break,
Announced the coming Prince of Hell!
But when his form obscured the cell,
1315   What words could paint, what tongue could tell,
    The terrors of his look!
The witch's heart, unused to shrink
Even at extremest danger's brink,
    With deadliest terror shook!
1320   And with their Prince were seen to rise
Spirits of every shape and hue, –
A hideous and infernal crew,
With hell-fires flashing from their eyes.
The cavern bellows with their cries,
1325   Which, echoing through a thousand caves,
Sound like as many tempest-waves.

Inspired and wrapped in bickering flame,
The strange and wild enchantress stood; –
Words unpremeditated came,
1330   In unintelligible flood,
From her black tumid lips – arrayed
In livid, fiendish smiles of joy –
Lips, which now dropped with deadly dew,
And now, extending wide, displayed
1335   Projecting teeth of mouldy blue.
As with a loud and piercing cry,
A mystic, harrowing lay she sang,
The rocks, as with a death-peal, rang,
And the dread accents, deep and drear,
1340   Struck terror on the dark night's ear!

1314–23. *Fraser* condenses these nine lines into six:
    His horrid form obscured the cell.
    Victorio shrunk, unused to shrink,
    E'en at extremest danger's brink;
    The witch then pointed to the ground,
    Infernal shadows flitted around,
    And with their prince were seen to rise,
1328. The strange, the awful being stood *Fraser*.
1335. *blue.*] hue, *Fraser*.
1338–40.   Along the rocks a death-peal rang.
    In accents hollow, deep and drear,
    They struck upon Victorio's ear. *Fraser*

As ceased the soul-appalling verse,
Obedient to its power, grew still
The hellish shrieks;–the mists disperse;–
Satan–a shapeless, hideous beast–
1345   In all his horrors stood confessed!
And as his vast proportions fill
The lofty cave, his features dire
Gleam with a pale and sulphurous fire;
From his fixed glance of deadly hate
1350   Even *she* shrunk back, appalled with dread–
For there contempt and malice sate,
And from his basiliskine eye
Sparks of living fury fly,
Which wanted but a being to strike dead.

1355   A wilder, a more awful spell
Now echoed through the long-drawn cell;
The demon bowed to its mandates dread.
'Receive this potent drug,' he cried,
'Whoever quaffs its fatal tide,
1360   Is mingled with the dead.'
Swept by a rushing sulphurous blast,
Which wildly through the cavern passed,
The fatal word was borne.
The cavern trembled with the sound,
1365   Trembled beneath his feet the ground;
With strong convulsions torn,
Victorio, shuddering, fell;
But soon awakening from his trance,
He cast around a fearful glance;
1370   Yet gloomy was the cell,
Save where a lamp's uncertain flare
Cast a flickering, dying glare.

WITCH

'Receive this dear-earned drug–its power
Thou, mortal, soon shalt know:
1375   This drug shall be thy nuptial dower,
This drug shall seal thy woe.

1341–54. *Omitted Fraser.*
1355–1425. *Omitted ELJ.*
1364.   "Death!
          Hell trembled at the hideous name and sighed
          From all its caves, and back resounded death."
                    –Paradise Lost [ii 787–9] (S.'s note).

Mingle it with Rosa's wine,
Victorio—Rosa then is thine.'

She spake, and, to confirm the spell,
1380 A strange and subterranean sound
Reverberated long around,
In dismal echoes—the dark cell
Rocked as in terror—through the sky
Hoarse thunders murmured awfully,
1385 And winged with horror, darkness spread
Her mantle o'er Victorio's head.
He gazed around with dizzy fear,
No fiend, no witch, no cave, was near;
But the blasts of the forest were heard to roar,
1390 The wild ocean's billows to dash on the shore.
The cold winds of Heaven struck chill on his frame,
For the cave had been heated by hell's blackening
                                        flame,
And his hand grasped a casket—the philtre was there!

★   ★   ★   ★   ★

Sweet is the whispering of the breeze
1395 Which scarcely sways yon summer trees;
Sweet is the pale moon's pearly beam,
Which sleeps upon the silver stream,
In slumber cold and still:
Sweet those wild notes of harmony,
1400 Which on the blast that passes by,
Are wafted from the hill:
So low, so thrilling, yet so clear,
Which strike enthusiast fancy's ear;
Which sweep along the moonlight sky,
1405 Like notes of heavenly symphony.

SONG

See yon opening flower
Spreads its fragrance to the blast;
It fades within an hour,
Its decay is pale, is fast.

1405. This line may have been followed by the 'pretty, affecting passage at the
end of the fourth canto', quoted in *Fraser's* Introduction (p. 536) but not
printed in the text:

'Tis mournful when the deadliest hate
Of friends, of fortune, and of fate
Is levelled at one fated head.

1410   Paler is yon maiden;
        Faster is her heart's decay;
        Deep with sorrow laden,
        She sinks in death away.

            ★   ★   ★   ★   ★

        'Tis the silent dead of night—
1415   Hark! hark! what shriek so low yet clear,
        Breaks on calm rapture's pensive ear,
        From Lara's castled height?
        'Twas Rosa's death-shriek fell!
        What sound is that which rides the blast,
1420   As onward its fainter murmurs passed?
        'Tis Rosa's funeral knell!
        What step is that the ground which shakes?
        'Tis the step of a wretch, nature shrinks from his tread;
        And beneath their tombs tremble the shuddering dead;
1425   And while he speaks the churchyard quakes.

                    PAULO

        'Lies she there for the worm to devour,
        Lies she there till the judgment hour,
        Is then my Rosa dead!
        False fiend! I curse thy futile power!
1430   O'er her form will lightnings flash,
        O'er her form will thunders crash,
        But harmless from my head
        Will the fierce tempest's fury fly,
        Rebounding to its native sky.—
1435   Who is the God of Mercy?—where
        Enthroned the power to save?
        Reigns he above the viewless air?
        Lives he beneath the grave?
        To him would I lift my suppliant moan,
1440   That power should hear my harrowing groan;—
        Is it then Christ's terrific Sire?
        Ah! I have felt his burning ire,
        I feel,—I feel it now,—
        His flaming mark is fixed on my head,
1445   And must there remain in traces dread;
        Wild anguish glooms my brow;

1417. *Lara's castled height*] Although the castle is in N. Italy, its name is apparently borrowed from the Castilian family concerned in the epic poems of the 'Cid'.

1436. *Enthroned*] Enthrones *Fraser*.

1443, 1446. These two lines are reversed in *Fraser*.

Oh! Griefs like mine that fiercely burn,
Where is the balm can heal!
Where is the monumental urn
1450 Can bid to dust this frame return,
Or quench the pangs I feel!'
As thus he spoke grew dark the sky,
Hoarse thunders murmured awfully,
'O Demon! I am thine!' he cried.
1455 A hollow fiendish voice replied,
'Come! for thy doom is misery.'

12 Olympia

Date of composition unknown, but probably c. April 1810. 'Olympia' is
eponymous with a character who makes a brief but violent appearance in ch. iv
of St Irvyne (written April–October 1810). Lady Olympia della Anzasca
develops a passion for Wolfstein, whose mistress Megalena demands her
murder; but Olympia commits suicide. The fragments were prefixed to chs. iv
and vii respectively of the romance (the chs. were contiguous, as no chs. were
numbered v or vi). The 'vengeance' of the first fragment must refer to
Megalena's. Ch. vii concerns Eloisa de St Irvyne's seduction by Nempere/
Ginotti, who is immortal and has sold his soul to Satan; Nempere (or his
Master) is presumably the 'fiend' of the second fragment, who fascinates Eloisa
and causes her remorse. Nothing more is known of a poem 'Olympia', and the
lines may have been purposely written as chapter-headings.
Text from St Irvyne, epigraphs to chs. iv and vii.
Previously uncollected.

——Nature shrinks back
Enhorrored from the lurid gaze of vengeance,
E'en in the deepest caverns, and the voice
Of all her works lies hushed.

     *   *   *   *   *

5 Yes! 'tis the influence of that sightless fiend
Who guides my every footstep, that I feel:
An iron grasp arrests each fluttering sense,
And a fell voice howls in mine anguished ear,
'Wretch, thou mayst rest no more.'

1447–51. Omitted Fraser.
¶ 12.2. Enhorror'd] Not in OED; but used in S.'s St Irvyne ch. i and a favourite
word in Charlotte Dacre's (Mrs Byrne's) prose and verse, e.g. in Zofloya ch.
xxxiii: 'his terrible eyes, from whose fiery glances Victoria turned enhorrored!'
5. sightless] invisible.
8. a fell voice] Like that which cried 'Macbeth shall sleep no more!' (Macbeth II ii
35–43).

13 The Revenge

Composed *c.* April 1810. The lines were included in a conspiratorial letter to Edward Fergus Graham dated 23 April in *L* i 9, and were prefixed to ch. ix of *St Irvyne*, that in which the innocent Eloisa is seduced by the satanic Nempere. Nothing is known of 'The Revenge', perhaps a title arbitrarily attached to a casual epigram.
Text from *St Irvyne*, epigraph to ch. ix.
Previously uncollected.

> If Satan had never fallen,
> Hell had been made for thee.

14 February 28th 1805: To St Irvyne

Following a speculation of Dowden's (*Dowden Life* i 48) that 'the title may refer to some incident of February in that year, which might be viewed as a starting-point in the course of [S.'s and Harriet Grove's] love', Cameron makes a good case (*Esd Nbk* 305–9) for dating this poem 1810. The most likely date is 24–25 Feb. The title-date cannot be that of composition: S. was then only twelve; and besides looking back to a love-episode in a previous August the poem echoes a line of Byron's published in 1807 (see note to line 1, below). But S. and Harriet G. were acquainted as children (*Medwin* i 66), and Harriet G.'s brother Charles remembered S.'s staying for the Easter holidays—which included part of February—at Fern near Shaftesbury, Wiltshire (the Groves's estate) in a year which may easily have been 1805 (*Hogg* ii 550). Moreover Harriet G. wrote in her diary on 28 February 1809 'sent my letter to [S.]', and on 1 March 'Received an immensely long letter from [S.]' (*SC* ii 514), which suggests an anniversary exchange (no earlier diary is extant to confirm this, and correspondence ceased from September 1809). There had been a high wind in the West Country on the night of 28 February 1805 (*GM* xxv (March 1805) 194), and it was 'stormy' throughout southern England on 24 and 25 February 1810, which could have prompted an 'anniversary' poem. There is some indication that Harriet G. had been to Field Place before her recorded visit in April 1810 (see her diary entries for 25 January and 4 August 1809, *SC* ii 511, 526); if so, the visit could plausibly have been in August 1808 (see note to No. 16) during S.'s Eton holidays. This poem, which is the last in *Esd*, is in the hand of Harriet S. who has written underneath it 'To H Grove'.
Text from *Esd* ff. 96ᵛ–97ʳ (*Esd* No. 58: quoted by permission of the Carl H. Pforzheimer Library).
Published in *Rogers* 38 (lines 17–20); *Esd Nbk* 171–2; *Esd Poems* 113; *SC* iv 1061–2 (transcript of *Esd*).

O'er thy turrets, St. Irvyne, the winter winds roar,
   The long grass of thy towers streams to the blast;
Must I never, St. Irvyne, then visit thee more?
   Are those visions of transient happiness past.

5   When with Harriet I sat on the mouldering height,
      When with Harriet I gazed on the star-spangled sky
   And the August moon shone through the dimness of
                            night?
   How swiftly the moment of pleasure fled by.

How swift is a fleeting smile chased by a sigh
10   This breast, this poor sorrow-torn breast must confess;
Oh Harriet, loved Harriet, though thou art not nigh
   Think not thy lover thinks of thee less.

How oft have we roamed, through the stillness of eve,
   Through St. Irvyne's old rooms that so fast fade away;
15   That those pleasure-winged moments were transient I
                            grieve,
   My soul like those turrets falls fast to decay.

My Harriet is fled like a fast-fading dream
   Which fades ere the vision is fixed on the mind,
But has left a firm love and a lasting esteem
20   That my soul to her soul must eternally bind.

¶ *14. Title.* The title and date are reversed in *Esd Nbk* and *Esd Poems.* 'St Irvyne'
was S.'s romantic name, presumably coined from that of its absentee owner
Lady Irvine (who preferred 'Irwin'), for Hills Place, a neglected 17th-century
mansion between Field Place and Horsham which had tall turret-like chimneys
(but no 'towers'). See illustrations in W. Albery, *A Parliamentary History of
Horsham 1295–1885* (1927) 39 and in *Esd Nbk* 201. Though a real house it is
semi-dramatized for poetic purposes, as it was to be for fictional purposes in
S.'s novel *St Irvyne* (1811).
1. Echoes the first line of Byron's 'On Leaving Newstead' in *Hours of Idleness*
(1807): 'Through thy battlements, Newstead, the hollow winds whistle'.
2. long grass] Hills Place became the Duke of Norfolk's property in December
1810, but it remained unoccupied, and was demolished in 1819. Cp. 'A
Summer Evening Churchyard' 11.
4. past] *Esd;* past– *Esd Nbk;* past? *Esd Poems.*
7. night?] night,– *Esd Poems.*
8. moment] moments *Esd Poems.*
9. sigh] *Esd;* sigh! *Esd Nbk.*
17–20. Echoing Cowper's 'Catharina' 5–8. 'Catharina has fled like a dream– /
(So vanishes pleasure, alas!) / But has left a regret and esteem, / That will not so
suddenly pass'.

When my mouldering bones lie in the cold chilling grave,
    When my last groans are borne o'er Strood's wide lea
And over my tomb the chill night tempests rave,
    Then, loved Harriet, bestow one poor thought on me.

15 Song

Dated 'April, 1810' in *V&C*; written on or immediately after 16–18 April when Harriet Grove was staying at Field Place, and connected with the poem following. Charles Grove recollected in 1857 (*Hogg* ii 550–1): 'Bysshe was at that time more attached to my sister Harriet than I can express, and I recollect well the moonlight walks we four had at Strode, and also at St. Irving's . . . (St. Irving's Hills, a beautiful place, on the right hand side as you go from Horsham to Field Place, laid out by the famous Capability Brown, and full of magnificent forest-trees, waterfalls, and rustic seats) . . . Bysshe was full of life and spirits, and very well pleased with his successful devotion to my sister' (the gloss in brackets was perhaps added by Hellen S.). Harriet G.'s diary for 17 April reads: '. . . Walked to Horsham saw the Old House St Irvyne   had a long conversation but more perplexed than ever   walked in the evening to Strood by moonlight' (*SC* ii 575). Harriet's perplexity may have been because it was probably her own father, not the Shelleys, who distrusted her intimacy with S. The poem is in the anapaestic measure of some of Cowper's best-known lyrics, e.g. 'The Poplar Field', 'Verses supposed to be written by Alexander Selkirk', and 'Catharina' I and II.
Text from *V&C* 17–18.
Published in *V&C*; *V&C (1898)* 17–18.

Come ——! sweet is the hour,
    Soft zephyrs breathe gently around,
The anemone's night-boding flower
    Has sunk its pale head on the ground.

5 'Tis thus the world's keenness hath torn
    Some mild heart that expands to its blast,
'Tis thus that the wretched forlorn
    Sinks poor and neglected at last. –

22. *Strood's wide lea*] Strood was the large estate adjoining Field Place to the NW and bordering the way to Warnham Church, where S.'s baby sister and other relatives were already buried.
¶ 15.3–4. *Anemone nemorosa*, the common white wood-anemone, closes its petals and droops its head in the evening.
6. *expands to its blast*] 'Pliny says [*Hist. Nat.* xxi sect. 165] this flower never opens its petals but when the wind blows; whence its name ["wind-flower"]' (E. Darwin, *Botanic Garden* (4th edn 1799) ii 41n.).

The world with its keenness and woe
10   Has no charms or attraction for me,
Its unkindness with grief has laid low
The heart which is faithful to thee.

The high trees that wave past the moon,
As I walk in their umbrage with you,
15 All declare I must part with you soon,
All bid you a tender adieu! –

Then ——! dearest, farewell,
You and I, love, may ne'er meet again;
These woods and these meadows can tell
20 How soft and how sweet was the strain. –

16 'How swiftly through Heaven's wide expanse'

Written immediately after Harriet Grove's visit to Field Place, 16–18 April 1810. The text below was included in a letter to Edward Fergus Graham (?1787–1852), who was a protégé of S.'s father, educated at the latter's expense and brought up at Field Place where he and S., according to a mutual friend, 'were like brothers' (*Dowden Life* i 52). G. was gifted musically and was a pupil of the German composer Woelff; his London apartment in 1810–11 was S.'s base whenever the latter was in town. See Nos. 56–7. S.'s letter, dated 22 April, begins: 'Enclosed I send you some lines which I can assure you are natural, & which I believe I owe you, as you wanted at Xmass to try your powers of composition with some Poetry of mine–' (*Pierpont Morgan Library MS*). Until very recently this, the only extant MS of the letter, was considered a forgery (see *L* i 8–9) because of its apparently irreconcilable differences from Forman's version (*Medwin (1913)* 452–4) of the original letter auctioned in 1909 (*Christie, Manson & Woods Cat.*, 31 March 1909, item 66 p. 18). Part of the prose conclusion of the letter had been found illegible when Forman saw it, and he also recorded gaps in the text of the poem, in line 30 ('line cut away with foot of leaf'), and in lines 20, 24, 26, 28, 32, 39, 40 (letters missing at the ends of lines). Neither the auction catalogue nor Forman recorded an (unpublished) postscript written vertically on f. 4 of the *PML MS*: 'If you have any thing to say, write by return of Post, if not I shall see you in Town–' (next day S.

18. Cameron comments (*SC* ii 493): 'The idea that they "may ne'er meet again" is, of course, fictitious.' Harriet G. and S. were together again for ten days in London a week later, but that was, in fact, their last recorded meeting. ¶ *16. Title.* Entitled 'Song' in *St Irvyne*. The title 'St Irvyne's Tower', introduced by *Rossetti 1870*, has no other authority.

arranged to meet Graham at Clapham on 25 April–: *L* i 9–10). However, that
the *PML MS* is both S.'s original letter and the auction copy seen by Forman is
probable for the following reasons: (a) the handwriting, as examined in
excellent bromide prints and ultraviolet enlargement, is indistinguishable in
any detail from S.'s; and the letter is on paper with the same watermark
('Wilmott 1808') as that of S.'s contemporary letters to Graham of 23 April
1810 (Berg Collection, N.Y. Pub. Lib.) and 10 May 1810 (*CHPL*). (b) Forman
reported the poem he saw to be 'much mutilated' whereas the text of the *PML
MS* is perfect, but the auction catalogue reproduced without comment all the
'missing final letters' bracketed by Forman, and it is possible these may only
have been curled under a tattered edge; line 30 whose absence in Forman's copy
is confirmed by the auction catalogue ('the 8th verse is incomplete') is at the
extreme foot of f. 2 in *PML MS* and may likewise have been curled or even
detached. The *PML MS* has subsequently been carefully repaired and 'silked'.
Thus the signature described in the auction catalogue as 'partially torn away' is
also in the middle of a repaired torn fold in *PML MS*. (c) the third 'outside'
panel of the double sheet of the *PML MS* now appears as blank as the two
found illegible by Forman, perhaps owing to physical repair; but ultraviolet
photography shows the beginnings of the words Forman deciphered as still
unmistakably present. (d) Forman in his two transcripts read two cancelled
words in lines 28 and 36 of the poem as *stop* and *take* respectively; both words
are in fact *still*, but the plausibility of the errors and the entirely characteristic
orthography that made them possible are almost conclusive evidence that the
PML MS is in S.'s hand and that it was also Forman's copy-text. That Forman
could have been so deceived by any other copy-text, or by a copy-text not in
S.'s hand, are equally inconceivable. By calculating the average number of
letters per line, the mutilated conclusion to the letter may be conjecturally
reconstructed from Forman's transcript as follows: 'Of course I communica[te
these lines to] you as to a friend [One in whom I con]fide will not shew [them
to any member] of my family or o[ffer them to be] published the t[wo
characters who] are addressed a[re indeed not without] individuality.–[The
lines were written I] assure you with [a strong and sincere] impulse on the
[scene of the occasion *or perhaps* night of the occasion] they describe–you may
set them to music if you think them worth it–.' (For an alternative partial
reconstruction see *Medwin (1913)* 453–4). Clearly this poem, though semi-
dramatized, reflects S.'s personal experience; the poem as published in *St
Irvyne*, though no doubt revised, represents a severely censored 'public' version, which S. rounded off with an irrelevant final stanza lifted from another
poem.
Text from *PML MS*.
Published in *St Irvyne* 132–3 (omitting stanzas 5–9 and with additional final
stanza); *Athenaeum* 5 June 1909, 674, reprinted *Medwin (1913)* 452–3.

> How swiftly through Heaven's wide expanse
> Bright day's resplendent colours fade,
> How sweetly does the moonbeam's glance
> With silver tint St. Irvyne's glade.

5 No cloud along the spangled air
   Is borne upon the evening breeze;
How solemn is the scene, how fair
   The moonbeam's rest upon the trees.

   Yon dark grey turret glimmers white,
10   Upon it sits the mournful owl;
Along the stillness of the night
   Her melancholy shriekings roll.

But not alone on Irvyne's tower
   The moonbeam pours its silver ray:
15 It gleams upon the ivied bower,
   It dances on the cascade's spray,

For there a youth with darkened brow
   His long lost love is heard to mourn.
He vents his swelling bosom's woe—
20   'Ah! when will hours like those return?

'O'er this torn soul, o'er this frail form
   Let feast the fiends of tortured love,
Let lower dire fate's terrific storm
   I would, the pangs of death to prove.

25 'Ah! why do prating priests suppose
   That God can give the wretch relief,
Can still the bursting bosom's woes
   Or calm the tide of frantic grief?

'Within me burns a raging Hell.
30   Fate, I defy thy farther power,
Fate, I defy thy fiercer spell,
   And long for stern death's welcome hour.

3–4. The moon was full on 19 April 1810. *tint*] *St Irvyne*; teint *PML MS.*
8. The moonbeam's rest] *PML MS*; The moonbeams rest *St Irvyne*. It is the *repose* of the moonlight that is so beautiful; lines 3 and 13–14 support the singular *moonbeam.*
14. The silver moonbeam pours her ray *St Irvyne.*
16. on] in *St Irvyne. the cascade's spray*] Charles Grove remembered Hills Place as 'full of . . . magnificent forest-trees, waterfalls, and rustic seats' (*Hogg* ii 551). *Stanzas 5–9.* Omitted in *St Irvyne*, with full stop after *spray* in line 16.
21–4. 'I would let the fiends feast over this torn soul, the storm of fate lower over this frail form, in order to experience the pangs of death'. In MS, commas after *soul* and *storm* constitute the only punctuation. If this reading is correct, the syntax is exceptionally distorted. But cp. *WJ* 510.
28. calm] stem *pencilled alternative in MS.*

'No power of Earth, of Hell or Heaven,
    Can still the tumults of my brain;
35   The power to none save ——'s given
    To calm my bosom's frantic pain.

'Ah, why do darkening shades conceal
    The hour when Man must cease to be?
Why may not human minds unveil
40   The dark shade of futurity?' –

17 'How eloquent are eyes!'

If the heading '1810' in *Esd* is reliable, probably inspired if not composed
between 16 April and 5 May when Harriet Grove was with S. on a visit to Field
Place and to her brother John Grove in London. A spring context fits lines
11–12, 23–4. S.'s relationship with Harriet at this time is accurately shown as
'passionate Friendship', and the poem implies an interval of close physical
propinquity in the midst of a long separation ('a waste of years'). The lovers
were much too young to think of marriage (S. was 17, Harriet only 15),
although Harriet's brother Charles recalled later that 'an engagement . . . had
. . . been permitted, both by his father and mine' (*Hogg* ii 551). Stanza 5, if not
composed later, must reflect either adolescent despondency or some awareness
of parental uncertainty on the Groves' side. *Zastrozzi* and *WJ*, sent earlier to
Harriet, had not been well received by her family; her mother had hesitated
before accepting the invitation to Field Place; and Harriet seemed perplexed by
the warmth of her welcome there (see *SC* ii 571–8). S. detached stanza 5 and
sent it (adapted in order to stress Hogg's situation in regard to the unresponsive
Elizabeth S.) at the foot of 'Hopes that swell in youthful breasts' to Hogg on
about 11 June 1811 (the accepted date, *c*. 19 June, is dubious). Hogg printed it
continuously with 'Hopes that swell', and it has formerly appeared as the last
stanza of that poem (see *SC* ii 814). Lines 1–13 were printed by Rossetti in 1870
as a 'poem extracted by Mr. Garnett from a MS book' and dated 'not later than

35. ——'s] 'Harriet's'.
Stanza 10. After this stanza (there the 5th) *St Irvyne* adds a stanza adapted from
the previous poem, 'Come —— ! sweet is the hour,':
        The keenness of the world hath torn
            The heart which opens to its blast;
        Despis'd, neglected, and forlorn,
            Sinks the wretch in death at last.
The anemone image is unfunctional in the present poem.
37–8. R. H. Shepherd first noted that these lines are lifted from 'Stanzas' ('I
would I were a careless child') 19–20, in Byron's *Poems Original and Translated*
(1808: the 2nd edn of *Hours of Idleness*).
40. The dim mists of futurity? *St Irvyne.*

1813' (*Rosetti 1870* ii 601). As these lines coincide exactly with one page of *Esd*, Garnett's source was probably the former 'governess in the Esdaile family' (*L about S* 87) who also copied for him two birthday sonnets. Only the more significant additions to the pointing have been noted.

Text from *Esd* ff. 52ᵛ–53ᵛ (*Esd* No. 34: quoted by permission of the Carl H. Pforzheimer Library).

Published in *Hogg* i 398 (lines 33–9 only); *Rossetti 1870* ii 530 (lines 1–13, entitled 'Eyes'); *Esd Nbk* 110–11; *Esd Poems* 64–6; *SC* iv 1000–2 (transcript of *Esd*).

> How eloquent are eyes!
> Not the rapt Poet's frenzied lay
> When the soul's wildest feelings stray
>   Can speak so well as they.
> 5   How eloquent are eyes!
> Not music's most impassioned note
> On which love's warmest fervours float
>   Like they bid rapture rise.
>
> Love! look thus again,
> 10 That your look may light a waste of years,
> Darting the beam that conquers cares
>   Through the cold shower of tears!
> Love! look thus again,
> That Time the victor as he flies
> 15 May pause to gaze upon thine eyes,
>   A victor then in vain!
>
> Yet no! arrest not Time.
> For Time, to others dear, we spurn;
> When Time shall *be* no more we burn,
> 20   When Love meets full return.

¶ *17.2. rapt*] 'entranced, enraptured, transported' *Concordance. frenzied*] frienzied *Esd*.

6–8. Harriet Grove played the piano; her stay with S. at her brother's included at least one musical evening (see diary entry for 1 May 1810, *SC* ii 577).

8. Like them bids rapture rise. *Rossetti 1870* and all editions except *Esd Nbk*. Rossetti's emendation is ambiguous ('awakens rapture comparable with eyes'); while 'Like they bids rapture rise' would be intolerable. The line resists grammatical adjustment.

10. light] lighten *Rossetti 1870* (first corrected *Dowden 1891*, from *Esd*).

17. Time.] Time *Esd*.

18. to others dear,] i.e. to conventional lovers who wish to prolong the passing moment.

19–20. Presumably: 'we burn for the time when Time no longer exists, when love is fully reciprocated'.

20. return.] return *Esd*.

> Ah no! arrest not Time,
> Fast let him fly on eagle wing
> Nor pause till Heaven's unfading spring
>   Breathes round its holy clime.

25   Yet quench that thrilling gaze
> Which passionate Friendship arms with fire,
> For what will eloquent eyes inspire
>   But feverish, false desire?
> Quench then that thrilling gaze,
30   For age may freeze the tremulous joy,
> But age can never *love* destroy.
>   It lives to better days.

> Age cannot love destroy.
> Can perfidy, then, blight its flower
35   Even when in most unwary hour
>   It blooms in fancy's bower?
> Age cannot love destroy.
> Can slighted vows, then, rend the shrine
> On which its chastened splendours shine
40   Around a dream of joy?

18 'Hopes that bud in youthful breasts'

Date of composition unknown, but probably contemporary with 'How eloquent are eyes!' (No. 17), which is associated with it in both MSS. S. sent a
version of stanzas 1–2 to Hogg on about 11 June 1811 (dated '*c.* 19 June 1811' in
L i 106) together with the final stanza of 'How eloquent are eyes!' and other
verses, as 'a strange mélange of maddened stuff which I wrote by the midnight
moon last night' (see headnote to previous poem); but another version in *Esd* is
headed '1810'. Cameron (*SC* ii 814) rightly suspects that S. sent Hogg an
assortment of old and recent poetry, pretending to have just improvised it all.
The copy sent to Hogg was influenced by S.'s resentment over his broken
engagement (e.g. in line 13, the petals of love's rose are riven 'by the frosts' in

28. desire?] desire *Esd*.
33. destroy.] destroy *Esd*.
34. But perfidy can blast the flower *Hogg MS*.
37. destroy.] destroy *Esd*.
38. shrine] shine *Esd*.
38–40. For these three lines *Hogg MS* has two:
> But perfidy can rend the shrine
> In which its vermeil splendours shine

Esd, 'by Earth's slaves' in *Hogg MS*), but if the Hogg version were the original
or the preferred one its variants would have been adopted when the poem was
copied into the Esdaile Notebook. They were not, and it is therefore safe to
assume that the poem predates S.'s entry to Oxford.
Text from *Esd* f. 54 (untitled; headed '1810'; *Esd* No. 35: quoted by permission
of the Carl H. Pforzheimer Library).
Published in *Hogg* i 397–8 (stanzas 1–2, untitled); *SC* ii 811 (transcript of *Hogg
MS*); *Esd Nbk* 112; *Esd Poems* 66–7; *SC* iv 1002–3 (transcript of *Esd.*).

Hopes that bud in youthful breasts
   Live not through the lapse of time:
Love's rose a host of thorns invests
   And ungenial is the clime
5   Where its blossoms blow.
Youth says–'The purple flowers are mine
   That fade the while they glow.'

Dear the boon to Fancy given,
   Retracted while 'tis granted.
10 Sweet the rose that breathes in Heaven,
   Although on Earth 'tis planted
   Where its blossoms blow,
Where by the frosts its leaves are riven
   That fade the while they glow.

15 The pure soul lives that heart within
   Which age cannot remove
If undefiled by tainting sin,
   A sanctuary of love

¶ *18.1. bud*] swell *Hogg MS.*
2. Live they thro' the waste of time? *Hogg MS.*
3. invests] invest *Esd.*
4. And] Cold *Hogg MS.*
5, 12. blossoms] honours *Hogg MS* (Lat. *honores*, 'finery'; a common classicism,
e.g. Akenside, *Pleasures of Imagination* (1744) i 461–2: 'the flowers / Their
purple honours, with the Spring, resume'); Cowper, *Task* (1785) i 320: 'the
woods, in scarlet honours bright').
6. purple] Lat. *purpureus*, 'bright'.
6–7. No quotation-marks in either MS, which leaves their scope uncertain.
9. 'tis] it's *Hogg MS.*
10. that breathes] which lives *Hogg MS.*
11. planted] planten *Esd.*
13. Where by the frosts its] Yet by Earth's slaves the *Hogg MS.*
14. That fade] Which die *Hogg MS.*
15–21. Omitted *Hogg MS.*
15–17. 'Purity of soul inhabits the kind of heart that is unchanged by time
because of its perfect sincerity'.

         Where its blossoms blow,
20   Where, in this unsullied shrine
         They fade not while they glow.

19 Song: Despair

Dated 'June, 1810' in *V&C*. The first of three poems subheaded respectively
'Despair', 'Sorrow', and 'Hope'; the last two, however, which are explicitly
linked, are dated August and are in the first person singular, so this poem seems
grouped with the others arbitrarily (see Nos. 23, 24). Garnett (*V&C (1898)*
xiv–xx) refers it to 'Victor' and to S.'s relationship with Harriet Grove; but it is
less fluent than is characteristic of S., with an awkward change of metre at line
18. Whether by 'Victor' or 'Cazire', however, it seems to concern death rather
than fickleness, and may be associated with Harriet's younger sister Louise,
who died on 19 June.
Text from *V&C*.
Published in *V&C*; *V&C (1898)* 19–20.

         Ask not the pallid stranger's woe,
             With beating heart and throbbing breast
         Whose step is faltering, weak, and slow,
             As though the body needed rest;

 5   Whose wildered eye no object meets,
             Nor cares to ken a friendly glance;
         With silent grief his bosom beats, –
             Now fixed, as in a deathlike trance;

         Who looks around, with fearful eye,
10   And shuns all converse with mankind,
         As though some one his griefs might spy,
             And soothe them with a kindred mind.

         A friend or foe to him the same,
             He looks on each with equal eye;
15   The difference lies but in the name,
             To none for comfort can he fly. –

         'Twas deep despair, and sorrow's trace,
             To him too keenly given,

¶ 19.2. *breast*] breast, *V&C*. The line describes the stranger, not the reader.
4. *rest;*] rest.– *V&C*.
6. *ken*] S. uses this verb only once elsewhere (*Q Mab* ii 86).
8. *trance;*] trance. *V&C*.

Whose memory time could not efface –
20   His peace was lodged in Heaven. –

He looks on all this world bestows,
   The pride and pomp of power,
As trifles best for pageant shows
   Which vanish in an hour. –

25   When torn is dear affection's tie,
   Sinks the soft heart full low;
It leaves without a parting sigh
   All that these realms bestow.

20 'Cold are the blasts'

Probably written July 1810, the date appended to the poem in *V&C*. The
version in *Esd*, however, which must be the latest and which furnishes the
present text, is headed '1808'. This is impossibly early, and may represent a
kind of title rather than a composition date; Harriet Grove may have visited
Field Place in 1808 (see headnote to No. 14). Despite the 'Gothic' narrative, the
theme of perjured love links the poem with others concerning Harriet G., and
the names Henry and Louisa (left blank in *V&C*) are those of Harriet's brother
and sister (cp. No. 7). Besides the *V&C* and *Esd* texts, S. wrote out this poem,
together with parts of Nos. 24 and 25, for Hogg, probably in November 1810,
as similar notepaper was used for letters written in November (*SC* ii 630), in
the cause of promoting an alliance between Hogg and S.'s sister Elizabeth.
'Bysshe wrote down these verses for me at Oxford from memory. I was to
have a complete and more correct copy of them some day. They were the
composition of his sister Elizabeth . . .' (*Hogg* i 201). The inclusion of 'Cold are
the blasts' in the Esdaile Notebook, however, shows that S. meant to publish it
as his own work, so as Cameron says (*Esd Nbk* 259), 'it is more likely . . . that S.
was simply pulling Hogg's leg on all occasions and that none of these poems or
any part of them was by Elizabeth.' The text of the MS given to Hogg, which
is almost identical with that of *V&C*, is printed below at the end of the notes.
The metre of the poem, and some of its phrasing, derives from Scott's
'Hellvellyn' (1805), 'a poem he greatly admired' (*Medwin (1913)* 52). Lines 1–8,
21–4 show that S.'s liking for repetitive structures, used in mature poems such
as 'Ode to the West Wind', 'Indian Serenade', and 'Remembrance', is not
wholly due to Calderòn's influence. Punctuation in *Esd* is almost entirely
lacking.
Text from *Esd* ff. 64ᵛ–65ᵛ (*Esd* No. 45: quoted by permission of the Carl H.
Pforzheimer Library).
Published in *V&C* 14–16; *Hogg* i 199–200; *V&C (1898)* 14–16; *Esd Nbk* 129–30;
Esd Poems 115–17 (Appendix); *SC* ii 625–6 (transcript of *Hogg MS*); *SC* iv
1019–21 (transcript of *Esd*).

¶ *20. Title*. Headed 'Song' in *V&C*, '1808' in *Esd*, and untitled in *Hogg MS*.

Cold are the blasts when December is howling,
　　Chill are the damps on a dying friend's brow,
Stern is the Ocean when tempests are rolling,
　　Sad is the grave where a brother lies low, –
5　But chillier is scorn from the false one that loved thee,
　　More stern is the sneer from the friend that has proved
　　　　　　　　　　　　　　　　　　　　thee,
　　More sad are the tears when these sorrows have moved
　　　　　　　　　　　　　　　　　　　　thee
　　　That envenomed by wildest delirium flow.

And alas! thou, Louisa, hast felt all this horror! . . .
10　　Full long the fallen victim contended with fate,
Till, a destitute outcast abandoned to sorrow,
　　She sought her babe's food at her ruiner's gate.
Another had charmed the remorseless betrayer,
He turned laughing away from her anguish-fraught
　　　　　　　　　　　　　　　　　　　　prayer;
15　She spoke not, but wringing the rain from her hair
　　Took the rough mountain path, though the hour was
　　　　　　　　　　　　　　　　　　　　late.

On the cloud-shrouded summit of dark Penmanmawr
　　The form of the wasted Louisa reclined;
She shrieked to the ravens loud croaking afar,
20　　She sighed to the gusts of the wild sweeping wind: –
'Ye storms o'er the peak of the lone mountain soaring,
Ye clouds with the thunder-winged tempest-shafts
　　　　　　　　　　　　　　　　　　　　lowering,

6. *proved*] Presumably 'found out in a falsehood'.

10–14. The deserted mother rejected by her seducer is an 18th-century stereotype recurring again in S.'s 'Ballad' (No. 31). The fate of Louisa's baby, however, is unclear.

15. Cp. Scott's 'Glenfinlas' 157–61, in *Tales of Wonder* (1800): 'All dropping wet her garments seem, / Chilled was her cheek, her bosom bare, / As bending o'er the dying gleam, / She wrung the moisture from her hair.'

17. *Penmanmawr*] The northernmost peak (1500 ft) of the Snowdon range, 'a huge, bare, overhanging rock, rising almost perpendicularly from the sea, and formerly the terror of travellers, from the numerous fatal accidents' (*Monthly Mag* xiv (1802) 304), much used in poetry as an extreme of wildness, e.g. by Thomson (*Summer* 1163–5), John Philips (*Cyder* (1708) i 105–9), Southey (*Madoc* (1805) i 26–7).

20–4. Cp. *Tales of Terror*, 'Albert of Werdendorff' 53–6:
　　　'Fall on, chilling mists! thou art cruel,' she said,
　　　　'But crueller far is Lord Albert to me!
　　　Blow on, thou bleak wind! o'er my woe-stricken head,
　　　　Thou'rt cold, but Lord Albert is colder than thee!' –

Thou wrath of black Heaven, I blame not thy pouring,
  But thee, cruel Henry, I call thee unkind.'

25 Then she wreathed a wild crown from the flowers of the
                                                mountain,
  And deliriously laughing, the heath-twigs entwined;
  She bedewed it with tear-drops, then leaned o'er the
                                                fountain
  And cast it a prey to the wild sweeping wind.
  'Ah, go,' she exclaimed, 'where the tempest is yelling;
30 'Tis unkind to be cast on the sea that is swelling—
  But I left, a pitiless outcast, my dwelling,
  My garments are torn—so they say is my mind.'

  Not long lived Louisa;—and over her grave
  Waved the desolate limbs of a storm-blasted yew;

25–8. The wreath made by a distracted girl on her faithless lover's account is a
stereotype deriving from Ophelia's (*Hamlet* IV v 174–85, IV vii 165–74); e.g.
Thomas Russell's 'The Maniac' (1789) 37–9: 'From every hedge a flower she
pluck'd, / And moss from every stone, / To make a garland for her love'.
34. a storm-blasted yew] A stock 'Gothic' property.
The *Hogg MS* reads:

  Cold cold is the blast when December is howling
    Cold are the damps on a dying mans brow
  Stern are the seas when the wild waves are rolling
    And sad the grave where a loved one lies low
5 But colder is scorn from the being who loved thee
  More stern is the sneer from the friend who has proved thee
  More sad are the tears when these sorrows have moved thee
    Which mixed with groans, anguish & wild madness flow.

  And ah! poor Louisa has felt all this horror
10   Full long the fallen victim contended with fate
  Till a destitute outcast abandoned to sorrow
    She sought her babe's food at her ruiner's gate
  Another had charmed the remorseless betrayer
  He turned callous aside from her moans & her prayer
15 She said nothing but wringing the wet from her hair
    Crossed the dark mountain side tho the hour it was late

  'Twas on the dark summit of huge Penmanmawr
    That the form of the wasted Louisa reclined,
  She shrieked to the ravens that croaked from afar
20   And she sighed to the gusts of the wild sweeping wind
  I call not yon clouds where the thunder peals rattle
  I call not yon rocks where the elements battle
    But thee perjured Henry I call thee unkind

35 Around it no demons or ghosts dare to rave
    But spirits of love steep her slumbers in dew.
    Then stay thy swift steps mid the dark mountain heather,
    Though bleak be the scene and severe be the weather,
    For perfidy, traveller, cannot bereave her
40   Of the tears to the tombs of the innocent due.

21 Song.
Translated from the Italian

Dated 'July, 1810' in *V&C*. These lines may well be by 'Cazire' (Elizabeth S.)
as Garnett first suggested (*V&C (1898)* xiv), and in any case are unlikely to be
really 'from the Italian'. Elizabeth, who was then sixteen, died unmarried in
1831.
Text from *V&C* 26.
Published in *V&C*; *V&C (1898)* 26.

    Oh! what is the gain of restless care,
      And what is ambition's treasure?
    And what are the joys that the modish share,
      In their sickly haunts of pleasure?

5 My husband's repast with delight I spread,
      What though 'tis but rustic fare?
    May each guardian angel protect his shed,
      May contentment and quiet be there.

────────────────────────────────────

    Then she wreathed in her hair the wild flowers of the mountain
25   And deliriously laughing a garland entwined
    She bedewed it with tears, then she hung oer the fountain
      And laving it, cast it a prey to the wind
    'Ah! go' she exclaimed, 'where the tempest is yelling
    'Tis unkind to be cast on the sea that is swelling
30 But I left a pityless outcast my dwelling
      My garments are torn so they say is my mind'

    Not long lived Louisa—but over her grave
      Waved the desolate form of a storm-blasted yew
    Around it no demons or ghosts dare to rave
35   But spirits of Peace steep her slumbers in dew
    Then stay thy swift steps mid the dark mountain heather
    Tho chill blow the wind & severe be the weather,
    For perfidy traveller cannot bereave her
      Of the tears to the tombs of the innocent due

¶ *21.2. ambition's*] ambitious *V&C*.

And may I support my husband's years,
10 May I soothe his dying pain,
And then may I dry my fast falling tears,
And meet him in Heaven again.

22 Fragment, or the Triumph of Conscience

Probably composed July or early August 1810. The poem first appeared in
V&C (completed 10 August 1810), and was probably then a recent composition, as it was included in ch. i of *St Irvyne* (published 18 December 1810),
where the high-born Wolfstein, who has just joined a band of Alpine banditti,
inscribes 'on a tablet the following lines: for the inaccuracy of which, the
perturbation of him who wrote them, may account.' (He then tears the poem
up.) It is explained only that 'before he had become an associate with the band
of robbers, the conscience of Wolfstein had been clear; clear, at least, from the
commission of any wilful and deliberate crime', but that 'an event almost too
dreadful for narration, had compelled him to quit his native country.' Wolfstein's lines are untitled; the present title is taken from *V&C*; all other titles are
editorial. Verbal differences only from *V&C* are recorded.
Text from *St Irvyne* 17–18.
Published *V&C* 63–4; *St Irvyne*; *V&C (1898)*.

'Twas dead of the night, when I sat in my dwelling;
One glimmering lamp was expiring and low;
Around, the dark tide of the tempest was swelling,
Along the wild mountains night-ravens were yelling, –
5   They bodingly presaged destruction and woe.

'Twas then that I started! – the wild storm was howling,
Nought was seen, save the lightning, which danced in
the sky;
Above me, the crash of the thunder was rolling,
And low, chilling murmurs the blast wafted by.

10 My heart sank within me – unheeded the war
Of the battling clouds on the mountain-tops broke; –
Unheeded the thunder-peal crashed in mine ear –
This heart, hard as iron, is stranger to fear,
But conscience in low, noiseless whispering spoke.

¶ *22.7. lightning, which*] lightning that *V&C*.
10. war] jar *V&C*.
13. is] was *V&C*.

15   'Twas then that her form on the whirlwind upholding,
       The ghost of the murdered Victoria strode;
     In her right hand, a shadowy shroud she was holding,
       She swiftly advanced to my lonesome abode.

     I wildly then called on the tempest to bear me –

               ★   ★   ★   ★   ★

23 Song: Sorrow

Dated 'August, 1810' in *V&C*, which was with the printers by the 11th, so presumably written 1–10 August. This poem forms a pair with No. 24 on the conventional themes of Sorrow and Hope, though they may be connected with the visit made by Harriet Grove to Field Place from 16–18 August. Text from *V&C* 21–3.
Published in *V&C*; *V&C (1898)* 21–3.

     To me this world's a dreary blank,
       All hopes in life are gone and fled,
     My high strung energies are sank,
       And all my blissful hopes lie dead. –

5   The world once smiling to my view
       Showed scenes of endless bliss and joy;
     The world I then but little knew,
       Ah! little knew how pleasures cloy:

     All then was jocund, all was gay,
10   No thought beyond the present hour,
     I danced in pleasure's fading ray,
       Fading, alas! as drooping flower.

     Nor do the heedless in the throng
       One thought beyond the morrow give,
15   They court the feast, the dance, the song,
       Nor think how short their time to live.

15. upholding,] uprearing, *V&C*. Presumably 'upholding itself'; *OED* recognizes no intransitive use of this verb.
16. The ghost] The dark ghost *V&C. Victoria*] A name borrowed from the female villain of *Zofloya*, who sells her soul to Satan and is finally destroyed by him.
17. Her right hand a blood reeking dagger was bearing, *V&C.*
18–19. V&C has no stanza-break between these lines.
¶ *23.3. sank*] S. only uses this form of the past participle (not admitted in *OED*) here, in No. 24 line 4, and in *L&C* I xiii 2.

The heart that bears deep sorrow's trace,
   What earthly comfort can console?
It drags a dull and lengthened pace,
20   Till friendly death its woes enroll. –

The sunken cheek, the humid eyes,
   E'en better than the tongue can tell
In whose sad breast deep sorrow lies,
   Where memory's rankling traces dwell. –

25 The rising tear, the stifled sigh,
   A mind but ill at ease display,
Like blackening clouds in stormy sky,
   Where fiercely vivid lightnings play.

Thus when souls' energy is dead,
30   When sorrow dims each earthly view,
When every fairy hope is fled,
   We bid the ungrateful world adieu.

24 Song: Hope

Written 1–10 August 1810 (see headnote to previous poem).
Text from *V&C* 24–5.
Published in *V&C*; *V&C (1898)* 24–5.

And said I that all hope was fled,
   That sorrow and despair were mine,
That each enthusiast wish was dead,
   Had sank beneath pale Misery's shrine? –

5 Seest thou the sunbeam's yellow glow,
   That robes with liquid streams of light
Yon distant mountain's craggy brow,
   And shows the rocks so fair, – so bright? –

'Tis thus sweet expectation's ray
10   In softer view shows distant hours,

32. the] Omitted V&C.
¶ *24.5–10.* The image derives from Campbell's *Pleasures of Hope* (1799) i 3–8:
       Why to yon mountain turns the musing eye,
       Whose sunbright summit mingles with the sky?
       Why do those cliffs of shadowy tint appear
       More sweet than all the landscape smiling near? –
       'Tis distance lends enchantment to the view,
       And robes the mountain in its azure hue.

And portrays each succeeding day
    As dressed in fairer, brighter flowers.—

The vermeil-tinted flowers that blossom
    Are frozen but to bud anew,
15 Then, sweet deceiver, calm my bosom,
    Although thy visions be not true,—

Yet true they are,—and I'll believe
    Thy whisperings soft of love and peace;
God never made thee to deceive,
20   'Tis sin that bade thy empire cease.

Yet though despair my life should gloom,
    Though horror should around me close,
With those I love, beyond the tomb,
    Hope shows a balm for all my woes.

25 Song: To———

Dated 'August 1810' in *V&C*; presumably written just after Harriet Grove's last visit to Field Place on 16–18 August. Lines 1–4 describe the estate of 'St Irvyne' (Hills Place, Horsham), 'full of magnificent forest-trees, waterfalls, and rustic seats' (*Hogg* ii 550–1), the setting of S.'s romance with Harriet, though the 'dimly-seen mountain' is poetic licence. S. included the first 4½ lines (there are no verbal variants) among related verses written out for Hogg at Oxford probably in November 1810 (see headnote to No. 20), pretending them to be the work of his sister Elizabeth (*Hogg* i 200–201). But it is now clear that the attribution to Elizabeth S. was a mere 'blind' (see *Esd Nbk* 258–9), which S.'s references to himself in the third person, after 'thy [Percy]' in line 8 of this poem, accidentally appear to support. Apparently Hogg was never allowed to know of the existence of *V&C*, from which the lines given him were taken.
Text from *V&C* 33–4.
Published in *V&C*; *V&C (1898)* 33–4. Lines 1–5: *SC* ii 627 (from SC 114).

Ah! sweet is the moonbeam that sleeps on yon fountain,
    And sweet the mild rush of the soft-sighing breeze,
And sweet is the glimpse of yon dimly-seen mountain,
    'Neath the verdant arcades of yon shadowy trees.

15. *Then, sweet deceiver,*] Then sweet deceivers *V&C*.
17. 'Yet true *they* are'–i.e. the real flowers renewed in spring.
¶ 25. *Title.* Presumably 'To [Harriet Grove]'.
1. There was a full moon on 15 August, the eve of Harriet G.'s arrival at Field Place.

5   But sweeter than all was thy tone of affection,
        Which scarce seemed to break on the stillness of eve;
    Though the time it is past! – yet the dear recollection
        For aye in the heart of thy ——— must live.

    Yet he hears thy dear voice in the summer winds sighing,
10   Mild accents of happiness lisp in his ear,
    When the hope-wingèd moments athwart him are flying,
        And he thinks of the friend to his bosom so dear. –

    And thou, dearest friend, in his bosom for ever
        Must reign unalloyed by the fast-rolling year;
15   He loves thee, and dearest one, never, oh, never
        Canst thou cease to be loved by a heart so sincere.

26 Song: To ———

Dated 'August, 1810' in *V&C*, where it follows No. 24 and evidently concerns the same occasion: the brief reunion with Harriet Grove on 16–18 August. Lines 9–15 and 17–18 were also among the verses written out for Hogg at Oxford as examples of Elizabeth S.'s work (see headnotes to Nos. 19 and 24), in this case with changes of pronoun and other alterations (noted below) designed to make her authorship plausible.
Text from *V&C* 35–6.
Published in *V&C*; *V&C (1898)* 35–6; *Hogg* i 200, *SC* ii 627 (lines 9–15, 17–18).

    Stern, stern is the voice of fate's fearful command,
        When accents of horror it breathes in our ear,
    Or compels us for aye bid adieu to the land
        Where exists that loved friend to our bosom so dear;
5   'Tis sterner than death o'er the shuddering wretch
                             bending,
    And in skeleton grasp his fell sceptre extending,
    Like the heart-stricken deer to that loved covert wending
        Which never again to his eyes may appear. –

8. Presumably 'thy [Percy]'. S. appears in Harriet G.'s diary as 'Bysshe' until 27 April 1810, and thereafter as 'Percy'.
9. Yet] i.e. 'Still'.
¶ *26. Title.* Presumably 'To [Harriet Grove]'.
7–8. S.'s first use of a favourite image, deriving primarily from *As You Like It* II i 33–5, 47–50, where: 'a poor sequestred stag, / That from the hunter's aim had ta'en a hurt, / Did come to languish . . . Left and abandoned of his velvet friends', secondarily from Cowper's *Task* iii 108–20: 'I was a stricken deer, that left the herd' etc., where the victim is associated with Christ. 'Heart-stricken' recalls Lear's 'heart-struck injuries' (III i 17).
8. appear. –] appear – *V&C*.

And ah! he may envy the heart-stricken quarry,
10   Who bids to the friend of affection farewell,
He may envy the bosom so bleeding and gory,
     He may envy the sound of the drear passing knell;
Not so deep is his grief on his death couch reposing,
When on the last vision his dim eyes are closing!
15   As the outcast whose love-raptured senses are losing
     The last tones of thy voice on the wild breeze that
                                                      swell!

Those tones were so soft, and so sad, that ah! never
     Can the sound cease to vibrate on Memory's ear;
In the stern wreck of nature for ever and ever
20   The remembrance must live of a friend so sincere.

27 Song: 'How stern are the woes'

Written shortly before its inclusion in a letter of 14 September 1810 to Edward
'Hesekiah' [Fergus] Graham, the music-teacher at Field Place and a protégé of
S.'s parents. S. hoped to have it set to music by the Austrian musician Joseph
Woelff (1772–1814), who had been Graham's own teacher, and S.'s introductory words, 'This is the other song', show that one or more poems had already
been submitted for this purpose. Likely ones are Nos. 26 ('Stern, stern is the
voice'), published in *V&C* as 'Song', and 28 ('Ah! faint are her limbs'), which is
given to Eloise to sing in ch. ix of *St Irvyne*. The incorporation of songs into the
novel was imitated from Mrs Radcliffe and 'Monk' Lewis. 'How stern are the
woes' is also sung by Eloise earlier in the same chapter, in memory of her
deceased mother, but explained as 'a song which Marianne [Eloise's elder
sister] had composed soon after her brother's death'. It is perhaps associated
therefore with Louisa Grove's death. S. commented to Graham: 'You well
know I am not much of a hand at *love* songs, you see I mingle metaphysics with
even this, but perhaps in this age of Philosophy that may be excused' (*L* i 16).
All three of these songs are in the metre of Scott's 'Hellvellyn'. Although the *St
Irvyne* version must be subsequent to that of the letter it is verbally inferior,

9. *he*] she *Hogg MS* (SC 114).
10. *the friend of affection*] the scenery of childhood *Hogg MS*.
9–10. An inversion: 'he . . . who bids . . . may envy . . .' etc.
11. *He*] She *Hogg MS*.
13. *is his grief*] are his woes *Hogg MS*.
13–15. 'The dying man's grief is not so deep as the outcast['s] whose . . .'
15–16. *Omitted after* outcast– *Hogg MS*.
17. *tones*] notes *Hogg MS*.
18. *Can*] May *Hogg MS*.
19–20. *Omitted Hogg MS*.

though almost unpointed. (*St Irvyne* was corrected for the printer on 14
November: *L* i 20).
Text from Bod. MS Shelley adds.b.2, f. 4.
Published in *St Irvyne* 171; *L* i 16.

I.

How stern are the woes of the desolate mourner
   As he bends in still grief o'er the hallowed bier,
As enanguished he turns from the laugh of the scorner
   And drops to Perfection's remembrance a tear;
5 When floods of despair down his pale cheek are
                         streaming,
When no blissful hope o'er his bosom is beaming,
Or if lulled for a time, soon he starts from his dreaming
   And finds torn the soft ties to affection so dear.

2.

Oh! when shall day dawn on the night of the grave,
10   Or summer succeed to the winter of Death?
Rest awhile, hapless victim, and Heaven will save
   The spirit that faded away with the breath.
Eternity points in its amaranth bower
Where no clouds of fate o'er the sweet prospect lower
15 Unspeakable pleasure, of goodness the dower,
   Where woe fades away like the mist on the heath.

¶ *27.2. hallowed*] The past participle is not accented in either text, and an accent
is metrically unnecessary.
6. o'er] on *St Irvyne*.
7. time] while *St Irvyne* (possibly an intended amendment).
9. Oh!] Ah! *St Irvyne*.
9–10. S.'s immediate source is Beattie's *Hermit* (1766) 31–2:
        But when shall spring visit the mouldering urn?
        O when shall it dawn on the night of the grave?
This was a much-used Romantic formula deriving from *Amos* v 8: 'Seek him
that . . . turneth the shadow of death into the morning' (see also *II Peter* i 19)
and revived by Ossian's 'Songs of Selma', first published in James Macpherson's *Fragments of Ancient Poetry collected in the Highlands of Scotland* (1760):
'When shall it be morn in the grave, to bid the slumberer awake?' It was a
favourite expression of S.'s at this time, e.g. 'Can the dead feel—dawns any
daybeam on the night of dissolution?' (to Hogg, 3 January 1811, *L* i 36); and
'Shall I say the time may come when happiness shall dawn upon a night of
wretchedness–' (to Hogg, 26 April 1811, *L* i 68).
13. points] 'points out' (*OED* sense III 2). The verb's object is *pleasure*. *amaranth*]
The immortal flower (Milton, *PL* iii 353).
14. lower] Omitted adds.b.2; supplied from *St Irvyne*.
16. Where] When *St Irvyne*. *on*] of *St Irvyne*.

28 Song: 'Ah! faint are her limbs'

Written August–September 1810, perhaps to be set to music (see headnote to
No. 27), and incorporated in ch. ix of *St Irvyne*, where Eloise sings it to her
future seducer, Nempere/Ginotti, calling it 'a melancholy song; my poor
brother wrote it, I remember, about ten days before he died. 'Tis a gloomy tale
concerning him; he ill deserved the fate he met.' Koszul ('The Sources of S.'s
Romances', *Athenaeum* 6 May 1905, 561–2) noted a similarity to the song of the
five bards added to Ossian's 'Croma' (*Fingal* (2nd edn 1762) 255): 'A maid sits
beside the rock, and eyes the rolling stream. Her lover promised to come. She
saw his boat, when yet it was light on the lake. Is this his broken boat on the
shore? Are these his groans on the wind?' But other drownings may have
contributed, e.g. Osric's in 'Osric and Ella' (*Tales of Terror*). The poem is
closely related to Nos. 26 and 27.
Text from *St Irvyne* 181–2.
Published in *St Irvyne*.

I.

Ah! faint are her limbs, and her footstep is weary,
    Yet far must the desolate wanderer roam;
Though the tempest is stern, and the mountain is dreary,
    She must quit at deep midnight her pitiless home.
5 I see her swift foot dash the dew from the whortle,
As she rapidly hastes to the green grove of myrtle;
And I hear, as she wraps round her figure the kirtle,
    'Stay thy boat on the lake, – dearest Henry, I come.'

2.

High swelled in her bosom the throb of affection,
10   As lightly her form bounded over the lea,
And arose in her mind every dear recollection:
    'I come, dearest Henry, and wait but for thee.'
How sad, when dear hope every sorrow is soothing,
When sympathy's swell the soft bosom is moving,
15 And the mind the mild joys of affection is proving,
    Is the stern voice of fate that bids happiness flee!

3.

Oh! dark lowered the clouds on that horrible eve,
    And the moon dimly gleamed through the tempested
                       air;
Oh! how could fond visions such softness deceive?
20   Oh! how could false hope rend a bosom so fair?

¶ *28*.5. Suggested by Scott, *Lady of the Lake* (1810) I xviii 12–13: 'A foot more
light, a step more true, / Ne'er from the heath-flower dash'd the dew'. The
'kirtle' (line 7) may derive from Scott or from a ballad, e.g. 'Tam Lin'.

Thy love's pallid corse the wild surges are laving,
O'er his form the fierce swell of the tempest is raving;
But fear not, parting spirit; thy goodness is saving,
    In eternity's bowers, a seat for thee there.

29 'Late was the night'

A draft belonging probably to autumn 1810. These verses exist only in Harriet
S.'s hand in *Esd*, dated '1815' at the foot, and their incoherence has cast doubt
on S.'s authorship. The well-educated, meticulous Harriet, however, cannot
possibly have concocted such lines and inserted them as a 'poem' into S.'s
obviously cherished collection. In theme, treatment, and vocabulary the lines
are wholly Shelleyan, relating closely to the opening of *St Irvyne* and to other
poems such as Nos. 20 and 30, while they bear the unmistakable features of a
hesitant transcript from one of S.'s rough drafts. The attached date must be
that of the transcription, as S. had been separated from Harriet S. since 28 July
1814, and this is a much earlier poem. It is a reasonable assumption, therefore,
that Harriet S. used the back of the notebook to transcribe all the poems and
fragments by her husband which she could find, and that all its contents are
S.'s. But Harriet S. had far less experience in reading S.'s hand than her
successor, and her copy fails to make consistent sense. Under these circumstances it seems defensible to attempt some conjectural reconstruction where
suggested by the known characteristics of S.'s orthography and style. This is
guesswork, however; and Harriet's original readings (where these are themselves legible) are kept in the notes.
Text from *Esd* ff. 95ᵛ–96ʳ (*Esd* No. 57: quoted by permission of the Carl H.
Pforzheimer Library).
Published in *Esd Nbk* 170; *Esd Poems* 118 (Appendix); *SC* iv 1060–1 (transcript
of *Esd*).

Late was the night, the moon shone bright,
It tinted the vale with a silver light,
And threw its wide uncertain beam
Upon the rolling mountain stream.

5   That stream so swift that rushes along
    Has oft heard yelling the murderers' song,

23–4. Here and in No. 27 the reward of virtue is said to be happiness in Heaven.
¶ 29.4. the] its *Esd*. Conjectural; an easy misreading.
6. oft heard yelling the] oft been dyed by the *Esd*. Conjectural: the meaningless
Esd reading could have arisen from misgrouping S.'s letters: 'oft beend yedby
the' is theoretically a possible error. Cameron's suggested reversal of the
rhyme-words in lines 6–7 (*Esd Nbk* 369) would give *murderous wave* and
exulting song, solving one problem but remaining unintelligible.   *murderers'*]
murderes *Esd*.

It oft has heard the exulting staves
Of one who oft the murderers braves.

The Alpine summits which, raised on high,
10   Peacefully frown on the valley beneath
And lift their huge forms to the sky,
Oft have heard the voices of death.

Now not a murmur floats on the air
Save the distant sounds of the torrent's tide;
15   Not a cloud obscures the moon so fair,
Not a shade is seen on the rocks to glide.

See that fair form that leans o'er [the wave];
Her garments are tattered, her bosom is bare;
She shrinks from the yawning watery grave,
20   And shivering, around her enwraps her dark hair.

Poor Emma has toiled o'er many a mile,
The victim of misery's own sad child;
Pale is her cheek; all trembling awhile,
She totters and falls on the cold-stricken wild.

30 'Ghosts of the dead!'

Apparently written for *St Irvyne*, September–October 1810. *St Irvyne* was
conceived and possibly begun by 1 April 1810 (*L* i 6), and was finished by 14
November (*L* i 20), but between these dates S. wrote and published two other
volumes; so it is likely that most if not all of the novel, which opens in late
autumn, was written at that season. In ch. i, Megalina de Metastasio, daughter

7. *staves*] wave *Esd*. Conjectural. Cp. *WJ* 858: 'And shriek amid their deadly
stave'.
8. *murderers braves.*] murderes braved *Esd*. Conjectural.
15. *moon*] *Esd Poems*; moors *Esd Nbk, SC*.
16. *on*] Possibly a misreading of *o'er*.
17. *leans o'er*] ?leans ore *Esd*; [?none] ?can save *Esd Poems*. The last two words
have been supplied for the rhyme.
18. *is*] so *Esd*. Conjectural; an easy misreading.
20–1. No stanza-break in *Esd*–further evidence of transcription from draft.
22. *victim*] victims *SC*. Probably corrupt; no plausible conjecture forthcoming.
The last four words are a Romantic formula: cp. Amos Cottle, 'To the Apple
Tree' 13, in Joseph Cottle's *Malvern Hills* (1798): 'Sad emblem thou of misery's
drooping child'; Thomas Penrose's *Poems* (1781), 'The Field of Battle' 8:
'Maria, Sorrow's early child'.
24. *cold-stricken*] ?cold-stricken *Esd*. 'Woe-stricken' occurs in *Tales of Terror*,
'Albert of Werdendorff' 55.

of an Italian Count, is captured while crossing the Alps by bandits who 'had inhumanly murdered him, and cast his lifeless body adown the yawning precipice'. Still uncertain of his fate, Megalina writes these lines on her cell-wall; then rubs them out, 'ashamed of the exuberance of her imagination'. Despite its Swiss setting, the poem is very Ossianic: '. . . from the top of the windy mountain, speak ye ghosts of the dead! . . . No feeble voice is on the wind: no answer half-drowned in the storms of the hill' etc. ('Songs of Selma', *Fingal* (2nd edn 1762) 212). S. was also influenced by Byron's *Hours of Idleness* (1807), which includes an imitation of Ossian, 'The Death of Calmar and Orla' (see notes below).
Text from *St Irvyne* 39.
Published in *St Irvyne*.

Ghosts of the dead! have I not heard your yelling
   Rise on the night-rolling breath of the blast,
When o'er the dark ether the tempest is swelling,
   And on eddying whirlwind the thunder-peal past?

5 For oft have I stood on the dark height of Jura,
   Which frowns on the valley that opens beneath;
Oft have I braved the chill night-tempest's fury,
   Whilst around me, I thought, echoed murmurs of
            death.

And now, whilst the winds of the mountain are howling,
10   O father! thy voice seems to strike on mine ear;
In air whilst the tide of the night-storm is rolling,
   It breaks on the pause of the elements' jar.

On the wing of the whirlwind which roars o'er the
            mountain
   Perhaps rides the ghost of my sire who is dead,
15 On the mist of the tempest which hangs o'er the
            fountain,
   Whilst a wreath of dark vapour encircles his head.

¶ *30.1–2.* R. H. Shepherd (*Shepherd 1871–5* iv 132) first noted the derivation from Byron's 'Lachin y Gair' 17–18, in *Hours of Idleness* (1807):
    'Shades of the dead! have I not heard your voices
      Rise on the night-rolling breath of the gale?'
Byron's ghosts, however, were of his Jacobite ancestors.
4. past] i.e. 'is past'–the ghosts are heard in the lull after a thunder-clap, while the storm is increasing.
5. Jura] Mountain-chain north of Geneva, on the Swiss–French border.
13. the wing of the whirlwind] Ossianic; Byron also uses 'the whirlwind's wing' in stanza 67 of 'Oscar of Alva' in *Hours of Idleness*.
14. ghost of my sire] 'It was long thought, in the North of Scotland, that storms were raised by the ghosts of the deceased' (note to James Macpherson's 'Conlath and Cuthona: a Poem', *Fingal* (2nd edn 1762) 123).

31 Ballad: 'The death-bell beats!'

Written probably September–October 1810 for *St Irvyne* (see headnote to No. 30), but possibly earlier in 1810, as it has clear connections both with *WJ* and with Coleridge's 'The Mad Monk' (1800; reprinted in *Wild Wreath*, 1804): the murdered nun's name is Rosa, like the novice's in *WJ* and like the murdered maiden's in Coleridge, and the remorseful Monk-murderer is released from a curse of immortality in line 46, while Coleridge's tormented monk cries 'Oh, let me die in peace, and be for ever dead!' (45). But the writing is dilute and the gothic thrills trite and mechanical, suggesting that the ballad is an exercise deriving from these sources rather than a variation that shares the impulse of *WJ*'s origin. To some degree, however, it anticipates *The Devil's Walk* and (more remotely) 'November, 1815' and 'The Sensitive Plant'. In ch. ii of *St Irvyne* Steindolph repeats the lines to his fellow-bandits, in response to their demand for 'metrical spectre tales', saying: 'I learnt it whilst in Germany; my old grandmother taught it me'. 'As Steindolph concluded, an universal shout of applause echoed through the cavern'.

Text from *St Irvyne* 47–51.
Published in *St Irvyne*.

1.

The death-bell beats! –
The mountain repeats
The echoing sound of the knell;
And the dark Monk now
5   Wraps the cowl round his brow,
As he sits in his lonely cell.

2.

And the cold hand of death
Chills his shuddering breath
As he lists to the fearful lay
10   Which the ghosts of the sky,
As they sweep wildly by,
Sing to departed day.
And they sing of the hour
When the stern fates had power
15   To resolve Rosa's form to its clay.

3.

But that hour is past;
And that hour was the last
Of peace to the dark Monk's brain.
Bitter tears from his eyes gushed silent and fast,
20   And he strove to suppress them in vain.

4.

Then his fair cross of gold he dashed on the floor,
When the death-knell struck on his ear,
  'Delight is in store
  For her evermore;
25 But for me is fate, horror, and fear.'

5.

  Then his eyes wildly rolled,
  When the death-bell tolled,
And he raged in terrific woe.
  And he stamped on the ground, –
30 But when ceased the sound,
Tears again began to flow.

6.

  And the ice of despair
  Chilled the wild throb of care,
And he sat in mute agony still;
35 Till the night-stars shone through the cloudless air,
And the pale moonbeam slept on the hill.

7.

  Then he knelt in his cell: –
  And the horrors of hell
Were delights to his agonized pain.
40 And he prayed to God to dissolve the spell
Which else must for ever remain.

8.

And in fervent pray'r he knelt on the ground,
  Till the abbey bell struck One:
His feverish blood ran chill at the sound:
45 A voice hollow and horrible murmured around–
  'The term of thy penance is done!'

9.

  Grew dark the night;
  The moonbeam bright
Waxed faint on the mountain high;
50 And, from the black hill,
  Went a voice cold and still, –
'Monk! thou art free to die.'

10.

  Then he rose on his feet,
  And his heart loud did beat,
55 And his limbs they were palsied with dread;

Whilst the grave's clammy dew
O'er his pale forehead grew;
And he shuddered to sleep with the dead.

11.

And the wild midnight storm
60   Raved around his tall form,
As he sought the chapel's gloom:
And the sunk grass did sigh
To the wind bleak and high
As he searched for the new-made tomb.

12.

65   And forms, dark and high,
Seemed around him to fly,
And mingle their yells with the blast:
And on the dark wall
Half-seen shadows did fall,
70   As enhorrored he onward passed.

13.

And the storm-fiends wild rave
O'er the new-made grave,
And dread shadows linger around.
The Monk called on God his soul to save,
75   And, in horror, sank on the ground.

14.

Then despair nerved his arm
To dispel the charm,
And he burst Rosa's coffin asunder.
And the fierce storm did swell
80   More terrific and fell
And louder pealed the thunder.

15.

And laughed, in joy, the fiendish throng
Mixed with ghosts of the mouldering dead:
And their grisly wings, as they floated along,
85   Whistled in murmurs dread.

16.

And her skeleton form the dead Nun reared
Which dripped with the chill dew of hell.
In her half-eaten eyeballs two pale flames appeared,
And triumphant their gleam on the dark Monk glared,
90   As he stood within the cell.

¶ 31.71–3. St Irvyne prints fiend's, with a comma after shadows, which makes an
unlikely sense rejected by all eds.

17.
And her lank hand lay on his shuddering brain;
But each power was nerved by fear. –
'I never, henceforth, may breathe again;
Death now ends my anguished pain. –
95   The grave yawns, – we meet there.'

18.
And her skeleton lungs did utter the sound,
So deadly, so lone, and so fell,
That in long vibrations shuddered the ground;
And as the stern notes floated around,
100   A deep groan was answered from hell.

32 'Ambition, power, and avarice'

Written between 10 October (the beginning of S.'s first term at Oxford) and 17
November 1810, when it was published as the first poem in *Posthumous
Fragments of Margaret Nicholson*. The publisher, Henry Slatter, recorded that
'the ease with which he composed many of the stanzas therein contained, is
truly astonishing; when surprised with a proof from the printers, in the
morning, he would frequently start off his sofa, exclaiming that that had been
his only bed, and, on being informed that the men were waiting for more
copy, he would sit down and write off a few stanzas, and send them to the press
without even revising or reading them, – this I have myself witnessed' (note in
Robert Montgomery's *Oxford, a Poem* (3rd edn 1833) 165). Hogg (*Hogg* i
260–9) gives a circumstantial but different account of the genesis of this book.
He was shown proofs of the poems, criticized their 'many irregularities and
incongruities', and declared they were publishable 'only as burlesque poetry'.
'The proofs lay in his rooms for some days, and we occasionally amused
ourselves during an idle moment by making them more and more ridiculous;
by striking out the more sober passages; by inserting whimsical conceits; and
especially by giving them what we called a dithyrambic character, which was
effected by cutting some lines in two, and joining the different parts together
that would agree in construction, but were the most discordant in sense'. Hogg
claimed credit for suggesting the title, which 'gave an object and purpose to
our burlesque; to ridicule the strange mixture of sentimentality with the
murderous fury of revolutionists, that was so prevalent in the compositions of
the day'. Margaret Nicholson was a local celebrity of Stockton-on-Tees, near
Hogg's family house at Norton, so she may have been his idea; but the poems
do not support the rest of his account. S. certainly thought highly enough of

98. Inversion: 'so deadly, etc. that the ground shuddered'.
¶ 32. Title. Untitled in *PFMN* (see S.'s 'Advertisement'); recommended to
Godwin as 'The Essay on War' on 16 January 1812 (*L* i 231).

this poem (which Hogg ascribed to 'some rhymester of the day' and dismissed as 'puling trash') to draw Godwin's attention to it fifteen months later (*L* i 231 with important note). It is much more likely that S.'s 'sly relish for a practical joke' expressed itself in exploiting this title (like that of *Q Mab*) as a publicity stunt and as a safeguard for doctrines which were—in essentials—seriously held (see *Cameron (1951)* 319). The volume ('with its expensive binding and grotesque gothic type set': *Holmes* 49) was published to raise money in support of the Irish journalist Peter Finnerty, a campaigner against the British government's Irish policies throughout the first decade of the 19th century (ibid. 49–51). The full title reads: *Posthumous Fragments of Margaret Nicholson; being poems found amongst the papers of that noted female who attempted the life of the King in 1786. Edited by John Fitzvictor.* Margaret Nicholson was a weak-minded seamstress who had menaced George III with a dessert-knife in 1786 and was confined to Bedlam for life (she outlived S. by six years). For further details see *SC* i 34–8. By posing as the nephew of a mad regicide, S. could voice outrageous sentiments without specifying the ones he shared. 'Fitzvictor', 'son of Victor', suggests the author's descent from Cazire's coadjutator. Hogg (i 268) and C. K. Sharpe (*Letters to and from Charles Kirkpatrick Sharpe, Esq.*, ed. Alexander Allardyce (1888) i 442–3) agree that the book enjoyed a limited vogue at Oxford, but the publisher (Montgomery, *Oxford* 165) remembered it as 'almost still-born'. It is S.'s only volume of verse that received no review. The 'Essay on War' combines several stock contemporary themes: the dying soldier's parting from his loved ones occurs e.g. in Campbell's 'Wounded Hussar', Scott's 'Maid of Toro', Cottle's 'War, a Fragment', and E. Darwin's *Loves of the Plants*; the devastation of war is stressed (if ironically) in Burke's *Vindication of Natural Society*; the inevitable fall of kings is a traditional commonplace. Writing to Godwin on 16 January 1812 S. affirms (*L* i 231): 'I have desired the publications of my earlier youth to be sent to you, you will perceive that *Zastrozzi* and *St Irvyne* were written prior to my acquaintance with your writings. The Essay on War a little Poem, since'. Probable direct influences include *Enquirer* Part II Essay V, Joseph Cottle's poem 'War, a Fragment', and especially Volney's *Ruins*. Cameron (*Cameron (1951)* 53–4) attributes the republicanism to Paine's *Rights of Man*, but Paine derides the importance of monarchy whereas S. here blames the sufferings of war exclusively on the power and vices of kings. His exculpation of the 'Almighty Power' derives from Volney, as also does the confident conclusion (see note to lines 85–9). The following 'Advertisement', purposely equivocal and pedantic, headed the poems:

> The energy and native genius of these Fragments, must be the only apology which the Editor can make for thus intruding them on the Public Notice. The FIRST I found with no title, and have left it so. It is intimately connected with the dearest interests of universal happiness; and much as we may deplore the fatal and enthusiastic tendency which the ideas of this poor female had acquired, we cannot fail to pay the tribute of unequivocal regret to the departed memory of genius, which, had it been rightly organized, would have made that intellect, which had since become the victim of frenzy and despair, a most brilliant ornament to society.

In case the sale of these Fragments evinces that the Public have any curiosity to be presented with a more copious collection of my unfortunate Aunt's Poems, I have other papers in my possession, which shall, in that case, be subjected to their notice. It may be supposed they require much arrangement; but I send the following to the press in the same state in which they came into my possession.

J.F.

Text from *PFMN*.
Published in *PFMN*.

Ambition, power, and avarice, now have hurled
Death, fate, and ruin, on a bleeding world.
See! on yon heath what countless victims lie,
Hark! what loud shrieks ascend through yonder sky;
5 Tell then the cause, 'tis sure the avenger's rage
Has swept these myriads from life's crowded stage:
Hark to that groan, an anguished hero dies,
He shudders in death's latest agonies;
Yet does a fleeting hectic flush his cheek,
10 Yet does his parting breath essay to speak—

'Oh God! my wife, my children—Monarch, thou
For whose support this fainting frame lies low,
For whose support in distant lands I bleed,
Let his friends' welfare be the warrior's meed.
15 He hears me not—ah! no—kings cannot hear,
For passion's voice has dulled their listless ear.
To thee, then, mighty God, I lift my moan,
Thou wilt not scorn a suppliant's anguished groan.
Oh! now I die—but still in death's fierce pain—
20 God hears my prayer—we meet, we meet again.'
He spake, reclined him on death's bloody bed,
And with a parting groan his spirit fled.

Oppressors of mankind, to *you* we owe
The baleful streams from whence these miseries flow;
25 For you how many a mother weeps her son,
Snatched from life's course ere half his race was run!
For you how many a widow drops a tear,
In silent anguish, on her husband's bier!

3. The 'heath' setting may derive from Campbell's 'Wounded Hussar' 7 (cp. line 71 below).
9. *hectic*] subst., 'a feverish colour'.
14. There was no provision for dependants of military casualties in 1810.
19. *still*] 'unchanging' (adv., *OED* sense 3).

'Is it then thine, Almighty Power,' she cries,
30   'Whence tears of endless sorrow dim these eyes?
Is this the system which thy powerful sway,
Which else in shapeless chaos sleeping lay,
Formed and approved?–it cannot be–but oh!
Forgive me, Heaven, my brain is warped by woe.'

35   'Tis not–he never bade the war-note swell,
He never triumphed in the work of hell–
Monarchs of earth! thine is the baleful deed,
Thine are the crimes for which thy subjects bleed.
Ah! when will come the sacred fated time,
40   When man unsullied by his leaders' crime,
Despising wealth, ambition, pomp, and pride,
Will stretch him fearless by his foemen's side?
Ah! when will come the time, when o'er the plain
No more shall death and desolation reign?
45   When will the sun smile on the bloodless field,
And the stern warrior's arm the sickle wield?
Not whilst some King, in cold ambition's dreams,
Plans for the field of death his plodding schemes;
Not whilst for private pique the public fall,
50   And one frail mortal's mandate governs all,
Swelled with command and mad with dizzying sway;
Who sees unmoved his myriads fade away,
Careless who lives or dies–so that he gains
Some trivial point for which he took the pains.
55   What then are Kings?–I see the trembling crowd,
I hear their fulsome clamours echoed loud;
Their stern oppressor pleased appears awhile,
But April's sunshine is a Monarch's smile–
Kings are but dust–the last eventful day
60   Will level all and make them lose their sway;
Will dash the sceptre from the Monarch's hand,
And from the warrior's grasp wrest the ensanguined
                                                            brand.

---

29. *thine*] i.e. 'thy system'. With lines 29–36 cp. *Ruins* ch. iii: '. . . has God
troubled the primitive and invariable order which he assigned to nature? . . . Is
it his pride that creates murderous wars; or the pride of kings and their
ministers?' etc.
37–8. *Monarchs of earth! thine . . . Thine*] Perhaps an extreme case of S.'s habit of
regarding a plural subject as a singular collective entity ('Monarchs of earth' =
'monarchy'); or of Margaret Nicholson's distracted mind.
53–4. Cp. Cottle's 'War, a Fragment' (1798) 173–4: '. . . heedless view your
subjects bleed and groan, / To add some bauble to a burthen'd throne'.

Oh! Peace, soft Peace, art thou for ever gone,
Is thy fair form indeed for ever flown?
65 And love and concord hast thou swept away,
As if incongruous with thy parted sway?
Alas I fear thou hast, for none appear.
Now o'er the palsied earth stalks giant Fear,
With War, and Woe, and Terror, in his train;
70 List'ning he pauses on the embattled plain,
Then speeding swiftly o'er the ensanguined heath,
Has left the frightful work to hell and death.
See! gory Ruin yokes his blood-stained car,
He scents the battle's carnage from afar;
75 Hell and destruction mark his mad career,
He tracks the rapid step of hurrying Fear;
Whilst ruined towns and smoking cities tell
That thy work, Monarch, is the work of hell.
'It is thy work!' I hear a voice repeat.
80 Shakes the broad basis of thy blood-stained seat;
And at the orphan's sigh, the widow's moan,
Totters the fabric of thy guilt-stained throne—
'It is thy work, O Monarch;' now the sound
Fainter and fainter yet is borne around,
85 Yet to enthusiast ears the murmurs tell
That heaven, indignant at the work of hell,
Will soon the cause, the hated cause remove,
Which tears from earth peace, innocence, and love.

33 Fragment. Supposed to be an Epithalamium of Francis Ravaillac and Charlotte Cordé

Placed second in *PFMN* and probably written between 10 October and 17 November 1810. S. told Fergus Graham on 21 November, after sending him the volume, that 'the latter part of the Epithalamium was composed in compliance with the desires of a poetical friend, & is omitted in the copy which I send to Field Place' (*L* i 22), but nine days later this account was expanded and modified: 'The part of the Epithalamium which you mention, (i.e. from the end of Satan's triumph) is the production of a friend's *mistress*; it had been concluded there but she thought it abrupt & added this; it is omitted in

73. Cp. Cottle, op. cit. 63: 'as Destruction roll'd his scythed car'.
85–8. Cp. *Ruins* ch. xiii: 'a new age will make its appearance, an age . . . of dread to tyrants . . . and of hope to the whole world'.

numbers of the copies,–that which I sent to my Mother of course did not
contain it . . . Of course to my Father Peg is a profound secret . . .' (*L* i 23). The
'poetical friend' must have been Hogg, and his '*mistress*' (in the Tudor sense)
Elizabeth S., but it is most unlikely that this attribution was anything but an
invention to titillate the interest of either Hogg or Graham or both; nor are
lines 82–102 (presumably the sensitive passage) omitted in any of the five
known copies of *PFMN*. S. relied heavily for sales on the sensational nature of
the 'Epithalamium', which 'will make it sell like wildfire, and as the *Nephew* is
kept a profound secret, there can arise no danger from the indelicacy of the
Aunt' (ibid.). C. K. Sharpe, however, a Christ Church contemporary, knew
the author's identity and said that his book 'though stuffed full of treason, is
extremely dull; . . . Shelley's style is much like that of Moore burlesqued; for
Frank is a very foul-mouthed fellow, and Charlotte, one of the most impudent
brides that I ever met with in a book' (*Letters to and from Charles Kirkpatrick
Sharpe, Esq.*, ed. Alexander Allardyce (1888) i 442–3). There are numerous
analogues in verse and prose of a visionary journey to a vantage-point from
which society or the universe can be contemplated. The sources of the poem,
an anticipation of *Q Mab*, include the archetype, Scipio's Dream (Cicero, *De
Re Publica* VI ix–xxvi) for the music of the spheres; Volney's *Ruins* ch. iv, and
Southey's *Joan of Arc* (1795) Bk ix, for the despondency over human society
before the vision; Pope's 'Eloisa to Abelard' for the gothic, sensual, equivocal-
ly Christian atmosphere (cp. 'Eloisa' 155–70); and Moore's 'The Grecian Girl's
Dream of the Blessed Islands' (*Odes and Epistles*, 1806), for the dream of
assumption into Paradise, the kissing, and many verbal parallels. See also N.
Crook and D. Guiton, *Shelley's Venomed Melody* (Cambridge 1986) 42–3. The
political content seems to be S.'s own invention. A. M. D. Hughes (*Hughes* 52)
pronounces the 'Epithalamium' to be the one 'unmistakable parody' in the
book; but the joke is aimed primarily at orthodox Christianity, seen at this
time as the main enemy. Tyrannicides are welcomed into Heaven by a chorus
of angels, while their victims go to Hell; such congenial minds will meet in
eternity, even when separated in life by several centuries; and although it will
clearly be spent in Heaven, not Moore's pagan Elysium, eternity's advantage is
that of limitless sensual indulgence. Charlotte Corday d'Armont (1768–93), a
Girondin descendent of Corneille, was guillotined after assassinating Marat for
his reputed part in the September massacres of 1792; François Ravaillac (1578–
1610) was quartered for the assassination of Henry IV.
Text from *PFMN*.
Published in *PFMN*.

> 'Tis midnight now–athwart the murky air,
>   Dank lurid meteors shoot a livid gleam;
> From the dark storm–clouds flashes a fearful glare,
>   It shows the bending oak, the roaring stream.
> 5   I pondered on the woes of lost mankind,

¶ *33.5.* Cp. Volney's *Ruins* ch. ii (before the Genius conducts the author aloft): 'I

I pondered on the ceaseless rage of Kings;
My rapt soul dwelt upon the ties that bind
    The mazy volume of commingling things,
When fell and wild misrule to man stern sorrow brings.

10   I heard a yell—it was not the knell,
    When the blasts on the wild lake sleep,
That floats on the pause of the summer gale's swell,
    O'er the breast of the waveless deep.

I thought it had been death's accents cold
15   That bade me recline on the shore;
I laid mine hot head on the surge-beaten mould,
    And thought to breathe no more.

        But a heavenly sleep
        That did suddenly steep
20   In balm my bosom's pain,
        Pervaded my soul,
        And free from control
        Did mine intellect range again.

Methought enthroned upon a silvery cloud,
25   Which floated mid a strange and brilliant light,
My form upborne by viewless ether rode,
    And spurned the lessening realms of earthly night.
What heavenly notes burst on my ravished ears,
    What beauteous spirits met my dazzled eye!
30   Hark! louder swells the music of the spheres,
    More clear the forms of speechless bliss float by,
And heavenly gestures suit etherial melody.

But fairer than the spirits of the air,
    More graceful than the Sylph of symmetry,
35   Than the enthusiast's fancied love more fair,
    Were the bright forms that swept the azure sky.

---

give myself up to the most gloomy meditations on human affairs'. So too the
Angel shows Joan of Arc the miseries in store for the unrighteous before
predicting the overthrow of tyranny in Southey's poem.

24–7. Cp. Volney's *Ruins* ch. iv: 'penetrated as with a celestial flame, the ties
that fix us to the earth seemed to be loosened; and lifted by the wing of the
genius, I felt myself like a light vapour conveyed in the uppermost region'.

30. *the music of the spheres*] Probably suggested directly by Cicero, *De Re Publica*
VI xviii.

34. *Sylph of symmetry*] After Pope's *Rape of the Lock* (1714), 'sylphs' (graceful
spirits of the air, originally male) were employed by many poets, e.g. Moore in
The Poetical Works of the Late Thomas Little (1801).

Enthroned in roseate light, a heavenly band
   Strewed flowers of bliss that never fade away;
They welcome virtue to its native land,
40   And songs of triumph greet the joyous day
When endless bliss the woes of fleeting life repay.

Congenial minds will seek their kindred soul,
   E'en though the tide of time has rolled between;
They mock weak matter's impotent control,
45   And seek of endless life the eternal scene.
At death's vain summons *this* will never die,
   In nature's chaos *this* will not decay—
These are the bands which closely, warmly, tie
   Thy soul, O Charlotte, 'yond this chain of clay,
50   To him who thine must be till time shall fade away.

Yes, Francis! thine was the dear knife that tore
   A tyrant's heart-strings from his guilty breast,
Thine was the daring at a tyrant's gore
   To smile in triumph, to contemn the rest;
55   And thine, loved glory of thy sex! to tear
   From its base shrine a despot's haughty soul,
To laugh at sorrow in secure despair,
   To mock, with smiles, life's lingering control,
And triumph mid the griefs that round thy fate did roll.

60   Yes! the fierce spirits of the avenging deep
   With endless tortures goad their guilty shades.
I see the lank and ghastly spectres sweep
   Along the burning length of yon arcades;
And I see Satan stalk athwart the plain;
65   He hastes along the burning soil of hell.
'Welcome ye despots, to my dark domain;
   With maddening joy mine anguished senses swell
To welcome to their home the friends I love so well.'

*   *   *   *   *

*   *   *   *   *

Hark! to those notes, how sweet, how thrilling sweet
70   They echo to the sound of angels' feet.

*   *   *   *   *

37–8. Cp. 'Eloisa to Abelard' 317–18: 'prepare your roseate bow'rs, / Celestial palms, and ever-blooming flow'rs'.

42. Cp. Moore's 'Grecian Girl's Dream' 99–100: 'how divinely sweet / Is the pure joy, when kindred spirits meet!'

66. Welcome ye despots,] Welcome thou despots, *PFMN.* (Possibly an intentional solecism.)

Oh haste to the bower where roses are spread,
For there is prepared thy nuptial bed.
Oh haste–hark! hark!–they're gone.'

★   ★   ★   ★   ★

CHORUS OF SPIRITS

Stay ye days of contentment and joy,
75   Whilst love every care is erasing,
Stay ye pleasures that never can cloy,
    And ye spirits that can never cease pleasing.

And if any soft passion be near,
    Which mortals, frail mortals, can know,
80   Let love shed on the bosom a tear,
    And dissolve the chill ice-drop of woe.

SYMPHONY

FRANCIS

'Soft, my dearest angel, stay,
Oh! you suck my soul away;
Suck on, suck on, I glow, I glow!
85   Tides of maddening passion roll,
And streams of rapture drown my soul.
Now give me one more billing kiss,
Let your lips now repeat the bliss,
Endless kisses steal my breath,
90   No life can equal such a death.'

CHARLOTTE

'Oh! yes, I will kiss thine eyes so fair,
    And I will clasp thy form;
Serene is the breath of the balmy air,
    But I think, love, thou feelest me warm.
95   And I will recline on thy marble neck

83–4. 'There were some verses, I remember, with a good deal about sucking in them; to these I objected, as unsuitable to the gravity of an university, but S. declared they would be the most impressive of all' (*Hogg* i 267). S. uses the convention of lovers exchanging souls as they kiss, generally before dying (with possible equivocation over 'dying'), as in Marlowe, *Faustus* 1357: 'Her lips suck forth my soul'; Dryden, *Don Sebastian* III i: 'Sucking each other's Souls while we expire'; Pope, 'Eloisa to Abelard' 324: 'Suck my last breath, and catch my flying soul'. S.'s purpose here is purely erotic; see 'Kissing Agathon' for a later Platonic usage.

Till I mingle into thee.
And I will kiss the rose on thy cheek,
    And thou shalt give kisses to me.
For here is no morn to flout our delight,
100   Oh! dost thou not joy at this?
And here we may lie an endless night,
    A long, long night of bliss.'

Spirits! when raptures move,
Say what it is to love,
105 When passion's tear stands on the cheek,
    When bursts the unconscious sigh;
And the tremulous lips dare not speak
    What is told by the soul-felt eye.
But what is sweeter to revenge's ear
110   Than the fell tyrant's last expiring yell?
Yes! than love's sweetest blisses 'tis more dear
    To drink the floatings of a despot's knell.
I wake—'tis done—'tis o'er . . .

      ★   ★   ★   ★   ★

      ★   ★   ★   ★   ★

34 Despair

The third poem in *PFMN*, written between 10 October and 17 November
1810. Though including summer imagery (lines 3–4), and probably connected
emotionally with S.'s broken engagement, the gothic exaggerations and delusions are dramatically contrived for Margaret Nicholson's utterance. In lines
25–36 the speaker becomes unmistakably related to the Wandering Jew. Only
the second is a regular Spenserian stanza.
Text from *PFMN*.
Published in *PFMN*.

And canst thou mock mine agony, thus calm
    In cloudless radiance, Queen of silver night?
Can you, ye flow'rets, spread your perfumed balm

96. *mingle*] One of S.'s habitual terms for sexual intercourse; here perhaps
suggested by Moore's 'Grecian Girl's Dream' 107: 'when he mingles with his
fountain-bride'.
110. *last expiring yell*] See line 10, and letter to Hogg, 26 December 1810 (*L* i 32):
'. . . that which injured me shall perish! I even now by anticipation hear the
expiring yell of intolerance!'
¶ 34.2. *cloudless radiance*] There was a full moon on the nights of October 13 and
November 11 in 1810.

Mid pearly gems of dew that shine so bright?
5 And you wild winds, thus can you sleep so still
Whilst throbs the tempest of my breast so high?
Can the fierce night-fiends rest on yonder hill,
And, in the eternal mansions of the sky,
Can the directors of the storm in powerless silence lie?

10 Hark! I hear music on the zephyr's wing,
Louder it floats along the unruffled sky;
Some fairy sure has touched the viewless string—
Now faint in distant air the murmurs die;
Awhile it stills the tide of agony.
15 Now—now it loftier swells—again stern woe
Arises with the awakening melody.
Again fierce torments, such as demons know,
In bitterer, feller tide, on this torn bosom flow.

Arise ye sightless spirits of the storm,
20 Ye unseen minstrels of the aërial song,
Pour the fierce tide around this lonely form,
And roll the tempest's wildest swell along.
Dart the red lightning, wing the forkèd flash,
Pour from thy cloud-formed hills the thunder's roar;
25 Arouse the whirlwind—and let ocean dash
In fiercest tumult on the rocking shore,
Destroy this life or let earth's fabric be no more.

Yes! every tie that links me here is dead;
Mysterious fate, thy mandate I obey,
30 Since hope and peace, and joy, for aye are fled,
I come, terrific power, I come away.
Then o'er this ruined soul let spirits of hell,
In triumph, laughing wildly, mock its pain;
And though with direst pangs mine heart-strings swell,
35 I'll echo back their deadly yells again,
Cursing the power that ne'er made aught in vain.

35 Fragment

The fourth poem in *PFMN*, written between 10 October and 17 November 1810. A theatrically exaggerated 'mad song', based (in the first two stanzas) on the conflict for Margaret's soul between Hell, symbolized by the yell of the fiends, and Heaven, symbolized by planetary music as in No. 33; and (in the second two stanzas) on the emotions of frustrated love that preoccupied S. at

9. *directors of the storm*] 'ghosts of deceased warriors, who were supposed in those times to rule the storms' (James Macpherson, *Fingal* (2nd edn 1762) iii 38*n*.). See also No. 30 and note; *WJ* 482–92 and note.

this time. The symbolism and the dialogue have an embryonic relationship
with those in 'Julian and Maddalo'.
Text from *PFMN*.
Published in *PFMN*.

> Yes! all is past—swift time has fled away,
>   Yet its swell pauses on my sickening mind;
> How long will horror nerve this frame of clay?
>   I'm dead, and lingers yet my soul behind.
> 5 Oh! powerful fate, revoke thy deadly spell,
>   And yet that may not ever, ever be,
> Heaven will not smile upon the work of hell;
>   Ah! no, for heaven cannot smile on me;
> Fate, envious fate, has sealed my wayward destiny.
>
> 10 I sought the cold brink of the midnight surge,
>   I sighed beneath its wave to hide my woes,
> The rising tempest sung a funeral dirge,
>   And on the blast a frightful yell arose.
> Wild flew the meteors o'er the maddened main,
> 15   Wilder did grief athwart my bosom glare;
> Stilled was the unearthly howling, and a strain
>   Swelled mid the tumult of the battling air,
> 'Twas like a spirit's song, but yet more soft and fair.
>
> I met a maniac—like he was to me,
> 20   I said—'Poor victim, wherefore dost thou roam?
> And canst thou not contend with agony,
>   That thus at midnight thou dost quit thine home?'
> 'Ah, there she sleeps: cold is her bloodless form,
>   And I will go to slumber in her grave;
> 25 And then our ghosts, whilst raves the maddened storm,
>   Will sweep at midnight o'er the wildered wave;
> Wilt thou our lowly beds with tears of pity lave?'
>
> 'Ah! no, I cannot shed the pitying tear,
>   This breast is cold, this heart can feel no more;
> 30 But I can rest me on thy chilling bier,
>   Can shriek in horror to the tempest's roar.'

★   ★   ★   ★   ★

¶ 35.11. 'I longed to escape my troubles by drowning myself'.
23–31. Cp. 'Julian and Maddalo' 291–6, 386–91.

36 The Spectral Horseman

The fifth poem in *PFMN*; probably written between 10 October and 17
November 1810. S. was evidently determined to pack as many miscellaneous
gothicisms as possible into this, his last published poem of the kind: Scottish
Banshee (line 5), Hungarian vampire (13), hints of Faustus (25–6), the 'wilde
Jäger' (37–8), the Wandering Jew (39–43), Finn or Cuchullin (47–52), and
nameless monsters (59). The supernatural huntsman figures in several Euro-
pean legends, and phantom riders abound in gothic ballads of the time, esp. in
S.'s favourite 'Lenore', in 'The Bleeding Nun', in Scott's 'The Wild Hunts-
men', and in Leyden's 'The Elfin-King', all in *Tales of Wonder* and all drawn on
for various materials. Moore's 'The Shield' also contributed (*Poetical Works of
Thomas Little*, 1801); but the most pervasive influence is Ossian. The metre,
unrhymed anapaestic tetrameters, is unusual, though still close to that of
Scott's 'Hellvellyn'.
Text from *PFMN*.
Published in *PFMN*.

> What was the shriek that struck fancy's ear
> As it sate on the ruins of time that is past?
> Hark! it floats on the fitful blast of the wind,
> And breathes to the pale moon a funeral sigh.
> 5   Is it the Benshie's moan on the storm,
> Or a shivering fiend that thirsting for sin
> Seeks murder and guilt when virtue sleeps,
> Winged with the power of some ruthless king,
> And sweeps o'er the breast of the prostrate plain?
> 10   It was not a fiend from the regions of hell
> That poured its low moan on the stillness of night;
> It was not a ghost of the guilty dead,
> Nor a yelling vampire reeking with gore;
> But aye at the close of seven years' end,

¶ *36.5. Is it*] It is *PFMN*. *the Benshie's moan*] The wail of the Banshee (*bean-sídhe*,
'fairy-woman') was supposed, in the Scottish Highlands and in Ireland, to
foretell death or disaster. The spelling suggests that S. found the word in
Scott's *Lady of the Lake* III vii 20 and note.
6. *shivering fiend*] Borrowed from Moore's 'The Shield' (*Poetical Works of
Thomas Little*, 1801).
9. *plain?*] plain. *PFMN*.
13 *vampire*] Perhaps introduced from Southey's *Thalaba* (1801) viii 9–10 and
note.
14, 16. seven years' end] The Knight in Green on his ghostly courser in J.
Leyden's 'The Elfin-King' (*Tales of Wonder* i) was seen 'At every seven years'
end'.

15   That voice is mixed with the swell of the storm,
      And aye at the close of seven years' end,
      A shapeless shadow that sleeps on the hill
      Awakens and floats on the mist of the heath.
      It is not the shade of a murdered man,
20   Who has rushed uncalled to the throne of his God,
      And howls in the pause of the eddying storm.
      This voice is low, cold, hollow, and chill,
      'Tis not heard by the ear, but is felt in the soul.
      'Tis more frightful far than the death-demon's scream,
25   Or the laughter of fiends when they howl o'er the corpse
      Of a man who has sold his soul to hell.
      It tells the approach of a mystic form,
      A white courser bears the shadowy sprite;
      More thin they are than the mists of the mountain,
30   When the clear moonlight sleeps on the waveless lake.
      More pale *his* cheek than the snows of Nithona
      When winter rides on the northern blast,
      And howls in the midst of the leafless wood.
      Yet when the fierce swell of the tempest is raving,
35   And the whirlwinds howl in the caves of Inisfallen,
      Still secure mid the wildest war of the sky,
      The phantom courser scours the waste,
      And his rider howls in the thunder's roar.
      O'er him the fierce bolts of avenging heaven
40   Pause, as in fear, to strike his head.
      The meteors of midnight recoil from his figure,
      Yet the wildered peasant that oft passes by
      With wonder beholds the blue flash through his form:
      And his voice, though faint as the sighs of the dead,
45   The startled passenger shudders to hear,
      More distinct than the thunder's wildest roar.
      Then does the dragon, who chained in the caverns
      To eternity, curses the champion of Erin,
      Moan and yell loud at the lone hour of midnight,
50   And twine his vast wreaths round the forms of the
                                                    demons;

31. *Nithona*] Apparently a combination of Inisthona, the Scandinavian 'island of waves' in Ossian's 'War of Inis-thona', and Ithona in his 'Conlath and Cuthóna'.
35. *Inisfallen*] Ireland ('island of the Fa-il, or Falans').
43. Ossian's ghosts are similarly thin and semi-transparent.
48. *champion of Erin*] During his qualifying ordeals for becoming Champion of Erin (Ulster), the legendary Cuchullin killed a worm or dragon which rose from a lake. S.'s source for this story is untraced.

Then in agony roll his death-swimming eyeballs,
Though wildered by death, yet never to die!
Then he shakes from his skeleton folds the nightmares,
Who, shrieking in agony, seek the couch
55   Of some fevered wretch who courts sleep in vain;
Then the tombless ghosts of the guilty dead
In horror pause on the fitful gale.
They float on the swell of the eddying tempest,
And scared seek the caves of gigantic ★ ★
60   Where their thin forms pour unearthly sounds
On the blast that sweeps the breast of the lake,
And mingles its swell with the moonlight air.

37 Melody to a Scene of Former Times

Sixth and last poem in *PFMN*; written between 10 October and 17 November
1810. It is virtually free from gothic sensationalism and seems to have less
relevance to Margaret Nicholson than to S.'s own feelings. His entry to
Oxford was evidently used by Harriet Grove and her parents as an opportunity
to end the relationship that had been precariously alive during the past year. S.
nowhere discloses details (his letter to Hogg of 26 December is unreliable: see
SC ii 675), sometimes complaining of 'fate', sometimes of 'perjured love'; but
he always blames religious prejudice as chiefly responsible for the break, which
therefore inaugurates a passionate and lasting revulsion from orthodox
Christianity.
Text from *PFMN*.
Published in *PFMN*.

Art thou indeed for ever gone,
    For ever, ever lost to me?
Must this poor bosom beat alone,
    Or beat at all, if not for thee?
5   Ah! why was love to mortals given,
To lift them to the height of heaven,
Or dash them to the depths of hell?
    Yet I do not reproach thee, dear!
Ah! no, the agonies that swell
10   This panting breast, this frenzied brain
    Might wake my ——'s slumb'ring tear.

59. *gigantic* ★ ★] noun omitted *PFMN*, no doubt for 'authenticity'.
¶ *37.11. my* ——'s] Presumably 'my Harriet's'.

Oh! heaven is witness I did love,
And heaven does know I love thee still,
Does know the fruitless sick'ning thrill,
15   When reason's judgment vainly strove
To blot thee from my memory;
But which might never, never be.
Oh! I appeal to that blest day
When passion's wildest ecstasy
20   Was coldness to the joys I knew,
When every sorrow sunk away.
Oh! I had never lived before,
But now those blisses are no more.
      And now I cease to live again,
25   I do not blame thee love; ah no!
The breast that feels this anguished woe
Throbs for thy happiness alone.
Two years of speechless bliss are gone,
I thank thee dearest for the dream.
30   'Tis night–what faint and distant scream
Comes on the wild and fitful blast?
It moans for pleasures that are past,
It moans for days that are gone by.
Oh! lagging hours how slow you fly!
35   I see a dark and lengthened vale,
The black view closes with the tomb;
But darker is the lowering gloom
    That shades the intervening dale.
In visioned slumber for awhile
40   I seem again to share thy smile,
I seem to hang upon thy tone.
    Again you say, 'Confide in me,
For I am thine, and thine alone,
    And thine must ever, ever be.'
45   But oh! awak'ning still anew,
Athwart my enanguished senses flew
    A fiercer, deadlier agony!

38 To Mary–I

The first of a group of four poems (Nos. 38, 39, 41, 42) in *Esd*, dated
'November 1810', and introduced by the following 'Advertisement':

18. *that blest day*] If line 28, 'Two years of speechless bliss are gone', is
autobiographical, the date would coincide approximately with Harriet G.'s
hypothetical visit to Field Place in August 1808, when S. was just sixteen.

The few poems immediately following are selected from many written during three weeks of an entrancement caused by hearing Mary's story——I hope that the delicate & discriminating genius of the friend who related it to me, will allow the publication of the heart breaking facts under the title of Leonora.—For myself at that time nondum amabam, et amare amabam, quaerebam quid amarem, amans amare*

Mary died three months [after canc.] before I heard her tale.—
     * Confess. St. Augustin.

One other poem evidently among the 'many written' (No. 40) was sent to Elizabeth Hitchener on 23 November 1811. Nothing more is known of 'Mary' than can be gleaned from these poems, except for S.'s comment of 3 January 1811 (L i 36) on Hogg's unpublished (and lost) novel Leonora: 'It is divine, is delightful not that I like yr. heroine, but the poor Mary is a character worthy of Heaven. I adore it.' Possibly S. 'heard her tale' read to him from the novel. It seems that Mary, a minor character, was deprived of her lover's esteem by another woman (?Leonora), and died of a broken heart (in August 1810, if she ever really existed) after attempting suicide. The poems show an imaginative projection on S.'s part, half possessive, half self-identifying, towards this other victim, real or fictional, of perjured love, but the emotion is decidedly second-hand. S.'s quotation from the opening of Bk III of St Augustine's Confessions ('I was not yet in love, and I loved to be in love, I sought what I might love, loving to be in love') suggests, as Cameron observes (Esd Nbk 245), that the 'Adver-tisement' was written after S.'s marriage to Harriet Westbrook. S. repeated the quotation inside a diary (1814) used by Claire Clairmont (see Claire Jnl 60–2), where it is apparently connected with Cornelia Turner; and again as the epigraph to Alastor (1816).

Text from Esd ff. 56ʳ–57ᵛ (Esd No. 37: quoted by permission of the Carl H. Pforzheimer Library).

Published in Esd Nbk 116–17; Esd Poems 69–70; SC iv 1005–8 (transcript of Esd).

Dear girl! thou art wildered by madness,
    Yet do not look so, sweet,
I could share in the sigh of thy sadness,
    Thy woe my soul could meet.

5   I loved a heart sincerely.
        Yes! dear it was to mine;
    Yet, Mary, I love more dearly
        One tender look of thine.

¶ 38.2. so, sweet,] so sweet Esd. The stanza seems to mean: 'if your affliction consisted merely in suffering, I could share it with you'.

Oh! do not say that Heaven
10   Will frown on errors past:
Thy faults are all forgiven,
Thy virtues ever last.

The cup with death o'erflowing
I'll drink, fair girl, to thee,
15   For when the storm is blowing
To shelter we may flee.

Thou canst not bear to languish
In this frail chain of clay,
And I am tired of anguish;
20   Love! let us haste away!

Like thee I fear to weather
Death's darksome wave alone.
We'll take the voyage together;
Come, Mary! let's begone.

25   Strange mists my woe efface, love,
And thou art pale in Death . . .
Give one, one last embrace, love,
And we resign our breath.

39 To Mary—II

Written November 1810 (see headnote to No. 38). Except for the longer last
line of each stanza the metre is that of the Minstrel's Song in Chatterton's *Aella*.
This funeral music haunted S., who used it again in 'Autumn: A Dirge'.
Text from *Esd* ff. 57ᵛ–58ʳ (*Esd* No. 38: quoted by permission of the Carl H.
Pforzheimer Library).
Published in *Esd Nbk* 118; *Esd Poems* 70–71; *SC* iv 1007–8 (transcript of *Esd*).

10. 'This opinion is of all others the most deeply rooted in my conviction. The
enquirer will laugh at it as a dream, the Christian will abhor it as a blasphemy. –
Mary, who repeatedly attempted suicide, yet was unwilling to die alone–Nor
is it probable that she would, had I instead of my friend been subjected to the
trial of sitting a summer night by her side, –whilst two glasses of poison stood
on the table, & she folded me to her tremulous bosom in extasies of friendship
& despair! [What are the Romances of Leadenhall Str. to this of real life? *canc.*]':
S.'s note, not keyed to the text but probably referring to line 10 (cp. *L&C* VIII
xxii; the irrelevance of punishment and of self-punishment was indeed one of
S.'s rooted convictions). Cameron argues convincingly (*Esd Nbk* 355) that S.
improvised this note while in process of copying the poem into the notebook.
The Minerva Press and its circulating library, established in Leadenhall Street
c. 1790, popularized the novel of gothic sensation (see Amy Cruse, *The
Englishman and his Books in the Early 19th Century* (1930) 93–107).

Fair one! calm that bursting heart . . .
 Dares then fate to frown on thee,
Lovely, spotless as thou art?
 Though its worst poison lights on me.
5 Then dry that tear;
  Thou needest not fear
These woes when thy limbs are cold on the bier.

Start not from winter's breathing, dearest,
 Though bleak is yonder hill . . .
10 As perjured love the blast thou fearest
 Is not half so deadly chill;
  Like these winds that blow
  No remorse does it know
And colder it strikes than the driving snow.

15 The tomb is damp and dark and low
 Yet with thee the tomb I do not dread;
There is not a place of frightful woe
 Where with thee I'd refuse to lay my head . . .
  But our souls shall not sleep
20 In the grave damp and deep
But in love and devotion their holy-day keep.

40 To Mary who died in this opinion

Presumably written in November 1810 with the other 'Mary' poems (see headnote to No. 38); if so, it fits logically before No. 41. S. sent it to Elizabeth Hitchener on 23 November 1811 (*L* i 190), commenting: 'I transcribe a little Poem I found this morning. It was written [?nearly three years *canc.*] some time ago, but as it appears to shew what I then thought of eternal life I send it.' 'Then' and throughout his life S. was sceptical of a future existence but realized that 'what we earnestly desire we are very much prejudiced in favor of' (to Eliz. Hitchener, 24 November 1811, *L* i 192).
Text from BL Add. MS 37496, f. 57.
Published in *Rossetti 1870* ii 525–6.

¶ *39. Stanza 2.* Echoes two Shakespearean dirges, that of the king's sons in *Cymbeline* (IV ii 258–60), and Amiens' in *As You Like It* (II vii 174–93).
21. devotion] 'The expression *devotion*, is not used in a religious sense, for which abuse of this lovely word, few have a greater horror than the Author' (S.'s note).

Maiden, quench the glare of sorrow
   Struggling in thine haggard eye:
Firmness dare to borrow
   From the wreck of destiny;
5 For the ray morn's bloom revealing
   Can never boast so bright an hue
As that which mocks concealing
   And sheds its loveliest light on you.

Yet is the tie departed
10 Which bound thy lovely soul to bliss;
Has it left thee broken-hearted
   In a world so cold as this?
Yet though, fainting fair one,
   Sorrow's self thy cup has given,
15 Dream thou'lt meet thy dear one
   Never more to part, in Heaven.

Existence would I barter
   For a dream so dear as thine,
And smile to die a martyr
20 On affection's bloodless shrine;
Nor would I change for *pleasure*
   That withered hand and ashy cheek
If my heart enshrined a treasure
   Such as forces thine to break.

41 To Mary—III

Written November 1810 (see headnote to No. 38).
Text from *Esd* ff. 58ᵛ–59ʳ (*Esd* No. 39: quoted by permission of the Carl H.
Pforzheimer Library).
Published in *Esd Nbk* 119–20; *Esd Poems* 71–2; *SC* iv 1009–10 (transcript of
Esd).

¶ *40.9. departed*] i.e. 'parted', 'broken' (arch. sense i 4 in *OED*).
9–10. Probably an inversion; but *Hutchinson* puts question marks at the ends of
lines 2 and 4.
20. shrine] shine *MS*.
21. pleasure] underlined in *MS*; pleasure *eds*.
21–4. 'If I had love like yours in my heart, I would willingly accept the physical
effects of suffering'.
23. enshrined] enshined *MS*.
24. Such as] *Rossetti 1870*. The words are torn out in *MS*, but may have been
present when R. saw it.

Mary, Mary! art thou gone
  To sleep in thine earthy cell?
Presses thy breast the death-cold stone?
Pours none the tear, the sob, the groan
5 Where murdered virtue sleeps alone,
  Where its first glory fell?

Mary, Mary, past is past!
  I submit in silence to fate's decree,
Though the tear of distraction gushes fast
10 And at night when the lank reeds hiss in the blast
  My spirit mourns in sympathy.

Thou wert more fair in mind than are
  The fabled heavenly train,
But thine was the pang of corroding care,
15 Thine cold contempt and lone despair
And thwarted love more hard to bear . . .
  And I, wretch! weep that such they were
  And I . . . still drag my chain.

Thou wert but born to weep, to die,
20 To feel dissolved the dearest tie,
Its fragments by the pitiless world
Adown the blast of fortune hurled
To strive with envy's wreckful storm;
Thou wert but born to weep and die,
25 Nor could thy ceaseless misery
Nor heavenly virtues aught avail,
Nor taintless innocence prevail
With the world's slaves thy love to spare,
Nor the magic unearthly atmosphere
30   That wrapped thine etherial form.

Such, loveliest Mary, was thy fate,
  And such is Virtue's doom . . .
Contempt, neglect and hatred wait
Where yawns a wide and dreary gate,
35   To drag its votaries to the tomb, –
Sweet flower! that blooms amid the weeds
  Where the rank serpent, interest, feeds.

¶ *41.6. its first glory*] 'virtue's foremost ornament'.
10. Cp. Southey, *Joan of Arc* (1796) ix 22–3: 'hoarse / The long reeds rustled to the gale of night'.
18. And] The conjunction has the force of 'whereas': 'I weep that I am still alive while you have suffered and died'.
19, 24. wert but born] i.e. 'wert born but'.
30. etherial] *above* heavenly *Esd canc.*
37. rank] dank *Esd Nbk, SC.*

42 To the Lover of Mary

Fourth and last of the 'Mary' group of poems in *Esd*, written in November
1810 (see headnote to No. 38). The frank dualism and belief in immortality of
stanzas 1–2 are neither endorsed nor rejected by the author, but portrayed as
attractive hypotheses ('O this were joy'). In stanza 3 S. recommends (with a
Biblical allusion) outsoaring Heaven by working for a Paradise on earth (cp.
PU III iv 202–3).
Text from *Esd* ff. 59ᵛ–60ʳ (*Esd* No. 40: quoted by permission of the Carl H.
Pforzheimer Library).
Published in *Esd Nbk* 121–2; *Esd Poems* 72–3; *SC* iv 1010–12 (transcript of *Esd*).

> Drink the exhaustless moonbeam where its glare
>   Wanly lights murdered virtue's funeral
>   And tremulous sheds on the corpse-shrouding pall
>   A languid, languid flare . . .
> 5   Hide thee, poor wretch, where yonder baleful yew
>   Sheds o'er the clay that now is tenantless,
>   Whose spirit once thrilled to thy warm caress,
>   Its deadly, deadly dew;
>   The moon-ray will not quench thy misery,
> 10 But the yew's death-drops will bring peace to thee,
>   And yonder clay-cold grave thy bridal bed shall be.
>
> And since the Spirit dear that breathes of Heaven
>   Has burst the powerless bondage of its clay
>   And soars an Angel to eternal day,
> 15   Purged of its earthly leaven,
>   Thy yearnings now shall bend thee to the tomb,
>   Oblivion blot a life without a stain
>   And death's cold hand round thy heart's ceaseless pain
>   Enfold its veil of gloom.
> 20 The wounds shall close of Misery's scorpion goad
>   When Mary greets thee in her blest abode
>   And worships holy Love, in purity thy God.
>
> O this were joy! and such as none would fear
>   To purchase by a life of passing woe,

¶ 42.20. i.e. the wounds inflicted by Misery's goad.
22. *Love, in purity thy God.*] Comma as in *Esd*. Love in purity, thy God *Esd
Poems*. The notion is that when Mary's lover attains the pure state of Heaven he
too will recognize Love as the God he worships (cp. lines 32–3 and S.'s note).
Stanza 3. S.'s line-count shows that this stanza was added after the final count
in the book, perhaps having been mislaid (*SC* iv 1011).
24. *passing*] surpassing.

25   For on this earth the sickly flowers that glow
         Breathe of perfection there.
      Yet live—for others barter thine own bliss,
         And living show what towering Virtue dares
         To accomplish even in this vale of tears:
30   Turn Hell to Paradise
      And spurning selfish joy soar high above
      The Heaven of Heavens, let ever eternal love,
      Despised awhile, thy sense of holier Virtue prove.

43 To Death

Composed in or shortly after December 1810. Though eligible in theme the poem was evidently written too late for inclusion in *PFMN*, published 17 November, while an untitled version of lines 1–48 (SC 120) was 'written at Oxford' and given to Hogg (*Hogg* i 198–9). S. and Hogg were sent down on 25 March 1811. But the poem is related in several respects to Volney's *Ruins* and to the first poem in *PFMN*; and its theatrical acceptance of Death matches S.'s black mood in the winter of 1810–11 over his broken relationship with Harriet Grove. It is a rhymed 'Pindaric' ode of the kind exemplified (less irregularly) by Gray's *Odes* (1757). Punctuation in both the Hogg and *Esd* MSS is almost non-existent, so that the meaning is sometimes very obscure: *Esd Nbk* and *Esd Poems* give divergent meanings through differing punctuation. In lines 1–17 the poet is boasting of his supremacy over Death: 'Where lies your sting, Death, if I triumph like this at the moment of dying? None of your bloody victories have equalled this of mine'. This grammatical structure is repeated in lines 32–8: 'If I die without capitulating to Pride, Envy, etc., no king in his glory triumphs as I do over Death'. Finally, the structure of lines 18–38 depends on a series of verbal infinitives following *must*: 'To know that everything but love must perish, that Pride's frown must fade, Envy's fires decay, all life's secret troubles subside—this would be true victory!'
Text from *Esd* ff. 28ᵛ–30ʳ (*Esd* No. 19: quoted by permission of the Carl H. Pforzheimer Library).
Published in *Hogg* i 198–9 (lines 1–48 only); *SC* ii 641–3 (transcript of *Hogg MS*); *Esd Nbk* 74–6; *Esd Poems* 34–6; *SC* iv 963–6 (transcript of *Esd*).

29. vale of tears] Cameron notes (*Esd Nbk* 246) that this famous expression, which originated (in English) in the Bishops' Bible translation (1568) of *Psalms* lxxxiv 6, recurs in 'Hymn to Intellectual Beauty' 17.
32. Heaven of Heavens] Alluding to *I Kings* viii 27: 'But will God indeed dwell on the earth? behold, the heaven and heaven of heavens cannot contain thee'.
32–3. eternal love . . . holier Virtue] 'as if they were not synonimous!' (S.'s note).

Death! where is thy victory?
    To triumph whilst I die,
    To triumph whilst thine ebon wing
    Enfolds my shuddering soul—
5   O Death, where is thy sting?
Not when the tides of murder roll,
When Nations groan that Kings may bask in bliss,
Death, couldst thou boast a victory such as this, —
    When in his hour
10   Of pomp and power
Thy slave, the mightiest murderer, gave
    Mid nature's cries
    The sacrifice
    Of myriads to glut the grave, —
15   When sunk the tyrant, sensualism's slave,
Or Freedom's life-blood streamed upon thy shrine, —
Stern despot, couldst thou boast a victory such as
                      mine.

To know, in dissolution's void,
    That earthly hopes and fears decay,
20   That every sense but Love, destroyed,
    Must perish with its kindred clay—
    Perish ambition's crown,
    Perish its sceptred sway,
From Death's pale front fade Pride's fastidious frown,
25   In death's damp vault the lurid fires decay
Which Envy lights at heaven-born Virtue's beam,
    That all the cares subside
    Which lurk beneath the tide
    Of life's unquiet stream . . .
30   Yes! this were victory!
And on some rock whose dark form glooms the sky
To stretch these pale limbs when the soul is fled,

¶ *43.1, 5.* Cp. *I Corinthians* xv 55: 'O death, where is thy sting? O grave, where
is thy victory?'
14. myriads] millions *Hogg MS.*
15. sensualism's] desolation's *Hogg MS.*
17. despot] tyrant *Hogg MS.*
19. That mortals [hopes & fears *canc.*] bubbles sank away *Hogg MS.*
20. sense] thing *Hogg MS* (a more intelligible reading, as Love is hardly a *sense*).
24. front] i.e. forehead.
25–6. 'the hatred of those who envy Virtue is quenched in death'.
27–9. Rogers notes (*Esd Poems* 123) that these images recur in 'Hymn to
Intellectual Beauty' 32–6.
31. some] yon *Hogg MS.*

To baffle the lean passions of their prey,
To sleep within the chambers of the dead!–
35 Oh! not the wretch around whose dazzling throne
His countless courtiers mock the words they say,
Triumphs amid the bud of glory blown
As I on Death's last pang and faint expiring groan.

Tremble, ye Kings whose luxury mocks the woe
40 That props thy column of unnatural state:
Ye, the curses deep though low
From misery's tortured breast that flow
Shall usher to your fate. –
Tremble, ye conquerors at whose fell command
45 The war-fiend riots o'er an happy land:
Ye, desolation's gory throng
Shall bear from victory along
To Death's mysterious strand.
'Twere Hell that Vice no pain should know
50 But every scene that memory gives,
Though from the selfsame fount might flow
The joy which Virtue aye receives . . .
It is the grave–no conqueror triumphs now;
The wreaths of bay that bound his head
55 Wither around his fleshless brow.
Where is the mockery fled
That fired the tyrant's gaze?
'Tis like the fitful glare that plays
On some dark-rolling thunder cloud–
60 Plays whilst the thunders roar,

35. wretch] King *Hogg MS.*
38. I on Death's last pang] I, in this cold bed *Hogg MS.*
39, 44. Tremble, ye Kings . . . Tremble, ye conquerors] Echoes the *Marseillaise,*
stanza 4: 'Tremblez, tyrans!', which S. translated in 1811; and Dr Richard
Price's *Discourse on the Love of our Country, delivered on Nov 4, 1789 . . . to the
Society for Commemorating the Revolution in Great Britain* (5th edn 1790, 50):
'Tremble all ye oppressors of the world! Take warning all ye supporters of
slavish governments, and slavish hierarchies!'.
41. curses deep though low] plainings faint & low *Hogg MS.* Cp. *Macbeth* V iii 27:
'Curses, not loud but deep'.
41-3. Cp. 'Ambition, power, and avarice' 81–2.
42. breast] soul *Hogg MS* (corrected from 'breast').
45. an happy] a peaceful *Hogg MS.*
48. Death's] that *Hogg MS. Hogg MS* ends with this line.
49-52. 'It would be a true Hell if the vicious were punished only by memories
[of their own misdeeds], although the reward of the virtuous might derive
from the same source [memories of their own benevolence]'. Cp. *Q Mab* iii

But when the storm is past
Fades like the warrior's name.
Death! in thy vault when Kings and peasants lie
Not power's stern rod or fame's most thrilling blasts
65   Can liberate thy captives from decay –
My triumph, their defeat; my joy, their shame.
Welcome then, peaceful Death, I'll sleep with thee:
Mine be thy quiet home, and thine my Victory.

44 To the Emperors of Russia and Austria

who eyed the battle of Austerlitz from the heights whilst
Buonaparte was active in the thickest of the fight.

The Battle of Austerlitz was fought on 2 December 1805, but lines 19–20
indicate that the 'game' of war had since been resumed elsewhere. Moreover,
lines 41–6 imply some measure of accommodation between Napoleon and the
other two Emperors ('The tyrant needs such slaves as you'). The Peace of
Schönbrunn on 14 October 1809 had ended hostilities with Austria and led to
Napoleon's marriage with Maria Louisa, the daughter of the Emperor Francis.
Napoleon had made peace with Russia at Tilsit as early as 1807, but by the end
of 1810 Alexander was again turning against France, and on 31 December the
reopening of Russian ports to neutral (and British) shipping, in defiance of
Napoleon's 'Continental System', made a resumption of war inevitable. For
lines 41–6 to be fully meaningful, therefore, the poem must have been written
between October 1809 and January 1811. S.'s political interests were relatively
unawakened before the autumn of 1810, however, and formal and stylistic
qualities also suggest this period. He was evidently reading up the earlier
campaigns of the war as part of his new enthusiasm for revolutionary France
and its literature. His information comes, directly or indirectly, from the

---

77–80 and note, the first hint of a Platonic doctrine important to S. which
reappears in *PU* (l 403–5: see note), where Justice is 'Too much avenged by
those who err'. Possibly influenced by the Marion episode at the end of Bk II of
Rousseau's *Confessions*, which S. had read by 14 May 1811 (*L* i 84).
63. *when Kings and peasants lie*] 'when Kings are reduced to an equality with
peasants'. The levelling effect of death was a neo-classical commonplace (via
e.g. Horace, *Odes* I iv 13–14), but S.'s triumph is over those who command
'power's rod' and 'fame's blasts'.
64. *fame's most thrilling blasts*] Imitated from Kirke White, 'Time' 170–72 (a
passage much quarried by S.).
68. 'May I appropriate your refuge and your triumph' (the phrasing risks
ambiguity).

French official Bulletin XXX, dated 3 December, which British journals printed in the absence of an official British report of the disaster. The translation in *GM* lxxvi (January 1806) 74–5 describes how Napoleon visited his posts in person on the eve of the battle, and again early on the morning of 2 December. During the fighting

> A battalion of the 4th of the line was charged by the Imperial Russian Guard on horseback, and routed; but the Emperor was at hand; he perceived this movement . . . in a moment the Russian guard was routed . . . From the heights of Austerlitz the two Emperors beheld the defeat of all the Russian guard.

Napoleon's activity in the battle is a fact, but Alexander also took part, and is said to have wept over the Russian dead when it was ended. Alexander and Francis were not, of course, primarily field officers as Napoleon was.
Text from *Esd* ff. 12ᵛ–13ʳ (*Esd* No. 7: quoted by permission of the Carl H. Pforzheimer Library).
Published in *Esd Nbk* 48–9; *Esd Poems* 12–14; *SC* iv 937–9 (transcript of *Esd*).

> Coward Chiefs! who while the fight
>   Rages in the plain below
> Hide the shame of your affright
>   On yon distant mountain's brow,
> 5 Does one human feeling creep
> Through your hearts' remorseless sleep?
> On that silence cold and deep
>   Does one impulse flow
> Such as fires the Patriot's breast,
> 10 Such as breaks the Hero's rest?
>
> No, cowards! ye are calm and still.
>   Keen frosts that blight the human bud
> Each opening petal blight and kill,
>   And bathe its tenderness in blood.
> 15 Ye hear the groans of those who die,
> Ye hear the whistling death-shots fly,
> And when the yells of Victory
>   Float o'er the murdered good
> Ye smile secure. – On yonder plain
> 20 The game, if lost, begins again.

¶ *44.6. remorseless sleep*] *Esd Nbk* puts the question-mark after *deep* in line 7.
18. the murdered good] A value-judgement not necessarily on the coalition opposing Napoleon so much as on the common soldiers constituting its forces sacrificed at Austerlitz
19. secure] carrying some sense of the Lat. *securus*, 'carefree' (cp. 41 below).
19–20. The Russians were defeated again near Warsaw in December 1806 and at Friedland in June 1807. The Austrians were defeated at Wagram on 5 July 1809.

Think ye the restless fiend who haunts
   The tumult of yon gory field,
Whom neither shame nor danger daunts,
   Who dares not fear, who cannot yield,
25 Will not with equalizing blow
Abase the high, exalt the low,
And in one mighty shock o'erthrow
   The slaves that sceptres wield,
Till from the ruin of the storm
30 Ariseth Freedom's awful form?

Hushed below the battle's jar
   Night rests silent on the heath—
Silent save when vultures soar
   Above the wounded warrior's death.
35 How sleep ye now, unfeeling Kings?
Peace seldom folds her snowy wings
On poisoned memory's conscience-stings
   Which lurk bad hearts beneath,
Nor downy beds procure repose
40 Where crime and terror mingle throes.

Yet may your terrors rest secure.
   Thou Northern chief why startest thou?
Pale Austria, calm those fears. Be sure
   The tyrant needs such slaves as you.
45 Think ye the world would bear his sway
Were dastards such as you away?
No! they would pluck his plumage gay
   Torn from a nation's woe,
And lay him in the oblivious gloom
50 Where Freedom now prepares your tomb.

21. *the restless fiend*] Probably the 'war-fiend' of No. 43, line 45, borrowed from Erasmus Darwin, *Botanic Garden* Pt I, iv 313–16.
26. Exalt the high, abase the low *Esd, Esd Nbk, Esd Poems*. Clearly a slip on S.'s part. He is drawing on *Ezekiel* xxi 26–7: 'Thus saith the Lord GOD; Remove the diadem, and take off the crown . . . exalt him that is low, and abase him that is high. I will overturn, overturn, overturn it: and it shall be no more, until he come whose right it is'. This quotation was said to be 'the watch-word of the Luddites' (*Quarterly Review* viii (December 1812) 348). All three of the 'slaves' contesting Austerlitz 'wielded sceptres'.
33. *when*] Perhaps *where* in *Esd*.
42. *Thou Northern chief*] Tsar Alexander I of Russia (1777–1825).
43. *Pale Austria*] Francis I of Austria (1768–1835).
44. *The tyrant*] Bonaparte, who had been crowned Emperor of France on 2 December 1804.

45 To Liberty

Undated in *Esd*, and date of composition unknown, but perhaps late 1810 or early 1811. Cameron (*Esd Nbk* 194–5) believes it 'was almost certainly written between the late fall of 1811 and the period of composition of *Queen Mab*', citing the verbal parallel of line 41 with *Q Mab* ii 129, the likeness in content of the final stanzas to the first half of *Q Mab* ix, and the anticipation in the final lines of the opening of *Q Mab* ix. This may be correct. But the likenesses may be due to the use of the same sources and subject-matter. The poem has similar links with poems much earlier than *Q Mab* (see note to lines 21–7). The argument for the earlier date is that if the tyrant of stanzas 1–3 is primarily Napoleon, as seems likely, the global scope of the poem and its impotent defiance ('A world's indignant cry') best fits the period in 1810–11 of Napoleon's almost unchallenged dominion over Europe, not the period beginning late in 1811 when the struggle was about to be renewed. The cherished flame of resistance (line 4), the proud independence (11–20), and the death of patriots (21–7) could most plausibly refer to the Spanish guerrillas, active during the discouraging months of the Peninsular War.

Text from *Esd* ff. 18ʳ–19ʳ (*Esd* No. 12: quoted by permission of the Carl H. Pforzheimer Library).

Published in *Dowden Life* i 348 (lines 26–30 only); *Esd Nbk* 58–9; *Esd Poems* 20–1; *SC* iv 946–8 (transcript of *Esd*).

    O let not Liberty
      Silently perish,
    May the groan and the sigh
      Yet the flame cherish,
5   Till the voice to Nature's bursting heart given,
      Ascending loud and high
      A world's indignant cry
      And startling on his throne
      The tyrant grim and lone,
10 Shall beat the deaf vault of Heaven.

    Say, can the Tyrant's frown
      Daunt those who fear not
    Or break the spirits down
      His badge that wear not?

¶ 45.5–10. The construction is: 'Till the voice . . . ascending . . . and startling . . . shall beat . . .'
9, 11. *the tyrant*] with Bonaparte almost certainly in mind.
10. Cp. Shakespeare's Sonnet 29: 'And trouble deaf Heaven with my bootless cries'.

15 Can chains or death or infamy subdue
        The pure and fearless soul
        That dreads not their control,
        Sees Paradise and Hell,
        Sees the Palace and the cell,
20 Yet bravely dares prefer the good and true.

    Regal pomp and pride
        The Patriot falls in scorning,
    The spot whereon he died
        Should be the despot's warning;
25 The voice of blood shall on his crimes call down
                                            Revenge!
        And the spirits of the brave
        Shall start from every grave,
        Whilst from her Atlantic throne
        Freedom sanctifies the groan
30 That fans the glorious fires of its change.

    Monarch! sure employer
        Of vice and want and woe,
    Thou conscienceless destroyer,
        Who and what art thou?–
35 The dark prison house that in the dust shall lie,
        The pyramid which guilt
        First planned, which man has built,
        At whose footstone want and woe
        With a ceaseless murmur flow
40 And whose peak attracts the tempests of the sky.

---

16. pure] *Esd, SC*; free *Esd Nbk, Esd Poems*.

23–4. Cp. 'Henry and Louisa' 304–15.

26–7. Dowden (*Dowden Life* i 348) notes the 'direct reminiscence' from 'Ye Mariners of England' (by Campbell) 11–12: 'The spirits of your fathers / Shall start from every wave!–'

28. *her Atlantic throne*] America. Cp. Volney's *Ruins* ch. xiii:
    Yes, continued [the Genius], a hollow noise already strikes my ear; the cry of liberty, uttered upon the farther shore of the Atlantic, has reached to the old continent. At this cry a secret murmur against oppression is excited in a powerful nation . . .

36–42. Volney's *Ruins* ch. xi footnote 4 stresses the oppressive waste represented by the pyramids, as does his *Travels Through Spain and Egypt, in the Years 1783, 1784, and 1785* (2nd edn 1788) i 283: 'we shudder at the numberless acts of injustice and oppression these tiresome labours must have cost . . . and we are inflamed with indignation at the tyranny of the despots who enforced these barbarous works'.

The pyramids shall fall . . .
 And Monarchs! so shall ye,
Thrones shall rust in the hall
 Of forgotten royalty,
45 Whilst Virtue, Truth and Peace shall arise
 And a Paradise on Earth
 From your fall shall date its birth,
 And human life shall seem
 Like a short and happy dream
50 Ere we wake in the daybeam of the skies.

46 The Solitary

Dated '1810' in *Esd*, which supplies the title. Cameron (*Esd Nbk* 199–200), noting that '1810' was first written '1811', assigns it to the Christmas vacation, but S.'s solitude amid a 'varied multitude', and his conformist draining of 'the genial bowl' (possibly even the 'busy beings' round him) suggest S.'s first term at Oxford, November 1810. Hogg notes that on first meeting S. he 'had no acquaintance with any one' (*Hogg* i 52), avoided 'all communication' during the mornings (i 91), missed College dinner whenever possible (i 85), welcomed the 'oak' (i 93), shunned his ex-schoolfellows (i 124), and disliked social gatherings (i 208–9). S. enjoyed companionship but was non-gregarious, and his numbed reaction to College life was exacerbated by the shock of his broken love-affair. Later both Hogg and S. affected singularity: 'These two young men gave up associating with anybody else some months since, never dined in College, dressed differently from all others, and did everything in their power to show singularity' (R. Clarke to John Hogg, 6 April 1811, quoted in *S in Eng* 221). Cp. S.'s criticism of 'self-centred seclusion' in the Preface and text of *Alastor*. Rossetti first printed this poem as 'Copied out by Mr. Garnett' (*Rossetti 1870* i 599), which Forman took to mean 'from the original MS at Boscombe' (*Forman 1876–7* iv 319). No such 'original MS' survives, and it is highly unlikely that a copy ever existed among the MSS descended from S.'s widow. The poem occupies just one page in *Esd*, whose existence was not generally known of in 1877: its text in *Rossetti 1870* supports the assumption that it was

41. The pyramids shall fall . . .] Cameron (*Esd Nbk* 195) cites *Q Mab* ii 129: 'Those pyramids shall fall'. Blair's *Grave* 190–218 associates the fall of pyramids with that of wide-wasting monarchs, as does Peacock's *Palmyra* (1806) xxii 9–10: 'ages, with insidious flow, / Shall lay those blood-bought fabrics low'.
43–4. Cp. *PU* III iv 131, 164–79; *Q Mab* ix 119–21 (though these are chains rusting, not thrones).
50. daybeam] A word not recognized by *OED*, but in current use (e.g. *Monthly Magazine* xxi (1806) 227). Cp. 'On Robert Emmet's Tomb' 25.

among the verses supplied to Garnett by a former 'governess in the Esdaile family' (*L about S* 87–8).

Text from *Esd* f. 23ᵛ (*Esd* No. 15: quoted by permission of the Carl H. Pforzheimer Library).

Published in *Rossetti 1870* ii 507–8; *Esd Nbk* 67; *Esd Poems* 27–8; *SC* iv 955–6 (transcript of *Esd*).

> Darest thou amid this varied multitude
> To live alone, an isolated thing,
> To see the busy beings round thee spring,
> And care for none?–in thy calm solitude
> 5   A flower that scarce breathes in the desert rude
>   To Zephyr's passing wing?
>
> Not the swarth Pariah in some Indian grove,
> Lone, lean, and hunted by his brothers' hate,
> Hath drunk so deep the cup of bitter fate
> 10   As that poor wretch who cannot, cannot love:
> He bears a load which nothing can remove,
>   A killing, withering weight.
>
> He smiles . . . 'tis sorrow's deadliest mockery;
> He speaks . . . the cold words flow not from his soul;
> 15   He acts like others, drains the genial bowl,
> Yet, yet he longs, although he fears, to die;
> He pants to reach what yet he seems to fly,
>   Dull Life's extremest goal.

47 The Monarch's Funeral: An Anticipation

Dated '1810' in *Esd*, which supplies the title; written probably in the second half of December. George III had lapsed into insanity after the death of his daughter Amelia on 2 November 1810, and although the bulletins disguised

¶ *46.5–6. Zephyr*] Zephyrus, the West Wind, said to produce flowers by his breath alone (Ovid, *Met.* i 107–8), can barely keep *this* flower alive.

7–8. Pariah] Cp. Volney's *Ruins* ch. xx: 'These men [Hindus] anxiously support hospitals for the reception of hawks, serpents, and rats, and look with horror upon their brethren of mankind! . . . with all this humanity in unintelligible cases, they think themselves obliged to let a Paria perish with hunger rather than relieve him! [Note on 'Paria':] . . . the name of a cast or tribe reputed unclean'.

his condition a Regency Bill was introduced in the Commons on 20 December, and passed on 5 February 1811. The poem anticipates his death and State funeral in Westminster Abbey, and is influenced by various writings on death, including Shakespeare's Sonnet 55, Gray's *Elegy*, Blair's *Grave* (esp. 208–31), and E. Darwin's *Temple of Nature* (1802) iv 273–90, 383–404. George did not in fact die until January 1820, and S. wrote a second anticipatory poem ('England in 1819') nine years later.

Text from *Esd* ff. 24^r–26^r (*Esd* No. 16: quoted by permission of the Carl H. Pforzheimer Library).

Published in *Esd Nbk* 68–70; *Esd Poems* 28–31; *SC* iv 956–9 (transcript of *Esd*).

> The growing gloom of eventide
>   Has quenched the sunbeam's latest glow
> And lowers upon the woe and pride
>   That blasts the city's peace below.
>
> 5 At such an hour how sad the sight
>   To mark a Monarch's funeral,
> When the dim shades of awful night
>   Rest on the coffin's velvet pall;
>
> To see the Gothic arches show
> 10   A varied mass of light and shade,
> While to the torches' crimson glow
>   A vast cathedral is displayed;
>
> To see with what a silence deep
>   The thousands o'er this death-scene brood,
> 15 As though some wizard's charm did creep
>   Upon the countless multitude;
>
> To see this awful pomp of death
>   For one frail mass of mouldering clay,
> When nobler men the tomb beneath
> 20   Have sunk unwept, unseen away.
>
> For who was he, the uncoffined slain,
>   That fell in Erin's injured isle
> Because his spirit dared disdain
>   To light his country's funeral pile?–

¶ 47.1. *growing*] glowing *Esd Nbk*.
20. Lines 25–32 identify this Irish martyr as Robert Emmet (1778–1803), executed after the failure of the rising he organized. Because all his friends were also implicated, his body was unclaimed and interred in 'Bully's Acre', the pauper burial-ground near Kilmainham Hospital, Dublin (R. R. Madden, *The United Irishmen; their Lives and Times*, 3rd ser. (1846) iii 285).

25   Shall he not ever live in lays
        The warmest that a Muse may sing
    Whilst monumental marbles raise
        The fame of a departed King?

     May not the Muse's darling theme
30   Gather its glorious garland thence,
    Whilst some frail tombstone's dotard dream
        Fades with a monarch's impotence?

    –Yes, 'tis a scene of wondrous awe
        To see a coffined Monarch lay,
35   That the wide grave's insatiate maw
        Be glutted with a regal prey!

    Who *now* shall public councils guide?
        Who rack the poor on gold to dine?
    Who waste the means of regal pride
40   For which a million wretches pine?

    It is a child of earthly breath,
        A being perishing as he,
    Who, throned in yonder pomp of death,
        Hath now fulfilled his destiny.

45   Now dust to dust restore! . . . O Pride,
        Unmindful of thy fleeting power,
    Whose empty confidence has vied
        With human life's most treacherous hour,

    One moment feel that in the breast
50   With regal crimes and troubles vexed
    The pampered earthworms soon will rest–
        One moment feel . . . and die the next.

---

25. *lays*] Including Southey's 'Written immediately after Reading the Speech of Robert Emmet' (1803), and Moore's 'Oh, breathe not his name' (1808).

25–32. As in Shakespeare's Sonnet 55, the contrast is between the gilded monuments of princes and the living record of Emmet's fame in poetry. His grave was left uninscribed in honour of the wish expressed in his final speech: 'Let no man write my epitaph . . . Let . . . my memory be left in oblivion, and my tomb remain uninscribed, until other times and other men can do justice to my character . . .' (Madden, op. cit., iii 246).

34. *lay*] A contemporary alternative for 'lie', not used by S. after 1818 (see 'Listen, listen, Mary mine' 9).

38. 'Who will extort wealth from the poor in order to eat off gold plate?'

45. *restore! . . . O Pride,*] restore, O Pride!– *Esd Poems.* 'Pride' is not, however, the subject of the vocative 'restore' but an aspect of the dying King.

Yet deem not in the tomb's control
The vital lamp of life can fail,
55 Deem not that e'er the Patriot's soul
Is wasted by the withering gale:

The dross which forms the *King* is gone
And reproductive earth supplies
As senseless as the clay and stone
60 In which the kindred body lies;

The soul which makes the *Man* doth soar,
And love alone survives to shed
All that its tide of bliss can pour
Of Heaven upon the blessed dead.

65 So shall the Sun forever burn,
So shall the midnight lightnings die,
And joy that glows at Nature's bourn
Outlive terrestrial misery.

And will the crowd who silent stoop
70 Around the lifeless Monarch's bier,
A mournful and dejected group,
Breathe not one sigh, or shed one tear?

Ah! no. 'Tis wonder, 'tis not woe;
Even royalists might groan to see
75 The *Father of the People* so
Lost in the Sacred Majesty.

48 The Wandering Jew's Soliloquy

Date of composition unknown, but probably December 1810 or January 1811.
The poem in *Esd* follows 'The Retrospect' (June 1812), which evidently was
once intended to be the final poem of the collection (see headnote to No. 79),

54. *lamp of life*] Cp. E. Darwin, *Origin of Society* ii 58: 'the golden lamp of life
and love'.
57–8. 'The kingly substance is dead and provides fertile soil'. King-Hele
(*KSMB* xvi (1965) 26–7) cites E. Darwin's *Temple of Nature* iv 383–99: 'Hence
when a monarch or a mushroom dies, / Awhile extinct the organic matter lies; /
. . . The wrecks of Death are but a change of forms; / Emerging matter from
the grave returns'.
74–5. Perhaps a sardonic comment on Pope's version of the origin of monarchy (*Essay on Man* iii 211–14): ''Twas VIRTUE ONLY . . . A Prince the Father
of a People made'.

and precedes the two sonnets to Harriet and Ianthe S. (July and September 1813), but this may simply be because for some reason it was not available earlier. The Jew it presents differs both from the gothic sufferer of *WJ* and from the hypothetical phantasm of *Q Mab*, so it seems to be an independent poem, and could not easily have formed part of the revisions S. was planning on 2 December 1810 of his original *WJ* (*L* i 23–4). Like S.'s letters of the winter of 1810–11 it is strongly anti-religious. The decisive influence, however, is that of Southey's *The Curse of Kehama* (1810), S.'s 'most favourite poem' by 11 June 1811 (*L* i 101), which he ordered from Stockdale on 18 December 1810 (*L* i 25). As it was published three days later (*New Letters of Robert Southey*, ed. K. Curry (1965) i 547) S. is likely to have read it before the end of the year. In *Kehama*, Ladurlad, having killed Arvalan to save his daughter from violation, is cursed in revenge by A.'s father Kehama, an evil mortal who has achieved near-omnipotence and seeks to supplant the Hindoo gods. The Curse entails exemption from death by any means, from sleep, and from relief from pain,

> And thou shalt seek Death
> To release thee, in vain;
> Thou shalt live in thy pain
> While Kehama shall reign

> (II xiv 17–20)

The Deity addressed by S.'s Jew is Kehama Christianized. The Jew's solicitation of Destruction (6–8, 27) recalls Ladurlad's solicitation of death by insulting Kehama (*Kehama* III viii-x); the imagery of suicide by burning (9–10) draws on that of the suttee episode (especially *Kehama* I x 1–3; see also XIV xiii); the designation 'Tyrant of Earth' (11) is repeatedly applied to Kehama (e.g. *Kehama* VI iv 34), as is that of 'Almighty Tyrant' (28) (e.g. *Kehama* VI iv 58); the notion of draining the cup of hate (29) recalls the last scene in *Kehama* when the tyrant drinks from the Amreeta-cup to consummate his triumph, and natural death simultaneously releases Ladurlad from the Curse (*Kehama* XXIV xiii-xxvi; see also II vi 16).

Text from *Esd* ff. 90ᵛ–91ʳ (*Esd* No. 51: quoted by permission of the Carl H. Pforzheimer Library).

Published in B. Dobell (ed.), *The Wandering Jew* (1887) 69–70; *Esd Nbk* 161–2; *Esd Poems* 107–8; *SC* iv 1054–5 (transcript of *Esd*).

     Is it the Eternal Triune, is it He
     Who dares arrest the wheels of destiny
     And plunge me in this lowest Hell of Hells?
     Will not the lightning's blast destroy my frame?
5   Will not steel drink the blood-life where it swells?
     No—let me hie where dark destruction dwells

¶ *48.2. wheels of destiny*] Perhaps suggested by *Kehama* VII xi 58, or by Southey's *Thalaba the Destroyer* (1801) XI i 1–3: 'O fool, to think thy human hand / Could check the chariot-wheels of Destiny!'

To rouse her from her deeply-caverned lair,
And taunting her cursed sluggishness to ire
Light long Oblivion's death-torch at its flame
10   And calmly mount Annihilation's pyre.

Tyrant of Earth! pale misery's jackal thou!
Are there no stores of vengeful violent fate
Within the magazines of thy fierce hate?
No poison in thy clouds to bathe a brow
15   That lowers on thee with desperate contempt?
Where is the noonday pestilence that slew
The myriad sons of Israel's favoured nation?
Where the destroying minister that flew
Pouring the fiery tide of desolation
20   Upon the leagued Assyrian's attempt?
Where the dark Earthquake-demon who engorged
At thy dread word Korah's unconscious crew,
Or the Angel's two-edged sword of fire that urged
Our primal parents from their bower of bliss
25   (Reared by thine hand) for errors not their own
By thine omniscient mind foredoomed, foreknown?
Yes! I would court a ruin such as this,
Almighty Tyrant! and give thanks to thee. –
Drink deeply–drain the cup of hate–remit, then I may
                                                    die.

16. *the noonday pestilence*] *II Samuel* xxiv 15: 'So the LORD sent a pestilence upon Israel from the morning even to the time appointed'; perhaps combined with *Psalms* xci 6.
20. *the leagued Assyrian*] Sennacherib, who sent 'a great host' against Jerusalem (*II Kings* xix 35).
21. *Earthquake-demon*] W. L. Bowles uses 'Earthquake's Demon' in his 'St Michael's Mount' (1798) 83, which was probably known to S. as it was published with 'Coombe Ellen' (Cwm Elan, Radnorshire, was an estate belonging to Harriet Grove's father, S.'s uncle). Cp. 'Letter to the Gisbornes' 60. The engulfment of Korah is described in *Numbers* xvi 31–3.
23. *two-edged sword of fire*] An embellishment of the Genesis account, possibly suggested by *Revelation* i 16.
24. *bower of bliss*] A phrase borrowed from Southey rather than Spenser: Indra's Paradise in *Kehama* VII vii 13, xi 39, etc., unlike Eden, was offered by the god at his own risk as a refuge for the persecuted.
29. *hate–remit, then*] hate–remit then *Esd*; hate–remit this *Dobell 1887*; hate, remit!... Then *Esd Poems*. 'The Jew means that if God will take back the curse He placed upon him he can die (which is what he wishes)' (Cameron, *Esd Nbk* 287).

49 'I will kneel at thine altar'

Headed '1809'—decoratively underlined—in *Esd*, but probably written December 1810 or January 1811. (i) The poem shows S. as 'wretched to the last degree' and angry at the religious intolerance he considered responsible for his enforced break with Harriet Grove in autumn 1810, and closely parallels contemporary letters to Hogg (see specific notes below). (ii) S.'s 'political' poems begin only in November 1810 with *PFMN*; if this poem belonged to 1809 it would be unique, and the reference to similar 'lays' in line 3 inexplicable. (iii) It is metrically almost identical to 'Dares the llama', sent to Hogg 20 April 1811, and very similar in mood and wording. (iv) Cameron (*Esd Nbk* 251–4) notes the influence of *Political Justice* while conceding that S. may not have read this book before 1810. (v) Cameron also notes the 'dedication' theme in stanzas 1 and 4, but rightly distinguishes this experience from that later described in the 'Hymn to Intellectual Beauty'. This 'dedication' is surely that expressed in letters to Hogg in the winter of 1810/11: 'I swear on the altar of perjured love to avenge myself on the hated cause of the effect which *even now* I can scarcely help deploring.—Indeed I think it is to the benefit of society to destroy the opinions which *can* annihilate the dearest of its ties.–' (20 December 1810, *L* i 27). The celebration of 'Love' or 'philanthropy' as superstition's adversary is not Godwinian, and owes something to Volney's *Ruins*. Volney (1757–1820), a Revolutionary deputy in 1790, was a steadfast libertarian who was imprisoned during the Terror and refused office under Napoleon. Volney's *Ruins* later became a 'textbook' of Harriet Westbrook's (*Hogg* ii 183). Text from *Esd* ff. 61ᵛ–62ʳ (*Esd* No. 42: quoted by permission of the Carl H. Pforzheimer Library).

Published in *Esd Nbk* 125–6; *Esd Poems* 75–6; *SC* iv 1014–15 (transcript of *Esd*).

> I will kneel at thine altar, will crown thee with bays,
>   Whether God, Love, or Virtue thou art
> Thou shalt live—aye! more long than these perishing
>   lays—
>   Thou shalt live in this high-beating heart;
> 5   Dear Love! from its life-strings thou never shall part

¶ 49.1. *thine altar*] Cp. S.'s *Proposals for an Association of Philanthropists* (1812): 'Reason points to the open gates of the Temple of Religious Freedom, Philanthropy kneels at the altar of the common God . . . do you hang upon his altar the garland of your devotion?' (*Mac-Carthy* 267–8). Love's altar in the heart derives ultimately from the altars erected at the various fêtes of revolutionary France (see note to *L&C* v 2071–88), but an immediate source is Volney's *Ruins* (ch. xvii), itself suggested by the Festival of the Federation on 14 July 1790: 'the people raised a mighty standard, varied with three colours, and upon which three words were written. They unfurled it over the throne of the legislators, and now for the first time the symbol of universal and equal justice

Though Prejudice clanking her chain,
Though Interest groaning in gain,
May tell me thou closest to Heaven the door,
May tell me that thine is the way to be poor.

10 The victim of merciless tyranny's power
May smile at his chains if with thee;
The most sense-enslaved loiterer in Passion's sweet
bower
Is a wretch if unhallowed by thee.
Thine, thine is the bond that alone binds the free.
15 Can the free worship bondage? nay, more,
What they feel not, believe not, adore?
What if felt, if believed, if existing, must give
To thee to create, to eternize, to live?–

For Religion more keen than the blasts of the North
20 Darts its frost through the self-palsied soul;
Its slaves on the work of destruction go forth:

---

appeared upon the earth. In front of the throne, the people built an altar . . .'
S.'s 'God, Love, or Virtue' are a significant variant on Volney's 'three words'
(Equality, Liberty, Justice). No doubt S. also had in mind the altar of the
Festival of Reason (10 November 1793), at which processions of young girls
crowned with flowers or leaves paid homage (F-A. Aulard, *Le Culte de la
Raison 1793–1794* (Paris 1892) 54). bays] bay-laurel (*Laurus nobilis*), hitherto the
traditional crown of victors in battle or poetry.
2. 'Love is Heaven, & Heaven is Love . . . Oh! that this Deity were the Soul of
the Universe, the spirit of universal imperishable love' (to Hogg, 12 January
1811, *L* i 44).
6–8. 'Prejudice pretends that those obedient to Love will forfeit salvation;
Interest that they will lose worldly advantage'. (This parallel construction is
frequent in S.; cp. 'The Invitation' 35–8).
12–13. 'What then shall happiness arise from? . . . Love! dear love . . . is not that
very agony to be preferred to the most thrilling sensualities of Epicurism' (to
Hogg, 1 January 1811, *L* i 34).
15–17.   nay more
               What they feel not, believe not adore
                         What if felt, if believed if existing *Esd*
                  Nay more,
               What they feel not, believe not? Adore
                         What, if felt, if believed, if existing, *Esd Poems*

The divinest emotions that roll
Submit to the rod of its impious control;
   At the venomous blast of its breath
25   Love, concord, lies gasping in death,
Philanthropy utters a war-drownèd cry
And selfishness, conquering, cries 'Victory!'

Can we, then, thus tame, thus impassive, behold
  That alone whence our life springs, destroyed?
30 Shall Prejudice, Priestcraft, Opinion, and Gold,
   Every passion with interest alloyed,
Where Love ought to reign fill the desolate void?
   But the Avenger arises, the throne
   Of selfishness totters, its groan
35 Shakes the nations. –It falls; Love seizes the sway,
The sceptre it bears unresisted away.

50 On an Icicle that clung to the grass of a grave

Headed '1809' above the title in *Esd*, but probably written between 31 December 1810 and 6 January 1811. The version in *Esd*, which supplies the title, seems complete although consisting only of stanzas 1, 3, and 4. S. sent the poem to Hogg in a letter of 6 January 1811, adding after it: 'I am very cold this morning, so you must excuse bad writing as I have been most of the night pacing a Church-yard . . . I must now engage in scenes of strong interest, You see the subject of the foregoing. I send because I think it may amuse [i.e. divert] you–.' (*SC* ii 690; text from MS). After receiving Hogg's (lost) reply, S. wrote on 11 January: 'The poetry w^h I sent you alluded not to [the] subject of my nonsensical ravings.–I hope that you are now publishing Leonora.' (*SC* ii 701). Hogg had therefore been expected to recognize the situation implied by the tear and the grave, but did not do so, and S. then dissociated the subject from that of his

22–5. 'I swear that never will I forgive Christianity! it is the only point on which I allow myself to encourage revenge . . . it encourages prejudice which strikes at the root of the dearest the tenderest of its ties' (to Hogg, 3 January 1811, *L* i 35). Cp. 'Dares the llama' 32–4: 'in vain from the grasp of religion I flee / The most tenderly loved of my soul / Are slaves to its hated control'.
28–9. 'Can we passively see destroyed that which is the sole source of our life?' (*springs* is a verb).
33–6. Cp. '. . . that which injured me shall perish! I even now by anticipation hear the expiring yell of intolerance!' (to Hogg, 26 December 1810, *L* i 32); '. . . do we not now see Superstition decaying, is not its influence weakened' (to Hogg, 12 January 1811, *L* i 45).

own 'non-sensical ravings'–presumably those concerning his loss of Harriet Grove. The rest of both letters mainly concerned Hogg's attempts to arouse Elizabeth S.'s interest. Though there may be some personal bearing in the poem (see especially lines 17–18), it is primarily a lament over the grave of a fair and virtuous but humble and unfortunate girl, and clearly belongs to the group of poems written about 'Mary' (see Nos. 38–42, and headnote to No. 38). There are parallels between it and those 'Mary' poems in which the girl is already dead, and three days before sending the poem S. had told Hogg: 'the poor Mary is a character worthy of Heaven. I adore it' (*L* i 36). The frost and snow suggest that it was written later than the others in the series (*GM* lxxxi (January 1811) 2; there was a period of hard frost between 31 December and 11 January, with snow on 1 and 3 January), and stanzas 2 and 5, which import an incongruous radicalism into the sentiment, may have been added for Hogg's benefit and dropped again when the poem was copied into *Esd*. S.'s hint about pacing a churchyard may also have been meant to convey the impression that the poem had been composed that very morning. The idea of the poem was probably found in Moore's 12-line lyric 'The Tear' (?1806), in which a girl weeps over her lover's grave, ending:

> A warm tear gush'd, the wintry air
> Congeal'd it as it flow'd away:
> All night it lay an ice-drop there,
> At morn it glitter'd in the ray!
>
> An angel, wandering from her sphere,
> Who saw this bright, this frozen gem,
> To dew-eyed Pity brought the tear,
> And hung it on her diadem!

Sydney Owenson in *The Lay of an Irish Harp; or Metrical Fragments* (1807) also has a 'fragment' called 'The Snow-Drop'; lines 17–20 are:

> And where the froze dew-drop once gem'd thy fair brow,
> That fair brow a dew drop more precious shall wear;
> Such a drop as the mild eyes of Pity bestow,
> When she sheds o'er the pale brow of SORROW her TEAR.

Text from SC 129 (*Hogg MS*: quoted by permission of the Carl H. Pforzheimer Library).
Published in *Hogg* i 160–61; *SC* ii 688–9 (transcript of *Hogg MS*); *Esd Nbk* 128 (stanzas 1, 3–4); *Esd Poems* 77–8 (stanzas 1, 3–4); *SC* iv 1017–18 (transcript of *Esd* ff. 63ᵛ–64ʳ, *Esd* No. 44).

> Oh! take the pure gem to where southernly breezes
>   Waft repose to some bosom as faithful as fair,
> In which the warm current of Love never freezes
>   As it rises unmingled with selfishness there,

¶ 50.1. *southernly*] southerly *Hogg* (an alternative form).
4. *rises unmingled with selfishness*] circulates freely & shamelessly *Esd*.

 5   Which untainted by Pride, unpolluted by care,
     Might dissolve the dim ice-drop, might bid it arise,
     Too pure for these regions, to gleam in the skies;

     Or where the stern warrior, his country defending,
       Dares fearless the dark-rolling battle to pour,
10   Or o'er the fell corpse of a dread Tyrant bending
       Where Patriotism, red with his guilt-reeking gore,
     Plants Liberty's flag on the slave-peopled shore,
     With Victory's cry, with the shout of the free
     Let it fly, taintless spirit, to mingle with thee.

15   For I found the pure gem when the day-beam returning
       Ineffectual gleams on the snow-covered plain,
     When to *others* the wished-for arrival of morning
       Brings relief to long visions of soul-racking pain;
     But regret is an insult—to grieve is in vain:
20   And why should we grieve that a spirit so fair
     Seeks Heaven to mix with its kindred there?

     But still 'twas some Spirit of kindness descending
       To share in the load of mortality's woe
     Who over thy lowly-built sepulchre bending
25   Bade sympathy's tenderest tear-drop to flow.
     Not for *thee* soft compassion celestials did know,
     But if *Angels* can weep, sure *Man* may repine,
     May weep in mute grief o'er thy low-laid shrine.

---

5. *Pride*] crime *Esd*.
6. *the dim*] this dim *Esd*; this dear *SC*.
Stanza 2. Omitted Esd.
9. *dark-rolling*] An Ossianic compound, used also by Campbell in 'The Wounded Hussar' 1.
10–12. 'Or (let it fly) where Patriotism, bending over a tyrant's corpse, plants the flag . . .'
14. *taintless spirit*] i.e. that of the grave's occupant. Cp. 'To Mary—III' 27
16. *snow-covered*] snow spangled *Esd*.
17. others] Underlining in *Esd* doubtful. *wished-for*] longed for *Esd*.
18. *visions*] night dreams *Esd*.
21. *Seeks*] Sought *Esd. mix*] meet *Esd. its kindred*] its own kindred *Hogg*.
22. *But still 'twas some Spirit*] Yet 'twas some Angel *Esd*.
25. *tear-drop*] tear drops *Esd*.
26. And consigned the rich gift to the Sister of Snow *Esd*. The text line means: 'Heaven showed you no mercy while you were alive'.
27. *But*] And *Esd. if Angels can weep*] Recalls *PL* i 620: 'Tears such as Angels weep, burst forth'. Man] I *Esd*.
28. And shed tear drops tho frozen to ice on thy shrine *Esd*.

And did I then say for the Altar of Glory
30   That the earliest, the loveliest flowers I'd entwine,
Though with millions of blood-reeking victims 'tis gory,
    Though the tears of the widow polluted its shrine,
Though around [it] the orphans, the fatherless pine,
Oh! fame, all thy glories I'd yield for a tear
35 To shed on the grave of an heart so sincere.

51 Fragment of a Poem

the original idea of which was suggested by the
cowardly and infamous bombardment of
Copenhagen

Probably composed shortly before 11 January 1811 when S. included stanzas
1–3 and 5, untitled, in a letter to Hogg. Following the lines he wrote: 'These
are Elisa's–she has written many more, & I will shew you at some future time
the whole of the composition. I like it very much if a Brother may be allowed
to praise a sister.' (*L* i 43; text from *Hogg MS*). This ambiguous attribution has
persuaded all editors to reject the poem as the work of Elizabeth S. It is,
however, characteristic of S. in every respect; the 16-year-old Elizabeth would
hardly have used such words as *dread-convulsed* (11) or *solium* (16); and S.
included stanzas 3, 1, 4 as his own, under the present title, in *Esd*. 'It is more
likely that the whole poem, in both versions, was by S. and that he was
representing the letter version as Elizabeth's in order to stimulate Hogg's
interest in her (as he did also with "Cold are the blasts")' (Cameron, *Esd Nbk*
256). Conceivably Elizabeth contributed to the final stanza, which is indebted
in doctrine and phrasing to the English translation of Volney's *Ruins*, and
possibly these seven lines (which follow a row of asterisks in *Hogg MS*) were all
that S. meant to include by the words 'These are Elisa's'. But it is still more
probable that S. himself composed what he could then plausibly ascribe to his
sister. The many compound adjectives suggest the influence of James Montgomery (see notes).

To forestall a takeover by Napoleon, Britain in 1807 had delivered a humi-
liating ultimatum to neutral Denmark, and when that was rejected, attacked
Copenhagen by land and sea for four days and three nights (2–5 September
1807), burning large areas of the city and inflicting heavy civilian casualties.
The Opposition outcry against this unprovoked aggression forced the King to

Stanza 5. Omitted Esd. The text construction is not interrogative but conditional: 'Had I ever, disregarding its bloody consequences, coveted Glory, I would
forgo it in return for a tear to shed on your grave'.
33. it] *Hogg*; omitted *Hogg MS*.

issue a long exculpatory statement on 25 September. Denmark thereafter sided with Napoleon.

Text from SC 132 (*Hogg MS*); supplemented by *Esd* f. 63ʳ, for stanza 4 (*Esd* No. 43). Quoted by permission of the Carl H. Pforzheimer Library. Published in *Hogg* i 165–6; *SC* ii 701–2 (transcript of *Hogg MS*); *Esd Nbk* 127 (stanzas 3, 1, 4); *Esd Poems* 114–15 (stanzas 3, 1, 4); *SC* iv 1016–17 (transcript of *Esd*).

> Yes! the arms of Britannia victorious are bearing
>   Fame, Triumph and Glory wherever they spread,
> Her Lion his crest o'er the nations is rearing:
>   Ruin follows! it tramples the dying and dead;
> 5 Thy countrymen fall, the blood-reeking bed
> Of the battle-slain sends a complaint-breathing sigh:
> It is mixed with the shoutings of Victory!
>
> Old Ocean to shrieks of Despair is resounding,
>   It washes the terror-struck nations with gore;
> 10 Wild horror the fear-palsied Earth is astounding
>   And murmurs of fate fright the dread-convulsed shore;
> The Andes in sympathy start at the roar,
> Vast Aetna, alarmed, leans his flame-glowing brow,
> And huge Teneriffe stoops with his pinnacled snow.
>
> 15 The ice-mountains echo, the Baltic, the Ocean
>   Where Cold sits enthroned on his solium of snow;

Stanza 1 (stanza 2 in *Esd*). S. seems indebted to stanza 12 of James Montgomery's 'The Ocean' (1805):

> For Britannia is wielding her trident to-day,
>   Consuming her foes in her ire,
> And hurling her thunder with absolute sway
>   From her wave-ruling chariots of fire.
> She triumphs; the winds and the waters conspire
>   To spread her invincible name;
>   The universe rings with her fame;
> But the cries of the fatherless mix with her praise,
> And the tears of the widow are shed on her bays!

¶ 51.2. *Triumph and Glory*] triumph & terror *Esd*. *spread*] spead *Hogg MS*; speed *Hogg*.

5. *Thy countrymen fall,*] But her countrymen fall . . . *Esd*.

Stanza 2. Omitted Esd.

Stanza 3. Stanza 1 in *Esd*.

15. *ice-mountains*] icebergs (the modern word was not generally used until after 1820).

16. *his*] its *Esd*. *solium*] chair of state (Lat.). In Kirke White's *Christiad* (I xii 1) Satan at the North Pole is raised 'High on a solium of the solid wave'.

E'en Spitzbergen perceives the terrific commotion,
  The roar floats on the whirlwinds of sleet as they
                                blow—
Blood tinges the streams as half frozen they flow,
20 The meteors of War lurid flame through the air,
They mix their bright gleam with the red Polar glare.

*   *   *   *   *

I see the lone female. The sun is descending,
  Dank carnage-smoke sheds an ensanguining glare,
Night its shades in the orient earlier is blending,
25   Yet the light faintly marks a wild maniac's stare:
She lists to the death-shrieks that came on the air,
The pride of her heart to her bosom she pressed,
Then sunk on his form in the sleep of the blest.

*   *   *   *   *

All are Brethren, – the [   ] African bending
30   To the stroke of the hard-hearted Englishman's rod,
The courtier at Luxury's Palace attending,
  The Senator trembling at Tyranny's nod,
 Each nation which kneels at the footstool of God–
All are Brethren; then banish Distinction afar.
35 Let concord and Love heal the miseries of War.

---

17. *Spitzbergen*] Norwegian island-group (Svalbard) bordering the Arctic ice-cap.
19. *Blood tinges*] Blood clots with *Esd.* (The first word is blotted in *Hogg MS.*)
20. Lurid flame oer the cities the meteors of war *Esd.*
21. And mix their deep gleam with the bright polar glare *Esd.* (The asterisks following this line, indicating omission, are from *Hogg MS.*)
Stanza 4. Omitted Hogg MS.
24. i.e. 'it is getting darker in the east sooner than is normal'.
Stanza 5. Omitted Esd (see headnote). The asterisks before this stanza are conjectural; the extent of the omission in *Hogg MS* is uncertain.
29. *Blank in Hogg MS.*
30, 33. Cp. Montgomery's picture of the West Indies in 'The Ocean' 71 2: 'Where man rules o'er man with a merciless rod, / And spurns at his footstool the image of GOD!'

52 A Translation of the Marseillaise Hymn

Date of composition unknown, but probably late 1810 or early 1811. When S. included stanza 4 in a letter of *c.* 20 June 1811 (*L* i 106) Edward Fergus Graham was evidently expected to recognize it, and line 39 of 'To Death' (No. 43), here assigned to November–December 1810, quotes a phrase from the same stanza. Cameron (*Esd Nbk* 272) compares 'pomp-fed Kings' (line 30) with 'pomp-fed despots' ('Henry and Louisa', No. 7, line 312) and dates the poem a year earlier. Words and music of 'La Marseillaise' were composed by Rouget de Lisle in 1792 and adopted as the French National Anthem on 14 July 1795. In this rather free version (his only translation from French) S. tried to widen its nationalism with a more universal revolutionary appeal. Thus 'contre nous' (3) is rendered 'Against thy rights'; 'nos fiers guerriers' (26) becomes 'the arm upraised for Liberty'; and 'La France' (38) becomes 'Our Mother Earth'. The extra line in each stanza corresponds to the repetition of each fourth line of the original; and S.'s form is stricter in that lines 2, 4 and 9 of each stanza rhyme throughout the poem. In places, however, S. misunderstands the original (e.g. 6, 41–2), and he evidently did not know the tune, as his words will not fit it.
Text from *Esd* ff. 76ʳ–77ᵛ (*Esd* No. 47: quoted by permission of the Carl H. Pforzheimer Library).
Published in *Forman 1876–7* iv 353 (stanza 4 only); A. Koszul, *La Jeunesse de Shelley* (1910) 402–4; *Esd Nbk* 144–6; *Esd Poems* 92–4; *SC* iv 1035–8 (transcript of *Esd*).

> Haste to battle, Patriot Band,
>   A day of Glory dawns on thee!
> Against thy rights is raised an hand –
>   The blood-red hand of tyranny!
> 5 See! the ferocious slaves of power
> Across the wasted country scour
> And in thy very arms destroy
> The pledges of thy nuptial joy,
>   Thine unresisting family.
>
>   *Chorus*
> 10 Then citizens, form in battle array,
>   For this is the dawn of a glorious day;
> March, march, fearless of danger and toil,
> And the rank gore of tyrants shall water your soil.

¶ 52. *Title:* Marsellois *Esd.*
5. *slaves of power*] translates 'soldats'.
6. *scour*] translates 'mugir' ('bellow'): perhaps a bad guess on S.'s part.
11–12. The original of these lines is merely 'Marchons! Marchons!'

2.

What wills the coward, traitorous train
15   Of Kings, whose trade is perfidy?
For whom is forged this hateful chain,
    For whom prepared this slavery?
For you. On you their vengeance rests . . .
What transports ought to thrill your breasts!
20   Frenchmen! this unhallowed train
To ancient woe would bind again
    Those souls whom valour has made free.

Chorus etc.

3.

What! shall foreign bands compel
    Us to the laws of tyranny?
25   Shall hired soldiers hope to quell
    The arm upraised for liberty?
Great God! by these united arms
Shall despots their own alarms
Pass neath the yoke made for our head;
30   Yea! pomp-fed Kings shall quake with dread,
    These masters of Earth's destiny!

Chorus etc.

4.

Tremble, Kings, despised of Man!
    Ye traitors to your country
Tremble! your parricidal plan
35   At length shall meet its destiny.
We all are soldiers fit for fight,
But if we sink in glory's night
Our Mother Earth will give ye new
The brilliant pathway to pursue
40   That leads to Death or Victory.

28–31. Renders: 'Nos fronts sous le joug se ploîraient; / De vils despotes deviendraient / Les maîtres de nos destinées! . . .' In 28 Koszul adds 'in' after 'despots'; Cameron sets 'their own alarms' in apposition to 'despots' by commas after 'despots' and 'alarms'; but no such changes are necessary: S.'s construction becomes an inversion in 28 in the plain future tense: 'their own terrors shall place despots under the yoke intended for us'.

36. *fit for*] fit to *Graham MS.*

38. *will give ye new*] i.e. will give you, Frenchmen, new soldiers.

Chorus etc.

5.

Frenchmen! on the guilty brave
Pour your vengeful energy –
Yet in your triumph pitying save
The unwilling slaves of tyranny;
45 But let the gore-stained despots bleed,
Be death fell Bouillé's bloodhound-meed,
Chase those unnatural fiends away
Who on their mother's vitals prey
With more than tiger cruelty.

Chorus etc.

6.

50 Sacred Patriotism! uphold
The avenging bands who fight with thee;
And thou more dear than meaner gold,
Smile on our efforts, Liberty!
Where conquest's crimson streamers wave
55 Haste thou to the happy brave,
Where at our feet thy dying foes
See as their failing eyes unclose
Our glory and thy Victory.

53 'Dares the llama'

Headed '1810' (underlined) in *Esd*, but a closely similar version, also without title, was sent to Hogg on 20 April 1811 (*L* i 73, misdated 28 April: see *SC* ii 757–8) as 'a mad effusion of this morning'. This *Hogg MS* is in the Mary Couts Burnett Library, Texas Christian University. The theme of persecution by

41–2. Renders 'Français, en guerriers magnanimes, / Portez ou retenez vos coups!' ('Deliver or withhold your blows, as befits generous fighters'). S. seems to have misunderstood the original.
46. Bouillé's] Boullie's *Esd*. 'Let death be the fit reward for a bloodhound such as B.' The marquis François-Claude de Bouillé (1739–1800) had planned the escape of Louis XVI from Paris in June 1791.
54. conquest's crimson streamers] Cp. Gray's 'Bard' 3: 'Conquest's crimson wing'. The French has 'nos drapeaux', but S.'s 'conquest' (like Gray's) is probably the oppressor's (cp. 'Henry and Louisa' 309: 'conquest's crimson glow').
57. unclose] i.e. Liberty's victory is what the enemy sees when he opens his eyes for the last time.

conventional Christianity links the poem with *WJ*, and it is rhythmically akin
to the poems of 1810 influenced by Scott's 'Hellvellyn'; but lines 33–4, 'The
most tenderly loved of my soul / Are slaves to its chilling control', must refer
to Harriet Grove and S.'s sister Elizabeth. Elizabeth S. had resisted all attempts
to interest her in Hogg's courtship. S.'s letters remain hopeful of Hogg's
prospects until mid-January 1811, and that of 20 April is the first to concede
defeat over Elizabeth, but both versions of the poem use the plural 'Are slaves'.
It must therefore have been written, or perhaps revised, shortly before the date
of this letter, and then revised again for copying into *Esd*.

Text from *Esd* ff. 60ᵛ–61ʳ (*Esd* No. 41: quoted by permission of the Carl H.
Pforzheimer Library).

Published in *Hogg* i 351–2; *Esd Nbk* 123–4; *Esd Poems* 74–5; *SC* iv 1012–14
(transcript of *Esd*).

> Dares the llama, most fleet of the sons of the wind,
>   The lion to rouse from his lair?
> When the tiger awakes, can the fast-fleeting hind
>   Repose trust in his footsteps of air?
> 5   No—abandoned it sinks in helpless despair:
>   The monster transfixes his prey,
>   On the sand flows its life-blood away,
> And the rocks and the woods to the death-yells reply,
> Protracting the horrible harmony.
>
> 10   Yet the fowl of the desert when danger encroaches
>   Dares dreadless to perish, defending her brood
> Though the fiercest of cloud-piercing tyrants approaches
>   Thirsting—aye, thirsting for blood,
> And demands, like mankind, his brother for food;
> 15   Yet more lenient, more gentle than they,
>   For hunger, not glory, the prey
> Must perish—revenge does not howl o'er the dead,
> Nor ambition with fame bind the murderer's head.

¶ 53.2. *lion*] The mountain lion (puma) of the Andes. *his lair*] his scull covered
lair *Hogg MS*.

5. *it*] he *Hogg MS*.

8. Whilst India's rocks to his death-yells reply *Hogg MS*.

10. *fowl of the desert*] If this is still India (see previous note), probably the
peafowl, reputed for its courage.

11. *dreadless*] fearless *Hogg MS*.

12. *cloud-piercing tyrants*] Vultures.

16. *hunger*] Underlined in *Hogg MS*. *the prey*] their prey *Hogg MS*.

18. *bind*] crown *Hogg MS*.

Though weak as the llama that bounds on the mountains
20   And endued not with fast-fleeting footsteps of air
Yet, yet will I draw from the purest of fountains,
    Though a fiercer than tigers is there,
Though more frightful than death it scatters despair,
    And its shadow eclipsing the day
25   Spreads the darkness of deepest dismay
O'er the withered and withering nations around,
And the war-mangled corpses that rot on the ground.

They came to the fountain to draw from its stream
    Waves too poisonously lovely for mortals to see;
30   They basked for awhile in the love-darting beam,
    Then perished—and perished like me.
For in vain from the grasp of Religion I flee;
    The most tenderly loved of my soul
    Are slaves to its chilling control . . .
35   It pursues me, it blasts me. Oh! where shall I fly,
    What remains but to curse it, to curse it and die?

54   A Dialogue

Headed 'A Dialogue–1809' in *Esd*, but more plausibly written January–April 1811. An untitled holograph version on a separate leaf, predating the *Esd* text, was sent by Hogg with a covering letter to Dawson Turner (MSO.14.12, f. 126a, Trinity College, Cambridge) on 30 May 1834, as 'a poem, or rather a rough draft of part of a poem' which Hogg believed 'was written in 1810,

21, 29. the purest of fountains . . . Waves too poisonously lovely] Cameron (*Esd Nbk* 250) explains: 'Religion is the poison in the waves of the fountain (of life?) which has corrupted those the poet loves and which has injured the poet himself'; but although the image is of animals caught at a water-hole, the fountain ('Waves too pure too celestial . . .' *Hogg MS*) is more likely to be Love, or Truth. Possibly the 'Waves too poisonously lovely for mortals to see' are the flattering delusions of Heaven, speedily transformed into threats of Hell ('despair').
22. i.e. 'Though something [conventional Christianity] fiercer than tigers is to be found there'.
23. frightful] dreadful *Hogg MS*.
24–7. Tho its shadow eclipses the day / And the darkness of deepest dismay / Spreads the influence of soul-chilling terror around / And lowers on the corpses that rot on the ground *Hogg MS*.
29. too poisonously lovely] too pure too celestial *Hogg MS*.
30. the love-darting] its silvery *Hogg MS*.
35. Oh! where shall] ah vain that *Hogg MS*.

when the young poet was but 17, or 18, years old'. The origins of the other
thirteen poems and fragments in Hogg's possession can be accounted for:
assuming, therefore, that he kept all the poetry S. gave him (which seems to be
the case), these may be 'some verses' otherwise unaccounted for, sent him in a
letter of 26 April 1811 (*L* i 68–70). This letter begins: 'You indulge despair, *why*
do you so?' and ends: 'You talk of the dead. Do we not exist after the tomb. It is
a natural question my friend, when there is nothing in life'. Echoes of the poem
occur in letters written to Hogg January–April 1811, and in other poems
written at this time. Cameron, while accepting the 1809 date (*Esd Nbk* 236–7),
notes of the revisions in lines 2–3 of *Esd* that S. 'changes a personal, philosophical reference to a social, anti-war reference', and points out that S.'s note
to line 25 quotes *Q Mab* and must have been added on transcription in 1812.
Text from *Esd* ff. 51ʳ–52ʳ (*Esd* No. 33: quoted by permission of the Carl H.
Pforzheimer Library).
Published in *Hogg* i 197–8; *Esd Nbk* 108–9; *Esd Poems* 62–4; *SC* iv 997–9
(transcript of *Esd*).

DEATH

Yes! my dagger is drenched with the blood of the brave,
I have sped with Love's wings from the battlefield grave
Where Ambition is hushed neath the peacegiving sod
And slaves cease to tremble at Tyranny's nod;
5 I offer a calm habitation to thee:
Victim of grief, wilt thou slumber with me?
Drear and damp is my hall, but a mild Judge is there
Who steeps in oblivion the brands of Despair.
Nor a groan of regret, nor a sigh, nor a breath
10 Dares dispute with grim Silence the empire of Death,
Nor the howlings of envy resound through the gloom
That shrouds in its mantle the slaves of the tomb.
I offer a calm habitation to thee:
Say, victim of grief, wilt thou slumber with me?

MORTAL

15 Mine eyelids are heavy, my soul seeks repose,
It longs in thy arms to embosom its woes,

¶ 54.1. *Yes!*] –For *Hogg MS. drenched with*] bathed in *Hogg MS.*
2. I come, care-worn tenant of life! from the grave *Hogg MS.*
3. *Ambition is hushed*] Innocence sleeps *Hogg MS.*
4. *slaves*] the good *Hogg MS.*
6. *Victim*] Say, victim *Hogg MS.*
7–8.   My mansion is damp, cold silence is there
        But it lulls in oblivion the fiends of despair *Hogg MS*
9. *Nor . . . nor . . . nor*] Not . . . not . . . not *Hogg MS.*
11–12. Omitted *Hogg MS.*
16. *arms*] cells *Hogg MS.*

It longs in that realm to deposit its load
Where no longer the scorpions of perfidy goad,
Where the phantoms of Prejudice vanish away
20 And Bigotry's bloodhounds lose scent of their prey.
Yet tell me, dark Death, when thine Empire is o'er
What awaits on futurity's mist-circled shore?

DEATH

Cease, cease, wayward mortal! I dare not unveil
The shadows that float o'er eternity's vale.
25 What thinkest thou will wait thee? A Spirit of Love
That will hail thy blest advent to mansions above.
For Love, mortal! gleams through the gloom of my sway
And the clouds that surround me fly fast at its ray.
Hast thou *loved*?–then depart from these regions of hate
30 And in slumber with me quench the arrows of fate
That canker and burn in the wounds of a heart
That urges its sorrows with me to depart.
I offer a calm habitation to thee:
Say, victim of grief, wilt thou slumber with me?

MORTAL

35 Oh, sweet is thy slumber, and sweeter the ray
Which after thy night introduces the day.

17. that realm] thy cells *Hogg MS.*
22. mist-circled] mist-covered *Hogg MS.*
25. Nought waits for the good but a spirit of love *Hogg MS.* *A Spirit of Love*]
'The author begs to be understood by this expression neither to mean the
Creator of the Universe, nor the Christian Deity.–When this little poem was
written the line stood thus: "What waits for the good?" but he has altered it on
transcription, because however his feelings may love to linger on a future state
of Happiness, neither justice, reason, nor passion can reconcile to his belief that
the crimes of this life, equally necessary and inevitable as its virtues, should be
punished in another.
                    Earth in itself
                Contains at once the evil & the cure
                And all sufficing Nature can chastize
                Those who transgress her law.'
                            [Q *Mab* iii 80–3. S.'s note in *Esd*]
26. thy] their *Hogg MS.*
27. Love, mortal!] *Love* Mortal! *Hogg MS.*
28. clouds that] shades which *Hogg MS.*
30. quench] blunt *Hogg MS.*
31–2. Omitted Hogg MS.
35. and sweeter] oh! sweet is *Hogg MS.*
35–6. Cp. S. to Hogg, 26 April 1811: 'Shall I say the time may come when
happiness shall dawn upon a night of wretchedness–' (*L* i 68).

How soft, how persuasive self-interest's breath
Though it floats to mine ear from the bosom of Death.
I hoped that I quite was forgotten by all,
40 Yet a lingering friend may be grieved at my fall,
And duty forbids, though I languish, to die
When departure might heave Virtue's breast with a sigh.
Yet, Death! oh! my friend, snatch this form to thy shrine,
And I fear, dear destroyer, I shall not repine.

55 'Why is it said thou canst but live'

Included, without title, in a letter to Hogg dated 8 May 1811, and probably contemporary with it. S., alone in London, has been replying to Hogg's reports from Ellesmere in Shropshire: 'The scenery excites mournful ideas. I am sorry to hear it. I hoped that it wd. have had a contrary effect.' (24 April; *L* i 67). He has argued that although Elizabeth S. was plainly lost to Hogg for the foreseeable future, still 'ought it not rather to be years, or rather ought *years* even to decide upon a question so important–'? (*c.* 25 April; *L* i 75). Hogg's eventual inheritance 'would possibly add to the happiness of some being to whom you cherish some remote hope of approximation, union–the indissoluble sacred union of love Why is it said', etc.–the poem running on without a break on the same line. S.'s poem may have been suggested by the reunion of Ladurlad with his dead wife Yedillian in the Bower of Bliss in Southey's *Kehama* X 10: 'They sin who tell us Love can die. / With life all other passions fly,' etc. Hogg's textual changes or inadvertencies, noted below, defeat the intended sense.

Rossetti (*Rossetti 1870* i 521) introduced the title 'Love', and it is Love who is addressed as 'thou' in lines 1–10. In 11–24, however, 'thou' becomes Hogg, or the reader of the poem.
Text from SC 157 (*Hogg MS*: quoted by permission of the Carl H. Pforzheimer Library).
Published in *Hogg* i 366; *SC* ii 776–7 (transcript of *Hogg MS*).

Why is it said thou canst but live
    In a youthful breast and fair,
Since thou eternal life canst give,
    Canst bloom forever there,
5 Since withering pain no power possesses,
    Nor Age, to blanch thy vermeil hue,

37. *soft*,] concealed *Hogg MS*. *self-interest's breath*] i.e. the selfish prompting to suicide.
40. *may*] might *Hogg MS*.
41. *duty*] *Hogg MS*; Virtue *Esd* (the repetition is weak and seems inadvertent).
43. *Yet, Death!*] Oh death, *Hogg MS*.
¶ 55.1. *thou*] Love. *but*] not *Hogg*.
5. *possesses*] possesst *Hogg*.

Since time's dread victor death confesses
      Though bathèd with his poison dew
Still thou retainst unchanging bloom
10 Fixed tranquil even in the tomb?–
And oh! when on the blest reviving
      The day-star dawns of love,
Each energy of soul surviving
      More vivid soars above–
15 Hast thou ne'er felt a rapturous thrill
      Like June's warm breath athwart thee fly
O'er each idea then to steal
      When other passions die,
Felt it in some wild noonday dream
20 When sitting by the lonely stream
Where Silence says, Mine is the dell,
      And not a murmur from the plain
And not an echo from the fell
      Disputes her silent reign?

56 Letter to Edward Fergus Graham

Written 14 or 15 May 1811 on returning to Field Place from Cuckfield,
probably sent with a prose letter of the same date (see *L* i 86 and note), in which
S. had told Graham: 'We had this morning a letter addressed to my Father
accusing him & my mother of getting drunk, & the latter of being more
intimate with *you* than with my father himself. We all laughed heartily &
thought it a good opportunity of making up. But he is as inveterate as ever'.
The poem exploits this scandal with 'a certain adolescent wantonness' (*Forman
1892* i xix). In October, however, the promotion by S.'s mother of a marriage
between Graham and Elizabeth S. caused S. suddenly to take the accusation
seriously–doubtless, as Jones suggests (*L* i 85*n.*), through his overreacting on
Hogg's behalf. He challenged his mother with this accusation, the unlikeli-
hood of which is the basis of the poem, causing his father to declare that had S.
'stay'd in Sussex I would have sworn in Especial Constables around me' (*S in
Eng* 347). Nothing came of Elizabeth's projected marriage to Graham. No
editor before Ingpen would print this *jeu d'esprit* ('which it were preferable the
sun had never seen'–*Forman 1892* loc. cit.), on the grounds of its 'referring to

7. *Since*] Nor *Hogg.* confesses] confess'd, *Hogg.*
11–14. The meaning seems to be: 'When the reviving sun of love rises on the
blest (and) soars, more vivid, above every surviving impulse, have you never
felt . . .?'
24. Echoing Gray's *Elegy* 12: 'Molest her ancient solitary reign'.

his father in odious terms' (*Dowden Life* i 131n.), though most earlier editors
(including Dowden) copied it. The title is Ingpen's.
Text from *Graham MS* (Berg Collection, NYPL).
Published in *L about S* 61 (lines 55–end); *London Mercury* vi (August 1922) 418
(lines 1–10, 18–28, 51–end); *Julian* i 92–4 (full text).

As you will see, I wrote to you
As is most fitting, right and due,
With Killjoy's frank; old Killjoy he
Is eaten up with Jealousy,
5   His brows so dark, his ears so blue!
And all this fury is for you.
Yes, Graham, thine is sure the name
On Spanish fields so dear to fame
Which sickening Killjoy scarce can hear
10 Without a mingled pang of fear.
Fierce hatred cowards always have,
But Gratitude usurps the brave,
And therefore, Graham, I will tell
You, if you don't as yet know well
15 Before I tell this tale to you,
That Killjoy hot with envy blue
Can neither bear, Graeme, me or you.
A good man bears his heaven about him,
An idiot's pride won't move without him,
20 And pride may justly be called Hell
Since 'twas from Pride that Satan fell,
From pride the mighty conquerors strode
O'er half the globe, from pride the abode
Of Peace becomes the poisoned cell
25 Where the fiends of Hatred dwell,
Suspicion always tracks its way,
Around the wretch what horrors play
And on his poisoned vitals prey.

¶ 56.3. *Killjoy's frank*] 'this killjoy, as I name him' (*L* i 93) was S.'s father, Sir
Timothy, who was angered by S.'s expulsion from Oxford and his attempt to
renounce the entail of the family estate, was trying to separate S. from Hogg,
and was discouraging S.'s influence over Elizabeth S. As MP he had the
privilege of franking letters for free delivery.
7–8. Graham's namesake, Gen. Thomas Graham, Lord Lynedoch (1748–
1843), had won a striking victory over the French at Barrosa on 5 March.
12. *usurps*] 'fills the feelings of' (*OED* 2c).
17. *Graeme*] The name was pronounced as a monosyllable in Scotland (see
Scott's note to *The Vision of Don Roderick* (1811) I ix 7).

Hence you, my Fargy, when we know
30   That you are never used to go
In courtship to the ancient dames
Who reverence claim instead of flames,
Since but once in an age is seen
Of forty-eight a peerless queen
35   Like Ninon famed, that girl of France
Who at ninety-two could dance
With such a grace as did impart
Improper flames to grandson's heart,
We fairly may acquit your soul—
40   Though your life's pulses fiercely roll—
Of having let one wild wish glow
Of cornuting old Killjoy's brow;
Heaven knows 'twere a courageous horn
That would this frowning brow adorn.
45   Oh! not the fiercest antler dare
To stretch its fell luxuriance there.
Safe mayst thou sin; although there's none
Of what is called temptation,
And I should think 'twere no mistake
50   To say you sinned for sinning sake.
Yet as this place no news affords
But secret damns and glossy words
Before your face, I bid adieu
And wish, my Graeme, good night to you.

P.S.
55   The wind is high and I have been
With little Jack upon the green,
A dear delightful red-faced brute,
And setting up a parachute
The wind beneath its bosom played.
60   Oh! Fargy, wondrous sport we made.

29. *Fargy*] Familiar form of 'Fergus'.
34. *forty-eight*] If this is the age of S.'s mother (otherwise unrecorded) she was born in 1762 or 1763 and so was about 10 years younger than her husband.
35. *Ninon*] Anne de Lenclos (1620–1705), wit and beauty, and a famous courtesan.
42. *cornuting*] adorning with horns, cuckolding.
52–3. i.e. outward politeness but covert hostility.
56. *little Jack*] S.'s five-year-old brother John. All the Shelleys had a very fresh complexion (see miniature of Elizabeth S., *KSMB* xiii (1962) frontispiece). *the green*] Probably Strood Green, just west of Field Place.
58. *parachute*] Parachutes were first demonstrated in 1802. This must have been some form of kite.
60. Following this line S. wrote: 'Are not human minds just like this little para' (*Julian* reads the last word as 'poem').

57 Second Letter to Edward Fergus Graham

Written untitled on a single sheet folded into a letter, dated 'Horsham June
Seven 1811' above the outside address (a complete facsimile is given by
Rogers, who first printed the poem, with commentary–see below). Graham
had evidently played up with a letter of mock-penitence to the scandal reported
of him in S.'s previous letters (see headnote to No. 56), and this poem follows
up the joke (such as it is) by pretending that S.'s father will accept no apologies.
S. had taken advantage of his father's absence to accompany his mother and
sister Elizabeth for a week's stay (his second recent visit) at his uncle's at
Cuckfield, and had picked up Graham's letter on his return on 2 June (*L* i 95).
    From the indentation of the rhyme-words in lines 3 and 8 it seems likely that
the poem was not improvised but copied from a draft; S. also made allowance
(though not quite enough) for the tear that would result when the seal was
broken. The epistolary doggerel is indebted to that of Christopher Anstey's
much-printed *New Bath Guide* (1766).
Text from facsimile in *KSMB* xxiv (1973) facing p. 20.
Published in *KSMB* xxiv (1973) 22–3.

> Dear dear dear dear dear dear Graeme!
> When back from Cuckfield here I came
>   I found your penitential letter,
>   But sackcloth cannot now prevail
> 5 Nor even ashes aught avail,
>   For I can see there's no relenting.
>   Indeed I fear that all repenting
>   Would act but as a temper-whetter,
>   For the more you repent, the more tears he demands,
> 10 The more you submit, the more the commands,
>   The more sighs that you breathe, the joy so divine!
>   The more will he want you to groan, gnash and whine.
>   They are food to his soul, and when the notes fall
>   'Tis like your beloved Catalani's squall:
> 15 The murmurs of grief are the music he hears
>   And discontent's groanings are balm to his ears.

¶ *57.1.* One 'dear' too few in *KSMB*. S. puns on 'dear, dear!' ('tut, tut!').
10. the more the] the more he *KSMB*.
11. so] to *KSMB*.
12. more will he want you] more he desires you *KSMB*.
14. Catalani's] Catalanis *MS*. Angelica Catalani (1780–1849) the great operatic
soprano lived in London 1806–13. S.'s objection to her voice was perhaps
influenced by her patronage of French émigrés (see *Reminiscences and Recollections of Captain Gronow 1810–1860* (1862–6; 1900 edn) i 122–3.

What wonder then happiness sounds to him woe,
What wonder that mirth bid satire to flow,
That his blue visage gleams with a blueness intenser
20   [When] happiness acts as a passion-condenser?
But give him a prison, and give him a throne,
And give him a world to reign in alone,
Full of death-groaning nations let it be crammed,
And I wish no worse place for the souls of the damned,
25   Or give him a daughter and give him a wife,
I'll engage he'll torment 'em just out of their life,
If so be't their peculiar wish lies this way
With exactness our squire will their wishes obey.
Have you found yet the horn that dares to adorn
30   A brow which no daring horn yet has attempted?–
And I will engage, for the rest of his age,
That from all further duty he shall be exempted.
I think that our squire does mainly desire
That an horn on his dark frowning brow were
                                                implanted–
35   I've hit it exactly; he'd get one directly,
But the worst is that things will not come when they're
                                                wanted;–
He wishes to drive from her own native hive
His wife who so merrily laughs at each odd whim.
And now I have done, for they say that this fun
40   Would look worse on the side of this letter than
                                                Godwin.

17. sounds] sound *KSMB*.
18. mirth bid satire to] mirth had [?] [?] to *KSMB*. Dubious reading: the line is
obscured by cancellations.
20. [When]] [?Than] *KSMB*. Conjectural: word removed by seal-tear.
passion-condenser] A 'condenser' normally converted vapour into liquid, but
was also used of a plate for concentrating electricity.
21. But] [ ]! *KSMB*.
30. daring] dancing *KSMB*.
35. he'd] he'll *KSMB*.
39–40. The last two lines are written overleaf, at right angles to the address; i.e.
they were readable on the inside of the fold without breaking the seal, and S.
acknowledges that his jesting would be found more offensive even than
political subversion.

58 Zeinab and Kathema

Date of composition unknown. Presumably written soon after S.'s reading of Sydney Owenson's (Lady Morgan's) *The Missionary: an Indian Tale* (1811), which he had 'just finished' on 11 June (*L* i 101), though the novel contributed only the contrast between the uncorrupted Indian character and scenery, centred on the Vale of Kashmir, and the corruptions of imperialism. The plot seems partly derived from 'The Poor Negro Sadi' in Charlotte Dacre's (Mrs Byrne's) *Hours of Solitude* (1805) i 117–22. Sadi is forced from wife and home into slavery, but escapes by swimming to an English ship:

> Soft, soft blew the gale, and the green billows swelling,
>> Gay sail'd the light vessel for Albion's shore;
> Poor Sadi sigh'd deep for his wife and his dwelling,
>> That wife and that dwelling he ne'er must see more. (37–40)

In England, he wanders desolate for several days, is dragged without pity from the doorway into which he crawls, and finally dies of cold and hunger. The Christianity that condones this treatment is specifically attacked; but S.'s social criticism and dismissal of 'God's holy plan' is far more uncompromising, while Zeinab's prostitution and gibbeting and Kathema's suicide have no parallels in 'Sadi'. The name 'Zeinab' is that of the (Arab) hero's mother in Southey's *Thalaba the Destroyer* (1801) I iii 2, etc., and 'Kathema' seems adapted from 'Kehama' in his *Curse of Kehama* (1810). It is tempting to surmise that Coleridge's 'Ancient Mariner' supplied the image of the vessel silhouetted against the evening sun ('AM' 149–52, 171–6; 'Z & K' 13–18) and its impulsion by 'some inward spirit' ('AM' 375–80; 'Z & K' 79–82); although Medwin says (*Medwin (1913)* 44) that about 1809 'Wordsworth's writings were at that time by no means to his taste . . . he wanted something more exciting', his phrasing implies that S. may at least have read *Lyrical Ballads* before 1811. The metre is one of Chatterton's (e.g. the Minstrels' interlude in 'The Tournament'; *Aella* xxvii–xxxiv), used also by Southey ('The Chapel Bell', 1793).

Dowden, who read the poem in MS, points out (*Dowden Life* i 348) that it was 'designed less as a piece of romantic art than as an indictment of widespread evils'–both domestic and colonial–and Cameron (*Esd Nbk* 279) notes some remarkable anticipations of *L&C*. The silhouetted ship recurs in *L&C* I vi 178–80; Kehama's childhood love of Zeinab in Laon's for Cythna (*L&C* II xxi–xlix); Zeinab's abduction in that of Cythna to the seraglio in *L&C* VII iii–vi; Kehama's awakening under the gibbet in Laon's delirious vision of Cythna's decayed corpse suspended by the hair in *L&C* III xxv–xxvi; the image of the star and the comet in *L&C* I xxvi. To these may be added comparison of Zeinab's waging of 'ruthless war' against her oppressors with S.'s own commitment to 'war with mankind' in *L&C* Ded. v 5–6, and other details. Clearly the poem's sensationalism, as later with *L&C*, is partly symbolic, and should not be allowed to obscure the marked advance in economy and technical skill of the narrative (e.g. 61–72, 79–80, 103–8). If the date is wrong it is more likely to be too early than too late.

Text from *Esd* ff. 81ʳ–85ᵛ (*Esd* No. 49: quoted by permission of the Carl H. Pforzheimer Library).
Published in *Dowden Life* i 347 (lines 79–84 only); *Esd Nbk* 148–54; *Esd Poems* 96–102; *SC* iv 1040–47 (transcript of *Esd*).

Upon the lonely beach Kathema lay,
   Against his folded arm his heart beat fast;
Through gathering tears the sun's departing ray
   In coldness o'er his shuddering spirit passed,
5   And all unfelt the breeze of evening came
   That fanned with quivering wing his wan cheek's feeble
                   flame.

'Oh!' cried the mourner, 'could this widowed soul
   But fly where yonder sun now speeds to dawn.'
He paused–a thousand thoughts began to roll,
10   Like waves they swept in restless tumult on,
   Like those fast waves that quick-succeeding beat
   Without one lasting shape the beach beneath his feet.

And now the beamless, broad and yellow sphere
   Half sinking lingered on the crimson sea;
15   A shape of darksome distance does appear
   Within its semicircled radiancy.
All sense was gone to his betrothèd one–
His eye fell on the form that dimmed the setting sun,–

He thought on his betrothèd . . . for his youth
20   With her that was its charm to ripeness grew.
All that was dear in love, or fair in truth,
   With her was shared as childhood's moments flew,
And mingled with sweet memories of her
Was life's unveiling morn with all its bliss and care,

25   A wild and lovely Superstition's spell:
   Love for the friend that life and freedom gave;
Youth's growing hopes that watch themselves so well,
   Passion so prompt to blight, so strong to save,
And childhood's host of memories combine
30   Her life and love around his being to entwine.

¶ 58.7–8. i.e. fly to England. A confusion perhaps attributable to Kathema's state of mind. He must have descended the Indus from Kashmir (92), and the sun will rise again some five hours earlier to him near Karachi than it will over London. He means 'if only I could follow the disappearing sun to where it is still high in the sky'.
13–14. *And now . . . crimson sea*] Cp. *Thalaba* X vi 1–2; 'Now sunk the Evening sun / A broad and beamless orb'.
25. *Superstition's spell*] 'unreasoning enchantment'.

And to their wishes with its joy-mixed pain
  Just as the veil of hope began to fall,
The Christian murderers over-ran the plain
  Ravaging, burning and polluting all.
35 Zeinab was reft to grace the robbers' land;
Each drop of kindred blood stained the invaders' brand.

Yes! they had come their holy book to bring
  Which God's own son's apostles had compiled
That charity and peace and love might spring
40   Within a world by God's blind ire defiled,
But rapine, war and treachery rushed before
Their hosts, and murder dyed Kathema's bower in
                         gore.

Therefore his soul was widowed, and alone
  He stood in the world's wide and drear expanse;
45 No human ear could shudder at his groan,
  No heart could thrill with his unspeaking glance,
One only hope yet lingering dared to burn,
Urging to high emprize and deeds that danger spurn.

The glow has failed on Ocean's western line,
50   Faded from every moveless cloud above;
The moon is up—she that was wont to shine
  And bless thy childish nights of guileless love,
Unhappy one, ere Christian rapine tore
All ties, and stained thy hopes in a dear mother's gore.

55 The form that in the setting sun was seen
  Now in the moonlight slowly nears the shore,
The white sails gleaming o'er the billows green
  That sparkle into foam its prow before;
A wanderer of the deep it seems to be
60 On high adventures bent, and feats of chivalry.

Then hope and wonder filled the mourner's mind;
  He gazed till vision even began to fail,
When to the pulses of the evening wind
  A little boat approaching gave its sail,
65 Rode o'er the slow-raised surges near the strand,
Ran up the beach and gave some stranger men to land.

33–4. The conquest of India in the interests of the E. India Co. had been swiftly
and often brutally prosecuted in the first decade of the century, but Kashmir
was not yet directly involved; S. has in mind bands of freebooters (lines 41–2)
who exploited the anarchy prevailing in Central and N. India.
54. *dear*] *possibly* dead *Esd.*
57. *billows*] billow *Esd.*

'If thou wilt bear me to far England's shore
   Thine is this heap [of gold], the Christians' God.'
The chief with gloating rapture viewed the ore,
70   And his pleased avarice gave the willing nod.
They reach the ship, the freshening breezes rise,
And smooth and fast they speed beneath the moonlight
                       skies.

What heart e'er felt more ardent longings now?
   What eye than his e'er beamed with riper hope
75 As curbed impatience on his open brow
   There painted fancy's unsuspected scope,
As all that's fair the foreign land appeared
By ever-present love, wonder and hope endeared?

Meanwhile through calm and storm, through night and
                       day,
80   Unvarying in her aim the vessel went
   As if some inward spirit ruled her way
   And her tense sails were conscious of intent,
Till Albion's cliffs gleamed o'er her plunging bow,
And Albion's river-floods bright sparkled round her
                       prow.

85 Then on the land in joy Kathema leaped
   And kissed the soil in which his hopes were sown–
These even now in thought his heart has reaped.
   Elate of body and soul he journeyed on,
And the strange things of a strange land passed by
90 Like motes and shadows pressed upon his charmèd eye.

Yet Albion's changeful skies and chilling wind
   The change from Kashmire's vale might well denote:
There Heaven and Earth are ever bright and kind,
   Here blights and storms and damp forever float,

---

68. *heap [of gold], the*] heap the *Esd* (an accidental omission); cp. James Ridley's
Tales of the Genii (1764), Tale VI, 'Misnar, Sultan of India': 'The Europeans . . .
acknowledge one God, who, they pretend, doth inhabit the heavens; but
whom *we* find buried in the entrails of the earth: gold, O prince, is their
god . . .' S. could have seen the same judgement made of Pizarro's Spaniards
in 1614: 'Some of them [Indians] showing a piece of Gold, will say, Lo here the
Christian's God . . . for this they . . . do whatsoever violence and lust'
(*Hakluytus Posthumus or Purchas His Pilgrimes* (Glasgow 1906 edn) xvii 299).
84. *Albion's river-floods*] Esp. the Thames.
90. *motes*] mites *Esd Nbk.*
93–100. Cp. the idealized description of Kashmir in *The Missionary* i 130–31.

95 Whilst hearts are more ungenial than the zone,
    Gross, spiritless, alive to no pangs but their own;

    There flowers and fruits are ever fair and ripe,
        Autumn there mingles with the bloom of spring,
    And forms unpinched by frost or hunger's gripe
100   A natural veil o'er natural spirits fling,
    Here, woe on all but wealth has set its foot:
    Famine, disease and crime even wealth's proud gates
                                                pollute.

    Unquiet death and premature decay,
        Youth tottering on the crutches of old age,
105 And ere the noon of manhood's riper day
        Pangs that no art of medicine can assuage,
    Madness and passion ever mingling flames,
    And souls that well become such miserable frames—

    These are the bribes which Art to man has given
110   To yield his taintless nature to her sway:
    So might dark night with meteors tempt fair Heaven
        To blot the sunbeam and forswear the day
    Till gleams of baleful light alone might show
    The pestilential mists, the darkness and the woe.

115 Kathema little felt the sleet and wind,
        He little heeded the wide-altered scene;
    The flame that lived within his eager mind
        There kindled all the thoughts that once had been.
    He stood alone in England's varied woe
120 Safe, mid the flood of crime that round his steps did
                                                flow.

    It was an evening when the bitterest breath
        Of dark December swept the mists along
    That the lone wanderer came to a wild heath.
        Courage and hope had stayed his nature long,
125 Now cold, and unappeasèd hunger, spent
    His strength; sensation failed in total languishment.

---

100. i.e. 'clothe healthy impulses in healthy bodies'.
109. bribes] Ironical. Human suffering, the Missionary found, resulted from
deserting Nature in pursuit of illusions (The Missionary iii 142).
111. dark] dank SC.
123. The heaths near London, Cameron notes (Esd Nbk 280), were a usual site
for gibbeting executed criminals. Gibbeting was practised up to 1832.

When he awaked to life cold horror crept
　　Even to his heart, for a damp deathy smell
　Had slowly come around him while he slept.
130　　He started . . . lo! the fitful moonbeams fell
　Upon a dead and naked female form
　That from a gibbet high swung to the sullen storm,

　And wildly in the wind its dark hair swung
　　Low mingling with the clangour of the chain,
135　Whilst ravenous birds of prey that on it clung
　　In the dull ear of night poured their sad strain,
　And ghastlily her shapeless visage shone
　In the unsteady light, half mouldered through the bone.

　Then madness seized Kathema, and his mind
140　　A prophecy of horror filled. He scaled
　The gibbet which swung slowly in the wind
　　High o'er the heath. – Scarcely his strength availed
　To grasp the chain, when by the moonlight's gleam
　His palsied gaze was fixed on Zeinab's altered frame.

145　Yes! in those orbs once bright with life and love
　　Now full-fed worms bask in unnatural light;
　That neck on which his eyes were wont to rove
　　In rapture, changed by putrefaction's blight
　Now rusts the ponderous links that creak beneath
150　Its weight, and turns to life the frightful sport of death.

　　Then in the moonlight played Kathema's smile
　Calmly. – In peace his spirit seemed to be.
　He paused even like a man at ease awhile,
　　Then spoke – 'My love! I will be like to thee,
155　A mouldering carcase, or a spirit blest,
　With thee corruption's prey, or Heaven's happy guest.'

　He twined the chain around his neck, then leaped
　　Forward, in haste to meet the life to come.
　An iron-souled son of Europe might have wept
160　　To witness such a noble being's doom,
　As on the death-scene Heaven indignant frowned
　And Night in horror drew her veil the dead around.

---

133. its] her *Esd Poems*. The two words are superimposed in *Esd*.
133–4. i.e. the wind whistling through her hair (a common Ossianic image)
mingles with the sound of the chain.
150. life] i.e. generated from corruption.

For they had torn his Zeinab from her home;
 Her innocent habits were all rudely shriven,
165 And dragged to live in love's untimely tomb
 To prostitution, crime and woe was driven;
The human race seemed leagued against her weal,
And indignation cased her naked heart in steel.

Therefore against them she waged ruthless war
170 With their own arms of bold and bloody crime,
Even like a mild and sweetly-beaming star
 Whose rays were wont to grace the matin prime
Changed to a comet horrible and bright
Which wild careers awhile then sinks in dark-red night.

175 Thus, like its God, unjust and pitiless,
 Crimes first are made and then avenged by man,
For where's the tender heart whose hope can bless
 Or man's, or God's, unprofitable plan?–
A universe of horror and decay,
180 Gibbets, disease, and wars, and hearts as hard as they.

59 'Sweet star!'

Included in a letter to Hogg dated 18–19 June by Cameron (*SC* ii 813–14). Cameron's persuasive dating is, however, open to objection. S. says in the letter that 'Sweet star!' was part of 'a strange mélange of maddened stuff which I wrote by the midnight moon last night', adding that 'last night . . . I saw the moon, just behind one of the chimneys' of Field Place. There was a new moon early on 21 June 1811, and the moon could not therefore have been seen at midnight–if at all–two days earlier. S. is normally accurate in such matters (see No. 4), and has reason to be so in this verse fragment, which aims to titillate Hogg's imagination by picturing Field Place as an ideal setting for romance (that Hogg responded is shown by his revealing mistranscription of the last word 'unnerved' as 'enamoured'). A proposal had been made by 2 June (*L* i 96) that Hogg should visit Field Place secretly in order to see S.'s sister Elizabeth–a visit actually carried out during the last days of the month (see *L* i 114–15, and original text of relevant letter in *KSMB* xv (1964) 43–4). S. was constantly writing to Hogg at this time: his letters during June still exist for 2 (Sunday), 4,

164. *shriven,*] riven *emend. Esd Poems.* Emendation is unnecessary because *shrive* can mean 'remove' (*OED* 8b), with an ironical religious connotation: 'given short shrift of her innocence, [she] was dragged . . .'
173. *a comet*] S.'s first use of these opposing symbols: cp. *L&C* I xxvi 5–6: 'A blood red Comet and the Morning Star / Mingling their beams in combat'.
175. *its God*] i.e. mankind's God.

16 (Sunday), 20, 23 (Sunday)–and this letter. The unlikely gap of twelve days from 4–16 June strongly suggests that at least one letter has been lost or suppressed. If this hypothetical letter were dated 9 June it could have been the 'violent' one referred to at the beginning of the 'Sweet star!' letter: 'I wrote you on Sunday'. The 'Sweet star!' letter may then belong to 13 or 14 June, which would account satisfactorily for the (waning) 'midnight moon'. If a letter really is missing, this may be because Hogg returned it (perhaps with annotations) to its sender, as S. told him on 16 June: 'Your letter came this morning, I burnt that one of mine, I shuddered even to look at a page of it, the flames destroyed it' (L i 103). The verse fragment 'Sweet star!', therefore, was very possibly written on the night of 13 or 14 June, and has an element of playful provocation.

Text from SC 166 (*Hogg MS*: quoted by permission of the Carl H. Pforzheimer Library).

Published in *Hogg* i 397; *SC* ii 810–11 (transcript of *Hogg MS*).

> Sweet star! which gleaming o'er the darksome scene
> Through fleecy clouds of silvery radiance, fling'st
> Spanglets of light on evening's shadowy veil
> Which shrouds the day-beam from the waveless lake,
> 5 Lighting the hour of sacred love, – more sweet
> Than the expiring Morn-star's paly fires:
> Sweet star! when wearied nature sinks to sleep
> And all is hushed, – all save the voice of love,
> Whose broken murmurings swell the balmy blast
> 10 Of soft Favonius, which at intervals
> Sighs in the ear of Stillness–art thou aught but love,
> Lulling the slaves of interest to repose
> With that mild pitying gaze? . . . oh! I could look
> On thy dear beam till every bond of sense
> 15 Became unnerved . . .

¶ 59.1. *Sweet star!*] The planet Venus as Evening Star, symbol and embodiment of Love.

2. *fling'st*] flyest *Hogg*.

3. *evening's shadowy veil*] Mist over the lake at Field Place.

6. *Morn-star's*] Venus as Morning Star (Venus does not appear both at morning and evening during the same period). Cp. 'To a Skylark' 21–5.

10. *Favonius*] The west wind.

11. *love,*] Accidentally omitted *Hogg*.

13. *could*] cd. *Hogg MS*; would *Hogg*.

15. *unnerved . . .*] enamoured– *Hogg*.

60 On a Fête at Carlton House

Written on or just after 20 June 1811. On 19 June 'the Prince Regent gave a splendid fête at Carlton House, in which the novelty was introduced of a stream of water, in imitation of a river, meandering down the middle of a very long table, in a temporary tent erected in Carlton Gardens . . . Bysshe . . . wrote a poem on the subject of about fifty lines, which he published immediately, wherein he apostrophized the Prince as sitting on the bank of his tiny river; and he amused himself with throwing copies into the carriages of persons going to Carlton House after the fête' (Charles Grove to Hellen S., quoted in *Hogg* ii 556–7). 'In the front of the Regent's seat there was a circular bason of water, with an enriched temple in the centre of it, from whence there was a meandering stream to the bottom of the table, bordered with green banks. Three or four fantastic bridges were thrown over it, one of them with a small tower upon it, which gave the little stream a picturesque appearance. It contained also a number of gold and silver fish' (*Annual Register* (1811), Chronicle p. 69). The fashionable public were admitted to view the decorations for a week after the fête, and came in large numbers; but the poem is lost, except for the following 'verses . . . which Mr Garnett has taken down from the mouth of the Rev. Mr. Grove', Harriet Grove's brother (*Rossetti 1870* ii 599). S. wrote derisively to Elizabeth Hitchener: '. . . it is said that this entertainment will cost 20,000£; nor will it be the last bauble which the nation must buy to amuse this overgrown bantling of regency' (*L* i 110). The fête had actually been given in lieu of the insane King's birthday-party.
Text from *Rossetti 1870* ii 523.
Published in *Rossetti 1870*.

> By the mossy brink,
> With me the Prince shall sit and think;
> Shall muse in visioned Regency,
> Rapt in bright dreams of dawning Royalty.

61 Written at Cwm Elan

Headed '1811' in *Esd*, composed between *c.* 8 July and *c.* 5 August, probably soon after S.'s arrival at Cwm Elan (for this visit, see headnote to No. 62). There was a full moon on 5 July, and if 'the yellow moonbeam' appeared not long after sunset the date is likely to have been 8–10 July; moreover the poem shows little sign of the emotional stresses that developed later in July as S.

¶ 60. *Title:* Rossetti's. Carlton House, which stood in what is now Waterloo Place until its demolition in 1827, was the Prince of Wales's Palace.
3–4. The Regency Act passed on 5 February 1811 did not confer full powers for another twelve months, in case George III should recover his sanity.

exchanged letters with Harriet Westbrook. The experimental metre–
'fourteeners' used in stanzas, with alternate feminine and masculine rhymes–is
very unusual.
Text from *Esd* f. 28ʳ (*Esd* No. 18: quoted by permission of the Carl H.
Pforzheimer Library).
Published in *Esd Nbk* 73; *Esd Poems* 33–4; *SC* iv 962 (transcript of *Esd*).

When the peasant hies him home, and the day-planet
      reposes
Pillowed on the azure peaks that bound the western
      sight,
When each mountain flower its modest petal tremulously
      closes
And sombre-shrouded twilight comes to lead her sister
      Night,
5 Vestal dark! how dear to me are then thy dews of
      lightness
That bathe my brow so withering, scorched beneath the
      daybeam's brightness,–
More dear to me, though day be robed in vest of dazzling
      whiteness,
Is one folding of the garment dusk that wraps thy form,
      O Night!

With thee I still delight to sit where dizzy Danger
      slumbers,
10 Where mid the rocks the fitful blast hath waked its
      wildest lay,
Till beneath the yellow moonbeam decay the dying
      numbers
And silence even in fancy's throne hath seized again the
      sway.
Again she must resign it, hark! for wildest cadence
      pouring,
Far, far amid the viewless glen beneath, the Elan roaring
15 Mid tangled woods, and shapeless rocks with moonlight
      summits soaring,
It mingles its magic murmuring with the blast that floats
      away.

¶ 61. *Title, 14. Elan*] Ellan *Esd*.
8. *garment dusk*] 'dusky garment', with a pun on 'dusk'.
11. *numbers*] 'song'.
15. *tangled*] tongued *Esd Nbk*; tangèd *Esd Poems*. The word in *Esd* looks like
'tungued', and *Esd Nbk* may be correct (= 'vocal').
16. *It*] i.e. the Elan; grammatically superfluous.

62 'Death-spurning rocks!'

Composed probably towards the end of July 1811. As Cameron shows (*Esd Nbk* 211–12), the setting and situation are those of S.'s first visit to Cwm Elan in Radnorshire, the summer estate of his cousin Thomas Grove, Harriet Grove's brother, who had invited him. The poet Bowles had stayed there, and in 1798 published a 350-line descriptive poem, 'Coombe-Ellen', which S. certainly knew. The river Elan, a tributary of the Wye, flowed through wild and wooded mountain scenery, and in this poem S. first uses the landscape allegorically with full consciousness. The rocky ascent symbolizes the course of his emotional life, part more constant (the rocks), part less so (the oak), but all at the mercy of Time. Memory shrinks from contemplating not only the dim mists of antiquity, geology and Druids, but also his associations with Harriet Grove, who knew the place well and had often described it to him (*Hogg* ii 554). Was his unhappiness over her prophetic of the future too, or was the sunlight (Harriet Westbrook) attainable? The ambiguous 'It burns!' (line 30) applies both to the sun and to the torment of S.'s uncertainty.
Text from *Esd* f. 33^{r-v} (*Esd* No. 22: quoted by permission of the Carl H. Pforzheimer Library).
Published in *Esd Nbk* 81–2; *Esd Poems* 40–1; *SC* iv 970–1 (transcript of *Esd*).

Death-spurning rocks! here have ye towered since Time
　　Sprung from Tradition's mist-encircled height
Which Memory's palsied pinion dreads to climb,
　　Awed by the phantoms of its beamless night.
5　　　Death-spurning rocks! each jagged form
　　Shall still arrest the passing storm
　　Whilst rooted there the aged Oak
　　Is shivered by the lightning's stroke.
Years shall fade fast, and centuries roll away,
10　Ye shall spurn death no more but like your Oak decay.

¶ *62.7. the aged Oak*] An Ossianic poetic property, but perhaps the capital indicates a real tree, which Bowles also took allegorically ('Coombe-Ellen' 54–66):

Upon the adverse bank, withered, and stripped
Of all its pleasant leaves, a scathed oak
Hangs desolate, once sovereign of the scene . . .
It seems to say . . . yet enjoy
Your pleasant prime, and lift your green heads high,
Exulting; but the storm will come at last,
That shall lay low your strength, and give your pride
To the swift-hurrying stream of age, like mine

See also *Q Mab* vii 259–61.

A maniac-sufferer soared with wild intent
  Where Nature formed these wonders. On the way
There is a little spot. Fiends would relent
  Knew they the snares that there for memory lay,
15   How many a hope and many a fear
    And many a vain and bitter tear –
    Whilst each prophetic feeling wakes
    A brood of mad and venomed snakes
To make the lifesprings of his soul their food,
20 To twine around his veins and fatten on his blood.

To quench his pangs he fled to the wild moor;
  One fleeting beam flashed but its gloom to show,
Turned was the way-worn wanderer from the door
  Where Pity's self promised to soothe his woe.
25   Shall he turn back? the tempest there
    Sweeps fiercely through the turbid air;
    Beyond a gulf before that yawns
    The daystar shines, the daybeam dawns. –
God! Nature! Chance! remit this misery.
30 It burns! – why need he live to weep who does not fear to
                                                          die?

11. *A maniac-sufferer*] S.'s prototype is probably Werter, who, distracted by his love, contemplates suicide from the summit of a towering rock (*The Sorrows of Young Werter* (1774; trans. 1802) Letter lxxxvii; see also Letter xxxiii). S. had read *Werter* by 2 June 1811 (*L* i 95).

13. *a little spot*] While under his suicidal impulse, Werter sees 'a little spot' associated with the memory of Charlotte (*Werter*, Letter lxxxvii).

24. *Pity's self*] Possibly S.'s sister Elizabeth, whom he believed to have failed him.

25–8. 'behind is the tempest; beyond the gulf that yawns ahead the sun is shining'. The punctuation of *Esd Nbk* and *Esd Poems* misses the point of the inversion. The analogy is with the dilemma S. had reached over committing himself with Harriet Westbrook: 'He . . . wrote me a letter concerning what he termed, his summons to link his fate with another, closing his communication thus: "Hear it not, Percy, for it is a knell, which summons thee to heaven or to hell"' (Charles Grove to Hellen S., 16 February 1857, *Hogg* ii 554).

27–8. The image of the 'daybeam' is in Bowles, 115–20: 'the heaven's pure beam, / That breaks above the sable mountain's brow . . . / Awakes the blissful confidence, that here, / Or in a world where sorrow never comes, / All shall be well.'

63 To Harriet ★ ★ ★ ★ ★ ★ ★ ★ ★

Date of composition unknown. The lines exist only in Harriet S.'s hand as the third entry (after Nos. 65 and 94) in her 'appendix' to *Esd*, and present mutually incompatible features. The lines are headed 'May 1813 To Harriet . . . .' and end 'Cum Elam) Adieu my love good night'. Neither S. nor Harriet was at Cwm Elan in 1813. S. was there alone in 1811, in July and early August, not May; they were near Cwm Elan together in May 1812, but Harriet was then no longer 'Westbrook' as the nine points in the title require. Finally, as Dowden and Garnett agreed (*L about S* 122–3), the doggerel manner seems to belong to a period before either date, suggesting that the lines concern Harriet Grove, not Westbrook. The problem is further obscured by indications that the lines were copied from a draft (e.g. the many unrhymed lines, especially the presumed work-draft alternative 'grief' in line 4 instead of 'joy', and the fact that lines 19–20 belong here logically rather than *in situ* despite the change of metre.) Two ultimately separate poems seem to be involved: 1–10, and 11–37; these groups are not, however, distinguished in *Esd* except by a stanza-break. *Any* suggested solution creates some improbability. Four possible dates present themselves.

(1) 1809 or earlier, hence involving Harriet Grove. 'My Harriet' (line 21) is no obstacle, as S. regarded his cousin as rightfully 'his', and the stylistic crudity would be explained; but though S. 'had heard much of Cwm Elan' from Harriet Grove, he had never been there with her (*Hogg* ii 554); Harriet S. must have guessed or faked the title; and the date is unexplained.

(2) May 1812 when Harriet S. was seriously ill and S. alarmed for her life (lines 15–18, 29–32 may imagine her death). The date could have been mistaken by a year, like that of No. 94; as two of the 'appendix' poems are dated '1815' Harriet could have transcribed the whole group in that year, possibly early in January which might explain her confusion. But her name was not then Westbrook, nor were the S.'s staying at Cwm Elan but at Nantgwillt, five miles away.

(3) The lines were addressed in May 1813 to Harriet S., but by Hogg, not S. This would account for the disclaimers of merely physical interest (11–14), the suicidal references (25–8), and lines 29–30 (Harriet's refusal to admit Hogg to her company). But it is inconceivable that Hogg should write doggerel so like S.'s, or that Harriet should preserve the amorous scribble of a man she detested; and 'Cum Elam' is unexplained. Moreover Harriet's name was no longer Westbrook.

(4) *c.* 3 August 1811, when S., alone at Cwm Elan, learned that Harriet Westbrook was willing to elope with him. 'Gratitude and admiration all demand that I should love her *forever*' (*L* i 131). Harriet's offer of herself left her open to betrayal (hence lines 11–14, disclaiming the reactions of a libertine); S. had been lonely and depressed at Cwm Elan ('I do not see a soul. all is gloomy

¶ 63. *Title.* Presumably the asterisks stand for 'Westbrook'.

& desolate'–*L* i 129: cp. line 19); his love has not attained 'its prime' (8) but is not merely fleeting; she is now 'my Harriet' (21); he would sacrifice his life to 'save' her ('. . . the misery of living where she could *love* no one. Suicide was with her a favorite theme . . . her letters became more & more gloomy; at length one assumed a tone of such despair, as induced me to quit Wales precipitately'–S. to Elizabeth Hitchener, 28 October 1811, *L* i 162); she has rescued him from the despair of his earlier disappointment (25–8), and the alternative to accepting her self-committal is unbearable (29–30). The conditional tenses in lines 10, 15–16, 19–20 suggest that the union is still speculative rather than actual. The emphasis on affectionate companionship accords well with S.'s known attitude to his future first wife; and the stylistic crudity can perhaps be ascribed to haste and confusion ('I am thinking at once of ten million things'–*L* i 131). Finally, the situation accords with that described later in 'The Retrospect' (No. 79). On the whole, then, this seems the least unacceptable hypothesis, although the date added or copied by Harriet, 'May 1813', remains inexplicable. The spelling of 'Cum Elam', bracketed off from the rest of line 37, suggests that this name (like 'Stanmore' in No. 65) was Harriet's own annotation to the transcribed lines. All the present punctuation is editorial; but the text is too uncertain for rearrangement, except for one word in line 4 and some indication that the two sections are in different metres. Lines 11–37 are in an 18th-century lyric measure; cp. Fielding's *Joseph Andrews* Bk II ch. xii:

> How can it thy dear image be
>   Which fills thus my bosom with woe?
> Can aught bear resemblance to thee
>   Which grief and not joy can bestow? (17–20)

Cp. also Cowper's 'Catharina' and 'Song. On Peace' (1783).
Text from *Esd* ff. 94ᵛ–95ᵛ (*Esd* No. 56: quoted by permission of the Carl H. Pforzheimer Library).
Published in *Esd Nbk* 168–9; *Esd Poems* 111–12; *SC* iv 1059–60 (transcript of *Esd*).

> Oh Harriet, love like mine that glows
> What rolling years can e'er destroy?
> Without thee can I tell my woes?
> And with thee can I speak my joy?
>
> 5   Ah no, past all the futile power
> Of words to tell is love like mine;
> My love is not the fading flower
> That fleets ere it attains its prime.
> A moment of delight with thee
> 10   Would pay me for an age of pain.

4. *my joy*] *conj.*; my grief *Esd*.

I'll tell not of Rapture and Joy
Which swells through the Libertine's frame;
That breast must feel bliss with alloy
That is scorched by so selfish a flame.

15   It were pleasure to die for my love,
It were rapture to sink in the grave
My eternal affection to prove,
My ever dear Harriet to save.

Without thee all pleasure were gloom,
20   And with thee all sorrow were joy;
Ere I knew thee, my Harriet, each year
Passed in mournful rotation away;
No friend to my bosom was dear,
Slow rolled the unvarying day.

25   Shall I wake then those horrors anew
That swelled in my desperate brain
When to death's darkened portals I flew
And sought misery's relief to my pain?

That hour which tears thee from me
30   Leaves nothing but death and despair,
And that, Harriet, never could be
Were thy mind less enchantingly fair.

'Tis not for the charms of thy form
Which decay with the swift rolling years—
35   Ah no, Heaven expands to my sight,
For Elysium with Harriet must be.
Adieu, my love, good night.

64 To November

Written probably on 1 November 1811 at York, where S. had just rejoined
Harriet after an absence in Sussex since 16 October (*L* i 149). The 'sullen brow'

12. *swells*] S. often uses a singular verb with paired nouns.
21–2. Cp. 'The Retrospect' 11–22.
23. *No friend*] i.e. no *chère amie*.
24–8. Cp. 'The Retrospect' 37–48, 116–23, and 'Death-spurning rocks!' 1–12.
All probably relate to S.'s stay at Cwm Elan in 1811.
28. *misery's*] miseries *Esd.*
29. *That hour which tears*] A conditional: 'that hour which were to separate us
would leave nothing . . .'
37. Cum Elam) Adieu my love good night *Esd.*

of November, presaging winter weather (lines 1–2), and line 25, 'Now thou
art here', point to the opening of the month. The carefree first and lightly-
flattering final stanzas indicate that Harriet had not yet disclosed to S., as she
did two or three days later, that Hogg had been trying to seduce her (see
headnote to No. 65). Southey had written two pieces, 'On the First of
December' (1793) and 'On the First of January' (1794), and Harriet's under-
standably warm response to her husband's return may have suggested a lyric in
optimistic contrast to these. A cross made against the title in *Esd* perhaps means
that S. intended to add a footnote about the emotional storm that November
actually brought.

Text from *Esd* ff. 13ᵛ–14ʳ (*Esd* No. 8: quoted by permission of the Carl H.
Pforzheimer Library).

Published in *Esd Nbk* 50–1; *Esd Poems* 14–15; *SC* iv 939–40 (transcript of *Esd*).

O month of gloom, whose sullen brow
   Bears stamp of storms that lurk beneath,
No care or horror bringest thou
   To one who draws his breath
5   Where Zephyrs play and sunbeams shine
   Unstained by any fog of thine.

Whilst thou obscur'st the face of day
   Her radiant eyes can gild the gloom,
Darting a soft and vernal ray
10   On Nature's leafless tomb;
Yes! though the landscape's beauties flee
My Harriet makes it spring to me.

Then raise thy fogs, invoke thy storms,
   Thy malice still my soul shall mar,
15 And whilst thy rage the heaven deforms
   Shall laugh at every care,
And each pure feeling shall combine
To tell its Harriet 'I am thine!'

It once was May; the Month of Love
20 Did all it could to yield me pleasure,
Waking each green and vocal grove
   To a many-mingling measure,
But warmth and peace could not impart
To such a cold and shuddering heart.

¶ 64.4. *draws*] draw *Esd Poems*.
14. An inversion: 'my soul will still frustrate your malice, and laugh . . .'
15. *thy rage*] the rage *Esd* (a slip of the pen).
19. *May*] S. had spent the latter half of May and most of June idling in Sussex,
following his expulsion. He told Elizabeth Hitchener on 5 June that his time
was 'totally vacant' (*L* i 98).

25   Now thou art here–come! do thy worst
       To chill the breast that Harriet warms;
     I fear me, sullen Month! thou'lt burst
       With envy of her charms,
     And finding nothing's to be done
30   Turn to December ere thou'st won.

65 'Full many a mind with radiant genius fraught'

Date of composition unknown, but conceivably *c.* November 1811. These stanzas exist only in Harriet S.'s handwriting in *Esd*, subscribed 'Stanmore. 1815', and their incoherence has led both Cameron (*Esd Nbk* 300–1) and Rogers (*Esd Poems* xxiv) to reject them as not by S. It is far less believable, however, that such illiterate verses by the educated, accomplished, scrupulously tidy Harriet S. could have been 'composed', or copied from a printed source, between two poems indisputably by S., into S.'s treasured notebook. In the last twelve pages of *Esd* she was clearly trying to salvage every available scrap of S.'s work, which necessarily consisted mainly of unfinished drafts, or poems whose intimacy had inhibited publication, or both. There is no reason whatever to suspect that *Esd* contains anything not by S. Harriet S. could have had no access to poems drafted in 1815, when S. was already living with Mary Godwin, so the date must be that of the transcription. Nor was the place of composition likely to be written on an incomplete, chaotic draft. The place-name is widely separated from the date in MS, so may well indicate (like Mary S.'s similar annotations on her own transcripts in Bod. MS Shelley adds.d.7 and d.9) a locality memorably linked by the transcriber with the genesis of the lines. On one of the first four days of November 1811, S. with Harriet S. and Eliza Westbrook fled from York to Keswick in order to avoid Hogg (see *White* i 170–4) who had been pressing his attentions on Harriet. Harriet might have visited the north-west as a child ('Harriet and her sister liked this part of the country, & I was at the moment of our sudden departure indifferent to all places'–S. from Keswick, *L* i 169). Their route via Richmond (letter to Hogg, 13 November 1811, best read in *SC* iii 46–8) took them close to Stanmore (now Stainmore), a famous mountain ridge on the Cumberland border; just possibly they even spent a night there (note xxxv to Scott's *Rokeby* (1813) mentions 'a small house of entertainment' near the summit). It is likely that the draft to which these lines belong was begun on this journey, which Harriet S. would remember vividly, and that they concern Hogg rather than S. Both S. and Hogg were in a very disturbed emotional state following their confrontation in York: Hogg wrote immediately declaring 'I *will* have Harriet's forgiveness or blow my brains out at her feet' (*L* i 181), and S. replied 'I am wretchedly miserable . . . Death comes–Cold, calm death, almost I would it were tomorrow' (*L* i 172). This affair is often misapprehended. S. did not modify his principles when faced by 'life': his revulsion arose, as he explained to Elizabeth Hitchener (*L* i 168–9, 181–3), from Hogg's commonplace attempt 'to *seduce my wife*'; that is, Hogg had solicited Harriet covertly, with 'arguments of detestable sophism' (e.g. 'There is no injury to him who knows it not'), and against her will and moral feelings. In respect of the marriage-laws it was Harriet who was 'prejudiced' (I fear her arguments were such as *could not* be logically superior to his'–*L* i 182); but Hogg had acted deceitfully, and Harriet's prejudices had to be respected. S. had thought Hogg exceptionally gifted; now in his first letter he urged him to master his misery accordingly: 'Stand *you* alone preeminent in suffering . . . Have I not known you the best the noblest of men . . . I did esteem you as a superior being. I took you for one who was to give laws to us poor beings who grovel beneath . . . Become yourself . . . bear pain' (S. to Hogg, 7–8 November 1811; text from *SC* iii 41–2). These sentiments repeat those of stanza 1, which reminds Hogg that many great men, though perhaps tempted to end their existence on earth (2–4), have had to learn to bear pain (1–2). Lines 5–8, in a different metre, *may* belong to a separate poem, as Cameron suspected; at any rate the conditional in line 5 surely implies a dramatic attribution of some kind; hence stanza 2 may be read in at least two ways: as a presentation of Harriet's viewpoint ('it must be wrong to think the marriage-laws obstruct Man's true happiness; [rather they] afford him peace of mind'), or as a recapitulation of Hogg's ('earthly laws cannot be allowed to stand in the way of suicide (or adultery)–cannot lead to true peace of mind'). The latter reading is assumed below; the MS has no pointing except the final stop, and lines 6/7 may be grammatically discontinuous. Harriet S. left one page blank before these stanzas, as if to leave room for earlier undeciphered lines; this also suggests that lines 7–8 were the final lines of S.'s draft. Text from *Esd* f. 94ʳ (*Esd* No. 55: quoted by permission of the Carl H. Pforzheimer Library).

Published in Louise Boas, *Harriet Shelley: Five Long Years* (1962) 179–80; *Esd Nbk* 167; *Esd Poems* 117; *SC* iv 1058 (transcript of *Esd*).

> Full many a mind with radiant genius fraught
> Is taught the dark scowl of misery to bear;
> How many a great soul has often sought
> To stem the sad torrent of wild despair:
>
> 5   'It could not be Earth's laws were given
>   To stand between Man, God and Heaven–
>   To teach him where to seek and truly find
>   That lasting comfort, peace of mind.'

¶ 65.*1–4*. Cp. Beattie, *Minstrel* i 3–4: 'Ah! who can tell how many a soul sublime / Has felt the influence of malignant star'.
5. could] GM conj.; would *Esd, SC, Esd Nbk, Esd Poems*.
6. Man, God] Man God *Esd*; Mankind *conj.*

66 Passion:
To the [Woody Nightshade]

Composed November or December 1811, depending on the epoch of S.'s first appreciation of Wordsworth. The sequence of questions in stanzas 2–5 derives from the first poem of Wordsworth's known to have impressed S., 'A Poet's Epitaph' (published 1800), which he quoted to Elizabeth Hitchener 2 January 1812 (*L* i 217). It is often assumed that S. was converted to Wordsworth's work by Southey, whom he first met at Keswick between 15 and 26 December 1811 (*L* i 208, 210–11); but before this he had made friends with William Calvert, brother of Wordsworth's patron Raisley Calvert, in the first week of December (*L* i 198), and may have been influenced by him. But S., always alert to connections between locality and literature, might well have begun re-reading Wordsworth (as well as Southey and Coleridge) prior to outside encouragement on settling in the Lakes, i.e. from *c*. 6 November. The subheading and parenthesis were left uncompleted in *Esd*; Cameron (*Esd Nbk* 180) quotes Dowden's comment in the latter's transcript of *Esd*: '?To the *deadly nightshade* only that Shelley c^d hardly have failed to insert this name'. S. knew, however, that the plant was a nightshade, because he puns with the word's supposed etymology in lines 29–30, and he must have known that one of its popular names was 'bittersweet' because the whole conduct of the poem rests on this oxymoron. (Its specific Latin name, *dulcamara*, also means 'bittersweet', as does the name used by Culpeper, *Amara dulcis*). According to *Hogg* (i 75) S.'s 'botanical knowledge was more limited than that of the least skilful of common observers', but the testimony of a native of County Durham who did not know the ragged robin (*New SL* 99) is worth little. The plant is, in fact, poisonous mainly by repute, but R. J. Thornton's *A New Family Herbal* (1810) warns that the berries 'are extremely dangerous for children, for thirty of them being given to a dog, killed it in less than three hours' (143). *Solanum dulcamara* acquired symbolic importance in S.'s poetry, and seems generally to be intended rather than *Atropa belladonna* when he refers to nightshade (cp. *Q Mab* viii 129–31: 'Like passion's fruit, the nightshade's tempting bane / Poisons no more the pleasure it bestows: / All bitterness is past'; *PU* III iv 78–82; etc.). Cameron (*Esd Nbk* 180–1), on botanical advice, proposed *Arum maculatum*; but a Sussex country boy must have known *one* of its many local names; November is already too late for it; and the plant does not fit the poem: line 47, 'thine Heaven-directed flight', would be ludicrous addressed to the chubby little cuckoo-pint. Bittersweet is a climber.

The poem clearly originates in Hogg's recent apostasy, and develops the feeling expressed in S.'s letter of 17–18 November: 'my soul is half sick at this terrible world where Nature seems to own no monster in her works but man!' (*L* i 184). The nature of 'passion' is a preoccupation in many of S.'s letters at this time–'Prime source of all that's lovely, good and great' when reciprocated, but 'Debasing man below the meanest brute' when selfish and treacher-

ous (see esp. *L* i 80–2). The unrhymed stanzas are modelled on Southey's 'To
Hymen' and 'Written on the First of January' (both 1794), and behind these on
Collins's 'Ode to Evening'.
Text from *Esd* ff. 7ʳ–8ʳ (*Esd* No. 4: quoted by permission of the Carl H.
Pforzheimer Library).
Published in *Esd Nbk* 41–2; *Esd Poems* 5–7; *SC* iv 929–31 (transcript of *Esd*).

> Fair are thy berries to the dazzled sight,
> Fair is thy chequered stalk of mingling hues,
>   And yet thou dost conceal
>   A deadly poison there,
> 5   Uniting good and ill.
>
> Art thou not like a lawyer whose smooth face
> Dost promise good, while hiding so much ill?
>   Ah! no. The semblance even
>   Of goodness lingereth not
> 10   Within that hollow eye.
>
> Art thou the tyrant whose unlovely brow
> With rare and glittering gems is contrasted?
>   No–thou mayst kill the body,
>   He withers up the soul;
> 15   Sweet thou when he is nigh.
>
> Art thou the wretch whose cold and sensual soul
> His hard–earned mite tears from the famished hind,
>   Then says that God hath willed
>   Many to toil and groan
> 20   That few may boast at ease?
>
> Art thou the slave whose mercenary sword
> Stained with an unoffending brother's blood
>   Deeper yet shows the spot
>   Of cowardice, whilst he
> 25   Who wears it talks of courage?

¶ 66. *Title.* Passion (to the   . *Esd.*
1–2. Woody nightshade berries are bright red when ripe, and its stem is
sometimes streaked with purple. The flower (line 37) is purple and orange.
6–7. Cp. S. to Hogg, ?14 November: 'I hope I have shewn you that I do not
regard you as a *smooth tongued traitor*' (*L* i 180). The Lawyer is the only specific
figure duplicated from Wordsworth's poem ('A Poet's Epitaph' 5–7). Did S.
know Hogg intended reading for the Bar the following spring?
Stanza 4. Recalls S.'s earlier horror at one of Hogg's arguments on 20 April:
'you say that millions of bad, are necessary to the existence of a few preeminent
in excellence. Is not this . . . the Asiatic tyrant who renders his territory
wretched to fill his seraglio?' (*L* i 71).

Ah no! else while I gaze upon thy bane
I should not feel unmingled with contempt
   This awful feeling rise:
   As if I stood at night
30   In some weird ruin's shade.

Thou art like youthful passion's quenchless fire
Which in some unsuspecting bosom glows,
   So wild, so beautiful,
   Possessing wondrous power
35   To wither or to warm.

Essence of Virtue blasting virtue's prime,
Bright bud of Truth producing Falsehood's fruit,
   Freedom's own soul that binds
   The human will in chains
40   Indissolubly fast—

Prime source of all that's lovely, good and great
Debasing man below the meanest brute,
   Spring of all healing streams
   Yet deadlier than the gall
45   Blackening a monarch's heart—

Why art thou thus, O Passion? Custom's chains
Have bound thee from thine Heaven-directed flight,
   Or thou wouldst never thus
   Bring misery to man,
50   Uniting good and ill.

67 A Winter's Day

Composed in the early winter of 1811 at Keswick, or—less probably—of 1812 at
Tanyrallt. *Early* winter seems indicated by lines 13–14 ('And winter reassume
the sway / That shall so long endure'). There were fine days, in south-west
England at least, through 1–3 December 1812 (*GM* lxxxii (December 1812)
498); if 'cascades' (4) was intended for a genitive singular this would support
the 1812 dating, as a cascade murmurs just outside the then front door of
Tanyrallt; and 'the moor' (12) may have been suggested by 'Traeth Mawr', the
wide expanse of the Glaslyn estuary behind the house, uncovered at low tide

30. weird] grey *canc. Esd.*
36. blasting virtue's] blushing virtues' *Esd Nbk.*
46–7. For S., 'passion' unperverted had no necessary conflict with 'reason' but
its expression was distorted by ruling prejudices (cp. *Q Mab* viii 231–4; *PU* III
iv 155–9, 193–9).

(though S. must have known that the name meant 'Great Sands'). But cascade
and moor are also compatible with the Keswick area, in December 1811, and
(as Cameron noted: *Esd Nbk* 194) the poem is close in style and content to other
poems certainly written at Keswick. The structure of successive questions
resembles that of 'Passion' (No. 66), and has the same origin in Wordsworth's
'A Poet's Epitaph' (published 1800), which S. quoted to Elizabeth Hitchener
from Keswick on 2 January 1812 (*L* i 217); moreover stanza 4 may well refer,
like 'Passion', to Hogg's infatuation with Harriet S. It is similar in theme to 'To
November' (No. 64), and both poems have a prosodic affinity with Wordsworth's 'The Green Linnet' (published 1807). The middle stanza dispenses
with a seventh line.
Text from *Esd* f. 17 (*Esd* No. 11: quoted by permission of the Carl H.
Pforzheimer Library).
Published in *Esd Nbk* 56–7; *Esd Poems* 18–19; *SC* iv 944–6 (transcript of *Esd*).

> O wintry day! that mockest spring
>   With hopes of the reviving year,
> That sheddest softness from thy wing
> And near the cascade's murmuring
> 5 Awakenest sounds so clear
> That peals of vernal music swing
>   Through the balm atmosphere, –
>
> Why hast thou given, O year! to May
>   A birth so premature,
> 10 To live one incompleted day
> That the mad whirlwind's sullen sway
>   May sweep it from the moor,
> And winter reassume the sway
>   That shall so long endure?
>
> 15 Art thou like Genius's matin bloom,
>   Unwelcome promise of its prime,
> That scattereth its rich perfume
> Around the portals of the tomb,
>   Decking the scar of time
> 20 In mockery of the early doom?
>
> Art thou like Passion's rapturous dream
>   That o'er life's stormy dawn
> Doth dart its wild and flamy beam,
> Yet like a fleeting flash doth seem

¶ 67.4. *cascade's*] cascades *Esd*, *Esd Poems* (see headnote).
7. *balm*] Not recorded in *OED* as adj.
10. *incompleted*] uncompleted *Esd Poems*.
15. *Genius's*] Genius *Esd Poems*. S. may have Hogg in mind rather than himself
(cp. 'Full many a mind', No. 65).

25 When many chequered years are gone
And tell the illusion of its gleam
Life's blasted springs alone?

Whate'er thou emblemest, I'll breathe
Thy transitory sweetness now,
30 And whether Health with roseate wreath
May bind mine head, or creeping Death
Steal o'er my pulse's flow,
Struggling the wintry winds beneath
I'll love thy vernal glow.

68 A Tale of Society as it is: from facts, 1811

Composed shortly before 7 January 1812. In *Esd* the poem is headed '1811', but lines 1–79 were sent untitled to Elizabeth Hitchener on 7 January (BL MS adds. 37496 f. 78: *Hitch. MS*) with the comment: 'the subject is not fictitious; it is the overflowings of the mind this morning. The facts are real; that recorded in the last fragment of a stanza is literally true. – The poor man said: – None of my family ever came *to parish*, and I wd. starve first. I am a poor man but I could never hold my head up after that.' S. added: 'Think of the Poetry which I have inserted as a picture of my feelings not a specimen of my art' (*L* i 223–4). Although it had long been fashionable to write humanitarian poems 'from facts' (see Robert Mayo, 'The Contemporaneity of the *Lyrical Ballads*', *PMLA* lxix (1954) 486–522), S.'s stay in Keswick had brought him into direct contact with the sufferings of the poor for the first time. He told Elizabeth Hitchener on 26 December 1811: 'I have been led into reasonings which make me *hate* more & more the existing establishment of every kind. I gasp when I think of plate & balls & tables & kings. – I have beheld scenes of misery. – The manufacturers [i.e. factory-hands] are reduced to starvation.' (*L* i 213). Again on 7 January: 'Keswick seems more like a suburb of London than a village of Cumberland. Children are frequently found in the River which the unfortunate women employed at the manufactory destroy' (*L* i 223). Keswick had a factory for making lead-pencils from the plumbago mined near Seathwaite, as well as a woollen mill. S.'s new style of sober narrative also reflects the

26–7. Cameron (*SC* iv 945) construes this as an additional question: 'And do Life's blasted springs dare tell (record) the illusion of its gleam'?, but a straight inversion is more likely: '[When many years are gone] and life's blasted springs alone reveal the illusion'. Cp. 'Passion' (No 66) 36–7: 'Essence of Virtue blasting Virtue's prime, / Bright bud of Truth producing Falsehood's fruit'.
32. *pulse's*] pulses *Esd*.

influence of Southey's 'English Eclogues' such as the well-known 'Hannah' and 'The Sailor's Mother', and of Wordsworth, especially 'The Affliction of Margaret' (published 1807; see notes), but S.'s radicalism is far more explicit. Text from *Esd* ff. 20ᵛ–23ʳ (*Esd* No. 14: quoted by permission of the Carl H. Pforzheimer Library).

Published in *Rossetti 1870* ii 526–8 (lines 1–79, from *Hitch. MS*, entitled 'Mother and Son' by Rossetti); *Dowden 1891* 679–80 (corrected from *Esd* and given its present title); *Esd Nbk* 62–6; *Esd Poems* 23–7; *SC* iv 950–5 (transcript of *Esd*).

> She was an aged woman, and the years
> Which she had numbered on her toilsome way
> Had bowed her natural powers to decay. –
> She was an aged woman, yet the ray
> 5 Which faintly glimmered through the starting tears
> Pressed from their beds by silent misery
> Hath soul's imperishable energy. –
> She was a cripple, and incapable
> To add one mite to golden luxury,
> 10 And therefore did her spirit clearly feel
> That Poverty, the crime of tainting stain,
> Would merge her in its depths never to rise again.
>
> One only son's love had supported her.
> She long had struggled with infirmity
> 15 Lingering from human life-scenes, for to die
> When fate has spared to rend some mental tie
> Not many wish, and surely fewer dare.
> But when the tyrant's bloodhounds forced her child

¶ 68.1–7. The old woman 'bowed . . . to decay' and crippled but firm-minded recalls the Leech-gatherer in Wordsworth's 'Resolution and Independence' (published 1807) 65–70, 138.
5. *through the*] through her *Hitch. MS*.
6. *from their beds*] into light *Hitch. MS*.
9. *golden*] gold-fed *Hitch. MS*.
10. *clearly*] dimly *Rossetti 1870*.
15. *Lingering from*] Lingering to *Hitch. MS* (a slip). 'Quitting reluctantly' (cp. 'Hymn of Apollo' 26).
16. *rend*] send *Esd Nbk*.
17. *Not*] Would *Rossetti 1870*.
18. *the tyrant's bloodhounds*] Press-gangs were used only by the Navy, and William seems to have been in the Army (lines 21, 103). But Castlereagh as War Minister in 1807 had introduced a scheme whereby home-defence militia could be forcibly inducted into the regular Army, and recruitment methods closely resembled impressment: 'So great was the pressure for recruits at this time [c. 1811] that very unfair means were frequently adopted to get men for the Army . . . During the protracted war in the Peninsula . . . no young man

For tyrant's power unhallowed arms to wield,
20   Bend to another's will, become a thing
More senseless than the sword of battlefield,
Then did she feel keen sorrow's keenest sting,
And many years had past ere comfort they would bring.

For seven years did this poor woman live
25   In unparticipated solitude.
Thou mightst have seen her in the desert rude
Picking the scattered remnants of its wood;
If human thou mightst then have learned to grieve.
The gleanings of precarious charity
30   Her scantiness of food did scarce supply;
The proofs of an unspeaking sorrow dwelt
Within her ghastly hollowness of eye:
Each arrow of the seasons' change she felt,
Yet still she yearned ere her sad course were run—
35   One only hope it was—once more to see her son.

It was an eve of June, when every star
Spoke peace from Heaven to those on Earth that live.
She rested on the moor . . . 'twas such an eve
When first her soul began indeed to grieve:
40   Then he was here . . . now he is very far.
The freshness of the balmy evening
A sorrow o'er her weary soul did fling,
Yet not devoid of rapture's mingled tear:

---

could safely go to London' ([William Silver Darter], *Reminiscences of Reading* [1888] 32, 35). *her*] the *Hitch. MS.*

20–1. 'A soldier is of all descriptions of men the most completely a machine . . . He is like the puppet of a showman, who . . . cannot assume the most insignificant gesture . . . but as he is moved by the exhibitor' (*Enquirer* ii 236). Quoted by S. in his notes to *Q Mab* iv 178–9. S. had read the *Enquirer* before 26 November 1811 (*L* i 195).

24. seven years] Margaret in Wordsworth's 'Affliction of Margaret' 8–9 was also 'seven years' without hearing from her son.

25. unparticipated solitude] Cp. 'Affliction of Margaret' 71–2: 'Beyond participation lie / My troubles'.

26. desert] forest *Hitch. MS, Esd Poems.* Taking wood from someone's forest might have brought her before a magistrate; on waste land she still had common rights.

28. then] there *Esd Nbk. grieve.*] feel *Hitch. MS.*

37. After *Heaven*, asterisks only in *Hitch. MS.*

41. freshness] sweetness *Hitch. MS.*

42. weary] aged *Hitch. MS.*

A balm was in the poison of the sting.
45   This aged sufferer for many a year
Had never felt such comfort . . . she suppressed
A sigh, and turning round clasped William to her breast.

And though his form was wasted by the woe
Which despots on their victims love to wreak,
50   Though his sunk eyeball and his faded cheek
Of slavery, violence and scorn did speak,
Yet did the aged woman's bosom glow;
The vital fire seemed reillumed within
By this sweet unexpected welcoming.
55   O! consummation of the fondest hope
That ever soared on Fancy's dauntless wing!
O! tenderness that foundst so sweet a scope!
Prince! who dost swell upon thy mighty sway,
When thou canst feel such love thou shalt be great as
                                                        they.

60   Her son, compelled, the tyrant's foes had fought,
Had bled in battle, and the stern control
That ruled his sinews and coerced his soul
Utterly poisoned life's unmingled bowl
And unsubduable evils on him wrought.
65   He was the shadow of the lusty child
Who, when the time of summer season smiled,
For her did earn a meal of honesty
And with affectionate discourse beguiled
The keen attacks of pain and poverty,
70   Till power, as envying this her only joy,
From her maternal bosom tore the unhappy boy.

And now cold charity's unwelcome dole
Was insufficient to support the pair,
And they would perish rather than would bear
75   The law's stern slavery and the insolent stare
With which law loves to rend the poor man's soul,
The bitter scorn, the spirit-sinking noise
Of heartless mirth which women, men and boys
Wake in this scene of legal misery . . .

49. *despots*] tyrants *Hitch. MS.*
56. *dauntless*] wildest *Hitch. MS.*
58. *swell upon*] pride thee on *Hitch. MS.*
62. *That*] Which *Hitch. MS.*
64. *wrought*] brought *Hitch. MS.*
75. *The law's stern slavery*] Parish assistance under the Poor Law of 1795.

80   Oh! William's spirit rather would rejoice
On some wild heath with his dear charge to die, –
The death that keenest penury might give
Were sweeter far than cramped by slavery to live.

And they have borne thus long the winter's cold,
85   The driving sleet, the penetrating rain;
It seemeth that their element is pain,
And that they never will feel life again,
For is it life to be so deathlike old? –
The sun's kind light feeds every living thing
90   That spreads its blossoms to the breath of spring,
But who feeds thee, unhappy wanderer?
With the fat slaves who from the rich man's board
Lick the fallen crumbs, thou scantily dost share
And mutterest for the gift a heartless prayer.
95   The flow'rs fade not thus, thou must poorly die;
The changeful year feeds them, the tyrant man feeds
                                          thee.

And is it life that in youth's blasted morn
Not one of youth's dear raptures are enjoyed,
All natural bliss with servitude alloyed,
100   The beating heart, the sparkling eye destroyed,
And manhood of its brightest glories shorn
Debased by rapine, drunkenness and woe,
The foeman's sword, the vulgar tyrant's blow,
Ruined in body and soul till Heaven arrive,
105   His health and peace insultingly laid low,
Without a fear to die or wish to live,
Withered and sapless, miserably poor,
Relinquished for his wounds to beg from door to door?

Seest thou yon humble sod where osiers bind
110   The pillow of the monumentless dead?
There since her thorny pilgrimage is sped
The aged sufferer rests on the cold bed
Which all who seek or who avoid must find.

86. *their element is pain*] Cp. Southey's *Curse of Kehama* XIII ix 7–9: 'The pious soul hath framed unto itself / A second nature, to exist in pain / As in its own allotted element' – remembered again by S. in *PU* I 477–8: 'Pain is my element, as hate is thine'.

89. *sun's*] same *Esd Nbk.*

94. *heartless*] spiritless (the normal sense before *c.* 1815).

95. The stress on *not* and *thou* preserves the metre.

97–108. i.e. the son's existence is no more truly 'life' than his mother's.

98. *are*] is *Esd Poems.* The verb is attracted into the plural by *raptures*.

O let her sleep! and there at close of eve
115   'Twere holiness in solitude to grieve
And ponder on the wretchedness of Earth.
With joy of melancholy I would leave
A spot that to such deep-felt thoughts gives birth,
And though I could not pour the useless prayer
120   Would weep upon the grave and leave a blessing there.

69   A Sabbath Walk

Composed late November or December 1811. The poem celebrates a fine
Sunday (ll. 28–9) in early winter (ll. 6–7: 'even when the frost has torn / All
save the ivy'); these conditions seem best met by 22 or 29 December, both of
which followed several days of frost, though snow had fallen on the hill-tops
before mid-December (*L* i 200). It is too close to Southey's work both in
matter and manner to belong to the following winter, which S. spent at
Tanyrallt. S. had learned from William Calvert that Southey's beliefs had
changed, so that 'He to whom Bigotry Tyranny and Law was hateful has
become the votary of these Idols . . . The Church of England it's Hell and all
has become the subject of his panygeric' (to Elizabeth Hitchener, 15 December
1811, *L* i 208), but though disappointed in Southey's reasoning-powers S.
found much that was congenial in his notions of Deity: 'he says I ought not to
call myself an Atheist, since in reality I believe that the Universe is God. – I tell
him I believe that God is another signification for the Universe . . . Southey
agrees in my idea of Deity, the mass of infinite intelligence' (to Elizabeth
Hitchener, 2 January 1812, *L* i 215). Thus the poem castigates Southey for his
tergiversation (39–42) but adopts a similar view of natural religion to that
expressed by Southey in 'The Chapel Bell' (1793), 'Written on Sunday Morning' (1795), and *Joan of Arc* iii 359, 389–91 (1796 edn):

> Gods priest-created, are to me unknown
> . . . 'Twas Nature taught my early youth
> Religion – Nature bade me see the God
> Confest in all that lives, and moves, and is.

S.'s rhymeless metre, like his sentiment, is close to that of 'Written on Sunday
Morning':

> Go thou and seek the 'House of Prayer!
> I to the woodlands wend, and there,
> In lovely Nature see the God of Love. (1–3)

117. *joy of melancholy*] An Ossianic concept that appealed to other poets besides
S.: 'Pleasant is the joy of grief' ('Carric-thura' 194, *Fingal* (1762)); 'There is a
joy in grief when peace dwells in the breast of the sad' ('Croma' 250, ibid.).

The poem is therefore an early example of S.'s habit of criticizing an admired predecessor by modifying the latter's vision of reality while following his metrical form or accepted 'myth' (for an account of this habit in S.'s later poetry see Earl R. Wasserman, *Prometheus Unbound: A Critical Reading* (Baltimore 1965) ch. ii, esp. 60–8).

Text from *Esd* ff. 5ʳ–6ʳ (*Esd* No. 2: quoted by permission of the Carl H. Pforzheimer Library).

Published in *Dowden Life* i 345 (lines 45–6); *Esd Nbk* 38–9; *Esd Poems* 2–4; *SC* iv 926–8 (transcript of *Esd*).

> Sweet are the stilly forest glades:
> Imbued with holiest feelings there
> I love to linger pensively
> And court seclusion's smile;
> 5   This mountain labyrinth of loveliness
> Is sweet to me even when the frost has torn
> All save the ivy clinging to the rocks
> Like friendship to a friend's adversity!
> Yes, in my soul's devotedness
> 10 I love to linger in the wilds;
> I have my God, and worship him,
> O vulgar souls, more ardently
> Than ye the Almighty fiend
> Before whose throne ye kneel.
>
> 15 'Tis not the soul pervading all,
> 'Tis not the fabled cause that framed
> The everlasting orbs of Heaven
> And this eternal earth,
> Nor the cold Christian's bloodstained King of Kings
> 20 Whose shrine is in the temple of my heart, –

¶ 69.7–8. A revision of Southey's ivy-simile in 'Written on the First of December' (1793) 25–6: 'So Virtue diffident of strength / Clings to religion's firmer aid'. S. probably has Hogg's apostasy in mind: 'Would that I could have rescued him! it is an unavailing wish–the last one that I shall breathe over departed excellence. – How I have loved him *you can feel*' (to Elizabeth Hitchener, 26 December 1811, *L* i 213).

13. the Almighty fiend] Cp. Mab's characterization of God as 'A vengeful, pitiless, and almighty fiend, / Whose mercy is a nickname for the rage / Of tameless tigers hungering for blood.' (*Q Mab* iv 211–13; cp. also vi 222–3).

15. the soul pervading all] The concept of God as 'the vital spirit, which, diffused through all beings, animated the vast body of the world' is outlined in *Ruins* ch. xxii, sect. 7. Southey's Joan of Arc claimed to have seen God when she 'saw th' eternal energy pervade / The boundless range of nature' (*Joan of Arc* iii 365–6).

19. Christian's] Christians *Esd*; Christians' *Esd Nbk*, *Esd Poems*.

20. shrine] shine *Esd*.

'Tis that divinity whose work and self
Is harmony and wisdom, truth and love,
   Who in the forests' rayless depth
   And in the cities' wearying glare,
25   In sorrow, solitude and death
      Accompanies the soul
      Of him who dares be free.

It is a lovely winter's day.
Its brightness speaks of Deity
30   Such as the good man venerates,
      Such as the Poet loves.
Ah, softly o'er the quiet of the scene
A pealing harmony is felt to rise:
The village bells are sweet but they denote
35   That spirits love by the clock, and are devout
   All at a stated hour. The sound
   Is sweet to sense but to the heart
   It tells of worship insincere,
   Creeds half believed, the ear that bends
40   To custom, prejudice and fear,
      The tongue that's bought to speak,
      The heart that's hired to feel.

But to the man sincerely good
Each day will be a sabbath day,
45   Consigned to thoughts of holiness
      And deeds of living love;
The God he serves requires no cringing creed,
No idle prayers, no senseless mummeries,
No gold, no temples and no hireling priests.
50   The winds, the pine-boughs and the waters make
   Its melody. The hearts of all
   The beings it pervadeth form
   A temple for its purity;
   The wills of those that love the right
55   Are offerings beyond
      Thanksgiving, prayers and gold.

39–42. By New Year 1812 S. was becoming disillusioned with Southey: 'Now
he is . . . contaminated by Custom' (to Elizabeth Hitchener, 7 January, *L* i 223)
and 'the servile champion of every abuse and absurdity' (to Godwin, 16
January, *L* i 231).

70 The Crisis

Composition probably contemporary with that of S.'s prose *An Address to the Irish People* (published February 1812) which was written at Keswick January 1812 to be printed in Ireland, the 'Crisis' of the title being the general moral and political crisis discussed in both his Irish pamphlets: 'A crisis is now arising which shall decide your fate . . . The crisis to which I allude as the period of your emancipation is not the death of the present King, or any circumstance that has to do with kings . . . it is the increase of virtue and wisdom which . . . will restore those rights which Government has taken away. Have nothing to do with force or violence, and things will safely and surely make their way to the right point' (*Address to the Irish People*, quoted from *Mac-Carthy* 197, 199). The poem's metre (Sapphics) evidently derives from that of Southey's 'The Widow' (1795), while its apocalyptic conclusion may draw on that of *Wat Tyler* (then unpublished, written 1794) which Southey could have shown S. in MS (see note to line 13). Christopher Ricks (*Guardian* 23 October 1964) points out a thematic tradition in S.'s choice of metre: 'by using Sapphics, Shelley was aligning his poem with eighteenth-century poems on future doom: Isaac Watts's "The Day of Judgment" ("When the fierce North wind with his airy forces"), and Cowper's "Lines Written During a Period of Insanity" ("Hatred and vengeance, my eternal portion")'. S. used the repetitive formula of lines 1–12 again in his unfinished fragments 'When a lover clasps his fairest'. Text from *Esd* f. 6ᵛ (*Esd* No. 3: quoted by permission of the Carl H. Pforzheimer Library). Published in *Dowden Life* i 347 (lines 13–16); *Esd Nbk* 40; *Esd Poems* 4–5; *SC* iv 928–9 (transcript of *Esd*).

When we see Despots prosper in their weakness,
When we see Falsehood triumph in its folly,
When we see Evil, Tyranny, Corruption,
    Grin, grow and fatten,–

5 When Virtue toileth through a world of sorrow,
When Freedom dwelleth in the deepest dungeon,
When Truth in chains and infamy bewaileth
    O'er a world's ruin,–

¶ *70.6.* 'A countryman of yours is now confined in an English gaol . . . Mr. Finnerty . . . was imprisoned for persisting in the truth . . . Such is the libel law: such the liberty of the Press' (*Address to the Irish People*, quoted from *Mac-Carthy* 216–17). From the actual or the anticipated profits on his (lost) poem 'A Poetical Essay on the Existing State of Things' S. contributed 'nearly an hundred pounds' to a fund for assisting Finnerty in prison (*Mac-Carthy* 255).

When Monarchs laugh upon their thrones securely
10   Mocking the woes which are to them a treasure,
        Hear the deep curse, and quench the Mother's hunger
                In her child's murder, –

        Then may we hope the consummating hour
        Dreadfully, sweetly, swiftly is arriving
15   When light from Darkness, peace from desolation
                Bursts unresisted, –

        Then mid the gloom of doubt and fear and anguish
        The votaries of virtue may raise their eyes to Heaven,
        And confident watch till the renovating day-star
20   Gild the horizon.

71 The Tombs

Presumably composed during S.'s first visit to Ireland, 12 February–4 April
1812; probably early, as S. does not identify Emmet's memorial (uninscribed
and so not a 'speaking stone') but introduces Emmet as an example while
speculating about death and immortality in the manner of his letters of summer
1811 and of Southey's 'The Dead Friend' (1799) 9–11:

> The Spirit is not there!
> It is but lifeless perishable flesh
> That moulders in the grave

The unrhymed metre is also inspired by Southey's. The tombs were probably
those in St Michan's churchyard, Dublin, the presumed final resting-place of
Robert Emmet, the Irish insurrectionary leader executed 20 September 1803,
who was caught while delaying for an answer to his declaration of love for
Sarah Curran. Sarah was the daughter of Godwin's friend John Philpot Curran
the barrister, who had defended several of the captured leaders of the 1798
rebellion and whom S. met in Dublin (and disliked). Strictly, line 23 ('When
blood and chains defiled the land') must refer to the hideous atrocities of 1798

11–12. S. seems to mean that the ruler whose régime condemns a woman to
poverty is responsible for the infanticide to which she may be driven. Cp. S.'s
letter to Elizabeth Hitchener, 7 January 1812: 'Children are frequently found
in the River which the unfortunate women employed at the manufactory
destroy' (*L* i 223).
13. the consummating hour] Probably 'the destined hour' predicted by the
doomed Tyler when 'The rays of truth shall emanate around, / And the whole
world be lighted' (Southey, *Wat Tyler* III ii 105, 113–14). Southey claimed
however (letter to *Courier*, 17 March 1817) that the MS of *Wat Tyler* had been
with his publishers since 1794. *hour*] Pronounced with two syllables (spelt
hower in 'Henry and Louisa' 111).

rather than the minor rising of 1803 associated with Emmet (lines 21–5), but
the romantic circumstances of the latter's arrest, and his moving final speech to
the court that condemned him, had made him a timeless national symbol (line
22) celebrated by many poets including Southey ('Written Immediately after
Reading the Speech of Robert Emmet') and Thomas Moore ('Oh! breathe not
his name', *Irish Melodies*, 1st ser. (1807), and 'She is far from the land', *Irish
Melodies*, 4th ser. (1811)).

Text from *Esd* f. 34^{r-v} (*Esd* No. 23: quoted by permission of the Carl H.
Pforzheimer Library).

Published in *Esd Nbk* 83–4; *Esd Poems* 41–2; *SC* iv 971–2 (transcript of *Esd*).

These are the tombs. O cold and silent Death
Thy Kingdom and thy subjects here I see:
   The record of thy victories
   Is graven on every speaking stone
5   That marks what once was man.

These are the tombs. Am I, who sadly gaze
On the corruption and the skulls around,
   To sum the mass of loathsomeness
   And to a mound of mouldering flesh
10   Say–'thou wert human life!

In thee once throbbed the Patriot's beating heart,
In thee once lived the Poet's soaring soul,
   The pulse of love, the calm of thought,
   Courage and charity and truth
15   And high devotedness,

All that could sanctify the meanest deeds,
All that might give a manner and a form
   To matter's speechless elements,
   To every brute and morbid shape
20   Of this phantasmal world'?

¶ 71.3. *thy*] the *Esd*.

10. life!] life!" *Esd, Esd Nbk, Esd Poems*. The premature closure of the inverted
commas in *Esd* must be inadvertent; the syntactical skeleton of lines 6–25 is:
'Am I to say [to this corpse] "*thou* wert life! in thee lived all that vitalizes
matter?" [Am I to say] that Emmet's true self lived in the body destroyed by
his murderers?'

13–15. Thomas Moore, who was at Trinity College Dublin with Emmet,
affirmed: 'Were I to number, indeed, the men, *among all I have ever known*, who
appear to me to combine, in the *greatest* degree, pure *moral worth* with *intellectual* power, I should among the highest of the few, place ROBERT
EMMETT' (quoted from 'Memoir of Robert Emmett and the Irish Insurrec-
tion of 1803', *English Chartist Circular* [*c.* 1838] 47).

    –That the high sense which from the stern rebuke
Of Erin's victim-patriot's death-soul shone
    When blood and chains defiled the land
    Lives in the torn uprooted heart
25   His savage murderers burn?

Ah no! else while these tombs before me stand
My soul would hate the coming of its hour,
    Nor would the hopes of life and love
    Be mingled with those fears of death
30   That chill the warmest heart.

72 On Robert Emmet's Tomb

Composed between S.'s arrival in Dublin 12 February 1812 and *c.* 16 April when, just after returning to England, he told Elizabeth Hitchener: 'I have written some *verses* on Robert Emmet which you shall see, & which I will insert in my book of Poems' (*L* i 282–3). As S. had not sent the verses earlier it seems likely that they had been recently written, especially as they are in the facile retrospective vein of Moore's rhymed *Irish Melodies* rather than the harsher manner of Southey (see especially stanza 3). The influence of Gray's *Elegy* is also apparent. For Robert Emmet, see headnote to No. 71.
Text from *Esd* ff. 19ᵛ–20ʳ (*Esd* No. 13: quoted by permission of the Carl H. Pforzheimer Library).
Published in *Dowden Life* i 268 (lines 21–end); *Esd Nbk* 60–1; *Esd Poems* 22–3; *SC* iv 948–9 (transcript of *Esd*).

    May the tempests of Winter that sweep o'er thy tomb
    Disturb not a slumber so sacred as thine;

22. *Erin's victim-patriot*] Robert Emmet (see headnote). His 'stern rebuke' was in his famous last speech, which concluded: 'Let no man write my epitaph; for as no man who knows my motives dare now vindicate them, let not prejudice or ignorance asperse them. Let them rest in obscurity and peace, my memory be left in oblivion, and my tomb remain uninscribed, until other times and other men can do justice to my character. When my country takes her place among the nations of the earth, then, and not till then, let my epitaph be written. I have done.' (R. R. Madden, *The United Irishmen; their Lives and Times*, 3rd ser., iii (1846) 238–46).
24–5. Emmet's body was apparently not mutilated after execution, but such mutilations were 'customary' in 1798 (Madden i 429). S. could have read an account (among others) of how, after killing one rebel leader, soldiers on the orders of Lord Mountnorris 'took out his heart, roasted his body and oiled their boots with the grease which dripped from it'. A British officer admitted 'that he himself had assisted in cutting open the breast with an axe, and pulling out the heart' (James Gordon, *History of the Rebellion in Ireland in the Year 1798* (1803) 258–9). Or S. may be imitating Southey's *Wat Tyler* (III ii 96) where the hero's execution, he is told, will include 'Your heart torn out, and burnt before your face–'.

May the breezes of summer that breathe of perfume
Waft their balmiest dews to so hallowed a shrine;

5 May the foot of the tyrant, the coward, the slave
Be palsied with dread where thine ashes repose,
Where that undying shamrock still blooms on thy grave
Which sprung when the dawnlight of Erin arose.

There oft have I marked the grey gravestones among,
10 Where thy relics distinguished in lowliness lay,
The peasant boy pensively lingering long
And silently weep as he passèd away.

And how could he not pause, if the blood of his sires
Ever wakened one generous throb in his heart:
15 How could he inherit a spark of their fires
If tearless and frigid he dared to depart?

Not the scrolls of a court could emblazon thy fame
Like the silence that reigns in the palace of thee,
Like the whispers that pass of thy dearly loved name,
20 Like the tears of the good, like the groans of the free.

No trump tells thy virtues—the grave where they rest
With thy dust shall remain unpolluted by fame,
Till thy foes, by the world and by fortune caressed,
Shall pass like a mist from the light of thy name.

25 When the storm-cloud that lowers o'er the daybeam is
                              gone,
Unchanged, unextinguished its life-spring will shine;
When Erin has ceased with their memory to groan
She will smile through the tears of revival on thine.

¶ *72.4. shrine*] shine *Esd.*
7. *shamrock*] Yellow Trefoil (*Trifolium dubium*), the national emblem of Ireland.
Stanza 3. The construction is: 'There have I seen . . . the peasant boy lingering, and [seen him] weep as he passed on'.
9–10. When Madden visited St Michan's *c.* 1845 he found Emmet's grave marked by a large horizontal slab, 'the only uninscribed one in the church-yard' (*The United Irishmen; their Lives and Times*, 3rd ser., iii (1846) 285).
12. *passèd*] passed *Esd.*
18. Esd is marked 'X' at the end of this line, as if S. had intended a note. Possibly he meant to quote from Emmet's last speech: 'I am going to my cold and silent grave . . . I have but one request to ask at my departure from this world; it is *the charity of its silence.*' (Quoted from Madden, op. cit. 244.)
20. the groans of the free] The lamentations of the emancipated over Emmet's fate.
21–4. See note to line 22 of 'The Tombs' (No. 71).
26. its] i.e. his name's.
27. their memory] i.e. that of Emmet's foes (line 23).

73 To the Republicans of North America

Substantially composed on or just before 14 February 1812 when an untitled version of the poem, minus stanza 4, was sent to Elizabeth Hitchener (BL add.MS 37496 f. 90: *Hitch. MS*) with the comment: 'Have you heard, a new republic is set up in Mexico. I have just written the following short tribute to its success' (*L* i 253). Stanza 4 may have been already written but tactfully omitted because in the same letter S. was acclaiming 'The society of peace and love!' and stressing the 'spirit of peace toleration and patience' of his Irish enterprise, then under way. In *Esd* the poem was originally headed 'To the Republicans of New Spain', but the last two words were altered to read 'North (lit. 'Nouth') America', no doubt to avoid any colonialist taint (Spain had conferred the viceregal title of 'New Spain' on her North and Central American possessions in 1535). No republic was proclaimed until 6 November 1813 in Mexico, where a bloody partisan war was still being waged by Morelos, and it is possible that S., or his source, had confused Mexico with Venezuela, who had declared her independence on 5 July 1811 in a proclamation later translated in full in *Annual Register* (1811), 'State Papers' 331–4. But Venezuela had been virtually independent since April 1810 whereas S.'s poem describes a desperate sacrificial struggle such as that taking place in Mexico (lines 6–10, 45–50); moreover the 'wild and winding shore' (line 4) suggests the long Mexican coastline. For details of American independence movements see John Lynch, *The Spanish American Revolutions 1808–1826* (1973) 312–15. S.'s information came from brief glances at American papers which may have anticipated Morelos's declaration. On 10 March S. wrote to Elizabeth Hitchener: 'The Republic of Mexico proceeds & extends. I have seen American papers, but have not had time to read them. – I only know that the spirit of Republicanism extends in South America, and that the prevailing opinion is that there will soon be no province which will recognize the ancient dynasty of Spain' (*L* i 272). Thus the poem comprehends all the anti-colonialist struggles in America (lines 21–2), perhaps including (as Cameron suggests: *Esd Nbk* 203) that of the United States against Britain. This war which began 18 June 1812 may have done so before the poem was copied into *Esd*, so influencing the title.

Text from *Esd* f. 26ᵛ–27ᵛ (*Esd* No. 17: quoted by permission of the Carl H. Pforzheimer Library).

Published in *Letters from Percy Bysshe Shelley to Elizabeth Hitchener* (1890) ed. T. J. Wise, ii 71–3 (*Hitch. MS*); *Rossetti 1870* ii 528–9 (*Hitch. MS*; Rossetti's title 'The Mexican Revolution' was corrected from *Esd* in *Dowden 1891*); *Esd Nbk* 71–2; *Esd Poems* 31–3; *SC* iv 959–61 (transcript of *Esd*).

> Brothers! between you and me
>   Whirlwinds sweep and billows roar,
> Yet in spirit oft I see
>   On the wild and winding shore

¶ *73.1. Brothers!*] The translation of the Venezuelan Declaration of Independ-

5   Freedom's bloodless banner wave,
    Feel the pulses of the brave
    Unextinguished by the grave,
      See them drenched in sacred gore,
    Catch the patriot's gasping breath
10 Murmuring 'Liberty' in death.

    Shout aloud! let every slave
      Crouching at corruption's throne
    Start into a man, and brave
      Racks and chains without a groan!
15 Let the castle's heartless glow
    And the hovel's vice and woe
    Fade like gaudy flowers that blow,
      Weeds that peep and then are gone,
    Whilst from misery's ashes risen
20 Love shall burst the Captive's prison.

    Cotopaxi! bid the sound
      Through thy sister mountains ring
    Till each valley smile around
      At the blissful welcoming,
25 And O! thou stern Ocean-deep
    Whose eternal billows sweep
    Shores where thousands wake to weep
      Whilst they curse some villain King,
    On the winds that fan thy breast
30 Bear thou news of freedom's rest.

---

ence refers several times to European republicans as 'our brethren in Europe' (*Annual Register* (1811), 'State Papers' 332).

4. *the wild*] thy wild *Hitch. MS.*

7. *by*] in *Hitch. MS.*

9. *patriot's*] Warriors *Hitch. MS.*

10. *'Liberty' in death.*] Liberty in death *Esd, Hitch. MS*; 'Liberty in death!' *Esd Poems* (the opposite meaning to the required one).

13. *brave*] bear *Hitch. MS.*

15–16. *the castle's . . . the hovel's*] S. is thinking partly of the Irish poor, ruled under the British Crown from Dublin Castle.

21. *Cotopaxi!*] A volcano in Ecuador, in the volcanic chain of the Andes. Cp. 'Ode to Liberty' 182–7.

26. *Whose eternal*] Thou, whose foamy *Hitch. MS.*

27. *Shores*] Ireland's, to which westerly winds will bring news of the successful struggles in America. *wake to weep*] S.'s first use of a persistent phrase.

28. *some*] a *Hitch. MS.*

Earth's remotest bounds shall start;
　　Every despot's bloated cheek,
Pallid as his bloodless heart,
　　Frenzy, woe and dread shall speak . . .
35　Blood may fertilise the tree
　　Of new bursting Liberty;
Let the guiltiness then be
　　On the slaves that ruin wreak,
On the unnatural tyrant brood
40　Slow to Peace and swift to blood.

Can the daystar dawn of love
　　Where the flag of war unfurled
Floats with crimson stain above
　　Such a desolated world?
45　Never! but to vengeance driven
When the patriot's spirit shriven
Seeks in death its native Heaven,
　　Then to speechless horror hurled
Widowed Earth may balm the bier
50　Of its memory with a tear.

74 'The Ocean rolls between us'

Composed on or shortly before 14 February 1812 when the lines were written
out as prose in a letter to Elizabeth Hitchener from Ireland, where S. and
Harriet S. had arrived two days earlier for a propaganda campaign, urging her

Stanza 4. Omitted Hitch. MS.
35–6. The phrase from the speech of Barère de Vieuzac (1755–1841) to the
French National Convention in 1792 had gained wide verbal and symbolic
currency: 'L'arbre de la liberté ne croît qu'arrosé par le sang des tyrans'.
Cameron (*Esd Nbk* 203n.) quotes Thomas Jefferson's letter of 13 November
1787: 'The tree of liberty must be refreshed from time to time with the blood of
patriots and tyrants'.
40. A sardonic inversion of a scriptural formula, e.g. *Psalms* ciii: 'The Lord is
merciful and gracious, slow to anger, and plenteous in mercy'.
41. *dawn*] Verb, not substantive.
44. The fabric of a ruined world *Hitch. MS*; world . . . *Esd.*
45–50. i.e. an ideal society cannot spring from bloodshed; but it is forgivable to
mourn the death of a partisan goaded into rebellion.
48–50.　　　　　　Then to desolation hurled
　　　　　　　　Widowed love may watch thy bier
　　　　　　　　Balm thee with its dying tear *Hitch. MS*
49. *Widowed Earth*] S. has in mind Sarah Curran, popularly regarded as
'widowed' by the execution of Emmet.

to come and stay with the S.'s the following summer (*L* i 250–5). The same letter includes the fragment 'Bear witness, Erin!' (No. 75) and 'Brothers! between you and me' (No. 73; see headnote). The first editor to print the two sets of lines concerning Ireland as a single poem in two parts, and to entitle it 'To Ireland', was G. E. Woodberry (*Woodberry 1893* iv 315–16), and this practice was followed by all subsequent editors (who reversed Woodberry's order of the parts). The two fragments have nothing in common, however, except for an Irish interest, and F. L. Jones rightly questions their connection (*L* i 254*n*.). Lines 14–25, as Dowden noted (*Dowden Life* i 248*n*.) were reworked later for *Q Mab* ix 23–37, and the passage is essentially a meditation on Time grafted in a complimentary way on to S.'s invitation for the summer (having only just arrived S. is unlikely to have been counting the moments until his return quite so eagerly). Such meditations were topical, and S. draws on various sources (see notes), but the quotation from Southey (line 23) shows that S. had transferred to the Conqueror Time some of the tyrannous characteristics of Kehama (see note). Some of the earlier lines are imperfect as blank verse, and *Julian* lineates by ending 3–7 with the words *arm, on!, amid, shall die, which*, respectively. A passage of similar imperfect blank verse occurs at the end of the fourth paragraph of *An Address to the Irish People* (February 1812):

> Oh Ireland!
> Thou emerald of the ocean, whose sons
> Are generous and brave, whose daughters are
> Honourable and frank and fair, thou art the isle
> On whose green shores I have desired to see
> The standard of liberty erected–a flag of fire–
> A beacon at which the world shall light
> The torch of Freedom!
>
> (prose text from *Mac-Carthy* 188)

Text from BL Add.MS 37496 f. 90 (*Hitch. MS*).
Published in *Mac-Carthy* 143 (lines 1–5); *Dowden Life* i 247–8 (lines 8–14, 22–5); T. J. Wise, *Letters of Percy Bysshe Shelley to Elizabeth Hitchener* (1890) ii 67–8; W. G. Kingsland, *Poet-Lore* iv (July 1892) 311 (lines 15–21); first printed in full as verse *Julian* iii 104–5.

The Ocean rolls between us.
     O thou Ocean,
Whose multitudinous billows ever lash
Erin's green isle, on whose shores
This venturous arm would plant the flag of liberty,
5 Roll on! and with each wave whose echoings die
Amid thy melancholy silentness
Shall die a moment too–one of those moments
Which part my friend and me.

¶ 74.2–4. Storms had driven the S.'s off-course during their crossing.

I could stand
Upon thy shores, O Erin, and could count
10   The billows that in their unceasing swell
Dash on thy beach, and every wave might seem
An instrument in Time the giant's grasp
To burst the barriers of Eternity.
Proceed, thou giant, conquering and to conquer,
15   March on thy lonely way—the Nations fall
Beneath thy noiseless footstep—pyramids
That for milleniums have defied the blast
And laughed at lightnings thou dost crush to nought.
Yon Monarch in his solitary pomp
20   Is but the fungus of a winter day
That thy light footstep presses into dust.—
Thou art a conqueror, Time! all things give way
Before thee, but *the fixed and virtuous will*,
The sacred sympathy of soul which was
25   When thou wert not, which *shall be* when thou perishest.

75 'Bear witness, Erin!'

Composed on or shortly before 14 February 1812, included in the same letter
of that date as Nos. 73 and 74 (see headnotes), and associated in ideas and
phrasing with both pieces. Although written, and always printed, continuously, the lines are clearly disjointed: the vocative pronoun addressing Erin in line
1 addresses the tree of Liberty in line 5, and in line 7 this tree (or another) is
referred to in the third person. S.'s apology following the lines suggests an

14. thou giant, conquering and to conquer] Cp. Kirke White, 'Time' 560–1:
'unvanquished Time, / The conqueror of conquerors'.
16–18. Cp. Blair's *Grave* 190–7: 'The tap'ring pyramid . . . whose spiky top . . .
Has . . . long outliv'd / The angry shaking of the winter's storm . . . At once
gives way'.
20. the fungus of a winter day] King-Hele (*The Essential Writings of Erasmus
Darwin* (1968) 173) quotes Darwin's *Temple of Nature* iv 383: 'When a Monarch
or a mushroom dies'. In *Q Mab* ix 31–2 the lines are: 'Yon monarch, in his
solitary pomp, / Was but the mushroom of a summer day', echoing Kirke
White on the vanity of man ('Time' 154): 'poor insect of a summer day'.
23. 'the fixed and virtuous will'] Jones (*L* i 251*n*.) cites *PL* ii 560: 'Fix'd fate,
free-will', but the relevant source is Southey's *Kehama* XXIV x 2–5: 'Almighty
as thou art, / Thou hast put all things underneath thy feet; / But still the resolute
heart / And virtuous will are free'. See also *Kehama* XVIII x 3–6; and *Q Mab* vii
257–8: 'Mocking my powerless tyrant's horrible curse / With stubborn and
unalterable will'.

improvisation: 'I find that I sometimes can write poetry when I feel. Such as it
is–' (*L* i 254).
Text from BL Add.MS 37496 f. 90 (*Hitch. MS*).
Published in *Rossetti 1870* ii 529–30.

Bear witness, Erin! when thine injured isle
Sees summer on its verdant pastures smile,
Its cornfields waving in the winds that sweep
The billowy surface of thy circling deep–

5   Thou tree whose shadow o'er the Atlantic gave
Peace, wealth and beauty to its friendly wave

–its blossoms fade,
And blighted are the leaves that cast its shade,
Whilst the cold hand gathers its scanty fruit
10 Whose chillness struck a canker to its root.

76 Falsehood and Vice: A Dialogue

Date of composition uncertain, but perhaps February–March 1812 in Dublin.
The 'famished nation' and 'unhappy land' of lines 2 and 12 suggest Ireland. It is
undated in *Esd*, which may indicate that it was a recent poem when transcribed
there, and S. still thought highly enough of it a year later to include a revised
version (the present text) in his notes to *Q Mab* as 'so strongly expressive of my
abhorrence of despotism and falsehood, that I fear lest it never again be
depictured so vividly. This opportunity is perhaps the only one that ever will
occur of rescuing it from oblivion' (see p. 362). The archetype of this and
contemporary dialogues like it was the second witches' scene in *Macbeth* (I iii
1–37), but Locock recognized Coleridge's War Eclogue, 'Fire, Famine, and
Slaughter' (1798) as the immediate inspiration (*Locock 1911* ii 553), in which the
three Sisters are incited to their evil deeds in Ireland and elsewhere by the then

¶ *75.1. Bear witness*] A hole has destroyed the third through the eighth letter [ar
witne], so that different words are theoretically possible. But the MS may have
been intact when Rossetti read it.
5. *Thou tree*] Presumably the Tree of Liberty (see No. 73, 35–6), influencing
Ireland from America and perhaps distinct from the Irish tree in lines 7–10.
Green was the symbolic colour of Ireland, and the insurrectionaries of 1798
frequently carried branches or Tree of Liberty insignia.
9. *the cold hand*] Either of the British Government or of the Irish landlord.
The construction of lines 9–10 is: 'the hand . . . whose chillness struck . . .
gathers . . .'

Prime Minister, Pitt. Coleridge's poem, in the same octosyllabic metre as S.'s, was reprinted in the *Annual Anthology* (1800). Where Coleridge's poem bears specifically on the policies of Pitt, S.'s much more sweeping assault is on the moral causes leading to the 'desolated globe' of 1811–12, when Napoleon's victories held nearly all the European monarchies in nominal subservience. S.'s school friend Andrew Amos remembered him singing the Witches' songs in *Macbeth* at Eton (*White* ii 495).

Text from *Q Mab* (1813), modified in some accidentals from *Esd* f. 9ʳ–11ᵛ (*Esd* No. 6).

Published in *Q Mab* 130–6; *Esd Nbk* 44–7; *Esd Poems* 8–12; *SC* iv 932–7 (transcript of *Esd*).

> Whilst monarchs laughed upon their thrones
> To hear a famished nation's groans,
> And hugged the wealth wrung from the woe
> That makes its eyes and veins o'erflow, –
> 5 Those thrones, high built upon the heaps
> Of bones where frenzied famine sleeps,
> Where slavery wields her scourge of iron
> Red with mankind's unheeded gore,
> And war's mad fiends the scene environ,
> 10 Mingling with shrieks a drunken roar,
> There Vice and Falsehood took their stand,
> High raised above the unhappy land.

FALSEHOOD

> Brother! arise from the dainty fare
>   Which thousands have toiled and bled to bestow;
> 15 A finer feast for thy hungry ear
>   Is the news that I bring of human woe.

VICE

> And, secret one, what hast thou done
>   To compare, in thy tumid pride, with me?
> I, whose career through the blasted year
> 20   Has been tracked by despair and agony.

¶ 76.4. *its eyes*] their eyes *Esd*.

5–6. Perhaps remembering Satan in Richard Cumberland's *Calvary* vii 423–5: 'about his throne, / If throne it might be call'd, which was compos'd / Of human bones, as in a charnel pil'd', and Coleridge, *Conciones ad Populum or Addresses to the People* (1795): 'The Temple of Despotism, like that of Tescalipoca, the Mexican Deity, is built of human skulls, and cemented with human blood' (quoted from *Collected Works* i, *Lectures 1795 On Politics and Religion*, ed. L. Patton and P. Mann (1971) 48).

7. *wields*] with *Esd*.

20. *tracked by despair and agony*] marked by ruin & misery *Esd*.

FALSEHOOD

What have I done!–I have torn the robe
From baby truth's unsheltered form,
And round the desolated globe
Borne safely the bewildering charm:
25 My tyrant-slaves to a dungeon-floor
Have bound the fearless innocent,
And streams of fertilizing gore
Flow from her bosom's hideous rent,
Which this unfailing dagger gave . . .
30 I dread that blood!–no more–this day
Is ours, though her eternal ray
    Must shine upon our grave.
Yet know, proud Vice, had I not given
To thee the robe I stole from heaven,
35 Thy shape of ugliness and fear
Had never gained admission here.

VICE

And know, that had I disdained to toil,
But sate in my loathsome cave the while,
And ne'er to these hateful sons of heaven
40 GOLD, MONARCHY, and MURDER given;
Hadst thou with all thine art essayed
One of thy games then to have played,
With all thine overweening boast,
Falsehood! I tell thee thou hadst lost!–
45 Yet wherefore this dispute?–we tend,
Fraternal, to one common end;
In this cold grave beneath my feet
Will our hopes, our fears, and our labours meet.

---

21. *I have*] I've *Esd*.
24. *Borne*] Worn *Esd* (possibly the better reading). The robe of Truth is 'bewildering' because worn as a disguise by Falsehood.
25. *tyrant-slaves*] Cp. *PU* II iv 110: 'All spirits are enslaved which serve things evil' and note.
26. *fearless*] dauntless *Esd*. The 'fearless innocent' is 'baby truth' of line 22.
34. *robe*] mask *Esd*.
37–8. *toil . . . while*] Still probably a good rhyme for S., as also in lines 101–2 (see H. C. Wyld, *Studies in English Rhymes from Surrey to Pope* (1923) 73–5).
38. *loathsome*] noisome *Esd*.
40. *and*] or *Esd*.
44. *hadst*] had *Esd*.
45. *Yet*] But *Esd*.

FALSEHOOD

I brought my daughter, RELIGION, on earth;
50 She smothered Reason's babes in their birth;
But dreaded their mother's eye severe, –
So the crocodile slunk off slily in fear,
And loosed her bloodhounds from the den . . .
They started from dreams of slaughtered men,
55 And by the light of her poison eye
Did her work o'er the wide earth frightfully:
The dreadful stench of her torches' flare,
Fed with human fat, polluted the air:
The curses, the shrieks, the ceaseless cries
60 Of the many-mingling miseries,
As on she trod, ascended high
And trumpeted my victory! –
Brother, tell what thou hast done.

VICE

I have extinguished the noon-day sun
65 In the carnage-smoke of battles won:
Famine, murder, hell and power
Were glutted in that glorious hour
Which searchless fate had stamped for me
With the seal of her security . . .
70 For the bloated wretch on yonder throne
Commanded the bloody fray to rise.
Like me he joyed at the stifled moan
Wrung from a nation's miseries;
While the snakes, whose slime *even him* defiled,
75 In ecstasies of malice smiled:
They thought 'twas theirs, – but mine the deed!
Theirs is the toil, but mine the meed –

50. *Reason's babes*] its sweetest buds *Esd.*
51. *their mother's*] Reasons *Esd.*
54. 'The dreams from which they woke were of religious massacres'.
57. *dreadful*] deathy *Esd.*
57–8. A recollection of Gibbon's paraphrase of Tacitus, *Annali* XV xliv 6, describing the persecution of the Christians under Nero: 'Some were nailed on crosses . . . others again, smeared over with combustible materials, were used as torches to illuminate the darkness of the night' (*Decline and Fall of the Roman Empire* (1776–88; 1897 edn) ch. xvi ii 85).
67. *glutted in that glorious*] sated in that joyous *Esd* (the first three letters of *sated* are canc. but not replaced).
74. The word italicized in Q *Mab* is *defiled*–probably a printer's slip.

Ten thousand victims madly bleed.
They dream that tyrants goad them there
80   With poisonous war to taint the air:
These tyrants, on their beds of thorn,
Swell with the thoughts of murderous fame,
And with their gains to lift my name
Restless they plan from night to morn:
85   I–I do all; without my aid
Thy daughter, that relentless maid,
Could never o'er a death-bed urge
The fury of her venomed scourge.
Brother, well:–the world is ours;
90   And whether thou or I have won,
The pestilence expectant lowers
On all beneath yon blasted sun.
Our joys, our toils, our honours meet
In the milk-white and wormy winding-sheet:
95   A short-lived hope, unceasing care,
Some heartless scraps of godly prayer,
A moody curse, and a frenzied sleep
Ere gapes the grave's unclosing deep,
A tyrant's dream, a coward's start,
100   The ice that clings to a priestly heart,
A judge's frown, a courtier's smile
Make the great whole for which we toil;
And, brother, whether thou or I
Have done the work of misery,
105   It little boots: thy toil and pain,
Without my aid, were more than vain;
And but for thee I ne'er had sate
The guardian of heaven's palace gate.

79. *dream*] think *Esd*.
Between lines 80–1: But hired assassins tis not vice–
                    Tis her sweet sister Cowardice . . . *Esd canc.*
82. *with the thoughts*] in their dreams *Esd*.
83. *name*] name. *Q Mab.*
86–8. Terror of hell was supposed to overpower atheists on their deathbeds. S.
may have in mind a recent account of Tom Paine's deathbed (*GM* xxxi
(November 1811) 435–7) in which a certain Dr. Manley, assailing the old man
at midnight when 'he was in great distress' two or three days before his death,
'took occasion . . . to test the strength of his opinions respecting the Revelation'
with a remorseless interrogation.

77 Written on a Beautiful Day in Spring

Composed in the spring of either 1811 or 1812, most probably just after reaching Nantgwillt, Radnorshire, on 14 April 1812, having 'traversed the whole of Wales, & heard no tidings of a house' (*L* i 281). A bad crossing from Ireland and a week's dispiriting search had ended in S.'s finding a rentable farm close to Thomas Grove's estate of Cwm Elan where he had spent the previous spring alone. Although ultimately disappointed here too (*White* i 230–1), S. probably wrote this poem in the initial relief of settling in surroundings which he described enthusiastically to Elizabeth Hitchener in a letter postmarked 18 April: 'Oh my friend what shall I say of the scenery but *you* will enjoy it with us, which is all that is wanting to render it a perfect heaven.–' (*L* i 281). As Peacock described the locality in 1857 (*Peacock Works* viii 246–7):

> One of the most beautiful scenes on the Wye is Nant Gwyllt, the Wild Brook, which runs into the Elan, which runs into the Wye, near Rhayader in Radnorshire. Above the confluence of the two upper streams, are two valleys, one called Cwm Elan, the other Nant Gwyllt. In each of these was a gentleman's house. Cwm Elan, in 1812–13, was occupied by its owner. Nant Gwyllt was occupied by a farmer, who let the greater part of it in lodgings. Shelley lodged there, and always spoke of the place with great delight.

For details and illustration see W. M. Rossetti, 'S. at Cwm Elan and Nant-gwilt' in R. Eustace Tickell's *The Vale of Nantgwilt: a Submerged Valley* (1894) 17–35. Perhaps because S. was likewise revisiting a familiar locality, the debt to Wordsworth seems to be mainly to 'Lines written a few miles above Tintern Abbey', lines 103–12 and especially 28–31:

> sensations sweet,
> Felt in the blood, and felt along the heart,
> And passing even into my purer mind
> With tranquil restoration

S. may also have recalled 'Lines written at a small distance from my house' 21–36; 'Lines written in early spring' (title and lines 5–6); 'Expostulation and Reply' 21–4; and 'The Tables Turned' 21–32; all in *Lyrical Ballads* (1798). But the poem draws on only one of the more obvious aspects of Wordsworth's ideas, which may have reached S. from indirect sources (see notes), celebrating a recovery of morale by submitting the mind, in a 'wise passiveness', to the sensational influences of Nature. Lines 12–13 owe more to Holbach (especially *Système de la Nature* I chs. i–viii) than to Wordsworth, and are Shelleyan in formulation (see note). S. had 'just finished reading' Holbach's *Système de la Nature* on 3 June 1812 (*L* i 303).

Text from *Esd* f. 14ᵛ (*Esd* No. 9: quoted by permission of the Carl H. Pforzheimer Library).
Published in *Esd Nbk* 52; *Esd Poems* 15–16; *SC* iv 940–1 (transcript of *Esd*).

> In that strange mental wandering when to live,
> To breathe, to be, is undivided joy,
> When the most woe-worn wretch would cease to grieve,
> When satiation's self would fail to cloy;
> 5 When unpercipient of all other things
> Than those that press around – the breathing Earth,
> The gleaming sky and the fresh season's birth –
> Sensation all its wondrous rapture brings,
> And to itself not once the mind recurs,
> 10 Is it foretaste of Heaven?
> So sweet as this the nerves it stirs,
> And mingling in the vital tide
>   With gentle motion driven
> Cheers the sunk spirits, lifts the languid eye,
> 15 And scattering through the frame its influence wide
> Revives the spirits when they droop and die,
> The frozen blood with genial beaming warms,
> And to a gorgeous fly the sluggish worm transforms.

¶ *77.1–2.* The 'Wordsworthian' opening seems more directly indebted to that of 'Fragment VII' in Sydney Owenson's *The Lay of an Irish Harp; or Metrical Fragments* (1807) 1–2:
> There was a day when simply but to BE,
> To live, to breathe, was purest ecstasy;

7. Cp. Wordsworth's 'Resolution and Independence' 9: 'The sky rejoices in the morning's birth'.

8. its] it *Esd.*

10. i.e. 'is this mental condition (the antecedent of *it* in line 11 and grammatical subject of the subsequent main verbs) a foretaste of Heaven?'

12–13. The mind's induced participation in the tide of life anticipates 'Mont Blanc' (Text B) 1–11, 37–40: 'my human mind . . . Holding an unremitting interchange / With the clear universe of things around'; and *PU* II ii 41–7.

15. Cp. Coleridge's 'Fears in Solitude' (1798) 20–1: 'from the sun, and from the breezy air, / Sweet influences trembled o'er his frame'.

16. die,] die *Esd*; die. *Esd Nbk.* The period was presumably to avoid making *Sensation* transform the caterpillar to a butterfly. But caterpillars do not literally turn into butterflies in spring: all the images of lines 14–18 concern the mind and are metaphorical (see note to lines 12–13, and cp. No. 78, lines 136–43).

17. Cp. Southey's 'Written on Sunday Morning' 22–3: 'The morning beams that life and joy impart, / Will with their influence warm my heart'.

78 'Dark Spirit of the desert rude'

Line 10 ('the pure Elan's foamy course') shows the poem to have been written during one of S.'s two stays in Wales, and Cameron (*Esd Nbk* 207–9) and Rogers (*Esd Poems* 123) assign it to summer 1811 on the grounds of its gloom and loneliness. Lines 30–3, however, establish the date of composition decisively as spring, and so probably *c*. 20 April 1812. The S.'s were then at Nantgwillt in the house they were trying to lease, only a mile or two from Cwm Elan, to which they moved from financial necessity on 6 June when the deal fell through. Harriet S.'s indisposition (perhaps originating in the bad crossing from Ireland), which worsened alarmingly between *c*. 20 April and *c*. 7 May, accounts for the gloom of this poem and of No. 79, and for S.'s unaccompanied rambles in the neighbourhood. On *c*. 16 April he wrote to Elizabeth Hitchener: 'We are now embosomed in the solitude of mountains woods & rivers, silent, solitary, and old' (*L* i 283), and on 24 April to his father: 'Your daughter in law is confined by a tedious intermittent fever, which considerably augments the gloomy feelings incident to our unsettled state' (*L* i 285). The former letter also contains strictures on the rapacity of the English monarchy that are reflected in the theme of the poem: 'That infernal wretch the P[rince] of Wales demands more money . . . if the murderer of Marrs family . . . deserves a gibbet, how much more does a Prince whose conduct destroys millions deserve it?' (*L* i 282).

The invocation in the first line, and some descriptive passages, derive from Bowles's poem 'Coombe-Ellen', written at Thomas Grove's residence fourteen years earlier (see notes); and 'Dark Spirit' also has close links with S.'s 'The Retrospect', written during S.'s same stay in Wales.

Text from *Esd* ff. 30ᵛ–31ᵛ (*Esd* No. 20: quoted by permission of the Carl H. Pforzheimer Library).

Published in *Esd Nbk* 77–8; *Esd Poems* 37–8; *SC* iv 966–8 (transcript of *Esd*).

> Dark Spirit of the desert rude
> That o'er this awful solitude,
> Each tangled and untrodden wood,
> Each dark and silent glen below
> 5 Where sunlight's gleamings never glow,
> Whilst jetty, musical and still
> In darkness speeds the mountain rill;
> That o'er yon broken peaks sublime,
> Wild shapes that mock the scythe of time,

¶ *78.1*. Cp. Bowles, 'Coombe-Ellen' 1–2: 'Call the strange spirit that abides unseen / In wilds, and wastes, and shaggy solitudes', and 18–19: 'Think that thou holdest converse with some Power / Invisible and strange'.

8–9. Cp. 'The Retrospect' 112–13: 'Ye jagged peaks that frown sublime, / Mocking the blunted scythe of Time'.

10   And the pure Elan's foamy course,
      Wavest thy wand of magic force,
      Art thou yon sooty and fearful fowl
        That flaps its wing o'er the leafless oak
      That o'er the dismal scene doth scowl,
15   And mocketh music with its croak?

      I've sought thee where day's beams decay
        On the peak of the lonely hill;
      I've sought thee where they melt away
        By the wave of the pebbly rill;
20   I've strained to catch thy murky form
      Bestride the rapid and gloomy storm;
      Thy red and sullen eyeball's glare
      Has shot in a dream through the midnight air,
        But never did thy shape express
25   Such an emphatic gloominess.

      And where art thou, O thing of gloom? . . .
      On nature's unreviving tomb
      Where sapless, blasted and alone
      She mourns her blooming centuries gone!–
30   From the fresh sod the violets peep,
      The buds have burst their frozen sleep,
        Whilst every green and peopled tree
      Is alive with Earth's sweet melody.
        But thou alone art here
35   Thou desolate Oak, whose scathèd head
      For ages has never tremblèd,
      Whose giant trunk dead lichens bind,
      Moaningly sighing in the wind,

10. *Elan's*] Ellans *Esd.*

12. *sooty and fearful fowl*] A raven (as in Chatterton's *Aella*, 'Minstrelles Song' cvi 1–2). Ravens still haunted the area eighty years later (see R. E. Tickell, *The Vale of Nantgwilt: a Submerged Valley* (1894) 17–35).

26. The 'dark Spirit' is associated with unnatural death, with a dying oak, with the Upas Tree, and finally with a King.

31. *their*] there *Esd.*

35. *Thou desolate Oak*] Cameron (*Esd Nbk* 208) regards the oak as 'perhaps a product of the poetic imagination', but it is the centre both of the natural and the symbolic scene, and may well have been the same tree that Bowles had described ('Coombe-Ellen' 54–66):

        Upon the adverse bank, withered, and stripped
        Of all its pleasant leaves, a scathed oak
        Hangs desolate, once sovereign of the scene

Cp. 'Death-spurning rocks!' 7–10.

40
With huge loose rocks beneath thee spread, –
Thou, Thou alone art here!
Remote from every living thing,
Tree, shrub, or grass, or flower,
Thou seemest of this spot the King,
And with a regal power
45
Suck like that race all sap away
And yet upon the spoil decay.

79 The Retrospect: Cwm Elan 1812

Composed in Wales between 14 April and *c.* 18 June 1812, probably early in
May. The contrast between Cwm Elan as it seemed to S. in 1811 and as it
seemed in 1812, a main theme of the poem, is described in a letter to Godwin of
25 April: 'Nantgwillt, the place where we now reside is in the neighbourhood
of scenes marked deeply on my mind by the thoughts which possessed it when
present among them. The ghosts of these old friends have a dim & strange
appearance when resuscitated in a situation so altered as mine is, since I felt that
they were alive' (*L* i 287). The other preoccupation in the poem, the nature of
true friendship, arises from S.'s efforts to induce Elizabeth Hitchener to leave
her school in Sussex and reside with them. Elizabeth's father strongly opposed
this move, and S.'s motives in urging it were distrusted locally (see headnote to
No. 80), for which S. blamed Capt. and Mrs Pilfold at Cuckfield, his uncle and
aunt. Miss Hitchener told him *c.* 3 May (*L* i 293*n.*) that she and Harriet
constituted 'a bliss an envious world cannot bear to see, & which they exert &
will continue to exert all their maliciousness to destroy, well may they say they
cannot understand it, disinterested friendship is indeed unintelligible to them,
& a friendship free from all worldly *influence & prejudice*, may well astonish
them'. S. replied 7 May (*L* i 294–5) with a passionate letter which provides a
gloss to lines 71–111: 'And so our dear friends are *determined* to *destroy our peace
of mind* if we live together . . . Now my friend are we or are we not to sacrifize

39. Cp. 'Coombe-Ellen' 99–100: 'all beneath it [the hill-brow] spread / With
massy fragments riven from its top'.
41–2. S. confers on the oak the deadly qualities of the Upas Tree as described in
Erasmus Darwin's Additional Note to *The Botanic Garden* Part II, iii 238: 'the
country round it, to the distance of ten or twelve miles from the tree, is entirely
barren. Not a tree nor a shrub, nor even the least plant or grass is to be seen'.
45–6. 'Like the race of Kings, [you] rob others of sustenance yet decay in the
midst of your plunder'. The switch from 'thou' to 'you' verb forms within a
single speech is common in Shakespeare (see E. A. Abbott, *A Shakespearian
Grammar* (1886) 153–60), but S. omits the second pronoun.

an attachment in which far more than you & I are immediately implicated, in which far more than these dear beings are remotely concerned; and to sacrifize to what? – To the *world*. – to the swinish multitude, to . . . such as continue this liberticide war . . . or (equal in unprincipled cowardice) the slaves who permit such things – for of these two classes is composed what may be called the *world* . . . My friend my dearest friend you must, you shall be with us – all our schemes even of walks or rides will be unfinished without you'. The passage on friendship was also influenced by Godwin's *Fleetwood* (see notes).

The title, and the strategy of contrasting impressions of the same scene experienced at dissimilar periods, recall Southey's 'The Retrospect' (*Poems*, Bath 1795); but whereas Southey's poem (esp. in its original, longer version) looks back with nostalgia on scenes endeared by childhood and now sadly changed, S.'s memory of Cwm Elan is of pain and solitude now converted to happiness by his wife's companionship. Of more direct influence on the content of the poem was Bowles's 'Coombe-Ellen', which describes the same scenery.

This is S.'s first poem of any real imaginative complexity, whose cryptic self-revelation anticipates that of *Epipsychidion*. It was probably once intended to conclude the poems collected in *Esd*, as Wordsworth's 'Tintern Abbey' lines had concluded *Lyrical Ballads*.

Text from *Esd* ff. 86ʳ–90ʳ (*Esd* No. 50: quoted by permission of the Carl H. Pforzheimer Library).

Published in *Dowden Life* i 270–4 (lines 15–end); *Esd Nbk* 155–60; *Esd Poems* 102–7; *SC* iv 1048–54 (transcript of *Esd*).

> To trace Duration's lone career,
> To check the chariot of the year
> Whose burning wheels forever sweep
> The boundaries of oblivion's deep –
> 5 To snatch from Time the monster's jaw
> The children which she just had borne,

¶ 79. *Title.* The date was altered from '1811' in *Esd*, supporting the assumption, as Cameron agrees (*SC* iv 1048*n*.), that 'Cwm Elan 1812' is part of the poem's title.

1–22. Esd Poems obscures the drift of this long paragraph, the basic structure of which is: 'It requires great objectivity (lines 11–12) to arrest and scrutinize the flux of experience (lines 1–10) – to compare past with present thoughts (lines 13–14), and a scene of past unhappiness with the same scene under changed circumstances (lines 15–22)'.

4. deep–] deep. . . . *Esd*.

5–6. Perhaps recalling Shakespeare's Sonnet 19, 1–2: 'Devouring Time blunt thou the lions paws / And make the earth devour her own sweet brood' – itself a reminiscence of Ovid's 'tempus edax rerum' (*Met.* xv 234–6) and of the Titan Saturn (Cronus), often depicted as an old man with a scythe, who swallowed his sons as soon as they were born (Hesiod, *Theog.* 453–73).

And ere entombed within her maw
To drag them to the light of morn
And mark each feature with an eye
10   Of cold and fearless scrutiny –
It asks a soul not formed to feel,
An eye of glass, a hand of steel,
Thoughts that have passed and thoughts that are
With truth and feeling to compare:
15   A scene which wildered fancy viewed
In the soul's coldest solitude
With that same scene when peaceful love
Flings rapture's colours o'er the grove,
When mountain, meadow, wood and stream
20   With unalloying glory gleam
And to the spirit's ear and eye
Are unison and harmony.

The moonlight was my dearer day: –
Then would I wander far away,
25   And lingering on the wild brook's shore
To hear its unremitting roar
Would lose in the ideal flow
All sense of overwhelming woe;
Or at the noiseless noon of night
30   Would climb some heathy mountain's height
And listen to the mystic sound
That stole in fitful gasps around.
I joyed to see the streaks of day
Above the purple peaks decay,
35   And watch the latest line of light
Just mingling with the shades of night,
For day with me was time of woe
When even tears refused to flow;
Then would I stretch my languid frame

10. *scrutiny –*] scrutiny. . . . . *Esd.*
14. *feeling to compare:*] feeling to compare; *Esd, Esd Nbk*; feeling, to compare *Esd Poems* (an impossible pointing).
23–48. A recapitulation of 'Written at Cwm Elan'. There had been a full moon on 5 July 1811, a few days before S.'s arrival.
25. *wild brook's*] 'Wild Brook' is a literal translation of 'Nant Gwyllt'.
31. *mystic sound*] Cp. the 'magic murmuring' of 'Written at Cwm Elan' 10–16.
37–48. Cp. Bowles, 'Coombe-Ellen' 36–7: 'Here Melancholy, on the pale crags laid, / Might muse herself to sleep'. Both poets follow the 'melancholy man' paradigm of Gray's *Elegy* 101–8, which in turn imitates the description of Jaques in *As You Like It* II i 29–52.

40 Beneath the wild-wood's gloomiest shade
 And try to quench the ceaseless flame
 That on my withered vitals preyed;–
 Would close mine eyes and dream I were
 On some remote and friendless plain,
45 And long to leave existence there
 If with it I might leave the pain
 That with a finger cold and lean
 Wrote madness on my withering mien.

 It was not unrequited love
50 That bade my wildered spirit rove;
 'Twas not the pride, disdaining life,
 That with this mortal world at strife
 Would yield to the soul's inward sense,
 Then groan in human impotence,
55 And weep, because it is not given
 To taste on Earth the peace of Heaven;
 'Twas not that in the narrow sphere
 Where Nature fixed my wayward fate
 There was no friend or kindred dear
60 Formed to become that spirit's mate
 Which, searching on tired pinion, found
 Barren and cold repulse around . . .
 Ah no! yet each one sorrow gave
 New graces to the narrow grave.

65 For broken vows had early quelled
 The stainless spirit's vestal flame.
 Yes! whilst the faithful bosom swelled
 Then the envenomed arrow came,
 And apathy's unaltering eye
70 Beamed coldness on the misery,
 And early I had learned to scorn
 The chains of clay that bound a soul
 Panting to seize the wings of morn,
 And where its vital fires were born

---

40. *wild-wood's*] wild-woods *Esd* wild-woods' *Dowden Life, Esd Nbk.*
59–62. Cp. Godwin's *Fleetwood* (1805) II xi: 'It is inconceivable in how deep and insurmountable a solitude that creature is involved, who looks every where around for sympathy, but looks in vain'.
60–1. i.e. 'the mate of that spirit which . . .' The spirit is S.'s own (as in line 66).
63. *Ah*] Oh *Dowden Life.*
64. *grave.*] grave: *Esd, Esd Nbk.*
65. *broken vows*] Those of Harriet Grove.

75   To soar, and spurn the cold control
     Which the vile slaves of earthly night
     Would twine around its struggling flight.
     O many were the friends whom fame
     Had linked with the unmeaning name
80   Whose magic marked among mankind
     The casket of my unknown mind,
     Which hidden from the vulgar glare
     Imbibed no fleeting radiance there.
     My darksome spirit sought. It found
85   A friendless solitude around. –
     For who, that might undaunted stand
     The saviour of a sinking land,
     Would crawl, its ruthless tyrant's slave,
     And fatten upon freedom's grave,
90   Though doomed with her to perish, where
     The captive clasps abhorred despair?

     They could not share the bosom's feeling
     Which, passion's every throb revealing,
     Dared force on the world's notice cold
95   Thoughts of unprofitable mould,
     Who bask in Custom's fickle ray,
     Fit sunshine of such wintry day!
     They could not in a twilight walk
     Weave an impassioned web of talk

78–111. This passage was influenced by the long digression on friendship at the opening of II xi of Godwin's *Fleetwood*, e.g.: 'This must be a friend, who is to me as another self, who joys in all my joys, and grieves in all my sorrows . . . I do not condemn the man, upon whom a wound through my vitals acts but as a scratch . . . But he is not the brother of my heart . . . I walk among these men as in an agreeable promenade . . . but they are nothing to me . . . If that which produces sensation in me, produces sensation no where else, I am substantially alone.' S. had read *Fleetwood* by 24 February 1812 (*L* i 260).

79. the unmeaning name] 'Love' or 'friendship' (see line 107). The obscure lines 78–83 seem to mean: 'I had many acquaintances whose intimacy was presumed to give them access to my deepest thoughts–but it was not so'. S. may have had in mind a letter from Elizabeth Hitchener *c*. 3 May which read: 'I am told, I cannot know you, but those who say it, know not the springs which open instantly the human heart & mind to the inspection of others, *I do know you*, & far better than those who say I know you not' (*L* i 293*n*.).

86–91. 'For who–even if doomed to share freedom's fate and die in despair– would choose to side with tyranny against freedom, when he might be the redeemer of his country?' S. may have been thinking of Miss Hitchener rather than of himself.

91. despair?] despair. *Esd, eds*.

95. 'Opinions that bring no worldly advantage'.

100   Till mysteries the spirit press
      In wild yet tender awfulness,
      Then feel within our narrow sphere
      How little yet how great we are!
      But they might shine in courtly glare,
105   Attract the rabble's cheapest stare,
      And might command where'er they move
      A thing that bears the name of love;
      They might be learned, witty, gay,
      Foremost in fashion's gilt array,
110   On Fame's emblazoned pages shine,
      Be princes' friends, but never mine!

      Ye jagged peaks that frown sublime,
      Mocking the blunted scythe of Time,
      Whence I would watch its lustre pale
115   Steal from the moon o'er yonder vale:

      Thou rock whose bosom black and vast,
      Bared to the stream's unceasing flow,
      Ever its giant shade doth cast
      On the tumultuous surge below!

120   Woods to whose depth retires to die
      The wounded echo's melody,
      And whither this lone spirit bent
      The footstep of a wild intent—

      Meadows! whose green and spangled breast
125   These fevered limbs have often pressed
      Until the watchful fiend despair
      Slept in the soothing coolness there!

      Have not your varied beauties seen
      The sunken eye, the withering mien,

112–13. Quoting his own 'Dark spirit' 8–9: 'yon broken peaks sublime, / Wild shapes that mock the scythe of time'.

116. Thou rock] Perhaps the rock identified by Bowles as 'Dole-Vinoc' in 'Coombe-Ellen' 255–60 (Graig Dolfaenog, on NE bank of what is now the Garreg Ddu Reservoir).

120–1. Woods . . . echo's melody] Perhaps recalling Mary Wollstonecraft's *Vindication of the Rights of Men* (2nd edn 1790) 152: 'the sick heart retires to die in lonely wilds, far from the abodes of men'.

123. a wild intent] A suicidal impulse. Cp. 'Death-spurning rocks!' 11–12: 'A maniac sufferer soared with wild intent / Where nature formed these wonders'; and Goethe, *Sorrows of Werter*, Letter lxxxvii.

127–8. No stanza-break in *Esd* or *eds.*, but it is likely that S. inadvertently left no interval here in a series of invocations intended as quatrains.

130   Sad traces of the unuttered pain
      That froze my heart and burned my brain?

      How changed since nature's summer form
      Had last the power my grief to charm,
      Since last ye soothed my spirit's sadness,
135   Strange chaos of a mingled madness!
      Changed!–not the loathsome worm that fed
      In the dark mansions of the dead,
      Now soaring through the fields of air
      And gathering purest nectar there,
140   A butterfly whose million hues
      The dazzled eye of wonder views
      Long lingering on a work so strange,
      Has undergone so bright a change!

      How do I feel my happiness?
145   I cannot tell, but they may guess
      Whose every gloomy feeling gone
      Friendship and passion feel alone,
      Who see mortality's dull clouds
      Before affection's murmur fly,
150   Whilst the mild glances of her eye
      Pierce the thin veil of flesh that shrouds
      The spirit's radiant sanctuary.

      O thou! whose virtues latest known,
      First in this heart yet claim'st a throne,
155   Whose downy sceptre still shall share
      The gentle sway with virtue there,
      Thou fair in form and pure in mind,
      Whose ardent friendship rivets fast
      The flowery band our fates that bind
160   Which incorruptible shall last

136–43. Cp. the butterfly-image of 'Written on a Beautiful Day in Spring' 18.

140. *A butterfly*] Literally, a vanessid butterfly (lines 140–1) whose larva was nourished on graveyard nettles (136–7); metaphorically, the psyche (Gk. 'soul', later 'butterfly') risen from the 'grave-worm' of folk-lore.

145–7. '. . . those who, no longer sorrowful, feel nothing but love may guess how I feel'. The dualism of lines 150–1 is partly attributive, continuing the corpse-soul image of lines 136–43, and so semi-metaphorical.

146. *feeling*] orig. passion *Esd canc.*

153. *whose virtues latest known*] An absolute construction: 'The meaning is 'O thou! who, thy virtues being latest known' (i.e. 'more recently than those of Harriet Grove')' (Rogers, *Esd Poems* 128).

159. *our fates that bind*] An inversion: 'that our fates bind [round us]'.

When duty's hard and cold control
Had thawed around the burning soul–
The gloomiest retrospects that bind
With crowns of thorn the bleeding mind,
165   The prospects of most doubtful hue
That rise on Fancy's shuddering view
Are gilt by the reviving ray
Which thou hast flung upon my day.

80 To Harriet

Date of composition unknown, but probably 24 April–7 May 1812, contemporary with No. 79. The story circulating locally in Sussex regarding Elizabeth Hitchener's move to join the S.'s was, as she informed him and as he incredulously repeated to her on 7 May, 'That you are to be *my Mistress*! that you refused it whilst I was single, but that my marriage takes away all objections that before stood in the way of this singular passion.–They certainly seem to have acquired a taste of fabricating the most whimsical & impossible crimes' (*L* i 294). Earlier (25 April) S. had assumed the objection to be the other way round, that Elizabeth might have tried to seduce him if she had joined his household. '*I* unfaithful to my Harriet! *You* a female Hogg! common sense should laugh such an idea to scorn, if indignation would wait till it could be looked upon!' (*L* i 288). Between these dates Harriet was so ill as to cause S. serious apprehension. 'Harriet will recover,' he reassured Elizabeth Hitchener (and himself) on 1 May, 'Oh certainly she will! Her illness is of a nature comparatively slight, & I am weak to think so gloomily of it, as I do sometimes.–Yet she has been ill a week' (*L* i 292). Cameron, arguing from the influence of Southey perceptible in the unrhymed form of the lyric, assigns the poem to the earlier Keswick period and the crisis with Hogg, but this forces him to attribute the second stanza to 'death-wish fantasies' (*Esd Nbk* 182). The warmth of 'yonder Sun', however, is a much more plausible allusion in late spring 1812 than in winter 1811; and the moon was full on 26 April 1812 (lines 5–6).

Text from *Esd* ff. 8ᵛ–9ʳ (*Esd* No. 5: quoted by permission of the Carl H. Pforzheimer Library).

Published in *Esd Nbk* 43; *Esd Poems* 7–8; *SC* iv 931–2 (transcript of *Esd*).

Never, O never shall yonder Sun
   Through my frame its warmth diffuse
When the heart that beats in its faithful breast
   Is untrue, fair girl, to thee,

164. With coronets of thorn the mind *orig. Esd canc.*
165. *prospects of most doubtful hue*] No doubt these included the unsettled contract for leasing the Nantgwillt house, and S.'s chronic shortage of money (he was still a minor).

5   Nor the beaming moon
       On its nightly voyage
   Shall visit this spirit with softness again
       When its soaring hopes
       And its fluttering fears
10 Are untrue, fair girl, to thee!

   O ever while this frail brain has life
       Will it thrill to thy love-beaming gaze,
   And whilst thine eyes with affection gleam
       It will worship the spirit within;
15   And when death comes
       To quench their fire
   A sorrowful rapture their dimness will shed,
       As I bind me tight
       With thine auburn hair
20 And die, as I lived, with thee.

81 Mary to the Sea-Wind

Date of composition unknown; very possibly July or August 1812 at Lynmouth. Except for the name 'Mary', the poem has no affinities with the group
of poems 'To Mary' of November 1811 (Nos. 38–41), from which it is widely
separated in Esd. The other name, 'Henry', occurs in the opening of Q Mab,
where it is associated with S. himself; the season is summer; the place a
sea-coast with trees near the shore and 'heath' inland (lines 6, 12). The atmosphere of sexual felicity suggests a song written with Harriet S. as the imaginary
singer, and with Moore's sentimental lyrics as inspiration. No song of
Moore's, however, much resembles it. Its unusual metre was used by Campion or Rosseter in 'When Laura smiles' (A Book of Ayres (1601) Part II, No.
ix), but employs alternate rhymes where Campion's are couplets.
Text from Esd f. 40ʳ (Esd No. 30: quoted by permission of the Carl H.
Pforzheimer Library).
Published in Esd Nbk 94; Esd Poems 49; SC iv 980–1 (transcript of Esd).

   I implore thee, I implore thee, softly swelling Breeze,
   Waft swift the sail of my lover to the shore,
   That under the shadow of yon darkly woven trees
   I may meet him, I may meet him to part with him no
                                              more.
5 For this boon, for this boon, sweet Sea Wind, will I
                                              weave
   A garland wild of heath flowers to breathe to thee
                                              perfume;

¶ 80.13–14. Cp. 'The Retrospect' 150–2.

Thou wilt kiss them, yet like Henry's thy kisses will but
leave
A more heaven-breathing fragrance and sense-
enchanting bloom.

And then on Summer evens I will hasten to inhale–
10   Remembering that thou wert so kind–thy balmy, balmy
breath,
And when thy tender pinions in the gloom begin to fail
I will catch thee to my bosom ere thou diest on the heath:

I will catch thee to my bosom–and if Henry's oaths are
true
A softer, sweeter grave thou wilt never find than there;
15   Nor is it, lovely Sea Wind, nor is it to undo
That my arms are so inviting, that my bosom is so fair.

82 Sonnet: To Harriet on her Birthday, August I 1812

Written at Lynmouth for Harriet S.'s seventeenth birthday–her first birthday since marriage.
Text from *Esd* f. 37ʳ (*Esd* No. 25: quoted by permission of the Carl H. Pforzheimer Library).
Published in *Dowden Life* i 286 (lines 9–12); *Esd Nbk* 88; *Esd Poems* 45; *SC* iv 976 (transcript of *Esd*).

O thou whose radiant eyes and beamy smile,
Yet even a sweeter somewhat indexing,
Have known full many an hour of mine to guile
Which else would only bitter memories bring,
5   O ever thus, thus! as on this natal day–
Though age's frost may blight those tender eyes,
Destroy that kindling cheek's transparent dyes,
And those luxuriant tresses change to grey–
Ever as now with Love and Virtue's glow
10   May thy unwithering soul not cease to burn,

¶ *81.13. oaths*] sworn praises.
15. undo] deceive.
¶ *82.2.* 'Indicating an even sweeter something' ('somewhat' is a subst.).
7–8. Peacock wrote to Harriet S., 'Her complexion was beautifully transparent; the tint of the blush rose shining through the lily' (*Peacock Works* viii 95); Hellen S. remembered her as 'a very handsome girl, with a complexion quite unknown in these days–brilliant in pink and white–with hair quite like a poet's dream, and Bysshe's peculiar admiration' (*Hogg* i 25).

Still may thine heart with those pure thoughts o'erflow
Which force from mine such quick and warm return,
And I must love thee even more than this
Nor doubt that Thou and I part but to meet in bliss.

83 The Devil's Walk:
A Ballad

An incomplete version of this poem had been drafted by winter 1811–12,
when S. sent 49 lines (BL Add.MS 37496 f. 80ᵛ) from Keswick to Elizabeth
Hitchener in a letter postmarked 20 January 1812 (see note to stanza 1), but it
was later revised and expanded as a broadsheet, probably in Barnstaple in July
or August. At the end of June the S.'s had moved to Lynmouth where S.
immediately began distributing propaganda. His landlady's niece, Mrs Mary
Blackmore, told Mathilde Blind in 1871 (Trinity College, Dublin, Dowden
Papers R.4.37):

> . . . he had a number of papers printed at Barnstaple, & when they came
> home he had me in to cut the printer's name off. . . He would then send his
> man, who was an Irishman called Daniel Healy, to Barnstaple with some
> of these papers to stick up about the town. The man was taken up
> afterwards & imprisoned for six months. The next day Mr S was sent for &
> on his arrival he asked the servant how he came to stick the papers up, &
> how he came by them; he said in his Irish accent, Sure & faith your honour
> I met the gentleman on the bridge, & he gave them me & told me to stick
> them up, & I thought it no harm. Mr S asked him how he came to be so
> foolish, & gave him one of the papers to read, & he held it upside down . . .
> This man was very fond of his master, & I have heard him say repeatedly
> that he would go through fire & water for him.

When Healy (who gave his name as Hill) was arrested on 19 August, copies of
The Devil's Walk were found in his possession, one of which was forwarded to
Lord Sidmouth and provides the present text. For details see *Mac-Carthy*
341–53; *Dowden Life* i 292–9; *Peck* i 269–74.

S.'s model was Coleridge/Southey's 'The Devil's Thoughts', published in
the *Morning Post* 6 September 1799 as a ballad of 14 stanzas, of which Coleridge
later ascribed stanzas 1–2 to Southey, and which Southey probably showed to
S. at Keswick. The original has the confusing textual history of a true ballad.
S.'s stanza 3 is closely imitated from the third stanza of the *Morning Post*
version, and many minor ingredients from the latter are also incorporated into
S.'s poem, e.g. the cormorant, the pig, and the 'General Conflagration' (see
notes below). But Southey seems to have shown S. a longer version, as S. also

13. must] 'am destined to'.

uses material first published (1830) in Southey's own version, including the title, the mention of London and of the Devil's Sunday clothes (see notes below). According to Southey (stanzas 37–9 of his 1838 published version), the original ballad was extemporized jointly by the two poets at Nether Stowey:

> There while the one was shaving
> Would he the song begin;
> And the other when he heard it at breakfast,
> In ready accord join in.

Thus Coleridge and Southey probably kept differing versions of the same improvisation, those they respectively published being selections from this material, so S. had access to material which may reflect the work of either poet.

S.'s poem lacks the deft satirical detail of the Coleridge/Southey ballad, but is more wholeheartedly subversive, openly attacking the oppression of Ireland, the Peninsular War, the King, the Regency, and Religion (where Coleridge's gibe is at Methodism only).

Text from Broadsheet in Public Record Office (H.O. 42/126).

Published by Shelley as broadsheet 1812; by W. M. Rossetti in *Fortnightly Review* xlix (1871) 67–85; *Forman 1876–7* iv 371–7 (broadsheet); *Letters from Percy Bysshe Shelley to Elizabeth Hitchener*, ed. T. J. Wise (1890) ii 26–30 (*Hitch. MS*).

> Once, early in the morning,
>   Beelzebub arose,
> With care his sweet person adorning,
> He put on his Sunday clothes.

¶ *83. Title.* The Coleridge/Southey ballad was first published under the present title in 1830 when it was attributed to Professor Porson, and this was also Southey's title. Coleridge called his version 'The Devil's Thoughts'. But the ballad was circulating as 'The Devil's Walk' much earlier than 1830, as Byron refers to it in his Journal for 17/18 December 1813 (*Byron L&J* iii 240).

Stanza 1. Cp. the opening of 'The Devil's Thoughts' (*Morning Post* 6 September 1799):

> From his brimstone bed at break of day,
>   A walking the Devil is gone,
> To look at his snug little farm the Earth,
>   And see how his stock went on.

The earlier version of S.'s poem (*Hitch. MS*) appears thus in the letter: 'Here follows a few stanzas which may amuse you. I was once rather fond of the Devil.

> The Devil went out a walking one day
>   Being tired of staying in Hell
> He dressed himself in his Sunday array
>   And the reason that he was drest so gay

5   Was to cunningly pry, whether under the sky
              The affairs of earth went well

           He poked his hot nose into corners so small
              One wd. think that the innocents there
           Poor creatures were just doing nothing at all
10   But settling some dress or arranging some ball
              – The Devil saw deeper there

           He peeped in each hole, to each chamber stole
              His promising live-stock to view
           Receiving applause, he just shews his claws
15   And Satan laughed in the mirth of his soul
           That they started with fright, from *his* ugly sight
              Whose works they delighted to do.

           A Parson with whom in the house of prayer
              The devil sate side by side
20   Bawled out that if the devil were [there]
           His presence he couldnt abide,
           Ha ha thought old Nick, thats a very stale trick
           For without the Devil, ô favorite of evil
           In thy carriage thou wouldst not ride

25   He saw the Devil [*for* a lawyer] a viper slay
              Under his brief-covered table
           It reminded the Devil marvellously
              Of the story of Cain and Abel

           Satan next saw a Brainless King
30   In a house as hot as his own
           Many imps he saw near there on the wing
           They flapped the black pennon & twirle[d] the sting
              Close to the very throne

           Ah! Ah cried Satan the pasture is good
35   My cattle will *here* thrive better than others
           They will have for their food, news of human blood
           They will drink the groans of the dying & dead
           And supperless never will go to bed
           Wch will make 'em as fat as their brothers.

40   The Devil was walking in the Park
              Dressed like a bond Street beau
           For tho his visage was rather dark
           And his mouth was wide his chin came out
           And something like Castlereagh was his snout
45   He might be calld so, so.

           Why does the Devil grin so wide
           & shew the Iron teeth within

 5 He drew on a boot to hide his hoof,
       He drew on a glove to hide his claw,
    His horns were concealed by *Bras Chapeau*,
    And the Devil went forth as natty a *Beau*
       As Bond Street ever saw.

10 He sate him down, in London town,
       Before earth's morning ray,
    With a favourite imp he began to chat
    On religion, and scandal, this and that,
       Until the dawn of day.

15 And then to St. James's court he went,
       And St. Paul's Church he took in his way,
    He was mighty thick with every Saint,
       Though they were formal and he was gay.

    The Devil was an agriculturist,
20   And as bad weeds quickly grow,
    In looking over his farm, I wist
       He wouldn't find cause for woe.

    He peeped in each hole, to each chamber stole,
       His promising livestock to view,
25 Grinning applause, he just showed them his claws,

       Nine & ninety on each side
          By the clearest reckoning–
Here the Poetry ends. the fact is he saw the Prince reviewing a regiment of
hussars–. Well is not this trifling a most teasing thing if you are not in a
laughing mood. But I can laugh or weep with you–'.
4. Cp. Coleridge, 'The Devil's Thoughts' (1828) 9–10: 'And how then was the
Devil drest? / Oh! he was in his Sunday best'. This stanza was not in *Morning
Post*, but appears also as stanza 3 in the version by Southey, to whom Coleridge
attributed it.
7. *by Bras*] by a *bras 1871*; by a *Bras 1972*. *Bras Chapeau*] A *chapeau bras* was 'A hat
made to fold, and carry beneath the arm, by beaux who feared to derange their
wigs' (H. A. Dillon, *Costume in England* (1896) ii 119). In S.'s day gentlemen
were refused admission to fashionable clubs and theatres without *chapeau bras*
(*Reminiscences and Recollections of Capt. Gronow 1810–1860* (1862–6; 1900 edn) i
32, 36).
10. Cp. Southey, 'The Devil's Walk' (1827, published 1838) 63: 'He walk'd
into London leisurely' (London is not mentioned in any of Coleridge's versions).
16 *in*] on *1871, 1972*.
19–22. Cp. 'The Devil's Thoughts' 3–4 above. Since writing *Hitch*. MS S. had
looked over a prospective farm of his own at Nantgwillt.
23–7. Cp. *Hitch*. MS 12–17 above.

And they shrunk with affright from his ugly sight
　　Whose works they delighted to do.

Satan poked his red nose into crannies so small
　　One would think that the innocents fair,
30　Poor lambkins! were just doing nothing at all
　　But settling some dress or arranging some ball,
　　　But the Devil saw deeper there.

A Priest, at whose elbow the Devil during prayer
　　Sate familiarly, side by side,
35　Declared, that if the tempter were there,
　　His presence he would not abide;
　Ah! Ah! thought Old Nick, that's a very stale trick,
For without the Devil, O! favourite of evil,
　　In your carriage you would not ride.

40　Satan next saw a brainless King,
　　　Whose house was as hot as his own,
Many imps in attendance were there on the wing,
They flapped the pennon and twirled the sting,
　　Close by the very Throne.

45　Ah, ha! thought Satan, the pasture is good,
　　My Cattle will here thrive better than others,
They dine on news of human blood,
　　They sup on the groans of the dying and dead,
　　And supperless never will go to bed;
50　Which will make them as fat as their brothers.

Fat as the fiends that feed on blood,
　　Fresh and warm from the fields of Spain,
　　　Where ruin ploughs her gory way
When the shoots of earth are nipped in the bud,

26–7. i.e. they shrank from him whom they nevertheless willingly served.
27. works] work 1871, 1972.
28–32. Cp. Hitch. MS 7–11 above.
33–9. Cp. Hitch. MS 18–24 above.
40. a brainless King] George III had been insane since November 1811.
40–4. Cp. Hitch. MS 29–33 above.
43. pennon] wing (as of Milton's Satan, PL ii 933: 'Fluttring his pennons vain
plumb down he drops'). twirled] Hitch. MS; twisted Broadsheet (a probable
misreading of S.'s hand: see line 112). Cp. Southey's 'The Devil's Walk' 46–7:
'And Satan gave thereat his tail / A twirl of admiration'.
45–50. Cp. Hitch. MS 34–9 above.
54. When] Where 1871, 1972.

55   Where Hell is the Victor's prey,
        Its glory the meed of the slain.

Fat—as the death-birds on Erin's shore,
That glutted themselves in her dearest gore,
        And flitted round Castlereagh,
60   When they snatched the Patriot's heart, that *his* grasp
     Had torn from its widow's maniac clasp,
        And fled at the dawn of day.

Fat—as the reptiles of the tomb,
        That riot in corruption's spoil,
65   That fret their little hour in gloom,
     And creep, and live the while.

Fat as that Prince's maudlin brain,
        Which addled by some gilded toy,
     Tired, gives his sweetmeat, and again
70   Cries for it, like a humoured boy.

For he is fat, his waistcoat gay,
     When strained upon a levee day,
        Scarce meets across his princely paunch,

55–6. These lines on Spain are not in *Hitch. MS*. S. may have had in mind the
capture of Badajos on 6 April 1812, where Wellington 'lost 5,000 men under a
downpour of masonry, steel, lead and fire' and where, after the victory, his
troops 'burst out from the discipline of their icy commander into a carnival of
greed and lust' (*Oxford History of England* xii (1960) 493).

59. *Castlereagh*] Viscount Castlereagh (1769–1822) was foreign secretary 1812–
22; see *The Mask of Anarchy*, headnote and 6*n*.

60. *the Patriot's heart*] Robert Emmet's. See note to 'The Tombs' (No. 71).

61. *its widow's*] Presumably Sarah Curran's, who was not, however, as devoted
to Emmet as legend pretended; nor was she his wife.

65. Cp. *Macbeth* V v 24–5: 'Life's but a walking shadow, a poor player / That
struts and frets his hour upon the stage'.

67. *that Prince's maudlin brain*] The vacillating Prince of Wales had let it appear he
would give places to his Whig favourites after acquiring full powers of Regency on 18 February 1812, but then took advantage of a false report of the King's
recovery to reverse his intentions and confirm the Tories in office (*Oxford
History of England* xii 490–2). S. laments this 'Unforeseen conduct of the
Regent of England' at the conclusion of his *Proposals for an Association of
Philanthropists* (published 2 March 1812).

71. *For he is fat*] Leigh Hunt's prose attack on the Prince Regent for which he
was later imprisoned, and which included the description 'a corpulent gentleman of fifty', had been published in *The Examiner* 22 March 1812.

And pantaloons are like half moons,
75　　Upon each brawny haunch.

How vast his stock of calf! when plenty
　　Had filled his empty head and heart,
Enough to satiate foplings twenty
　　Could make his pantaloon seams start.

80　The Devil (who sometimes is called nature)
　　For men of power provides thus well,
Whilst every change, and every feature,
　　Their great original can tell.

Satan saw a lawyer a viper slay,
85　　That crawled up the leg of his table,
It reminded him most marvellously
　　Of the story of Cain and Abel.

The wealthy yeoman, as he wanders
　　His fertile fields among,
90　And on his thriving cattle ponders,
　　Counts his sure gains, and hums a song;
Thus did the Devil, through earth walking,
　　Hum low a hellish song.

For they thrive well, whose garb of gore
95　　Is Satan's choicest livery,
And they thrive well, who from the poor
　　Have snatched the bread of penury,
And heap the houseless wanderer's store
　　On the rank pile of luxury.

100　The Bishops thrive, though they are big,
　　The Lawyers thrive, though they are thin;
For every gown, and every wig,
　　Hides the safe thrift of Hell within.

Thus pigs were never counted clean,
105　　Although they dine on finest corn;
And cormorants are sin-like lean,
　　Although they eat from night to morn.

84–7. Cp. *Hitch.* MS 25–8 above. Both versions derive from 'The Devil's Thoughts' (1799) 9–12:

　　　He saw a Lawyer killing a viper
　　　　On a dunghill beside his stable;
　　　'Oh–oh,' quoth he, for it put him in mind
　　　　Of the story of Cain and Abel.

104–6. *pigs . . . cormorants*] Both creatures featured in 'The Devil's Thoughts' (1799): the swimming pig cutting its own throat (Victory crippling itself with

Oh! why is the Father of Hell in such glee,
　　As he grins from ear to ear?
110　Why does he doff his clothes joyfully,
　　As he skips, and prances, and flaps his wing,
　　As he sidles, leers, and twirls his sting,
　　And dares, as he is, to appear?

A Statesman passed—alone to him
115　The Devil dare his whole shape uncover,
To show each feature, every limb,
　　Secure of an unchanging lover.

At this known sign, a welcome sight,
　　The watchful demons sought their King,
120　And every fiend of the Stygian night
　　Was in an instant on the wing.

Pale Loyalty, his guilt-steeled brow
　　With wreaths of gory laurel crowned:
The hell-hounds, Murder, Want and Woe,
125　For ever hungering flocked around;
From Spain had Satan sought their food,
'Twas human woe and human blood!

Hark, the earthquake's crash I hear,
　　Kings turn pale, and Conquerors start,
130　Ruffians tremble in their fear,
　　For their Satan doth depart.

This day fiends give to revelry,
　　To celebrate their King's return,
And with delight its sire to see,
135　Hell's adamantine limits burn.

But were the Devil's sight as keen
　　As Reason's penetrating eye,
His sulphurous Majesty I ween
　　Would find but little cause for joy.

140　For the sons of Reason see
　　That ere fate consume the Pole,
The false Tyrant's cheek shall be
　　Bloodless as his coward soul.

Taxation) in lines 37–40; and Milton's image of Satan sitting 'like a Cormorant' (*PL* iv 196) in lines 19–20.
120. the Stygian] thy Stygian *Broadsheet.*
135. burn] i.e. with bonfires of welcome.
141. ere fate consume the Pole] A faint echo of the conclusion of 'The Devil's
Thoughts' (1799) 53–7, where the Devil mistakes an unnamed General's red
face for 'General Conflagration'.

84 Sonnet: On Launching some Bottles filled with *Knowledge* into the Bristol Channel

Written at Lynmouth, mid-August 1812, a period when S. was distributing propaganda, including his prose *Declaration of Rights* and *The Devil's Walk* (No. 83), by all available means. As the niece of S.'s landlady recalled to Mathilde Blind sixty years later, S. 'had a number of papers printed at Barnstaple, & when they came home he had me in to cut the printer's name off. He would then put them into small boxes & bottles & cork up the latter & put them off to sea . . . Some ladies were lodging at the place at the time, & they used to watch him put the bottles out to sea, & wrote to a friend of theirs in Barnstaple who was a lawyer. Some bottles were picked up, & that is how it came to be found out. – ' (Dowden papers, Trinity College Dublin, MS. R.4.37). Henry Drake, Town Clerk at Barnstaple, informed Lord Sidmouth on 20 August that 'Mr. Shelley has been seen frequently to go out in a Boat a short distance from Land and drop some Bottles into the Sea, and that at one time he was observed to wade into the Water and drop a Bottle which afterwards drifting ashore was picked up, and on being broken was found to contain a seditious paper, the Contents of which the Mayor has not yet been able to ascertain' (*Peck* i 271). The paper was *The Devil's Walk* (*Fortnightly Review* xlix (1871) 78), and a copy of *Declaration of Rights* was also later picked up by a Revenue Officer 'in a Sealed Wine Bottle, floating near the Entrance of Milford Haven on 10th' September (*Hughes* 156). The officer thought these papers were aimed at 'the Sea-faring part of the People, many hundreds of which may thus reach that Class and do incalculable mischief among them' (ibid.). The Home Office was sufficiently disturbed to put S. under surveillance, but he was soon alarmed into leaving Devon for Wales, perhaps on 27 August (*Esd Nbk* 224), more probably on 30 (see headnote to No. 88). The facts were first revealed by W. M. Rossetti in *Fortnightly Review* xlix (1871) 67–85; see also *Peck* i 269–74 and *White* i 248–52.

Text from *Esd* f. 38ʳ (*Esd* No. 27: quoted by permission of the Carl H. Pforzheimer Library).

Published in *Dowden Life* i 294; *Esd Nbk* 90; *Esd Poems* 46–7; *SC* iv 977 (transcript of *Esd*).

> Vessels of Heavenly medicine! may the breeze
> Auspicious waft your dark green forms to shore;

¶ *84. Title. Knowledge*] political enlightenment.

. *1. Vessels*] A pun: phials + boats. Some of S.'s containers were actually rigged with sails (*Peck* i 273).

2. dark green forms] Bottle-glass in 1812 was normally dark green or amber (the 'emerald group' of line 7 refers to the cluster of bottles, not to Ireland).

Safe may ye stem the wide surrounding roar
Of the wild whirlwinds and the raging seas:
5 And oh! if Liberty e'er deigned to stoop
From yonder lowly throne her crownless brow
Sure she will breathe around your emerald group
The fairest breezes of her west that blow.
Yes! she will waft ye to some freeborn soul
10 Whose eyebeam, kindling as it meets your freight,
Her heaven-born flame on suffering Earth will light
Until its radiance gleams from pole to pole,
And tyrant-hearts with powerless envy burst
To see their night of ignorance dispersed.

85 Sonnet: To a Balloon, Laden with *Knowledge*

See headnote to No. 84. Written at Lynmouth in August 1812, a period when S. was distributing propaganda, including his prose *Declaration of Rights* and *The Devil's Walk* (No. 83), by all available means. In the fifth of the lectures given by the peripatetic science lecturer Adam Walker at Syon House Academy and at Eton (*White* i 22–4, 40), S. had received instructions for making the type of hot-air balloon introduced by the Montgolfier brothers in 1782, using a paper bag and a sponge soaked in spirits (A. Walker, *A System of Familiar Philosophy* (1799) 241). John Moultrie, who entered Eton just after S. had left, records his launching of such balloons, among traditions of his school exploits:

> oft at eve the fire-balloon,
> Inflated by his skill, would mount on high

(*Gray's Poetical Works, English and Latin, Illustrated: with introductory Stanzas by the Rev. John Moultrie*, etc., 1853 (4th ed.), 11). Richard Holmes comments (*Holmes* 150): 'In this poem, every image is shot through by the presence of flame, and the fire-balloon itself becomes a metaphor of the life of the revolu-

3. *stem*] stern *Esd Nbk*, SC (Cameron explains *stern* as meaning to 'steer through'–an improbable archaism, though the word in *Esd* resembles *stern*).
8. *fairest breezes of her west*] '. . . why did [S.] call for westerly breezes instead of easterly ones?' (Robert Graves, *Mammon and the Black Goddess* (1965) 82). Because crownless Liberty's throne was in America, not St James's Palace. *blow.*] blow, *Esd*, *Esd Poems*.
10–12. i.e. 'his eye, kindled to fire by the message you carry, will spread the flame of Liberty over the whole earth'.

tionary or philanthropist, whose body is burnt away and destroyed, but whose message survives and kindles those around'.

Text from *Esd* f. 37ᵛ (*Esd* No. 26: quoted by permission of the Carl H. Pforzheimer Library).

Published in *Dowden Life* i 294; *Esd Nbk* 89; *Esd Poems* 45–6; *SC* iv 976–7 (transcript of *Esd*).

> Bright ball of flame that through the gloom of even
> Silently takest thine etherial way
> And with surpassing glory dimm'st each ray
> Twinkling amid the dark blue depths of Heaven,
> 5 Unlike the Fire thou bearest, soon shalt thou
> Fade like a meteor in surrounding gloom,
> Whilst that, unquenchable, is doomed to glow
> A watch-light by the patriot's lonely tomb,
> A ray of courage to the oppressed and poor,
> 10 A spark, though gleaming in the hovel's hearth,
> Which through the tyrant's gilded domes shall roar,
> A beacon in the darkness of the Earth,
> A Sun which o'er the renovated scene
> Shall dart like Truth where Falsehood yet has been.

86 A Retrospect of Times of Old

Date of composition unknown; possibly prompted by S.'s reading of Peacock's *Palmyra* (1806), the 2nd edn of which (1812) S. acknowledged 18 August 1812, calling it 'far beyond mediocrity in genius & versification' and its conclusion 'the finest piece of poetry I ever read' (*L* i 325). Verbal links are slight, however, and many other sources were available to describe the downfall of temporal power, including Volney's *Ruins*, Robert Wood's *The Ruins of Palmyra* (1753), Kirke White's 'Time', Blair's *Grave*. S.'s poem is distinctive in its emphasis on the destruction of earthly rulers rather than on Time the universal destroyer, and in assuming the relativity of all religions ('New gods . . . changing in ceaseless flow, / Ever at hand as ancient ones decay'). It may be a by-product of S.'s work on *Q Mab* begun some four months earlier (*L* i 324), as it covers broadly similar ground to *Q Mab* iii 131–213; iv 227–65; ix 23–37. Text from *Esd* ff. 40ᵛ–43ʳ (*Esd* No. 31: quoted by permission of the Carl H. Pforzheimer Library).

Published in *Rogers* 28 (lines 1–4, 71–83); *Esd Nbk* 95–7; *Esd Poems* 50–3; *SC* iv 981–5 (transcript of *Esd*).

¶ *85. Title.* Knowledge] political enlightenment.
5. the Fire thou bearest] The cargo of 'knowledge'. *shalt*] shall *Esd Nbk* (a possibly correct reading).
7. doomed] destined.
14. yet] as yet.

The mansions of the Kings are tenantless . . .
Low lie in dust their glory and their shame.
No tongue survives their virtuous deeds to bless;
No tongue with execration blasts their fame;
5   But on some ruined pile, where yet the gold
Casts purple brilliance o'er colossal snow,
Where sapphire eyes in breathing statues glow,
And the tainted blast sighs mid the reeds below
Where grim effigies of the Gods of old
10 In mockery stand of ever-changing men
(Their ever-changing worship, ah how vain!
Yet baubles aye must please the multitude),
There Desolation dwells! – Where are the Kings,
Why sleep they now if sleep be not eternal?
15 Cannot Oblivion's silent tauntings call
The kings and heroes from their quietude
Of Death, to snatch the scrolls from her palsying hand
To tell the world how mighty once they were? –
They dare not wake . . . thy Victory is here,
20 O Death! – Yet I hear unearthly voices cry
'Death, thou'lt be swallowed up in Victory!'

Yes, Dream of fame! the halls are desolate
Where whitened skeletons of thine heroes lie . . .
Stillness keeps watch before each grass-grown gate,

¶ 86.1. Cp. Q Mab iii 134–6: 'the gorgeous throne / Shall stand unnoticed in the regal hall, / Fast falling to decay'; PU III iv 131: 'And behold, thrones were kingless'.

5. on] in Esd Nbk.   where yet the gold] 'Gilding yet remains on the cornices of the ruined palace of Persepolis–' [S.'s note].

6. purple] bright red (Lat. purpureus).   colossal snow] huge white edifices. Many travellers were struck by the whiteness of the Palmyra ruins, e.g. James Bruce, Travels, Between the Years 1768 and 1773 . . . to discover the source of the Nile (1805) 38: '. . . these magnificent remains of antiquity . . . all composed of white stones, which at a distance appeared like marble'.

8. the tainted blast] The Simoon of line 25: a hot desert wind, reputedly poisonous (see Southey, Thalaba (1801) II xi 5–9; Bruce, Travels (1805) 380, 416). Erasmus Darwin calls the Simoon 'tainted air' (Botanic Garden Pt I, iv 67).

11–12. Only line 12 is bracketed in Esd, but both lines are parenthetical.

13–14. Sardonically recalling I Corinthians xv 12–29, on the resurrection of the dead.

17. Unmetrical and unrhymed; perhaps an inadvertent telescoping of two lines.

19–21. Quoting I Corinthians xv 54: 'So when this corruptible shall have put on incorruption . . . then shall be brought to pass the saying that is written, Death is swallowed up in victory'.

25 Save where amid thy towers the Simoon's sigh
    Wakes the lone lyre whose mistress sleeps below,
    And bids it thrill to notes of awfulness and woe.

    Here, ages since, some Royal Bloodhound crept,
    When on these pillared piles a midnight lay
30 Which but from visioned memories long has fled,
    To work ambition whilst his brother slept,
    And reckless of the peaceful smile that played
    Around his dream-fraught features when, betrayed,
    They told each innocent secret of the day,
35 Wakened the thoughtless victim, bade him stare
    Upon the murderous steel . . . the chaste pale glare
    Of the midnight moonbeam kissed its glittering blade
    A moment! and its brightness quenched in blood
    Distained with murder the moon's silver flood.
40 The blushing moon wide-gathering vapours shrouded.
    One moment did he triumph; – but remorse,
    Suspicion, anguish, fear, all triumph clouded;
    Destruction . . . suicide . . . his last resource . . .
    Wide yawned the torrent. The moon's stormy flash
45 Disclosed its black tumultuousness . . . the crash

26. *the lone lyre*] Evidently visualized as a type of Aeolian Harp, perhaps
suggested by the statue of Memnon, whose lyre produced music at sunrise (see
Erasmus Darwin, *Botanic Garden* Pt I, Addn.n. viii). Cp. No. 7, 260n.
28. *Here*] There *Esd Nbk*.   *some Royal Bloodhound*] See S.'s note to line 47
below. Cameron observes (*Esd Nbk* 228) that S.'s example 'seems generally
similar to the story of Cambyses', the deranged Persian king who out of
jealousy had his brother Smerdis murdered only to realize before his own death
that it was to no purpose (Herodotus, *History* iii 28–68); and many other
stories, true or fictional, could have supplied particular details, e.g. the
murderer's 'remorse, suspicion, anguish, fear' from Caracalla's murder of
Geta in A.D. 212 (Gibbon, *Decline and Fall of the Roman Empire* (1776–88; 1897
edn) i 132–3), the sleep of the victim from *Hamlet* (I v 74–5), etc.
38. *Esd Poems* adds commas after *and* and *blood*, a parenthesis which makes the
glare of the moon itself distain the moonlight. The subject is *brightness* ('its
brightness, reddened with blood, stained . . .'). S.'s source is the massacre of
the thousand archers in Southey's *Curse of Kehama* VIII xi: 'Ten thousand
scymitars at once uprear'd, / Flash up, like waters sparkling to the sun; / A
second time the fatal brands appear'd / Lifted aloft, . . . they glitter'd then no
more, / Their light was gone, their splendour quench'd in gore.'
44. *Wide*] Wider *Esd Nbk*.

Of rocks and boughs mixed with its roarings hoarse
A moment! and he dies: hark to the awful dash!

Such were thy works, Ambition, even amid
The darksome times of generations gone
50 Which the dark veil of viewless hours has hid,
The veil of hours forever onward flown.
Swift roll the waves of Time's eternal tide,
The peasant's grave marked by no tribute stone
Not less remembered than the gilded bed
55 On which the hero slept! now ever gone
Passion, and will and power, flesh, heart, and brain, and
bone.

Each trophied bust where gore-emblazoned Victory
In breathing marble shook the ensanguined spear,
Flinging its heavy purple canopy
60 In cold expanse o'er martyred Freedom's bier—
Each gorgeous altar where the victims bled
And grim Gods frowned above their human prey,
Where the high temple echoed to the yell
Of death pangs, to the long and shuddering groan,
65 Whilst sacred hymns along the aisles did swell
And pitiless priests drowned each discordant moan—
All, all have faded in past time away,
New Gods, like men changing in ceaseless flow,
Ever at hand as ancient ones decay;
70 Heroes, and Kings, and laws have plunged the world in
woe.

---

47. 'I believe it was only in those early times when Monarchy was in its
apprenticeship that its compunction for evil deeds was unendurable . . . There
is no instance upon record parallel to that related above, but I know that neither
men nor sets of men become vicious but slowly & step by step, each less
difficult than the former' [S.'s note, unkeyed but evidently relating to this
line].
63. echoed] echoing Esd, edd. A main vb. is indispensable; perhaps the participle
was due to shuddering (64).
67. Cp. Q Mab viii 44–6: 'The present now is past, / And those events that
desolate the earth / Have faded from the memory of Time'.
68.   New Gods like men, changing in ceaseless flow Esd
           New Gods, like men, changing in ceaseless flow, Esd Nbk
70. the world] this world Esd Nbk.

Sesostris, Caesar, and Pizarro, come!
Thou, Moses! and Mahommed, leave that gloom;
Destroyers! never shall your memory die.
Approach, pale Phantom, to yon mouldering tomb
75 Where all thy bones, hopes, crimes and passions lie;
And thou, poor peasant, when thou pass't the grave
Where deep enthroned in monumental pride
Sleep low in dust the mighty and the brave,
Where the mad conqueror, whose gigantic stride
80 The Earth was too confined for, doth abide
Housing his bones amid a little clay,
In gratitude to Nature's Spirit bend
And wait in still hope for thy better end.

87 To Harriet

Date of composition very possibly end of August 1812. Cameron notes (*Esd Nbk* 224–5) that in *Esd* it is grouped with poems of the Lynmouth period and that 'the final stanza could refer most appropriately to Shelley's anti-government activities in Devon'. Cameron further notes the 'discord' implicit in it, attributing this to friction with Harriet's sister Eliza. The discord, however, points not inward to the household but towards the world outside, for whose evil and pain Harriet's love is felt to compensate. S.'s determination to sustain his country's cause at the cost of personal sacrifice (28–9), and the feeling of insecurity on Harriet's part as well as his (9–10, 20), suggest an affirmation of mutual love under the threat of political persecution following Daniel Healey's arrest on 19 August. The 'adieu to all vice and care' of line 17,

71. *Sesostris*] Semi-legendary Egyptian king and world-conqueror. *Pizarro*] Francisco Pizarro (1478–1541), Spanish conqueror of Peru and destroyer of the Inca empire: 'A mighty realm / He overran, and with relentless arm / Slew or enslaved its unoffending sons' (Southey, 'Inscription XIII', 1796).
72. *Mahommed*] 'To this innumerable list of legal murderers our own age affords numerous addenda. Frederic of Prussia, Buonaparte, Suwarroff, Wellington & Nelson are the most skilful & notorious scourges of their species of the present day–' [S.'s note]. Alexander Suvorov (d. 1800) had suppressed the Polish rising of 1792 and fought the Revolutionary armies in Italy in 1799.
73. *Destroyers!*] S. is thinking of acts such as Moses' slaughter and enslavement of the Midianites (*Numbers* xxxi 1–18), and Mohammed's establishment of Islam by military conquest. Cp. his account of human 'scourges' in *The Triumph of Life* 208–95.
74. *mouldering*] mouldring *Esd*.
76. *pass't*] *Esd*, *Esd Nbk*; pass'st *Esd Poems*.

and the lines immediately following, may foreshadow their flight to Wales on
or about 29 August.

   The metre is one used several times by Moore in his *Irish Melodies*, e.g. in
'Oh, blame not the bard' (3rd ser., 1810).

Text from *Esd* f. 39^{r-v} (*Esd* No. 29: quoted by permission of the Carl H.
Pforzheimer Library).

Published in *Esd Nbk* 92–3; *Esd Poems* 48–9; *SC* iv 979–80 (transcript of *Esd*).

> Harriet! thy kiss to my soul is dear,
>   At evil or pain I would never repine
> If to every sigh and to every tear
>   Were added a look and a kiss of thine:
> 5 Nor is it the look when it glances fire,
>   Nor the kiss when bathed in the dew of delight,
> Nor the throb of the heart when it pants desire
>   From the shadows of eve to the morning light,
>
> But the look when a lustre of joy-mingled woe
> 10   Has faintly obscured all its bliss-beaming Heaven,
> Such a lovely, benign and enrapturing glow
>   As sunset can paint on the clouds of even,
> And a kiss, which the languish of silent love,
>   Though eloquent, faints with the toil of expressing,
> 15 Yet so light that thou canst not refuse, my dove!
>   To add this one to the debt of caressing.
>
> Harriet! adieu to all vice and care,–
>   Thy love is my Heaven, thy arms are my world;
> While thy kiss and thy look to my soul remain dear
> 20   I should smile though Earth from its base be hurled.
> For a heart as pure and a mind as free
>   As ever gave lover, to thee I give,
> And all that I ask in return from thee
>   Is to love like me, and with me to live.
>
> 25 This heart that beats for thy love and bliss,
>   Harriet! beats for its country too,
> And it never would thrill with thy look or kiss
>   If it dared to that country's cause be untrue.
> Honour, and wealth and life it spurns,
> 30   But thy love is a prize it is sure to gain,
> And the heart that with love and virtue burns
>   Will never repine at evil or pain.

88 Sonnet: On Waiting for a Wind to Cross the Bristol Channel from Devonshire to Wales

Written at Lynmouth or Ilfracombe in late August (probably 29 or 30) 1812. When Godwin arrived in Lynmouth to visit S. he wrote on 19 September: 'The Shelleys are gone! have been gone these three weeks . . . They lived here nine weeks and three days' (C. Kegan Paul, *William Godwin, his Friends and Contemporaries* (1876) ii 211–12). 'Three weeks' taken literally would mean the S.'s left on 29–30 August. 'Nine weeks and three days' is precise, but the date of S.'s arrival in Lynmouth is not known. His last letter from Cwm Elan is dated 18 June (*L* i 308), and Harriet S.'s first letter from Lynmouth ('Now that we are again settled') is dated 30 June (*L* i 309). 27 June is thus a very reasonable assumption for their arrival. The Barnstaple Town Clerk, who went to Lynmouth to inquire into S.'s activities and returned on 7 September, 'found he, with his family, after attempting in vain to cross the Channel to Swansea from that place, had lately left Lynmouth for Ilfracombe' (*Fortnightly Review* xlix (1871) 78). High winds were recorded at Bristol for 19 through 23 August, and again for 29–30 August (*GM* lxxxii (September 1812) Part II, 202), blowing from north or north-east (*Philosophical Transactions* (1813), Met. Jnl. p. 17). The likelihood is, therefore, that S. tried to hire a boat to cross the Bristol Channel from Lynmouth on 29 August, was foiled by northerly gales and wrote this sonnet, then travelled to Ilfracombe to catch the regular packet-boat to Swansea on Monday 31 August (Paterson, *A New & Accurate Description of all the Direct & Principal Cross Roads in England and Wales* (15th edn 1811) 64). Cameron (*Esd Nbk* 224) dates the sonnet between 24 and 27 August, but takes no account of the weather.

Text from *Esd* f. 38ᵛ (*Esd* No. 28: quoted by permission of the Carl H. Pforzheimer Library).

Published in *Dowden Life* i 298–9 (lines 5–8, 9–10); *Esd Nbk* 91; *Esd Poems* 47; *SC* iv 978 (transcript of *Esd*).

> Oh! for the South's benign and balmy breeze!
> Come, gentle Spirit! through the wide Heaven sweep,
> Chase inauspicious Boreas from the seas,
> That gloomy tyrant of the unwilling deep.
> 5   These wilds where Man's profane and tainting hand
> Nature's primeval loveliness has marred
> And some few souls of the high bliss debarred
> Which else obey her powerful command,

¶ *88.3. Boreas*] The north wind.
5–8. i.e. political persecution has made the enjoyment of Nature impossible for the S. household and their intended guests the Godwins, who habitually

I leave without a sigh. Ye mountain piles
10   That load in grandeur Cambria's emerald vales,
Whose sides are fair in cultivation's smiles,
Around whose jagged heads the storm cloud sails,
A heart that's all thine own receive in me
With Nature's fervour fraught and calm in purity.

89 The Voyage. A Fragment . . . Devonshire–August 1812

Dated as above in *Esd*, and probably written during or immediately after S.'s passage from Ilfracombe to Swansea in the regular packet-boat on 31 August 1812 (see headnote to No. 88). The disjointed structure and diffuse style suggest that its composition might have occupied S. during the actual 30-mile crossing. However, as Cameron assumes in his full account of the poem (*Esd Nbk* 229–35), the occasion was probably a composite one. S.'s title was altered from an earlier 'The Journey', which could imply that at one stage the poem had contained some description of overland as well as oversea travel. His 'voyages' had so far consisted in: (a) a crossing from Whitehaven to Dublin via the Isle of Man, February 1812, which took several days through his being 'driven by a storm quite to the North of Ireland' (*L* i 250); (b) the return crossing Dublin–Holyhead (again a long one) in April, followed by ten days' journey through Wales, including a coastal voyage 'from Barmouth to Aberystwyth 30 miles in an open boat' (*L* i 281); (c) the crossing of the Bristol Channel, 31 August, followed by a journey through the length of Wales to Tremadoc in September. Any or all of these could have contributed details: thus the description of the storm (lines 74–111) in an 'arctic clime' (88) may draw on S.'s experiences 'to the North of Ireland'.

A main interest of the poem (again imitated in its formal features from Southey's *Thalaba* and *Kehama*) lies in its projection of the situation which had driven S. from Lynmouth and in its curious rehearsal of the physical attack which was soon to drive him from Tanyrallt. Cameron (op. cit.) identifies the two sailors (70–95), the landsman (114), and the 'idealist' (149–50), as the four passengers of a boat crewed by the sailor who whistles (64). A more natural reading seems to be that the packet-boat crew is made up of the two sailors, one

---

acknowledge only Nature's laws. Cp. Peacock, 'The Genius of the Thames' (1810) xxi 1–11: 'For what avails the myrtle-bower . . . / Fit dwelling for primeval love; / If man defile the beauteous scene'. S. had just read, on 17 August, two vols. of Peacock's poems including the 2nd edn of 'The Genius of the Thames' sent him by Hookham (*L* i 324–5).

10. *Cambria*] Wales: the Latinized version of *cymry*, 'Welshmen'.

14. *fraught . . . purity*] Both words uncertain in *Esd*; the last perhaps *piety*.

of whom whistles for a wind, and that the storm described belongs to their seafaring past, while there are four other souls as passengers: the landsman, the 'idealist', and the persons individualized in the idealist's dream, namely 'She whom he loved' (198) and 'A bleeding Sister' (210). These four correspond to the Government agent whose attentions had caused S.'s flight, S. himself, Harriet S., and Harriet's sister Eliza, the last three of whom (plus Elizabeth Hitchener) comprise 'The young and happy spirits' of line 40. Thus the dreamer's struggle with the landsman enacts S.'s unavailing contest with a sinister and all-powerful Establishment. A strong case has been made for the reality of the assassination-attempt on S. at Tanyrallt on 26 February 1813 (H. M. Dowling, 'The Attack at Tanyrallt', *KSMB* xii (1961) 28–36; *Holmes* 184–98), yet some features of it seem foreshadowed in the details of this dream: e.g. the Tanyrallt assailant's 'By God I will be revenged! I will murder your wife. I will ravish your sister' (Harriet S. to Hookham, 12 March 1813, *L* i 355) resembles line 190: 'His smile of dastardly revenge' and lines 210–11: 'A bleeding Sister lay / Beside this wretched pair'. Even the effect of the assailant's kneeling on S. during their struggle (Thornton Hunt, 'Shelley, by One who Knew Him', *Atlantic Monthly* xi (February 1863) 185–6) is anticipated by the rock piled on the dreamer's breast (lines 178, 182–3). That the attack predates the poem – or a revision of the poem – is most unlikely.

Text from *Esd* ff. 43ʳ–50ᵛ (*Esd* No. 32: quoted by permission of the Carl H. Pforzheimer Library).

Published in *Rogers* 91–2 (lines 40–62), 29 (lines 102–11 and note, 120–8); *Esd Nbk* 98–107; *Esd Poems* 53–62; *SC* iv 985–96 (transcript of *Esd*).

> Quenched is old Ocean's rage;
> Each horrent wave that flung
> Its neck that writhed beneath the tempest's scourge
> Indignant up to Heaven,
> 5 Now breathes in its sweet slumber
> To mingle with the day
> A spirit of tranquillity.
> Beneath the cloudless sun
> The gently swelling main
> 10 Scatters a thousand colourings,
> And the wind that wanders vaguely through the void,
> With the flapping of the sail, and the dashing at the
>   prow
> And the whistle of the sailor in that shadow of a calm
> A ravishing harmony makes.

¶ *89. Title.* Cancellations in *Esd* show that S. hesitated over calling the poem 'The Journey'.

2. horrent] puissant *Esd Nbk*. 'Bristling'; app. coined by Milton (*PL* ii 513) from Lat. *horreo*.

2–4. Cp. *Alastor* 323–5: 'The waves arose. Higher and higher still / Their fierce necks writhed beneath the tempest's scourge / Like serpents struggling in a vulture's grasp'.

15 O! why is a rapt soul e'er recalled
        From the palaces of visioned bliss
        To the cells of real sorrow!

    That little vessel's company
    Beheld the sight of loveliness:
20 The dark grey rocks that towered
        Above the slumbering sea,
        And their reflected forms
    Deep in its faintly-waving mirror given;
        They heard the low breeze sighing
25   The listless sails and ropes among,
    They heard the music at the prow,
    And the hoarse, distant clash
    Sent from yon gloomy caves
    Where Earth and Ocean strive for mastery.

30 A mingled mass of feeling
        Those human spirits pressed
    As they heard, and saw, and felt
    Some fancied fear, and some real woe
    Mixed with those glimpses of heavenly joy
35   That dawned on each passive soul.
    Where is the woe that never sees
    One joybeam illumine the night of the mind?
        Where is the bliss that never feels
    One dart from the quiver of earthly pain?

40 The young and happy spirits now
        Along the world are voyaging:
    Love, friendship, virtue, truth,
    Simplicity of sentiment and speech,
        And other sensibilities
45 Known by no outward name,
    Some faults that Love forgives,
    Some flaws that Friendship shares,
        Hearts passionate and benevolent,
        Alive, and urgent to repair
50 The errors of their brother heads—
        All voyage with them too.

27–9. In a letter from Lynmouth 5 July 1812 S. described 'the sea, which dashes
against a rocky & caverned shore' (L i 312).
40. *The young and happy spirits*] For Cameron (*Esd Nbk* 230) this 'is a general
reference to people on the voyage of life'. It must, however, refer to the
passengers primarily, as 'They look to land . . . they look to Sea' (52). The]
Tho' *Esd Nbk*.
50. *heads—*] heads; *Esd*.

They look to land . . . they look to Sea:
Bounded one is, and palpable
Even as a noonday scene . . .
55 The other indistinct and dim,
Spangled with dizzying sunbeams,
Boundless, untrod by human step,
Like the vague blisses of a midnight dream
Or Death's immeasurable main
60 Whose lovely islands gleam at intervals
Upon the Spirit's visioned solitude
Through Earth's wide-woven and many-coloured veil.

It is a moveless calm.
The sailor's whistle shrill
65 Speeds clearly through the sleeping atmosphere, –
As country curates pray for rain
When drought has frustrated full long
He whistles for a wind
With just the same success.
70 Two honest souls were they
And oft had braved in fellowship the storm,
Till from that fellowship had sprung
A sense of right and liberty.
Unbending, undismayed, aye they had seen
75 Where danger, death and terror played
With human lives in the boiling deep,
And they had seen the scattered spray
Of the green and jagged mountain-wave,
Hid in the lurid tempest-cloud
80 With lightnings tinging all its fleeting form,

51–2. No paragraph-break in *Esd Poems*.
62. The first occurence of S.'s 'painted veil' image. The land represents temporal reality, the sea eternity glimpsed through the veil of the material present. The 'lovely islands' derive from those of Elysium in the river Oceanus, the abode of the favoured dead in classical myth.
73–4.   liberty
                Unbending undismayed, aye they had seen *Esd*
                       liberty
                Unbending undismayed, –aye they had seen *Esd Poems*
77–81. No punct. before the period in *Esd*; *Esd Nbk* has commas after *tempest-cloud* and *form* only. But as the wave itself is 'Hid' it must be the fleeting form of the cloud that is 'tinged'.
78. *the green and jagged mountain-wave*] Cp. the storm in Southey, *Madoc in Wales* (1805) iv 165–6: 'The mountain wave incumbent with its weight / Of bursting waters o'er the reeling bark'.

Rolled o'er their fragile bark.
A dread and hopeless month
Had they participated once
In that diminutive bark:–
85   Their tearless eyes uplifted unto Heaven
      So fruitlessly for aid!
Their parchèd mouths oped eager to the shower
So thin and sleety in that arctic clime.
      Their last hard crust was shared
90   Impartial in equality,
And in the dreadful night
Where all had failed . . . even hope,
Together they had shared the gleam
      Shot from yon lighthouse tower
95   Across the waste of waves;
And therefore are they brave, free, generous,
For who that had so long fought hand to hand
With famine, toil and hazard, smiled at Death
When leaning from the bursting billow's height
100 He stares so ghastly terrible, would waste
One needless word for life's contested toys?

88. clime.] *Esd Nbk*; clime *Esd*; clime, *Esd Poems*. The Bristol Channel cannot be 'that arctic clime', which shows the composite nature of 'The Voyage' (see headnote).
94. yon lighthouse tower] Perhaps suggested by the Skerries light near the approaches to Holyhead which S. had passed at night on returning from Ireland in April, or the Mumbles Head beacon beyond Swansea.
96. 'It is remarkable that few are more experimentally convinced of the doctrine of necessity than old sailors, who have seen much & various service. The peculiarly engaging, & frank generosity of seafaring men probably is an effect of this cause. Those employed in small & ill equipped trading vessels seem to posess this generosity in a purer degree than those of a King's ship. The habits of subjection & coercion imbued into the latter may suffice to explain the cause of the difference'. (S.'s unkeyed note, begun at foot of lines 95–110). *Esd Nbk* refers it plausibly to line 109; *Esd Poems* to 112 (on the wrong p.). Godwin, summarizing Hume, wrote (*Political Justice* Bk IV ch. vii, i 375): 'Hence it appears that the most uninstructed peasant or artisan is practically [i.e. in practice] a necessarian'. But S.'s wording argues a direct debt to Hume (*Enquiry Concerning Human Understanding* VIII Pt i): '. . . this experimental inference and reasoning concerning the actions of others enters so much into human life that no man . . . is ever a moment without employing it. Have we not reason, therefore, to affirm that all mankind have always agreed in the doctrine of necessity . . .?' It is Godwin, however, who goes on to say that the doctrine encourages tranquillity of mind.

Who that had shared his last and nauseous crust
With Famine and a friend, would not divide
A landsman's meal with one who needed it?
105 Who that could rule the elements and spurn
Their fiercest rage, would bow before a slave
Decked in the fleetingness of Earthly power?
Who that had seen the soul of Nature work—
Blind, changeless and eternal in her paths—
110 Would shut his eyes and ears, quaking before
The bubble of a Bigot's blasphemy?

    The faintly moving prow
Divided Ocean's smoothness languidly.
    A landsman there reclined,
115   With lowering close-contracted brow
And mouth updrawn at intervals,
As fearful of his fluctuating bent
    His eyes wide-wandering round
    In insecure malignity,
120 Rapacious, mean, cruel and cowardly,
    Casting upon the loveliness of day
    The murkiness of villainy . . .
By other nurses than the battling storm,
    Friendship, Equality and Sufferance,
125   His manhood had been cradled, —
Inheritor to all the vice and fear
Which Kings and laws and priests and conquerors
                       spread
    On the woe-fertilized world.
    Yes! in the dawn of life
130 When guileless confidence and unthinking love
    Dilate all hearts but those
Which servitude or power has cased in steel,
He bound himself to an unhappy woman,
Not of those pure and heavenly links that Love
135   Twines round a feeling to Freedom dear,
But of vile gold, cankering the breast it binds,
Corroding and inflaming every thought
    Till vain desire, remorse and fear
    Envenom all the being.

---

104. A landsman's meal] i.e. any meal taken after retiring from the sea.
117. 'As if nervous of his own erratic purposes'. No end-of-line punct. in *Esd*
114–19; *Esd Nbk* and *Esd Poems* place a comma after *bent*, but the landsman's
nerves are better represented by his restless eyes than by his pursed mouth.
128. woe-fertilized] nourished by the blood of victims. Not specifically recorded
in *OED*; perhaps the participle should be accented.
136. cankering] cankring *Esd*.

140   Yet did this chain, though rankling in the soul
      Not bind the grosser body; he was wont
          All means to try of thriving:
      To those above him, the most servile cringe
      That ignorance e'er gave to titled Vice
145   Was simperingly yielded;
      To those beneath, the frown which Commerce darts
      On cast-off friends, unprofitably poor,
          Was less severe than his.

          There was another too . . .
150   One of another mould.
      He had been cradled in the wildest storm
      Of Passion, and though now
      The feebler light of worn-out energies
          Shone on his soul, yet ever and anon
155   A flash of tempests long passed by
          Would wake to pristine visions.
      Now he was wrapped in a wild, woeful dream.
          Deeply his soul could love,
      And as he gazèd on the boundless sea
160   Chequered with sunbeams and with shade
          Alternate to infinity,
              He fell into a dream:

      He dreamed that all he loved
      Across the shoreless wastes were voyaging
165   By that unpitying landsman piloted,
          And that at length they came
      To a black and barren island rock.
      Barren the isle . . . no egg
      Which sea-mews leave upon the wildest shore;
170   Barren the isle . . . no blade
      Of grass, no seaweed, not the vilest thing
          For human nutriment . . .

---

142. thriving] striving *Esd Nbk.*
146. Commerce] S. always disliked 'commerce' (by which he meant bourgeois capitalism) more than aristocracy because the former was vulgar, predatory, and cultureless: 'Vile as aristocracy is, commerce, purse-proud ignorance & illiterateness is more contemptible' (S. to Elizabeth Hitchener, 16 October 1811, *L* i 151). See also the long attacks in *Q Mab* iv 38–93, and in 'A Philosophical View of Reform' (1819), *Prose* 245.
150. mould.] *Esd Nbk*; mould *Esd, Esd Poems.*
156. i.e. 'would wake [him]'.
167. barren] sullen *Esd Poems* (the word is overwritten and uncertain in *Esd*).

He struggled with the pitiless landsman then
   But nervèd though his frame with love,
175   Quenchless, despairing love,
It nought availed . . . strong Power
Truth, love and courage vanquished;
A rock was piled upon his feeble breast,
   All was subdued, but that
180   Which is immortal, unsubduable.

He still continued dreaming . . .
The rock upon his bosom quenched not
   The frenzy and defiance of his eye,
But the strong and coward landsman laughed to scorn
185   His unprevailing fortitude,
And in security of malice stabbed
One who accompanied his voyagings.
The blood gushed forth, the eye grew dim,
The nerve relaxed, the life was gone.
190   His smile of dastardly revenge
     Glared upon [a] dead frame.
Then back the Victim flung his head
   In horror insupportable
   Upon the jagged rock whereon he lay,
195   And human Nature paused awhile
     In pity to his woe.

When he awaked to life
She whom he loved was bending over him;
   Haggard her sunken eye . . .
200   Bloodless her quivering lips . . .
   She bended to bestow
The burning moisture from her feverish tongue
   To lengthen out his life
   Perhaps till succour came! . . .
205   But more her dear soft eyes in languid love
When life's last gleam was flickering in decay
   The waning spark rekindled,

---

173. *the pitiless landsman*] The dream-villain becomes a 'displacement' of arbitrary Power embodied in the Government agent who was actually driving the S. household from Devon (see headnote). *then*] there *Esd Poems*.

187. *One*] Presumably the 'bleeding Sister' of line 210 (see headnote).

191. *upon [a] dead*] upon dead *Esd, Esd Nbk*; upon [the] dead *Esd Poems*. The text is evidently faulty, but satisfactory emendation is not easy. Possibly S. intended *Glared on a dead frame*.

195. *human Nature paused*] 'he became unconscious'.

And the faint lingering kiss of her withered lips.
Mingled a rapture with his misery.
210   A bleeding Sister lay
            Beside this wretched pair,
And He, the dastard of relentless soul,
In moody malice lowered over all.

            And this is but a dream!
215   For yonder—see! the port in sight
            The vessel makes towards it!
            The sight of their safety then,
            And the hum of the populous town,
        Awakened them from a night of horror
220   To a day of secure delights.

Lo! here a populous Town
Two dark rocks either side defend,
The quiet water sleeps within
            Reflecting every roof and every mast.
225   A populous town! it is a den
Where wolves keep lambs to fatten on their blood.
'Tis a distempered spot. Should there be one,
Just, dauntless, rational, he would appear
            A madman to the rest.
230   Yes! smooth-faced tyrants chartered by a Power
Called King, who in the castellated keep
Of a far distant land wears out his days
Of miserable dotage, pace the quay
And by the magic of that dreadful word,
235   Hated though dreadful, shield their impotence,
Their lies, their murders, and their robberies.
            See, where the sailor absent many years,

213. Cp. 'On Leaving London for Wales' 36: 'And Tyranny, high raised, stern
lowers over all'.
215. *sight*] *Esd, Esd Poems*; sight! *Esd Nbk*. An absolute construction: 'The port
being in sight, the vessel makes towards it'.
219. *a night of horror*] i.e. as if from a night of horror—from a waking nightmare.
It is still daytime in reality (223–4); the sailor's return by moonlight (237–46) is
again an imaginary scene. The plural *them* seems to implicate the whole party
in the dream (see headnote).
220. *delights*] delight *Esd*.
221. *Town*] Town; *Esd Nbk*; town *Esd Poems*. An inversion: 'Here two rocks
defend a populous Town'.
230. *smooth-faced tyrants*] The press-gang.
237. *sailor*] sailors *Esd*.

With Heaven in his rapture-speaking eyes
Seeks the low cot where all his wealth reposes
240   To bring himself for joy, and his small store
Hard earned by years of peril and of toil,
For comfort to his famine-wasted babes.
Deep in the dark blue Sea the unmoving moon
Gleams beautifully quiet . . . such a night
245   When the last kiss from Mary's quivering lips
Unmanned him. To the well-known door he speeds,
His faint hand pauses on the latch . . . His heart
Beats eagerly. – When suddenly the gang
Dissolves his dream of rapture–no delay!
250   No pity! unexpostulating power
Deals not in human feelings . . . he is stripped
By those low slaves whose master's names inflict
Curses more fell than even themselves would give;
The Indian muslins and the Chinese toys,
255   These for small gain, and those for boundless love
Thus carefully concealed, are torn away;
The very handkerchief his Mary gave
Which in unchanging faithfulness he wore,
Rent from his manly neck! his kindling eye
260   Beamed vengeance, and the tyrant's manacles
Shook on his struggling arm; 'Where is my Wife?
Where are my Children?'–close beside him stood
A sleek and pampered townsman–'Oh! your wife
'Died this time year in the House of Industry;
265   'Your young ones all are dead, except one brat
'Stubborn as you–Parish apprentice now.'

They have appropriated human life
And human happiness, but these weigh nought
In the nice-balanced Politician's scale,
270   Who finds that murder is expedient
And that vile means can answer glorious ends.

---

245. *When*] Where *Esd Nbk.*

250. *unexpostulating*] Lit. 'making no appeal', hence by hypallage 'permitting no appeal'. Recorded in *OED* only from *The Cenci* (II ii 150).

252. *master's names*] masters names *Esd*; masters' names *Esd Poems*. The press-gang acted in the King's name, but 'King' for S. subsumed many titles of oppression: cp. line 260, 'the tyrant's manacles', and *PU* III iv 180–3.

263. *townsman*] town's man *Esd, SC, Esd Nbk.*

264. *this time year*] last year *Esd Poems*. 'This time last year': a recognized locution (*OED Year* 1b).

266–7. No paragraph break in *Esd Nbk.*

Wide Nature has outstretched her fertile Earth
In commonage to all–but they have torn
Her dearest offspring from her bleeding breast,
275 Have disunited Liberty and life,
Severed all right from duty, and confused
Virtue with selfishness. –The grass-green hills,
The fertile valleys and the limpid streams,
The beach on the seashore, the sea itself,
280 The very snow-clad mountain peaks, whose height
Forbids all human footstep, the ravines
Where cataracts have roared ere Monarchs were,
Nature, fair Earth, and Heaven's untainted air
Are all apportioned out . . . some bloated Lord
285 Some priestly pilferer, or some Snake of Law,
Some miserable mockery of a man,
Some slave without a heart, looks over these
And calls them *Mine*–in self-approving pride;
The millionth of the produce of the vale
290 He sets apart for *charity*. Vain fool!
He gives in mercy, while stern Justice cries
'Be thou as one of them–resign thine hall
Brilliant with murder's trophies, and the board
Loaded with surfeiting viands, and the gems
295 Which millions toil to buy thee. –Get thee hence
And dub thyself a man, then dare to throw
One act of usefulness, one thought of love
Into the balance of thy past misdeeds!'

90 On Leaving London for Wales

Written on or about 13 November 1812, when the S.'s left London to return to
Tanyrallt (Harriet S. to Catherine Nugent, 14 November, *L* i 331). S.'s only
other departure from London for Wales was early July 1811, but that journey
to Cwm Elan did not take him to within 60 miles of Snowdon (lines 26–31). S.
had been in London since 4 October for the sake of the Tremadoc embankment, 'in the hopes', Harriet wrote, 'of raising a subscription that would finish
it; but as yet nothing is done. Bysshe's being a minor lays us under many
unpleasant affairs, and makes us obliged to depend upon in a great measure the
will of others, in the manner of raising money' (*L* i 327). He failed to enlist the
Duke of Norfolk's help (*Hogg* ii 173), and had no better success in Sussex

283. *Nature, fair*] Nature's fair *Esd Nbk*.
295. *buy*] bring *Esd Nbk*.

where, he told John Williams, overseer of the embankment works, on 7
November: 'I meet with no encouragement, they are a parcel of cold selfish &
calculating animals who seem to have no other aim or business on Earth but to
eat drink & sleep' (*L* i 330). This ill-success may account for S.'s expressed
revulsion from the rich and privileged, as Cameron suggests (*Esd Nbk* 192),
but it seems from lines 8–9, 60–3, that there may have been some particular
claim on his sympathies from the poor (30–1 show that he cannot mean the
Welsh poor). Nothing significant, however, is known of his activities in
London, except that he visited the Godwins (*Dowden Life* i 304–6), sent
Elizabeth Hitchener home to Sussex, and renewed contact with Hogg shortly
before leaving town (*Hogg* ii 165–76). Writing to Hogg on 27 December, S.
reported that his health had been much improved by a vegetarian diet, 'tho
partly perhaps by my removal from your nerve racking & Spirit quelling
metropolis' (*L* i 347). For S.'s association with the Tremadoc embankment
project, see Elizabeth Beazley, *Madocks and the Wonder of Wales* (1967), especially 190–7.
Text from *Esd* ff. 15ʳ–16ᵛ (*Esd* No. 10: quoted by permission of the Carl H.
Pforzheimer Library).
Published in *Dowden Life* i 317–18 (lines 19–45, 55–63); *Esd Nbk* 53–5; *Esd
Poems* 16–18; *SC* iv 941–4 (transcript of *Esd*).

> Thou miserable city! where the gloom
>   Of penury mingles with the tyrant's pride,
> And virtue bends in sorrow o'er the tomb
>   Where Freedom's hope and Truth's high courage died,
> 5 May floods and vales and mountains me divide
>   From all the taints thy wretched walls contain,
> That life's extremes in desolation wide
>   No more heap horrors on my beating brain
> Nor sting my shuddering heart to sympathy with pain.
>
> 10 With joy I breathe the last and full farewell
>   That long has quivered on my burdened heart;
> My natural sympathies to rapture swell
>   As from its day thy cheerless glooms depart,
> Nor all the glare thy gayest scenes impart
> 15   Could lure one sigh, could steal one tear from me,
>   Or lull to languishment the wakeful smart
>   Which virtue feels for all 'tis forced to see,
> Or quench the eternal flame of generous Liberty.

¶ *90.3. the tomb*] Probably London itself (line 6): instead of the Whigs, the
Prince Regent had unexpectedly called Lord Liverpool to office in June; and
war with the United States had followed during the same month.
10. full] poss. free *Esd* (so read by Dowden; see *Esd Nbk* 338).
13. its day] i.e. the day of farewell.

Hail to thee, Cambria, for the unfettered wind
20   Which from thy wilds even now methinks I feel
Chasing the clouds that roll in wrath behind
    And tightening the soul's laxest nerves to steel.
True! Mountain Liberty alone may heal
    The pain which Custom's obduracies bring,
25 And he who dares in fancy even to steal
    One draught from Snowdon's ever-sacred spring
Blots out the unholiest rede of worldly witnessing.

And shall that soul, to selfish peace resigned,
    So soon forget the woe its fellows share?
30 Can Snowdon's Lethe from the freeborn mind
    So soon the page of injured penury tear?
Does this fine mass of human passion dare
    To sleep unhonouring the patriot's fall,
Or life's sweet load in quietude to bear
35   While millions famish even in Luxury's hall
And Tyranny high raised stern lowers over all?

No, Cambria! never may thy matchless vales
    A heart so false to hope and virtue shield,
Nor ever may thy spirit-breathing gales
40   Waft freshness to the slaves who dare to yield.

22. *tightening*] tightning *Esd*.
23. *True! Mountain Liberty*] *Esd, Esd Nbk*; True mountain Liberty *Dowden Life*, *Esd Poems*. To Rogers (*Esd Poems* xxix) the *Esd* reading is 'quite irrational' and 'could only make sense if [S.] meant "It is true that . . ." ' But that is almost certainly what S. did mean (what is *false* mountain Liberty?). S. is endorsing the sentiment of Southey's *Madoc* (1805), 'Madoc in Wales' xii 51–7:

> Among the hills of Gwyneth and its wilds
> And mountain glens, perforce he cherish'd still
> The hope of mountain liberty; they braced
> And knit the heart and arm of hardihood; . . .
> But here . . . his spirit yielded.

The English source is Milton, 'L'Allegro' 36: 'The Mountain Nymph, sweet Liberty'.
26. The river Glaslyn which flows over the Traeth Mawr near Tanyrallt rises on Snowdon. The road to London 'passes at the foot of Snowdon' (*L* i 352). In the Glaslyn S. unites associations of the fountain Hippocrene near Mount Helicon, sacred to the Muses (hence to *Q Mab*), with those of Lethe, the Underworld river that conferred oblivion of the past (line 30).
27. *rede*] counsel; perhaps inverting Spenser's 'holesome reede' (*FQ* VI vi 5).
33. *the patriot's fall*] Possibly that of Leigh Hunt, due for trial in December for libelling the Prince Regent.
36. *lowers*] poss. towers *Esd*; but cp. 'The Voyage' 213: 'In moody malice lowered over all'.

For me! . . . the weapon that I burn to wield
   I seek amid thy rocks to ruin hurled,
That Reason's flag may over Freedom's field,
   Symbol of bloodless victory, wave unfurled
45 A meteor-sign of love effulgent o'er the world.

Hark to that shriek! my hand had almost clasped
   The dagger that my heart had cast away,
When the pert slaves whose wanton power had grasped
   All hope that springs beneath the eye of day
50 Pass before Memory's gaze in long array.
   The storm fleets by and calmer thoughts succeed;
Feelings once more mild reason's voice obey.
   Woe be the tyrants' and the murderers' meed,
But Nature's wound alone should make their Conscience
                                      bleed.

55 Do thou, wild Cambria, calm each struggling thought,
   Cast thy sweet veil of rocks and woods between
That by the soul to indignation wrought
   Mountains and dells be mingled with the scene.
Let me forever be what I have been,
60   But not forever at my needy door
Let Misery linger, speechless, pale and lean.

41. *For me!*] 'As for me'. *the weapon that I burn to wield*] *Q Mab*, which S. had been writing among the mountains at Tanyrallt.

42. *amid thy rocks to ruin hurled*] 'line 42 must refer to the rocks that are being rolled down the mountains in order to build the embankment' (Cameron, *Esd Nbk* 192). But those rocks were not hurled to ruin but drawn by railway to a construction site. More probably S. implies 'amid geological signs of the working of Necessity' (cp. 'Mont Blanc' (Text B) 69–74).

47. *away,*] away *Esd, Esd Nbk*. The comma, needed to avoid the construction *had cast away When*, invites the ambiguity of making the procession of slaves consequent on the clasping of the dagger. S. intends: 'When I remember those oppressors, I feel like using the violence I have renounced'.

53. *the tyrants' and the murderers'*] the tyrants and the murderers *Esd*; the tyrant's and the murderer's *Esd Poems*; the tyrants' and murderers' *Esd Nbk*.

54. *Nature's wound*] Cameron (*Esd Nbk* 192) says the phrase 'does not make sense unless it is taken as a reference to the embankment'. But S. is revising Milton's account of the Fall (*PL* ix 782–4): 'Earth felt the wound, and Nature from her seat / Sighing through all her Works gave signs of woe, / That all was lost'; tyranny for S. constituted the primal injury to the order of Nature (cp. *Q Mab* iii 196–200).

58. *the scene*] i.e. the mental scene depicted in 48–50.

62. Cp. the Maniac's words in *Julian and Maddalo* 449–50: '*Me*–who am as a nerve o'er which do creep / The else unfelt oppressions of this earth'.

I am the friend of the unfriended poor:
Let me not madly stain their righteous cause in gore.

No more! the visions fade before my sight
65   Which Fancy pictures in the waste of air,
Like lovely dreams ere morning's chilling light:
And sad realities alone are there.
Ah! neither woe, nor fear, nor pain can tear
Their image from the tablet of my soul,
70   Nor the mad floods of despotism where
Lashed into desperate furiousness they roll,
Nor passion's soothing voice, nor interest's cold control.

91 To Harriet

Date of composition uncertain; perhaps November or December 1812 at
Tanyrallt. Cameron (*Esd Nbk* 217–18) assigns the poem to summer 1812,
endorsing Dowden, who suggests (*Dowden Life* i 288n.): 'The reader cannot
fail to note that this poem contains several reminiscences of Wordsworth's
'Tintern Abbey', which it resembles in the general treatment of the blank verse
. . . in passing through Chepstow, Shelley may have visited Tintern Abbey,
and have read Wordsworth's poem, and . . . this may have been written soon
after reaching Lynmouth'. This dating is plausible. It is possible, however, that
what influenced S. was not Tintern itself but the fact that Wordsworth's poem
marked a return from 'the din / Of towns and cities' (26–7) to a known
landscape in company with one he loved–a return such as S. made with Harriet
on about 16 November 1812, from his disenchanting visit to London (*L* i 331).
Passing or visiting Valle Crucis Abbey near Llangollen, two miles off the
London road, could have reminded S. of Wordsworth's 'Lines'. In further
support of the later date: (a) the heavily stressed contrast between 'the frigid
intercourse / Of common souls', the corrupting custom and cold forms of an
unthinking world, and the 'Warm, tranquil, spirit-healing' communion with
Harriet; (b) the image in lines 22–3, 'that untainted seed / Which springeth here
beneath such love as ours', which suggests an awareness of Harriet's pregnancy, which must have been apparent by November or December 1812; (c) the
wintry imagery of lines 25–9; (d) the similarity of phrasing to 'On Leaving
London for Wales' (see notes below); (e) S.'s use of lines 58–69 virtually
unaltered in *Q Mab*, which argues for recent composition. Features such as the
flood imagery of 58–63 and the 'thirst for action' (64) would suit Tremadoc
equally as well as Lynmouth.

68–70. An echo of *Hamlet* I v 98–104: 'Yea, from the table of my memory / I'll
wipe away all trivial fond records' etc.
72. *soothing*] self-flattering. *nor interest's*] not Interest's *Esd Poems*.

Text from *Esd* ff. 35ʳ–36ᵛ (*Esd* No. 24: quoted by permission of the Carl H. Pforzheimer Library).
Published in *Q Mab* (1813), note to viii 203–7 (lines 58–69); *Rossetti 1870* ii 523–4 (lines 5–13); *Dowden Life* i 286–8 (complete); *Esd Nbk* 85–7; *Esd Poems* 42–4; *SC* iv 973–5 (transcript of *Esd*).

> It is not blasphemy to hope that Heaven
> More perfectly will give those nameless joys
> Which throb within the pulses of the blood
> And sweeten all that bitterness which Earth
> 5   Infuses in the heaven-born soul – O Thou
> Whose dear love gleamed upon the gloomy path
> Which this lone spirit travelled, drear and cold
> Yet swiftly leading to those awful limits
> Which mark the bounds of Time and of the space
> 10   When Time shall be no more: wilt thou not turn
> Those spirit-beaming eyes and look on me,
> Until I be assured that Earth is Heaven
> And Heaven is Earth? – will not thy glowing cheek,
> Glowing with soft suffusion, rest on mine
> 15   And breathe magnetic sweetness through the frame
> Of my corporeal nature, through the soul
> Now knit with these fine fibres? I would give
> The longest and the happiest day that fate
> Has marked on my existence, but to feel
> 20   *One* soul-reviving kiss . . . oh thou most dear,

¶ *91.2–3.* An echo of Wordsworth's 'Tintern Abbey' 28: '. . . sensations sweet, / Felt in the blood, and felt along the heart'; and 35–6: 'His little, nameless, unremembered acts / Of kindness and of love'.

5–13. O Thou . . . Earth?] It is most unlikely that Rossetti's source for these lines was, as he claimed (*Forman 1876–7* iv 359*n*.), 'one of the Boscombe MSS'; it was almost certainly *Esd*, deriving from the 'lady, formerly a governess in the Esdaile family' (*L about S* 87) who also gave him the texts of Nos. 95–6.

6–10. Foreshadowing *Epipsychidion* 72: 'She met me, Stranger, upon life's rough way' (Emilia Viviani); 277–80: 'One stood on my path' etc. (Mary Godwin).

7. cold] *Esd*; cold, *eds*.

8. those awful limits] The boundary between Life and Eternity. The implications of S.'s path 'swiftly leading' to eternity before his knowing Harriet may not be suicidal, however, as Cameron claims (*Esd Nbk* 220), but merely purposeless: life is brief when it contains no worthwhile experience (lines 59–69).

9. Time] time *Dowden Life*.

17. these fine fibres] Cp. 'On Leaving London for Wales' 32: 'this fine mass of human passion' – both expressions denoting the poet's physical self.

17–20. It seems needless to conjecture with Cameron (*Esd Nbk* 219) that these lines presuppose an earlier 'quarrel or misunderstanding': S. means that *at any time* he would exchange his happiest day for a kiss.

'Tis an assurance that this Earth is Heaven,
And Heaven the flower of that untainted seed
Which springeth here beneath such love as ours.
Harriet! let death all mortal ties dissolve,
25   But ours shall not be mortal—the cold hand
Of Time may chill the love of Earthly minds,
Half frozen now; the frigid intercourse
Of common souls lives but a summer's day,
It dies where it arose, upon this Earth,
30   But ours! oh, 'tis the stretch of fancy's hope
To portray its continuance as now
Warm, tranquil, spirit-healing. Nor when age
Has tempered these wild ecstasies, and given
A soberer tinge to the luxurious glow
35   Which blazing on devotion's pinnacle
Makes virtuous passion supersede the power
Of reason, nor when life's aestival sun
To deeper manhood shall have ripened me,
Nor when some years have added judgment's store
40   To all thy woman sweetness, all the fire
Which throbs in thine enthusiast heart,—not then
Shall holy friendship (for what other name
May love like ours assume?)—not even then
Shall custom so corrupt, or the cold forms

22–3. See headnote.
27. now;] now, Esd, Esd Nbk.
32–7. Cp. 'Tintern Abbey' 139–47: 'When these wild ecstasies shall be matured / Into a sober pleasure, when thy mind / Shall be a mansion for all lovely forms,' etc.
37. aestival] summer.
38. me,] me. Esd.
39. Nor] Now SC.
41. heart,—] heart, Esd.
43. assume?)—not] assume?) not Esd, Esd Nbk.
43–55. Grammatically obscure. Possibly so harden us (45) refers back to the fate of Earthly minds in lines 25–9, thus requiring (or implying) a full stop; and the clauses introduced by As (46) are postulated examples of how true minds cannot so deteriorate: 'As, for instance: can we make hollow compliments?' etc. Esd Poems remakes the text by emending to: 'so harden us . . . That when we think . . . we can say'; this further necessitates a stop after Virtue and a new question beginning in line 52. In any case the passage behind S.'s seems to be 'Tintern Abbey' 126–133:

> [Nature] can so inform
> The mind that is within us, so impress
> With quietness and beauty, and so feed
> With lofty thoughts, that neither evil tongues,

45   Of this desolate world so harden us
     As, when we think of the dear love that binds
     Our souls in soft communion, while we know
     Each other's thoughts and feelings, can we say
     Unblushingly a heartless compliment,
50   Praise, hate or love with the unthinking world,
     Or dare to cut the unrelaxing nerve
     That knits our love to Virtue?—can those eyes,
     Beaming with mildest radiance on my heart
     To purify its purity, e'er bend
55   To soothe its vice or consecrate its fears?
     Never, thou second self! is confidence
     So vain in virtue that I learn to doubt
     The mirror even of Truth?—Dark Flood of Time,
     Roll as it listeth thee. I measure not
60   By months or moments thy ambiguous course.
     Another may stand by me on thy brink
     And watch the bubble whirled beyond his ken
     Which pauses at my feet—the sense of love,
     The thirst for action, and the impassioned thought
65   Prolong my being. If I wake no more
     My life more actual living will contain
     Than some grey veteran's of the world's cold school

        Rash judgments, nor the sneers of selfish men,
        Nor greetings where no kindness is, nor all
        The dreary intercourse of daily life,
        Shall e'er prevail against us

46. *As, when*] As when *Esd, Esd Nbk, Dowden Life*; That, when *Esd Poems*.
48. *can we say*] we can say *Esd Poems*.
52. *Virtue?—can*] Virtue—can *Esd, Esd Nbk*; virtue. Can *Esd Poems*; Virtue. Can *Dowden Life*.
55. *To soothe its vice*] Cp. 'On Leaving London for Wales' 72: 'Nor Passion's soothing voice'.
58–69. These lines on Time are quoted in S.'s note to *Q Mab* viii 203–7, where reference is made to Godwin, *Political Justice* i 411[–12] (Bk IV ch. ix): 'It seems to be consciousness, rather than succession of ideas, that measures time to the mind . . . The indolent man reclines for hours in the shade; and, though his mind be perpetually at work, the silent progress of time is unobserved. But, when acute pain, or uneasy expectation, obliges consciousness to recur with unusual force, the time appears insupportably long'. Godwin here modifies the conclusions of Condillac (*Traité des Sensations* (1754) I iv 17–18): 'La notion de la durée est donc toute relative: chacun n'en juge que par la succession de ses idées: et vraisemblablement il n'y a pas deux hommes qui, dans un temps donné, comptent un égal nombre d'instans'. But S. may also be indebted to

Whose listless hours unprofitably roll
By one enthusiast feeling unredeemed.
70 Virtue and Love! unbending Fortitude,
Freedom, Devotedness and Purity!
That life my spirit consecrates to you.

92 Queen Mab

S. wrote the bulk of *Q Mab* between mid-April 1812 and mid-February 1813
(i.e. when aged 19–20), mainly in Wales, in the Elan Valley at Nantgwillt and
at Tanyrallt; the notes were mostly written after the poem and were probably
complete when printing began (*L* i 368) three months later. D. L. Clark ('The
Date and Sources of S.'s *A Vindication of Natural Diet*', *SP* xxxvi (January 1939)
70–1) and Cameron (*Cameron (1951)* 375–7) argue that *A Vindication* was
written before the notes in *Q Mab* and that, despite its sub-heading 'being one
in a series of notes to Queen Mab (a philosophical poem)', it was indeed
published earlier. The arguments for this are dubious: the internal evidence
which suggests revision of *A Vindication* for *Q Mab* more plausibly indicates
modification and corruption of the *Q Mab* text in printing *A Vindication* from it
(see notes to S.'s note to viii 211–12). There has been much confusion over the
composition dates of the poem, some of it intentional. S. asserted in his letter
to the *Examiner* 22 June 1821, dissociating himself from the recent piracy of the
poem (*L* ii 304), 'A poem, entitled 'Queen Mab', was written by me at the age
of eighteen', and this date, 1810, was accepted by Mary in her Note to the
poem (*1839* i 96) and by Medwin, who wrote of the period following S.'s
expulsion from Oxford (25 March 1811): 'He reverted to his *Queen Mab*,
commenced a year and a half before, and converted what was a mere imaginative poem into a systematic attack on the institutions of society. He not only

William Smellie's popular *Philosophy of Natural History* (1790), which also
elaborates on Condillac: 'It is certain that the natural measure of time depends
solely on the succession of our ideas. Were it possible for the mind to be totally
occupied with a single idea for a day, a week, or a month, these portions of
time would appear to be nothing more than so many instants. Hence a
philosopher often lives as long in one day, as a clown or a savage does in a week
or a month spent in mental inactivity and want of thought' (i 519). Characteristically, S. substitutes a reactionary worldling for Godwin's indolent man and
Smellie's clown.

67. *veteran's*] veterans *Esd, Dowden Life*; veterans' *Q Mab*.

70–2. The punctuation of *Esd* could signify 'My spirit consecrates to Virtue and
Love a life of unbending Fortitude' etc. But S. has stressed '*my life*' in the
preceding lines, so the meaning seems to be: 'That life of mine I consecrate to
Virtue, Love, Fortitude' etc.

71. *Purity!*] *Dowden Life*; Purity *Esd*; Purity– *Esd Nbk, Esd Poems*.

corrected the versification with great care, but more than doubled its length, and appended to the text the Notes, which were at that time scarcely, if at all begun, even if they were contemplated' (*Medwin (1913)* 91–2). Medwin added, however, that 'Shelley never showed me a line of *Queen Mab*' (ibid. 93), which makes his account improbable, unless Dowden's speculation (*Dowden Life* i 110–11) is well-founded, that the poem may have originated in the lost 'Poetical Essay on the Existing State of Things' advertised in the *Oxford Herald* on 9 March (*Mac-Carthy* 100) and in the leading journals in May 1811. Early in 1817 S.'s solicitor Longdill prepared 'Observations' in defence of his client's claim to the custody of his children by Harriet S., presumably with S.'s collaboration; these affirm of *Q Mab* that 'It was . . . written and printed by Mr Shelley when he was only 19' (*White* ii 515). It was to S.'s advantage to be made to appear as young as possible, but the date could be checked and so is fairly accurate: some of the poem was written when S. was 19, though he was 20 when it was printed. The embryonic notion was first mentioned in a letter of *c.* 10 December 1811 to Elizabeth Hitchener: 'I have now my dear friend in contemplation a Poem. I intend it to be by anticipation a picture of the manners, simplicity and delights of a perfect state of society; tho still earthly. –Will you assist me. I only thought of it last night.' (*L* i 201). He added: 'I think I shall also make a selection of my younger Poems for publication' (ibid. 202). Conversations with Southey, however, had deflected S.'s purpose by 26 December when he told Miss Hitchener: 'I do not proceed with my poem, the subject is not *now* to my mind . . . The minor Poems I mentioned you will see soon. They are about to be sent to the Printers' (*L* i 213–14). From Dublin on 14 February 1812 S. sent Miss Hitchener some verse (No. 74) written out as prose, which was later revised and incorporated in *Q Mab* ix 23–37. By 18 August S. was able to send Hookham part of his MS from Lynmouth: 'I enclose . . . by way of specimen all that I have written of a little poem begun since my arrival in England [from Ireland, 6 April 1812, though S. did not settle at Nantgwillt until 14 April]. I conceive I have matter enough for 6 more cantos. You will perceive that I have not attempted to temper my constitutional enthusiasm in that Poem. Indeed a Poem is safe, the iron-souled Attorney general would scarcely dare to attack 'genus irritabile vatum'[.] The Past, the Present, & the Future are the grand & comprehensive topics of this Poem. I have not yet half exhausted the second of them' (*L* i 324). If the poem was written consecutively, S.'s description would mean that Hookham received approximately four cantos; but the opening at least of Canto iv must have been written during the winter of 1812–13, after S. had received news of Bonaparte's retreat from Moscow. News of the burning of Moscow in the 19th and 20th Bulletins of the French Grand Army (16–17 September 1812) appears in *GM* lxxxii (October 1812) 382–3; the evacuation (19 October) and later Russian victories in the snow are retailed from Bulletins 28–9 (11 November and 3 December) in *GM* lxxxii (Dec 1812) 570–4. The severe weather began early in November. S.'s lines, however, also describe clear, cold weather with snow on the Welsh hills (iv 8–9) and a near-full moon (iv 6, 12). In London snow fell on 17 December after a week of clear, cold weather (*GM* lxxxii

(December 1812) 498) and the moon was full the following night. This, then, could be the date of the opening of Canto iv (an alternative is *c*. 17 January 1813). In the New Year (letter to Hookham, 26 January 1813) S. was approaching the end of his poem: 'I expect to have Queen Mab, & the other Poems finished by March. Queen Mab will be in ten cantos [it was in fact completed in nine] & contain about 2800 lines. The other poems probably contain as much more. The notes to Q.M. will be long & philosophical. I shall take that opportunity which I judge to be a safe one of propagating my principles, which I decline to do syllogistically in a poem. A poem very didactic is I think very stupid' (*L* i 350). On 7 February S. wrote to Hogg: '*Mab* has gone on but slowly altho she is nearly finished. They have teazed me out of all poetry. With some restrictions I have taken your advice, tho I have not been able to bring myself to rhyme. The didactic is in blank heroic verse, & the descriptive in blank lyrical measure. If authority is of any weight in support of this singularity, Miltons Samson Agonistes, the Greek Choruses, & (you will laugh) Southeys Thalaba may be adduced . . . Since I wrote the above I have finished the rough sketch of my Poem . . . I mean to subjoin copious philo-sophical notes' (*L* i 352–3). Some ten days later S. told Hookham: 'Queen Mab is finished and transcribed.—I am now preparing the Notes which shall be long & philosophical.–You will receive it with the other poems. I think that the whole should form one volume, but of that we can speak hereafter.–' (*L* i 354). The sequence of S.'s creative activities may thus have been as follows: an *Ur-Mab* conceived and possibly begun in December 1811 was abandoned when conversations with Southey turned his mind in new directions. *Q Mab* was begun seriously at Nantgwillt *c*. 14 April 1812 and carried through at least to the end of Canto iii by mid-August; these cantos were sent to his publisher as a specimen (and possibly not reclaimed before printing: only two notes (to i 242–3, 252–3) are attached to the first three cantos). There was then an intermission caused by the flight from Lynmouth and by S.'s practical duties on the embankment works at Tremadoc. After S.'s return to Tanyrallt from London in mid-November 1812 he first put his minor poems in order (i.e. copied out the Esdaile Notebook; see *L* i 340); then resumed work on *Q Mab* Canto iv in mid-December and completed the poem on 7 February 1813. The last-composed poem in *Esd* that can be dated with certainty (No. 90; *Esd* No. 10) was written *c*. 13 November 1812, and the next datable group belongs to summer 1813 and to *Esd*'s 'appendix'; it seems, then, that S. gave up writing minor poems for about six months between December 1812 and *c*. May 1813 in order to finish the long one. S. sent the poem to his publisher early in March 1813, from Dublin, with the comment: 'The notes are preparing & shall be forwarded before the completion of the printing of the Poem. I have many other Poems which shall also be sent' (*L* i 361). He added: 'Do not let the title page be printed before the body of the Poem. I have a motto to introduce from Shakespeare, & a Preface [neither eventually included; the Shakespeare motto would perhaps have been from *Romeo and Juliet* I iv 50–3: *R*. I dreamt a dream tonight. *M*. And so did I. / *R*. Well, what was yours? *M*. That dreamers often lie. / *R*. In bed asleep while they do dream things true. / *M*. O then I see Queen

Mab hath been with you.]. I expect no success.–Let only 250 Copies be printed. A small neat Quarto, on fine paper & so as to catch the aristocrats: They will not read it, but their sons and daughters may' (*L* i 361). Printing had begun by 21 May (letter of Harriet S. to Catherine Nugent, *L* i 367*n.*), and S. probably received copies about the end of June. The book (subtitled 'A Philosophical Poem with Notes' on the title-page) was privately distributed, and not published in the normal way until pirated by William Clark in 1821, by which date 70 of the 250 copies had been disposed of; for its later publication history see H. B. Forman, *The Shelley Library* (1886) 35–58 and 'The Vicissitudes of Queen Mab', *Shelley Society Papers*, Part I (1888) 19–35. 'In the twenty-five years from its first printing, [*Q Mab*] was undoubtedly the most widely read, the most notorious, and the most influential of all Shelley's works . . . and established itself as a basic text in the self-taught working-class culture from which the early trade union movement of the 1820s, and the Chartism of the thirties and forties was to spring' (*Holmes* 208). Clark's pirated edition of 1821 coincided with the first American edition (by W. Baldwin & Co., New York 1821), and was followed by a series of very widely circulated editions by Richard Carlile (in 1822, 1823, and 1826) and others (including, after Carlile's imprisonment, an edition by his wife and sons in 1832), culminating in the 'Chartist' edition of Heatherington and Watson in 1839. The much-quoted description of the poem as 'the Chartists' Bible' originates in G. B. Shaw's essay of 1892, 'Shaming the Devil about Shelley'. For *Q Mab* as 'the gospel of the sect' of the Owenites, see *Medwin (1913)* 100. In spite of the predominantly eighteenth-century idiom of its style and egalitarianism, *Q Mab* places S.'s intellectual and artistic development on an entirely new level. 'Many features of *Queen Mab* have a continuous development throughout Shelley's subsequent work [most notably in *L&C* and *PU*]. Human society is always seen in a cosmic setting, and human history as inseparable from the history of stars and insects' (GM). The influence of Godwin is less pervasive in the thought of the poem than has been argued; the major influences are Painite radicalism in politics and religion, and, above all, the writings of the eighteenth-century French materialists, particularly Holbach (see notes, *passim*). Many literary sources have been proposed for the poem's structure of a dream-vision (Cantos i, ii 1–96) in which past (ii 97–end), present (comprehending monarchy, iii; political tyranny, iv; economic corruption, v; religion, vi and vii), and future (viii and ix) are surveyed. Volney's *Ruins* is a clear influence, but the temporal survey structure has a number of possible forebears in the English poetic tradition, including Thomson's *Liberty* (1735–36) which itself recalls the device in *Paradise Lost* (see ii 69*n.*). The machinery of the poem's opening has been compared with that of Sir William Jones's 'The Palace of Fortune' (2nd edn 1777), but the influence in fact appears slight; a possible alternative is Southey's *Vision of the Maid of Orleans*, originally part of Bk ix of *Joan of Arc* (1795), in which an 'angel guide' takes the Maid to the planet Venus to see futurity, when tyrants shall fall and virtue and equality restore Earth as Paradise. S.'s title, designed to camouflage the poem's atheism and radicalism, probably derives from the numerous children's stories in the eighteenth cen-

tury which employed the Queen of the Fairies as a character; see for example
Marie Catherine La Mothe, Countess D'Aulnoy, *Queen Mab: A Select Collection of the Tales of the Fairies* (3rd edn 1782; there was an edition in 1799). For
critical accounts of *Q Mab*, see *Hughes* 184–92; *Baker* 21–40; *Cameron (1951)*
239–74; *Holmes* 200–11.

Text from *Queen Mab* (1813).

Published in *1813*; *1839* (omitting dedicatory poem, iv 203–20, vi 54–238, vii,
viii 165, ix 48); *1840* (with all omissions in *1839* restored except ix 48, presumably an oversight). S. reworked parts of the poem for publication in *1816* as
'The Daemon of the World' (No. 115); variants for S.'s reworking for *Daemon*
are given in the notes to that poem.

ECRASEZ L'INFAME!
Correspondance de Voltaire.

Avia Pieridum peragro loca, nullius ante
Trita solo; juvat integros accedere fonteis;
Atque haurire: juvatque novos decerpere flores.

. . . . . .

Unde prius nulli velarint tempora musae.
Primum quod magnis doceo de rebus; et arctis
Religionum animos nodis exsolvere pergo.

Lucret.lib.iv.

Δὸς ποῦ στῶ, καὶ κόσμον κινήσω.

Archimedes.

¶ *92. Epigraph 1.* 'Crush the infamous thing!' (Voltaire's notorious slogan).
Epigraph 2. From Lucretius, *De Rerum Naturae* iv 1–7: 'I wander through a
pathless region of poetry, trodden by no other foot before; it delights me to
approach untainted springs, and to drink: and it delights me to pick unfamiliar
flowers . . . [S. omits line 4: 'and to seek a distinguished crown for my head
from there'] whence the Muses have hitherto adorned no one's brows. First,
because I teach great matters; and I go on to set minds free from the hard knots
of superstition'. Line 3: *juvatque*] juratque *1813* (a misprint).
Epigraph 3. The famous saying was often used figuratively in radical writing,
e.g. the first sentence of Paine's *Rights of Man* Part II (1792: *Paine Writings* ii
401): 'What Archimedes said of the mechanical powers may be applied to
reason and liberty. "*Had we,*" said he, "*a place to stand upon, we might raise the
world.*"'; and James Mackintosh, *Vindiciae Gallicae* (1791) 124: 'The philosophers of antiquity did not, like ARCHIMEDES, want [i.e. lack] a spot on
which to fix their engines, but they wanted an engine to move the moral
world. The press is that engine, which has subjected the powerful to the wise,
by governing the opinions of mankind'.

To Harriet ★★★★★.

Whose is the love that, gleaming through the world,
Wards off the poisonous arrow of its scorn?
　　Whose is the warm and partial praise,
　　Virtue's most sweet reward?

5　Beneath whose looks did my reviving soul
　Riper in truth and virtuous daring grow?
　　Whose eyes have I gazed fondly on,
　　And loved mankind the more?

Harriet! on thine:–thou wert my purer mind;
10　Thou wert the inspiration of my song;
　　Thine are these early wilding flowers,
　　Though garlanded by me.

Then press into thy breast this pledge of love,
And know, though time may change and years may roll,
15　　Each flowret gathered in my heart
　　It consecrates to thine.

I.

How wonderful is Death,
Death and his brother Sleep!
One, pale as yonder waning moon
　With lips of lurid blue;
5　The other, rosy as the morn
　When throned on ocean's wave

Dedicatory poem. An earlier version of *Esd* No. 1 (see No. 97 and headnote). Here the five stars and period invite the name 'GROVE'. Harriet's niece Mrs Hussey had 'always understood from relations it [*Q Mab*] was dedicated to my Aunt Harriet Grove', 'the tradition of the Grove family certainly is, that it was to Harriet Grove' (Irving Massey, 'Some Letters of S. Interest', *KSMB* xix (1968) 14–15). Mrs Hussey also claimed that her father (Harriet's brother and S.'s friend John Grove) had owned the MS of *Q Mab* (ibid. 15), but this might be through confusion with *WJ*. The present poem is certainly addressed to Harriet S., S. himself acknowledging the 'foolish dedication to my late wife' (Letter to Ollier, 11 June 1821, *L* ii 298); but some equivocation may still have been intended by his asterisks.

i 2. Death and Sleep were children of Night in classical mythology (Hesiod, *Theogony* 202, 758–9) and their brotherhood was a commonplace (e.g. *Iliad* xiv 231; *Aeneid* vi 278: 'consanguineus Leti Sopor').

i 4. *lurid*] ghastly pale. The gothic colour, not used elsewhere by S., was perhaps borrowed from Peacock's *Genius of the Thames* (1810) I xx 11, I xxiii 1, which S. read 17–18 August 1812 (*L* i 324–5).

It blushes o'er the world:
Yet both so passing wonderful!

Hath then the gloomy Power
10   Whose reign is in the tainted sepulchres
Seized on her sinless soul?
Must then that peerless form
Which love and admiration cannot view
Without a beating heart, those azure veins
15   Which steal like streams along a field of snow,
That lovely outline, which is fair
As breathing marble, perish?
Must putrefaction's breath
Leave nothing of this heavenly sight
20   But loathsomeness and ruin?
Spare nothing but a gloomy theme,
On which the lightest heart might moralize?
Or is it only a sweet slumber
Stealing o'er sensation,
25   Which the breath of roseate morning
Chaseth into darkness?
Will Ianthe wake again,
And give that faithful bosom joy
Whose sleepless spirit waits to catch
30   Light, life and rapture from her smile?

Yes! she will wake again,
Although her glowing limbs are motionless,
And silent those sweet lips,
Once breathing eloquence
35   That might have soothed a tiger's rage,
Or thawed the cold heart of a conqueror.
Her dewy eyes are closed,
And on their lids, whose texture fine
Scarce hides the dark blue orbs beneath,
40   The baby Sleep is pillowed:
Her golden tresses shade
The bosom's stainless pride,

i 8. *passing*] surpassingly.
i 12–17. *that peerless form . . . breathing marble*] Beach Langston (*HLQ* xii (1948–9) 189) cites Shakespeare's *Rape of Lucrece* 418–20: 'With more than admiration he admired / Her azure veins, her alabaster skin, / Her coral lips, her snow-white dimpled chin'.
i 27. *Ianthe*] For possible sources of the name, see *Baker* 26. S. gave the name Ianthe to his first child (b. 23 June 1813) by his first wife Harriet. Harriet herself has been claimed as a model for the character in the poem (e.g. in *Reiman* (1977)).

Curling like tendrils of the parasite
Around a marble column.

45   Hark! whence that rushing sound?
'Tis like the wondrous strain
That round a lonely ruin swells,
Which, wandering on the echoing shore,
The enthusiast hears at evening:
50   'Tis softer than the west wind's sigh;
'Tis wilder than the unmeasured notes
Of that strange lyre whose strings
The genii of the breezes sweep:
Those lines of rainbow light
55   Are like the moonbeams when they fall
Through some cathedral window, but the tints
Are such as may not find
Comparison on earth.

Behold the chariot of the Fairy Queen!
60   Celestial coursers paw the unyielding air;
Their filmy pennons at her word they furl,
And stop obedient to the reins of light:
These the Queen of spells drew in,
She spread a charm around the spot,

i 43. *parasite*] Any climbing plant, not necessarily exploitative, could be called a 'parasite' in S.'s day (e.g. Mary Wollstonecraft, 'Letters to Imlay', Letter xvi, *Posthumous Works* (1798) iii 42: 'I have thrown out some tendrils to cling to the elm by which I wish to be supported . . . But, knowing that I am not a parasite-plant . . .'). The popularity of the word probably derives from Rousseau's description of the famous 'bosquet' in *Julie, ou la Nouvelle Héloise* (1761) Part IV Letter xi: '. . . ces ombrages verds et touffus . . . n'étoient formés que de ces plantes rampantes et parasites . . .'

i 45–9. *Hark! . . . hears at evening*] Cp. Peacock, *Palmyra* (2nd edn 1812) ii 11–15: 'Whence rose that dim, mysterious sound, / That breath'd in hollow murmurs round' etc.

i 52. *that strange lyre*] The Aeolian harp.

i 53. *genii*] Spirits fabled as powers of Nature (see *PU* IV 539–42 and headnote). From Arab. *djinn*.

i 54–8. *Those lines . . . Comparison on earth*] The imagery of light through stained windows was a Romantic favourite, a visual equivalent of Aeolian harp-imagery. S.'s immediate sources were probably Southey, *Joan of Arc* (1796) iii 269–74, and Scott, *Lay of the Last Minstrel* (1805) II xi, which ends: 'The moon-beam kiss'd the holy pane, / And threw on the pavement a bloody stain'.

i 61. *pennons*] wings (cp. *The Devil's Walk* 43).

65 And leaning graceful from the etherial car,
    Long did she gaze, and silently,
      Upon the slumbering maid.

    Oh! not the visioned poet in his dreams,
    When silvery clouds float through the wildered brain,
70 When every sight of lovely, wild and grand
      Astonishes, enraptures, elevates,
        When fancy at a glance combines
        The wondrous and the beautiful, –
    So bright, so fair, so wild a shape
75   Hath ever yet beheld,
    As that which reined the coursers of the air,
      And poured the magic of her gaze
        Upon the maiden's sleep.

      The broad and yellow moon
80   Shone dimly through her form –
    That form of faultless symmetry;
    The pearly and pellucid car
      Moved not the moonlight's line:
    'Twas not an earthly pageant:
85 Those who had looked upon the sight,
      Passing all human glory,
      Saw not the yellow moon,
      Saw not the mortal scene,
      Heard not the night-wind's rush,
90   Heard not an earthly sound,
      Saw but the fairy pageant,
      Heard but the heavenly strains
      That filled the lonely dwelling.

    The Fairy's frame was slight, yon fibrous cloud,
95   That catches but the palest tinge of even,
    And which the straining eye can hardly seize
    When melting into eastern twilight's shadow,
    Were scarce so thin, so slight; but the fair star
    That gems the glittering coronet of morn,

---

i 78. *maiden's sleep*] sleeping maid, *1839*, *1840*. (Presumably rephrased by Mary
S. to make concrete the object of the Fairy's gaze.)
i 81. *symmetry*] The essential requirement of female beauty in gothic novels,
including S.'s; e.g. Megalena de Metastasio in *St Irvyne* ch. i, whose figure was
'cast in the mould of most exact symmetry'.
i 83. i.e. 'by refraction' (Locock).
i 94. *fibrous*] i.e. cirrus.
i 98. *Were*] Subj., 'would be'.

100   Sheds not a light so mild, so powerful,
       As that which, bursting from the Fairy's form,
       Spread a purpureal halo round the scene,
            Yet with an undulating motion,
            Swayed to her outline gracefully.

105   From her celestial car
            The Fairy Queen descended,
            And thrice she waved her wand
       Circled with wreaths of amaranth:
            Her thin and misty form
110   Moved with the moving air,
            And the clear silver tones,
            As thus she spoke, were such
       As are unheard by all but gifted ear.

                    FAIRY
       Stars! your balmiest influence shed!
115   Elements! your wrath suspend!
       Sleep, Ocean, in the rocky bounds
            That circle thy domain!
       Let not a breath be seen to stir
       Around yon grass-grown ruin's height,
120   Let even the restless gossamer
            Sleep on the moveless air!
            Soul of Ianthe! thou,
       Judged alone worthy of the envied boon
       That waits the good and the sincere; that waits
125   Those who have struggled, and with resolute will
       Vanquished earth's pride and meanness, burst the
                                            chains,
       The icy chains of custom, and have shone
       The day-stars of their age;–Soul of Ianthe!
            Awake! arise!

130   Sudden arose
            Ianthe's Soul; it stood
       All beautiful in naked purity,

i 102. purpureal] bright, beautiful (Lat. purpureus).
i 108. amaranth] Legendary unfading flower.
i 123. boon] 1839, 1840; boon, 1813.
i 130–4. Sudden arose . . . beauty and grace.] The separation of soul from body is a
device borrowed from Volney, Ruins ch. iv: 'Then approaching me, and
placing his hand upon my head, rise, mortal, said he, and disengage yourself
from that corporeal frame with which you are encumbered'. Plato's dualism
denied the beauty of the body (Phaedo 67–8).

The perfect semblance of its bodily frame,
Instinct with inexpressible beauty and grace.
135   Each stain of earthliness
             Had passed away, it reassumed
             Its native dignity, and stood
             Immortal amid ruin.

             Upon the couch the body lay
140   Wrapped in the depth of slumber:
             Its features were fixed and meaningless,
             Yet animal life was there,
             And every organ yet performed
             Its natural functions: 'twas a sight
145   Of wonder to behold the body and soul.
             The self-same lineaments, the same
             Marks of identity were there:
             Yet, oh, how different! One aspires to Heaven,
             Pants for its sempiternal heritage,
150   And ever changing, ever rising still,
             Wantons in endless being.
             The other, for a time the unwilling sport
             Of circumstance and passion, struggles on;
             Fleets through its sad duration rapidly:

i *133–4. frame, . . . grace.*] *1951*; frame, . . . grace; *Locock 1911, 1972*; frame. / . . . grace, *1813, 1839, 1840* ('punctuation which evidently yields no sense' – Locock).

i *142. animal life*] Nervous or sensitive vitality, as distinct from 'Brute life' (which informed inanimate Nature), 'Vegetable life' (which moved vegetables), and 'Intellectual life' (imagination). 'The Animal life, by which [man] has Sensations, Appetites, and Desires, and feels Pleasure and Pain', 'The Animal Principle operates by nerves' (James Burnett, Lord Monboddo, *Ancient Metaphysics; or, the Science of Universals* (Edinburgh 1779) iii 6, 18). Cp. *PU* I 484.

i *145. body and soul*] The dualist passage to line 156 derives from Blair's *Grave* 377–382: '. . . body and soul must part! / Fond couple! link'd more close than wedded pair. / This wings its way to its Almighty Source, / . . . That drops into the dark and noisome grave, / Like a disabled pitcher of no use.'

i *150. ever changing, ever rising*] ever-changing, ever-rising *1839, 1840*, Hutchinson. About the beginning of 1812 S. sketched to Southey a theory of progressive reincarnation: ' "I think reason and analogy seem to countenance the opinion that life is infinite – that as the soul which now animates this frame was once the vivifying principle of the *infinitely* lowest link in the Chain of existence, so is it ultimately destined to attain the highest . . . that every thing is animation . . . and in consequence being infinite we can never arrive at its termination" ' (letter to Elizabeth Hitchener, 2 January 1812, *L* i 215).

155   Then like an useless and worn-out machine,
              Rots, perishes, and passes.

                        FAIRY
              Spirit! who hast dived so deep;
              Spirit! who hast soared so high;
              Thou the fearless, thou the mild,
160   Accept the boon thy worth hath earned,
              Ascend the car with me.

                        SPIRIT
              Do I dream? is this new feeling
              But a visioned ghost of slumber?
              If indeed I am a soul,
165   A free, a disembodied soul,
              Speak again to me.

                        FAIRY
              I am the Fairy Mab: to me 'tis given
              The wonders of the human world to keep:
              The secrets of the immeasurable past,
170   In the unfailing consciences of men,
              Those stern, unflattering chroniclers, I find:
              The future, from the causes which arise
              In each event, I gather: not the sting
              Which retributive memory implants
175   In the hard bosom of the selfish man;
              Nor that ecstatic and exulting throb
              Which virtue's votary feels when he sums up
              The thoughts and actions of a well-spent day,
              Are unforeseen, unregistered by me:
180   And it is yet permitted me, to rend
              The veil of mortal frailty, that the spirit
              Clothed in its changeless purity, may know
              How soonest to accomplish the great end
              For which it hath its being, and may taste
185   That peace, which in the end all life will share.
              This is the meed of virtue; happy Soul,
              Ascend the car with me!

i 155. an] a 1839, 1840.
i 162. is] Is 1839, 1840, eds.
i 180. yet] 'In addition to this' (Locock).
i 181. spirit] spirit, 1839, 1840, Hutchinson.
i 185. in the end] i.e. when earth is revolutionized.

The chains of earth's immurement
    Fell from Ianthe's spirit;
190 They shrank and brake like bandages of straw
    Beneath a wakened giant's strength.
    She knew her glorious change,
    And felt in apprehension uncontrolled
    New raptures opening round:
195 Each day-dream of her mortal life,
    Each frenzied vision of the slumbers
    That closed each well-spent day,
    Seemed now to meet reality.

    The Fairy and the Soul proceeded;
200   The silver clouds disparted;
And as the car of magic they ascended,
    Again the speechless music swelled,
    Again the coursers of the air
Unfurled their azure pennons, and the Queen
205   Shaking the beamy reins
    Bade them pursue their way.

    The magic car moved on.
    The night was fair, and countless stars
    Studded heaven's dark blue vault, –
210   Just o'er the eastern wave
    Peeped the first faint smile of morn: –
    The magic car moved on –
    From the celestial hoofs
The atmosphere in flaming sparkles flew,
215   And where the burning wheels
Eddied above the mountain's loftiest peak,
    Was traced a line of lightning.
    Now it flew far above a rock,
    The utmost verge of earth,
220   The rival of the Andes, whose dark brow
    Lowered o'er the silver sea.

    Far, far below the chariot's path,
    Calm as a slumbering babe,
    Tremendous Ocean lay.
225   The mirror of its stillness showed
    The pale and waning stars,
    The chariot's fiery track,

i *188–9. The chains . . . Ianthe's spirit*] Cp. Volney, *Ruins* ch. iv: 'Instantly,
penetrated as with a celestial flame, the ties that fix us to the earth seemed to be
loosened'.

And the grey light of morn
Tinging those fleecy clouds
230   That canopied the dawn.
Seemed it, that the chariot's way
Lay through the midst of an immense concave,
Radiant with million constellations, tinged
With shades of infinite colour,
235   And semi-circled with a belt
Flashing incessant meteors.

The magic car moved on.
As they approached their goal
The coursers seemed to gather speed;
240   The sea no longer was distinguished; earth
Appeared a vast and shadowy sphere;
The sun's unclouded orb
Rolled through the black concave;
Its rays of rapid light
245   Parted around the chariot's swifter course,
And fell, like ocean's feathery spray
Dashed from the boiling surge
Before a vessel's prow.

The magic car moved on.
250   Earth's distant orb appeared
The smallest light that twinkles in the heaven;
Whilst round the chariot's way
Innumerable systems rolled,
And countless spheres diffused
255   An ever-varying glory.

i *232–4. an immense concave . . . infinite colour*] '. . . these luminaries, dispersed through space at infinite distances from one another, fill the universe with light of various colours' (Walker, *A System of Familiar Philosophy* (1799) 3).

i *235. a belt*] The Milky Way, 'is splendidissimo candore inter flammas circus elucens' (Cicero, *De Re Publica* VI xvi 16).

i *242–3. The sun's . . . black concave*] See S.'s note.

i *244–8. Its rays . . . a vessel's prow*] The cleavage of the sun's light by the magic car as a boat cleaves water may derive from Lucretius, who treated light as a matter which could be impeded by denser or outstripped by more volatile matter (*De Rerum Natura* ii 150–6; iv 183–208), but Walker's view was also Lucretian: 'Light can be proved to be real matter; to have motion, and, of course momentum . . . a feeble light is capable of being absorbed, turned back, or retarded, in its motion, by stronger light' (*A System of Familiar Philosophy* 4, 3).

i *252–3.* See S.'s note.

It was a sight of wonder: some
Were hornèd like the crescent moon;
Some shed a mild and silver beam
Like Hesperus o'er the western sea;
260 Some dashed athwart with trains of flame,
Like worlds to death and ruin driven;
Some shone like suns, and as the chariot passed,
Eclipsed all other light.

Spirit of Nature! here!
265 In this interminable wilderness
Of worlds, at whose immensity
Even soaring fancy staggers,
Here is thy fitting temple.
Yet not the lightest leaf
270 That quivers to the passing breeze
Is less instinct with thee:
Yet not the meanest worm
That lurks in graves and fattens on the dead
Less shares thy eternal breath.
275 Spirit of Nature! thou!
Imperishable as this scene,
Here is thy fitting temple.

II.
If solitude hath ever led thy steps
To the wild ocean's echoing shore,

i *257. hornèd*] *1840*; horned *1813, 1839*.
i *259. Hesperus*] Venus, the Evening Star.
i *260. Some dashed athwart*] Comets, that move across the 'fixed' constellations.
The 'spheres' thus include planets, comets, and stars.
i *264–77. Spirit of Nature! . . . thy fitting temple.*] In the theistic version of the
Great Chain of Being it was a commonplace that lowly equally with noble
creatures were an expression of God's power, e.g. in Pope's *Essay on Man*
(1733–34) i 267, 270: 'All are but parts of one stupendous whole . . . / Great in
the earth, as in th'ethereal frame'. S. quoted the former line on 3 January 1811
as 'something more than Poetry, it has ever been my favourite theory' (*L* i 35).
Lines 269–74 are a pantheistic rendering of Kirke White's 'Time' 486–9: 'He
has thought of man; / Yea, compassed round with countless worlds, has
thought / Of us poor worms, that batten in the dews / Of morn, and perish ere
the noonday sun'.
i *269. lightest*] *1813, 1840*; slightest *1839*.
ii *1–12*. The opening passage echoes Southey's 'Madoc in Wales', *Madoc* (1805)
Part I, lii 276–81:
'When evening came, toward the echoing shore
I and Cadwallon walk'd together forth:

And thou hast lingered there,
Until the sun's broad orb
5   Seemed resting on the burnished wave,
Thou must have marked the lines
Of purple gold, that motionless
Hung o'er the sinking sphere:
Thou must have marked the billowy clouds
10   Edged with intolerable radiancy
Towering like rocks of jet
Crowned with a diamond wreath.
And yet there is a moment,
When the sun's highest point
15   Peeps like a star o'er ocean's western edge,
When those far clouds of feathery gold,
Shaded with deepest purple, gleam
Like islands on a dark blue sea;
Then has thy fancy soared above the earth,
20   And furled its wearied wing
Within the Fairy's fane.

Yet not the golden islands
Gleaming in yon flood of light,
Nor the feathery curtains
25   Stretching o'er the sun's bright couch,
Nor the burnished ocean waves
Paving that gorgeous dome,
So fair, so wonderful a sight
As Mab's etherial palace could afford.
30   Yet likest evening's vault, that faery Hall!
As Heaven, low resting on the wave, it spread
Its floors of flashing light,
Its vast and azure dome,
Its fertile golden islands
35   Floating on a silver sea;
Whilst suns their mingling beamings darted
Through clouds of circumambient darkness,
And pearly battlements around
Looked o'er the immense of Heaven.

40   The magic car no longer moved.
The Fairy and the Spirit

Bright with dilated glory shone the west;
But brighter lay the ocean-flood below,
The burnish'd silver sea, that heaved and flash'd
Its restless rays, intolerably bright'.
ii 21. *fane*] temple (a common Romantic poeticism).

Entered the Hall of Spells:
Those golden clouds
That rolled in glittering billows
45   Beneath the azure canopy
With the etherial footsteps trembled not:
The light and crimson mists,
Floating to strains of thrilling melody
Through that unearthly dwelling,
50 Yielded to every movement of the will.
Upon their passive swell the Spirit leaned,
And, for the varied bliss that pressed around,
Used not the glorious privilege
Of virtue and of wisdom.

55   Spirit! the Fairy said,
And pointed to the gorgeous dome,
This is a wondrous sight
And mocks all human grandeur;
But, were it virtue's only meed, to dwell
60 In a celestial palace, all resigned
To pleasurable impulses, immured
Within the prison of itself, the will
Of changeless nature would be unfulfilled.
Learn to make others happy. Spirit, come!
65 This is thine high reward: – the past shall rise;
Thou shalt behold the present; I will teach
The secrets of the future.

The Fairy and the Spirit
Approached the overhanging battlement. –
70   Below lay stretched the universe!
There, far as the remotest line
That bounds imagination's flight,

ii 45–6. canopy . . . footsteps] Locock 1911; canopy . . . footsteps, 1813, Forman 1876–7; canopy, . . . footsteps 1839, 1840.

ii 52. for] Locock glosses for as 'on account of', and explains: 'The "privilege" is that of resisting "pleasurable impulses".' But virtue's reward (though not its only reward: lines 59–64) is to enjoy the beauties of the Fairy's palace, so it seems more natural to take for as meaning 'for all', 'despite' (OED vii 4a; cp. TL 214) and to interpret: 'Despite the blisses at her command, Ianthe did not immerse herself in them as she was entitled'.

ii 59. meed] reward.

ii 69. overhanging battlement] The Fairy's prototype here is Milton's God surveying space and time from the walls of Heaven (PL iii 56–79): 'from his prospect high, / Wherein past, present, future he beholds . . .'

Countless and unending orbs
In mazy motion intermingled,
75   Yet still fulfilled immutably
Eternal nature's law.
Above, below, around
The circling systems formed
A wilderness of harmony;
80   Each with undeviating aim,
In eloquent silence, through the depths of space
Pursued its wondrous way.

There was a little light
That twinkled in the misty distance:
85   None but a spirit's eye
Might ken that rolling orb;
None but a spirit's eye,
And in no other place
But that celestial dwelling, might behold
90   Each action of this earth's inhabitants.
But matter, space and time
In those aërial mansions cease to act;
And all-prevailing wisdom, when it reaps
The harvest of its excellence, o'erbounds
95   Those obstacles, of which an earthly soul
Fears to attempt the conquest.

ii 73. *unending orbs*] The extent of the universe was disputed in S.'s day (*Grabo* (1930) 80–7), but S.'s most accessible sources assumed its infinity. Pierre Simon Laplace (*The System of the World* (1796; translated by J. Pond 1809) i 290–1) postulated 'a space without bounds, immovable and penetrable to matter', and was followed by Walker (*A System of Familiar Philosophy* 538): 'Our telescopes have their limits, as well as our eyes, but the space we explore has no limits!'. The infinity of space is also assumed in Paine's *Age of Reason*, Part I (1794). S. was studying Laplace in November 1813 (*L* i 380) and referred to his book in a note to *Q Mab* vi 45–6.

ii 74. *In mazy motion intermingled*] Suggested by *PL* v 620–7: 'mazes intricate, / Eccentric, intervolv'd, yet regular' etc. *mazy motion* occurs in Coleridge's 'Kubla Khan' 25, but there is no evidence that S. knew the poem (unpublished until 1816) at this time.

ii 79. *wilderness of harmony*] Cp. Pope's *Essay on Man* i 6: 'A mighty maze! but not without a plan'. The space-traveller in Young's *The Complaint; or, Night-Thoughts* (1742–45) sees beyond the planets 'A wilderness of wonders burning round' (Night ix 1730).

ii 81. *eloquent silence*] An endorsement of Addison's 'The Spacious Firmament on High' (*Spectator* 23 August 1712, quoted in Paine, *Age of Reason* Part I; *Paine Writings* iv 48) 17–24: 'What though, in solemn Silence, all / Move round the dark terrestrial Ball? / . . . In Reason's Ear they all rejoice . . .'

The Fairy pointed to the earth.
The Spirit's intellectual eye
Its kindred beings recognized.
100   The thronging thousands, to a passing view,
Seemed like an anthill's citizens.
How wonderful! that even
The passions, prejudices, interests,
That sway the meanest being, the weak touch
105   That moves the finest nerve,
And in one human brain
Causes the faintest thought, becomes a link
In the great chain of nature.

Behold, the Fairy cried,
110   Palmyra's ruined palaces!-
Behold! where grandeur frowned;
Behold! where pleasure smiled;
What now remains?-the memory
Of senselessness and shame-
115   What is immortal there?
Nothing-it stands to tell
A melancholy tale, to give
An awful warning: soon
Oblivion will steal silently
120   The remnant of its fame.
Monarchs and conquerors there
Proud o'er prostrate millions trod-

ii 98. *intellectual eye*] 'By "intellectual eye" S. simply means the eye of a creature
endowed with mind' (*Cameron (1974)* 237). See headnote to 'Hymn to Intellectual Beauty'.
ii *102–8. How wonderful! . . . chain of nature.*] Paraphrasing Holbach, *Système de
la Nature* i 56–7 (see S.'s note to *Q Mab* vi 171–3).
ii *110. Palmyra's ruined palaces!-*] Palmyra, wrongly identified by Gibbon
(*Decline and Fall of the Roman Empire* (1776–88; 1897 edn) i 306) with the
Biblical Tadmor, was a powerful caravan city in the Syrian desert, destroyed
by Aurelian in 273 A.D. Its ruins are still among the most impressive in the
world. Lines 109–25 owe much to Peacock's *Palmyra* (1806; 2nd edn 1812) esp.
sections xi, xvii, and to Volney's *Ruins*, chs i and ii. Where S.'s Fairy voices
moral and social criticism, however, Volney's traveller merely laments the
changes of Time: 'Within those walls, where a mournful silence reigns, the
noises of the arts and the shouts of joy and festivity continually resounded.
These heaps of marble formed regular palaces, these prostrate pillars were the
majestic ornaments of temples, these ruinous galleries present the outlines of
public places . . . And now a mournful skeleton is all that subsists of this
opulent city, and nothing remains of its powerful government but a vain and
obscure remembrance!' (ch. ii).

The earthquakes of the human race;
Like them, forgotten when the ruin
125   That marks their shock is past.

Beside the eternal Nile,
The Pyramids have risen.
Nile shall pursue his changeless way:
Those pyramids shall fall;
130   Yea! not a stone shall stand to tell
The spot whereon they stood;
Their very site shall be forgotten,
As is their builder's name!

Behold yon sterile spot;
135   Where now the wandering Arab's tent
Flaps in the desert-blast.
There once old Salem's haughty fane
Reared high to heaven its thousand golden domes,
And in the blushing face of day
140   Exposed its shameful glory.
Oh! many a widow, many an orphan cursed
The building of that fane; and many a father,
Worn out with toil and slavery, implored
The poor man's God to sweep it from the earth,
145   And spare his children the detested task
Of piling stone on stone, and poisoning
The choicest days of life,
To soothe a dotard's vanity.

ii *123. race;*] race, – *1839, 1840.*
ii *129–33. Those pyramids . . . their builder's name!*] A commonplace; but perhaps
recalling Kirke White's 'Time' 173–7: 'Who lies inhumed in the terrific gloom
/ Of the gigantic pyramid? or who / Reared its huge walls? Oblivion laughs,
and says, / The prey is mine. – They sleep, and never more / Their names shall
strike upon the ear of man'.
ii *131. stood;*] *1813, 1839, 1840;* stood! *Forman 1876–7, Hutchinson, 1972.*
ii *132. site*] scite *1813.*
ii *137. old Salem's haughty fane*] The building of Solomon's temple (Hebrew
Shalom, 'peace') in Jerusalem in the 9th century B.C. is described in *I Kings*
v–viii and *II Chronicles* iii–v. It was said to have taken 20 years to complete, out
of pre-dressed stone, cedarwood, and gold.
ii *141–8. Oh! many a widow . . . a dotard's vanity.*] 'And king Solomon raised a
levy out of all Israel; and the levy was thirty thousand men. And he sent them
to Lebanon, ten thousand a month by courses: a month they were in Lebanon,
and two months at home: and Adoniram was over the levy. And Solomon had
threescore and ten thousand that bare burdens, and fourscore thousand hewers
in the mountains; Beside the chief of Solomon's officers which were over the
work, three thousand and three hundred, which ruled over the people that
wrought in the work' (*I Kings* v 13–16). S. took the same view of York

There an inhuman and uncultured race
150 Howled hideous praises to their Demon-God;
They rushed to war, tore from the mother's womb
The unborn child, -old age and infancy
Promiscuous perished; their victorious arms
Left not a soul to breathe. Oh! they were fiends:
155 But what was he who taught them that the God
Of nature and benevolence had given
A special sanction to the trade of blood?
His name and theirs are fading, and the tales
Of this barbarian nation, which imposture
160 Recites till terror credits, are pursuing
Itself into forgetfulness.

Minster: '. . . when I contemplate these gigantic piles of superstition, when I consider too the leisure for the exercise of mind, which the labor which erected them annihilated, I set them down as so many retardations of the period when truth becomes omnipotent' (16 October 1811: L i 151).

ii *149. an inhuman and uncultured race*] The Old Testament Hebrews. Radical attacks on the Jews were essentially theological rather than racialist, assailing the religion which had enjoined the vengeful cruelties of the O.T., and so, indirectly, contemporary Christianity which acknowledged the same God. 'Could we permit ourselves to suppose that the Almighty would distinguish any nation of people by the name of *his chosen people*, we must suppose that people to have been an example to all the rest of the world of the purest piety and humanity, and not such a nation of ruffians and cut-throats as the ancient Jews were: a people who . . . had distinguished themselves above all others on the face of the known earth for barbarity and wickedness' (Paine, *The Age of Reason* Pt II; *Paine Writings* iv 114–15). '. . . le Dieu des Juifs, c'est-à-dire, du peuple le plus stupide, le plus crédule, le plus sauvage, le plus insociable qui fut jamais sur la terre . . .' (Holbach, *Le Bon Sens du Curé Jean Meslier* (1733) ch. cxxi).

ii *151–4. They rushed to war . . . they were fiends*] S.'s example, from *Numbers* xxxi, is the same as Paine's in *The Age of Reason*, and S. cites it again, with other Biblical texts, in *A Refutation of Deism* (1814), where his Deist spokesman Theosophus says: '. . . it is blasphemy of a more hideous and unexampled nature to maintain that the Almighty God expressly commanded Moses to invade an unoffending nation; and . . . utterly to destroy every human being it contained, to murder every infant and unarmed man in cold blood, to massacre the captives, to rip up the matrons, and to retain the maidens alone for concubinage and violation' (*Prose* 122–3).

ii *155. what was he*] 'Among the detestable villains that in any period of the world have disgraced the name of man, it is impossible to find a greater than Moses . . .' (Paine, *Age of Reason* Pt II; *Paine Writings* iv 102).

ii *156. had*] *1813, 1839, 1840*; hath *Forman 1876–7, Hutchinson, Locock 1911, 1972* (a perpetuated misprint).

ii *159–60. which imposture / Recites*] i.e. which are repeated by priests.

Where Athens, Rome, and Sparta stood,
There is a moral desert now:
The mean and miserable huts,
165   The yet more wretched palaces,
Contrasted with those ancient fanes
Now crumbling to oblivion;
The long and lonely colonnades,
Through which the ghost of Freedom stalks,
170   Seem like a well-known tune,
Which in some dear scene we have loved to hear,
Remembered now in sadness.
But, oh! how much more changed,
How gloomier is the contrast
175   Of human nature there!
Where Socrates expired, a tyrant's slave,
A coward and a fool, spreads death around—
Then, shuddering, meets his own.
Where Cicero and Antoninus lived,
180   A cowled and hypocritical monk
Prays, curses and deceives.

Spirit! ten thousand years
Have scarcely passed away,
Since, in the waste where now the savage drinks
185   His enemy's blood, and aping Europe's sons,
Wakes the unholy song of war,
Arose a stately city,

ii *166. fanes*] fanes, *1813, eds.* The decay towards oblivion must be that of the
classical monuments, not the modern huts and palaces, in order to parallel the
extinction of Socrates and Cicero.
ii *171. Which*] Which, *1813, 1839, 1840* (possible only with a second comma after
scene).
ii *176. a tyrant's slave*] Characterizing the Greek puppets who in 1813 were
serving Turkish overlords.
ii *179. Antoninus*] Titus Antoninus (d. A.D. 161), humane and enlightened
successor to the Emperor Hadrian. The Papacy now ruled Rome.
ii *187. a stately city*] Probably suggested by Tenochtitlán (Mexico City), the
14th-century Aztec capital described in D. F. S. Clavigero's *History of Mexico*
(1787; 2nd edn 1807) i 4 as 'the most renowned of all the cities of the new
world, and capital of the empire'. Aztec religion centred on human sacrifice
and cannibalism (lines 184–5); but this whole culture was destroyed by Cortes
in the 16th century (lines 191–2). Montezuma's extensive botanical and zoolo-
gical gardens (line 195) at Tenochtitlán astonished the Spaniards (Clavigero ii
71–4); S. had read a description of the city and gardens of Southey's composite
'Aztlan' in *Madoc* (Part I, vi 107–63 and notes). Tenochtitlán was built on
islands in Lake Texcoco, which had other cities on its banks, hence the 'ships'
of line 201 ('Aztlan' was also on a great lake). S.'s 'ten thousand years' must be
fanciful; perhaps he was also thinking of Tollan ('Tula'), a famous ancient

Metropolis of the western continent:
There, now, the mossy column-stone,
190 Indented by time's unrelaxing grasp,
Which once appeared to brave
All, save its country's ruin;
There the wide forest scene,
Rude in the uncultivated loveliness
195 Of gardens long run wild,
Seems, to the unwilling sojourner, whose steps
Chance in that desert has delayed,
Thus to have stood since earth was what it is.
Yet once it was the busiest haunt,
200 Whither, as to a common centre, flocked
Strangers, and ships, and merchandise:
Once peace and freedom blessed
The cultivated plain:
But wealth, that curse of man,
205 Blighted the bud of its prosperity:
Virtue and wisdom, truth and liberty,
Fled, to return not, until man shall know
That they alone can give the bliss
Worthy a soul that claims
210 Its kindred with eternity.

There's not one atom of yon earth
But once was living man;

Mexican site abandoned in the 10th century.

ii *196. Seems*] Column-stone and rude forest are alternative and separate signs of ancientness, hence perhaps the singular verb.

ii *211–15. There's not one atom . . . human veins*] An old speculation in part (see *Hamlet* V i 198–210), but also a logical extension of Holbach's necessitarianism in which the universe consisted of particles circulating endlessly through transient material forms (*Système de la Nature* i 42–6): 'Les animaux, les plantes & les minéraux rendent au bout d'un certain tems à la nature, c'est-à-dire à la masse générale des choses, au magasin universel, les élémens ou principes qu'ils en ont empruntés . . . Les parties élémentaires de l'animal ainsi désunies, dissoutes, élaborées, dispersées, vont former de nouvelles combinaisons; elles servent à nourrir, à conserver ou à détruire de nouveaux êtres . . . Telle est la marche constante de la nature; tel est le cercle éternel que tout ce qui existe est forcé de décrire' (see also ii 188). Erasmus Darwin explained the Pythagorean transmigration of souls as deriving from this reconstitution of elements: 'How the same organs, which today compose / The poisonous henbane, or the fragrant rose, / May with tomorrow's sun new forms compile, / Frown in the Hero, in the Beauty smile' (*Temple of Nature* iv 421–4). S. may have been influenced by James Montgomery's 48-stanza poem on this theme, 'The Mole-Hill' (1810): 'Once every atom of this mound / Lived, breathed, and felt like me' (lines 11–12).

Nor the minutest drop of rain,
That hangeth in its thinnest cloud,
215   But flowed in human veins:
And from the burning plains
Where Libyan monsters yell,
From the most gloomy glens
Of Greenland's sunless clime,
220   To where the golden fields
Of fertile England spread
Their harvest to the day,
Thou canst not find one spot
Whereon no city stood.

225   How strange is human pride!
I tell thee that those living things,
To whom the fragile blade of grass,
That springeth in the morn
And perisheth ere noon,
230   Is an unbounded world;
I tell thee that those viewless beings,
Whose mansion is the smallest particle
Of the impassive atmosphere,

ii *223–4. Thou canst not find . . . city stood*] Cp. Young's *Complaint: or, Night-Thoughts* (Night ix 92, 98): 'Where is the dust that has not been alive? / . . . Whole bury'd towns support the dancer's heel'. Cuvier's hypothesis, that earth had experienced a long series of geophysical 'revolutions', and Hutton's, that the processes of decay and renovation of the earth's surface had had no beginning and would have no end, had recently stimulated ideas of vast historical cycles. In a letter from Keswick of 23 November 1811 S. speculated: 'Imagination is resistlessly compelled to look back when, perhaps this retirement of peace and mountain simplicity, was the Pandemonium of druidical imposture, the scene of Roman Pollution, the resting place of the savage denizen of these solitudes with the wolf.—Still, still further!—strain thy reverted Fancy when . . . a vast populous and licentious city stood in the midst of an immense plain . . .' (*L* i 189).
ii *227. blade of grass*] Referring to *Psalms* xc 5–6: 'In the morning they are like grass which groweth up. In the morning it flourisheth, and groweth up; in the evening it is cut down, and withereth'.
ii *231. those viewless beings*] The microscopic world had been popularized by Bernard de Fontenelle, *Entretiens sur la Pluralité des Mondes* (1686), transl. Elizabeth Gunning as *Conversations on the Plurality of Worlds* (1808) 99–100: '. . . our world contains as many species of animals that are invisible to us, as of those that we discern . . . The leaf of a tree is a world, inhabited by worms

Think, feel and live like man;
235 That their affections and antipathies,
     Like his, produce the laws
     Ruling their moral state;
     And the minutest throb
     That through their frame diffuses
240   The slightest, faintest motion,
     Is fixed and indispensable
     As the majestic laws
     That rule yon rolling orbs.

     The Fairy paused. The Spirit,
245 In ecstacy of admiration, felt
     All knowledge of the past revived; the events
         Of old and wondrous times,
     Which dim tradition interruptedly
     Teaches the credulous vulgar, were unfolded
250   In just perspective to the view;
         Yet dim from their infinitude.
         The Spirit seemed to stand
     High on an isolated pinnacle;
     The flood of ages combating below,
255 The depth of the unbounded universe
         Above, and all around
     Nature's unchanging harmony.

---

imperceptibly small, to which it appears an amazing extent . . .', and in England by Addison (*Spectator* 519) and (among many others) Paine (*Age of Reason, Paine Writings* iv 67–8): '. . . we find every part of [creation] (the earth, the waters, and the air that surrounds it) filled, and, as it were, crowded with life, down from the largest animals . . . to others still smaller, and totally invisible without the assistance of the microscope. Every tree, every plant, every leaf, serves not only as a habitation, but as a world, to some numerous race, till animal existence becomes so exceedingly refined that the effluvia of a blade of grass would be food for thousands'. King-Hele (*Shelley: His Thought and Work* (2nd edn 1971) 37–8) and Rogers (*1972* 383–4) assume that by beings whose 'mansion' is a particle S. means the particles themselves, a possible but less likely reading of this passage. See below, *Q Mab* iv 143–50 and note. The paradoxical materialist doctrine that molecules of matter can feel and think, put forward by Pierre-Louis Moreau de Maupertuis in *Essai sur la Fonction des Corps organisés* (1754; retitled *Système de la Nature* in 1768) and in less extreme form by others in S.'s day, is discussed by H. W. Piper, *The Active Universe* (1962) 16–21. Lucretius did not, as King-Hele and Rogers claim, believe in sentient atoms (*De Rerum Natura* ii 865–990).

III.

Fairy! the Spirit said,
And on the Queen of spells
Fixed her etherial eyes,
I thank thee. Thou hast given
5 A boon which I will not resign, and taught
A lesson not to be unlearned. I know
The past, and thence I will essay to glean
A warning for the future, so that man
May profit by his errors, and derive
10   Experience from his folly:
For, when the power of imparting joy
Is equal to the will, the human soul
          Requires no other heaven.

MAB

Turn thee, surpassing Spirit!
15   Much yet remains unscanned.
Thou knowest how great is man,
Thou knowest his imbecility:
Yet learn thou what he is;
Yet learn the lofty destiny
20   Which restless time prepares
          For every living soul.

Behold a gorgeous palace, that, amid
Yon populous city, rears its thousand towers
And seems itself a city. Gloomy troops
25 Of sentinels, in stern and silent ranks,
Encompass it around: the dweller there
Cannot be free and happy; hearest thou not
The curses of the fatherless, the groans
Of those who have no friend? He passes on:
30 The King, the wearer of a gilded chain
That binds his soul to abjectness, the fool

iii 6–10. *I know . . . his folly*] The moral of *Ruins* ch. xiii: 'By force of experience
he [man] will become enlightened; by force of errors he will set himself right'.
iii *11–13. For, when the power . . . no other heaven*] Volney, like Holbach, based all
voluntary action, including benevolent action, on self-interest; Godwin,
however (*Political Justice* Bk IV ch. x, i 424 ff.), argued that 'agreeable sensation' was merely the superficial motive of benevolence, which could become
disinterested and provide 'an uncommonly exquisite source of happiness'.
iii *17. imbecility*] weakness.
iii *21*. 'For all humanity' (not 'for everyone now living').
iii *30. The King*] S.'s attack on monarchy belongs to a tradition of which later
examples include Cowper's *Task* (1785) v 246–382; Paine's *Common Sense*

Whom courtiers nickname monarch, whilst a slave
Even to the basest appetites–that man
Heeds not the shriek of penury; he smiles
35   At the deep curses which the destitute
Mutter in secret, and a sullen joy
Pervades his bloodless heart when thousands groan
But for those morsels which his wantonness
Wastes in unjoyous revelry, to save
40   All that they love from famine: when he hears
The tale of horror, to some ready-made face
Of hypocritical assent he turns,
Smothering the glow of shame, that, spite of him,
Flushes his bloated cheek.

                            Now to the meal
45   Of silence, grandeur, and excess, he drags
His palled unwilling appetite. If gold,
Gleaming around, and numerous viands culled
From every clime, could force the loathing sense
To overcome satiety,–if wealth
50   The spring it draws from poisons not,–or vice,
Unfeeling, stubborn vice, converteth not
Its food to deadliest venom; then that king
Is happy; and the peasant who fulfils
His unforced task, when he returns at even,

(1776) i 11–18 (*Paine Writings* i 75–84); *Ruins* ch. vi; and *Political Justice* Bk V chs
i–xiii, ii 1–113. John Ball's speech in Southey's *Wat Tyler* (II i 104–12) seems
especially relevant:

> When I gaze
> On the proud palace, and behold one man
> In the blood-purpled robes of royalty,
> Feasting at ease and lording over millions,
> Then turn me to the hut of poverty,
> And see the wretched labourer worn with toil,
> Divide his scanty morsel with his infants,
> I sicken, and indignant at the sight,
> 'Blush for the patience of humanity'.

iii 32–3. *a slave / Even to the basest appetites*] Cp. *Ruins* ch. xi: '. . . kings, in the
weariness of satiety, followed the dictates of every factitious and depraved
taste'.

iii 49–50. *if wealth . . . poisons not*] An inversion: 'if the source from which it
comes does not poison the king's wealth'.

iii 50–2. *or vice, . . . deadliest venom*] 'If selfish vice does not entail disease' (cp. Q
Mab ix 87–8: 'No longer prostitution's venomed bane / Poisoned the springs of
happiness and life').

55   And by the blazing faggot meets again
      Her welcome for whom all his toil is sped,
      Tastes not a sweeter meal.

                             Behold him now
      Stretched on the gorgeous couch; his fevered brain
      Reels dizzily awhile: but ah! too soon
60   The slumber of intemperance subsides,
      And conscience, that undying serpent, calls
      Her venomous brood to their nocturnal task.
      Listen! he speaks! oh! mark that frenzied eye—
      Oh! mark that deadly visage.

                    KING
                             No cessation!
65   Oh! must this last for ever! Awful death,
      I wish, yet fear to clasp thee!—Not one moment
      Of dreamless sleep! O dear and blessed peace!
      Why dost thou shroud thy vestal purity
      In penury and dungeons? wherefore lurkest
70   With danger, death, and solitude; yet shunn'st
      The palace I have built thee? Sacred peace!
      Oh visit me but once, but pitying shed
      One drop of balm upon my withered soul.

                    MAB
      Vain man! that palace is the virtuous heart,
75   And peace defileth not her snowy robes
      In such a shed as thine. Hark! yet he mutters;
      His slumbers are but varied agonies,
      They prey like scorpions on the springs of life.
      There needeth not the hell that bigots frame
80   To punish those who err: earth in itself
      Contains at once the evil and the cure;
      And all-sufficing nature can chastise
      Those who transgress her law,—she only knows

iii 65. ever!] *1813, 1839, 1840*; ever? *Hutchinson, 1972*.
iii 66–73. *Not one moment . . . withered soul.*] The 'care of Kings' was a
commonplace: e.g. Shakespeare, *Henry IV Pt. II* III i 31; *Henry V* IV i 263–4:
'Not all these, laid in bed majestical, / Can sleep so soundly as the wretched
slave'. A recent influence may have been Southey's *Wat Tyler* I 99–102: '. . .
sounder sleep / Waits on the weary ploughman's lowly bed, / Than on the
drowsy couch of luxury / Lulls the rich slave of pride and indolence'.
iii 74. *Change of speaker omitted 1813.*
iii 80–1. *earth in itself . . . the cure*] Adapted from Mohareb's sophistry in
Southey's *Thalaba* IX xiv 11–12: 'The same Earth / Bears fruit and poison'.

How justly to proportion to the fault
85 The punishment it merits.

                                        Is it strange
That this poor wretch should pride him in his woe?
Take pleasure in his abjectness, and hug
The scorpion that consumes him? Is it strange
That, placed on a conspicuous throne of thorns,
90 Grasping an iron sceptre, and immured
Within a splendid prison, whose stern bounds
Shut him from all that's good or dear on earth,
His soul asserts not its humanity?
That man's mild nature rises not in war
95 Against a king's employ? No—'tis not strange.
He, like the vulgar, thinks, feels, acts and lives
Just as his father did; the unconquered powers
Of precedent and custom interpose
Between a *king* and virtue. Stranger yet,
100 To those who know not nature, nor deduce
The future from the present, it may seem,
That not one slave, who suffers from the crimes
Of this unnatural being; not one wretch,
Whose children famish, and whose nuptial bed
105 Is earth's unpitying bosom, rears an arm
To dash him from his throne!

                                    Those gilded flies
That, basking in the sunshine of a court,
Fatten on its corruption!—what are they?
—The drones of the community; they feed

iii *85–106. Is it strange . . . dash him from his throne!*] Cowper (*Task* v 268–334)
had found similar facts 'strange': 'Such dupes are men to custom'.
iii *88–93. Is it strange . . . its humanity?*] S. seems indebted partly to Milton,
Paradise Regained ii 458–480, especially 'a Crown, / Golden in shew, is but a
wreath of thorns, / Brings dangers, troubles, cares, and sleepless nights / To
him who wears a royal diadem'; partly to Godwin, *Political Justice* Bk V chs.
ii–iii, ii 10, 16, 24–5: 'It is perhaps impossible, that a man [i.e. a King] shut up
in a cabinet, can ever be wise . . . It would be unreasonable to expect from him
any thing generous and humane . . . The man, who . . . may . . . be precluded
from that very intercourse and knowledge it is most important for him to
possess, whatever name he may bear, is, in reality, a prisoner'.
iii *109. drones of the community*] 'The aristocracy are not the farmers who work
the land, and raise the produce, but are the mere consumers of the rent; and . . .
are the drones . . . who neither collect the honey nor form the hive, but exist
only for lazy enjoyment' (Paine, *Rights of Man* Pt II; *Paine Writings* ii 471).

110   On the mechanic's labour: the starved hind
      For them compels the stubborn glebe to yield
      Its unshared harvests; and yon squalid form,
      Leaner than fleshless misery, that wastes
      A sunless life in the unwholesome mine,
115   Drags out in labour a protracted death,
      To glut their grandeur; many faint with toil,
      That few may know the cares and woe of sloth.

      Whence, thinkest thou, kings and parasites arose?
      Whence that unnatural line of drones, who heap
120   Toil and unvanquishable penury
      On those who build their palaces, and bring
      Their daily bread?—From vice, black loathsome vice;
      From rapine, madness, treachery, and wrong;
      From all that genders misery, and makes
125   Of earth this thorny wilderness; from lust,
      Revenge, and murder . . . And when reason's voice,
      Loud as the voice of nature, shall have waked
      The nations; and mankind perceive that vice
      Is discord, war, and misery; that virtue
130   Is peace, and happiness and harmony;
      When man's maturer nature shall disdain
      The playthings of its childhood;—kingly glare

iii *110. mechanic's*] manual worker's.

iii *111. stubborn glebe*] 'stiff soil', echoing Gray's *Elegy* 26: 'Their furrow oft the stubborn glebe has broke'.

iii *118. thinkest*] *1813, 1839, 1840*; think'st Hutchinson, Locock *1911, 1972*.

iii *122–34. From vice, . . . silently pass by*] '. . . it is more than probable that we should find the first of them [Kings] nothing better than the principal ruffian of some restless gang, whose savage manners, or pre-eminence in subtilty, obtained him the title of chief among plunderers; and who, by increasing in power, and extending his depradations, overawed the quiet and defenceless to purchase their safety by frequent contributions' (Paine, *Common Sense* (1776) i 15; *Paine Writings* i 80). Volney (*Ruins* chs viii, xi) had seen the origin of class-oppression in man's 'ignorance and love of accumulation'. 'Since then it was from his own bosom all the evils proceeded that have vexed the life of man, it was there also he ought to have sought the remedies, where only they are to be found'. S. did not necessarily regard these two accounts as incompatible (see *Q Mab* iii 201–3 below).

iii *124–5. makes / Of earth this thorny wilderness*] Recalling *Isaiah* xiv 16–17: 'Is this the man . . . That made the world as a wilderness . . . ?'

iii *132. playthings of its childhood*] The childishness of titles was Paine's particular line of attack: 'There is no occasion to take titles away, for they take themselves away when society concurs to ridicule them' (*Rights of Man* Pt I; *Paine Writings* ii 320).

Will lose its power to dazzle; its authority
Will silently pass by; the gorgeous throne
135   Shall stand unnoticed in the regal hall,
Fast falling to decay; whilst falsehood's trade
Shall be as hateful and unprofitable
As that of truth is now.

                   Where is the fame
Which the vain-glorious mighty of the earth
140   Seek to eternize? Oh! the faintest sound
From time's light footfall, the minutest wave
That swells the flood of ages, whelms in nothing
The unsubstantial bubble. Aye! to-day
Stern is the tyrant's mandate, red the gaze
145   That flashes desolation, strong the arm
That scatters multitudes. To-morrow comes!
That mandate is a thunder-peal that died
In ages past; that gaze, a transient flash
On which the midnight closed, and on that arm
150   The worm has made his meal.

                 The virtuous man,
Who, great in his humility, as kings
Are little in their grandeur; he who leads
Invincibly a life of resolute good,
And stands amid the silent dungeon-depths
155   More free and fearless than the trembling judge,
Who, clothed in venal power, vainly strove
To bind the impassive spirit;—when he falls,
His mild eye beams benevolence no more:

iii 134–6. *the gorgeous throne . . . falling to decay*] S.'s vision of monarchy as a
historical relic recalls 'A Retrospect of Times of Old': 'The mansions of the
Kings are tenantless'. It also prefigures the conclusion of *PU* Act III.
iii 143–50. *Aye! to-day . . . has made his meal*] Evidently suggested by Kirke
White's 'Time' 134–50, especially 139–45:
               The warrior's arm
    Lies nerveless on the pillow of its shame;
    Hushed is his stormy voice, and quenched the blaze
    Of his red eyeball.—Yesterday his name
    Was mighty on the earth.—To-day—'tis what?
    The meteor of the night of distant years,
    That flashed unnoticed
iii 151. *Who, great*] As great *Rossetti 1870*. Emended because 'who, great has no
proper syntactical sequence'; but the repetitive build-up 'The virtuous man
who . . . he who . . . who . . . when *he* falls' is rhetorically plausible.
iii 157. *impassive*] invulnerable.

Withered the hand outstretched but to relieve;
160 Sunk reason's simple eloquence, that rolled
But to appal the guilty. Yes! the grave
Hath quenched that eye, and death's relentless frost
Withered that arm: but the unfading fame
Which virtue hangs upon its votary's tomb;
165 The deathless memory of that man, whom kings
Call to their mind and tremble; the remembrance
With which the happy spirit contemplates
Its well-spent pilgrimage on earth,
Shall never pass away.

170 Nature rejects the monarch, not the man;
The subject, not the citizen: for kings
And subjects, mutual foes, for ever play
A losing game into each other's hands,
Whose stakes are vice and misery. The man
175 Of virtuous soul commands not, nor obeys.
Power, like a desolating pestilence,
Pollutes whate'er it touches; and obedience,
Bane of all genius, virtue, freedom, truth,
Makes slaves of men, and, of the human frame,
180 A mechanized automaton.

                              When Nero,
High over flaming Rome, with savage joy
Lowered like a fiend, drank with enraptured ear

iii *170–1. Nature rejects . . . not the citizen*] 'The romantic and barbarous
distinction of men into Kings and subjects, though it may suit the conditions of
courtiers, cannot that of citizens . . . Every citizen is a member of the
sovereignty, and, as such, can acknowledge no personal subjection: and his
obedience can be only to the laws' (Paine, *Rights of Man* Pt I; *Paine Writings* ii
386). See also *PU* III iv 193–7 and note.

iii *174–5. The man . . . nor obeys*] An absence of 'the mingled voice / Of slavery
and command' is a sign of successful revolution in *PU* III ii 30–1.

iii *176–7. Power . . . whate'er it touches*] An anticipation of Lord Acton's dictum
'Power tends to corrupt, and absolute power corrupts absolutely'.

iii *177–80. obedience . . . mechanized automaton*] These lines follow the uncompromising first version (1793) of *Political Justice* Bk III ch. vi, iii 266 ff.: '. . . one
man can in no case be bound to yield obedience to any other man or set of men
upon earth . . . Man, when he surrenders his reason, and becomes the partisan
of implicit faith and blind obedience, is the most mischievous of all animals . . .
He is, in the instant of submission, the blind instrument of every nefarious
purpose of his principal; and, when left to himself, is open to the seduction of
injustice, cruelty and profligacy'.

iii *180. Nero*] S. greatly exaggerates even the least favourable account of Nero's
behaviour at the fire: 'Watching this conflagration from the Maecenatian
Tower and exulting, as he put it, "in the beauty of the flames", he sang "The

The shrieks of agonizing death, beheld
The frightful desolation spread, and felt
185 A new created sense within his soul
Thrill to the sight, and vibrate to the sound;
Thinkest thou his grandeur had not overcome
The force of human kindness? and, when Rome,
With one stern blow, hurled not the tyrant down,
190 Crushed not the arm red with her dearest blood,
Had not submissive abjectness destroyed
Nature's suggestions?

                    Look on yonder earth:
The golden harvests spring; the unfailing sun
Sheds light and life; the fruits, the flowers, the trees,
195 Arise in due succession; all things speak
Peace, harmony, and love. The universe,
In nature's silent eloquence, declares
That all fulfil the works of love and joy, –
All but the outcast, man. He fabricates
200 The sword which stabs his peace; he cherisheth
The snakes that gnaw his heart; he raiseth up
The tyrant, whose delight is in his woe,
Whose sport is in his agony. Yon sun,
Lights it the great alone? Yon silver beams,

Sack of Ilium" in his theatrical costume' (Suetonius, *De Vita Caesarum* VI
xxxviii 3). But he was rumoured to have started the fire himself.
iii *199. the outcast, man.*] the outcast man. *1813*; the outcast, Man. *1839, 1840,*
Hutchinson, *1972*. The theme of man's disorder amid an orderly Nature has
scriptural and classical origins: S.'s immediate influence seems to have been
James Thomson's *Castle of Indolence* (1748) I xi 1: ' "Outcast of Nature, man!" '
The moral and political viewpoint of stanzas ix–xi is close to S.'s: the wizard
Indolence declares 'all but man with unearned pleasures gay', while Man is the
victim of his own vices, 'That all proceed from savage thirst of gain' and lead to
injustices and war. Charlotte Smith's *The Emigrants* (1793) i 32–4 has the same
moral: 'Yet Man, misguided Man, / Mars the fair work that he was bid enjoy, /
And makes himself the evil he deplores.' (Part of the poem is quoted in Mrs
Radcliffe's *Mysteries of Udolpho*, which S. had read.) On 24 December 1812 S.
ordered 'Poems by Clio Rickman' (*L* i 345) from the author, whose *Poetical
Scraps* (2 vols, 1803) includes 'An Extempore Effusion on the Times' (dated
1800): 'Nature, prolific! bountiful to all! / . . . Rejoice and sing; alas! in vain!
man mars / The splendid scene, full fraught with happiness! / Repays the
bounteous earth with seas of blood!' (ii 74). See note on *Q Mab* vii 48.
iii *203–6. Yon sun . . . dome of kings?*] Beach Langston (*HLQ* xii (1948–49) 173)
quotes *The Winter's Tale* IV iv 441–3: 'The self-same sun that shines upon his
court / Hides not his visage from our cottage, but / Looks on alike'. Cp. *Wat
Tyler* ii 82–3: 'Shines not the sun / With equal ray on both?'

205   Sleep they less sweetly on the cottage thatch,
       Than on the dome of kings? Is mother earth
       A step–dame to her numerous sons, who earn
       Her unshared gifts with unremitting toil;
       A mother only to those puling babes
210   Who, nursed in ease and luxury, make men
       The playthings of their babyhood, and mar,
       In self important childishness, that peace
       Which men alone appreciate?

              Spirit of Nature! no.
215   The pure diffusion of thy essence throbs
          Alike in every human heart.
              Thou, aye, erectest there
          Thy throne of power unappealable:
          Thou art the judge beneath whose nod
220   Man's brief and frail authority
              Is powerless as the wind
              That passeth idly by.
          Thine the tribunal which surpasseth
              The show of human justice,
225   As God surpasses man.

              Spirit of Nature! thou
       Life of interminable multitudes;
          Soul of those mighty spheres
       Whose changeless paths through Heaven's deep silence
                                                    lie;
230   Soul of that smallest being,
              The dwelling of whose life
              Is one faint April sun-gleam;–
              Man, like these passive things,
          Thy will unconsciously fulfilleth:
235   Like theirs, his age of endless peace,
              Which time is fast maturing,
              Will swiftly, surely come;
          And the unbounded frame, which thou pervadest,
              Will be without a flaw
240   Marring its perfect symmetry.

                          IV.
       How beautiful this night! the balmiest sigh,
       Which vernal zephyrs breathe in evening's ear,
       Were discord to the speaking quietude

iii *217. aye*] ever.
iii *220.* A line imitated from *Measure for Measure* II ii 117–18: 'man, proud man,
/ Drest in a little brief authority . . .'
iii *221–2. powerless . . . idly by*] Beach Langston (op. cit.) quotes *Julius Caesar* IV
iii 67–8: 'they pass by me as the idle wind / Which I respect not'.

That wraps this moveless scene. Heaven's ebon vault,
5   Studded with stars unutterably bright,
Through which the moon's unclouded grandeur rolls,
Seems like a canopy which love had spread
To curtain her sleeping world. Yon gentle hills,
Robed in a garment of untrodden snow;
10 Yon darksome rocks, whence icicles depend,
So stainless, that their white and glittering spires
Tinge not the moon's pure beam; yon castled steep,
Whose banner hangeth o'er the time-worn tower
So idly, that rapt fancy deemeth it
15 A metaphor of peace;–all form a scene
Where musing solitude might love to lift
Her soul above this sphere of earthliness;
Where silence undisturbed might watch alone,
So cold, so bright, so still.

                    The orb of day,
20 In southern climes, o'er ocean's waveless field
Sinks sweetly smiling: not the faintest breath
Steals o'er the unruffled deep; the clouds of eve
Reflect unmoved the lingering beam of day;
And vesper's image on the western main
25 Is beautifully still. To-morrow comes:
Cloud upon cloud, in dark and deepening mass,
Roll o'er the blackened waters; the deep roar
Of distant thunder mutters awfully;
Tempest unfolds its pinion o'er the gloom
30 That shrouds the boiling surge; the pitiless fiend,
With all his winds and lightnings, tracks his prey;
The torn deep yawns,–the vessel finds a grave
Beneath its jagged gulf.

               Ah! whence yon glare
That fires the arch of heaven?–that dark red smoke
35 Blotting the silver moon? The stars are quenched

iv 12. *yon castled steep*] Harlech Castle can be seen on a rocky height six miles
across the estuary from Tanyrallt.

iv 19–33. *The orb of day . . . jagged gulf*] Apparently a recollection of William
Falconer, *The Shipwreck* (1762) i 196–207: 'Now, in the southern hemisphere,
the sun / Thro' the bright virgin and the scales had run . . . / And not a breeze
awakes the silent deep . . . / This . . . / The watchful mariner, whom heaven
informs, / Oft deems the prelude of approaching storms'. The poem was stock
reading in S.'s boyhood.

iv 33–70. *Ah! whence yon glare . . . Waves o'er a warrior's tomb*] A passage based on
the occupation and burning of Moscow (lines 33–58), announced in the 19th
and 20th French Grand Army Bulletins reported in *GM* lxxxii (October 1812)
382–3, and on Bonaparte's subsequent costly retreat (lines 62–7). See headnote. Battles in the snow during the retreat were described in *GM* lxxxii

In darkness, and the pure and spangling snow
Gleams faintly through the gloom that gathers round!
Hark to that roar, whose swift and deaf'ning peals
In countless echoes through the mountains ring,
40   Startling pale midnight on her starry throne!
Now swells the intermingling din; the jar
Frequent and frightful of the bursting bomb;
The falling beam, the shriek, the groan, the shout,
The ceaseless clangor, and the rush of men
45   Inebriate with rage;—loud, and more loud
The discord grows; till pale death shuts the scene,
And o'er the conqueror and the conquered draws
His cold and bloody shroud.—Of all the men
Whom day's departing beam saw blooming there,
50   In proud and vigorous health; of all the hearts
That beat with anxious life at sun-set there;
How few survive, how few are beating now!
All is deep silence, like the fearful calm
That slumbers in the storm's portentous pause;
55   Save when the frantic wail of widowed love
Comes shuddering on the blast, or the faint moan
With which some soul bursts from the frame of clay
Wrapped round its struggling powers.

                                        The grey morn
Dawns on the mournful scene; the sulphurous smoke
60   Before the icy wind slow rolls away,
And the bright beams of frosty morning dance
Along the spangling snow. There tracks of blood
Even to the forest's depth, and scattered arms,
And lifeless warriors, whose hard lineaments
65   Death's self could change not, mark the dreadful path
Of the outsallying victors: far behind,
Black ashes note where their proud city stood.
Within yon forest is a gloomy glen—
Each tree which guards its darkness from the day,
70   Waves o'er a warrior's tomb.

                                        I see thee shrink,
Surpassing Spirit!—wert thou human else?
I see a shade of doubt and horror fleet
Across thy stainless features: yet fear not;
This is no unconnected misery,

(December 1812) 570–4. S. dramatizes these events not in the exultant strains
of Wordsworth's later 'French Army in Russia' poems (published 1816) but as
a self-inflicted human disaster illustrating the argument of Q *Mab* iii 192–203.

75   Nor stands uncaused, and irretrievable.
      Man's evil nature, that apology
      Which kings who rule, and cowards who crouch, set up
      For their unnumbered crimes, sheds not the blood
      Which desolates the discord-wasted land.
80   From kings, and priests, and statesmen, war arose,
      Whose safety is man's deep unbettered woe,
      Whose grandeur his debasement. Let the axe
      Strike at the root, the poison-tree will fall;
      And where its venomed exhalations spread
85   Ruin, and death, and woe, where millions lay
      Quenching the serpent's famine, and their bones
      Bleaching unburied in the putrid blast,
      A garden shall arise, in loveliness
      Surpassing fabled Eden.

iv 76–82. Man's evil nature . . . his debasement] 'Kings' were commonly blamed as
originators of war, but Godwin looked behind these agents to economic
motives (Political Justice Bk VIII ch. iii, ii 453–67). Paine, like S., blamed Kings
and exonerated Man: 'it is Kings, Courts, and Cabinets that must sit for the
portrait. Man, naturally as he is, with all his faults about him, is not up to the
character' (Rights of Man Pt II; Paine Writings ii 413). The trenchancy of S.'s
judgement, however, seems to be his own.
iv 82–3. Let the axe . . . will fall] A very common image in Radical literature,
reinforced after 1783 by the legend of the Upas Tree, with scriptural and
classical origins (e.g. Matthew iii 10: 'And now also the axe is laid unto the root
of the tree'; Virgil, Eclogue iv 24–5: 'fallax herba veneni / occidet', 'The false
poison-plant shall perish'). Examples that influenced S. include Paine, Rights of
Man Pt I; Paine Writings ii 295: 'Lay then the axe to the root, and teach
Governments humanity'; and Holbach, Système de la Nature ii 452: 'ce n'est
qu'en extirpant jusqu'aux racines l'arbre empoisonné qui depuis tant de siècles
obombre l'univers, que les yeux des habitans du monde apperçevront la
lumière propre à les éclairer, à les guider, à réchauffer leurs âmes'.
iv 86. the serpent's famine] (a) The Upas-tree's hunger for victims (Erasmus
Darwin describes the tree as a predatory 'scaly monster' with roots like 'a
thousand vegetative serpents' (Botanic Garden II iii 239–44)); (b) the contemporary system of society.
iv 86–7. their bones . . . in the putrid blast] The dead shepherd in Thomson's
'Winter' 320–1 is described as 'Stretched out, and bleaching in the northern
blast'. In The Botanic Garden (II iii 250) the Upas-tree strews 'With human
skeletons the whiten'd plain'.
iv 88. A garden] Perhaps recalling Mary Wollstonecraft's A Vindication of the
Rights of Men (1790) 147: 'What salutary dews might not be shed to refresh this
thirsty land, if men were more enlightened? . . . –A garden more inviting than
Eden would then meet the eye, and springs of joy murmur on every side'.
iv 89–91. Nature's soul . . . with plenty] Recalling Wordsworth's 'Immortality

                                    Hath Nature's soul,
90   That formed this world so beautiful, that spread
     Earth's lap with plenty, and life's smallest chord
     Strung to unchanging unison, that gave
     The happy birds their dwelling in the grove,
     That yielded to the wanderers of the deep
95   The lovely silence of the unfathomed main,
     And filled the meanest worm that crawls in dust
     With spirit, thought, and love; on Man alone,
     Partial in causeless malice, wantonly
     Heaped ruin, vice, and slavery; his soul
100 Blasted with withering curses; placed afar
     The meteor–happiness, that shuns his grasp,
     But serving on the frightful gulf to glare,
     Rent wide beneath his footsteps?

                                    Nature!–no!
     Kings, priests, and statesmen, blast the human flower
105 Even in its tender bud; their influence darts
     Like subtle poison through the bloodless veins
     Of desolate society. The child,
     Ere he can lisp his mother's sacred name,
     Swells with the unnatural pride of crime, and lifts
110 His baby-sword even in a hero's mood.

Ode' 78: 'Earth fills her lap with pleasures of her own', besides Gray's *Elegy*
117 and its source in *Aeneid* iii 509: 'optatae gremio telluris', 'in the lap of
welcome Earth'.

iv *101. The meteor–happiness*] The meteor-happiness *1813, eds.* The meteor
happiness *1839, 1840*. The *1813* compound coinage may be defended as meaning
'meteor-like [i.e. delusive] happiness' (*meteor* = will-of-the-wisp), but the *1839*
correction suggests that the hyphen was a misprinted dash in S.'s MS.

iv *102.* 'Serving merely to highlight his grim destiny'.

iv *107–20. The child . . . all natural good*] Locke had stressed the role of early
conditioning in the creation of social prejudices: 'All the entertainment of talk
and history is of nothing almost but fighting and killing; and the honour and
renown that is bestowed on conquerors, (who for the most part are but the
great butchers of mankind) further mislead growing youths, who by this
means come to think slaughter the laudable business of mankind, and the most
heroic of virtues. By these steps unnatural cruelty is planted in us; and what
humanity abhors, custom reconciles and recommends to us, by laying it in the
way to honour' (*Some Thoughts Concerning Education* (1690), *Works* (1823) ix
113). S. had been impressed by Locke's work at Oxford (*Hogg* i 99, 269–70).
William Smellie's popular *Philosophy of Natural History* adopted the same line:
'. . . what are the sentiments which strike in the most forcible manner the
unsuspicious, and, as yet, uninformed minds. They are of the most diabolical
kind. *Animosity, battles, treachery, cruelty*, and *murders!* The successful perpetra-

This infant-arm becomes the bloodiest scourge
Of devastated earth; whilst specious names,
Learnt in soft childhood's unsuspecting hour,
Serve as the sophisms with which manhood dims
115 Bright reason's ray, and sanctifies the sword
Upraised to shed a brother's innocent blood.
Let priest-led slaves cease to proclaim that man
Inherits vice and misery, when force
And falsehood hang even o'er the cradled babe,
120 Stifling with rudest grasp all natural good.

Ah! to the stranger-soul, when first it peeps
From its new tenement, and looks abroad
For happiness and sympathy, how stern
And desolate a tract is this wide world!
125 How withered all the buds of natural good!
No shade, no shelter from the sweeping storms
Of pitiless power! On its wretched frame,
Poisoned, perchance, by the disease and woe
Heaped on the wretched parent whence it sprung
130 By morals, law, and custom, the pure winds
Of heaven, that renovate the insect tribes,

---

tors of these horrid crimes are celebrated, both by their own *historians*, and by
unthinking *pedagogues*, under the grand appellation of HEROES! . . . What
monstrous *lessons* to young and tender minds!' (i (1790) 447). In 1811 S. had
proposed rearing two four-year-olds in solitude to ascertain 'what the impressions of the world are upon the mind when it has been veiled from human
prejudice' ([Joseph Gibbons Merle], 'A Newspaper Editor's Reminiscences',
Fraser's Magazine XXIII (June 1841) 707).

iv 115. *sanctifies*] Rossetti 1870 proposes *sanctify* on the grounds (approved by
Locock) that 'the word "names" (rather than manhood) appears to be the right
nominative'. But S.'s point is that in *childhood* the sophisms are learned which
manhood uses to sanctify war.

iv 121–7. *Ah! to the stranger-soul . . . Of pitiless power!*] This passage, which does
not imply pre-existence but points the contrast between the potential and the
actual environment of the newly-born child, is indebted to Beattie's 'Ode to
Hope' (1761) 42–5, 104–6: 'When first on childhood's eager gaze / Life's varied
landscape, stretched immense around, / Starts out of night profound, / Thy
voice incites to tempt th'untrodden maze . . . / Ill-fated youth, then whither
wilt thou fly? / No friend, no shelter now is nigh, / And onward rolls the
storm'. Other probable influences include Gray, 'Ode on a Distant Prospect of
Eton College' 41–90; Wordsworth, 'Immortality Ode' 58–68.

iv 127–38. *On its wretched frame . . . abjectness and bondage!*] The account of the
Manchester factory-children helps to explain 'the very harrowing effect which
Southey's *Don Espriello's Letters* produced on [Shelley] in 1810 or 1811' (*Med-
win (1913)* 190). 'They are deprived in childhood of all instruction and all

        May breathe not. The untainting light of day
        May visit not its longings. It is bound
        Ere it has life: yea, all the chains are forged
135   Long ere its being: all liberty and love
        And peace is torn from its defencelessness;
        Cursed from its birth, even from its cradle doomed
        To abjectness and bondage!

        Throughout this varied and eternal world
140   Soul is the only element, the block
        That for uncounted ages has remained
        The moveless pillar of a mountain's weight
        Is active, living spirit. Every grain

---

enjoyment; . . . of fresh air by day and of natural sleep by night. Their health physical and moral is alike destroyed; they die of diseases induced by unremitting task work, by confinement in the impure atmosphere of crowded rooms; . . . or they live to grow up without decency, without comfort, and without hope . . . and bring forth slaves like themselves to tread in the same path of misery. The dwellings of the labouring manufacturers [workers] are in narrow streets and lanes, blocked up from light and air . . . because every inch of land is of such value, that room for light and air cannot be afforded them' (*Letters from England: by Don Manuel Alvarez Espriella* [Southey] (1807), ed. Jack Simmons (1951) 209–10). The exploitation of young children in Vaublanc's spinning-mill in Godwin's *Fleetwood* (1805) caused the hero to exclaim: 'I know that the earth is the great Bridewell of the universe, where spirits descended from heaven are committed to drudgery and hard labour' (ch. xi).

iv *140–1. element, . . . remained*] element, . . . remained. *1813, 1839, 1840*; element: . . . remained *Hutchinson, 1972.* J. R. Tutin's proposal to delete the full stop after *remained* (*Nbk of the Shelley Soc.* (1888) 21) makes much better sense and has been generally accepted. This passage (lines 139–53) is in fact S.'s materialist answer to Young's aggressive theism in *The Complaint: or, Night-Thoughts*. In Night ix, the climactic book, Young demands: Who gave motion to dead matter? Can matter think and imagine? Unless every block of matter is creative and wise, then God exists:

        Who, motion, foreign to the smallest grain,
        Shot thro' vast masses of enormous weight?
        . . . Has matter more than motion? Has it thought,
        Judgment and genius? . . .
        If art, to form; and counsel, to conduct;
        And that with greater far than human skill;
        Resides not in each block;–a Godhead reigns. –

To which S. replies: Yes, matter has its own life and sentience, both in single atoms and in large aggregates, and it is from this that the universe is made. The un-Lucretian hylozoic idea that matter itself is active and sentient was shared by many materialists (see H. W. Piper, *The Active Universe* (1962) especially ch. i), and was debated even by Holbach (*Système de la Nature* i 127): 'Quelques

Is sentient both in unity and part,
145   And the minutest atom comprehends
A world of loves and hatreds; these beget
Evil and good: hence truth and falsehood spring;

philosophes pensent que la sensibilité est une qualité universelle de la matière
. . . la sensibilité est ou une qualité qui se communique comme le mouvement
& qui s'acquiert par la combinaison, ou cette sensibilité est une qualité in-
hérente à toute matière'. Pierre Jean Georges Cabanis (*Rapports du Physique et du
Moral de l'Homme* (Paris 1802; 8th edn 1844) 471–2) declared: '. . . nous sommes
dès aujourd'hui suffisamment fondés à regarder comme chimérique cette
distinction que Buffon s'est efforcé d'établir de la matière morte et de la matière
vivante, ou des corpuscules inorganiques et des corpuscules organisés . . . il
faut nécessairement avouer que . . . la matière inanimée est capable de s'orga-
niser, de vivre, de sentir'. S. ordered this work on 17 December 1812 (*L* i 342)
and quoted it in his notes to *Q Mab*.

iv *144. sentient both in unity and part*] Robert Forsyth (a theist) concluded in his
Principles of Moral Science (Edinburgh 1805) i 421 that 'enough seems known to
prove that matter is neither a solid nor an inactive substance, but on the
contrary that its minutest particles, as well as its greatest masses, are powerful
and energetic'. S. quoted this work in his Preface to *PU*, and its appendix 'The
Vision of Hystaspes' may have contributed to the scheme of *Q Mab*. A more
extreme view was expressed by Maupertuis in *Essai sur la Fonction des Corps
organisés* (1754), summarized by Denis Diderot (*Pensées sur l'Interpretation de la
Nature* (1754), *Oeuvres complètes* (Paris 1875) ii 46): 'De ces perceptions d'élé-
ments rassemblés et combinés, il en résultera une perception unique, prop-
ortionée à la masse et à la disposition; et ce système de perceptions dans lequel
chaque élément aura perdu la mémoire du *soi* et concourra à former la conscience du *tout*, sera l'âme de l'animal'. Diderot pointed out that the outcome of this
hypothesis would be to identify the total universe with God, 'âme du monde'.
S. told Southey *c.* 2 January 1812: 'I believe that God is another signification for
the Universe' (*L* i 215); he ordered Diderot's Works from Clio Rickman on 24
December 1812 (*L* i 345).

iv *146. A world of loves and hatreds*] The connection between physical and moral
sympathies and antipathies was made by Holbach in the chapter from which S.
quoted his note to *Q Mab* vi 171–3: 'Les êtres primitifs ou les élémens des corps
ont besoin de s'étayer, pour ainsi dire, les uns les autres, afin de se conserver,
d'acquérir de la consistance et de la solidité; verité également constante dans ce
qu'on appelle le *physique* et dans ce qu'on appelle le *moral*. C'est sur cette
disposition des matières et des corps . . . que sont fondées les façons d'agir que
les physiciens désignent sous le nom d'*attraction* et de *répulsion*, de *sympathie* et
d'*antipathie*, d'*affinités* ou de *rapports*. Les moralistes désignent cette disposition, et les effets qu'elle produit, sous le nom d'*amour* ou de *haine*, d'*amitié* ou
d'*aversion*'. In a note to the penultimate sentence Holbach declared: 'L'amour, à
qui les anciens attribuaient le débrouillement du *chaos*, ne paraît être que
l'attraction personnifiée'. Diderot represented Maupertuis as arguing (op. cit.)

Hence will and thought and action, all the germs
Of pain or pleasure, sympathy or hate,
150 That variegate the eternal universe.
Soul is not more polluted than the beams
Of heaven's pure orb, ere round their rapid lines
The taint of earth-born atmospheres arise.

Man is of soul and body, formed for deeds
155 Of high resolve, on fancy's boldest wing
To soar unwearied, fearlessly to turn
The keenest pangs to peacefulness, and taste
The joys which mingled sense and spirit yield.
Or he is formed for abjectness and woe,
160 To grovel on the dunghill of his fears,
To shrink at every sound, to quench the flame
Of natural love in sensualism, to know
That hour as blessed when on his worthless days
The frozen hand of death shall set its seal,
165 Yet fear the cure, though hating the disease.
The one is man that shall hereafter be;
The other, man as vice has made him now.

War is the statesman's game, the priest's delight,
The lawyer's jest, the hired assassin's trade,
170 And, to those royal murderers, whose mean thrones
Are bought by crimes of treachery and gore,
The bread they eat, the staff on which they lean.
Guards, garbed in blood-red livery, surround

---

that physical substance ('L'être corporel') possessed the attributes of 'le *désir*,
l'*aversion*, la *mémoire* et l'*intelligence*; en un mot, toutes les qualités que nous
reconnaissons dans les animaux, que les Anciens comprenaient sous le nom
d'*âme sensitive*, et que [Maupertuis] admet . . . dans la particule la plus petite de
matière, comme dans le plus gros animal'.

iv *151–3. Soul is not more polluted . . . atmospheres arise*] i.e. a soul is as pure as the
rays of the rising sun, before clouds obscure them. Fontenelle, among others,
had taught that if 'our air be considered only a mist, it must necessarily alter the
colour of the sky, sun and stars. The celestial fluid alone could give us light and
colours in their original state' (*Conversations on the Plurality of Worlds*, translated
by Elizabeth Gunning (1808) 86–7). It is not clear, however, that S. is saying
the soul is polluted by matter; he seems to be saying that the 'element' of matter
is pure until tainted by moral evil.

iv *168. War is the statesman's game*] 'War is the Pharo table of Governments, and
Nations the dupes of the games' (Paine, *Rights of Man* Pt II; *Paine Writings* ii
413).

Their palaces, participate the crimes
175 That force defends, and from a nation's rage
Secure the crown, which all the curses reach
That famine, frenzy, woe and penury breathe.
These are the hired bravos who defend
The tyrant's throne—the bullies of his fear:
180 These are the sinks and channels of worst vice,
The refuse of society, the dregs
Of all that is most vile: their cold hearts blend
Deceit with sternness, ignorance with pride,
All that is mean and villainous, with rage
185 Which hopelessness of good, and self-contempt,
Alone might kindle; they are decked in wealth,
Honour and power, then are sent abroad
To do their work. The pestilence that stalks
In gloomy triumph through some eastern land
190 Is less destroying. They cajole with gold,
And promises of fame, the thoughtless youth
Already crushed with servitude: he knows
His wretchedness too late, and cherishes
Repentance for his ruin, when his doom
195 Is sealed in gold and blood!
Those too the tyrant serve, who, skilled to snare
The feet of justice in the toils of law,
Stand, ready to oppress the weaker still;
And, right or wrong, will vindicate for gold,
200 Sneering at public virtue, which beneath
Their pitiless tread lies torn and trampled, where
Honour sits smiling at the sale of truth.

iv 176. *Secure*] *1839, 1840, eds.*; Secures *1813*.

iv 178-9. See S.'s note.

iv 190. *They*] Press-gangs for Army or Navy. In this passage (lines 173–202), *these, they*, do not refer only to 'Guards' but to different categories of Crown agents.

iv 195. *gold and blood!*] A recurrent phrase in S.'s poetry.

iv 199. *And, right or wrong,*] *1813, 1839, 1840, Forman 1876–7*; And right or wrong *mod. eds*. The words *right* and *wrong* are not nouns but adjectives qualifying *tyrant* (line 196) and the meaning is: 'Those too serve the tyrant . . . and will vindicate him for gold, whether he is right or wrong'. The reference is to spies and informers employed to incriminate the Luddites (see E. P. Thompson, *The Making of the English Working Class* (1963) 1968, 532–42). S. championed the Luddites to Elizabeth Hitchener in December 1811 (*L* i 213). 'Honour' (line 202) represents the Justices who accepted the evidence of informers.

Then grave and hoary-headed hypocrites,
Without a hope, a passion, or a love,
205 Who, through a life of luxury and lies,
Have crept by flattery to the seats of power,
Support the system whence their honours flow . . .
They have three words:—well tyrants know their use,
Well pay them for the loan, with usury
210 Torn from a bleeding world!—God, Hell, and Heaven.
A vengeful, pitiless, and almighty fiend,
Whose mercy is a nick-name for the rage
Of tameless tigers hungering for blood.
Hell, a red gulf of everlasting fire,
215 Where poisonous and undying worms prolong
Eternal misery to those hapless slaves
Whose life has been a penance for its crimes.
And Heaven, a meed for those who dare belie
Their human nature, quake, believe, and cringe
220 Before the mockeries of earthly power.

These tools the tyrant tempers to his work,
Wields in his wrath, and as he wills destroys,
Omnipotent in wickedness: the while
Youth springs, age moulders, manhood tamely does
225 His bidding, bribed by short-lived joys to lend
Force to the weakness of his trembling arm.

They rise, they fall; one generation comes
Yielding its harvest to destruction's scythe.
It fades, another blossoms: yet behold!
230 Red glows the tyrant's stamp-mark on its bloom,
Withering and cankering deep its passive prime.
He has invented lying words and modes,
Empty and vain as his own coreless heart;
Evasive meanings, nothings of much sound,
235 To lure the heedless victim to the toils
Spread round the valley of its paradise.

---

iv *203–20. Omitted 1839.*
iv *203. hypocrites*] Leaders of the Established Church.
iv *215. undying worms*] Echoing *Isaiah* lxvi 24: 'for their worm shall not die,
neither shall their fire be quenched'.
iv *216–17. Eternal misery . . . for its crimes*] Holbach had sardonically postulated
'un dieu que l'on suppose tendre des pièges aux hommes, les inviter à pécher,
permettre qu'ils commettent des crimes qu'il pourrait empêcher, afin d'avoir le
barbare plaisir de les en punir sans mesure' (*Système de la Nature* ii 82).
iv *227–9.* See S.'s note on v 1–2.

Look to thyself, priest, conqueror, or prince!
Whether thy trade is falsehood, and thy lusts
Deep wallow in the earnings of the poor,
240 With whom thy master was:–or thou delightst
In numbering o'er the myriads of thy slain,
All misery weighing nothing in the scale
Against thy short-lived fame: or thou dost load
With cowardice and crime the groaning land,
245 A pomp-fed king. Look to thy wretched self!
Aye, art thou not the veriest slave that e'er
Crawled on the loathing earth? Are not thy days
Days of unsatisfying listlessness?
Dost thou not cry, ere night's long rack is o'er,
250 'When will the morning come?' Is not thy youth
A vain and feverish dream of sensualism?
Thy manhood blighted with unripe disease?
Are not thy views of unregretted death
Drear, comfortless, and horrible? Thy mind,
255 Is it not morbid as thy nerveless frame,
Incapable of judgment, hope, or love?
And dost thou wish the errors to survive
That bar thee from all sympathies of good,
After the miserable interest
260 Thou holdst in their protraction? When the grave
Has swallowed up thy memory and thyself,
Dost thou desire the bane that poisons earth
To twine its roots around thy coffined clay,
Spring from thy bones, and blossom on thy tomb,
265 That of its fruit thy babes may eat and die?

V.

Thus do the generations of the earth
Go to the grave, and issue from the womb,
Surviving still the imperishable change

iv 240. *thy master*] Jesus. Lines 238–45 concern 'priest, conqueror, or prince' in rotation.
iv 252. *unripe*] premature.
iv 259–60. *After . . . in their protraction?*] 'After taking what advantage you can from prolonging those errors'.
iv 262. *the bane*] See note to iv 82–3 above.
v 1–2. See S.'s note.
v 3, *the imperishable change*] Despite the apparent parallel with *Hellas* 197–206, these lines do not concern metempsychosis but the recycling of material components in successive lives, as described by Holbach (ii 139–40): 'La nature entière ne subsiste & ne se conserve que par la circulation, la transmigration,

That renovates the world; even as the leaves
5   Which the keen frost-wind of the waning year
Has scattered on the forest soil, and heaped
For many seasons there, though long they choke,
Loading with loathsome rottenness the land,
All germs of promise, yet when the tall trees
10   From which they fell, shorn of their lovely shapes,
Lie level with the earth to moulder there,
They fertilize the land they long deformed,
Till from the breathing lawn a forest springs
Of youth, integrity, and loveliness,
15   Like that which gave it life, to spring and die.
Thus suicidal selfishness, that blights

---

l'échange & le déplacement perpétual des molécules & des atômes insensibles
ou des parties sensibles de la matière. C'est par cette *palingénésie* que subsiste le
grand tout'. Erasmus Darwin had applied the principle to organic life (*Temple
of Nature* iv 338–428, especially 397–400): 'While Nature sinks in Time's
destructive storms, / The wrecks of Death are but a change of forms; /
Emerging matter from the grave returns, / Feels new desires, with new
sensations burns'. Classical sources include Lucretius, *De Rerum Natura* i
215–64; Ovid, *Metamorphoses* xv 252–8.

v *4–6*. See S.'s note. The image of the falling leaves was a Romantic favourite,
and occurs in Ossian: 'The people are like . . . the leaves of woody Morven,
they pass away in the rustling blast, and other leaves lift their green heads'
(*Berrathon: A Poem*). In *Proposals for an Association* (1812) S. had used the foliage
of trees as illustration and asked: 'Do we not see that the laws of nature
perpetually act by disorganization and reproduction, each alternately becoming cause and effect [?]' (*Prose* 68–9).

v *9. promise, yet*] Rossetti 1870, eds.; promise. Yet *1813, 1839, 1840, Forman
1876–7, Locock 1911*. As Locock notes, the emendation is not essential, but the
continuity intended is seriously compromised by the full stop.

v *13. lawn*] Open glade in a forest.

v *16. suicidal selfishness*] S. parts company with those moralists who regarded
self-love or self-interest as the basis of all human action, including Helvétius
('La plus haute vertue, comme le vice le plus honteux, est en nous l'effet du
plaisir plus ou moins vif que nous trouvons à nous y livrer'–*De l'Esprit* (1758)
III ch. xvi; *Oeuvres* iv 148); Volney ('Self-love, the desire of happiness, and an
aversion to pain, are the essential and primary laws that nature herself imposed
on man . . . and these laws . . . are the simple and prolific principle of every
thing that takes place in the moral world'–*Ruins* ch. v); and Holbach ('il est de
l'essence de l'homme de s'aimer lui-même, de vouloir se conserver, de chercher à rendre son existence heureuse; ainsi l'intérêt ou le désir du bonheur est
l'unique mobile de toutes ses actions'–*Système de la Nature* i 343). Such a
doctrine did not of course efface the distinction between virtue and vice, but it
precluded a belief in *disinterested virtuous action*, which S. shared with Hume;

The fairest feelings of the opening heart,
Is destined to decay, whilst from the soil
Shall spring all virtue, all delight, all love,
20 And judgment cease to wage unnatural war
With passion's unsubduable array.

Twin-sister of religion, selfishness!
Rival in crime and falsehood, aping all
The wanton horrors of her bloody play;
25 Yet frozen, unimpassioned, spiritless,
Shunning the light, and owning not its name:
Compelled, by its deformity, to screen
With flimsy veil of justice and of right,

---

with Godwin ('The system of disinterested benevolence proves to us, that it is possible to be virtuous, and not merely to talk of virtue . . . and that, when we call upon mankind to divest themselves of selfish and personal considerations, we call upon them for something they are able to practise'–*Political Justice* Bk IV ch. x, i 436–7); and with Cabanis ('l'intérêt de chaque individu ne saurait jamais être véritablement séparé de l'intérêt des autres hommes'–*Rapports du Physique et du Moral de l'Homme* (1802) Preface (1844 edn) 51). To Godwin on 29 July 1812 S. avowed himself to be 'an irreconcileable enemy to the system of self love, both from a feeling of its deformity & a conviction of its falsehood' (*L* i 316).

v 20–1. *And judgment . . . unsubduable array.*] Helvétius (*De l'Esprit* III ch. vi) had vindicated passion as the driving-force of human betterment, and even of rational thought (but it is not known if and when S. read him, as the allusions in S.'s letters of 1811–12 are really to Holbach). Godwin distinguished three senses of the word 'passion': (1) 'the ardour and vehemence of mind with which any object is pursued', (2) deluded enthusiasms, (3) urges arising from physical needs; in Sense (1) 'passion is so far from being incompatible with reason, that it is inseparable from it', and of passions in Sense (3) 'it seems sufficiently reasonable to say that no attempt ought to be made to eradicate them' (*Political Justice* Bk I ch. v, i 80–3). Approval of sexual passion and the compatibility of reason with true passion (Godwin's Senses (1) and (2)) were cardinal points for S. In a letter to Hogg announcing the completion of *Q Mab* (7 February 1813) he wrote: 'Reason is only an assemblage of our better feelings, passion considered under a peculiar mode of its operation . . . A more elevated spirit has begun to diffuse itself which . . . scarce suffers true Passion & true Reason to continue at war' (*L* i 352). This follows Godwin: 'reason is nothing more than a collation and comparison of various emotions and feelings' (*Political Justice* Bk VII ch. iii, ii 341), and 'It is a mistake to suppose that sensible pleasures and intellectual ones are by any means incompatible' (*Enquirer* 244). Cp. 'Passion' 31–50; *Q Mab* viii 231; *PU* III iv 157–8, 197–8.

v 22. *Twin-sister of religion*] Religion offered Heaven as the selfish motive for virtue.

v 26. *name:*] *1839, 1840*; name *1813*; name, *eds*.

Its unattractive lineaments, that scare
30   All, save the brood of ignorance: at once
The cause and the effect of tyranny;
Unblushing, hardened, sensual, and vile;
Dead to all love but of its abjectness,
With heart impassive by more noble powers
35   Than unshared pleasure, sordid gain, or fame;
Despising its own miserable being,
Which still it longs, yet fears to disenthrall.

Hence commerce springs, the venal interchange
Of all that human art or nature yield;
40   Which wealth should purchase not, but want demand,
And natural kindness hasten to supply
From the full fountain of its boundless love,
For ever stifled, drained, and tainted now.
Commerce! beneath whose poison-breathing shade
45   No solitary virtue dares to spring,
But poverty and wealth with equal hand
Scatter their withering curses, and unfold
The doors of premature and violent death

v 34. *impassive*] 'Not susceptible of impression' (OED 2).

v 38. *commerce*] The widespread Radical attacks on 'commerce' were directed
(a) against the new philistine and callous ethos of industrial capitalism, (b)
against luxury trade which widened the gap between rich and poor. Cowper
had noted (*Task* (1785) iv 678–83) how kindly men, once entered on commercial life, 'seem at once to lose / Their nature; and, disclaiming all regard / For
mercy and the common rights of man, / Build factories with blood, conduct-
ing trade / At the sword's point, and dyeing the white robe / Of innocent
commercial justice red'. In 1807 Southey described the condition of child
labour in a Manchester cotton-factory, and commented: 'the commercial spirit
. . . extends to every thing, and poisons every thing:–literature, arts, religion,
government are alike tainted, it is a *lues* which has got into the system of the
country, and is rotting flesh and bone' (*Letters from England*, Letters xxxviii,
lx). In *A Vindication of Natural Diet*, contemporary with *Q Mab*, S. wrote that
'it is the direct influence of commerce to make the interval between the richest
and the poorest man wider and more unconquerable . . . it is a foe to everything
of real worth in the human character' (*Prose* 88), and to Elizabeth Hitchener he
had written on 16 October 1811: 'Vile as aristocracy is, commerce, purse-
proud ignorance & illiterateness is more contemptible' (*L* i 151).

v 40–2. *Which wealth . . . boundless love*] Godwin had argued that if his
neighbour needed ten pounds which could be spared, he was entitled to be
given them. 'It is therefore impossible for me to confer upon any man a favour;
I can only do him right' (*Political Justice* Bk II ch. ii, i 136). S. embraces the
principle, but the gift is to be made out of 'boundless love' rather than impartial
justice.

v 48. *death*] Rossetti *1870*; death, *1813*.

To pining famine and full-fed disease,
50 To all that shares the lot of human life,
Which, poisoned body and soul, scarce drags the chain
That lengthens as it goes and clanks behind.

Commerce has set the mark of selfishness,
The signet of its all-enslaving power
55 Upon a shining ore, and called it gold:
Before whose image bow the vulgar great,
The vainly rich, the miserable proud,
The mob of peasants, nobles, priests, and kings,
And with blind feelings reverence the power
60 That grinds them to the dust of misery.
But in the temple of their hireling hearts
Gold is a living god, and rules in scorn
All earthly things but virtue.

Since tyrants, by the sale of human life,
65 Heap luxuries to their sensualism, and fame

v 50. 'To all the evil that attends humanity'.
v 51. *Which, poisoned*] *Woodberry 1893, Locock 1911*; Which poisoned *1813, 1839*; Which poisoned, *Dowden 1891, Hutchinson, 1972*. *chain*] *1839, 1840*; chain, *1813, eds*.
v 51-2. *the chain . . . clanks behind*] Locock cites 'Julian and Maddalo' 302-3: 'To drag life on–which like a heavy chain / Lengthens behind with many a link of pain!' and *PU* II iv 20-2. S. could have adopted the image from Goldsmith's *The Traveller* (1764; 1774 edn) 8-10): 'My heart . . . drags at each remove a lengthening chain'.
v 55-63. *gold: . . . but virtue*] This passage seems prompted by *Daniel* iii 1-18, where Nebuchadnezzar's image of gold is worshipped by all his underlings except the three steadfast servants of God.
v 58. See S.'s note.
v 61-2. *But in the temple . . . living god*] Cp. *Timon of Athens* V i 46-8: 'What a god's gold, / That he is worshipped in a baser temple / Than where swine feed!'
v 64-5. *Since tyrants . . . their sensualism*] In 1805 Jamaican slavery alone produced nearly 100,000 tons of cane-sugar, the most topical item of 'luxury'. Helvétius had attached an influential note to his discussion of luxury-trades (*De l'Esprit* I iii): 'Si l'on suppute le nombre d'hommes qui périt, tant par les guerres que dans la traverée d'Afrique en Amérique; qu'on y ajoute celui des nègres qui, arrivés à leur destination, deviennent la victime des caprices, de la cupidité et du pouvoir arbitraire d'un maître . . . on conviendra qu'il n'arrive point de barrique de sucre en Europe qui ne soit teinte de sang humain'. Cp. also on the sugar-cane Montgomery, *The West Indies* (1810) ii 15-18: 'While with vain wealth it gorged the master's hoard, / And spread with manna his luxurious board, / Its culture was perdition to the slave, / It sapped his life, and flourished on his grave'.

To their wide-wasting and insatiate pride,
Success has sanctioned to a credulous world
The ruin, the disgrace, the woe of war.
His hosts of blind and unresisting dupes
70 The despot numbers; from his cabinet
These puppets of his schemes he moves at will,
Even as the slaves by force or famine driven,
Beneath a vulgar master, to perform
A task of cold and brutal drudgery;—
75 Hardened to hope, insensible to fear,
Scarce living pulleys of a dead machine,
Mere wheels of work and articles of trade,
That grace the proud and noisy pomp of wealth!

The harmony and happiness of man
80 Yields to the wealth of nations; that which lifts
His nature to the heaven of its pride,
Is bartered for the poison of his soul;
The weight that drags to earth his towering hopes,
Blighting all prospect but of selfish gain,
85 Withering all passion but of slavish fear,
Extinguishing all free and generous love
Of enterprise and daring, even the pulse

v 67. *Success*] Re-conquest of British possessions in the West Indies was almost complete in 1813, after long military struggles with Spain, Holland, and France.

v 72–8. *Even as the slaves . . . pomp of wealth!*] Probably 'wage-slaves', regarded by S. as being as much in the power of factory-owners as regular soldiers were of their rulers. Godwin had written of the child-operatives of M. Vaublanc's spinning-mill in *Fleetwood* (ch. xi): 'There was a kind of stupid and hopeless vacancy in every face . . . I am ashamed to tell you by what expedients they are brought to this unintermitted vigilance, this dead life, this inactive and torpid industry!' S. had some first-hand acquaintance with factory conditions in the lead-pencil manufactories at Keswick (*L* i 223), and with the situation of the agricultural labourer in North Wales (*L* i 334).

v 80. *Yields*] S.'s normal singular verb when governed by conjunctive nouns. *the wealth of nations*] Usually taken as referring to Adam Smith's *An Inquiry into the Nature and Causes of the Wealth of Nations* (1776). S. mentions Adam Smith's name on 6 February 1811 (*L* i 51); but his phrase may derive from the translation of Volney's *Ruins* ch. xi: 'And all the force and wealth of nations were converted into a supply for individual expense and personal caprice . . .'

v 87–9. *even the pulse . . . it destroys*] i.e. it destroys even the romantic component of sexual love. Cp. 'To thirst and find no fill' 3–4: 'To feel the blood run through the veins and tingle / Where busy thought and blind sensation mingle'.

That fancy kindles in the beating heart
To mingle with sensation, it destroys,–
90 Leaves nothing but the sordid lust of self,
The grovelling hope of interest and gold,
Unqualified, unmingled, unredeemed
Even by hypocrisy.

                                    And statesmen boast
Of wealth! The wordy eloquence that lives
95 After the ruin of their hearts, can gild
The bitter poison of a nation's woe,
Can turn the worship of the servile mob
To their corrupt and glaring idol fame,
From virtue, trampled by its iron tread,
100 Although its dazzling pedestal be raised
Amid the horrors of a limb-strewn field,
With desolated dwellings smoking round.
The man of ease, who, by his warm fire-side,
To deeds of charitable intercourse
105 And bare fulfilment of the common laws
Of decency and prejudice, confines
The struggling nature of his human heart,
Is duped by their cold sophistry; he sheds
A passing tear perchance upon the wreck
110 Of earthly peace, when near his dwelling's door
The frightful waves are driven,–when his son
Is murdered by the tyrant, or religion
Drives his wife raving mad. But the poor man,
Whose life is misery, and fear, and care;
115 Whom the morn wakens but to fruitless toil;
Who ever hears his famished offspring's scream,
Whom their pale mother's uncomplaining gaze
For ever meets, and the proud rich man's eye
Flashing command, and the heart-breaking scene

v 93–4. See S.'s note.
v 98. *idol fame*] An image suggested by the Hindu idol of Juggernaut which is
dragged along in a chariot in Southey's *Curse of Kehama* XIV iii–v: 'There
throned aloft in state / The Image of the seven-headed God / Came forth from
his abode . . . / Prone fall the frantic votaries in its road . . . / The ponderous Car
rolls on and crushes all' (iii 5–7; v 5, 10).
v 106. *prejudice*] 'Conventionality' (Locock).
v 112–13. See S.'s note.
v 116. *offspring's*] *1839, eds.*; offsprings *1813*; offspring *1840*. The *1813* plural
form is possible (*OED* 1b) but unlikely.

120   Of thousands like himself;–he little heeds
      The rhetoric of tyranny; his hate
      Is quenchless as his wrongs; he laughs to scorn
      The vain and bitter mockery of words,
      Feeling the horror of the tyrant's deeds,
125   And unrestrained but by the arm of power,
      That knows and dreads his enmity.

      The iron rod of penury still compels
      Her wretched slave to bow the knee to wealth,
      And poison, with unprofitable toil,
130   A life too void of solace, to confirm
      The very chains that bind him to his doom.
      Nature, impartial in munificence,
      Has gifted man with all-subduing will.
      Matter, with all its transitory shapes,
135   Lies subjected and plastic at his feet,
      That, weak from bondage, tremble as they tread.
      How many a rustic Milton has passed by,
      Stifling the speechless longings of his heart,
      In unremitting drudgery and care!
140   How many a vulgar Cato has compelled
      His energies, no longer tameless then,
      To mould a pin, or fabricate a nail!
      How many a Newton, to whose passive ken
      Those mighty spheres that gem infinity
145   Were only specks of tinsel, fixed in heaven
      To light the midnights of his native town!

      Yet every heart contains perfection's germ:
      The wisest of the sages of the earth,

v 127–8. Recalling Gray's *Elegy* 51–2: 'Chill Penury repressed their noble rage,
/ And froze the genial current of the soul', with a sharper social protest.
v 130. solace,] *Rossetti 1870, Locock 1911*; solace *1813, eds*. The comma is essential:
'Poverty makes its victim embitter a life that has all too few alleviations by toil
so badly paid that it worsens his situation'.
v 135. plastic] 'Susceptible of being moulded'. S. took the word from Erasmus
Darwin, *Botanic Garden* II ii 291–2: 'Etruria! next beneath thy magic hands /
Glides the quick wheel, the plastic clay expands'–the first recorded use of the
word in this sense, of Nature subject to control by science.
v 140. vulgar] Of the common people (not pejorative). The passage continues to
recall Gray's *Elegy* 45–60. Cato's activity was famous. Cicero has him say, in
his 84th year: 'The senate and the popular assembly never find my vigour
wanting, nor do my friends, my dependants, or my guests' (*De Senectute* x 32).
v 147. perfection's germ] 'The potential for growth towards perfection'. Perfecti-
bility, for S. as for Godwin, meant unlimited improvement. 'Lastly, man is
perfectible ... By perfectible, it is not meant that he is capable of being brought

That ever from the stores of reason drew
150   Science and truth, and virtue's dreadless tone,
Were but a weak and inexperienced boy,
Proud, sensual, unimpassioned, unimbued
With pure desire and universal love,
Compared to that high being, of cloudless brain,
155   Untainted passion, elevated will,
Which death (who even would linger long in awe
Within his noble presence, and beneath
His changeless eyebeam) might alone subdue.
Him, every slave now dragging through the filth
160   Of some corrupted city his sad life,
Pining with famine, swoln with luxury,
Blunting the keenness of his spiritual sense
With narrow schemings and unworthy cares,
Or madly rushing through all violent crime,
165   To move the deep stagnation of his soul, –
Might imitate and equal.

               But mean lust
Has bound its chains so tight around the earth,
That all within it but the virtuous man
Is venal: gold or fame will surely reach
170   The price prefixed by selfishness, to all
But him of resolute and unchanging will;
Whom, nor the plaudits of a servile crowd,
Nor the vile joys of tainting luxury,
Can bribe to yield his elevated soul
175   To tyranny or falsehood, though they wield
With blood-red hand the sceptre of the world.

All things are sold: the very light of heaven
Is venal; earth's unsparing gifts of love,

to perfection. But the word seems sufficiently adapted to express the faculty of being continually made better and receiving perpetual improvement . . . The term perfectible . . . not only does not imply the capacity of being brought to perfection, but stands in express opposition to it. If we could arrive at perfection, there would be an end to our improvement. There is however one thing of great importance that it does imply: every perfection or excellence that human beings are competent to conceive, human beings . . . are competent to attain' (*Political Justice* Bk I ch. v, i 92–3). 'Ridicule *perfection* as impossible . . . still a strenuous tendency towards this principle *however* unattainable cannot be considered as wrong' (S. to Elizabeth Hitchener, 25 July 1811, *L* i 125).
v *158. eyebeam*)] eyebeam,) *1813*.
v *177–8. the very light of heaven / Is venal*] In 1797 Pitt had trebled his tax on windows to help finance the war with revolutionary France.
v *178–88. earth's unsparing gifts . . . of her reign*] Southey's *Letters from England*

The smallest and most despicable things
180   That lurk in the abysses of the deep,
All objects of our life, even life itself,
And the poor pittance which the laws allow
Of liberty, the fellowship of man,
Those duties which his heart of human love
185   Should urge him to perform instinctively,
Are bought and sold as in a public mart
Of undisguising selfishness, that sets
On each its price, the stamp-mark of her reign.
Even love is sold; the solace of all woe
190   Is turned to deadliest agony, old age
Shivers in selfish beauty's loathing arms,
And youth's corrupted impulses prepare
A life of horror, from the blighting bane
Of commerce; whilst the pestilence that springs
195   From unenjoying sensualism, has filled
All human life with hydra-headed woes.

Falsehood demands but gold to pay the pangs
Of outraged conscience; for the slavish priest
Sets no great value on his hireling faith:
200   A little passing pomp, some servile souls,
Whom cowardice itself might safely chain,
Or the spare mite of avarice could bribe
To deck the triumph of their languid zeal,
Can make him minister to tyranny.
205   More daring crime requires a loftier meed:
Without a shudder, the slave-soldier lends

---

gives abundant examples of commercialization that could fit S.'s list, including
flowers, sea-shells (Letter xxi), payment of informers ('even life itself'), and
workhouses for the poor and helpless (Letter xxvi): 'It is not in the nature of
things that the superintendents of such institutions as these should be gentle-
hearted, when the superintendence is undertaken merely for the sake of the
salary'.

v *189. Even love is sold*] See S.'s note.

v *190–4. old age . . . bane / Of commerce*] i.e. material interest degrades marriage
by impelling young girls to marry old men, and young men to marry old
women.

v *193. horror,*] *Rossetti 1870*; horror *1813, eds.* The bane of commerce corrupts all
such unions, not merely the last-specified.

v *194. the pestilence*] Venereal disease.

v *200–3. some servile souls . . . languid zeal*] i.e. the prelate's underlings could be
kept loyal from pure cowardice, or else bribed to put on a show of support.

His arm to murderous deeds, and steels his heart
When the dread eloquence of dying men,
Low mingling on the lonely field of fame,
210   Assails that nature, whose applause he sells
For the gross blessings of a patriot mob,
For the vile gratitude of heartless kings,
And for a cold world's good word, – viler still!

There is a nobler glory, which survives
215   Until our being fades, and, solacing
All human care, accompanies its change;
Deserts not virtue in the dungeon's gloom,
And, in the precincts of the palace, guides
Its footsteps through that labyrinth of crime;
220   Imbues his lineaments with dauntlessness,
Even when, from power's avenging hand, he takes
Its sweetest, last and noblest title – death;
– The consciousness of good, which neither gold,
Nor sordid fame, nor hope of heavenly bliss,
225   Can purchase; but a life of resolute good,
Unalterable will, quenchless desire
Of universal happiness, the heart
That beats with it in unison, the brain,
Whose ever wakeful wisdom toils to change
230   Reason's rich stores for its eternal weal.

This commerce of sincerest virtue needs
No mediative signs of selfishness,
No jealous intercourse of wretched gain,
No balancings of prudence, cold and long;
235   In just and equal measure all is weighed,
One scale contains the sum of human weal,
And one, the good man's heart.

                      How vainly seek
The selfish for that happiness denied
To aught but virtue! Blind and hardened, they,
240   Who hope for peace amid the storms of care,

v *207. heart*] *Rossetti 1870*; heart, *1813, eds.* It is after the soldier's murderous deeds that he must steel his heart to the eloquence of his victims.

v *210. nature*] i.e. true human nature.

v *219. Its*] *1813, eds.*; His *Rossetti 1870.* The pronouns in this passage are confusing and Rossetti's emendation is graphically plausible. But *Its* (line 222) must again mean 'virtue's'; hence by *his* (line 220) it is best to understand 'that man's'. In line 216 *its* refers to *our being.*

v *231. This commerce*] i.e. this true 'commerce' – the trading of the good life for human happiness.

Who covet power they know not how to use,
And sigh for pleasure they refuse to give, –
Madly they frustrate still their own designs;
And, where they hope that quiet to enjoy
245 Which virtue pictures, bitterness of soul,
Pining regrets, and vain repentances,
Disease, disgust, and lassitude, pervade
Their valueless and miserable lives.

But hoary-headed selfishness has felt
250 Its death-blow, and is tottering to the grave:
A brighter morn awaits the human day,
When every transfer of earth's natural gifts
Shall be a commerce of good words and works;
When poverty and wealth, the thirst of fame,
255 The fear of infamy, disease and woe,
War with its million horrors, and fierce hell
Shall live but in the memory of time,
Who, like a penitent libertine, shall start,
Look back, and shudder at his younger years.

VI.

All touch, all eye, all ear,
The Spirit felt the Fairy's burning speech.
O'er the thin texture of its frame,
The varying periods painted changing glows,
5   As on a summer even,
When soul-enfolding music floats around,
The stainless mirror of the lake
Re-images the eastern gloom,
Mingling convulsively its purple hues
10   With sunset's burnished gold.

Then thus the Spirit spoke:
It is a wild and miserable world!

vi 4. *periods*] Sentences.
vi 9. *convulsively*] *Concordance* 124 glosses: 'With rapid fitful motion', but the
adverb must be figurative, of the eastern sky; perhaps 'With agitated effect'.
The lake-surface, like the Spirit, is coloured but unruffled.
vi *11–22. Then thus . . . limb of Heaven?*] The Spirit's despairing question
imitates that asked of the Genius by the traveller in Volney's *Ruins*: ' "O
Genius, since my reason is free, I strive in vain to welcome the flattering hope
with which you would console me . . . The more I meditate on the nature of
man, the more I examine the present state of society, the less possible does it
appear to me that a world of wisdom and felicity should ever be realised" ' (ch.
xiv). The Fairy's response also follows that of Volney's Genius: ' "Let us revive
the hope of this man; for if he who loves his fellow-creatures be suffered to

Thorny, and full of care,
Which every fiend can make his prey at will.
15   O Fairy! in the lapse of years,
         Is there no hope in store?
      Will yon vast suns roll on
      Interminably, still illuming
      The night of so many wretched souls,
20   And see no hope for them?
      Will not the universal Spirit e'er
      Revivify this withered limb of Heaven?

      The Fairy calmly smiled
      In comfort, and a kindling gleam of hope
25   Suffused the Spirit's lineaments.
      Oh! rest thee tranquil; chase those fearful doubts,
      Which ne'er could rack an everlasting soul,
      That sees the chains which bind it to its doom.
      Yes! crime and misery are in yonder earth,
30   Falsehood, mistake, and lust;
         But the eternal world
      Contains at once the evil and the cure.
      Some eminent in virtue shall start up,
         Even in perversest time:
35   The truths of their pure lips, that never die,
      Shall bind the scorpion falsehood with a wreath
         Of ever-living flame,
      Until the monster sting itself to death.

      How sweet a scene will earth become!
40   Of purest spirits a pure dwelling-place,

despair, what is to become of nations? The past is perhaps but too much
calculated to deject him. Let us then anticipate futurity; let us unveil the
astonishing age that is about to arise, that virtue . . . may redouble its efforts to
hasten the accomplishment of it"' (ch. xiv).
vi 31. *the eternal world*] Not 'the world of eternity' but 'this everlasting universe'. From the speakers' standpoint 'yonder earth' is one remote planet
among millions (cp. *Q Mab* i 250–1). The Fairy is endorsing Holbach (*Système
de la Nature* i 266): 'N'accusons donc point la nature d'être inexorable pour
nous; il n'existe point en elle de maux dont elle ne fournisse le remède à ceux
qui ont le courage de le chercher & de l'appliquer'. Cp. Southey's *Thalaba* (IX
xiv 11–12): 'The same Earth / Bears fruit and poison'.
vi 33. 'Let but a virtuous chief arise, a powerful and just people appear, and the
earth will arrive at supreme power' (*Ruins* ch. xiii). Perhaps also recalling
Enoch, shown to Adam as a virtuous dissident in *PL* xi 665–6: 'one rising,
eminent / In wise deport, spake much of Right and Wrong'.
vi 40. *spirits*] Rossetti *1870*; spirits, *1813*, *1839*, *1840*.

Symphonious with the planetary spheres;
When man, with changeless nature coalescing,
Will undertake regeneration's work,
When its ungenial poles no longer point
45   To the red and baleful sun
That faintly twinkles there.

Spirit! on yonder earth,
Falsehood now triumphs; deadly power
Has fixed its seal upon the lip of truth!
50   Madness and misery are there!
The happiest is most wretched! Yet confide,
Until pure health-drops, from the cup of joy,
Fall like a dew of balm upon the world.
Now, to the scene I show, in silence turn,
55   And read the blood-stained charter of all woe,
Which nature soon, with recreating hand,
Will blot in mercy from the book of earth.
How bold the flight of passion's wandering wing,
How swift the step of reason's firmer tread,
60   How calm and sweet the victories of life,
How terrorless the triumph of the grave!
How powerless were the mightiest monarch's arm,
Vain his loud threat, and impotent his frown!
How ludicrous the priest's dogmatic roar!
65   The weight of his exterminating curse,
How light! and his affected charity,
To suit the pressure of the changing times,
What palpable deceit!–but for thy aid,
Religion! but for thee, prolific fiend,
70   Who peoplest earth with demons, hell with men,
And heaven with slaves!

---

vi *41*. Metaphorically, 'in cosmic harmony'. It was anciently believed that the seven immortal planets produced harmonious music in their revolutions; the earth, motionless at the centre or bottom of the universe, was alone silent and corruptible (see Aristotle, *De Caelo* II ix; Cicero, *De Republica* VI xvii–xviii).

vi *45–6*. See S.'s note.

vi *51. most*] 'Very'.

vi *54–238* (end). *Omitted 1839*.

vi *57*. Cp. *Richard II* I iii 201–2: 'No Bolingbroke, if ever I were traitor, / My name be blotted from the book of life'.

vi *70–1. Who peoplest . . . heaven with slaves!*] Orthodox Christianity implied that those on earth were born sinners, those in hell were men undergoing eternal punishment, and those in heaven were serving the Supreme Author of this arrangement.

Thou taintest all thou lookest upon!–the stars,
Which on thy cradle beamed so brightly sweet,
Were gods to the distempered playfulness
75 Of thy untutored infancy: the trees,
The grass, the clouds, the mountains, and the sea,
All living things that walk, swim, creep, or fly,
Were gods: the sun had homage, and the moon
Her worshipper. Then thou becam'st, a boy,
80 More daring in thy frenzies: every shape,
Monstrous or vast, or beautifully wild,
Which, from sensation's relics, fancy culls;
The spirits of the air, the shuddering ghost,
The genii of the elements, the powers
85 That give a shape to nature's varied works,
Had life and place in the corrupt belief
Of thy blind heart: yet still thy youthful hands
Were pure of human blood. Then manhood gave
Its strength and ardour to thy frenzied brain;
90 Thine eager gaze scanned the stupendous scene,
Whose wonders mocked the knowledge of thy pride:
Their everlasting and unchanging laws
Reproached thine ignorance. Awhile thou stoodst

vi 72–102. *Thou taintest . . . called it GOD!*] These lines, with modifications, were published separately in *1816* under the title 'Superstition'.

vi 72. *upon!–the stars,*] upon! The stars *1816*.

vi 74. *gods*] Throughout this passage S. follows Holbach's account of the development of ideas of God: 'La premiere Théologie de l'homme lui fit d'abord craindre & adorer les élémens même, des objets matériels & grossiers; il rendit ensuite ses hommages à des agens présidans aux élémens, à des génies puissans, à des génies inférieurs . . . A force de réfléchir il crut simplifier les choses en soumettant la nature entière à un seul agent, à une intelligence souveraine, à un esprit, à une ame universelle qui mettoit cette nature & ses parties en mouvement.' (*Système de la Nature* ii 16–17).

vi 75. *infancy:*] infancy; *1816*.

vi 82. *sensation's relics*] 'This *decaying sense*, when wee would express the thing itself, (I mean *fancy* it selfe,) wee call *Imagination* . . .' (Hobbes, *Leviathan* (1651) I ch. ii). Presumably S. had read Hobbes at Oxford; but it had been a commonplace of contemporary materialist doctrine since Condillac that all ideas were derived from sensation, e.g. Cabanis: 'Nous ne sommes pas sans doute réduits encore à prouver que la sensibilité physique est la source de toutes les idées et de toutes les habitudes qui constituent l'existence morale de l'homme, . . , il n'en est maintenant aucune [personne] quie puisse élever le moindre doute à cet égard' (*Rapports du Physique et du Moral de l'Homme* (1802) IIme Mémoire, para. 1). See also *Système de la Nature* i ch. viii.

vi 93. *stoodst*] stoodest *1816*.

Baffled and gloomy; then thou didst sum up
95   The elements of all that thou didst know;
The changing seasons, winter's leafless reign,
The budding of the heaven-breathing trees,
The eternal orbs that beautify the night,
The sun-rise, and the setting of the moon,
100   Earthquakes and wars, and poisons and disease,
And all their causes to an abstract point
Converging, thou didst bend, –and called it GOD!
The self-sufficing, the omnipotent,

vi *101–2.*   And all their causes, to an abstract point,
Converging, thou didst bend, and called it GOD! *1813*

And all their causes, to an abstract point
Converging, thou didst bend, and call'd it God! *1840*

And all their causes, to an abstract point
Converging , thou didst bend and called it God!

Hutchinson, *1972*

And all their causes, to an abstract point
Converging, thou didst give it name, and form,
Intelligence, and unity, and power. *1816*

Locock's long discussion of this crux (*Locock 1911* ii 551–2) is invalidated by a
misreading of *1813* (comma omitted after *bend*) which apparently originated in
Forman 1876–7. The sense seems plain, though difficult to convey lucidly by
the pointing; there are as many different ways of punctuating these lines as
there have been editors: 'Superstition distorted the real causes of phenomena so
as to make them appear to coincide in one abstract cause, which it then labelled
"God" '. Hence *converging* is transitive (*OED* vb. 3): 'causing to come together'
(in *1816* the syntax is changed to an absolute construction, and *converging* is
intransitive). *Called* is a euphonic simplification of 'calledst' – common practice
with S. in a series of 2nd-person-singular verbs. The passage continues to
reword Holbach's account of the origin of the idea of God: '. . . par le mot *Dieu*
les hommes n'ont jamais pu désigner que la cause la plus câchée, la plus
éloignée, la plus inconnue des effets qu'ils voyoient: ils ne font usage de ce mot
que lorsque le jeu des causes naturelles & connues cesse d'être visible pour eux;
dès qu'ils perdent le fil des causes, ou dès que leur esprit ne peut plus en suivre la
chaîne, ils tranchent la difficulté, & terminent leurs recherches en appelant *Dieu*
la dernière des causes, c'est à dire, celle qui est au-delà de toutes les causes qu'ils
connoissent; ainsi ils ne font qu'assigner une dénomination vague à une cause
ignorée, à laquelle leur paresse ou les bornes de leurs connoissances les forcent
de s'arrêter' (*Système de la Nature* ii 17).

The merciful, and the avenging God!
105 Who, prototype of human misrule, sits
High in heaven's realm, upon a golden throne,
Even like an earthly king; and whose dread work,
Hell, gapes for ever for the unhappy slaves
Of fate, whom he created, in his sport,
110 To triumph in their torments when they fell!
Earth heard the name; earth trembled, as the smoke
Of his revenge ascended up to heaven,
Blotting the constellations; and the cries
Of millions, butchered in sweet confidence
115 And unsuspecting peace, even when the bonds
Of safety were confirmed by wordy oaths
Sworn in his dreadful name, rung through the land;
Whilst innocent babes writhed on thy stubborn spear,
And thou didst laugh to hear the mother's shriek
120 Of maniac gladness, as the sacred steel
Felt cold in her torn entrails!

vi 105. *prototype of human misrule*] 'C'est ainsi qu'en usent les tyrans de la terre, et leur conduite arbitraire servit de modèle à celle que l'on prêta à la divinité . . . D'où l'on voit que les plus méchans des hommes ont servi de modèles à Dieu, et que le plus injuste des gouvernemens fut le modèle de son administration' (*Système de la Nature* ii 56).

vi 108–10. *Hell, gapes . . . when they fell!*] 'Ne vaudrait-il pas mieux mille fois dépendre de la matière aveugle . . . que d'un dieu que l'on suppose tendre des pièges aux hommes, les inviter à pécher, permettre qu'ils commettent des crimes qu'il pourrait empêcher, afin d'avoir le barbare plaisir de les en punir sans mesure . . . ?' (*Système de la Nature* ii 82).

vi 111. *Earth heard the name; earth trembled*] An ironical echo of *PL* ii 787–9: 'I fled, and cry'd out *Death*; / Hell trembled at the hideous Name, and sigh'd / From all her Caves, and back resounded *Death*'.

vi 118. On the strength of this line (and the occurrence elsewhere of the name 'Ianthe') reference has been made to William Thompson's *Sickness* (1745) Bk iii 494–5: 'Man, courageous in his guilt, / Smiles at the infant writhing on his spear'. S. might have read this poem, but he had certainly read *Henry V* III iii 38–40: 'Your naked infants spitted upon pikes, / Whiles the mad mothers with their howls confused / Do break the clouds', and Southey's *Joan of Arc* (1796) i 412–14: '. . . the invader's savage fury / Spares not gray age, and mocks the infant's shriek / As he doth writhe upon his cursed lance'.

vi 120. *the sacred steel*] Perhaps recalling Helvétius, *De l'Esprit* (1758) II xxiv: '. . . partout on voit le couteau sacré de la religion levé sur le sein des femmes, des enfants, des vieillards; et la terre, fumante du sang des victimes immolées aux faux dieux où à l'Être suprême, n'offrir de toutes parts que le vaste, le dégoûtant et l'horrible charnier de l'intolérance'.

Religion! thou wert then in manhood's prime:
But age crept on: one God would not suffice
For senile puerility; thou framedst
125   A tale to suit thy dotage, and to glut
Thy misery-thirsting soul, that the mad fiend
Thy wickedness had pictured, might afford
A plea for sating the unnatural thirst
For murder, rapine, violence, and crime,
130   That still consumed thy being, even when
Thou heardst the step of fate;—that flames might light
Thy funeral scene, and the shrill horrent shrieks
Of parents dying on the pile that burned
To light their children to thy paths, the roar
135   Of the encircling flames, the exulting cries
Of thine apostles, loud commingling there,
      Might sate thine hungry ear
      Even on the bed of death!

But now contempt is mocking thy grey hairs;
140   Thou art descending to the darksome grave,
Unhonoured and unpitied, but by those
Whose pride is passing by like thine, and sheds,
Like thine, a glare that fades before the sun
Of truth, and shines but in the dreadful night
145   That long has lowered above the ruined world.

Throughout these infinite orbs of mingling light,
Of which yon earth is one, is wide diffused
A spirit of activity and life,

vi *123. one God would not suffice*] The Christian doctrine of the Trinity was fiercely and sometimes bloodily contested during the first four centuries A.D.

vi *125. A tale*] The Fall and the Redemption, involving the doctrine of eternal punishment and leading to institutions such as the Inquisition. The 'mad fiend' of line 126 is God, as conceived by superstition.

vi *129.* 'What is it the Bible teaches us? Rapine, cruelty, and murder' (Paine, *Age of Reason* Pt II; *Paine Writings* iv 186).

vi *132. horrent*] shuddering.

vi *133–4. parents dying . . . to thy paths*] The children are guided to the true faith by the *auto-da-fé* of their parents. Locock thought line 134 'one of the few really striking lines in *Queen Mab*' (*Locock 1911* ii 552).

vi *137. thine*] thy *1840*.

vi *146. mingling light*] Fontenelle had described how sunlight, reflected from every planet, 'proceeds in bright streams that intermix, and cross each other in a thousand directions, forming a splendid tissue of the richest materials' (*Conversations on the Plurality of Worlds*, translated by Elizabeth Gunning (1808) 116). S.'s 'infinite orbs' extends this idea to include starlight.

That knows no term, cessation, or decay;
150 That fades not when the lamp of earthly life,
Extinguished in the dampness of the grave,
Awhile there slumbers, more than when the babe
In the dim newness of its being feels
The impulses of sublunary things,
155 And all is wonder to unpractised sense:
But, active, steadfast, and eternal, still
Guides the fierce whirlwind, in the tempest roars,
Cheers in the day, breathes in the balmy groves,
Strengthens in health, and poisons in disease;
160 And in the storm of change, that ceaselessly
Rolls round the eternal universe, and shakes
Its undecaying battlement, presides,
Apportioning with irresistible law
The place each spring of its machine shall fill;
165 So that, when waves on waves tumultuous heap
Confusion to the clouds, and fiercely driven
Heaven's lightnings scorch the uprooted ocean-fords,
Whilst, to the eye of shipwrecked mariner,
Lone sitting on the bare and shuddering rock,
170 All seems unlinked contingency and chance:

vi 150. *lamp of earthly life*] A metaphor from Erasmus Darwin, *Temple of Nature* ii 47–60: 'Emblem of Life, to change eternal doom'd, / The beauteous form of fair Adonis bloom'd. – / . . . Soon from the yawning grave the bursting clay / Restored the Beauty to delighted day; / . . . Pleased for a while the assurgent youth above / Relights the golden lamp of life and love'. In *Botanic Garden* Pt I, i 403 the Nymphs of Fire 'Life's holy lamp with fires successive feed'.

vi 152–5. *when the babe . . . unpractised sense*] Hogg relates that at Oxford S. 'was vehemently excited by the striking doctrines which Socrates unfolds, especially by that which teaches that all our knowledge consists of reminiscences of what we had learned in a former existence'–i.e. in *Phaedo* 70–7 (*Hogg* i 103); but the sensations of the reincarnated soul seem to be mediated through Wordsworth's 'Immortality Ode' 58–64 and 142–6: '. . . those obstinate questionings / Of sense and outward things, / . . . Blank misgivings of a Creature / Moving about in worlds not realised'.

vi 154. *sublunary*] i.e. mortal. 'Infra autem iam nihil est nisi mortale et caducum . . . supra lunam sunt aeterna omnia': 'for below the moon is nothing that is not mortal and perishable . . . above it, all things are eternal' (Cicero, *De Re Publica* VI xvii 17).

vi 160. *storm of change*] Echoed from Erasmus Darwin (*Temple of Nature* ii 43–4): 'Immortal matter braves the transient storm, / Mounts from the wreck, unchanging but in form'; (ibid. iv 397–8): 'While Nature sinks in Time's destructive storms, / The Wrecks of Death are but a change of forms'.

No atom of this turbulence fulfils
A vague and unnecessitated task,
Or acts but as it must and ought to act.
Even the minutest molecule of light,
175   That in an April sunbeam's fleeting glow
Fulfils its destined, though invisible work,
The universal Spirit guides; nor less,
When merciless ambition, or mad zeal,
Has led two hosts of dupes to battle-field,
180   That, blind, they there may dig each other's graves,
And call the sad work glory, does it rule
All passions: not a thought, a will, an act,
No working of the tyrant's moody mind,
Nor one misgiving of the slaves who boast
185   Their servitude, to hide the shame they feel,
Nor the events enchaining every will,
That from the depths of unrecorded time
Have drawn all-influencing virtue, pass
Unrecognized, or unforeseen by thee,
190   Soul of the Universe! eternal spring
Of life and death, of happiness and woe,
Of all that chequers the phantasmal scene
That floats before our eyes in wavering light,
Which gleams but on the darkness of our prison,

vi *171–3*. See S.'s note.

vi *174. molecule of light*] The Newtonian theory of light as consisting of material particles was still the orthodox one. The word *molecule* (= particle) was a recent introduction (1794).

vi *188. virtue*] efficacy.

vi *190. Soul of the Universe!*] 'God himself is nothing more than the principal mover, the occult power diffused through every thing that has being, the sum of its laws and its properties, the animating principle; in a word, the soul of the universe' (*Ruins* ch. xxi). This view, attributed to Chinese Buddhists, was denounced as 'rank materialism' by 'theologians of every sect'.

vi *192–6. the phantasmal scene . . . cannot see.*] Many possible indirect sources of this passage were available to S., including Young's *The Complaint; or, Night-Thoughts* (Night vii 954–67): 'Who would be born to such a phantom world, / Where nought substantial, but our misery? / . . . Being, a shadow! consciousness, a dream!' etc., but the details suggest that S. is drawing directly on Plato's allegory of phenomenal life (*Republic* vii 514A–21B): 'Imagine men living in a kind of subterraneous cave . . . Suppose them to have been in this cave from childhood, with chains both on their legs and necks, obliged to remain there, and only able to look before them . . . Suppose there be likewise the light of a fire, burning far above and behind them; and that between the fire and the fettered men there is a raised road. Along this road, observe a low wall built . . . Behold now, along this wall, men bearing all sorts of utensils, raised above the wall, and human statues, and other animals, in wood and stone, and furniture

195   Whose chains and massy walls
           We feel, but cannot see.

           Spirit of Nature! all-sufficing Power,
           Necessity! thou mother of the world!
           Unlike the God of human error, thou
200   Requirest no prayers or praises; the caprice
           Of man's weak will belongs no more to thee
           Than do the changeful passions of his breast
           To thy unvarying harmony: the slave,
           Whose horrible lusts spread misery o'er the world,
205   And the good man, who lifts, with virtuous pride,
           His being, in the sight of happiness
           That springs from his own works; the poison-tree,
           Beneath whose shade all life is withered up,
           And the fair oak, whose leafy dome affords
210   A temple where the vows of happy love
           Are registered, are equal in thy sight:
           No love, no hate thou cherishest; revenge
           And favouritism, and worst desire of fame
           Thou knowest not: all that the wide world contains
215   Are but thy passive instruments, and thou
           Regardst them all with an impartial eye,

---

of every kind . . . do you think that such [prisoners] as these see anything of themselves, or of one another, but the shadows formed by the fire, falling on the opposite part of the cave?' (Thomas Taylor's translation (1784)). This Allegory of the Cave furnished S. with some of his most persistent imagery.
vi *198*. See S.'s note. S. is quoting Holbach i 59n.: 'Platon dit que *la matière & la nécessité sont la même chose, & que cette nécessité est la mère du monde'*. Holbach may have had in mind *Timaeus* 48A: 'For the generation of this universe was a mixed result of the combination of Necessity and reason' (i.e. a combination of given materials and a shaping intelligence). Plato nowhere specifically identifies matter with Necessity (by which he seems to have meant 'randomness'). See F. M. Cornford, *Plato's Cosmology* (1937) 159–77.
vi *206. happiness*] Rossetti *1870*; happiness, *1813*.
vi *211. equal in thy sight*] 'Tout est toujours dans l'ordre rélativement à la nature . . . Il est entré dans son plan que de certaines terres produiroient des fruits délicieux, tandis que d'autres ne fourniroient que des épines, des végétaux dangereux. Elle a voulu que quelques sociétés produisent des sages, des héros, des grands hommes; elle a réglé que d'autres ne feroient naître que des hommes abjects . . . en un mot elle répand, par la nécessité de son être, & le bien & le mal dans le monde que nous habitons' (Holbach, *Système de la Nature* i 265).
vi *215. thy passive instruments*] '. . . tout auroit dû convaincre l'homme qu'il est dans chaque instant de sa durée un instrument passif entre les mains de la nécessité' (*Système de la Nature* i 81); 'Man is in reality a passive and not an active being' (Godwin, *Political Justice* Bk IV ch. viii; i 389). That is, for both Holbach and Godwin, man's actions are invariably determined by the strongest motive.

      Whose joy or pain thy nature cannot feel,
        Because thou hast not human sense,
        Because thou art not human mind.

220   Yes! when the sweeping storm of time
      Has sung its death-dirge o'er the ruined fanes
      And broken altars of the almighty fiend
      Whose name usurps thy honours, and the blood
      Through centuries clotted there, has floated down
225   The tainted flood of ages, shalt thou live
      Unchangeable! A shrine is raised to thee,
        Which, nor the tempest breath of time,
        Nor the interminable flood
         Over earth's slight pageant rolling,
230   Availeth to destroy, –
      The sensitive extension of the world,
        That wondrous and eternal fane,
      Where pain and pleasure, good and evil join,
      To do the will of strong necessity,
235   And life, in multitudinous shapes,
      Still pressing forward where no term can be,
        Like hungry and unresting flame
      Curls round the eternal columns of its strength.

VII.

SPIRIT

      I was an infant when my mother went
      To see an atheist burned. She took me there:

vi *220. storm of time*] See note to vi 160 above.

vi *222. fiend*] *1840*; fiend, *1813*.

vi *226. shrine*] 'Here, high in air, unconscious of the storm, / Thy temple, Nature, rears its mystic form' (Erasmus Darwin, *Temple of Nature* i 65–6).

vi *227–8.* 'Neither the violent attacks nor the endless attrition of Time'.

vi *228. flood*] Rossetti *1870*; flood, *1813*.

vi *231. sensitive extension*] i.e. sentient life, evolved from matter by Necessity and culminating in Man with his moral sense–the subject of Erasmus Darwin's *The Temple of Nature*. Cp. *Ruins* ch. v: 'When the secret power that animates the universe formed the globe of the earth, . . . [to man, whom] he decreed to expose to the encounter of so many substances, and yet wished to preserve his frail existence, he gave the faculty of perception. By this faculty, every action injurious to his life gives him a sensation of pain and evil, and every favourable action a sensation of pleasure and good'. *world,*] world. *1813, 1840, Hutchinson, 1972*.

vi *236. term*] conclusion.

The whole of *Q Mab* vii is omitted in *1839*.

vii. *2. an atheist burned*] S. cited Lucilio Vanini ('Giulio Cesare'; 1585–1619) as an example of persecution in his *Letter to Lord Ellenborough* (1812), probably

The dark-robed priests were met around the pile;
The multitude was gazing silently;
5   And as the culprit passed with dauntless mien,
Tempered disdain in his unaltering eye,
Mixed with a quiet smile, shone calmly forth:
The thirsty fire crept round his manly limbs;
His resolute eyes were scorched to blindness soon;
10   His death-pang rent my heart! the insensate mob
Uttered a cry of triumph, and I wept.
Weep not, child! cried my mother, for that man
Has said, There is no God.

FAIRY

                    There is no God!
Nature confirms the faith his death-groan sealed:
15   Let heaven and earth, let man's revolving race,
His ceaseless generations tell their tale;
Let every part depending on the chain
That links it to the whole, point to the hand
That grasps its term! let every seed that falls
20   In silent eloquence unfold its store
Of argument: infinity within,
Infinity without, belie creation;
The exterminable spirit it contains
Is nature's only God; but human pride

---

because Vanini was imprisoned in England as a freethinker before being
burned at Toulouse. But Giordano Bruno the pantheist philosopher (1548–
1600), burned in Rome, would have been an apt example, as suggested in *The
Theological Inquirer or Polemical Magazine* for May 1815 (Louise Boas, *Harriet
Shelley* 178–9). There is a prevented burning by Christians in *Ruins* ch. xxi, but
the victim is a Jewish Rabbi.

vii *13. There is no God!*] A repetition possibly provoked by Bowles's reiterated
assertion 'There is a God!' in 'The Sylph of Summer' (223, 229, 290). See S.'s
note.

vii *17–19. Let every part . . . its term!*] i.e. just try to show how any God could
comprehend a chain of causality that is infinite. Cameron (*Cameron (1951)* 257)
quotes S.'s letter of 2 January 1812 (*L* i 215): '. . . as the soul which now
animates this frame was once the vivifying principle of the *infinitely* lowest link
in the Chain of existence, so it is ultimately destined to attain the highest . . .
and in consequence being infinite we can never arrive at its termination. How,
on this hypothesis are we to arrive at a first cause?'

vii *23. exterminable*] *1813, 1840, eds.*; inexterminable *Rossetti 1870 conj.* The text
seems to give a sense opposite to that required, i.e. 'susceptible of expulsion or
annihilation' (see line 47), and the anonymous author of *Reply to the Anti-
Matrimonial Hypothesis and Supposed Atheism of P.B.S. as Laid Down in Queen
Mab* (1821) ch. ii (*Unextinguished Hearth* 87–9) discusses Q *Mab* vii 1–30 on the
assumption that the word is really *inexterminable*. *Concordance* 213 glosses

25   Is skilful to invent most serious names
      To hide its ignorance.

                The name of God
      Has fenced about all crime with holiness,
      Himself the creature of his worshippers,
      Whose names and attributes and passions change,
30   Seeva, Buddh, Foh, Jehovah, God, or Lord,
      Even with the human dupes who build his shrines,
      Still serving o'er the war-polluted world
      For desolation's watch-word; whether hosts
      Stain his death-blushing chariot-wheels, as on
35   Triumphantly they roll, whilst Brahmins raise
      A sacred hymn to mingle with the groans;
      Or countless partners of his power divide
      His tyranny to weakness; or the smoke
      Of burning towns, the cries of female helplessness,
40   Unarmed old age, and youth, and infancy,
      Horribly massacred, ascend to heaven
      In honour of his name; or, last and worst,
      Earth groans beneath religion's iron age,
      And priests dare babble of a God of peace,
45   Even whilst their hands are red with guiltless blood,
      Murdering the while, uprooting every germ
      Of truth, exterminating, spoiling all,
      Making the earth a slaughter-house!

'indestructible' (derivation not given); *OED* defines as 'illimitable', which must be the right meaning though S.'s is the unique example. S. evidently coined the word from Lat. *ex + terminare*, 'to end', intending 'beyond the limits', 'unconfinable'. He is here contrasting infinite with finite (*term* in line 19), and this line makes a paradox: the only God Nature *contains* is *exterminable*, uncontainable.

vii *30. Ruins* ch. xx discusses 'one God, who under various names, is acknowledged by the nations of the East. The Chinese worship him under the name of *Fôt* . . . the people of Thibet, *Budd* and *La*'. Siva (spelt 'Seeva' in Southey's *Curse of Kehama*, 'Chiven' in *Ruins*) is the Destroyer or transmuter in the Hindu Trinity (with Brahma and Vishnu).

vii *43. religion's iron age*] i.e. the present. Volney, writing in 1791 of the recent (1783) conquest of the Crimea from the Turks, represents the latter as praying: 'Indulgent God! grant us the favour to exterminate these Christians . . .', while the Russians pray: 'Beneficent God! . . . permit us to exterminate these impious Mahometans . . .' (*Ruins* ch. xii).

vii *48.* King-Hele (*Erasmus Darwin* (1963) 145) quotes *The Temple of Nature* iv 66: 'And one great Slaughter-house the warring world!' S. had also read Clio Rickman's 'An Extempore Effusion on the Times' (*Poetical Scraps* 1803) ii 74: '[Man] Repays the bounteous earth with seas of blood! / . . . Transforms a

O Spirit! through the sense
50 By which thy inner nature was apprised
     Of outward shows, vague dreams have rolled,
     And varied reminiscences have waked
       Tablets that never fade;
     All things have been imprinted there,
55   The stars, the sea, the earth, the sky,
     Even the unshapeliest lineaments
       Of wild and fleeting visions
       Have left a record there
       To testify of earth.

60 These are my empire, for to me is given
     The wonders of the human world to keep,
     And fancy's thin creations to endow
     With manner, being, and reality;
     Therefore a wondrous phantom, from the dreams
65 Of human error's dense and purblind faith,
     I will evoke, to meet thy questioning.
       Ahasuerus, rise!

---

world, created for his bliss, / Into a slaughterhouse!' Both poets may, however, be indebted to William Smellie's influential *Philosophy of Natural History* i
(1790) ch. xiv, which depicts 'the general system of carnage established by
Nature', the 'instinctive slaughter' to ensure the survival of the fittest, in which
'Of all rapacious animals, *Man* is the most universal destroyer'.

vii *49–59. O Spirit! . . . testify of earth*] Plato's *Phaedo* is here drawn on to suggest
that the visions evoked by the Fairy merely remind Ianthe of eternal truths (line
53) forgotten at birth (see also *Q Mab* ix 155–6): '. . . did we not, as soon as we
were born, see and hear, and possess our other senses? . . . But . . . before we
possessed these, we must have had a knowledge of abstract equality . . . the
beautiful itself, the good, the just, and the holy . . . So that we must necessarily
have had a knowledge of all these before we were born . . . But if, having had it
before we were born, we lose it at our birth, and afterwards, through exercis-
ing the senses about these things, we recover the knowledge which we once
before possessed, would not that which we call learning be a recovery of our
own knowledge?' (*Phaedo* 75; Cary's translation).

vii *53. Tablets*] 'Memoranda'. Tablets were originally a pair of hinged surfaces
for note-taking; in the early 19th century the word could still be applied to any
pocket-notebook.

vii *60–3. to me is given . . . reality*] The Fairy can conjure up anything from Man's
past, including his past delusions.

vii *67. Ahasuerus*] See S.'s note, and headnote to *WJ*. Although only a superstitious legend (lines 64–5, 274–5), A. is a convenient interpreter of a creed
(Christianity) which in S.'s view logically entailed injustice and malice on the
part of its deity.

A strange and woe-worn wight
Arose beside the battlement,
70   And stood unmoving there.
His inessential figure cast no shade
Upon the golden floor;
His port and mien bore mark of many years,
And chronicles of untold ancientness
75   Were legible within his beamless eye:
Yet his cheek bore the mark of youth;
Freshness and vigour knit his manly frame;
The wisdom of old age was mingled there
With youth's primaeval dauntlessness;
80   And inexpressible woe,
Chastened by fearless resignation, gave
An awful grace to his all-speaking brow.

SPIRIT
Is there a God?

AHASUERUS
Is there a God!—aye, an almighty God,
85   And vengeful as almighty! Once his voice
Was heard on earth: earth shuddered at the sound;
The fiery-visaged firmament expressed
Abhorrence, and the grave of nature yawned
To swallow all the dauntless and the good
90   That dared to hurl defiance at his throne,
Girt as it was with power. None but slaves
Survived,—cold-blooded slaves, who did the work
Of tyrannous omnipotence; whose souls
No honest indignation ever urged
95   To elevated daring, to one deed
Which gross and sensual self did not pollute.
These slaves built temples for the omnipotent fiend,
Gorgeous and vast: the costly altars smoked
With human blood, and hideous paeans rung

vii 71–2. Ahasuerus is purely fictitious, like the Persian city of resurrection
described in *Ruins* ch. xxii sect. 5, 'distinguished from all other cities by this
singular attribute, that the bodies of its inhabitants cast no shade'.
vii 85–96. *Once his voice . . . did not pollute*] A.'s illustration is from *Numbers* xvi,
where Korah, Dathan, Abiram and their families are swallowed up alive by the
earth for objecting to Moses' assumption of princely authority over the people,
and fire consumes their followers. When the Israelites protest at this injustice,
14,700 of the malcontents are consumed by a plague.

100   Through all the long-drawn aisles. A murderer heard
       His voice in Egypt, one whose gifts and arts
       Had raised him to his eminence in power,
       Accomplice of omnipotence in crime,
       And confidant of the all-knowing one.
105   These were Jehovah's words:

       From an eternity of idleness
       I, God, awoke; in seven days' toil made earth
       From nothing; rested, and created man:
       I placed him in a paradise, and there
110   Planted the tree of evil, so that he
       Might eat and perish, and my soul procure
       Wherewith to sate its malice, and to turn,
       Even like a heartless conqueror of the earth,
       All misery to my fame. The race of men
115   Chosen to my honour, with impunity
       May sate the lusts I planted in their heart.

vii *100. A murderer*] Moses, whose first recorded adult act was to kill an
Egyptian (*Exodus* ii 11-12).
vii *105. words:*] *Locock 1911*; words. *1813, 1840*. The first five books of the Old
Testament were traditionally ascribed to Moses, Genesis containing what was
known as the Mosaic account of creation.
vii *106-14. From an eternity . . . to my fame*] S.'s tendentious version of Genesis
derives from *Ruins* ch. xxi, wherein a Catholic divine explains to the protagon-
ists of rival faiths that 'God (after having passed an eternity without doing
anything), conceived at length the design (without apparent motive) of forming the world out of nothing: that having in six days created the whole
universe, he found himself tired on the seventh: that having placed the first pair
of human beings in a delightful garden to make them completely happy, he
nevertheless forbade them to taste of the fruit of one tree which he planted
within their reach: that these first parents having yielded to temptation, all
their race (as yet unborn), were condemned to suffer the penalty of a fault
which they had no share in committing . . . permitting the human species to
damn themselves for four or five thousand years . . .' Ahasuerus's imputation
of 'malice' to God is from Holbach: 'Une théologie qui assure que Dieu a pu
créer des hommes pour les rendre éternellement malheureux, ne nous montre
qu'un génie malfaisant, dont la malice est un abîme inconcevable, et surpasse
infiniment la cruauté des êtres les plus dépravés de notre espèce' (*Système de la
Nature* ii 82).
vii *107-8. in seven days' toil . . . created man*] Earth was created in six days,
followed by a day of rest (*Genesis* i, ii 1-3). As Voltaire noted (*Dictionnaire
philosophique* (1764) art. 'Genèse') Man was created either on the sixth day
(*Genesis* i 26-7), or after the day of rest (*Genesis* ii 7).

Here I command thee hence to lead them on,
Until, with hardened feet, their conquering troops
Wade on the promised soil through woman's blood,
120 And make my name be dreaded through the land.
Yet ever burning flame and ceaseless woe
Shall be the doom of their eternal souls,
With every soul on this ungrateful earth,
Virtuous or vicious, weak or strong, – even all
125 Shall perish, to fulfil the blind revenge
(Which you, to men, call justice) of their God.

                  The murderer's brow
Quivered with horror.

                  God omnipotent,
Is there no mercy? must our punishment
130 Be endless? will long ages roll away,
And see no term? Oh! wherefore hast thou made
In mockery and wrath this evil earth?
Mercy becomes the powerful – be but just:
O God! repent and save.

vii *119. through woman's blood*] No doubt S. had in mind *Numbers* xxxi 7–18:
'And the children of Israel took all the women of Midian captives, and their
little ones . . . And Moses was wroth with the officers of the host . . . and Moses
said unto them, Have ye saved all the women alive? . . . Now therefore . . . kill
every woman that hath known man by lying with him. But all the women
children, that have not known a man by lying with him, keep alive for
yourselves'. S. quotes this passage in *A Refutation of Deism* (1814), *Prose* 123n.;
Paine also quotes it (*Age of Reason* Pt II; *Paine Writings* iv 102).

vii *124–5. all / Shall perish*] Only 'after permitting the human species to damn
themselves for four or five thousand years' had God authorized the Redemption (*Ruins* ch. xxi). S. could have seen the morality of this delay challenged by
several authors, including Rousseau (*Émile ou de l'Éducation* (1762) iv, 'Profession de Foi du Vicaire Savoyard') and Holbach (*Le Bon Sens du Curé Jean Meslier*
(1733) 'Testament', ch. v (1892 edn) 360): 'Qu'est-ce donc qu'un Dieu qui
vient se faire crucifier et mourir pour sauver tout le monde, et qui laisse tant de
nations damnées? Quelle pitié et quelle horreur!' In *A Refutation of Deism* S.
causes the Deist Theosophus to say of those who lived before Christ: 'In vain
will you assure me with amiable inconsistency that the mercy of God will be
extended to the virtuous and that the vicious will alone be punished . . . A
subterfuge thus palpable plainly annihilates the necessity of the incarnation of
God for the redemption of the human race . . .' (*Prose* 124).

vii *125–6. the blind revenge . . . of their God*] 'Moral justice cannot take the
innocent for the guilty, even if the innocent would offer itself . . . It is then no
longer justice. It is indiscriminate revenge' (Paine, *Age of Reason* Pt I; *Paine
Writings* iv 43).

One way remains:
135 I will beget a son, and he shall bear
The sins of all the world; he shall arise
In an unnoticed corner of the earth,
And there shall die upon a cross, and purge
The universal crime; so that the few
140 On whom my grace descends, those who are marked
As vessels to the honour of their God,
May credit this strange sacrifice, and save
Their souls alive: millions shall live and die,
Who ne'er shall call upon their Saviour's name,
145 But, unredeemed, go to the gaping grave.
Thousands shall deem it an old woman's tale,
Such as the nurses frighten babes withal:
These in a gulf of anguish and of flame
Shall curse their reprobation endlessly.
150 Yet tenfold pangs shall force them to avow,
Even on their beds of torment, where they howl,
My honour, and the justice of their doom.
What then avail their virtuous deeds, their thoughts
Of purity, with radiant genius bright,
155 Or lit with human reason's earthly ray?
Many are called, but few will I elect.
Do thou my bidding, Moses!

Even the murderer's cheek
Was blanched with horror, and his quivering lips
Scarce faintly uttered–O almighty one,
160 I tremble and obey!

O Spirit! centuries have set their seal
On this heart of many wounds, and loaded brain,
Since the Incarnate came: humbly he came,
Veiling his horrible Godhead in the shape
165 Of man, scorned by the world, his name unheard,

vii 135–6. See S.'s note.
vii 137. an unnoticed corner] The Theist in Holbach's Le Bon Sens is mocked for his belief that 'le Dieu de l'univers a pu se changer en homme et mourir sur une croix dans un coin d'Asie (1829 edn, 170). It is not known whether S. read this work; but the objection to the obscurity of Palestine as scene for the Incarnation was widespread.
vii 156. Quoting the parable of the wedding-feast, Matthew xxii 14: 'For many are called, but few are chosen'.
vii 164. his horrible Godhead] Ahasuerus's account is (like himself) a pure fiction for S.: if the incredible Redemption story were true, Godhead would necessarily have the characteristics described.

Save by the rabble of his native town,
Even as a parish demagogue. He led
The crowd; he taught them justice, truth, and peace,
In semblance; but he lit within their souls
170 The quenchless flames of zeal, and blessed the sword
He brought on earth to satiate with the blood
Of truth and freedom his malignant soul.
At length his mortal frame was led to death.
I stood beside him: on the torturing cross
175 No pain assailed his unterrestrial sense;
And yet he groaned. Indignantly I summed
The massacres and miseries which his name
Had sanctioned in my country, and I cried,
Go! go! in mockery.
180 A smile of godlike malice reillumined
His fading lineaments. – I go, he cried,
But thou shalt wander o'er the unquiet earth
Eternally.――――The dampness of the grave

vii 170–1. *the sword / He brought*] 'Think not that I am come to send peace on earth: I came not to send peace, but a sword' (*Matthew* x 34). S. commented in *A Refutation of Deism* (*Prose* 124–5): 'I will admit that one prediction of Jesus Christ has been indisputably fulfilled: *I come not to bring peace upon earth, but a sword* . . . Eleven millions of men, women and children have been killed in battle, butchered in their sleep, burned to death at public festivals of sacrifice, poisoned, tortured, assassinated, and pillaged in the spirit of the religion of Peace, and for the glory of the most merciful God'. Paine with others likewise observed that 'no sooner were the professors of Christianity sufficiently powerful to employ the sword than they did so, and the stake and the faggot too' (*Age of Reason* Pt II; *Paine Writings* iv 185).

vii 175. 'If Jesus Christ was the being which those mythologists tell us he was . . . the only real suffering he could have endured would have been *to live*. His existence here was a state of exilement or transportation from heaven, and the way back to his original country was to die' (*Age of Reason* Pt I; *Paine Writings* iv 41).

vii 176–83. *Indignantly . . . Eternally.*] This episode, drawn from Roger of Wendover's *Flowers of History* (1849 edn, ii 513), is re-told from *WJ* (ii 581–9 and note), where Ahasuerus's insult is quite gratuitous. Here A. has proleptic knowledge of events after the Crucifixion (lines 176–8) and Christ himself reacts vindictively instead of 'with a severe countenance'.

vii 180. *godlike malice*] S.'s object, like Holbach's, is to destroy the credibility of orthodox Christian doctrines by exposing their moral implications: 'Un Dieu assez perfide et malin pour créer un seul homme, et pour le laisser ensuite exposé au péril de se damner, ne peut pas être regardé comme un être parfait, mais comme un monstre de déraison, d'injustice, de malice et d'atrocité' (*Le*

Bathed my imperishable front. I fell,
185 And long lay tranced upon the charmèd soil.
When I awoke hell burned within my brain,
Which staggered on its seat; for all around
The mouldering relics of my kindred lay,
Even as the Almighty's ire arrested them,
190 And in their various attitudes of death
My murdered children's mute and eyeless skulls
Glared ghastily upon me.

                              But my soul,
From sight and sense of the polluting woe
Of tyranny, had long learned to prefer
195 Hell's freedom to the servitude of heaven.
Therefore I rose, and dauntlessly began
My lonely and unending pilgrimage,
Resolved to wage unweariable war
With my almighty tyrant, and to hurl
200 Defiance at his impotence to harm
Beyond the curse I bore. The very hand
That barred my passage to the peaceful grave
Has crushed the earth to misery, and given
Its empire to the chosen of his slaves.
205 These have I seen, even from the earliest dawn

Bon Sens ch. lxii 90). *reillumined*] reillumed *1840, Hutchinson, 1972*. The change is as likely to be a printer's error as an emendation by Mary S. and is unneeded metrically.

vii *186*. Ladurlad in Southey's *Curse of Kehama* describes how Kehama's curse 'Hath sent a fire into my heart and brain, / A burning fire, for ever there to be' (III x 8–11).

vii *188*. In the *Belle Assemblée* translation of Schubart's 'Ewige Jude' (see S.'s note on Q *Mab* vii 67) the skulls of Ahasuerus's kinsfolk signify only his punishment by survival ('THEY COULD DIE! but I, reprobate wretch, alas, I *cannot* die'); here his kindred have apparently been destroyed by God in a separate act of vengeance.

vii *192. ghastily*] ghastly *1840* (a misprint).

vii *195*. Echoing Milton's Satan: 'Better to reign in hell, than serve in heav'n' (*PL* i 263).

vii *198–9. Resolved . . . tyrant*] Milton's Satan resolves 'To wage by force or guile eternal Warr, / Irreconcileable to our grand Foe . . .' (*PL* i 121–2).

vii *200. impotence to harm*] In Southey's *Kehama* the curse on Ladurlad, intended to ensure everlasting punishment, defeats its own object as it provides immunity from death at critical points in the action.

Of weak, unstable and precarious power,
Then preaching peace, as now they practise war;
So, when they turned but from the massacre
Of unoffending infidels, to quench
210   Their thirst for ruin in the very blood
That flowed in their own veins, and pitiless zeal
Froze every human feeling, as the wife
Sheathed in her husband's heart the sacred steel,
Even whilst its hopes were dreaming of her love;
215   And friends to friends, brothers to brothers stood
Opposed in bloodiest battle-field, and war
Scarce satiable by fate's last death-draught waged,
Drunk from the winepress of the Almighty's wrath;
Whilst the red cross, in mockery of peace,
220   Pointed to victory! When the fray was done,
No remnant of the exterminated faith
Survived to tell its ruin, but the flesh,
With putrid smoke poisoning the atmosphere,
That rotted on the half-extinguished pile.

vii *206–7. power, . . . war;*] *Rossetti 1870*; power; . . . war, *1813*, *1840*. Perhaps S.'s
printer transposed these stops.

vii *207.* Rival theologians in Volney's *Ruins* ch. xxi accuse the Christians of
hypocrisy: 'When weak, you have preached liberty, toleration, and peace;
when power has been in your hands, you have practised violence and persecution!'

vii *208. So,*] i.e. 'So also have I seen them' (*Locock 1911*). But it may mean
'Unchanged in nature', i.e. turning merely from the conquest of infidels to
wars among themselves.

vii *216. war*] war, *1813*.

vii *218.* The image is from *Revelation* xiv 19–20: 'And the angel thrust in his
sickle into the earth, and gathered the vine of the earth, and cast it into the great
winepress of the wrath of God. And the winepress was trodden without the
city, and blood came out of the winepress, even unto the horse bridles . . .'

vii *219. the red cross*] This passage (lines 208–24) may be based on Gibbon's
account of the conflicts arising from the Arian and Donatist heresies under the
rule of Constantine's son Constantius (*Decline and Fall* chs. xx–xxi). In ch. xx
Gibbon relates Eusebius's version of the miracle which led Constantine to
adopt the Cross as his military standard: 'Christ appeared before his eyes; and,
displaying the same celestial sign of the cross, he directed Constantine to frame
a similar standard, and to march, with an assurance of victory, against Maxen-
tius [a pagan] and all his enemies' (1776–88; 1897 edn, ii 304).

vii *221. the exterminated faith*] Gibbon (ch. xxi) quotes Constantius's successor
Julian as admitting that 'Whole troops of those who were styled heretics were
massacred . . . In Paphlagonia, Bithynia, Galatia, and in many other provinces,
towns and villages were laid waste and utterly destroyed' (ii 387).

225 Yes! I have seen God's worshippers unsheathe
The sword of his revenge, when grace descended,
Confirming all unnatural impulses,
To sanctify their desolating deeds;
And frantic priests waved the ill-omened cross
230 O'er the unhappy earth: then shone the sun
On showers of gore from the upflashing steel
Of safe assassination, and all crime
Made stingless by the spirits of the Lord,
And blood-red rainbows canopied the land.

235 Spirit! no year of my eventful being
Has passed unstained by crime and misery,
Which flows from God's own faith. I've marked his
slaves,
With tongues whose lies are venomous, beguile
The insensate mob, and, whilst one hand was red
240 With murder, feign to stretch the other out
For brotherhood and peace; and that they now
Babble of love and mercy, whilst their deeds
Are marked with all the narrowness and crime
That freedom's young arm dare not yet chastise,
245 Reason may claim our gratitude, who now
Establishing the imperishable throne
Of truth, and stubborn virtue, maketh vain
The unprevailing malice of my foe,
Whose bootless rage heaps torments for the brave,
250 Adds impotent eternities to pain,
Whilst keenest disappointment racks his breast
To see the smiles of peace around them play,
To frustrate or to sanctify their doom.

Thus have I stood—through a wild waste of years
255 Struggling with whirlwinds of mad agony,
Yet peaceful, and serene, and self-enshrined,

vii 233. *Made stingless*] i.e. absolved from the sting of remorse.   *spirits*] Spirits
eds (a perpetuated error).
vii 234. *blood-red rainbows*] This striking image may have been suggested by the
'celestial cross encircled with a splendid rainbow; which . . . had appeared over
the Mount of Olives' to presage Constantius's bloody victory at the Battle of
Mursa against the pagan Magnentius, said to have cost a total of 54,000 lives
(Gibbon chs. xviii, xxi; ii 239–41, 358–9).
vii 237. *flows*] S.'s characteristic singular verb for paired nouns.   *slaves,*] *1840*;
slaves *1813*.
vii 241–8. *that they now . . . malice of my foe*] The construction is: 'That they now
talk of mercy . . . is thanks to Reason, who makes God's malice vain'.

Mocking my powerless tyrant's horrible curse
With stubborn and unalterable will,
Even as a giant oak, which heaven's fierce flame
260   Had scathèd in the wilderness, to stand
A monument of fadeless ruin there;
Yet peacefully and movelessly it braves
The midnight conflict of the wintry storm,
    As in the sunlight's calm it spreads
265   Its worn and withered arms on high
To meet the quiet of a summer's noon.

        The Fairy waved her wand:
        Ahasuerus fled
Fast as the shapes of mingled shade and mist,
270   That lurk in the glens of a twilight grove,
        Flee from the morning beam:
    The matter of which dreams are made
    Not more endowed with actual life
    Than this phantasmal portraiture
275   Of wandering human thought.

                    VIII.
The present and the past thou hast beheld:
It was a desolate sight. Now, Spirit, learn
    The secrets of the future. – Time!
Unfold the brooding pinion of thy gloom,
5   Render thou up thy half-devoured babes,
And from the cradles of eternity,
Where millions lie lulled to their portioned sleep
By the deep murmuring stream of passing things,

vii 258. An echo of Kailyal's defiance of the tyrant in Southey's *Curse of Kehama* (XXIV x 2–5): 'Almighty as thou art, / Thou hast put all things underneath thy feet; / But still the resolute heart / And virtuous will are free'. (See *Q Mab* ix 35 below.)

vii 259–63. *Even as a giant oak . . . wintry storm*] A passage adapted (as Medwin noted, *Medwin (1913)* 42) from the epigraph to ch. x of *St Irvyne*, which in turn was taken from *WJ* (see iii 783–91 and note). One source of the image is Milton, *PL* i 612–15; 'As when heaven's fire / Hath scathed the forest oaks or mountain pines / With singèd top their stately growth, though bare, / Stands on the blasted heath'.

vii 272–5. An absolute construction: 'the stuff of dreams being no more real than this hypothetical figure'.

viii 5. *half-devoured babes*] In classical mythology Cronus (Time) devoured his own sons as soon as they were born (Hesiod, *Theognis* 453–74).

Tear thou that gloomy shroud. – Spirit, behold
10   Thy glorious destiny!
        Joy to the Spirit came.
Through the wide rent in Time's eternal veil,
Hope was seen beaming through the mists of fear:
        Earth was no longer hell;
15   Love, freedom, health, had given
Their ripeness to the manhood of its prime.
        And all its pulses beat
Symphonious to the planetary spheres:
        Then dulcet music swelled
20 Concordant with the life-strings of the soul;
It throbbed in sweet and languid beatings there,
Catching new life from transitory death, –
Like the vague sighings of a wind at even,
That wakes the wavelets of the slumbering sea
25 And dies on the creation of its breath,
And sinks and rises, fails and swells by fits,
        Was the pure stream of feeling
        That sprung from these sweet notes,
And o'er the Spirit's human sympathies
30 With mild and gentle motion calmly flowed.

        Joy to the Spirit came, –
        Such joy as when a lover sees
The chosen of his soul in happiness,
        And witnesses her peace
35 Whose woe to him were bitterer than death,
        Sees her unfaded cheek
Glow mantling in first luxury of health,
        Thrills with her lovely eyes,
Which like two stars amid the heaving main
40   Sparkle through liquid bliss.

Then in her triumph spoke the Fairy Queen:
I will not call the ghost of ages gone
To unfold the frightful secrets of its lore;

viii *18*. See note to vi 41 which this line repeats.

viii *20*. Indebted to Akenside's account (*Pleasures of the Imagination* (1744) i 109–24) of how Nature attunes the mind to external things, 'till now the soul / At length discloses every tuneful spring, / To that harmonious movement from without / Responsive'.

viii *26*. *fits,*] *Rossetti 1870*; fits: *1813, eds.*

viii *27*. *stream of feeling*] Cp. *PU* II ii 34; the whole stanza has an affinity with lines 19–30.

The present now is past,
45 And those events that desolate the earth
Have faded from the memory of Time,
Who dares not give reality to that
Whose being I annul. To me is given
The wonders of the human world to keep,
50 Space, matter, time, and mind. Futurity
Exposes now its treasure; let the sight
Renew and strengthen all thy failing hope.
O human Spirit! spur thee to the goal
Where virtue fixes universal peace,
55 And midst the ebb and flow of human things,
Show somewhat stable, somewhat certain still,
A lighthouse o'er the wild of dreary waves.

The habitable earth is full of bliss;
Those wastes of frozen billows that were hurled
60 By everlasting snow-storms round the poles,
Where matter dared not vegetate or live,
But ceaseless frost round the vast solitude
Bound its broad zone of stillness, are unloosed;
And fragrant zephyrs there from spicy isles
65 Ruffle the placid ocean-deep, that rolls
Its broad, bright surges to the sloping sand,
Whose roar is wakened into echoings sweet
To murmur through the heaven-breathing groves
And melodize with man's blessed nature there.

70 Those deserts of immeasurable sand,
Whose age-collected fervours scarce allowed
A bird to live, a blade of grass to spring,
Where the shrill chirp of the green lizard's love
Broke on the sultry silentness alone,
75 Now teem with countless rills and shady woods,
Corn-fields and pastures and white cottages;
And where the startled wilderness beheld
A savage conqueror stained in kindred blood,

viii 56. *Show*] A reflexive imperative (*OED* iv 3a): 'Show yourself to be as firm-minded as you can'.
viii 58. i.e. 'The whole earth is habitable and full of bliss' (King-Hele, *S. His Thought & Work* 44).
viii 61. *or*] nor *1839, 1840*.
viii 73. Adapted from *Thalaba* IV v 16: 'the grey Lizard's chirp'. The gecko, widespread in warm climates, is a grey-green lizard whose name derives from the sound it makes (most lizards are silent).

A tigress sating with the flesh of lambs
80   The unnatural famine of her toothless cubs,
Whilst shouts and howlings through the desert rang,
Sloping and smooth the daisy-spangled lawn,
Offering sweet incense to the sunrise, smiles
To see a babe before his mother's door,
85   Sharing his morning's meal
With the green and golden basilisk
That comes to lick his feet.

Those trackless deeps, where many a weary sail
Has seen above the illimitable plain
90   Morning on night, and night on morning rise,
Whilst still no land to greet the wanderer spread
Its shadowy mountains on the sun-bright sea,
Where the loud roarings of the tempest-waves
So long have mingled with the gusty wind
95   In melancholy loneliness, and swept
The desert of those ocean solitudes,

viii 79. The tigress and the conqueror are parallels in perversity: the 'natural' food of the cubs is milk, but habit has conditioned them to demand flesh. *lambs*] *1839*; lambs, *1813*.

viii 86. *basilisk*] i.e. deadly crested serpent. The legendary basilisk (= cockatrice) was hatched by a snake from a cock's egg, and its look killed (cp. 'Ode to Naples' 83–4: 'Be thou like the imperial Basilisk / Killing thy foe with unapparent wounds!'). *OED* cites *Q Mab* viii 86 as the first occurrence in English of modern *basilisk* (= iguana lizard), which is impossible. The point is the child's friendship with a previously lethal creature; S. elaborates the picture of Man's reconcilement with Nature in *Isaiah* xi 8: 'And the sucking child shall play on the hole of the asp, and the weaned child shall put his hand on the cockatrice' den'. The translation *basilisk* did not appear until the Revision of 1888, although Luther had rendered the Vulgate version 'in caverna reguli' as 'in die Höhle des Basilisken' (1545), and S. had not yet met *basiliscus* ('kingsnake'), in Lucan's *Pharsalia* (ix 726), which he apparently did not read until 1815 (*L* i 429, 432); so his use of the word probably derives from Pope's paraphrase of *Isaiah* ('Messiah' 81–4): 'The smiling infant in his hand shall take / The crested basilisk and speckled snake, / Pleas'd the green lustre of the scales survey, / And with their forky tongues shall innocently play'. Cp. also Bowles's picture of primitive innocence in 'Spirit of Discovery' (1805) i 212–14: '. . . in the sun / A naked infant playing, stretched his hand / To reach a speckled snake . . .', and the conclusion of S.'s 1814 fragment 'The Assassins' (*Prose* 153–4).

viii 88–92. *many a weary sail . . . the sun-bright sea*] Recalling the voyage to Mexico in Southey's *Madoc* Pt I iv 75–8: 'I saw / The sun still sink below the endless waves, / And still at morn, beneath the farthest sky, / Unbounded ocean heaved' etc.

viii 89. *plain*] plain, *1813*.

But vocal to the sea-bird's harrowing shriek,
The bellowing monster, and the rushing storm,
Now to the sweet and many-mingling sounds
100 Of kindliest human impulses respond.
Those lonely realms bright garden-isles begem,
With lightsome clouds and shining seas between,
And fertile valleys, resonant with bliss,
Whilst green woods overcanopy the wave,
105 Which like a toil-worn labourer leaps to shore,
To meet the kisses of the flowrets there.

All things are recreated, and the flame
Of consentaneous love inspires all life:
The fertile bosom of the earth gives suck
110 To myriads, who still grow beneath her care,
Rewarding her with their pure perfectness:
The balmy breathings of the wind inhale
Her virtues, and diffuse them all abroad:
Health floats amid the gentle atmosphere,
115 Glows in the fruits, and mantles on the stream:
No storms deform the beaming brow of heaven,
Nor scatter in the freshness of its pride
The foliage of the ever verdant trees;
But fruits are ever ripe, flowers ever fair,
120 And autumn proudly bears her matron grace,
Kindling a flush on the fair cheek of spring,
Whose virgin bloom beneath the ruddy fruit
Reflects its tint and blushes into love.

viii 97. *but vocal to*] 'filled only with the sound of' (*OED* ii 5).
viii 99. *many-mingling*] Rossetti 1870; many mingling 1813, 1839, 1840.
viii 101. *bright garden-isles*] Borrowed from Erasmus Darwin's glowing description of the formation of earth's primeval islands (*Botanic Garden* Pt I, ii 33–46): 'O'er those blest isles no ice-crown'd mountains tower'd, / No lightnings darted, and no tempests lower'd / . . . Sweet breathed the zephyrs, just perceived and lost, / And brineless billows only kiss'd the coast'. The Huttonian theory posited the elevation of new lands from the sea as an inevitable geological process (*Theory of the Earth* (1785) i 198–200), and Humphry Davy publicized it in his Geological Lectures vi (1811): 'In the Azores, in the different Asiatic Archipelagoes, Islands have been often raised. That near Santerin, which rose out of the bosom of the sea in 1707, is now covered in many parts with vegetables. The Lipari Islands were probably all of them elevated by submarine volcanoes. Fertile fields now exist, where before there was a comparatively useless expanse of sea' (*Works* (1840) viii 236–7).
viii 108. *consentaneous*] accordant.
viii 120–1. i.e. winter will be eliminated. See S.'s note to vi 45–6.

The lion now forgets to thirst for blood:
125 There might you see him sporting in the sun
Beside the dreadless kid; his claws are sheathed,
His teeth are harmless, custom's force has made
His nature as the nature of a lamb.
Like passion's fruit, the nightshade's tempting bane
130 Poisons no more the pleasure it bestows:
All bitterness is past; the cup of joy
Unmingled mantles to the goblet's brim,
And courts the thirsty lips it fled before.

But chief, ambiguous man, he that can know
135 More misery, and dream more joy than all;
Whose keen sensations thrill within his breast
To mingle with a loftier instinct there,
Lending their power to pleasure and to pain,
Yet raising, sharpening, and refining each;
140 Who stands amid the ever-varying world,
The burthen or the glory of the earth;

viii *124–6. The lion . . . dreadless kid*] Imitating *Isaiah* ii 6–7: 'The wolf also shall dwell with the lamb, and the leopard shall lie down with the kid; and the calf and the young lion and the fatling together . . . the lion shall eat straw like the ox'. Cp. Pope's 'Messiah' 79: 'The steer and lion at one crib shall meet', and Virgil's *Eclogue* iv 22 (quoted by Pope): 'nec magnos metuent armenta leones' ('nor shall the herds fear huge lions').

viii *127. custom's force*] S. argued in his contemporary 'On the Vegetable System of Diet' that meat-eating was an unnatural addictive habit in human beings, who are not physically adapted to it, whereas 'if a lion were fed on grass, or a cow on flesh, the health of these animals would be materially injured'. Nevertheless these diets may themselves result only from habit of longer standing: 'Custom has been found to reconcile the animal system to habits the most unnatural and pernicious . . . No argument can therefore be adduced in favour of any system of diet from the mere fact of its being generally used, so long as disease and meagreness and misery are observed among its unfailing concomitants' (*V&P* 100). In the coming reconcilement of Man and Nature the lion's aggressive habits would change with its relinquishment of a flesh diet (see *PU* III iv 78–82 and note).

viii *129–32. Like passion's fruit . . . goblet's brim*] The elimination of vegetable poison is not in *Isaiah* or Pope but occurs in Virgil, *Ecl.* iv 24–5: 'fallax herba veneris occidet' ('the false poison-plant shall perish'). For S., however, the plant becomes harmless without perishing. He normally used the woody nightshade, *solanum dulcamara*, as an analogue of sexual passion as its Latin and alternative English name ('bittersweet') enabled him to exploit the oxymoron (line 131, *bitterness . . . joy*). See 'Passion' and note, and 'Lines: "That moment is gone for ever"' 13–14: 'In the cup of its joy was mingled / Delusion too sweet, though vain'.

He chief perceives the change, his being notes
The gradual renovation, and defines
Each movement of its progress on his mind.

145 Man, where the gloom of the long polar night
Lowers o'er the snow-clad rocks and frozen soil,
Where scarce the hardiest herb that braves the frost
Basks in the moonlight's ineffectual glow,
Shrank with the plants, and darkened with the night;
150 His chilled and narrow energies, his heart,
Insensible to courage, truth, or love,
His stunted stature and imbecile frame,
Marked him for some abortion of the earth,
Fit compeer of the bears that roamed around,
155 Whose habits and enjoyments were his own:
His life a feverish dream of stagnant woe,
Whose meagre wants, but scantily fulfilled,

viii *145–86. Man . . . name of God*] I. J. Kapstein (*PMLA* lii (1937) 238–43) refers
this section to Cabanis's *Rapports du Physique et du Moral de l'Homme* (Paris
1802), which is quoted in S.'s notes. Cabanis demonstrates the correlation
between man's physical and moral being, but his generalities assert only that
'Le tempérament, caracterisé par l'aisance et la liberté de toutes les fonctions,
par la tournure heureuse de tous les penchans et de toutes les idées, se développe
pe rarement et mal dans les pays très-froids et dans les pays très-chauds . . .
l'homme de ces pays [froids] sera supérieur à celui des pays chauds dans tous les
travaux qui demandent un corps robuste: il lui sera souvent inférieur . . . dans
les travaux qui tiennent à la culture de l'esprit, particulièrement dans les arts
d'imagination'–while a temperate climate normally coincides with a well-
balanced human temperament (9ᵐᵉ Mém., xiv; 1844 edn, 457). Kapstein also
quotes Jean Sylvain Bailly's *Lettres sur l'Origine des Sciences, et sur Celle des
Peuples de l'Asie* (Paris 1777, 114), also named in S.'s notes: 'Il faut à la
constitution parfaite de l'homme un degré de chaleur moyen, à peu près égal
peut-être à celui que nous éprouvons dans nos climats, lesquels, par cette
raison, ont été nommés tempérés'. S. goes much further than either Cabanis or
Bailly in claiming that men's moral state and physical environment are not
merely correlated but are linked aspects of the same cosmic harmony: the
argument of lines 163–4 is not that men infringe Nature's law by living in polar
or in tropical regions, but that such regions only exist while her moral laws are
infringed. See *PU* II iv 49–58; III iii 115–23. Godwin, by contrast to all three
writers, thought climate irrelevant to human progress: 'There is no state of
mankind that renders them incapable of the exercise of reason' (*Political Justice*
Bk I ch. vi, i 104).

viii *154. Fit compeer of the bears*] S.'s impression of life in the far north seems
indebted to that of western Siberia in Thomson's 'Winter' 936–45, especially:
'Here human nature wears its rudest form . . . / . . . immersed in furs / Doze the
gross race–nor sprightly jest, nor song, / Nor tenderness they know, nor
aught of life / Beyond the kindred bears that stalk without–'.

Apprised him ever of the joyless length
Which his short being's wretchedness had reached;
160 His death a pang which famine, cold and toil
Long on the mind, whilst yet the vital spark
Clung to the body stubbornly, had brought:
All was inflicted here that earth's revenge
Could wreak on the infringers of her law;
165 One curse alone was spared—the name of God.

Nor where the tropics bound the realms of day
With a broad belt of mingling cloud and flame,
Where blue mists through the unmoving atmosphere
Scattered the seeds of pestilence, and fed
170 Unnatural vegetation, where the land
Teemed with all earthquake, tempest and disease,
Was man a nobler being; slavery
Had crushed him to his country's bloodstained dust;
Or he was bartered for the fame of power,
175 Which all internal impulses destroying,
Makes human will an article of trade;
Or he was changed with Christians for their gold,
And dragged to distant isles, where to the sound
Of the flesh-mangling scourge, he does the work
180 Of all-polluting luxury and wealth,
Which doubly visits on the tyrants' heads
The long-protracted fulness of their woe;
Or he was led to legal butchery,
To turn to worms beneath that burning sun
185 Where kings first leagued against the rights of men,
And priests first traded with the name of God.

viii *165*. According to Volney (*Ruins* ch. xx) many primitive peoples 'entertaining none of these ideas of civilised countries respecting God, the soul, and a future state, exercise no species of worship'.

viii *165*. Omitted 1839.

viii *166–72*. *Nor where the tropics . . . a nobler being*] Again borrowing from Thomson's picture in 'Summer' of the tropics where 'The parent sun himself / Seems o'er this world of slaves to tyrannise' (884–5), and 'Where putrefaction into life ferments / And breathes destructive myriads, or from woods . . . / In vapours rank and blue corruption wrapt / . . . then wasteful forth / Walks the dire power of pestilent disease' (1029–35).

viii *183*. *led to legal butchery*] i.e. inducted into the Egyptian campaigns of the Napoleonic War, 1798–1807.

viii *184–6*. *that burning sun . . . name of God*] '. . . the vast, complicated, and learned, theological system, which from the banks of the Nile, conveyed from country to country by commerce, war, and conquest, invaded the whole world' (*Ruins* ch. xxii sect. 3). *sun*] *1839*, *1840*; sun, *1813*, eds.

Even where the milder zone afforded man
A seeming shelter, yet contagion there,
Blighting his being with unnumbered ills,
190 Spread like a quenchless fire; nor truth till late
Availed to arrest its progress, or create
That peace which first in bloodless victory waved
Her snowy standard o'er this favoured clime:
There man was long the train-bearer of slaves,
195 The mimic of surrounding misery,
The jackal of ambition's lion-rage,
The bloodhound of religion's hungry zeal.

Here now the human being stands adorning
This loveliest earth with taintless body and mind;
200 Blessed from his birth with all bland impulses,
Which gently in his noble bosom wake
All kindly passions and all pure desires.
Him (still from hope to hope the bliss pursuing,
Which from the exhaustless lore of human weal
205 Draws on the virtuous mind) the thoughts that rise
In time-destroying infiniteness, gift
With self-enshrined eternity, that mocks

viii *190. till late*] i.e. until the future which the Fairy is now about to reveal.
viii *194. train-bearer of slaves*] 'toady of potentates'.
viii *203–5.* See S.'s note.

Him, still from hope to hope the bliss pursuing,
Which from the exhaustless lore of human weal
Draws on the virtuous mind, *1813 text*

Him, (still from hope to hope the bliss pursuing,
Which, from the exhaustless lore of human weal
Dawns on the virtuous mind,) *1813 notes*

1839 reads as *1813 text*, but emends *lore* to *store*.
1840 reads as the present text, but emends *lore* to *store*.
store . . . Dawns *Rossetti 1870*
store . . . Draws *Woodberry 1893*
lore . . . Dawns *Hutchinson, Locock 1911, 1972* (all these eds misstate the *1813* text
reading). The context requires not a single revelation but an unending process,
consequently the misprint is likely to be *Dawns* in *1813 notes*. The very difficult
lines 203–7 may be paraphrased: 'Man's illimitable thoughts endow him—as he
goes on hopefully pursuing the happiness which, by the inexhaustible study of
human welfare, lures the virtuous mind along—with a self-sufficient immortality that mocks old age'. The main construction is: 'The thoughts . . . gift . . .
him . . . with eternity'.

The unprevailing hoariness of age,
And man, once fleeting o'er the transient scene
210 Swift as an unremembered vision, stands
Immortal upon earth: no longer now
He slays the lamb that looks him in the face,
And horribly devours his mangled flesh,
Which still avenging nature's broken law,
215 Kindled all putrid humours in his frame,
All evil passions, and all vain belief,
Hatred, despair, and loathing in his mind,
The germs of misery, death, disease, and crime.
No longer now the wingèd habitants,
220 That in the woods their sweet lives sing away,
Flee from the form of man; but gather round,
And prune their sunny feathers on the hands
Which little children stretch in friendly sport
Towards these dreadless partners of their play.
225 All things are void of terror: man has lost
His terrible prerogative, and stands
An equal amidst equals: happiness
And science dawn though late upon the earth;
Peace cheers the mind, health renovates the frame;
230 Disease and pleasure cease to mingle here,
Reason and passion cease to combat there;
Whilst each unfettered o'er the earth extend
Their all-subduing energies, and wield
The sceptre of a vast dominion there;
235 Whilst every shape and mode of matter lends
Its force to the omnipotence of mind,
Which from its dark mine drags the gem of truth
To decorate its paradise of peace.

viii *211. Immortal upon earth*] See S.'s note to lines 203–7, and commentary.
viii *211–12. no longer now . . . in the face*] See S.'s note.
viii *222. prune*] preen (an obsolete form, probably from Spenser, *FQ* II iii 36).
viii *226. His terrible prerogative*] 'His special privilege to kill other animals'. Cp.
Southey's *Letters from England* lv: 'When man shall cease to be the tyrant of
inferior beings he may truly become their lord'.
viii *230. Disease*] i.e. venereal disease (cp. v 194–6; viii 129–30; ix 87–8).
viii *232–3. each unfettered . . . extend / Their*] *1813, eds.*; each unfettered . . .
extends / Its *1839, 1840, 1972.* 'Each unfettered' is a parenthetic absolute, and the
subject of 'extend' is 'energies': 'Reason and passion being each unfettered,
their all-subduing energies extend over the earth'.

IX.

O happy Earth! reality of Heaven!
To which those restless souls that ceaselessly
Throng through the human universe, aspire;
Thou consummation of all mortal hope!
5   Thou glorious prize of blindly-working will!
Whose rays, diffused throughout all space and time,
Verge to one point and blend for ever there:
Of purest spirits thou pure dwelling-place!
Where care and sorrow, impotence and crime,
10   Languor, disease, and ignorance dare not come:
O happy Earth, reality of Heaven!

Genius has seen thee in her passionate dreams,
And dim forebodings of thy loveliness
Haunting the human heart, have there entwined
15   Those rooted hopes of some sweet place of bliss
Where friends and lovers meet to part no more.
Thou art the end of all desire and will,
The product of all action; and the souls
That by the paths of an aspiring change
20   Have reached thy haven of perpetual peace,
There rest from the eternity of toil
That framed the fabric of thy perfectness.

Even Time, the conqueror, fled thee in his fear;
That hoary giant, who, in lonely pride,
25   So long had ruled the world, that nations fell
Beneath his silent footstep. Pyramids,
That for millenniums had withstood the tide
Of human things, his storm-breath drove in sand
Across that desert where their stones survived
30   The name of him whose pride had heaped them there.
Yon monarch, in his solitary pomp,
Was but the mushroom of a summer day,

---

ix *1–3*. i.e. un͟ ˡy millennium actualizes what was real in the hope of
Heaven, which has always had a universal appeal.

ix *9–10*. Cp. S.'s 'Essay on Christianity' (1817): 'We die, says Jesus Christ, and
when we awaken from the languor of disease the glories and the happiness of
Paradise are around us . . . How delightful a picture even if it be not true!' (*Prose*
205).

ix *21*. Necessity's 'eternity of toil' contrasts with God's 'eternity of idleness'
before creation (vii 106).

ix *23*. *Time*] Lines 23–37 are a revision of 'The Ocean rolls between us' 12–25
(see notes).

ix *27*. *millenniums*] 'thousands of years' (the normal plural).

ix *29–30*. An anticipation of 'Ozymandias' 3–8.

That his light-wingèd footstep pressed to dust:
Time was the king of earth: all things gave way
35   Before him, but the fixed and virtuous will,
The sacred sympathies of soul and sense,
That mocked his fury and prepared his fall.

Yet slow and gradual dawned the morn of love;
Long lay the clouds of darkness o'er the scene,
40   Till from its native heaven they rolled away:
First, crime triumphant o'er all hope careered
Unblushing, undisguising, bold and strong;
Whilst falsehood, tricked in virtue's attributes,
Long sanctified all deeds of vice and woe,
45   Till done by her own venomous sting to death
She left the moral world without a law,
No longer fettering passion's fearless wing,
Nor searing reason with the brand of God.
Then steadily the happy ferment worked;
50   Reason was free; and wild though passion went
Through tangled glens and wood-embosomed meads,
Gathering a garland of the strangest flowers,
Yet like the bee returning to her queen,
She bound the sweetest on her sister's brow,
55   Who meek and sober kissed the sportive child,
No longer trembling at the broken rod.

Mild was the slow necessity of death:
The tranquil spirit failed beneath its grasp,

ix 45. *death*] death, *1813*.

ix 48. *Omitted 1839, 1840* (presumably a censored line missed when passages were restored in *1840*).

ix 53. In the honey-bee, queen and workers are both female.

ix 54. *her sister's*] Reason's. See note to v 20–1.

ix 57–9. Milton's Michael tells Adam that he must live temperately 'till like ripe Fruit thou drop / Into thy Mother's lap, or be with ease / Gatherd, not harshly pluckt, for death mature' (*PL* xi 535–7). It was a Christian commonplace that 'virtuous men pass mildly away' (Donne, 'A Valediction Forbidding Mourning' 1), but in 1812 the virtuous and the natural were often identified: 'Were there a country where the inhabitants led lives entirely natural and virtuous, few of them would die without measuring out the whole period of present existence allotted to them; pain and distemper would be unknown among them, and death would come upon them like a sleep, in consequence of no other cause than gradual and unavoidable decay' (Dr Richard Price, quoted by Malthus in *An Essay on the Principle of Population* (1798) 338–9). S. first referred to Malthus's *Essay* in his *Proposals for an Association of Philanthropists* (2 March 1812).

ix 58. *spirit*] Spirit *1813, 1839, 1840*. The capital would invite confusion with Ianthe.

Without a groan, almost without a fear,
60   Calm as a voyager to some distant land,
And full of wonder, full of hope as he.
The deadly germs of languor and disease
Died in the human frame, and purity
Blessed with all gifts her earthly worshippers.
65   How vigorous then the athletic form of age!
How clear its open and unwrinkled brow!
Where neither avarice, cunning, pride, or care,
Had stamped the seal of grey deformity
On all the mingling lineaments of time.
70   How lovely the intrepid front of youth!
Which meek-eyed courage decked with freshest grace;
Courage of soul, that dreaded not a name,
And elevated will, that journeyed on
Through life's phantasmal scene in fearlessness,
75   With virtue, love, and pleasure, hand in hand.

Then, that sweet bondage which is freedom's self,
And rivets with sensation's softest tie
The kindred sympathies of human souls,
Needed no fetters of tyrannic law:
80   Those delicate and timid impulses
In nature's primal modesty arose,
And with undoubting confidence disclosed
The growing longings of its dawning love,
Unchecked by dull and selfish chastity,
85   That virtue of the cheaply virtuous,
Who pride themselves in senselessness and frost.

ix *60–1.* Recalling Swift's Houyhnhnms who, when dying, 'take a solemn leave of their friends, as if they were going to some remote part of the country, where they designed to pass the rest of their lives' (*Gulliver's Travels* Bk IV ch. ix).

ix *62. germs*] 'seeds' (a metaphor).

ix *72. a name*] i.e. a conventional authority.

ix *74. life's phantasmal scene*] See note to vi 192.

ix *76. that sweet bondage*] sexual love.

ix *82. undoubting*] *1813, 1839, 1840*; undoubted *Forman 1876–7, Hutchinson, 1972* (an error).

ix *84. chastity*] See S.'s note to v 189. He explained to Byron on 26 May 1820 that 'as things are' he thought 'a regard to chastity is quite necessary . . . to a young female–that is, to her happiness–and at any time a good habit' (*L* ii 199).

ix *86. senselessness*] lack of sensual and emotional feeling. S. is agreeing with Mary Wollstonecraft: 'When novelists or moralists praise as a virtue, a woman's coldness of constitution, and want of passion . . . I am disgusted.

No longer prostitution's venomed bane
Poisoned the springs of happiness and life;
Woman and man, in confidence and love,
90 Equal and free and pure together trod
The mountain-paths of virtue, which no more
Were stained with blood from many a pilgrim's feet.

Then, where, through distant ages, long in pride
The palace of the monarch-slave had mocked
95 Famine's faint groan, and penury's silent tear,
A heap of crumbling ruins stood, and threw
Year after year their stones upon the field,
Wakening a lonely echo; and the leaves
Of the old thorn, that on the topmost tower
100 Usurped the royal ensign's grandeur, shook
In the stern storm that swayed the topmost tower
And whispered strange tales in the whirlwind's ear.

Low through the lone cathedral's roofless aisles
The melancholy winds a death-dirge sung:
105 It were a sight of awfulness to see
The works of faith and slavery, so vast,
So sumptuous, yet so perishing withal!
Even as the corpse that rests beneath its wall.
A thousand mourners deck the pomp of death
110 To-day, the breathing marble glows above
To decorate its memory, and tongues
Are busy of its life: to-morrow, worms
In silence and in darkness seize their prey.

Within the massy prison's mouldering courts,
115 Fearless and free the ruddy children played,
Weaving gay chaplets for their innocent brows
With the green ivy and the red wall-flower,
That mock the dungeon's unavailing gloom;
The ponderous chains, and gratings of strong iron,
120 There rusted amid heaps of broken stone
That mingled slowly with their native earth:

They may be good women, in the ordinary acceptation of the phrase, and do
no harm; but they appear to me not to have those "finely fashioned nerves,"
which render the senses exquisite . . . They want that fire of the imagination,
which produces *active* sensibility, and *positive* virtue' (*The Wrongs of Woman* ch.
x, *Posth. Works* ii 29–30).
ix 93–137. Cp. the similar prophetic description in *PU* III iv 130–204.
ix 103–7. S. had seen Tintern Abbey on the way from Cwm Elan to Chepstow
at the end of June 1812. See note to ii 141–8.

> There the broad beam of day, which feebly once
> Lighted the cheek of lean captivity
> With a pale and sickly glare, then freely shone
125 On the pure smiles of infant playfulness:
> No more the shuddering voice of hoarse despair
> Pealed through the echoing vaults, but soothing notes
> Of ivy-fingered winds and gladsome birds
> And merriment were resonant around.

130 These ruins soon left not a wreck behind:
> Their elements, wide scattered o'er the globe,
> To happier shapes were moulded, and became
> Ministrant to all blissful impulses:
> Thus human things were perfected, and earth,
135 Even as a child beneath its mother's love,
> Was strengthened in all excellence, and grew
> Fairer and nobler with each passing year.

> Now Time his dusky pennons o'er the scene
> Closes in steadfast darkness, and the past
140 Fades from our charmèd sight. My task is done:
> Thy lore is learned. Earth's wonders are thine own,
> With all the fear and all the hope they bring.
> My spells are past: the present now recurs.
> Ah me! a pathless wilderness remains
145 Yet unsubdued by man's reclaiming hand.

> Yet, human Spirit, bravely hold thy course,
> Let virtue teach thee firmly to pursue
> The gradual paths of an aspiring change:
> For birth and life and death, and that strange state
150 Before the naked soul has found its home,
> All tend to perfect happiness, and urge

ix *128. ivy-fingered*] First recorded in S. *Concordance* 363 explains as 'gently rustling through ivy', but the meaning is more likely to be 'winds fingered by ivy', i.e. winds played on as if they were instruments by the ivy-leaves (an ivy-leaf has five angles or 'fingers').

ix *130*. An echo of *The Tempest* IV i 152–6: '. . . the gorgeous palaces, / The solemn temples . . . / . . . shall dissolve, / And . . . / Leave not a rack behind'.

ix *138. pennons*] wings.

ix *139. the past*] the future *Rossetti 1870 emend*. But the whole vision has now become the past for Ianthe and Henry (line 143).

ix *148*. By repeating ix 19, S. stresses that the change will be slow and will result from human purpose.

ix *149. that strange state*] i.e. after conception and before birth. Harriet S. was about five months pregnant with her first child, later named after *Q Mab*'s heroine, at the time this Canto was written.

The restless wheels of being on their way,
Whose flashing spokes, instinct with infinite life,
Bicker and burn to gain their destined goal:
155 For birth but wakes the spirit to the sense
Of outward shows, whose unexperienced shape
New modes of passion to its frame may lend;
Life is its state of action, and the store
Of all events is aggregated there
160 That variegate the eternal universe;
Death is a gate of dreariness and gloom,
That leads to azure isles and beaming skies
And happy regions of eternal hope.
Therefore, O Spirit! fearlessly bear on:
165 Though storms may break the primrose on its stalk,
Though frosts may blight the freshness of its bloom,

ix *152–4*. Cp. the description of the Spirit of the Earth in *PU* IV 270–6: 'And from a star upon its forehead, shoot . . . / Vast beams like spokes of some invisible wheel / Which whirl as the orb whirls, swifter than thought, / Filling the abyss with sun-like lightenings'.

ix *155–7*. Notopoulos (*Notopoulos* 185) considers lines 146–63 'the most important Platonic passage in *Q Mab*', and refers 155–6 to the *Phaedo*, but the lines are Pythagorean rather than Platonic, concerned with the transience of forms and the adjustment of the newly-born soul to an unfamiliar world. Ovid has Pythagoras say: 'nascique vocatur / incipere esse aliud, quam quod fuit ante, morique / desinere illud idem'–'What we call birth is but a beginning to be other than what one was before; and death is but cessation of a former state' (*Met.* xv 255–7). S. is indebted also to the 'obstinate questionings / Of sense and outward things' of the new-born child in Wordsworth's 'Immortality Ode' 144–8. S.'s own earlier speculations were Pythagorean: 'as I conceive . . . that nothing can be annihilated, but that everything appertaining to nature . . . is in a continual change, then do I suppose . . . that neither will soul perish; that in a future existence it will lose all consciousness of having formerly lived elsewhere, – will begin life anew, possibly under a shape of which we have now no idea. But we have no right to make hypotheses–this is not one . . .' (letter to Elizabeth Hitchener, 20 June 1811, *L* i 110).

ix *161–3*. Notopoulos refers to Plato's *Phaedo*; but S.'s immediate source is Blair's *Grave* 689–96: 'Death only lies between, a gloomy path! / . . . why, like ill-condition'd children, / Start we at transient hardships in the way / That leads to purer air and softer skies, / And a ne'er-setting sun?'

ix *165–70*. Perhaps recalling 'The Brahmin' in James Montgomery's *Prison Amusements* (1797), e.g. 23–6: 'In every animal inspired with breath, / The flowers of life produce the seeds of death;– / The seeds of death, though scattered in the tomb, / Spring with new vigour, vegetate and bloom' etc. S. referred to the religion of Brahma in the letter quoted in the note to ix 155–7 above.

Yet spring's awakening breath will woo the earth,
To feed with kindliest dews its favourite flower,
That blooms in mossy banks and darksome glens,
170 Lighting the green wood with its sunny smile.

Fear not then, Spirit, death's disrobing hand,
So welcome when the tyrant is awake,
So welcome when the bigot's hell-torch burns;
'Tis but the voyage of a darksome hour,
175 The transient gulf-dream of a startling sleep.
Death is no foe to virtue: earth has seen
Love's brightest roses on the scaffold bloom,
Mingling with freedom's fadeless laurels there,
And presaging the truth of visioned bliss.
180 Are there not hopes within thee, which this scene
Of linked and gradual being has confirmed?
Whose stingings bade thy heart look further still,
When to the moonlight walk by Henry led,
Sweetly and sadly thou didst talk of death?
185 And wilt thou rudely tear them from thy breast,
Listening supinely to a bigot's creed,
Or tamely crouching to the tyrant's rod,
Whose iron thongs are red with human gore?
Never: but bravely bearing on, thy will
190 Is destined an eternal war to wage
With tyranny and falsehood, and uproot
The germs of misery from the human heart.
Thine is the hand whose piety would soothe
The thorny pillow of unhappy crime,

ix 170. *green wood*] greenwood *1839, 1840, eds.*

ix 175. *gulf-dream*] 'Sensation of drowning or falling' (*Concordance* 306).

ix 184. Harriet S. often spoke of ending her own life, including during the period of her pregnancy with Ianthe (*Hogg* ii 7–8, 283–4).

ix 193–5. According to the doctrine of Necessity, crime resulted from a chain of inevitable causes and could be corrected only by the proposal of an apter motivation (see Holbach, *Système de la Nature* i 245–50; Godwin, *Political Justice* Bk IV ch. viii, i 392–5; Bk VII chs. i–vi, ii 321–93). Godwin wrote: 'I view the assassin with more disapprobation than the dagger, because he is more to be feared, and it is more difficult to change his vicious structure . . . Except in the articles here specified, the two causes are exactly parallel. The assassin cannot help the murder he commits, any more than the dagger' (*Political Justice* Bk VII ch. i, ii 324). Holbach conceded that punishment could be of utility, but argued that the law was unjust to punish 'ceux à qui elle n'a point présenté les motifs nécessaires pour influer sur leurs volontés' (*Système de la Nature* i 248). The further inference that the criminal is *ipso facto* unhappy is in Plato: '. . . wrong-doing is the worst harm that can befall a wrong-doer' (*Gorgias* sect. 508–9). S. held these beliefs all his life (see *PU* I 405 and note).

195 Whose impotence an easy pardon gains,
Watching its wanderings as a friend's disease:
Thine is the brow whose mildness would defy
Its fiercest rage, and brave its sternest will,
When fenced by power and master of the world.
200 Thou art sincere and good; of resolute mind,
Free from heart-withering custom's cold control,
Of passion lofty, pure and unsubdued.
Earth's pride and meanness could not vanquish thee,
And therefore art thou worthy of the boon
205 Which thou hast now received: virtue shall keep
Thy footsteps in the path that thou hast trod,
And many days of beaming hope shall bless
Thy spotless life of sweet and sacred love.
Go, happy one, and give that bosom joy
210 Whose sleepless spirit waits to catch
Light, life and rapture from thy smile.

The Fairy waves her wand of charm.
Speechless with bliss the Spirit mounts the car,
That rolled beside the battlement,
215 Bending her beamy eyes in thankfulness.
Again the enchanted steeds were yoked,
Again the burning wheels inflame
The steep descent of heaven's untrodden way.
Fast and far the chariot flew:
220 The vast and fiery globes that rolled
Around the Fairy's palace-gate
Lessened by slow degrees, and soon appeared
Such tiny twinklers as the planet orbs
That there attendant on the solar power
225 With borrowed light pursued their narrower way.

Earth floated then below:
The chariot paused a moment there;
The Spirit then descended:
The restless coursers pawed the ungenial soil,
230 Snuffed the gross air, and then, their errand done,
Unfurled their pinions to the winds of heaven.

The Body and the Soul united then,
A gentle start convulsed Ianthe's frame:
Her veiny eyelids quietly unclosed;
235 Moveless awhile the dark blue orbs remained:

ix 196. *as a friend's disease*] '. . . our disapprobation of vice, will be of the same
nature, as our disapprobation of an infectious distemper' (*Political Justice* Bk IV
ch. viii, i 392).

> She looked around in wonder and beheld
> Henry, who kneeled in silence by her couch,
> Watching her sleep with looks of speechless love,
> And the bright beaming stars
> 240   That through the casement shone.

NOTES

i. *242–3*

> The sun's unclouded orb
> Rolled through the black concave.

1   Beyond our atmosphere the sun would appear a rayless orb of
fire in the midst of a black concave. The equal diffusion of its
light on earth is owing to the refraction of the rays by the
atmosphere, and their reflection from other bodies. Light consists
5   either of vibrations propagated through a subtle medium, or of
numerous minute particles repelled in all directions from the
luminous body. Its velocity greatly exceeds that of any substance
with which we are acquainted: observations on the eclipses of
Jupiter's satellites have demonstrated that light takes up no more
10   than 8′ 7″ in passing from the sun to the earth, a distance of
95,000,000 miles. – Some idea may be gained of the immense
distance of the fixed stars, when it is computed that many years
would elapse before light could reach this earth from the nearest
of them; yet in one year light travels 5,422,400,000,000 miles,
which is a distance 5,707,600 times greater than that of the sun
15   from the earth.

i. *252–3*

> Whilst round the chariot's way
> Innumerable systems rolled.

1   The plurality of worlds, – the indefinite immensity of the
universe is a most awful subject of contemplation. He who
rightly feels its mystery and grandeur, is in no danger of
seduction from the falsehoods of religious systems, or of deifying
5   the principle of the universe. It is impossible to believe that the

i 242–3. Line 11] The sun is about 93,000,000 miles from the earth. S.'s
astronomical facts are 'without serious error, apart from two arithmetical
lapses', noted below (King-Hele, *Shelley: His Thought & Work* 39).

Spirit that pervades this infinite machine, begat a son upon the
body of a Jewish woman; or is angered at the consequences of
that necessity, which is a synonym of itself. All that miserable tale
of the Devil, and Eve, and an Intercessor, with the childish
10   mummeries of the God of the Jews, is irreconcileable with the
knowledge of the stars. The works of his fingers have borne
witness against him.

The nearest of the fixed stars is inconceivably distant from the
earth, and they are probably proportionably distant from each
15   other. By a calculation of the velocity of light, Sirius is supposed
to be at least 54,224,000,000,000 miles from the earth.[1] That
which appears only like a thin and silvery cloud streaking the
heaven, is in effect composed of innumerable clusters of suns,
each shining with its own light, and illuminating numbers of
20   planets that revolve around them. Millions and millions of suns
are ranged around us, all attended by innumerable worlds, yet
calm, regular, and harmonious, all keeping the paths of
immutable necessity.

[1] See Nicholson's Encyclopedia, art. Light.

iv. *178–9*

            These are the hired bravos who defend
            The tyrant's throne.

1   To employ murder as a means of justice, is an idea which a man
of an enlightened mind will not dwell upon with pleasure. To
march forth in rank and file, and all the pomp of streamers and

i *252–3*. Line 11] An ironical echo of *Psalms* viii 3–9: 'When I consider thy
heavens, the work of thy fingers,' etc.
Line 16] S.'s figure for the distance of Sirius is 'quite near the correct value of
about 51 billion miles'–but only by a lucky mistake (*Shelley: His Thought &
Work* 39).
Footnote] S. ordered William Nicholson's *The British Encyclopedia* (6 vols,
1807–9) *c.* 17 December 1812 (*L* i 343).
iv *178–9*.] The whole of this note is quoted (with one page omitted) from
Enquirer Pt II Essay v, 234–6. S. had recommended *The Enquirer* to Elizabeth
Hitchener on 26 November 1811 as 'very good' (*L* i 195). The verbal variants
are as follows:
as a means] as the means *Enquirer* (hereafter cited as *E*)   *of enlightened*] of an
enlightened *E*   *and all*] with all *E*   *as a mark*] as at a mark *E*   *wound*]
wounds *E*   *we suppose*] we will suppose *E*. [One *Enquirer* page omitted
between S.'s para. 1 and para. 2, in which Godwin argues that a soldier 'has no
duty but that of murder' and consequently 'must learn ferocity'.]   *that the
soldier*] that a soldier *E*   *by his exhibitor*] by the exhibitor *E*.

trumpets, for the purpose of shooting at our fellow-men as a
5 mark; to inflict upon them all the variety of wound and anguish;
to leave them weltering in their blood; to wander over the field of
desolation, and count the number of the dying and the dead, – are
employments which in thesis we may maintain to be necessary,
but which no good man will contemplate with gratulation and
10 delight. A battle we suppose is won: – thus truth is established,
thus the cause of justice is confirmed! It surely requires no
common sagacity to discern the connection between this
immense heap of calamities and the assertion of truth or the
maintenance of justice.

15   Kings, and ministers of state, the real authors of the calamity,
sit unmolested in their cabinet, while those against whom the
fury of the storm is directed are, for the most part, persons who
have been trepanned into the service, or who are dragged
unwillingly from their peaceful homes into the field of battle. A
20 soldier is a man whose business it is to kill those who never
offended him, and who are the innocent martyrs of other men's
iniquities. Whatever may become of the abstract question of the
justifiableness of war, it seems impossible that the soldier should
not be a depraved and unnatural being.

25   To these more serious and momentous considerations it may
be proper to add a recollection of the ridiculousness of the
military character. Its first constituent is obedience: a soldier is, of
all descriptions of men, the most completely a machine; yet his
profession inevitably teaches him something of dogmatism,
30 swaggering, and self-consequence: he is like the puppet of a
showman, who, at the very time he is made to strut and swell and
display the most farcical airs, we perfectly know cannot assume
the most insignificant gesture, advance either to the right or the
left, but as he is moved by his exhibitor. – *Godwin's Enquirer,
Essay*
35 v.
      I will here subjoin a little poem, so strongly expressive of my
abhorrence of despotism and falsehood, that I fear lest it never
again may be depictured so vividly. This opportunity is perhaps
the only one that ever will occur of rescuing it from oblivion.
40   [A version follows of 'Falsehood and Vice: a Dialogue' revised
from *Esd*. For both texts see No. 76]

v. *1–2*

                Thus do the generations of the earth
                Go to the grave and issue from the womb.

Line 37. *This opportunity . . . from oblivion*] Evidently S. had now abandoned the
idea of publishing *Esd* (*c*. March/April 1813).
v *1–2*] Quoted accurately from *Ecclesiastes* i 4–7 except that the A.V. reads:
'unto the place from whence the rivers come, thither they return again'.

1 One generation passeth away and another generation cometh,
   but the earth abideth for ever. The sun also ariseth and the sun
   goeth down, and hasteth to his place where he arose. The wind
   goeth toward the south and turneth about unto the north, it
5 whirleth about continually, and the wind returneth again
   according to his circuits. All the rivers run into the sea, yet the sea
   is not full; unto the place whence the rivers come, thither shall
   they return again.

                                              Ecclesiastes, chap. i

v. *4–6*

                        Even as the leaves
            Which the keen frost-wind of the waning year
            Has scattered on the forest soil.

   Οἴη περ φύλλων γενεὴ, τοιήδε καὶ αυδρῶν.
   Φύλλα τὰ μέυ τ' ἄυεμος καμάδις κέει, ἄλλα δέ θ'ὕλη
   Τηλεθόωσα φύει, ἔαρος δ'ἐπιγίγνεται ὥρη
   ῀Ως ἀυδρῶν γενεὴ, ἡ μὲν φύει, ἡδ' ἀπολήγει.

                                         ΙΛΙΑΔ. Z'. l. 146.

v. *58*

            The mob of peasants, nobles, priests, and kings.

1 Suave mari magno turbantibus æquora ventis
   E terrâ magnum alterius spectare laborem;
   Non quia vexari quemquam 'st jucunda voluptas,
   Sed quibus ipse malis careas quia cernere suave'st.
5 Suave etiam belli certamina magna tueri,
   Per campos instructa, tua sine parte pericli;

v *4–6*] Quoted accurately from the *Iliad* vi 146–9: 'As with the generations of
leaves, so with those of men. The wind showers the leaves on the ground, yet
the flourishing wood puts out buds, the season of spring follows. So with the
generations of men, one brings forth, and one ceases'.
v *58*] Quoted accurately from Lucretius. *De Rerum Natura* ii 1–14: 'It is
pleasant, when winds are raging over a great sea, to watch from shore the
strenuous efforts of another; not because anyone's distress is an enjoyable
entertainment, but because it is pleasant to see what misfortunes you yourself
are free from. It is pleasant, too, to witness great contests of war drawn up on
the plains, without having any part in the danger: but nothing is sweeter than
to occupy high, calm sanctuaries well fortified by the teachings of wise men;
from which you can look down on others and see them everywhere astray,
trying to find the path of life; clashing wits; struggling for precedence; striving
night and day with egregious effort to get to the top in wealth and power. O
unhappy minds of men, o blind understandings!'

Sed nil dulcius est bene quam munita tenere
Edita doctrina sapientum templa serena;
Despicere unde queas alios, passim que videre
10   Errare atque viam palanteis quærere vitæ;
Certare ingenio; contendere nobilitate;
Nocteis atque dies niti præstante labore
Ad summas emergere opes, rerum que potiri.
O miseras hominum menteis! O pectora cæca!

                                                 Luc. lib. ii.

v. *93–4*

                    And statesmen boast
             Of wealth!

1   There is no real wealth but the labour of man. Were the
        mountains of gold and the valleys of silver, the world would not
        be one grain of corn the richer; no one comfort would be added to
        the human race. In consequence of our consideration for the
5   precious metals, one man is enabled to heap to himself luxuries at
        the expense of the necessaries of his neighbour; a system
        admirably fitted to produce all the varieties of disease and crime,
        which never fail to characterize the two extremes of opulence and
        penury. A speculator takes pride to himself as the promoter of his
10   country's prosperity, who employs a number of hands in the
        manufacture of articles avowedly destitute of use, or subservient
        only to the unhallowed cravings of luxury and ostentation. The
        nobleman, who employs the peasants of his neighbourhood in
        building his palaces, until *'jam pauca aratro jugera, regiæ moles*
15   *relinquunt,'* flatters himself that he has gained the title of a patriot
        by yielding to the impulses of vanity. The show and pomp of
        courts adduces the same apology for its continuance; and many a
        fête has been given, many a woman has eclipsed her beauty by
        her dress, to benefit the labouring poor and to encourage trade.
20   Who does not see that this is a remedy which aggravates, whilst it

v *93–4.* Line 1] Modified from *Enquirer* 177: 'There is no wealth in the world
except this, the labour of man'. Godwin himself had made a more cautious
claim in the chapter added to the second edition of *Political Justice* (1796): 'There
is scarcely any species of wealth . . . that is not, in some way, produced, by the
express manual labour . . . of the inhabitants . . . (Bk VIII ch. ii, ii 435).
Line 14] By changing the tense from future to present, S. adapts Horace, *Odes*
II xv 1–2: 'Now splendid mansions leave few acres for the plough'.
Line 17. *its continuance*] i.e. that of the 'show and pomp'. The two nouns
collectively govern a singular verb, which cannot be 'corrected' without
obscuring the sense.
Lines 20–21. *Who does not see . . . society?*] 'The country-gentleman who, by

palliates the countless diseases of society? The poor are set to
labour, – for what? Not the food for which they famish: not the
blankets for want of which their babes are frozen by the cold of
their miserable hovels: not those comforts of civilization without
25   which civilized man is far more miserable than the meanest
savage; oppressed as he is by all its insidious evils, within the
daily and taunting prospect of its innumerable benefits
assiduously exhibited before him:–no; for the pride of power, for
the miserable isolation of pride, for the false pleasures of the
30   hundredth part of society. No greater evidence is afforded of the
wide extended and radical mistake of civilized man than this fact:
those arts which are essential to his very being are held in the
greatest contempt; employments are lucrative in an inverse ratio
to their usefulness[1]: the jeweller, the toyman, the actor gains fame
35   and wealth by the exercise of his useless and ridiculous art; whilst
the cultivator of the earth, he without whom society must cease
to subsist, struggles through contempt and penury, and perishes
by that famine which, but for his unceasing exertions, would
40   annihilate the rest of mankind.
    I will not insult common sense by insisting on the doctrine of
the natural equality of man. The question is not concerning its
desirableness, but its practicability: so far as it is practicable, it is
desirable. That state of human society which approaches nearer to
45   an equal partition of its benefits and evils should, *cæteris paribus*,
be preferred: but so long as we conceive that a wanton
expenditure of human labour, not for the necessities, not even for
the luxuries of the mass of society, but for the egotism and
ostentation of a few of its members, is defensible on the ground

[1] See Rousseau, 'De l'Inegalité parmi les Hommes,' note 7.

---

levelling an eminence, or introducing a sheet of water into his park, finds work
for hundreds of industrious poor, is the enemy, and not, as has commonly
been imagined, the friend, of his species . . . All that is luxury and superfluity,
would increase the accommodations of the rich . . . But it would afford no
alleviation to the great mass of the community' (*Political Justice* Bk VIII ch. ii, ii
436–7).
Footnote.] S.'s footnote cites Rousseau's *Discours sur l'Origine et les Fondements
de l'Inégalité parmi les Hommes* (1755; Cambridge 1941) 121 *n*.7: '. . . l'agricul-
ture doit être le moins lucratif de tous les arts, parce que, son produit étant de
l'usage le plus indispensable pour tous les hommes, le prix en doit être
proportionné aux facultés des plus pauvres. Du même principe on peut tirer
cette règle qu'en général les arts sont lucratifs en raison inverse de leur utilité, et
que les plus nécessaires doivent enfin devenir les plus négligés. (Cameron
(*Cameron (1951)* 403) and Rogers (*1972* i 392) are mistaken in saying that S.'s
reference is wrong.)

50   of public justice, so long we neglect to approximate to the
     redemption of the human race.
         Labour is required for physical, and leisure for moral
     improvement: from the former of these advantages the rich, and
     from the latter the poor, by the inevitable conditions of their
55   respective situations, are precluded. A state which should
     combine the advantages of both, would be subjected to the evils
     of neither. He that is deficient in firm health, or vigorous
     intellect, is but half a man: hence it follows, that, to subject the
     labouring classes to unnecessary labour, is wantonly depriving
60   them of any opportunities of intellectual improvement; and that
     the rich are heaping up for their own mischief the disease,
     lassitude and ennui by which their existence is rendered an
     intolerable burthen.
         English reformers exclaim against sinecures, – but the true
65   pension list is the rent-roll of the landed proprietors: wealth is a
     power usurped by the few, to compel the many to labour for
     their benefit. The laws which support this system derive their
     force from the ignorance and credulity of its victims: they are the
     result of a conspiracy of the few against the many, who are
70   themselves obliged to purchase this pre-eminence by the loss of
     all real comfort.
         The commodities that substantially contribute to the
     subsistence of the human species form a very short catalogue:
     they demand from us but a slender portion of industry. If these
75   only were produced, and sufficiently produced, the species of
     man would be continued. If the labour necessarily required to
     produce them were equitably divided among the poor, and, still
     more, if it were equitably divided among all, each man's share of
     labour would be light, and his portion of leisure would be ample.
80   There was a time when this leisure would have been of small
     comparative value: it is to be hoped that the time will come,

Lines 52–63. *Labour is required . . . intolerable burthen*] 'Accumulated property
treads the powers of thought in the dust, extinguishes the sparks of genius, and
reduces the great mass of mankind to be immersed in sordid cares, besides
depriving the rich . . . of the most salubrious and effectual motives to activity'
(*Political Justice* Bk VIII ch. iii, ii 460).
Lines 64–7. *English reformers . . . their benefit*] 'But the rent-roll of the lands of
England is a much more formidable pension-list . . . All riches, and especially
hereditary riches, are to be considered as the salary of a sinecure office, where
the labourer and the manufacturer [i.e. factory-hand] perform the duties, and
the principal spends the income in luxury and idleness' (*Political Justice* Bk VIII
ch. iii, ii 458–9).
Lines 72–86. *The commodities . . . enjoyment*] This paragraph is quoted accurately from *Enquirer* Pt II Essay ii, 174–5.

when it will be applied to the most important purposes. Those
hours which are not required for the production of the necessaries
of life, may be devoted to the cultivation of the understanding,
85   the enlarging our stock of knowledge, the refining our taste, and
thus opening to us new and more exquisite sources of enjoyment.

*   *   *   *   *

It was perhaps necessary that a period of monopoly and
oppression should subsist, before a period of cultivated equality
90   could subsist. Savages perhaps would never have been excited to
the discovery of truth and the invention of art, but by the narrow
motives which such a period affords. But surely, after the savage
state has ceased, and men have set out in the glorious career of
discovery and invention, monopoly and oppression cannot be
95   necessary to prevent them from returning to a state of
barbarism. – *Godwin's Enquirer, Essay II. See also Pol. Jus., book
VIII. chap. II.*
    It is a calculation of this admirable author, that all the
conveniences of civilized life might be produced, if society would
100   divide the labour equally among its members, by each individual
being employed in labour two hours during the day.

v. *112–13*

or religion
Drives his wife raving mad.

1   I am acquainted with a lady of considerable accomplishments,
and the mother of a numerous family, whom the Christian
religion has goaded to incurable insanity. A parallel case is, I
believe, within the experience of every physician.

5   Nam jam sæpe homines patriam, carosque parentes
    Prodiderunt, vitare Acherusia templa petentes.

Lucretius.

Lines 87–96. *It was perhaps . . . barbarism*] This paragraph is quoted accurately
from *Enquirer* Pt II Essay ii, 175–6.
Lines 98–101. *It is a calculation . . . during the day*] In *Political Justice* Bk VIII ch.
vi, ii 484 Godwin had in fact concluded 'that half an hour a day, employed in
manual labour by every member of the community, would sufficiently supply
the whole with necessaries' (see also ii 493).
v *112–13*] The identity of this lady is unknown. King-Hele (*Erasmus Darwin*
55–6) cites cases of religious mania reported in *Zoonomia, or the Laws of Organic
Life* (1794–6) ii 379. The quotation is from Lucretius, *De Rerum Natura* ii 85–6:
'For often before now men have betrayed their country and their beloved
parents, in seeking to avoid the domains of hell'.

v. *189*

Even love is sold.

1   Not even the intercourse of the sexes is exempt from the
despotism of positive institution. Law pretends even to govern
the indisciplinable wanderings of passion, to put fetters on the
clearest deductions of reason, and, by appeals to the will, to
5   subdue the involuntary affections of our nature. Love is
inevitably consequent upon the perception of loveliness. Love
withers under constraint: its very essence is liberty: it is
compatible neither with obedience, jealousy, nor fear: it is there
most pure, perfect, and unlimited, where its votaries live in
10   confidence, equality, and unreserve.
How long then ought the sexual connection to last? what law
ought to specify the extent of the grievances which should limit
its duration? A husband and wife ought to continue so long
united as they love each other: any law which should bind them
15   to cohabitation for one moment after the decay of their affection,
would be a most intolerable tyranny, and the most unworthy of
toleration. How odious an usurpation of the right of private
judgment should that law be considered, which should make the
ties of friendship indissoluble, in spite of the caprices, the
20   inconstancy, the fallibility, and capacity for improvement of the
human mind. And by so much would the fetters of love be
heavier and more unendurable than those of friendship, as love is
more vehement and capricious, more dependent on those delicate
peculiarities of imagination, and less capable of reduction to the
25   ostensible merits of the object.

v *189*] Cameron *(Cameron (1951)* 266–70) illustrates three principal influences
on S.'s note: *Political Justice* Bk VIII ch. viii, ii 506–13; James Lawrence's *Love:
an Allegory* (1802), and *The Empire of the Nairs; or, the Rights of Women: An
Utopian Romance* (1811); and Mary Wollstonecraft's *A Vindication of the Rights
of Woman* (1792). To these should be added the latter's *The Wrongs of Woman:
or, Maria (Posthumous Works* (1798) i–iii). Godwin argued against cohabitation
(as prejudicing independence) as well as against formal marriage (as an unreasonable contract, and a pernicious monopoly), while adding, in the 2nd
edn, his rejection of promiscuity. Lawrence's romance of the Malabar coast
sought to show 'the possibility of a nation's reaching the highest civilization
without marriage' *(Empire of the Nairs* 2), commended the social and sexual
emancipation of women, and argued a close relationship between the cult of
chastity in Britain and the prevalence of prostitution (see Walter Graham, 'S.
and *The Empire of the Nairs*', *PMLA* xl (1925) 881–91). S. shared all these views
except Godwin's on cohabitation, and for the most part re-states them more
trenchantly. The basis of his attitude was his equalitarianism: 'I could not
endure the bare idea of marriage even if I had no arguments in favor of my

The state of society in which we exist is a mixture of feudal
savageness and imperfect civilization. The narrow and
unenlightened morality of the Christian religion is an aggravation
of these evils. It is not even until lately that mankind have
30   admitted that happiness is the sole end of the science of ethics, as
of all other sciences; and that the fanatical idea of mortifying the
flesh for the love of God has been discarded. I have heard, indeed,
an ignorant collegian adduce, in favour of Christianity, its
35   hostility to every worldly feeling![1]

> [1] The first Christian emperor made a law by which seduction was punished
> with death: if the female pleaded her own consent, she also was punished with
> death; if the parents endeavoured to screen the criminals, they were banished and
> their estates were confiscated; the slaves who might be accessary were burned
> alive, or forced to swallow melted lead. The very offspring of an illegal love were
> involved in the consequences of the sentence. – *Gibbon's Decline and Fall, &c.* vol.
> ii, page 210. See also, for the hatred of the primitive Christians to love and even
> marriage, page 269.

dislike . . . For God's sake if you want more argument read the marriage service
before you *think* of allowing an amiable beloved female to submit to such
degradation' (letter to Hogg, 9 May 1811, *L* i 80–1). Cp. also S.'s review of
Hogg's novel *Memoirs of Prince Alexy Haimatoff* (1814): 'No man can rise pure
from the poisonous embraces of a prostitute, or sinless from the desolated
hopes of a confiding heart. Whatever may be the claims of chastity, whatever
the advantages of simple and pure affection, these ties, these benefits are of
equal obligation to either sex. Domestic relations depend for their integrity
upon a complete reciprocity of duties' (*Prose* 304). S. was strongly influenced
by Mary Wollstonecraft, and the assumption of a male viewpoint in his note is
merely a grammatical convenience.
Lines 13–17. *A husband and wife . . . unworthy of toleration*] 'I will do you justice,
sir', Southey wrote to S. in 1820, 'While you were at Keswick you told your
bride that you regarded marriage as a mere ceremony, and would live with her
no longer than you liked her' (*L* ii 232). In the 1st and 2nd edns of *Political Justice*
Godwin held that 'We ought to dismiss our mistake as soon as it is detected; but
we are taught to cherish it' (Bk VIII ch. vi), but he dropped this passage in 1798
(iii 219). See *Cameron (1951)* 266–70.
S.'s footnote] Constantine's edict is correctly summarized (*Decline and Fall of
the Roman Empire*, ed. J. B. Bury (1897) i 434). Gibbon went on to attribute to
the primitive Christians the opinion that 'if Adam had preserved his obedience
to the Creator, he would have lived for ever in a state of virgin purity, and that
some harmless mode of vegetation might have peopled paradise with a race of
innocent and immortal beings. The use of marriage was permitted only to his
fallen posterity, as a necessary expedient to continue the human species, and as
a restraint, however imperfect, on the natural licentiousness of desire' (ibid. ii
36). The edition of Gibbon used by S. was Cadell & Davies's 12-vol. edn of
1807 (*L* i 342, 433).

But if happiness be the object of morality, of all human unions
and disunions; if the worthiness of every action is to be estimated
by the quantity of pleasurable sensation it is calculated to
produce, then the connection of the sexes is so long sacred as it
40   contributes to the comfort of the parties, and is naturally
dissolved when its evils are greater than its benefits. There is
nothing immoral in this separation. Constancy has nothing
virtuous in itself, independently of the pleasure it confers, and
partakes of the temporizing spirit of vice in proportion as it
45   endures tamely moral defects of magnitude in the object of its
indiscreet choice. Love is free: to promise for ever to love the
same woman, is not less absurd than to promise to believe the
same creed: such a vow, in both cases, excludes us from all
enquiry. The language of the votarist is this: The woman I now
50   love may be infinitely inferior to many others; the creed I now
profess may be a mass of errors and absurdities; but I exclude
myself from all future information as to the amiability of the one
and the truth of the other, resolving blindly, and in spite of
conviction, to adhere to them. Is this the language of delicacy and
55   reason? Is the love of such a frigid heart of more worth than its
belief?
       The present system of constraint does no more, in the majority
of instances, than make hypocrites or open enemies. Persons of
delicacy and virtue, unhappily united to one whom they find it
60   impossible to love, spend the loveliest season of their life in
unproductive efforts to appear otherwise than they are, for the
sake of the feelings of their partner or the welfare of their mutual
offspring: those of less generosity and refinement openly avow
their disappointment, and linger out the remnant of that union,
65   which only death can dissolve, in a state of incurable bickering
and hostility. The early education of their children takes its colour

Lines 36–41. *But if happiness . . . greater than its benefits*] 'Pleasure or happiness is
the sole end of morality': 'Morality is nothing more than a calculation of
pleasures: nothing therefore which is connected with pleasurable sensation,
can be foreign to, or ought to be despised in, a question of morality' (Godwin,
Enquirer Part II 243; Part I 104). The principle derives from the French materialists, especially Helvétius.
Lines 57–8. *The present system of constraint . . . open enemies*] This paragraph
draws on the argument of Mary Wollstonecraft's *Wrongs of Woman*, summarized in Maria Venables's plea at her trial (ch. xvii, *Posth. Works* ii 145–55): '. . .
because I had, before arriving at what is termed years of discretion, pledged my
faith, I was treated by the world, as bound for ever to a man whose vices were
notorious . . . A false morality is even established, which makes all the virtue of
women consist in chastity, submission, and the forgiveness of injuries'.
Lines 66–8. *The early education . . . falsehood*] The effect on the children of
parental incompatibility is stressed throughout *Wrongs of Woman*.

from the squabbles of the parents; they are nursed in a systematic
school of ill humour, violence, and falsehood. Had they been
suffered to part at the moment when indifference rendered their
70   union irksome, they would have been spared many years of
misery: they would have connected themselves more suitably,
and would have found that happiness in the society of more
congenial partners which is for ever denied them by the
despotism of marriage. They would have been separately useful
75   and happy members of society, who, whilst united, were
miserable, and rendered misanthropical by misery. The
conviction that wedlock is indissoluble holds out the strongest of
all temptations to the perverse: they indulge without restraint in
acrimony, and all the little tyrannies of domestic life, when they
80   know that their victim is without appeal. If this connection were
put on a rational basis, each would be assured that habitual ill
temper would terminate in separation, and would check this
vicious and dangerous propensity.
85   Prostitution is the legitimate offspring of marriage and its
accompanying errors. Women, for no other crime than having
followed the dictates of a natural appetite, are driven with fury
from the comforts and sympathies of society. It is less venial than
murder; and the punishment which is inflicted on her who
90   destroys her child to escape reproach, is lighter than the life of
agony and disease to which the prostitute is irrecoverably

Line 85. *Prostitution is the legitimate offspring of marriage*] 'Where marriage is a
profession love will be a trade' (*Empire of the Nairs* ii 4). Mary Wollstonecraft
had castigated hypocritical attitudes to 'fallen' women in *A Vindication of the
Rights of Woman* chs iv, vii–ix and in *Wrongs of Woman*, exposing the salacity
underlying contemporary emphasis on 'chastity', but it was Lawrence who
explicitly blamed prostitution on the conventions of marriage: 'In Britain,
female chastity is more general than in any other European country, but what
are the consequences of the preposterous estimation in which it is held? To this
may be ascribed the number of involuntary courtesans who infest the metropolis; some of whom, women of family and education, and free from every
crime, though unable to resist the dictates of nature, have been banished from
the protection and endearments of their home, and obliged to seek a precarious
livelihood by a loathsome profession' (ibid. i xxv), while the obligatory
chastity of 'every creditable female' drives young men to seek less creditable
ones. 'The number of virgins in Europe enable the courtesans to be polyan-
drists' (ibid. i xxxi). S. told Lawrence (17 August 1812): 'Your 'Empire of the
Nairs', which I read this spring, succeeded in making me a perfect convert to
its doctrines. I then retained no doubts of the evils of marriage,–Mrs Wollstonecraft reasons too well for that; but I had been dull enough not to perceive
the greatest argument against it, until developed in the 'Nairs', viz., prostitution both *legal* and *illegal*' (*L* i 323). About May 1813 Lawrence called on S. in
London (*Hogg* ii 314).

doomed. Has a woman obeyed the impulse of unerring nature;–
society declares war against her, pitiless and eternal war: she must
be the tame slave, she must make no reprisals; theirs is the right of
95   persecution, hers the duty of endurance. She lives a life of infamy:
the loud and bitter laugh of scorn scares her from all return. She
dies of long and lingering disease: yet *she* is in fault, *she* is the
criminal, *she* the froward and untameable child,–and society,
forsooth, the pure and virtuous matron, who casts her as an
100   abortion from her undefiled bosom! Society avenges herself on
the criminals of her own creation; she is employed in
anathematizing the vice to-day, which yesterday she was the
most zealous to teach. Thus is formed one tenth of the population
of London: meanwhile the evil is twofold. Young men, excluded
105   by the fanatical idea of chastity from the society of modest and
accomplished women, associate with these vicious and miserable
beings, destroying thereby all those exquisite and delicate
sensibilities whose existence cold-hearted worldlings have
denied; annihilating all genuine passion, and debasing that to a
110   selfish feeling which is the excess of generosity and devotedness.
Their body and mind alike crumble into a hideous wreck of
humanity; idiotcy and disease become perpetuated in their
miserable offspring, and distant generations suffer for the bigoted
morality of their forefathers. Chastity is a monkish and
115   evangelical superstition, a greater foe to natural temperance even
than unintellectual sensuality; it strikes at the root of all domestic
happiness, and consigns more than half of the human race to
misery, that some few may monopolize according to law. A
system could not well have been devised more studiously hostile
120   to human happiness than marriage.
    I conceive that, from the abolition of marriage, the fit and

Lines 114–16. *Chastity is a monkish . . . unintellectual sensuality*] 'But though
neither sex should be condemned to a monastic chastity, both should observe a
natural chastity. The first may be compared to starvation, the second to
temperance' (*Empire of the Nairs* i xxxiii). The distinction made by both S. and
Lawrence between virginity-fetishism and 'natural chastity' stemmed from
Mary Wollstonecraft, with some difference of emphasis in all three.
Line 118. . . . *that some few may monopolise according to law*] During Hogg's
pursuit of Harriet S., S. assured him: 'I attach little value to the monopoly of
exclusive cohabitation' (c. 12 November 1812, *L* i 175). Godwin also held that
marriage was an undesirable form of property: '. . . marriage, as now understood, is a monopoly, and the worst of monopolies . . . so long as I seek, by
despotic and artificial means, to maintain my possession of a woman, I am
guilty of the most odious selfishness' (*Political Justice* Bk VIII ch. viii, ii 508.
The words *monopoly*, *monopolies*, were not used in the first edition).
Lines 121–9. *I conceive that . . . exempted from restraint*] Here S. diverges from
Lawrence to follow Godwin and Mary Wollstonecraft: 'The abolition of the

natural arrangement of sexual connection would result. I by no
means assert that the intercourse would be promiscuous: on the
contrary; it appears, from the relation of parent to child, that this
125   union is generally of long duration, and marked above all others
with generosity and self-devotion. But this is a subject which it is
perhaps premature to discuss. That which will result from the
abolition of marriage, will be natural and right, because choice
and change will be exempted from restraint.
130   In fact, religion and morality, as they now stand, compose a
practical code of misery and servitude: the genius of human
happiness must tear every leaf from the accursed book of God,
ere man can read the inscription on his heart. How would
morality, dressed up in stiff stays and finery, start from her own
135   disgusting image, should she look in the mirror of nature!

vi. *45–6*

To the red and baleful sun
That faintly twinkles there.

1   The north polar star, to which the axis of the earth, in its
present state of obliquity, points. It is exceedingly probable, from
many considerations, that this obliquity will gradually diminish,

---

present system of marriage, appears to involve no evils . . . It is a question of
some moment, whether the intercourse of the sexes, in a reasonable state of
society, would be promiscuous, or whether each man would select for himself
a partner, to whom he will adhere, as long as that adherence shall continue to
be the choice of both parties. Probability seems to be greatly in favour of the
latter' (*Political Justice* Bk VIII ch. viii, ii 508–9. The passage after *evils* was
added in the second edition).
vi 45–6] Paine's account of the precession of the equinox (*Age of Reason* Part I;
Paine Writings iv 69) added correctly: 'If the earth turned round itself in a
position perpendicular to the plane or level of the circle it moves in around the
sun . . . the days and nights would be always of the same length . . . and the
season would be uniformly the same throughout the year'. Cp. Milton, *PL* x
678–9: 'else had the Spring / Perpetual smil'd on Earth with vernant Flours'
etc. John Frank Newton (*The Return to Nature* (1811) 9–11) considered it
indisputable 'that the poles of the earth were at some distant period perpendicular to its orbit', identifying this period with the Golden Age, and speculated upon a time when 'a second change will be accomplished, which shall
bring back equal seasons and perpetual spring'. But Laplace knew (*Exposition
du Système du Monde* (1796) Bk IV ch. xiii) that the precession *is* an oscillation
only, with a period of about 26,000 years. S. did not read Laplace seriously
until November 1813 (*I.* i 380). S.'s footnote reference to Cabanis is wrong: his
last two references are both to J. S. Bailly, *Lettres sur l'Origine des Sciences*
(1777): (a) 'Leibnitz avait déjà reconnu quelque feuilles de plantes des Indes,
imprimées sur des pierres d'Allemagne' (315), while the discovery of elephant-

until the equator coincides with the ecliptic: the nights and days
5   will then become equal on the earth throughout the year, and
probably the seasons also. There is no great extravagance in
presuming that the progress of the perpendicularity of the poles
may be as rapid as the progress of intellect; or that there should be
a perfect identity between the moral and physical improvement of
10   the human species. It is certain that wisdom is not compatible
with disease, and that, in the present state of the climates of the
earth, health, in the true and comprehensive sense of the word, is
out of the reach of civilized man. Astronomy teaches us that the
earth is now in its progress, and that the poles are every year
15   becoming more and more perpendicular to the ecliptic. The
strong evidence afforded by the history of mythology, and
geological researches, that some event of this nature has taken
place already, affords a strong presumption that this progress is
not merely an oscillation, as has been surmised by some late
20   astronomers.[1] Bones of animals peculiar to the torrid zone have
been found in the north of Siberia, and on the banks of the river
Ohio. Plants have been found in the fossil state in the interior of
Germany, which demand the present climate of Hindostan for
their production.[2] The researches of M. Bailly[3] establish the
25   existence of a people who inhabited a tract in Tartary 49° north
latitude, of greater antiquity than either the Indians, the Chinese,
or the Chaldeans, from whom these nations derived their sciences
and theology. We find, from the testimony of ancient writers,
that Britain, Germany and France were much colder than at
30   present, and that their great rivers were annually frozen over.
Astronomy teaches us also, that since this period the obliquity of
the earth's position has been considerably diminished.

[1] Laplace, Système du Monde.
[2] Cabanis, Rapports du Physique et du Moral de l'Homme, vol. ii. page 406.
[3] Lettres sur les Sciences, à Voltaire. Bailly.

vi. *171–3*

No atom of this turbulence fulfils
A vague and unnecessitated task,
Or acts but as it must and ought to act.

---

bones in Siberia meant that 'Il est impossible de n'en pas conclure que le climat
de la Sibérie était alors moins froid qu'il n'est aujourd'hui' (320–3); (b) 'Cet
*ancien peuple paraît avoir habité dans l'Asie, vers le parallèle de 49°. Il semble que la
lumière des sciences & la population se soient étendues sur la terre du nord au midi*'
(Heading to Letter viii, 224).
vi *171–3*] Holbach, *Système de la Nature* (1774 edn) i 56, quoted accurately
except for agreements, accents, etc. Sir William Drummond virtually translated this passage (*Academical Questions* 263–5). *infalliblement*] infailliblement
Holbach.

1   Deux exemples serviront à nous rendre plus sensible le principe
      qui vient d'être posé; nous emprunterons l'une du physique et
      l'autre du moral. Dans un tourbillon de poussière qu'éleve un
      vent impetueux, quelque confus qu'il paroisse à nos yeux; dans la
5   plus affreuse tempête excité par des vents opposés qui soulèvent
      les flots, il n'y a pas une seule molécule de poussière ou d'eau qui
      soit placé au *hazard*, qui n'ait sa cause suffisante pour occuper le
      lieu où elle se trouve, et qui n'agisse rigoureusement de la
      manière dont elle doit agir. Une géomètre qui connoîtroit
10   exactement les différentes forces qui agissent dans ces deux cas, et
      les propriétés des molécules qui sont mues, demontreroit que
      d'après des causes donnés, chaque molécule agit précisément
      comme elle doit agir, et ne peut agir autrement qu'elle ne fait.
      Dans les convulsions terribles qui agitent quelquefois les
15   sociétés politiques, et qui produisent souvent le renversement
      d'un empire, il n'y a pas une seule action, une seule parole, une
      seule pensée, une seule volonté, une seule passion dans les agens
      qui concourent à la révolution comme destructeurs ou comme
      victimes, qui ne soit nécessaire, qui n'agisse comme elle doit agir,
20   qui n'opère infailliblement les effets qu'elle doit opérer, suivant la
      place qu'occupent ces agens dans ce tourbillon moral. Cela
      paroîtroit évident pour une intelligence qui sera en état de saisir et
      d'apprécier toutes les actions et reactions des esprits et des corps
25   de ceux qui contribuent à cette révolution.
                                   Système de la Nature, vol i. page 44.

vi. *198*

                  Necessity, thou mother of the world!

1   He who asserts the doctrine of Necessity, means that,
      contemplating the events which compose the moral and material
      universe, he beholds only an immense and uninterrupted chain of
      causes and effects, no one of which could occupy any other place
5   than it does occupy, or acts in any other place than it does act.
      The idea of necessity is obtained by our experience of the
      connection between objects, the uniformity of the operations of
      nature, the constant conjunction of similar events, and the
      consequent inference of one from the other. Mankind are
10   therefore agreed in the admission of necessity, if they admit that
      these two circumstances take place in voluntary action. Motive is,
      to voluntary action in the human mind, what cause is to effect in

vi *198*] Cameron (*Cameron (1951)* 270–3) stresses the predominant influence of
Hume, Holbach, and Godwin on this note. Clark (*Prose* 109–12) adds that of
Spinoza, but although much in the note can be reconciled with Spinoza's
teaching (e.g. that 'Necessity' is another name for the power of God) there
seems little if any direct influence.
Lines 11–13. *Motive is, to voluntary action . . . material universe*] '. . . the

the material universe. The word liberty, as applied to mind, is
analogous to the word chance, as applied to matter: they spring
15   from an ignorance of the certainty of the conjunction of
antecedents and consequents.

   Every human being is irresistibly impelled to act precisely as he
does act: in the eternity which preceded his birth a chain of causes
was generated, which, operating under the name of motives,
20   make it impossible that any thought of his mind, or any action of
his life, should be otherwise than it is. Were the doctrine of
Necessity false, the human mind would no longer be a legitimate
object of science; from like causes it would be in vain that we
should expect like effects; the strongest motive would no longer
25   be paramount over the conduct; all knowledge would be vague
and undeterminate; we could not predict with any certainty that
we might not meet as an enemy tomorrow him with whom we
have parted in friendship tonight; the most probable inducements
and the clearest reasonings would lose the invariable influence
30   they possess. The contrary of this is demonstrably the fact.
Similar circumstances produce the same unvariable effects. The
precise character and motives of any man on any occasion being
given, the moral philosopher could predict his actions with as
much certainty as the natural philosopher could predict the effects
35   of the mixture of any particular chemical substances. Why is the

conjunction between motives and voluntary actions is as regular and uniform
as that between the cause and effect in any part of nature' (Hume, *An Enquiry
Concerning Human Understanding* (1748) Section VIII Part i).
Lines 17–21. *Every human being . . . otherwise than it is*] 'In the life of every
human being there is a chain of events, generated in the lapse of ages which
preceded his birth, and going on in regular procession through the whole
period of his existence, in consequence of which it was impossible for him to
act in any instance otherwise than he has acted' (*Political Justice* Bk IV ch. viii, i
384). It is very doubtful whether, as F. E. L. Priestley affirms in his edition (iii.
108–9), S. used the first edition of *Political Justice* for this and the following
quotation.
Lines 31–5. *The precise character and motives . . . chemical substances*] 'He who
affirms that all actions are necessary, means that the man, who is acquainted
with all the circumstances under which a living or intelligent being is placed
upon any given occasion, is qualified to predict the conduct he will hold, with
as much certainty as he can predict any of the phenomena of inanimate nature'
(*Political Justice* Bk IV ch. vii, i 363).
Lines 35–42. *Why is the aged husbandman . . . to be effectual*] 'Why is the aged
husbandman more skilful in his calling than the young beginner, but because
there is a certain uniformity in the operation of the sun, rain and earth towards
the production of vegetables, and experience teaches the old practitioner the
rules by which this operation is governed and directed?' (Hume, loc. cit.).

aged husbandman more experienced than the young beginner?
Because there is a uniform, undeniable necessity in the operations
of the material universe. Why is the old statesman more skilful
than the raw politician? Because, relying on the necessary
40 conjunction of motive and action, he proceeds to produce moral
effects, by the application of those moral causes which experience
has shown to be effectual. Some actions may be found to which
we can attach no motives, but these are the effects of causes with
which we are unacquainted. Hence the relation which motive
45 bears to voluntary action is that of cause to effect; nor, placed in
this point of view, is it, or ever has it been the subject of popular
or philosophical dispute. None but the few fanatics who are
engaged in the herculean task of reconciling the justice of their
God with the misery of man, will longer outrage common sense
50 by the supposition of an event without a cause, a voluntary action
without a motive. History, politics, morals, criticism, all
grounds of reasoning, all principles of science, alike assume the
truth of the doctrine of Necessity. No farmer carrying his corn to
market doubts the sale of it at the market price. The master of a
55 manufactory no more doubts that he can purchase the human
labour necessary for his purposes, than that his machinery will act
as they have been accustomed to act.
    But, whilst none have scrupled to admit necessity as
influencing matter, many have disputed its dominion over mind.
60 Independently of its militating with the received ideas of the
justice of God, it is by no means obvious to a superficial enquiry.
When the mind observes it own operations, it feels no connection
of motive and action: but as we know 'nothing more of causation
than the constant conjunction of objects and the consequent
65 inference of one from the other, as we find that these two
circumstances are universally allowed to have place in voluntary
action, we may be easily led to own that they are subjected to the
necessity common to all causes.' The actions of the will have a
regular conjunction with circumstances and characters; motive is,
70 to voluntary action, what cause is to effect. But the only idea we
can form of causation is a constant conjunction of similar objects,
and the consequent inference of one from the other: wherever this
is the case necessity is clearly established.

Lines 53–7. *No farmer carrying his corn . . . accustomed to act*] The illustration of the
farmer and his corn derives from *Political Justice* Bk IV ch. vii, i 375; that of the
manufacturer and his machinery from Hume, loc. cit. *machinery*] 'Machines
taken collectively' (*OED* 2): hence perhaps S.'s plural verb.
Lines 63–8. *'nothing more of causation . . . to all causes'*] S.'s quotation is taken,
with minor changes, from Hume, loc. cit.

75   The idea of liberty, applied metaphorically to the will, has
          sprung from a misconception of the meaning of the word power.
          What is power?–*id quod potest*, that which can produce any given
          effect. To deny power, is to say that nothing can or has the power
          to be or act. In the only true sense of the word power, it applies
80   with equal force to the loadstone as to the human will. Do you
          think these motives, which I shall present, are powerful enough
          to rouse him? is a question just as common as, Do you think this
          lever has the power of raising this weight? The advocates of free-
          will assert that the will has the power of refusing to be
85   determined by the strongest motive: but the strongest motive is
          that which, overcoming all others, ultimately prevails; this
          assertion therefore amounts to a denial of the will being
          ultimately determined by that motive which does determine it,
90   which is absurd. But it is equally certain that a man cannot resist
          the strongest motive, as that he cannot overcome a physical
          impossibility.
              The doctrine of Necessity tends to introduce a great change
          into the established notions of morality, and utterly to destroy
95   religion. Reward and punishment must be considered, by the
          Necessarian, merely as motives which he would employ in order
          to procure the adoption or abandonment of any given line of
          conduct. Desert, in the present sense of the word, would no
          longer have any meaning; and he, who should inflict pain upon
100   another for no better reason than that he deserved it, would only
          gratify his revenge under pretence of satisfying justice. It is not
          enough, says the advocate of free-will, that a criminal should be
          prevented from a repetition of his crime: he should feel pain, and
          his torments, when justly inflicted, ought precisely to be

Lines 75–8. *The idea of liberty . . . any given effect*] 'In examining what we mean
to express by the word *power*, it would be difficult to show, that we understand
any thing else by it, than that which may, or does, produce change' (William
Drummond, *Academical Questions* (1805) i 176). S. apparently had this work
with him in Edinburgh at the end of 1813 (Letter to William Laing, 27
September 1815, *L* i 433).
Lines 83–92. *The advocates of free-will . . . a physical impossibility*] The argument
that the strongest motive must prevail is in Hume, loc. cit., Holbach (i
206–13), and Godwin (Bk IV ch. vii, i 368–82).
Lines 93–127. *The doctrine of Necessity . . . delusions of free-will*] That the doctrine
of Necessity makes punishment meaningless, while in no way legitimizing
vice, is argued by Hume (*Enquiry* Section VIII Part ii); by Holbach (i, chs
xii–xiii); and by Godwin (Bk VII chs. i–v, ii 321–77). *Damiens*] 'When
[Robert-Francois] Damiens, the maniac, was arraigned [1757] for his abortive
attempt on the life of Louis XV of France, a council of anatomists was
summoned, to deliberate how a human being might be destroyed with the
longest protracted and most diversified agony' (*Political Justice* Bk I ch. ii, i 13).

105   proportioned to his fault. But utility is morality; that which is
incapable of producing happiness is useless; and though the crime
of Damiens must be condemned, yet the frightful torments
which revenge, under the name of justice, inflicted on this
unhappy man, cannot be supposed to have augmented, even at

110   the long run, the stock of pleasurable sensation in the world. At
the same time, the doctrine of Necessity does not in the least
diminish our disapprobation of vice. The conviction which all
feel, that a viper is a poisonous animal, and that a tiger is
constrained, by the inevitable condition of his existence, to

115   devour men, does not induce us to avoid them less sedulously,
or, even more, to hesitate in destroying them: but he would
surely be of a hard heart, who, meeting with a serpent on a desert
island, or in a situation where it was incapable of injury, should
wantonly deprive it of existence. A Necessarian is inconsequent

120   to his own principles, if he indulges in hatred or contempt; the
compassion which he feels for the criminal is unmixed with a
desire of injuring him: he looks with an elevated and dreadless
composure upon the links of the universal chain as they pass
before his eyes; whilst cowardice, curiosity and inconsistency

125   only assail him in proportion to the feebleness and indistinctness
with which he has perceived and rejected the delusions of free-
will.

      Religion is the perception of the relation in which we stand to
the principle of the universe. But if the principle of the universe

130   be not an organic being, the model and prototype of man, the
relation between it and human beings are absolutely none.
Without some insight into its will respecting our actions, religion
is nugatory and vain. But will is only a mode of animal mind;
moral qualities also are such as only a human being can possess; to

135   attribute them to the principle of the universe, is to annex to it
properties incompatible with any possible definition of its nature.
It is probable that the word God was originally only an
expression denoting the unknown cause of the known events
which men perceived in the universe. By the vulgar mistake of a

140   metaphor for a real being, of a word for a thing, it became a man,
endowed with human qualities and governing the universe as an
earthly monarch governs his kingdom. Their addresses to this
imaginary being, indeed, are much in the same style as those of

Lines 137–45. *It is probable that the word God . . . supplicate his favour*] S.'s account
of the development of the idea of God from unknown cause to monarch-
prototype follows Holbach (ii 19–20). The responsibility of God for the evils
as well as the benefits of life is discussed by Hume at the end of *Enquiry* Section
VIII Part i.

145   subjects to a king. They acknowledge his benevolence, deprecate
      his anger, and supplicate his favour.
         But the doctrine of Necessity teaches us, that in no case could
      any event have happened otherwise than it did happen, and that,
      if God is the author of good, he is also the author of evil; that, if
      he is entitled to our gratitude for the one, he is entitled to our
150   hatred for the other; that, admitting the existence of this
      hypothetic being, he is also subjected to the dominion of an
      immutable necessity. It is plain that the same arguments which
      prove that God is the author of food, light, and life, prove him
      also to be the author of poison, darkness, and death. The wide-
155   wasting earthquake, the storm, the battle, and the tyranny, are
      attributable to this hypothetic being in the same degree as the
      fairest forms of nature, sunshine, liberty, and peace.
         But we are taught, by the doctrine of Necessity, that there is
      neither good nor evil in the universe, otherwise than as the events
160   to which we apply these epithets have relation to our own
      peculiar mode of being. Still less than with the hypothesis of a
      God, will the doctrine of Necessity accord with the belief of a
      future state of punishment. God made man such as he is, and then
      damned him for being so: for to say that God was the author of all
165   good, and man the author of all evil, is to say that one man made
      a straight line and a crooked one, and another man made the
      incongruity.
         A Mahometan story, much to the present purpose, is recorded,
      wherein Adam and Moses are introduced disputing before God in
170   the following manner. Thou, says Moses, art Adam, whom God
      created, and animated with the breath of life, and caused to be
      worshipped by the angels, and placed in Paradise, from whence
      mankind have been expelled for thy fault. Whereto Adam
      answered, Thou art Moses, whom God chose for his apostle, and
175   entrusted with his word, by giving thee the tables of the law, and

Lines 164–7. *to say that God . . . made the incongruity*] 'If a man doe an action of
Injustice, that is to say, an action contrary to the Law, God they say is the prime
cause of the Law, and also the prime cause of that, and all other Actions; but no
cause at all of the Injustice; which is the Inconformity of the Action to the Law.
This is Vain Philosophy. A man might as well say, that one man maketh both a
streight line, and a crooked, and another maketh their Incongruity' (Hobbes,
Leviathan (1651) Part IV ch. xlvi, 376). S. may be quoting Hobbes's aphorism,
which he uses again in *A Refutation of Deism* (1814), from Sir William Drummond (*Academical Questions* 275).
Line 168. *A Mahometan story*] The narrator was Mohammed himself (*The
Koran, translated into English . . .* by George Sale (1801 edn) Preliminary
Discourse Section VIII, i 164).

whom he vouchsafed to admit to discourse with himself. How
many years dost thou find the law was written before I was
created? Says Moses, Forty. And dost thou not find, replied
Adam, these words therein, And Adam rebelled against his Lord
180 and transgressed? Which Moses confessing, Dost thou therefore
blame me, continued he, for doing that which God wrote of me
that I should do, forty years before I was created, nay, for what
was decreed concerning me fifty thousand years before the
creation of heaven and earth?—*Sale's Prelim. Disc. to the Koran*,
185 *page* 164.

vii. *13*

There is no God!

1 This negation must be understood solely to affect a creative
Deity. The hypothesis of a pervading Spirit coeternal with the
universe, remains unshaken.
A close examination of the validity of the proofs adduced to
5 support any proposition, is the only secure way of attaining
truth, on the advantages of which it is unnecessary to descant: our
knowledge of the existence of a Deity is a subject of such
importance, that it cannot be too minutely investigated; in
consequence of this conviction we proceed briefly and impartially
10 to examine the proofs which have been adduced. It is necessary
first to consider the nature of belief.
When a proposition is offered to the mind, it perceives the
agreement or disagreement of the ideas of which it is composed.
A perception of their agreement is termed *belief*. Many obstacles
15 frequently prevent this perception from being immediate; these
the mind attempts to remove, in order that the perception may be
distinct. The mind is active in the investigation, in order to
perfect the state of perception of the relation which the

vii *13*] From the second paragraph to that ending 'no proof of the existence of a
Deity' this note reproduces (except where recorded below) *The Necessity of
Atheism* (*NA*), published in 1811 by Hogg and S. at Oxford. The additions seek
(a) to limit the earlier argument to non-belief in a *creative* God, (b) to incorporate Hume's argument that causality involves only a habitual sequence, not a
connection, of events. Hogg, probably the chief author of *NA* (see *Cameron*
(1951) 328–30), had described that essay as 'carrying perhaps a little too far
some of the arguments of Locke' (draft letter to Lady Elizabeth S., July 1811,
SC ii 821).
Lines 17–20. *The mind is active . . . which is passive:*] *NA* reads only: 'The mind is
active in the investigation, in order to perfect the state of perception which is
passive;'.

component ideas of the proposition bear to each, which is

20   passive: the investigation being confused with the perception, has
induced many falsely to imagine that the mind is active in belief—
that belief is an act of volition,—in consequence of which it may
be regulated by the mind. Pursuing, continuing this mistake,
they have attached a degree of criminality to disbelief; of which,

25   in its nature, it is incapable: it is equally incapable of merit.

Belief, then, is a passion, the strength of which, like every
other passion, is in precise proportion to the degrees of
excitement.

The degrees of excitement are three.

30   The senses are the sources of all knowledge to the mind;
consequently their evidence claims the strongest assent.

The decision of the mind, founded upon our own experience,
derived from these sources, claims the next degree.

The experience of others, which addresses itself to the former

35   one, occupies the lowest degree.

(A graduated scale, on which should be marked the capabilities
of propositions to approach to the test of the senses, would be a
just barometer of the belief which ought to be attached to them.)

Consequently no testimony can be admitted which is contrary

40   to reason; reason is founded on the evidence of our senses.

Every proof may be referred to one of these three divisions: it is
to be considered what arguments we receive from each of them,
which should convince us of the existence of a Deity.

1st. The evidence of the senses. If the Deity should appear to

45   us, if he should convince our senses of his existence, this
revelation would necessarily command belief. Those to whom
the Deity has thus appeared have the strongest possible
conviction of his existence. But the God of Theologians is
incapable of local visibility.

50   2d. Reason. It is urged that man knows that whatever is, must
either have had a beginning, or have existed from all eternity: he
also knows, that whatever is not eternal must have had a cause.
When this reasoning is applied to the universe, it is necessary to
prove that it was created: until that is clearly demonstrated, we

55   may reasonably suppose that it has endured from all eternity. We
must prove design before we can infer a designer. The only idea
which we can form of causation is derivable from the constant
conjunction of objects, and the consequent inference of one from
the other. In a case where two propositions are diametrically

---

Lines 36–8. The bracketed passage is not in *NA*.
Lines 48–9. *But the God of Theologians is incapable of local visibility*] Not in *NA*.
Lines 55–9. *We must prove design . . . inference of one from the other*] Not in *NA*.

60   opposite, the mind believes that which is least
        incomprehensible;—it is easier to suppose that the universe has
        existed from all eternity, than to conceive a being beyond its
        limits capable of creating it: if the mind sinks beneath the weight
        of one, is it an alleviation to increase the intolerability of the
65   burthen?
            The other argument, which is founded on a man's knowledge
        of his own existence, stands thus. A man knows not only that he
        now is, but that once he was not; consequently there must have
        been a cause. But our idea of causation is alone derivable from the
70   constant conjunction of objects and the consequent inference of
        one from the other; and, reasoning experimentally, we can only
        infer from effects, causes exactly adequate to those effects. But
        there certainly is a generative power which is effected by certain
        instruments: we cannot prove that it is inherent in these
75   instruments; nor is the contrary hypothesis capable of
        demonstration: we admit that the generative power is
        incomprehensible; but to suppose that the same effect is produced
        by an eternal, omniscient, omnipotent being, leaves the cause in
        the same obscurity, but renders it more incomprehensible.
80   3d. Testimony. It is required that testimony should not be
        contrary to reason. The testimony that the Deity convinces the
        senses of men of his existence can only be admitted by us, if our
        mind considers it less probable that these men should have been
        deceived, than that the Deity should have appeared to them. Our
85   reason can never admit the testimony of men, who not only
        declare that they were eye-witnesses of miracles, but that the
        Deity was irrational; for he commanded that he should be
        believed, he proposed the highest rewards for faith, eternal

Line 60. *least*] less *NA*.
Lines 62–3. *a being beyond its limits capable*] a being capable *NA*.
Lines 69–71. *But our idea of causation . . . reasoning experimentally,*] But what does
this prove? *NA*.
Line 78. *omnipotent being*] Almighty Being *NA*.
Lines 81–4. *The testimony that the Deity . . . have appeared to them*] A more
cautious version of Paine's demand: 'Is it more probable that nature should go
out of her course, or that a man should tell a lie?' (*Age of Reason* Part I; *Paine
Writings* iv 79). Paine discusses the inadequacy of personal revelation at the
beginning of Part I and in the Conclusion.
Lines 87–9. *for he commanded . . . punishments for disbelief*] John iii 16, 18: 'God so
loved the world, that he gave his only begotten Son, that whosoever believeth
in him should not perish, but have everlasting life . . . he that believeth not is
condemned already'; viii 24: 'if ye believeth not that I am *he*, ye shall die in your
sins'.

punishments for disbelief. We can only command voluntary
90   actions; belief is not an act of volition; the mind is even passive, or
involuntarily active; from this it is evident that we have no
sufficient testimony, or rather that testimony is insufficient to
prove the being of a God. It has been before shown that it cannot
be deduced from reason. They alone, then, who have been
95   convinced by the evidence of the senses, can believe it.
      Hence is is evident that, having no proofs from either of the
three sources of conviction, the mind *cannot* believe the existence
of a creative God: it is also evident, that, as belief is a passion of
the mind, no degree of criminality is attachable to disbelief; and
100   that they only are reprehensible who neglect to remove the false
medium through which their mind views any subject of
discussion. Every reflecting mind must acknowledge that there is
no proof of the existence of a Deity.
      God is an hypothesis, and, as such, stands in need of proof: the
105   *onus probandi* rests on the theist. Sir Isaac Newton says: *Hypotheses*
non fingo, quicquid enim ex phænomenis non deducitur, hypothesis
vocanda est, et hypothesis vel metaphysicæ, vel physicæ, vel qualitatum
occultarum, seu mechanicæ, in philosophiâ locum non habent. To all
proofs of the existence of a creative God apply this valuable rule.
110   We see a variety of bodies possessing a variety of powers: we
merely know their effects; we are in a state of ignorance with
respect to their essences and causes. These Newton calls the
phenomena of things; but the pride of philosophy is unwilling to
admit its ignorance of their causes. From the phenomena, which
115   are the objects of our senses, we attempt to infer a cause, which
we call God, and gratuitously endow it with all negative and

Lines 89–91. *We can only command . . . or involuntarily active*] This favourite
principle of S. is in Drummond, *Academical Questions* 21: 'will cannot be
changed, while sentiment remains unaltered . . . Belief cannot be forced, nor
can conviction be coerced'.   *or involuntarily active*] These words not in NA.
Line 98. *the existence of a creative God*] The word *creative* not in NA.
Line 102. *Every reflecting mind . . .*] Before this sentence NA has: 'It is almost
unnecessary to observe, that the general knowledge of the deficiency of such
proof, cannot be prejudicial to society: Truth has always been found to
promote the best interests of mankind. –'
Lines 105–8. *Hypotheses non fingo . . . non habent*] 'I do not make hypotheses, for
whatever is not deduced from the phenomena must be called a hypothesis, and
hypotheses, whether in metaphysics, or physics, or occult qualities, or mecha-
nics, have no place in philosophy' (Sir Isaac Newton, conclusion of *Philo-*
sophiae Naturalis Principia Mathematica (1687; 3rd edn 1726) Lib. III 530). S.'s
second '*hypothesis*' should be plural. Newton wrote: 'hypotheses seu metaphy-
sicae, seu phisicae, seu qualitatum occultarum, seu mechanicae, in *philosophia*
experimentali locum non habent'.

contradictory qualities. From this hypothesis we invent this
general name, to conceal our ignorance of causes and essences.
The being called God by no means answers with the conditions
120   prescribed by Newton; it bears every mark of a veil woven by
philosophical conceit, to hide the ignorance of philosophers even
from themselves. They borrow the threads of its texture from the
anthropomorphism of the vulgar. Words have been used by
sophists for the same purposes, from the occult qualities of the
125   peripatetics to the *effluvium* of Boyle and the *crinities* or *nebulæ* of
Herschel. God is represented as infinite, eternal,
incomprehensible, he is contained under every prædicate in non
that the logic of ignorance could fabricate. Even his worshippers
allow that it is impossible to form any idea of him: they exclaim
130   with the French poet,

> *Pour dire ce qu'il est, il faut être lui-même.*

Lord Bacon says, that 'atheism leaves to man reason,
philosophy, natural piety, laws, reputation, and every thing that
can serve to conduct him to virtue; but superstition destroys all

Line 125. *the peripatetics*] School of philosophy founded by Aristotle, named
after his habit of walking up and down while teaching.   *the* effluvium *of
Boyle*] Robert Boyle (1626–91), great Irish chemist, held that e.g. magnetism
resulted from an 'effluvium' of material particles.   *the* crinities *or* nebulæ *of
Herschel*] In 1791 Frederick William Herschel (1738–1822) had announced his
discovery of what came to be known as gaseous nebulae. *Crinis* ('hair') had
been used in Latin to mean a comet.
Lines 126–8. *God is represented . . . ignorance could fabricate*] S. told Godwin on 29
July 1812: 'I have read Berkeley, & the perusal of his arguments tended more
than anything to convince me that immaterialism & other words of general
usage deriving all their force from mere *predicates* in *non* [= negative proposi-
tions] were invented by the pride of philosophers to conceal their ignorance
even from themselves' (*L* i 316).
Line 131. Pour dire ce qu'il est, il faut être lui-même] S. lifted this quotation
from Holbach, *Système de la Nature* ii 275, where it is attributed to 'un Poète
moderne' as footnote to the sentence 'Si Dieu est tel que la théologie moderne
nous le dépeint, il faut être soi-même un Dieu pour s'en former un idée!' The
original poet is unidentified.
Lines 132–8. *Lord Bacon says . . . the present life.'*] S. translates Bacon from the
French of Holbach (ii 384–5). Bacon's actual words (*Essayes or Counsels Civill
& Morall* xvii, 'Of Superstition') were: '*Atheisme* leaves a Man to Sense; to
Philosophy; to Naturall Piety; to Lawes; to Reputation; All which may be
Guides to an outward Morall vertue, though *Religion* were not; but *Superstition*
dismounts all these, and erecteth an absolute Monarchy, in the Mindes of Men.
Therefore *Atheism* did never perturbe *States*; For it makes Men wary of
themselves, as looking no further'.

135　these, and erects itself into a tyranny over the understandings of
　　　men: hence atheism never disturbs the government, but renders
　　　man more clear-sighted, since he sees nothing beyond the
　　　boundaries of the present life.'

Bacon's Moral Essays

140　La première théologie de l'homme lui fit d'abord craindre et
　　　adorer les élémens même, des objets matériels et grossiers; il
　　　rendit ensuite ses hommages à des agens présidens aux élémens, à
　　　des génies inférieurs, à des héros, ou à des hommes doués de
　　　grands qualités. A force de réfléchir il crut simplifier les choses en
145　soumettant la nature entière à un seul agent, à un esprit, à une
　　　âme universelle, qui mettoit cette nature et ses parties en
　　　mouvement. En remontant des [= de] causes en causes, les
　　　mortels ont fini par ne rien voir; et c'est dans cette obscurité qu'ils
　　　ont placé leur Dieu; c'est dans cette abîme ténébreux que leur
150　imagination inquiète travaille toujours à se fabriquer des
　　　chimères, que [= qui] les affligeront jusqu'à ce que la
　　　connoissance de la nature les détrompe des phantômes qu'ils ont
　　　toujours si vainement adorés.

　　　　　Si nous voulons nous rendre compte de nos idées sur la
155　Divinité, nous serons obligés de convenir que, par le mot *Dieu*,
　　　les hommes n'ont jamais pu désigner que la cause la plus cachée,
　　　la plus éloignée, la plus inconnue des effets qu'ils voyoient: ils ne
　　　font usage de ce mot, que lorsque le jeu des causes naturelles et
　　　connues cesse d'être visible pour eux; dès qu'ils perdent le fit [=
160　fil] de ces causes, ou dès que leur esprit ne peut plus en suivre la
　　　chaîne, ils tranchent leur difficulté, et terminent leur recherches
　　　en appellant Dieu la dernière des causes, c'est-à-dire celle qui est
　　　au-delà de toutes les causes qu'ils connoissent; ainsi ils ne font
　　　qu'assigner une dénomination vague à une cause ignorée, à
165　laquelle leur paresse ou les bornes de leurs connoissances les
　　　forcent de s'arrêter. Toutes les fois qu'on nous dit que Dieu est
　　　l'auteur de quelque phénomène, cela signifie qu'on ignore
　　　comment un tel phénomène a pu s'opérer par le secours des forces
　　　ou des causes que nous connoissons dans la nature. C'est ainsi que
170　le commun des hommes, dont l'ignorance est la partage, attribue
　　　à la Divinité non seulement les effets inusités qui les frappent,

Lines 140–317. *La première théologie . . .*] This long quotation consists of
selections from Holbach's *Système de la Nature* ii 16–18, 27, 319–26. The
significant variants are noted.
Lines 142–3. *aux élémens, à des génies inférieurs*] aux élémens, à des génies
puissans, à des génies inférieurs SN.
Line 145. *à un seul agent, à un esprit,*] à un seul agent, à une intelligence
souveraine, à un esprit SN.
Line 161. *leur difficulté*] la difficulté SN.

mais encore les évènemens les plus simples, dont les causes sont
les plus faciles à connoître pour quiconque a pu les méditer. En un
mot, l'homme a toujours respecté les causes inconnues des effets
175 surprenans, que son ignorance l'empêchoit de démêler. Ce fut sur
les debus [= débris] de la nature que les hommes élevèrent le
colosse imaginaire de la Divinité.

Si l'ignorance de la nature donna la naissance aux dieux, la
connoissance de la nature est faite pour les detruire. A mésure que
180 l'homme s'instruit, ses forces et ses ressources augmentent avec
ses lumières; les sciences, les arts conservateurs, l'industrie, lui
fournissent des secours; l'expérience le rassûre ou lui procure des
moyens de résister aux efforts de bien des causes qui cessent de
l'alarmer dès qu'il les a connues. En un mot, ses terreurs se
185 dissipent dans la même proportion que son esprit s'éclaire.
L'homme instruit cesse d'être superstitieux.

Ce n'est jamais que sur parole que des peuples entiers adorent le
Dieu de leurs pères et de leurs prêtres: l'autorité, la confiance, la
soumission, et l'habitude leur tiennent lieu de conviction et de
190 preuves; ils se prosternent et prient, parce que leurs pères leur ont
appris à se prosterner et prier: mais pourquoi ceux-ci se sont-ils
mis à genoux? C'est que dans les temps éloignés leurs legislateurs
et leurs guides leur en ont fait un devoir. 'Adorez et croyez,' ont-
ils dit, 'des dieux que vous ne pouvez comprendre; rapportez-
195 vous en à notre sagesse profonde; nous en savons plus que vous
sur la divinité.' Mais pourquoi m'en rapporterois-je à vous? C'est
que Dieu le veut ainsi, c'est que Dieu vous punira si vous osez
résister. Mais ce Dieu n'est-il donc pas la chose en question?
Cependant les hommes se sont toujours payés de ce cercle
200 vicieux; la paresse de leur esprit leur fit trouver plus court de s'en
rapporter au jugement des autres. Toutes les notions religieuses
sont fondées uniquement sur l'autorité; toutes les religions du
monde défendent l'examen et ne veulent pas que l'on raisonne;
c'est l'autorité qui veut qu'on crire [= croie] en Dieu; ce Dieu
205 n'est lui-même fonde que sur l'autorité de quelques hommes qui
prétendent le connoître, et venir de sa part pour l'anoncer à la
terre. Un Dieu fait par les hommes, a sans doute besoin des
hommes pour se faire connoître aux hommes.

Ne seroit-ce donc que pour des prêtres, des inspirés, des
210 metaphysiciens que seroit reservée la conviction de l'existence
d'un Dieu, que l'on dit neanmoins si necessaire à tout le genre-
humain? Mais trouvons-nous de l'harmonie entre les opinions
théologiques des differens inspirés, ou des penseurs repandus sur

Line 175. *démêler. Ce*] Between these two words S. jumps from p. 18 to p. 27.
Lines 186–7. *superstitieux. Ce*] Between these two words S. jumps from p. 27
to p. 319.

la terre? Ceux même que [= qui] font profession d'adorer le
215   même Dieu, sont-ils d'accord sur son compte? Sont-ils contents
des preuves que leurs collègues apportent de son existence?
Souscrivent-ils unanimement aux idées qu'ils présentent sur sa
nature, sur sa conduite, sur la façon d'entendre ses prétendus
oracles? Est-il une contrée sur la terre, où la science de Dieu se soit
220   réellement perfectionné? A-t-elle pris quelque part la consistence
et l'uniformité que nous voyons prendre aux connoissances
humaines, aux arts les plus futiles, aux métiers les plus meprisés?
les mots *d'esprit, d'immatérialité*, de *création*, de *prédestination*, de
grace; cette foule de distinctions subtiles dont la théologie s'est
225   partout remplie dans quelques pays, ces inventions si ingénieuses,
imaginées par des penseurs que se sont succédés depuis tant de
siècles, n'ont fait, helas! qu'embrouilles [= qu'embrouiller] les
choses, et jamais le science le plus nécessaire aux hommes n'a
jusqu'ici pu acquérir la moindre fixité. Depuis des milliers
230   d'années, ces reveurs oisifs se sont perpétuellement relayés pour
méditer la Divinité, pour deviner ses voies cachées, pour inventer
des hypotheses propres à développer cette enigme importante.
Leur peu de succés n'a point découragé la vanité théologique;
toujours on a parlé de Dieu: on s'est égorgé pour lui, et cet être
235   sublime demeure toujours le plus ignoré et le plus discuté.
        Les hommes auroient été trop heureux, si, se bornant aux
objets visibles qui les intéressent, ils eussent employé à
perfectionner leurs sciences réelles, leurs loix, leur morale, leur
éducation, la moitié des efforts qu'ils ont mis dans leurs
240   recherches sur la Divinité. Ils auroient été bien plus sages encore,
et plus fortunés, s'ils eussent pu consentir à laisser leurs guides
désœuvrés se quereller entre eux, et sonder des profondeurs
capables de les étourdir, sans se mêler de leurs disputes insensées.
Mais il est de l'essence de l'ignorance d'attacher de l'importance à
245   ce qu'elle ne comprend pas. La vanité humaine fait que l'esprit se
roidit contre des difficultés. Plus un objet se derobe à nos yeux,
plus nous faisons d'efforts pour le saisir, parce que dès-lors il
aiguillone notre orgueil, il excite notre curiosité, il nous paroit
intéressant. En combattant pour son Dieu chacun ne combattit en
250   effet que pour les intérêts de sa propre vanité, qui de toutes les
passions produits par la mal organization de la societé, est la plus

Line 234. *Dieu: on s'est égorgé*] Dieu: on s'est disputé, on s'est égorgé *SN*.
Line 248. *il excite notre curiosité*] il irrite notre curiosité *SN*.
Line 249. *intéressant. En*] S. omits two sentences between these two words.
Lines 250–52. *qui de toutes les passions produits par la mal organization de la societé,
est la plus prompte à s'allarmer*] qui de toutes les passions humaines, est la plus
prompte à s'allarmer *SN*. S. seems to have interpolated these words on his own
account.

prompte à s'allarmer, et la plus propre à produire des tres grands folies.

Si écartant pour un moment les idées facheuses que la théologie
255 nous donne d'un Dieu capricieux, dont les décrets partaux[=
partiaux] et despotiques décident du sort des humains, nous ne
voulons fixer nos yeux que sur la bonté prétendue, que tous les
hommes, même en tremblant devant ce Dieu, s'accordent à lui
donner; si nous lui supposons le projet qu'on lui prête, de n'avoir
260 travaillé que pour sa propre gloire, d'exiger les hommages des
êtres intelligens; de ne chercher dans ses œuvres que le bien-être
du genre-humain; comment concilier ses vues et ses dispositions
avec l'ignorance vraiment invincible dans lequelle ce Dieu, si
glorieux et si bon, laisse la plupart des hommes sur son compte?
265 Si Dieu veut être connu, chéri, remercié, que ne se montre-t-il
sous des traits favorables à tous ces êtres intelligens dont il veut
être aimé et adoré? Pourquoi ne point se manifester à toute la terre
d'une façon non équivoque, bien plus capable de nous
convaincre, que ces révélations particuliers qui semblent accuser
270 la Divinité d'une partialité facheuse pour quelqu'uns de ses
créatures? Le tout-puissant n'auroit-il donc pas des moyens plus
convainquans de se montrer ceux [= aux] hommes que ces
métamorphoses ridicules, ces incarnations prétendues, qui nous
sont attestées par des écrivains si peu d'accord entre eux dans les
275 récits qu'ils en font? Au lieu de tant de miracles, inventés pour
prouver la mission divine de tant de législateurs, révérés par les
différens peuples du monde, le souverain des esprits ne pouvoit-il
pas convaincre tout d'un coup l'esprit humain des choses qu'il a
voulu lui faire connoître? Au lieu de suspendre un soleil dans la
280 voûte du firmament; au lieu de repandre sans ordre les étoiles, et
les constellations qui remplissent l'espace, n'eut-il pas été plus
conforme aux vues d'un Dieu si jaloux de sa gloire et si bien
intentionné pour l'homme; d'écrire d'une façon non sujette à
dispute, son nom, ses attributs, ses volontés permanentes en
285 caractères ineffaçables, et lisibles également pour tous les
habitants de la terre? Personne alors n'auroit pu douter de
l'existence d'un Dieu, de ses volontés claires, de ses intentions
visibles. Sous les yeux de ce Dieu si terrible personne n'auroit eu
l'audace de violer ses ordonnances; nul mortel n'eût osé se mettre
290 dans le cas d'attirer sa colère: enfin nul homme n'eût eu le front
d'en imposer en son nom, ou d'interpréter ses volontés suivant
ses propres phantasies.

En effet, quand même on admetteroit l'existence du Dieu
théologique, et la réalité des attributs si discordans qu'on lui

Lines 293–6. *En effet . . . de lui rendre*] In *SN*, this sentence occurs after the next two.

295 donne, l'on ne peut en rien conclure, pour autorizer la conduite
     ou les cultes qu'on prescrit de lui rendre. La théologie est
     vraiment *le tonneau des Danaïdes*. A force de qualités
     contradictoires et d'assertions hazardées, elle a, pour ainsi dire,
     tellement garroté son Dieu qu'elle a [= l'a] mis dans
300 l'impossibilité d'agir. S'il est infiniment bon qu'elle [= quelle]
     raison aurions-nous de le craindre? S'il est infiniment sage, de
     quoi nous inquieter sur notre sort? S'il sait tout, pourquoi
     l'avertir de nos besoins et le fatiguer de nos prières? S'il est
     partout, pourquoi lui élever des temples? S'il est maître de tout,
305 pourquoi lui faire des sacrifices et des offrandes? S'il est juste,
     comment croire qu'il punisse des créatures qu'il a rempli de
     foiblesses? Si la grace fait tout en elles, quelle raison auroit-il de
     les recompenser? S'il est tout-puissant, comment l'offenser,
     comment lui resister? S'il est raisonnable comment se mettroit-il
310 en colère contre des aveugles, à qui il a laissé la liberté de
     déraisonner? S'il est immuable, de quel droit prétendrions-nous
     faire changer ses decrets? S'il est inconcevable, pourquoi nous en
     occuper? S'IL A PARLÉ, POURQUOI L'UNIVERS N'EST-IL
     PAS CONVAINCU? Si la connoissance d'un Dieu est la plus
315 necessaire, pourquoi n'est-elle pas la plus évidente, et la plus
     claire.

                              Système de la Nature, London, 1781.

     The enlightened and benevolent Pliny thus publicly professes
     himself an atheist:–Quapropter effigiem Dei, formamque
320 quærere, imbecillitatis humanæ reor. Quisquis est Deus (si modo
     est alius) et quacunque in parte, totus est sensus, totus est visus,
     totus auditus, totus animæ, totus animi, totus sui. ★ ★ ★ ★ ★
     Imperfectæ vero in homine naturæ præcipua solatia ne deum
     quidem posse omnia. Namque nec sibi potest mortem
325 consciscere, si velit, quod homini dedit optimum in tantis vita
     pœnis: nec mortales æternitate donare, aut revocare defunctos;
     nec facere ut qui vixit non vixerit, qui honores gessit non gesserit,
     nullumque habere in præteritum jus, præterquam oblivionis,
     atque (ut facetis quoque argumentis societas hæc cum deo
330 copuletur) ut bis dena viginti non sint, et multa similiter efficere
     non posse.–Per quæ, declaratur haud dubie, naturæ potentiam id
     quoque esse, quod Deum vocamus.

                              Plin. Nat. His. cap. de Deo.

Lines 313–14. *S'IL A PARLÉ . . . CONVAINCU?*] Not capitalized in *SN*.
Lines 318–33. The quotation from Pliny is from *Naturalis Historia* II v 14, 27:
'For this reason I think it is a mark of human folly to seek the appearance and
shape of God. Whoever God is (if indeed he is a separate being) and in whatever
place, he is all sense, he is all seeing, all hearing, all spirit, all mind, all himself
. . . But the main consolations for nature's shortcomings in man are that not
even God can do everything. For he cannot kill himself if he wants to, which he

335   The consistent Newtonian is necessarily an atheist. See *Sir W.*
Drummond's Academical Questions, chap. iii.—Sir W. seems to
consider the atheism to which it leads, as a sufficient presumption
of the falsehood of the system of gravitation: but surely it is more
consistent with the good faith of philosophy to admit a deduction
from facts than an hypothesis incapable of proof, although it
340   might militate with the obstinate preconceptions of the mob. Had
this author, instead of inveighing against the guilt and absurdity
of atheism, demonstrated its falsehood, his conduct would have
been more suited to the modesty of the sceptic and the toleration
of the philosopher.

345   Omnia enim per Dei potentiam facta sunt: imo, quia natura
[naturae] potentia nulla est nisi ipsa Dei potentia, artem [certum]
est nos catemus [eatenus] Dei potentiam non intelligere,
quatemus [quatenus] causas naturales ignoramus; adeoque stulte
ad eandem Dei potentiam recurritur, quando rei alicujus, causam
350   naturalem, sive est, ipsam Dei potentiam ignoramus.
                Spinosa, Tract. Theologico-Pol. chap. i. *page* 14.

---

gave to man as the supreme blessing of life amid great sufferings: nor can he
confer immortality on mortals, or call back the dead; nor can he make a man
who has lived not to have lived, or one who has held honours not to have held
them, nor has he any power over the past, except of forgetting it, nor (to make
common case with God by a joking argument) of making twice ten not to be
twenty, nor can he do many things of the same kind.—By these facts the power
of nature is proclaimed to be that which we call God'. S. is said to have
translated much of this work by 'his beloved Pliny' while at Eton (*Hogg* i 461).
Line 334. *The consistent Newtonian is necessarily an atheist*] Drummond had said
(*Academical Questions* Bk II ch. iii, 211): 'The material law is the governing law
of our universe. In vain, then, shall we speak of providence ... of a Diety who
ordained, and who abandoned his world . . . We are taught by our rules of
philosophising to seek for no more causes, than are sufficient to explain the
phaenomena. We find all necessary causes in the properties of matter; and there
is no reason to believe, that what now sustains, has not always preserved, the
existence of nature and the world. Such are the arguments, which, I think, an
atheist might plausibly maintain, if the physical doctrines of the Newtonians
be true'.
Lines 345–50. *Omnia enim . . . ignoramus*] From Benedict de Spinoza, *Tractatus
Theologico-Politicus* ch. i, here translated from *Opera*, ed. J. van Vloten and J. P.
N. Land (The Hague 1895) i 370: 'For everything has happened through the
power of God: indeed, since the power of nature is nothing but that very
power of God, it is certain that we fail to understand the power of God insofar
as we are ignorant of natural causes; so it is very silly to refer something to the
power of God when we are ignorant of its natural cause—if that is itself the
power of God'. Spinoza's text reads 'hoc est', not 'sive est'; S.'s Latin, unintelligible in *1813*, was emended in the 'pirate' editions of 1821 and 1829.

vii. 67

Ahasuerus, rise!

1   Ahasuerus the Jew crept forth from the dark cave of Mount
Carmel. Near two thousand years have elapsed since he was first
goaded by never-ending restlessness to rove the globe from pole
to pole. When our Lord was wearied with the burthen of his
5   ponderous cross, and wanted to rest before the door of
Ahasuerus, the unfeeling wretch drove him away with brutality.
The Saviour of mankind staggered, sinking under the heavy load,

vii 67] This note is a translation of C. F. D. Schubart's 'Der ewige Jude. Eine
lyrische Rhapsodie' (1783) and closely follows a text in *La Belle Assemblée; or,
Bell's Court and Fashionable Magazine* vol. VI no. xli (January 1809) 19–20 (see
White i 580–1), which in turn is based on the translation by 'P. W.' in *The
German Museum* vol. III (June 1801) 424–6. It is clear that neither the *Belle
Assemblée* contributor nor S. knew the original German text, though S. must
have known its author's name, as this appears on the verso of a printed sentence
he copied. S.'s holograph of the passage from 'did the Elephant trample' to the
end of Schubart's poem is transcribed in *SC* ii 650; see also *Hogg* i 194–6. From
the variants between the text in *BA* and in S.'s note, and also between the
holograph and S.'s note, Cameron inclined to think (*SC* ii 656–7) that the
reader is 'confronted with not one but two unknown direct sources, one for the
. . . manuscript and one for the *Queen Mab* note'. The variants are not,
however, inconsistent with the probability that all three of S.'s texts – the note
to *WJ* 765, this note, and the Hogg MS – derive from *La Belle Assemblée* with
greater or less deliberate embellishment by S. according to requirement. S.
could make excuse for these changes by the romantic pretence, or fact, that the
fragment was found by accident, 'dirty and torn', about 1809 – a story repeated
by Mary S. (*1839* i 102). Medwin's characteristic attempt to involve himself in
its discovery (*Medwin (1913)* 42, 489–91) was rightly derided by Hogg (*Hogg* i
194). Schubart's complete poem has a further 8 lines, which are translated both
in *GM* and *BA*. S. had transcribed this conclusion, but may have suppressed it
because the ultimate forgiveness of Ahasuerus was not to his purpose. His
evidently hasty copy of *BA* ends as follows (*SC* ii 650): 'And Ahasuerus
dropped down Night covered his bristly eyelids. The angel bore me [carried
him *BA*, *GM*] back to the cavern Sleep here said the Angel, [said the Angel to
Ahasuerus, *BA*, *GM*] sleep in peace, the wrath of thy Judge is appeased, when
thou shalt awake he will be arrived he whose blo[o]d thou sawest flow upon
Golgotha whose mercy is extended even [is also extended *BA*, *GM*] to thee'.
All verbal variants from *La Belle Assemblée* (quoted as *BA*) are recorded below.
Line 1. *the dark cave*] a dark cave *BA*.
Line 2. *have elapsed*] are elapsed *BA*.
Line 3. *never-ending*] ever-increasing *BA* (no adjective in *Schubart*).
Line 4. *our Lord*] our blessed Lord *BA*; Jesus Christ *GM*.

but uttered no complaint. An angel of death appeared before
Ahasuerus, and exclaimed indignantly, 'Barbarian! thou hast
10 denied rest to the Son of Man: be it denied thee also, until he
comes to judge the world.'

A black demon, let loose from hell upon Ahasuerus, goads him
now from country to country: he is denied the consolation which
death affords, and precluded from the rest of the peaceful grave.

15 Ahasuerus crept forth from the dark cave of Mount Carmel—he
shook the dust from his beard—and taking up one of the skulls
heaped there, hurled it down the eminence: it rebounded from the
earth in shivered atoms. This was my father! roared Ahasuerus.
Seven more skulls rolled down from rock to rock; while the
20 infuriate Jew, following them with ghastly looks, exclaimed—
And these were my wives! He still continued to hurl down skull
after skull, roaring in dreadful accents—And these, and these, and
these were my children! They *could die*; but I! reprobate wretch,
alas! I cannot die! Dreadful beyond conception is the judgment
25 that hangs over me. Jerusalem fell—I crushed the sucking babe,
and precipitated myself into the destructive flames. I cursed the
Romans—but, alas! alas! the restless curse held me by the hair,—
and I could not die!

Rome the giantess fell—I placed myself before the falling
30 statue—she fell, and did not crush me. Nations sprung up and
disappeared before me;—but I remained and did not die. From
cloud-encircled cliffs did I precipitate myself into the ocean; but
the foaming billows cast me upon the shore, and the burning

Line 10. *denied thee*] denied to thee *BA*.
Line 15. *from the dark*] from dark *BA*.
Line 17. *heaped there*] heaped up there *BA*.
Line 18. *earth*] ground *BA*. *in shivered atoms*] and was shivered to pieces *BA*
(Und splitterte *Schubart*).
Line 19. *while*] whilst *BA*.
Line 23. *They could die*] THEY COULD DIE! *BA*.
Line 24. *cannot*] cannot *BA*.
Lines 27–8. *hair,—and*] hair, and—I *BA*.
Lines 29–30. *the falling statue*] the falling giantess *BA* (die stürzende Riesin
Schubart). S. still continues 'she fell', which suggests that the statue was his
own invention. *she fell, and*] she fell; but *BA*.
Line 32. *cloud-encircled cliffs*] cloud capp'd cliffs *BA*, *GM* (wolkengegürteten
Klippen *Schubart*). S. may have been avoiding the Shakespearean echo, just as
his source was exploiting it.
Lines 32–3. *but the foaming*] but foaming *BA*.

arrow of existence pierced my cold heart again. I leaped into
35   Etna's flaming abyss, and roared with the giants for ten long
months, polluting with my groans the Mount's sulphureous
mouth–ah! ten long months. The volcano fermented, and in a
fiery stream of lava cast me up. I lay torn by the torture-snakes of
hell amid the glowing cinders, and yet continued to exist. – A
40   forest was on fire: I darted on wings of fury and despair into the
crackling wood. Fire dropped upon me from the trees, but the
flames only singed my limbs; alas! it could not consume them. – I
now mixed with the butchers of mankind, and plunged in the
tempest of the raging battle. I roared defiance to the infuriate
45   Gaul, defiance to the victorious German; but arrows and spears
rebounded in shivers from my body. The Saracen's flaming
sword broke upon my skull: balls in vain hissed upon me: the
lightnings of battle glared harmless around my loins: in vain did
the elephant trample on me, in vain the iron hoof of the wrathful
50   steed! The mine, big with destructive power, burst upon me, and
hurled me high in the air–I fell on heaps of smoking limbs, but
was only singed. The giant's steel club rebounded from my body;
the executioner's hand could not strangle me, the tiger's tooth
could not pierce me, nor would the hungry lion in the circus
55   devour me. I cohabited with poisonous snakes, and pinched the
red crest of the dragon. The serpent stung, but could not destroy
me. – The dragon tormented, but dared not to devour me. – I now

Line 34. *pierced my cold heart again*] pierced me again *BA, GM* (durchstach mich
wieder *Schubart*).
Line 36. *months, polluting*] months in accents of despair, polluting *BA*; months
in accents of despair, lashing *GM* (zehn Monden lang / Mein Angstgeheul, und
geisselte *Schubart*).
Line 37. *ah!*] Ha! *BA.*
Lines 38–9. *lay torn by the torture-snakes of hell amid*] lay midst tortures of hell in
BA; lay convulsed with tortures of hell in *GM* (Ich zuckt in Asch *Schubart*). *and
yet*] but *BA.*
Line 42. *flames*] flame *BA* (die Flamme *Schubart*). *could not consume them*] could
not destroy me *BA, GM* (verzehrte mich nicht *Schubart*).
Line 43. *plunged in*] plunged into *BA.*
Line 49. *trample on*] trample upon *BA.*
Line 50. *burst upon me*] burst under me *BA.*
Line 51. *high in*] high into *BA. fell on*] fell down upon *BA. limbs, but*] limbs, and
BA.
Line 54. *pierce me*] hurt me *BA.*
Lines 51–2. *destroy me.–*] kill me: *BA.*

provoked the fury of tyrants. I said to Nero, Thou art a
bloodhound! I said to Christiern, Thou art a bloodhound! I said
60 to Muley Ismail, Thou art a bloodhound!–The tyrants invented
cruel torments, but did not kill me.——Ha! not to be able to die–
not to be able to die–not to be permitted to rest after the toils of
life–to be doomed to be imprisoned for ever in the clay-formed
dungeon–to be for ever clogged with this worthless body, its
65 load of diseases and infirmities–to be condemned to hold for
millenniums that yawning monster Sameness, and Time, that
hungry hyena, ever bearing children, and ever devouring again
her offspring!–Ha! not to be permitted to die! Awful avenger in
heaven, hast thou in thine armoury of wrath a punishment more
70 dreadful? then let it thunder upon me, command a hurricane to
sweep me down to the foot of Carmel, that I there may lie
extended; may pant, and writhe, and die!

This fragment is the translation of part of some German work,
whose title I have vainly endeavoured to discover. I picked it up,
75 dirty and torn, some years ago, in Lincoln's-Inn Fields.

vii. *135–6*

I will beget a Son, and he shall bear
The sins of all the world.

1   A book is put into our hands when children, called the Bible,
the purport of whose history is briefly this: That God made the
earth in six days, and there planted a delightful garden, in which
he placed the first pair of human beings. In the midst of the
5   garden he planted a tree, whose fruit, although within their reach,

Line 59. *I said to Christiern*] said to Christiern *BA*. Christiern was an alternative
spelling for Christian II of Denmark and Norway (1481–1559), known as
'Christian the Cruel'.
Line 60. *Muley Ismail*] Mulei Ismail *BA*. Moulay Ismail, Emperòr of Morocco
(1672–1727), known as 'the Bloodthirsty'.
Lines 65–6. *to hold*] to behold *BA*.
Line 68. *offspring!*] offsprings! *BA*.
Line 69. *thine armoury*] thy armory *BA*.
Line 72. *die!*] die! *BA*.
vii *135–6*] This note draws mainly on Hume's *Enquiry*, Paine's *Age of Reason*,
and Volney's *Ruins*, and incorporates material from S.'s *Letter to Lord Ellenbor-
ough* (1812).
Lines 1–18. *A book is put into our hands . . . everlasting fire*] The ironical summary
is based on that in *Ruins* ch. xxi; its final sentence refers to *Mark* xvi 14–16:
'Afterward he appeared unto the eleven . . . and upbraided them with their
unbelief . . . And he said unto them . . . he that believeth not shall be damned'.

they were forbidden to touch. That the Devil, in the shape of a
snake, persuaded them to eat of this fruit; in consequence of
which God condemned both them and their posterity yet unborn,
to satisfy his justice by their eternal misery. That, four thousand
10 years after these events, (the human race in the meanwhile having
gone unredeemed to perdition,) God engendered with the
betrothed wife of a carpenter in Judea (whose virginity was
nevertheless uninjured), and begat a Son, whose name was Jesus
Christ; and who was crucified and died, in order that no more
15 men might be devoted to hell-fire, he bearing the burthen of his
Father's displeasure by proxy. The book states, in addition, that
the soul of whoever disbelieves this sacrifice will be burned with
everlasting fire.
        During many ages of misery and darkness this story gained
20 implicit belief; but at length men arose who suspected that it was
a fable and imposture, and that Jesus Christ, so far from being a
God, was only a man like themselves. But a numerous set of
men, who derived and still derive immense emoluments from
this opinion, in the shape of a popular belief, told the vulgar, that,
25 if they did not believe in the Bible, they would be damned to all
eternity; and burned, imprisoned, and poisoned all the unbiassed
and unconnected enquirers who occasionally arose. They still
oppress them, so far as the people, now become more
enlightened, will allow.
30   The belief in all that the Bible contains, is called Christianity. A
Roman governor of Judea, at the instances of a priest-led mob,
crucified a man called Jesus eighteen centuries ago. He was a man
of pure life, who desired to rescue his countrymen from the
tyranny of their barbarous and degrading superstitions. The
35 common fate of all who desire to benefit mankind awaited him.
The rabble, at the instigation of the priests, demanded his death,
although his very judge made public acknowledgement of his
innocence. Jesus was sacrificed to the honour of that God with
whom he was afterwards confounded. It is of importance,
40 therefore, to distinguish between the pretended character of this
being as the Son of God and the Saviour of the world, and his real
character as a man, who, for a vain attempt to reform the world,
paid the forfeit of his life to that overbearing tyranny which has
since so long desolated the universe in his name. Whilst the one is

Lines 39–52. *It is of importance, therefore, to distinguish . . . the cause of suffering
humanity*] Paine discriminates at the opening of *Age of Reason* Part I between
'the *real* character of Jesus . . . This virtuous reformer and revolutionist' and the
'amphibious fraud' of the superstition constructed round him. Such a distinction is crucial in the account of Ahasuerus in vii 64–275, where Christ is the
false invention of 'human error's dense and purblind faith'.

45   a hypocritical demon, who announces himself as the God of
compassion and peace, even whilst he stretches forth his blood-
red hands with the sword of discord to waste the earth, having
confessedly devised this scheme of desolation from eternity; the
other stands in the foremost list of those true heroes, who have
50   died in the glorious martyrdom of liberty, and have braved
torture, contempt, and poverty, in the cause of suffering _
humanity.[1]

    The vulgar, ever in extremes, became persuaded that the
crucifixion of Jesus was a supernatural event. Testimonies of
55   miracles, so frequent in unenlightened ages, were not wanting to
prove that he was something divine. This belief, rolling through
the lapse of ages, met with the reveries of Plato and the
reasonings of Aristotle, and acquired force and extent, until the
divinity of Jesus became a dogma, which to dispute was death,
60   which to doubt was infamy.

    Christianity is now the established religion: he who attempts to
impugn it, must be contented to behold murderers and traitors
take precedence of him in public opinion; though, if his genius be
equal to his courage, and assisted by a peculiar coalition of
65   circumstances, future ages may exalt him to a divinity and
persecute others in his name, as he was persecuted in the name of
his predecessor in the homage of the world.

    The same means that have supported every other popular
belief, have supported Christianity. War, imprisonment,
70   assassination, and falsehood; deeds of unexampled and
incomparable atrocity have made it what it is. The blood shed by
the votaries of the God of mercy and peace, since the
establishment of his religion, would probably suffice to drown all
other sectaries now on the habitable globe. We derive from our
75   ancestors a faith thus fostered and supported: we quarrel,
persecute, and hate for its maintenance. Even under a
government which, whilst it infringes the very right of thought

    [1] Since writing this note I have seen reason to suspect, that Jesus was an
ambitious man, who aspired to the throne of Judea.

Lines 53–146. *The vulgar . . . essential to their being*] These 7 paragraphs follow,
often very closely, paras 8, 19–part of 22 of *A Letter to Lord Ellenborough*.
Line 57. *the reveries of Plato*] A phrase borrowed from Holbach's dismissive
'rêveries Platoniciennes' (*Système de la Nature* ii 131), and not in *Letter to Lord E.*
Lines 76–80. *Even under a government . . . outraged humanity*] Daniel Isaac Eaton
had been sentenced to the pillory and imprisonment on 15 May 1812 for
publishing Paine's *Age of Reason* Part III, and S. had published *A Letter to Lord
Ellenborough* in protest (July 1812). See *Cameron (1951)* 180–6.
S.'s footnote] Clark (*Prose* 104) quotes Paine, *Age of Reason* ch. iii: 'Neither is it
improbable that Jesus Christ had in contemplation the delivery of the Jewish
Nation from the bondage of the Romans' (*Paine Writings* iv 28).

and speech, boasts of permitting the liberty of the press, a man is
pilloried and imprisoned because he is a deist, and no one raises
80   his voice in the indignation of outraged humanity. But it is ever a
proof that the falsehood of a proposition is felt by those who use
coercion, not reasoning, to procure its admission; and a
dispassionate observer would feel himself more powerfully
interested in favour of a man, who, depending on the truth of his
85   opinions, simply stated his reasons for entertaining them, than in
that of his aggressor, who, daringly avowing his unwillingness or
incapacity to answer them by argument, proceeded to repress the
energies and break the spirit of their promulgator by that torture
and imprisonment whose infliction he could command.
90   Analogy seems to favour the opinion, that as, like other
systems, Christianity has arisen and augmented, so like them it
will decay and perish; that, as violence, darkness and deceit, not
reasoning and persuasion, have procured its admission among
mankind, so, when enthusiasm has subsided, and time, that
95   infallible controverter of false opinions, has involved its
pretended evidences in the darkness of antiquity, it will become
obsolete; that Milton's poem alone will give permanency to the
remembrance of its absurdities; and that men will laugh as
heartily at grace, faith, redemption, and original sin, as they now
100 do at the metamorphoses of Jupiter, the miracles of Romish
saints, the efficacy of witchcraft, and the appearance of departed
spirits.
        Had the Christian religion commenced and continued by the
mere force of reasoning and persuasion, the preceding analogy
105 would be inadmissible. We should never speculate on the future
obsoleteness of a system perfectly conformable to nature and
reason: it would endure so long as they endured; it would be a
truth as indisputable as the light of the sun, the criminality of
murder, and other facts, whose evidence, depending on our
110 organization and relative situations, must remain acknowledged
as satisfactory so long as man is man. It is an incontrovertible
fact, the consideration of which ought to repress the hasty
conclusions of credulity, or moderate its obstinacy in maintaining
them, that, had the Jews not been a fanatical race of men, had
115 even the resolution of Pontius Pilate been equal to his candour,
the Christian religion never could have prevailed, it could not
even have existed: on so feeble a thread hangs the most cherished
opinion of a sixth of the human race! When will the vulgar learn
humility? When will the pride of ignorance blush at having
120 believed before it could comprehend?
        Either the Christian religion is true, or it is false: if true, it
comes from God, and its authenticity can admit of doubt and
dispute no further than its omnipotent author is willing to allow.

Either the power or the goodness of God is called in question, if
125 he leaves those doctrines most essential to the well being of man
in doubt and dispute; the only ones which, since their
promulgation, have been the subject of unceasing cavil, the cause
of irreconcileable hatred. *If God has spoken, why is the universe not
convinced?*
130 There is this passage in the Christian Scriptures: 'Those who
obey not God, and believe not the Gospel of his Son; shall be
punished with everlasting destruction.' This is the pivot upon
which all religions turn: they all assume that it is in our power to
believe or not to believe; whereas the mind can only believe that
135 which it thinks true. A human being can only be supposed
accountable for those actions which are influenced by his will.
But belief is utterly distinct from and unconnected with volition:
it is the apprehension of the agreement or disagreement of the
ideas that compose any proposition. Belief is a passion, or
140 involuntary operation of the mind, and, like other passions, its
intensity is precisely proportionate to the degrees of excitement.
Volition is essential to merit or demerit. But the Christian
religion attaches the highest possible degrees of merit and demerit
to that which is worthy of neither, and which is totally
145 unconnected with the peculiar faculty of the mind, whose
presence is essential to their being.
Christianity was intended to reform the world: had an all-wise
Being planned it, nothing is more improbable than that it should
have failed: omniscience would infallibly have foreseen the
150 inutility of a scheme which experience demonstrates, to this age,
to have been utterly unsuccessful.
Christianity inculcates the necessity of supplicating the Deity.
Prayer may be considered under two points of view;—as an
endeavour to change the intentions of God, or as a formal
155 testimony of our obedience. But the former case supposes that
the caprices of a limited intelligence can occasionally instruct the
Creator of the world how to regulate the universe; and the latter,

Lines 128–9. If God has spoken, why is the universe not convinced?] A
translation of Holbach (ii 326), already quoted in S.'s note to vii 13, and used
also in the *Letter to Lord Ellenborough.*
Line 130. *There is this passage* . . .] Presumably *II Thessalonians* i 7–9: '. . .
when the Lord Jesus shall be revealed from heaven with his mighty angels, In
flaming fire taking vengeance on them that know not God, and that obey not
the gospel of our Lord Jesus Christ: Who shall be punished with everlasting
destruction . . .'
Lines 132–45. *This is the pivot* . . . *essential to their being*] The argument that
belief is involuntary, which derives from Locke (*Essay Concerning Human
Understanding* Bk IV ch. xviii, 'Faith and Reason') is also pleaded in S.'s *Letter.*

a certain degree of servility analogous to the loyalty demanded by
earthly tyrants. Obedience indeed is only the pitiful and cowardly
160   egotism of him who thinks that he can do something better than
       reason.
          Christianity, like all other religions, rests upon miracles,
       prophecies, and martyrdoms. No religion ever existed, which
       had not its prophets, its attested miracles, and, above all, crowds
165   of devotees who would bear patiently the most horrible tortures
       to prove its authenticity. It should appear that in no case can a
       discriminating mind subscribe to the genuineness of a miracle. A
       miracle is an infraction of nature's law, by a supernatural cause;
       by a cause acting beyond that eternal circle within which all
170   things are included. God breaks through the law of nature, that
       he may convince mankind of the truth of that revelation which,
       in spite of his precautions, has been, since its introduction, the
       subject of unceasing schism and cavil.
          Miracles resolve themselves into the following question:[1] –
175   Whether it is more probable the laws of nature, hitherto so
       immutably harmonious, should have undergone violation, or
       that a man should have told a lie? Whether it is more probable
       that we are ignorant of the natural cause of an event, or that we
       know the supernatural one? That, in old times, when the powers
180   of nature were less known than at present, a certain set of men
       were themselves deceived, or had some hidden motive for
       deceiving others; or that God begat a son, who, in his legislation,
       measuring merit by belief, evidenced himself to be totally
       ignorant of the powers of the human mind – of what is voluntary,
185   and what is the contrary?
          We have many instances of men telling lies; – none of an
       infraction of nature's laws, those laws of whose government
       alone we have any knowledge or experience. The records of all
       nations afford innumerable instances of men deceiving others
190   either from vanity or interest, or themselves being deceived by
       the limitedness of their views and their ignorance of natural
       causes: but where is the accredited case of God having come upon

          [1] See Hume's Essay, vol. ii. page 121.

S.'s footnote] S.'s reference is to Hume's *Enquiry Concerning Human Understanding* Section X Part i, 'Of Miracles', but the wording is much closer to
Paine's *Age of Reason* Part I; *Paine Writings* iv 79: '. . . it raises a question in the
mind . . . which is: Is it more probable that nature should go out of her course
or that a man should tell a lie? We have never seen, in our time, nature go out of
her course, but we have good reason to believe that millions of lies have been
told in the same time'. S. also follows Paine in exemplifying modern 'miracles'
from chemistry and from the restoration of people apparently drowned. See
also Holbach, *Système de la Nature* ii 18–20.

earth, to give the lie to his own creations? There would be
something truly wonderful in the appearance of a ghost; but the
195   assertion of a child that he saw one as he passed through the
church-yard is universally admitted to be less miraculous.

    But even supposing that a man should raise a dead body to life
before our eyes, and on this fact rest his claim to being considered
the son of God;–the Humane Society restores drowned persons,
200   and because it makes no mystery of the method it employs, its
members are not mistaken for the sons of God. All that we have a
right to infer from our ignorance of the cause of any event is that
we do not know it: had the Mexicans attended to this simple rule
when they heard the cannon of the Spaniards, they would not
205   have considered them as gods: the experiments of modern
chemistry would have defied the wisest philosophers of ancient
Greece and Rome to have accounted for them on natural
principles. An author of strong common sense has observed, that
'a miracle is no miracle at second-hand;' he might have added,
210   that a miracle is no miracle in any case; for until we are acquainted
with all natural causes, we have no reason to imagine others.

    There remains to be considered another proof of Christianity–
Prophecy. A book is written before a certain event, in which this
event is foretold; how could the prophet have foreknown it
215   without inspiration; how could he have been inspired without
God? The greatest stress is laid on the prophecies of Moses and
Hosea on the dispersion of the Jews, and that of Isaiah concerning
the coming of the Messiah. The prophecy of Moses is a collection
of every possible cursing and blessing; and it is so far from being
220   marvellous that the one of dispersion should have been fulfilled,
that it would have been more surprising if, out of all these, none
should have taken effect. In Deuteronomy, chap. xxviii, ver. 64,
where Moses explicitly foretells the dispersion, he states that they
shall there serve gods of wood and stone: 'And the Lord shall
225   scatter thee among all people, from the one end of the earth even
to the other, *and there thou shalt serve other gods, which neither thou
nor thy fathers have known, even gods of wood and stone.*' The Jews are

Line 208. *An author of strong common sense*] Probably Paine himself, who while
nowhere using these exact words repeats the principle in several places, e.g. at
the opening of *Age of Reason* Part I; *Paine Writings* iv 24: 'It is a contradiction in
terms and ideas to call anything a revelation that comes to us at second hand'.
Lines 222–40. *In Deuteronomy . . . clear and circumstantial*] Apparently S.'s own
venture in Biblical criticism. Paine's *Age of Reason* Part III had suggested the
method, but does not deal with any prophecy quoted here except that in *Isaiah*
liii. Part II had questioned the authenticity of the O.T. books. *subjected to these
curses*] *1840*; subjected to these causes *1813*. *The indelicate type*] i.e. that of
'mother turned wanton' (Israel).

at this day remarkably tenacious of their religion. Moses also
declares that they shall be subjected to these curses for
230   disobedience to his ritual: 'And it shall come to pass if thou wilt
not hearken unto the voice of the Lord thy God, to observe to do
all the commandments and statutes which I command you this
day, that all these curses shall come upon thee and overtake thee.'
Is this the real reason? The third, fourth and fifth chapters of
235   Hosea are a piece of immodest confession. The indelicate type
might apply in a hundred senses to a hundred things. The fifty-
third chapter of Isaiah is more explicit, yet it does not exceed in
clearness the oracles of Delphos. The historical proof, that
Moses, Isaiah and Hosea did write when they are said to have
240   written, is far from being clear and circumstantial.

   But prophecy requires proof in its character as a miracle; we
have no right to suppose that a man foreknew future events from
God, until it is demonstrated that he neither could know them by
his own exertions, nor that the writings which contain the
245   prediction could possibly have been fabricated after the event
pretended to be foretold. It is more probable that writings,
pretending to divine inspiration, should have been fabricated after
the fulfilment of their pretended prediction, than that they should
have really been divinely inspired; when we consider that the
250   latter supposition makes God at once the creator of the human
mind and ignorant of its primary powers, particularly as we have
numberless instances of false religions, and forged prophecies of
things long past, and no accredited case of God having conversed
with men directly or indirectly. It is also possible that the
255   description of an event might have foregone its occurrence; but
this is far from being a legitimate proof of a divine revelation, as
many men, not pretending to the character of a prophet, have
nevertheless, in this sense, prophesied.

   Lord Chesterfield was never yet taken for a prophet, even by a
260   bishop, yet he uttered this remarkable prediction: 'The despotic
government of France is screwed up to the highest pitch; a
revolution is fast approaching; that revolution, I am convinced,
will be radical and sanguinary.' This appeared in the letters of the
prophet long before the accomplishment of this wonderful

Lines 259–67. *Lord Chesterfield . . . foreknown them without inspiration?*] The
famous prediction of 25 December 1753 was not as striking as S. thought he
remembered: '. . . the affairs of France; they grow serious, and, in my opinion,
will grow more and more so every day . . . in short, all the symptoms which I
have ever met with in history, previous to great changes and revolutions in
Government, now exist, and daily increase in France' (*The Letters of Philip
Dormer Stanhope, 4th Earl of Chesterfield*, ed. B. Dobrée (1932) v 2065–6).

265   prediction. Now, have these particulars come to pass, or have
they not? If they have, how could the Earl have foreknown them
without inspiration? If we admit the truth of the Christian
religion on testimony such as this, we must admit, on the same
strength of evidence, that God has affixed the highest rewards to
270   belief, and the eternal tortures of the never-dying worm to
disbelief; both of which have been demonstrated to be
involuntary.

    The last proof of the Christian religion depends on the
influence of the Holy Ghost. Theologians divide the influence of
275   the Holy Ghost into its ordinary and extraordinary modes of
operation. The latter is supposed to be that which inspired the
Prophets and Apostles; and the former to be the grace of God,
which summarily makes known the truth of his revelation, to
those whose mind is fitted for its reception by a submissive
280   perusal of his word. Persons convinced in this manner, can do
anything but account for their conviction, describe the time at
which it happened, or the manner in which it came upon them. It
is supposed to enter the mind by other channels than those of the
senses, and therefore professes to be superior to reason founded
285   on their experience.

    Admitting, however, the usefulness or possibility of a divine
revelation, unless we demolish the foundations of all human
knowledge, it is requisite that our reason should previously
demonstrate its genuineness; for, before we extinguish the steady
290   ray of reason and common sense, it is fit that we should discover
whether we cannot do without their assistance, whether or no
there be any other which may suffice to guide us through the
labyrinth of life[1]: for, if a man is to be inspired upon all occasions,
if he is to be sure of a thing because he is sure, if the ordinary
295   operations of the spirit are not to be considered very
extraordinary modes of demonstration, if enthusiasm is to usurp
the place of proof, and madness that of sanity, all reasoning is
superfluous. The Mahometan dies fighting for his prophet, the
Indian immolates himself at the chariot-wheels of Brahma, the
300   Hottentot worships an insect, the Negro a bunch of feathers, the
Mexican sacrifices human victims! Their degree of conviction
must certainly be very strong: it cannot arise from conviction, it
must from feelings, the reward of their prayers. If each of these
should affirm, in opposition to the strongest possible arguments,
305   that inspiration carried internal evidence, I fear their inspired

    [1] See Locke's Essay on the Human Understanding, book iv. chap xix, on
Enthusiasm.

Line 302. *arise from conviction*] arise from reasoning *Rossetti 1870, eds.* Perhaps a
dittography; but 'conviction' may have two different senses here: (a) settled
persuasion (*OED* 7); (b) formal proof (*OED* 1).

brethren, the orthodox Missionaries, would be so uncharitable as
to pronounce them obstinate.

Miracles cannot be received as testimonies of a disputed fact,
because all human testimony has ever been insufficient to
310 establish the possibility of miracles. That which is incapable of
proof itself, is no proof of any thing else. Prophecy has also been
rejected by the test of reason. Those, then, who have been
actually inspired, are the only true believers in the Christian
religion.

315   Mox numine viso
            Virginei tumuere sinus, innuptaque mater
            Arcano stupuit compleri viscera partu
            Auctorem peritura suum. Mortalia corda
            Artificem texere poli, latuitque sub uno
320   Pectore, qui totum late complectitur orbem.
                                    Claudian, Carmen Paschali.

Does not so monstrous and disgusting an absurdity carry its
own infamy and refutation with itself?

viii. *203–7*

            Him, (still from hope to hope the bliss pursuing,
            Which, from the exhaustless lore of human weal
            Draws on the virtuous mind,) the thoughts that rise
            In time-destroying infiniteness, gift
            With self-enshrined eternity, &c.

1   Time is our consciousness of the succession of ideas in our
         mind. Vivid sensation, of either pain or pleasure, makes the time

Lines 315–20. *Mox numine viso* . . .] 'Soon, after the deity's visit, the virgin's
breasts swelled, and the unmarried mother was secretly astonished that, about
to experience her own maker, her vitals were filling with child. A mortal
womb hid the author of the sky, and under one bosom lay he who encircles the
whole wide globe' (Claudian, *Carmen Paschale* ('Easter Hymn'), now better
known as *De Salvatore* ('On the Saviour'), 7–13). S. omits two half-lines
between *poli* and *latuitque*: 'mundique repertor / Pars fuit humani generis'–
'and the inventor of the world became part of the human race'. Modern texts
have *paritura* in line 4 ('about to bring forth'). Claudian was a fifth-century
pagan poet, and the lines are almost certainly ironical. Alan Cameron comments (*Claudian: Poetry and Propaganda at the Court of Honorus* (Oxford 1970)
450–1): 'What a curious irony that Shelley should have seen the last great pagan
poet of Rome not as an ally, but, judged by this one *tour de force*, as the epitome
of all that was worst in Christianity'.
viii 203–7] *Draws*] Dawns *1813* (see note on text).
Lines 1–27. *Time* . . .] S. had learnt from Locke that 'we have no perception of

seem long, as the common phrase is, because it renders us more
acutely conscious of our ideas. If a mind be conscious of an
5   hundred ideas during one minute, by the clock, and of two
hundred during another, the latter of these spaces would actually
occupy so much greater extent in the mind as two exceed one in
quantity. If, therefore, the human mind, by any future
improvement of its sensibility, should become conscious of an
10   infinite number of ideas in a minute, that minute would be
eternity. I do not hence infer that the actual space between the
birth and death of a man will ever be prolonged; but that his
sensibility is perfectible, and that the number of ideas which his

---

Duration, but by considering the train of *Ideas*, that take their turns in our
Understandings . . . So that to me it seems, that the *constant and regular
Succession of Ideas* in a waking Man, *is*, as it were, *the Measure* and Standard of *all
other Successions* . . .' (*Essay Concerning Human Understanding* (1690) Bk II ch. xiv
paras 4, 12). Condillac and others stressed the relativity of this standard of
Time: 'L'idée de la durée n'est point absolue, et lorsque nous disons que le
temps coule rapidement ou lentement, cela ne signifie autre chose, sinon que
les révolutions qui servent à le mesurer, se font avec plus de rapidité ou avec
plus de lenteur que nos idées ne se succèdent . . . La notion de la durée est donc
toute relative: chacun n'en juge que par la succession de ses idées: et vraisemblablement il n'y a pas deux hommes qui, dans un temps donné, comptent un
égal nombre d'instans'. Hence 'eternity' may be conceived in terms of relatively speeded-up or slowed-down perception. (Condillac, *Traité des Sensations*
(1754) I iv 11–18). It followed that true length of life depended on mental
activity: 'It is certain that the natural measure of time depends solely on the
succession of our ideas. Were it possible for the mind to be totally occupied
with a single idea for a day, a week, or a month, these portions of time would
appear to be nothing more than so many instants. Hence a philosopher often
lives as long in one day, as a clown or a savage does in a week or a month spent
in mental inactivity and want of thought' (Smellie, *The Philosophy of Natural
History* i 519). S.'s references are to *Political Justice* Bk IV ch. ix, i 410–14, and to
Condorcet's Époque X, not IX. Godwin thought 'It seems to be consciousness
rather than the succession of ideas, that measures time to the mind . . . time
seems, in our apprehension, to flow, now with a precipitated, and now with a
tardy course', and he concluded: 'If we can have a series of three hundred and
twenty ideas in a second of time, why should it be supposed that we may not
hereafter arrive at the skill of carrying on a great number of contemporaneous
processes without disorder?' This and other mental adjustments could mean
that 'the term of human life may be prolonged, and that by the immediate
operation of intellect, beyond any limits which we are able to assign' (*Political
Justice* Bk VIII ch. ix, ii 525, 527). Condorcet also forecast an indefinite
extension to average human life, but purely by the elimination of disease and
other physical disabilities. *ephemeron*] May-fly.

mind is capable of receiving is indefinite. One man is stretched on
15   the rack during twelve hours; another sleeps soundly in his bed:
the difference of time perceived by these two persons is immense;
one hardly will believe that half an hour has elapsed, the other
could credit that centuries had flown during his agony. Thus, the
life of a man of virtue and talent, who should die in his thirtieth
20   year, is, with regard to his own feelings, longer than that of a
miserable priest-ridden slave, who dreams out a century of
dulness. The one has perpetually cultivated his mental faculties,
has rendered himself master of his thoughts, can abstract and
generalize amid the lethargy of every-day business;—the other can
25   slumber over the brightest moments of his being, and is unable to
remember the happiest hour of his life. Perhaps the perishing
ephemeron enjoys a longer life than the tortoise.

>   Dark flood of time!
>   Roll as it listeth thee—I measure not
> 30   By months or moments thy ambiguous course.
>   Another may stand by me on the brink
>   And watch the bubble whirled beyond his ken
>   That pauses at my feet. The sense of love,
>   The thirst for action, and the impassioned thought
> 35   Prolong my being: if I wake no more,
>   My life more actual living will contain
>   Than some grey veteran's of the world's cold school,
>   Whose listless hours unprofitably roll,
>   By one enthusiast feeling unredeemed.

40   *See Godwin's Pol. Jus. vol. i. page 411;—and Condorcet, Esquisse d'un*
Tableau Historique des Progrès de l'Esprit Humain, Epoque ix.

viii. *211—12*

>   No longer now
>   He slays the lamb that looks him in the face.

1   I hold that the depravity of the physical and moral nature of
man originated in his unnatural habits of life. The origin of man,
like that of the universe of which he is a part, is enveloped in
impenetrable mystery. His generations either had a beginning, or

Line 28. *Dark flood of time! . . .*] This passage forms lines 58–69 of 'To Harriet'
('It is not blasphemy to hope'): see headnote to this poem. *on the brink*] on thy
brink *Esd. That pauses*] Which pauses *Esd. veteran's*] *1829*; veterans' *1813*;
veterans *Esd.*
viii *211—12*] This note is almost identical with S.'s 1813 pamphlet *A Vindication
of Natural Diet* (see headnote). Major variants are recorded below. On 14
March 1812 Harriet S. wrote: '. . . we have forsworn meat & adopted the
Pithagorean system; about a fortnight has elapsed since the change and we do
not find ourselves any the worse for it' (*L* i 274–5). Thus S. became a

5   they had not. The weight of evidence in favour of each of these
suppositions seems tolerably equal; and it is perfectly
unimportant to the present argument which is assumed. The
language spoken however by the mythology of nearly all
religions seems to prove, that at some distant period man forsook

10   the path of nature, and sacrificed the purity and happiness of his

---

vegetarian from about 1 March 1812 (*Hogg* ii 414 is a year out), and remained
one, generally speaking, for the rest of his life (see D. L. Clark, 'The Date &
Source of S.'s Vindication of Natural Diet', *SP* xxxvi (January 1939) 70–6).
Horace Smith recalled that in 1816 'For several years Shelley had scrupulously
refrained from the use of animal food, not upon the Pythagorean or Brahmi-
nical doctrine that such diet necessitates a wanton, and, therefore, a cruel,
destruction of God's creatures, but from an impression that to kill the native
"burghers of the wood", or tenants of the flood and sky . . . tends to fiercen and
animalise both the slaughterer and devourer' ('A Greybeard's Gossip about his
Literary Acquaintance', *New Monthly Magazine* lxxi (October 1847) 289). This
is the purport of Joseph Ritson's *An Essay on Abstinence from Animal Food as a
Moral Duty* (1802), a main influence on S.'s note. S.'s general 'recognition of
the important relation between man's physical life and his moral and intellectual life' may owe much, as I. J. Kapstein argues (*PMLA* lii (March 1937)
238–43), to Pierre Jean George Cabanis, *Rapports du Physique et du Moral de
l'Homme* (Paris 1802). The second rational basis for S.'s vegetarianism was its
salubrity, the main theme of John Frank Newton's *The Return to Nature; or, a
Defence of the Vegetable Regimen* (1811), which was deeply influenced by Dr
Lambe's clinical experience (William Lambe, *Reports on the effect of a peculiar
regimen on scirrhous tumours and cancerous ulcers*, 1809). S. also drew directly on
Lambe's *Reports*: all his citations of Cuvier's *Leçons d'Anatomie Comparée* are
from Lambe, and he evidently did not read Cuvier himself (see below). S.'s
third incentive was economic and social: in a world where the poor starved,
agricultural land was wasted in raising animal food for the rich.

Lines 2–13. *The origin of man . . . an obvious correspondence*] No authentic human
fossils had yet been found, and non-literalist opinion was reserved on the
subject of man's origins. Georges Cuvier (*Theory of the Earth* (1813; 4th English
edn 1822) 133) declared: 'Every circumstance . . . contributes to establish this
position–That the human race did not exist in the countries in which the fossil
bones of animals have been discovered . . . I do not presume, however, to
conclude that man did not exist at all before these epochs. He may have then
inhabited some narrow regions, whence he went forth to re-people the earth
after the cessation of these terrible revolutions and overwhelmings'. Holbach
also reserved judgement, while assuming a link between changes in the earth's
condition, past and future, and in that of its human inhabitants: 'Si l'on nous
oblige de remonter, par l'imagination, à l'origine des choses et au berceau du
genre humain, nous dirons qu'il est probable que l'homme fut une suite
nécessaire du debrouillement de notre globe . . . que son existence est coordi-
née avec celle de ce globe . . . En supposant donc des changemens dans la
position de notre globe, l'homme primitif différoit, peut-être, plus de l'hom-

being to unnatural appetites. The date of this event seems to have
also been that of some great change in the climates of the earth,
with which it has an obvious correspondence. The allegory of
Adam and Eve eating of the tree of evil, and entailing upon their
15 posterity the wrath of God, and the loss of everlasting life, admits
of no other explanation than the disease and crime that have
flowed from unnatural diet. Milton was so well aware of this,
that he makes Raphael thus exhibit to Adam the consequence of
his disobedience.

20   Immediately a place
Before his eyes appeared: sad, noisome, dark:
A lazar-house it seem'd; wherein were laid
Numbers of all diseased: all maladies
Of ghastly spasm, or racking torture, qualms
25 Of heart-sick agony, all feverous kinds,
Convulsions, epilepsies, fierce catarrhs,
Intestine stone and ulcer, cholic pangs,
Dæmoniac frenzy, moping melancholy,
And moon-struck madness, pining atrophy,
30 Marasmus, and wide-wasting pestilence,
Dropsies, and asthmas, and joint-racking rheums.

And how many thousands more might not be added to this
frightful catalogue!
The story of Prometheus is one likewise which, although

---

me actuel, que le quadrupede ne diffère de l'insecte' (*Système de la Nature* i
91–2). Cuvier surveys the mythological accounts and concludes: 'Thus all the
nations which possess any records or ancient traditions, uniformly declare that
they have been recently renewed, after a grand revolution in nature' (loc. cit.
167). Rousseau and J. F. Newton associate the renewal with a climatic change:
'"Dicéarque, dit saint Jérôme, rapporte, dans ses livres des antiquités grec-
ques, que, sous le règne de Saturne, où la terre étoit encore fertile par elle-
même, nul homme ne mangeoit de chair, mais tous vivoient des fruits et des
légumes qui croissoient naturellement"' (*Discours sur l'Origine et les Fondements
de l'Inégalité parmi les Hommes* (1753) n.3); '. . . the poles of the earth were at
some distant period perpendicular to its orbit, as those of the planet Jupiter
now are, whose inhabitants must therefore enjoy a perpetual spring. We can
scarcely look around us without being struck by the proofs of violence and
convulsion which prevailed throughout this our ruined planet at the great
catastrophe of which the fable of Phaeton was intended to perpetuate the
memory' (*Return to Nature* 10).
Line 17. *Milton*] *PL* xi 477–88. Michael (not Raphael) is showing Adam what
results from 'Intemperance . . . in Meats and Drinks'.
Line 34. *The story of Prometheus*] Taken from J. F. Newton, *Return to Nature*
6–9.

35 universally admitted to be allegorical, has never been
satisfactorily explained. Prometheus stole fire from heaven, and
was chained for this crime to mount Caucasus, where a vulture
continually devoured his liver, that grew to meet its hunger.
Hesiod says, that, before the time of Prometheus, mankind were
40 exempt from suffering; that they enjoyed a vigorous youth, and
that death, when at length it came, approached like sleep, and
gently closed their eyes. Again, so general was this opinion, that
Horace, a poet of the Augustan age, writes—

Audax omnia perpeti,
45 Gens humana ruit per vetitum nefas;
Audax Iapeti genus
Ignem fraude mala gentibus intulit:
Post ignem ætheriâ domo
Subductum, macies et nova febrium
50 Terris incubuit cohors,
Semotique prius tarda necessitas
Lethi corripuit gradum.

How plain a language is spoken by all this. Prometheus (who
represents the human race) effected some great change in the
55 condition of his nature, and applied fire to culinary purposes; thus
inventing an expedient for screening from his disgust the horrors
of the shambles. From this moment his vitals were devoured by
the vulture of disease. It consumed his being in every shape of its
loathsome and infinite variety, inducing the soul-quelling
60 sinkings of premature and violent death. All vice arose from the
ruin of healthful innocence. Tyranny, superstition, commerce,
and inequality, were then first known, when reason vainly
attempted to guide the wanderings of exacerbated passion. I
conclude this part of the subject with an extract from Mr
65 Newton's Defence of Vegetable Regimen, from whom I have
borrowed this interpretation of the fable of Prometheus.
   'Making allowance for such transposition of the events of the
allegory as time might produce after the important truths were

Line 39. *Hesiod*] *Works and Days* 110–23, also taken from *Return to Nature* 9.
Lines 44–52. *Audax omnia . . . gradum*] Horace, *Odes* I iii 25–33: 'Daring to
suffer everything, the human race rushes through forbidden crime. The daring
son of Iapetus [Prometheus] brought fire to humanity by wicked deceit. After
fire had been stolen from its heavenly home, famine and a new host of fevers
invested the earth, and inevitable death, hitherto slow and distant, quickened
its step'. S. took this quotation from *Return to Nature* 9.
Lines 67–86. *'Making allowance . . . to his grave.'*] Not quoted but summarized
from *Return to Nature* 6–9, as is the passage on wild and domestic animals
immediately following.

forgotten, which this portion of the ancient mythology was
70   intended to transmit, the drift of the fable seems to be this:—Man
at his creation was endowed with the gift of perpetual youth; that
is, he was not formed to be a sickly suffering creature as we now
see him, but to enjoy health, and to sink by slow degrees into the
bosom of his parent earth without disease or pain. Prometheus
75   first taught the use of animal food (primus bovem occidit
Prometheus[1]) and of fire, with which to render it more digestible
and pleasing to the taste. Jupiter, and the rest of the gods,
foreseeing the consequences of these inventions, were amused or
irritated at the short-sighted devices of the newly-formed
80   creature, and left him to experience the sad effects of them.
Thirst, the necessary concomitant of a flesh diet,' (perhaps of all
diet vitiated by culinary preparation,) 'ensued; water was resorted
to, and man forfeited the inestimable gift of health which he had
received from heaven: he became diseased, the partaker of a
85   precarious existence, and no longer descended slowly to his
grave.'[2]

> But just disease to luxury succeeds,
> And every death its own avenger breeds;
> The fury passions from that blood began,
90 > And turned on man a fiercer savage—man.

Man, and the animals whom he has infected with his society,
or depraved by his dominion, are alone diseased. The wild hog,
the mouflon, the bison, and the wolf, are perfectly exempt from
malady, and invariably die either from external violence, or
95   natural old age. But the domestic hog, the sheep, the cow, and
the dog, are subject to an incredible variety of distempers; and,
like the corrupters of their nature, have physicians who thrive
upon their miseries. The supereminence of man is like Satan's, a
supereminence of pain; and the majority of his species, doomed
100   to penury, disease and crime, have reason to curse the untoward
event, that by enabling him to communicate his sensations, raised
him above the level of his fellow animals. But the steps that have

[1] Plin. Nat. Hist. lib. vii. sect. 57.
[2] Return to Nature. Cadell, 1811.

Lines 75–6. *(primus bovem occidit Prometheus)*] Pliny, *Historia Naturalis* VII lvi
209: '"Animal occidit primus Hyperbius Martis filius, Prometheus bovem".
Hyperbius, the son of Mars, first killed an animal, Prometheus first slew an ox'
(quotation and translation in full from *Return to Nature* 8).
Lines 87–90. *But just disease . . . savage—man*] Pope (*Essay on Man* iii 165–8)
laments man's decline from the state of Nature, when 'No murder cloth'd him,
and no murder fed'.

been taken are irrevocable. The whole of human science is
comprised in one question:–How can the advantages of intellect
105 and civilization be reconciled with the liberty and pure pleasures
of natural life? How can we take the benefits, and reject the evils
of the system, which is now interwoven with all the fibres of our
being?–I believe that abstinence from animal food and spirituous
liquors would in a great measure capacitate us for the solution of
110 this important question.

It is true, that mental and bodily derangement is attributable in
part to other deviations from rectitude and nature than those
which concern diet. The mistakes cherished by society respecting
the connection of the sexes, whence the misery and diseases of
115 unsatisfied celibacy, unenjoying prostitution, and the premature
arrival of puberty necessarily spring; the putrid atmosphere of
crowded cities; the exhalations of chemical processes; the
muffling of our bodies in superfluous apparel; the absurd
treatment of infants:–all these, and innumerable other causes,
120 contribute their mite to the mass of human evil.

Comparative anatomy teaches us that man resembles
frugivorous animals in every thing, and carnivorous in nothing;
he has neither claws wherewith to seize his prey, nor distinct and
pointed teeth to tear the living fibre. A Mandarin of the first class,
125 with nails two inches long, would probably find them alone
inefficient to hold even a hare. After every subterfuge of
gluttony, the bull must be degraded into the ox, and the ram into
the wether, by an unnatural and inhuman operation, that the
flaccid fibre may offer a fainter resistance to rebellious nature. It is
130 only by softening and disguising dead flesh by culinary
preparation, that it is rendered susceptible of mastication or
digestion; and that the sight of its bloody juices and raw horror
does not excite intolerable loathing and disgust. Let the advocate
of animal food force himself to a decisive experiment on its
135 fitness, and, as Plutarch recommends, tear a living lamb with his
teeth, and plunging his head into its vitals, slake his thirst with
the steaming blood; when fresh from the deed of horror, let him
revert to the irresistible instincts of nature that would rise in
judgment against it, and say, Nature formed me for such work as
140 this. Then, and then only, would he be consistent.

Lines 103–8. *The whole of human science . . . fibres of our being?*] Cp. 'Essay on
Christianity' (1817): 'Nothing is more obviously false than that the remedy for
the inequality among men consists in their return to the condition of savages
and beasts' (*Prose* 210).

Lines 111–20 *It is true, that mental . . . the mass of human evil.*] Not in *A
Vindication*.

Lines 117–18. *the muffling of our bodies in superfluous apparel*] Newton practised
nudism with his family; an excellent account is in *Hogg* ii 287–91.

Man resembles no carnivorous animal. There is no exception,
unless man be one, to the rule of herbivorous animals having
cellulated colons.

The orang-outang perfectly resembles man both in the order
145   and number of his teeth. The orang-outang is the most
anthropomorphous of the ape tribe, all of which are strictly
frugivorous. There is no other species of animals, which live on
different food, in which this analogy exists.[1] In many frugivorous
animals, the canine teeth are more pointed and distinct than those
150   of man. The resemblance also of the human stomach to that of
the orang-outang, is greater than to that of any other animal.

The intestines are also identical with those of herbivorous
animals, which present a larger surface for absorption and have
ample and cellulated colons. The cœcum also, though short, is
155   larger than that of carnivorous animals; and even here the orang-
outang retains its accustomed similarity.

The structure of the human frame then is that of one fitted to a
pure vegetable diet, in every essential particular. It is true, that the
reluctance to abstain from animal food, in those who have been
160   long accustomed to its stimulus, is so great in some persons of
weak minds, as to be scarcely overcome; but this is far from

[1] Cuvier, Leçons d'Anat. Comp. tom. iii. pages 169, 373, 443, 465, 480. Rees's
Cyclopædia, article Man.

Lines 141–56. *Man resembles . . . accustomed similarity*] S. himself cannot have
read Cuvier's *Leçons d'Anatomie Comparée* (Paris 1805) as the page-numbers he
quotes from vol. iii are all quoted by Lambe in his *Reports* and are not all
correct, or in correct order. A selection is itemized below. *Man resembles . . .
cellulated colons*] From Lambe's *Reports* 27, or from *Return to Nature* 11, quoting
Lambe. *The orang-outang perfectly . . . number of his teeth*] Cuvier's chart (*Leçons
d'Anatomie* iii 144–not 169, as given in Lambe and S.) does not positively
support S.'s statement, but shows only that the type and number of teeth are
identical in men and monkeys. S. is quoting Lambe's *Reports* 28: 'The teeth . . .
Here again, the ape tribe perfectly resembles man, both in order and number;
nor is there any other species of animals, in which this analogy exists . . . In the
form of the canine teeth he agrees with the orang very nearly'. Cuvier (*Leçons
d'Anatomie* 156–7) actually remarks that the *form* of the canines differs in men,
in monkeys, and in orang-outangs. *The resemblance also of the human stomach . . .
any other animal*] Quoted from Lambe's *Reports*, whose reference to Cuvier's
Leçons 373 is correct. *The intestines . . . cellulated colons*] From Lambe's *Reports*,
including the wrong page reference to Cuvier (448 for 441). *The cœcum also . . .
similarity*] S.'s (and Lambe's) references to Cuvier pp. 465 and 480 are correct,
but it is Lambe S. quotes (p. 31): '. . . even in this point the orang species of ape
retains its accustomed similarity'.
Line 141. *exception, unless man*] exception, except man *A Vindication*.
Lines 147–8. *animals, which live on different food, in which*] animals in which *A
Vindication*.

bringing any argument in its favour. A lamb, which was fed for
some time on flesh by a ship's crew, refused its natural diet at the
end of the voyage. There are numerous instances of horses,
165 sheep, oxen, and even wood-pigeons, having been taught to live
upon flesh, until they have loathed their natural aliment. Young
children evidently prefer pastry, oranges, apples, and other fruit,
to the flesh of animals; until, by the gradual depravation of the
digestive organs, the free use of vegetables has for a time
170 produced serious inconveniences; *for a time*, I say, since there
never was an instance wherein a change from spirituous liquors
and animal food to vegetables and pure water, has failed
ultimately to invigorate the body, by rendering its juices bland
and consentaneous, and to restore to the mind that cheerfulness
175 and elasticity, which not one in fifty possesses on the present
system. A love of strong liquors is also with difficulty taught to
infants. Almost every one remembers the wry faces which the
first glass of port produced. Unsophisticated instinct is invariably
unerring; but to decide on the fitness of animal food, from the
180 perverted appetites which its constrained adoption produces, is to
make the criminal a judge in his own cause: it is even worse, it is
appealing to the infatuated drunkard in a question of the salubrity
of brandy.
    What is the cause of morbid action in the animal system? Not
185 the air we breathe, for our fellow denizens of nature breathe the
same uninjured; not the water we drink, (if remote from the

Lines 166–70. *Young children . . . serious inconveniences*] From Rousseau's *Émile
ou de l'Éducation* (1762; Paris 1964) 168: 'Une des preuves que le goût de la
viande n'est pas naturel à l'homme, est l'indifférence que les enfants ont pour ce
mets-là, et la préférence qu'ils donnent tous à des nourritures végétales, telles
que le laitage, la pâtisserie, les fruits, etc. Il importe surtout de ne pas dénaturer
ce goût primitif, et de ne point rendre les enfants carnassiers; si ce n'est pour
leur santé, c'est pour leur caractère; car, de quelque manière qu'on explique
l'expérience, il est certain que les grands mangeurs de viande sont en général
cruels et féroces plus que les autres hommes; cette observation est de tous les
lieux et de tous les temps'. The edition used by S. is uncertain. Lambe (*Reports*
9–10) follows this passage closely.
Lines 176–9. *A love of strong liquors . . . invariably unerring*] A variant of *Émile*
165: 'La première fois qu'un sauvage boit du vin, il fait la grimace et le rejette . .
. nous serions tous abstèmes si l'on ne nous eût donné du vin dans nos jeunes
ans'.
Line 186. *not the water we drink*] J. F. Newton inveighs against the evils of
undistilled water (*Return to Nature* 20–30) on the authority of Lambe, who did
in fact assert that 'the practice of all drinking whatever is equally unnatural'
(*Reports* 3). Much drinking water was indeed heavily polluted; but S. draws
back here from this extreme position.

pollutions of man and his inventions,[1]) for the animals drink it
too; not the earth we tread upon; not the unobscured sight of
glorious nature, in the wood, the field, or the expanse of sky and
190   ocean; nothing that we are or do in common with the undiseased
inhabitants of the forest. Something then wherein we differ from
them: our habit of altering our food by fire, so that our appetite is
no longer a just criterion for the fitness of its gratification. Except
in children, there remain no traces of that instinct which
195   determines, in all other animals, what aliment is natural or
otherwise; and so perfectly obliterated are they in the reasoning
adults of our species, that it has become necessary to urge
considerations drawn from comparative anatomy to prove that
we are naturally frugivorous.
200   Crime is madness. Madness is disease. Whenever the cause of
disease shall be discovered, the root, from which all vice and
misery have so long overshadowed the globe, will lie bare to the
axe. All the exertions of man, from that moment, may be
considered as tending to the clear profit of his species. No sane
205   mind in a sane body resolves upon a real crime. It is a man of
violent passions, bloodshot eyes, and swollen veins, that alone
can grasp the knife of murder. The system of a simple diet
promises no Utopian advantages. It is no mere reform of
legislation, whilst the furious passions and evil prope. ˙ ˜ of the
210   human heart, in which it had its origin, are still unassua₂
strikes at the root of all evil, and is an experiment which n , be
tried with success, not alone by nations, but by small societies,
families, and even individuals. In no cases has a return to
vegetable diet produced the slightest injury; in most it has been
215   attended with changes undeniably beneficial. Should ever a
physician be born with the genius of Locke, I am persuaded that
he might trace all bodily and mental derangements to our
unnatural habits, as clearly as that philosopher has traced all
knowledge to sensation. What prolific sources of disease are not
220   those mineral and vegetable poisons that have been introduced
for its extirpation! How many thousands have become murderers
and robbers, bigots and domestic tyrants, dissolute and
abandoned adventurers, from the use of fermented liquors; who,
had they slaked their thirst only with pure water, would have
225   lived but to diffuse the happiness of their own unperverted
feelings. How many groundless opinions and absurd institutions

[1] The necessity of resorting to some means of purifying water, and the disease
which arises from its adulteration in civilized countries, is sufficiently apparent—
See Dr. Lambe's Reports on Cancer. I do not assert that the use of water is in itself
unnatural, but that the unperverted palate would swallow no liquid capable of
occasioning disease.

Line 224. *thirst only with pure water*] thirst only at the mountain stream *A
Vindication.*

have not received a general sanction from the sottishness and
intemperance of individuals! Who will assert that, had the
populace of Paris satisfied their hunger at the ever-furnished table
230   of vegetable nature, they would have lent their brutal suffrage to
the proscription-list of Robespierre? Could a set of men, whose
passions were not perverted by unnatural stimuli, look with
coolness on an auto da fè? Is it to be believed that a being of gentle
feelings, rising from his meal of roots, would take delight in
235   sports of blood? Was Nero a man of temperate life? could you
read calm health in his cheek, flushed with ungovernable
propensities of hatred for the human race? Did Muley Ismael's
pulse beat evenly, was his skin transparent, did his eyes beam
with healthfulness, and its invariable concomitants, cheerfulness
240   and benignity? Though history has decided none of these
questions, a child could not hesitate to answer in the negative.
Surely the bile-suffused cheek of Buonaparte, his wrinkled brow
and yellow eye, the ceaseless inquietude of his nervous system,
speak no less plainly the character of his unresting ambition than
245   his murders and his victories. It is impossible, had Buonaparte
descended from a race of vegetable feeders, that he could have
had either the inclination or the power to ascend the throne of the
Bourbons. The desire of tyranny could scarcely be excited in the
individual, the power to tyrannize would certainly not be
250   delegated by a society neither frenzied by inebriation nor
rendered impotent and irrational by disease. Pregnant indeed
with inexhaustible calamity is the renunciation of instinct, as it
concerns our physical nature; arithmetic cannot enumerate, nor
reason perhaps suspect, the multitudinous sources of disease in
255   civilized life. Even common water, that apparently innoxious
pabulum, when corrupted by the filth of populous cities, is a
deadly and insidious destroyer.[1] Who can wonder that all the
inducements held out by God himself in the Bible to virtue
should have been vainer than a nurse's tale; and that those
260   dogmas, by which he has there excited and justified the most

[1] Lambe's Reports on Cancer.

Lines 228–9. *had the populace of Paris satisfied*] had the populace of Paris drank at
the pure source of the Seine, and satisfied *A Vindication*.
Lines 255–7. *Even common water . . . insidious destroyer*] 'Common Water is the
vehicle, in which the poison of Cancer is introduced into the system' (Lambe's
Reports 57).
Lines 257–66. *Who can wonder . . . original and universal sin*] i.e. the eating habits
of Christians have predisposed them to obey the bloodthirsty rather than the
gentler precepts of the Bible.
Lines 260–1. *dogmas, by which . . . should*] dogmas, apparently favourable to the
intolerant and angry passions, should *A Vindication*.

ferocious propensities, should have alone been deemed essential;
whilst Christians are in the daily practice of all those habits,
which have infected with disease and crime, not only the
reprobate sons, but these favoured children of the common
265   Father's love? Omnipotence itself could not save them from the
consequences of this original and universal sin.

There is no disease, bodily or mental, which adoption of
vegetable diet and pure water has not infallibly mitigated,
wherever the experiment has been fairly tried. Debility is
270   gradually converted into strength, disease into healthfulness;
madness, in all its hideous variety, from the ravings of the
fettered maniac, to the unaccountable irrationalities of ill temper,
that make a hell of domestic life, into a calm and considerate
evenness of temper, that alone might offer a certain pledge of the
275   future moral reformation of society. On a natural system of diet,
old age would be our last and our only malady; the term of our
existence would be protracted; we should enjoy life, and no
longer preclude others from the enjoyment of it; all sensational
delights would be infinitely more exquisite and perfect; the very
280   sense of being would then be a continued pleasure, such as we
now feel it in some few and favoured moments of our youth. By
all that is sacred in our hopes for the human race, I conjure those
who love happiness and truth, to give a fair trial to the vegetable
system. Reasoning is surely superfluous on a subject whose
285   merits an experience of six months would set for ever at rest. But
it is only among the enlightened and benevolent that so great a
sacrifice of appetite and prejudice can be expected, even though
its ultimate excellence should not admit of dispute. It is found
easier, by the short-sighted victims of disease, to palliate their
290   torments by medicine, than to prevent them by regimen. The
vulgar of all ranks are invariably sensual and indocile; yet I cannot
but feel myself persuaded, that when the benefits of vegetable diet
are mathematically proved; when it is as clear, that those who live
naturally are exempt from premature death, as that nine is not
295   one, the most sottish of mankind will feel a preference towards a
long and tranquil, contrasted with a short and painful life. On the
average, out of sixty persons, four die in three years. Hopes are
entertained that, in April 1814, a statement will be given, that
sixty persons, all having lived more than three years on
300   vegetables and pure water, are then *in perfect health*. More than

Lines 297–305. *Hopes are entertained . . . without the slightest illness*] These sixty
persons must all have become vegetarians at the latest by March 1811, a year
before the S.'s, but S. makes no claim to be among them. Presumably the
number would be assembled from cases of varying seniority, as the Lambe and
Newton families were already veterans of seven years' standing.

two years have now elapsed; *not one of them has died*; no such
example will be found in any sixty persons taken at random.
Seventeen persons of all ages (the families of Dr Lambe and Mr
Newton) have lived for seven years on this diet without a death,
305 and almost without the slightest illness. Surely, when we
consider that some of these were infants, and one a martyr to
asthma now nearly subdued, we may challenge any seventeen
persons taken at random in this city to exhibit a parallel case.
Those who may have been excited to question the rectitude of
310 established habits of diet, by these loose remarks, should consult
Mr Newton's luminous and eloquent essay.[1]
When these proofs come fairly before the world, and are clearly
seen by all who understand arithmetic, it is scarcely possible that
abstinence from aliments demonstrably pernicious should not
315 become universal. In proportion to the number of proselytes, so
will be the weight of evidence: and when a thousand persons can
be produced, living on vegetables and distilled water, who have
to dread no disease but old age, the world will be compelled to
regard animal flesh and fermented liquors as slow but certain
320 poisons. The change which would be produced by simpler habits
on political economy is sufficiently remarkable. The
monopolizing eater of animal flesh would no longer destroy his
constitution by devouring an acre at a meal, and many loaves of
bread would cease to contribute to gout, madness and apoplexy,
325 in the shape of a pint of porter, or a dram of gin, when appeasing
the long-protracted famine of the hard-working peasant's hungry
babes. The quantity of nutritious vegetable matter, consumed in
fattening the carcase of an ox, would afford ten times the
sustenance, undepraving indeed, and incapable of generating

---

[1] Return to Nature, or Defence of Vegetable Regimen. Cadell, 1811.

Line 311. *eloquent essay.*] After these words, *A Vindication* adds: 'It is from that
book and from the conversation of its excellent and enlightened author that I
have derived the materials which I here present to the public'.
Lines 320–33. *The change . . . incapable of calculation*] 'Many ranks of people,
whose ordinary diet was, in the last century, prepare'd allmost entirely from
milk, roots and vegetables, now require, every day, a considerable portion of
the flesh of animals. Hence a great part of the richest lands of the country are
converted to pasturage. Much, allso, of the bread-corn, which went directly to
the nourishment of human bodys, now onely contributes to it, by fatening the
flesh of sheep and oxen. The mass and volume of provisions are hereby
diminish'd; and what is gain'd in the melioration of the soil is lost in the quality
of the produce' (Joseph Ritson, *An Essay on Abstinence from Animal Food, as a
Moral Duty* (1802) 84–5, quoting William Paley, *Principles of Moral and Political
Philosophy* (1788) ii 361. The spelling is Ritson's).

330   disease, if gathered immediately from the bosom of the earth.
       The most fertile districts of the habitable globe are now actually
       cultivated by men for animals, at a delay and waste of aliment
       absolutely incapable of calculation. It is only the wealthy that can,
       to any great degree, even now, indulge the unnatural craving for
335   dead flesh, and they pay for the greater licence of the privilege by
       subjection to supernumerary diseases. Again, the spirit of the
       nation that should take the lead in this great reform, would
       insensibly become agricultural; commerce, with all its vice,
       selfishness and corruption, would gradually decline; more natural
340   habits would produce gentler manners, and the excessive
       complication of political relations would be so far simplified, that
       every individual might feel and understand why he loved his
       country, and took a personal interest in its welfare. How would
       England, for example, depend on the caprices of foreign rulers, if
345   she contained within herself all the necessaries, and despised
       whatever they possessed of the luxuries of life? How could they
       starve her into compliance with their views? Of what
       consequence would it be that they refused to take her woollen
       manufactures, when large and fertile tracts of the island ceased to
350   be allotted to the waste of pasturage? On a natural system of diet,
       we should require no spices from India; no wines from Portugal,
       Spain, France, or Madeira; none of those multitudinous articles of
       luxury, for which every corner of the globe is rifled, and which
       are the causes of so much individual rivalship, such calamitous
355   and sanguinary national disputes. In the history of modern times,
       the avarice of commercial monopoly, no less than the ambition of
       weak and wicked chiefs, seems to have fomented the universal
       discord, to have added stubbornness to the mistakes of cabinets,
       and indocility to the infatuation of the people. Let it ever be
360   remembered, that it is the direct influence of commerce to make
       the interval between the richest and the poorest man wider and
       more unconquerable. Let it be remembered, that it is a foe to
       every thing of real worth and excellence in the human character.
       The odious and disgusting aristocracy of wealth is built upon the
365   ruins of all that is good in chivalry or republicanism; and luxury is
       the forerunner of a barbarism scarce capable of cure. Is it
       impossible to realize a state of society, where all the energies of
       man shall be directed to the production of his solid happiness?
       Certainly, if this advantage (the object of all political speculation)
370   be in any degree attainable, it is attainable only by a community,
       which holds out no factitious incentives to the avarice and
       ambition of the few, and which is internally organized for the
       liberty, security and comfort of the many. None must be
       entrusted with power (and money is the completest species of
375   power) who do not stand pledged to use it exclusively for the

general benefit. But the use of animal flesh and fermented liquors, directly militates with this equality of the rights of man. The peasant cannot gratify these fashionable cravings without leaving his family to starve. Without disease and war, those sweeping
380 curtailers of population, pasturage would include a waste too great to be afforded. The labour requisite to support a family is far lighter[1] than is usually supposed. The peasantry work, not only for themselves, but for the aristocracy, the army, and the manufacturers.
385 The advantage of a reform in diet is obviously greater than that of any other. It strikes at the root of the evil. To remedy the abuses of legislation, before we annihilate the propensities by which they are produced, is to suppose, that by taking away the effect, the cause will cease to operate. But the efficacy of this
390 system depends entirely on the proselytism of individuals, and grounds its merits, as a benefit to the community, upon the total change of the dietetic habits in its members. It proceeds securely from a number of particular cases to one that is universal, and has this advantage over the contrary mode, that one error does not
395 invalidate all that has gone before.
Let not too much, however, be expected from this system. The healthiest among us is not exempt from hereditary disease. The most symmetrical, athletic, and long-lived, is a being inexpressibly inferior to what he would have been, had not the
400 unnatural habits of his ancestors accumulated for him a certain portion of malady and deformity. In the most perfect specimen of

[1] It has come under the author's experience, that some of the workmen on an embankment in North Wales, who, in consequence of the inability of the proprietor to pay them, seldom received their wages, have supported large families by cultivating small spots of sterile ground by moonlight. In the notes to Pratt's Poem, 'Bread, or the Poor,' is an account of an industrious labourer, who, by working in a small garden, before and after his day's task, attained to an enviable state of independence.

Line 396. *Let not too much . . . from this system*] S.'s caution is taken from Newton's *Return to Nature* 33.
Lines 401–3. *In the most perfect specimen . . . physiological critic*] 'It cannot be truly said that we have ever seen *real men and women*' (*Return to Nature* 19).
S.'s footnote: *It has come under the author's experience . . .*] S. had assisted with the embankment project at Tremadoc in North Wales from September 1811 through February 1812 (see Elizabeth Beazley, *Madocks and the Wonder of Wales* (1967) 192–7). Samuel Jackson Pratt's *Bread; or, The Poor* (1802), once a very popular poem, gives the history of Joseph Smith of Wolvercot who, from renting one acre during twenty years, 'has reared eight children and buried three . . . and is now possessed of live stock worth at least 70£. and has lately purchased the cottage he lives in, and the one adjoining it' (Note k, p. 77).

civilized man, something is still found wanting by the
physiological critic. Can a return to nature, then, instantaneously
eradicate predispositions that have been slowly taking root in the
405   silence of innumerable ages?—Indubitably not. All that I contend
for is, that from the moment of the relinquishing all unnatural
habits, no new disease is generated; and that the predisposition to
hereditary maladies gradually perishes, for want of its
accustomed supply. In cases of consumption, cancer, gout,
410   asthma, and scrofula, such is the invariable tendency of a diet of
vegetables and pure water.

   Those who may be induced by these remarks to give the
vegetable system a fair trial, should, in the first place, date the
commencement of their practice from the moment of their
415   conviction. All depends upon breaking through a pernicious
habit resolutely and at once. Dr Trotter[1] asserts, that no drunkard
was ever reformed by gradually relinquishing his dram. Animal
flesh, in its effects on the human stomach, is analogous to a dram.
It is similar in the kind, though differing in the degree, of its
420   operation. The proselyte to a pure diet must be warned to expect
a temporary diminution of muscular strength. The subtraction of
a powerful stimulus will suffice to account for this event. But it is
only temporary, and is succeeded by an equable capability for
exertion, far surpassing his former various and fluctuating
425   strength. Above all, he will acquire an easiness of breathing, by
which such exertion is performed, with a remarkable exemption
from that painful and difficult panting now felt by almost every
one, after hastily climbing an ordinary mountain. He will be
equally capable of bodily exertion, or mental application, after as
430   before his simple meal. He will feel none of the narcotic effects of
ordinary diet. Irritability, the direct consequence of exhausting
stimuli, would yield to the power of natural and tranquil
impulses. He will no longer pine under the lethargy of ennui, that
unconquerable weariness of life, more to be dreaded than death
435   itself. He will escape the epidemic madness, which broods over
its own injurious notions of the Deity, and 'realizes the hell that
priests and beldams feign.' Every man forms as it were his god
from his own character; to the divinity of one of simple habits no
offering would be more acceptable than the happiness of his
440   creatures. He would be incapable of hating or persecuting others
for the love of God. He will find, moreover, a system of simple

   [1] See Trotter on the Nervous Temperament.

Line 416. *Dr. Trotter*] Thomas Trotter, *A View of the Nervous Temperament* (2nd
edn 1807) 38.
Lines 420–2. *The proselyte . . . for this event*] 'All these latter appearances,
however, are merely temporary, the natural consequences of withdrawing
from the system a powerful and habitual stimulus' (Lambe's *Reports* 13).

diet to be a system of perfect epicurism. He will no longer be
incessantly occupied in blunting and destroying those organs
from which he expects his gratification. The pleasures of taste to
445 be derived from a dinner of potatoes, beans, peas, turnips,
lettuces, with a dessert of apples, gooseberries, strawberries,
currants, raspberries, and, in winter, oranges, apples and pears, is
far greater than is supposed. Those who wait until they can eat
this plain fare with the sauce of appetite will scarcely join with the
450 hypocritical sensualist at a lord-mayor's feast, who declaims
against the pleasures of the table. Solomon kept a thousand
concubines, and owned in despair that all was vanity. The man
whose happiness is constituted by the society of one amiable
woman, would find some difficulty in sympathizing with the
455 disappointment of this venerable debauchee.

I address myself not only to the young enthusiast, the ardent
devotee of truth and virtue, the pure and passionate moralist, yet
unvitiated by the contagion of the world. He will embrace a pure
system, from its abstract truth, its beauty, its simplicity, and its
460 promise of wide-extended benefit; unless custom has turned
poison into food, he will hate the brutal pleasures of the chase by
instinct; it will be a contemplation full of horror and
disappointment to his mind, that beings capable of the gentlest
and most admirable sympathies, should take delight in the death-
465 pangs and last convulsions of dying animals. The elderly man,
whose youth has been poisoned by intemperance, or who has
lived with apparent moderation, and is afflicted with a variety of
painful maladies, would find his account in a beneficial change
produced without the risk of poisonous medicines. The mother,
470 to whom the perpetual restlessness of disease, and unaccountable
deaths incident to her children, are the causes of incurable
unhappiness, would on this diet experience the satisfaction of
beholding their perpetual healths and natural playfulness.[1] The

[1] See Mr Newton's book. His children are the most beautiful and healthy
creatures it is possible to conceive; the girls are perfect models for a sculptor; their
dispositions are also the most gentle and conciliating; the judicious treatment,
which they experience in other points, may be a correlative cause of this. In the
first five years of their life, of 18,000 children that are born, 7,500 die of various
diseases; and how many more of those that survive are not rendered miserable by
maladies not immediately mortal? The quality and quantity of a woman's milk are
materially injured by the use of dead flesh. In an island near Iceland, where no
vegetables are to be got, the children invariably die of tetanus, before they are
three weeks old, and the population is supplied from the main land. – Sir G.
Mackenzie's Hist. of Iceland. See also Emile, chap. i. pages 53, 54, 56.

Line 451. *Solomon*] Three hundred of Solomon's thousand were wives (*I Kings*
xi 3). He declared that all was vanity in *Ecclesiastes* i and ii.
S.'s footnote: *His children . . . correlative cause of this*] Hogg confirms this account
of J. F. Newton's five children: 'These young innocents were remarkably

most valuable lives are daily destroyed by diseases, that it is
475 dangerous to palliate and impossible to cure by medicine. How
much longer will man continue to pimp for the gluttony of death,
his most insidious, implacable and eternal foe?

'Αλλὰ δρακώντας ἀγρίους καλεῖτε καὶ παρδελέις καὶ
λέοντας, αὐτοὶδέ μιαφονεῖτέ εἰς ὠμοτητα καταλιπόντες
480 ἐκέινοις οὐδέν. ἐκέινοις μὲν ὁ φόνος τροφὴ, ἡμῖν δὲ ὄψον ἐστίν.

* * * * *

Ὅτι γὰρ οὐκ ἔστιν ανθρώπῳ κατὰ φὺσιν τὸ σαρκοφαγεῖν,
πρῶτον μὲν ἀπὸ των σωμοτων δηλοῦται τῆς κατασκεῦης.
Οὐδεν γὰρ ἔοικε τὸ ἀνθρώπου σῶμα των ἐπὶ σαρκοφαγίᾳ
γεγονότων, οὐ, χρωπότης χείλους, οὐκ ὀξύτης ὄνυχος οὐ
485 τραχύτης ὀδὸντων πρόσεστιν, οὐ κοιλίας ευτονία, καὶ

---

healthy, happy, beautiful and intelligent; whether they would have been less so
if they had always worn their clothes like other children, it is not easy to
determine' (*Hogg* ii 290). *In an island near Iceland* . . .] George Steuart Mackenzie
(*Travels in the Island of Iceland, during the Summer of the Year MDCCCX*,
Edinburgh 1811) mentions 'the disease, called . . . the Tetanus . . . which
invades children at a very early age, and almost invariably proves fatal'
(412–13). One of the Vestmannaeyjar islands 'is almost entirely supported by
migration from the mainland; scarcely a single instance having been known,
during the last twenty years, of a child surviving the period of infancy . . . Of
vegetable food the inhabitants have none . . .' (412–13). S.'s figure of three
weeks is drawn from a table on p. 414. *See also Emile* . . .] Rousseau recommended a vegetarian diet for a nurse or nursing mother:
'Les paysannes mangent moins de viande et plus de légumes que les femmes de
la ville; et ce régime végétal paraît plus favorable que contraire à elles et à leurs
enfants . . . Je ne puis croire qu'un enfant qu'on ne sèvrerait point trop tôt, ou
qu'on ne sèvrerait qu'avec des nourritures végétales, et dont la nourrice ne
vivrait aussi que de végétaux, fût jamais sujet aux vers . . . le maigre, loin
d'échauffer la nourrice, lui fournira du lait en abondance et de la meilleure
qualité. Se pourrait-il que le régime végétal étant reconnu le meilleur pour
l'enfant, le régime animal fût le meilleur pour la nourrice?' (*Émile* 35–6).
Line 477. *eternal foe?*] After these words *A Vindication* adds: 'The proselyte to a
simple and natural diet who desires health must from the moment of his
conversion attend to these rules: NEVER TAKE ANY SUBSTANCE INTO
THE STOMACH THAT ONCE HAD LIFE. DRINK NO LIQUID BUT
WATER RESTORED TO ITS ORIGINAL PURITY BY DISTILLA-
TION.' An Appendix then gives a list of centenarians, and concludes: 'It may
be here remarked that the author and his wife have lived on vegetables for eight
months. The improvements of health and temper here stated is the result of his
own experience'.

πνέυματος θερμότης, τρέψαι, καὶ κατεργάσασθαι δυνατὴ τό
βαρὺ καὶ κρεῶδες; ἀλλ᾽ αὐτόθεν ἡ φύσις τῇ λειότητι των
ὀδόντων, καὶ τῇ σμικρότητι τοῦ σοματος, καὶ τῇ μαλακότητι
τῆς γλώσσης, καὶ τῇ πρὸς πέψιν ἀμβλύτητι τοῦ πνέυματος,
490   ἐξόμινυται τὴν σαρκοφαγιὰν. Ει δὲ λεγείς πεφυκέναι σεαυτὸν
ἐπὶ τοιαύτην ἐδώδην, ὅ βούλει φαγεῖν, πρῶτον αὐτός
ἀπόκτεινον. ἀλλ᾽ αὐτός, διὰ σεαυτοῦ μὴ χρησάμενος κοπίδῃ,
μηδὲ τυμπανῳ μηδὲ πελέκει. ἀλλὰ ὡς λύκοι, καὶ ἄρκτοι, καὶ
λεόνες αὐτόι ὡς ἐσθιούσι φόνευουσιν, ἄνελε δήγματι βοῦν, ἤ
495   σώματι σῦν, ἤ ἄρνα ἤ λαγὼον διάρρηξον, καὶ φὰγε προσπεσὼν
ἔτι ξῶντος ὡς ἐκεῖνα.

*   *   *   *   *

Ημεῖς δὲ οὕτως ἐν τῷ μιαιφόνῳ τρυφῶμεν, ὥστε ὤφον τὸ
κρέας προσαγορέυομεν, εἶτα ὄψων πρὸς ἀυτὸ τὸ κρέας δέομεθα,
ἀναμιγνύντες ἔλαιον, οἶνον, μέλι, γάρον, ὄξος. ἡ δύσμασι
500   Συριακοῖς, Ἀρραβικοῖς, ὥσπερ ὄντως νεκρὸν, ἐνταφίαξοντες.
Καὶ γὰρ ὅτως αὐτων διαλυθέντων καὶ μαλαχθέντων καὶ τρόπον
τινὰ κρευσαπέυντων ἔργον ἐστὶ τὴν πέψιν κρατῆσαι καὶ
διακρατηθείσης δὲ δεινὰς βαρύτητας ἐμποιεῖ καὶ νοσώδεις
ἀπεψιάς.

*   *   *   *   *

505   Οὕτω τὸ πρῶτον ἄγριόν τι ξῶον ἐβρώθη καὶ κακοῦργον εἶτα
ὄρνις τις ἤ ἰχθύς ἕλκυστο καὶ γέυομενον, οὗτο καὶ
προμελέτησαν εν ἐκεῖνοις τὸ νικοῦν ἐπι βοῦν ἐργάτην ἦλθε,
καὶ τὸ κοσμον πρόβατον καὶ τὸν οἰκουρον ἀλεκτρὺονα. καὶ
καταμικρὸν οὗτο τὴν ἀπληστιάν τονώσαντες, ἐπὶσφαγὰς
510   ανθρώπων, καὶ φονους καὶ πολέμους προῆλθον.
                    Πλουτ. περι της σαρκοφαγιας.

Lines 478–511. quotation from Plutarch] 'You call serpents and panthers and
lions savage, but you yourselves, by your own foul slaughters, leave them no
room to outdo you in cruelty; for their slaughter is their living, yours is a mere
appetizer . . .
A man's frame is in no way similar to those creatures who were made for
flesh-eating: he has no ravenous beak or sharp nails or jagged tooth, no strong
stomach or warmth of vital fluids able to conduct and assimilate a heavy diet of
flesh. It is from this very fact, the evenness of our teeth, the smallness of our
mouths, the softness of our tongues, our possession of vital fluids too inert to
digest meat that Nature disavows our eating of flesh. If you declare that you are
naturally designed for such a diet, then first kill yourself what you want to eat.
Do it, however, only through your own resources, unaided by cleaver or
cudgel or any kind of axe. Rather, just as wolves and bears and lions them-

93 'The pale, the cold, and the moony smile'

There is no work, nor device, nor knowledge, nor wisdom, in
the grave whither thou goest. – *Ecclesiastes*.

Date of composition unknown. The poem is the only one from *Esd* for which
S. for some reason must have kept a MS after his elopement with Mary
Godwin, and the only *Esd* poem separately published by him (untitled, in
1816). These facts, together with a maturer style noted by several editors and
some traces of Platonism detected by Rogers (*Esd Poems* 123–4), suggest that it
may be among the later poems of the collection. If so it could belong to S.'s
'nervous & unsettled' state of mind (*L* i 360) following the attack at Tanyrallt
on the night of 26 February 1813. Perhaps the 'very tedious & stormy' crossing
to Dublin on 7–9 March (*L* i 360) contributed to the imagery of stanza 1;
certainly 'the fears and the love for that which we see' (30) points to some kind
of anxiety over Harriet, not merely over the sensible world. The poem is in
keeping with the others in *1816*, which are chiefly meditations on death, waste,
and mutability; and it could reflect the disillusionment with Harriet that began

selves slay what they eat, so you are to fell an ox with your fangs or a bear with
your body, or tear a lamb or hare in bits. Fall upon it and eat it still living, as
animals do . . .
But we are so refined in our blood-letting that we term flesh a supplementary
food; and then we need "supplements" for the flesh itself, mixing oil, wine,
honey, fish paste, vinegar, with Syrian and Arabian spices, as though we were
really embalming a corpse for burial. The fact is that meat is so softened and
dissolved and, in a way, putrified that it is hard for digestion to cope with it;
and if digestion loses the battle, the meats affect us with dreadful pains and
malignant forms of indigestion . . .' (Plutarch, *Moralia*, 'On the Eating of
Flesh', I 944–5. Loeb translation, modified to accord with S.'s text, in which
three misprints are corrected). 'Just so, at the beginning it was some wild and
harmful animal that was eaten, then a bird or fish that had its flesh torn. And so
when our conquering instincts had tasted blood and grew practised on wild
animals, they advanced to the labouring ox and the well-behaved sheep and the
house-warding cock; thus, little by little extending our insatiable appetite, they
have advanced to wars and the slaughter and murder of human beings' (ibid. II
998).

¶ *93. Epigraph.* From *Ecclesiastes* ix 10 (not in *Esd*).

to reveal itself shortly after the completion of Q *Mab* in mid-February. It is therefore here tentatively assigned to S.'s stay in Dublin, early March 1813. On the other hand the poem could well belong to the period of Harriet's illness in April–May 1812; it has thematic and verbal affinities with 'The Retrospect' (No. 79) and other contemporary poems; and in *Esd* it follows 'Dark Spirit of the desert rude', written at that time. For *1816* it was revised less towards Platonism than towards a more comprehensive necessitarianism (cp. lines 11–12 in the two versions). In both versions S.'s attitude towards an afterlife is—as usual—desirous but non-committal.

Text from *1816*.

Published in *1816*; *Dowden Life* i 349 (lines 1–6; *Esd* version); *Esd Nbk* 79–80; *Esd Poems* 38–40 (*1816* version); *SC* iv 968–9 (transcript of *Esd* f. 32, *Esd* No. 21).

The pale, the cold, and the moony smile
   Which the meteor beam of a starless night
Sheds on a lonely and sea-girt isle,
   Ere the dawning of morn's undoubted light,
5 Is the flame of life so fickle and wan
That flits round our steps till their strength is gone.

O man! hold thee on in courage of soul
   Through the stormy shades of thy worldly way,

1. moony] resembling moonlight (*OED* 3). The modern sense of *moony* ('foolishly dreamy') was unknown until the mid-19th century.
2. meteor beam] A hyphen would ensure that the words were taken as a compound noun (as in Burns, 'The Vision' ii 105: 'Misled by Fancy's meteor-ray') but S. may be exploiting an ambiguity. Any atmospheric phenomenon was a 'meteor', from *aurora borealis* to *ignis fatuus*: the former seems intended in lines 1–4 (*Esd* reads '*Till* the dawning . . .'), the latter in lines 5–6. An *ignis fatuus* was generally described as pale and without heat, e.g. in Southey, *Thalaba* VI viii 1–15: 'A meteor in the hazy air / Play'd before his path . . . / And wrapt him in its pale innocuous fire'. S. refers to the *aurora borealis* in 'The Assassins' (August–September 1814), *Prose* 147: 'Meteoric shapes, more effulgent than the moonlight, hung on the wandering clouds . . .' *starless*] stormy *Esd*.
4. Ere] Till *Esd*.
5. flame] taper *Esd*.
Stanzas 2–3 in *Esd* are as follows:

And the billows of cloud that around thee roll
10   Shall sleep in the light of a wondrous day,
Where hell and heaven shall leave thee free
To the universe of destiny.

This world is the nurse of all we know,
    This world is the mother of all we feel,
15 And the coming of death is a fearful blow
    To a brain unencompassed with nerves of steel;
When all that we know, or feel, or see,
Shall pass like an unreal mystery.

The secret things of the grave are there
20   Where all but this frame must surely be,
Though the fine-wrought eye and the wondrous ear
    No longer will live to hear or to see
All that is great and all that is strange
In the boundless realm of unending change.

Oh! Man, hold thee on with courage of soul
    Thro the long long night of thy doubtful way
And the billows of cloud that around thee roll
Shall subside in the calm of eternal day
For all in this world we can surely know
    Is a little delight & a little woe

All we behold we feel that we know
    All we perceive we know that we feel
And the coming of death is a fearful blow
    To a brain unencompassed by nervestrings of steel
When all that we know, we feel & we see
Shall fleet by like an unreal mystery

11–12. The weak platitude of *Esd* is revised in *1816* to mean 'Freed from superstitious fables, you will be able to enter whatever future it is that Necessity has in store'.

13–14. The *Esd* version means: 'We seem to have direct cognition of the sensible world, and we do have direct cognition of our own ideas—yet when we die both worlds vanish as if equally unreal'.

19. *there*] *Esd*; there, *1816* (the comma may simply represent contemporary practice before a relative clause). 'There' means 'in the universe-after-death'.

20. *frame*] body *Esd*.

23. *great*] bright *Esd*.

24. *boundless realm*] gradual path *Esd*.

25   Who telleth a tale of unspeaking death?
     Who lifteth the veil of what is to come?
   Who painteth the shadows that are beneath
     The wide-winding caves of the peopled tomb?
   Or uniteth the hopes of what shall be
30 With the fears and the love for that which we see?

94 To Harriet

Transcribed in Harriet S.'s hand in *Esd* and dated 'May 1814' at the foot, with
'Cook's Hotel' inserted between stanzas 3 and 4 (a facsimile is given in *Esd
Poems* 110). All editors have hitherto read this poem as a desperate appeal by S.
for his wife's tolerance, in order to save their threatened marriage–a reading
which throws the responsibility for the marriage's failure largely on Harriet's
obdurate lack of understanding. Dowden, recognizing difficulties in the syntax, gave a full paraphrase (*Dowden Life* i 413):

> In this piteous appeal Shelley declares that he has now no grief but one–the
> grief of having known and lost his wife's love; if it is the fate of all who
> would live in the sunshine of her affection to endure her scorn, then let him
> be scorned above the rest, for he most of all has desired that sunshine; let not
> the world and the pride of life harden her heart; it is better that she should be
> kind and gentle; if she has something to endure, it is not much, and all her
> husband's weal hangs upon her loving endurance; for, see, how pale and
> wildered anguish has made him; oh! in mercy do not cure his malady by the
> fatal way of condemning him to exile beyond all hope or further fear; oh!
> trust no erring guide, no unwise counsellor, no false pride; rather learn that a
> nobler pride may find its satisfaction in and through love; or if love be for
> ever dead, at least let pity survive in its room.

25. *a tale . . . death?*] the tales . . . Death? *Esd*.
25–8. The unanswerable questions are modelled on *Job* xxxviii, especially 17:
'Have the gates of death been opened unto thee? or hast thou seen the doors of
the shadow of death?'
27. *shadows*] beings *Esd*. (The change in *1816* may be Biblical rather than
Platonic: see note above).
28. *wide-winding caves*] wide stretching realms *Esd*.
29. *Or*] And *Esd*.
¶ 94. *Title*. Here and in line 7 Harriet S. has added a second 't' to her name–
possibly to differentiate lines addressed to her from any associated with
Harriet Grove during her collection of scraps for the final pages of *Esd*. When
preparing a marriage-settlement T. C. Medwin was instructed by S. on 21
October 1811 that Harriet's 'maiden name was Harriet*t* Westbrook, with two
*t*s to Harriet*t*' (*L* i 154), but neither S. nor Harriet normally spelt her name that
way.

Louise Boas, also quoting the poem in full (*Harriet Shelley: Five Long Years* (1962) 145–6) attributes the crisis and the appeal to S.'s attraction to Cornelia Boinville at Bracknell; but she too was puzzled: 'The first two stanzas are not immediately clear, and have been subject to misconstruction. S. was giving voice to a fear of having lost her love; alone, he grieves that the blessings of her love *have been* his; it is the Horatian use of the perfect tense, expressing a cessation'. Cameron, noting that S. had already met Mary Godwin in May 1814 (*Esd Nbk* 296–9), argues that the poem 'reveals him in a turmoil of conflicting emotions as his loyalty to Harriet was being overwhelmed by his growing passion for Mary' (*Cameron (1974)* 6). The objections to this dating and these interpretations are, however, insuperable: (a) S. was in London in May 1814 but not, so far as is otherwise known, at Cook's Hotel; (b) it is quite impossible so to distort lines 5–6 as to make them mean 'My only grief is that I have *lost* your love', when what they plainly say is 'My only grief is that I *and no one else* have enjoyed your love'; (c) stanza 2 is pointless: why should S. argue that if his wife dislikes those who love her she must dislike her husband more than anyone? (d) if S. is in the frantic state described in lines 19–22, what 'slight endurance' on Harriet's part could possibly ensure his 'lasting weal'? (e) why is S. a 'fellow-being' in line 18, rather than a husband or a lover? (f) of what use to S. would be his wife's 'pity' if what so overturns him is the loss of her love? All these problems vanish once it is assumed that Harriet wrote '1814' instead of '1813' at the end of the poem–either mistakenly, or as the date of transcription. All ten of S.'s known letters addressed from Cook's Hotel belong to 1813, and all are dated between 18 May and 9 July in *L*.

After returning from Dublin on 5 April the S.'s certainly lived for some time at Cook's, keeping at least the use of a room there until their move to Bracknell towards the end of July, after Ianthe's birth. Harriet also probably added the words 'Cook's Hotel' (which are unlikely to have been in the middle of S.'s original holograph) at the foot of the page in *Esd* (momentarily thinking the bottom of the page was the end of the poem) because the poem was memorably associated by her with that place. In November 1812 S. had called on Hogg in London to repair the estrangement caused by Hogg's pursuit of Harriet a year earlier (see headnote to No. 65), and Hogg himself has described his uncomfortable reception by Eliza Westbrook, 'who smiled faintly upon me in silence, and Harriet, who received me cordially and with much shaking of hands' (*Hogg* ii 169). Harriet was evidently trying hard to be civil, to please her husband, who, though in practice he had responded to his wife's distress, had never theoretically accepted the doctrine of 'the monopoly of exclusive cohabitation' (*L* i 175). But in May next year, when the S.'s were in Cook's Hotel, Hogg's blandishments had again become very distasteful to Harriet, who later refused to admit him to their lodgings after the birth of Ianthe (*Hogg* ii 461–2: 'I never set foot in the house; my visits did not extend beyond the door . . . I often asked Harriet to let me see her little girl, but she always made some excuse'). An undated note, assigned by F. L. Jones to 2 June, but possibly of 19 or 26 May, reads (*L* i 370):

Cooke's Hotel Wednesday Mor.

My dearest Friend,

[*Deleted by Hogg*: I have felt myself extremely hurt by Harriet's conduct towards you.]

She writes in this. I only desire that she were as anxious to confer on you all possible happiness as I am. She tells you that she invites you this evening. It will be better than our lonesome and melancholy interviews.

Your very affectionate
P. B. Shelley

I am very sure that Harriet will be as kind as ever. I could see when I spoke to her (if my eyes were not blinded by love) that it was an error not of the feelings but of reason. I entreat you to come this evening . . .

The poem evidently arises from the same situation as the note, and is thus an appeal to Harriet, not for himself, but on Hogg's behalf, written probably at the end of May 1813. A brief paraphrase might run as follows:

1. To me, your love is tranquillizing and consoling, and I have no regret except that I have been the only one to enjoy those privileges.

2. If all who desire your company deserve to be rejected, then I, your chosen husband, merit rejection more than anyone.

3. Be one of the few humane and generous people in the world, then; and by making this small concession ensure another human being's happiness,

4. for, truly, he is desperately in love with you–don't be so cruel as to destroy him by a summary rejection.

5. Don't listen to Eliza; this ill-natured attitude isn't the real *you*. Show your self-respect in a more admirable way, and treat Hogg with compassion even if you can't return his love.

The poem therefore provides no evidence of any weakening in S.'s love for Harriet (a month or so later it is followed by the tender 'To Ianthe', No. 95) though Harriet's refusal (doubtless encouraged by Eliza) to receive S.'s friends may have exasperated him; nor is it evidence of any coldness or lack of sympathy whatever toward S. on Harriet's part. Except for one exclamation mark (7) there is no punctuation in *Esd*.

Text from *Esd* ff. 92ᵛ–93ʳ (*Esd* No. 54, in Harriet S.'s hand: quoted by permission of the Carl H. Pforzheimer Library).

Published in *Dowden Life* i 413–14; *Esd Nbk* 165–6; *Esd Poems* 110–11; (with facsimile of lines 1–18); *SC* iv 1057–8 (transcript of *Esd*).

Thy look of love has power to calm
The stormiest passion of my Soul,
Thy gentle words are drops of balm
In life's too bitter bowl;
5 No grief is mine but that alone
These choicest blessings I have known.

Harriet! if all who long to live
In the warm sunshine of thine eye
That price beyond all pain must give
10   Beneath thy scorn to die,
Then hear thy chosen own too late
His heart most worthy of thy hate.

Be thou then one among mankind
Whose heart is harder not for state,
15   Thou only virtuous, gentle, kind
Amid a world of hate,
And by a slight endurance seal
A fellow-being's lasting weal.

For pale with anguish is his cheek,
20   His breath comes fast, his eyes are dim,
Thy name is struggling ere he speak,
Weak is each trembling limb;
In mercy let him not endure
The misery of a fatal cure.

25   O trust for once no erring guide,
Bid the remorseless feeling flee:
'Tis malice, 'tis revenge, 'tis pride,
'Tis anything but thee;
O deign a nobler pride to prove,
30   And pity if thou canst not love.

95 To Ianthe

The date '[Oct *canc.*] Septr 1813' written after the title in *Esd* is in a different ink from the poem, and probably refers (as in No. 96) to the time of transcription. Possibly these two sonnets were added to the main body of poems in *Esd* as a

14. i.e. 'whose heart is not hardened out of pride'.
18. weal] welfare. Below this line Harriet has written 'Cook's Hotel'.
23. mercy] misery SC.
25. erring guide] Presumably Eliza Westbrook. Ten months later S. told Hogg: 'I certainly hate her with all my heart and soul . . . I sometimes feel faint with the fatigue of checking the overflowings of my unbounded abhorrence for this miserable wretch' (*L* i 384).
30. Below this line Harriet S. has written 'May 1814'.
¶ *95. Title.* S.'s daughter was christened Eliza Ianthe (Louise Boas, *Harriet Shelley: Five Long Years* (1962) 176)—Eliza after Harriet's sister—but later evidently preferred to be known as Ianthe: *Esd* is inscribed 'Ianthe E. Esdaile'

kind of appendix on the last day of September shortly before S. left Bracknell for the Lakes. This poem to Ianthe S. was inserted just before No. 96, which is dated 31 July at the foot, so may well have been composed between 23 June (the day of the baby's own birth) and 31 July (the eve of her mother's birthday), perhaps nearer the former date (line 10). 'He was extremely fond of his child', according to Peacock; but he soon felt less than the perfect contentment that the sonnet reflects. Peacock adds (*Peacock Works* viii 70): 'to this first-born there were accompaniments which did not please him. The child had a wet-nurse whom he did not like, and was much looked after by his wife's sister, whom he intensely disliked.'

Text from *Esd* f. 91ᵛ (*Esd* No. 52: quoted by permission of the Carl H. Pforzheimer Library).

Published in *Dowden Life* i 376; *Esd Nbk* 163; *Esd Poems* 108–9; Sotheby & Co., *Sale Catalogue of Printed Books* (2 July 1962) 88 (facsimile of *Esd*); SC iv 1056 (transcript of *Esd*).

> I love thee, Baby! for thine own sweet sake:
> Those azure eyes, that faintly dimpled cheek,
> Thy tender frame so eloquently weak
> Love in the sternest heart of hate might wake;
> 5 But more, when o'er thy fitful slumber bending
> Thy mother folds thee to her wakeful heart,
> Whilst love and pity in her glances blending,
> All that thy passive eyes can feel, impart;
> More, when some feeble lineaments of her
> 10 Who bore thy weight beneath her spotless bosom
> As with deep love I read thy face, recur,
> More dear art thou, O fair and fragile blossom,
> Dearest, when most thy tender traits express
> The image of thy mother's loveliness. –

96 Evening: To Harriet

Dated 'July 31st 1813' (altered from 'July 30:') at foot of sonnet–presumably the date of composition, as this was the eve of Harriet S.'s eighteenth birthday; the date 'Sep. 1813' following the title must be that of transcription, as with No. 95. This is the last poem in S.'s hand in *Esd*. S. was at High Elms,

and the names are similarly reversed on her tombstone. The heroine of *Q Mab*, whose eyes are described as 'dark blue orbs' (i 39), had been named Ianthe (Gk. ἰανθενος, 'violet-coloured'). See note to line 27, *Q Mab* i. Ianthe S., who inherited *Esd* from her mother, married Edward Jeffries Esdaile in 1837 and died 16 June 1876 at Cothelstone in Somerset.

Bracknell, at this time, so 'the dark blue line / Of western distance' cannot be a sea horizon. The house High Elms was visited and described by Louise Boas (*Harriet Shelley: Five Long Years* (1962) x, 130) just before its destruction in 1962 to make way for a roundabout. The poem relies on a parallel between the setting sun, on which the 'astronomic' eye might detect spots, and S.'s conjugal happiness in which it would be equally invidious to note defects. Although the 11-year cycle was still unrecognized, 1813 was a year of maximum sun-spot activity; and as S. doubtless knew, 'A large groupe of spots have recently been observed advancing from the Sun's Eastern limb, which are at present near the centre of his disc . . . They appear to be nearly twice as large as any groupe of the same kind that has been observed on the Sun's disc for years' (*GM* lxxxiii (November 1813) 496). Strains within S.'s marriage were now equally apparent, including (a) Harriet's intolerance of Hogg (see No. 94 and headnote); (b) S.'s intolerance of Eliza Westbrook (see *White* i 287–8); (c) S.'s intimacy with Mrs Boinville and her daughter Cornelia–an important motive for the move to High Elms; and (d) Harriet's refusal to suckle Ianthe, now a month old. According to a story deriving from Peacock 'S. . . . thought that nature was violated by her refusal and abhorred a hired nurse. The nurse's soul would enter the child. All day he tried to persuade Harriet to do her duty, walking up and down the room, crooning old songs to the child in his arms. At last, in his despair, and thinking that the passion in him would make a miracle, he pulled his shirt away and tried himself to suckle the child' (Lawrence Pearsall Jacks, *Life and Letters of Stopford Brooke* (1917) ii 506–7).

Text from *Esd* f. 92ʳ (*Esd* No. 53: quoted by permission of the Carl H. Pforzheimer Library).

Published in *Dowden Life* i 385–6; *Esd Nbk* 164; *Esd Poems* 109; Sotheby & Co., *Sale Catalogue of Printed Books* (2 July 1962) 88 (facsimile of *Esd*); *SC* iv 1056–7 (transcript of *Esd*).

> O thou bright Sun! beneath the dark blue line
> Of western distance that sublime descendest,
> And gleaming lovelier as thy beams decline
> Thy million hues to every vapour lendest,
> 5 And over cobweb lawn and grove and stream
> Sheddest the liquid magic of thy light,
> Till calm Earth with the parting splendour bright
> Shows like the vision of a beauteous dream,
> What gazer now with astronomic eye
> 10 Could coldly count the spots within thy sphere?

¶ *96.5. cobweb lawn*] Grass covered with spiders' gossamers, lit up by the low sun. The phrase was earlier used of 'transparent linen' (as in Drayton's *Muses Elizium* (1630) vi 3–4: 'Thin clouds like scarfs of cobweb lawn / Veil'd heaven's most glorious eye'), and this connotation seems intended (cp. line 14, 'close-woven happiness').

Such were thy lover, Harriet, could he fly
The thoughts of all that makes his passion dear
And turning senseless from thy warm caress
Pick flaws in our close-woven happiness.

97 To Harriet

This version of the poem, entitled 'To Harriet' in Harriet S.'s hand, precedes
the main collection in *Esd*; another version headed 'To Harriet ★★★★★.' was
published as the dedication to *Q Mab* (No. 92). Because both versions are given
in full here, they are uncollated. Cameron argues (*Esd Nbk* 29) and Rogers
assumes (*Esd Poems* 119) that the published version is the later one, the
argument depending partly on style and partly on the fact that 'The phrase
"early wilding flowers" [line 11 in both versions] is appropriate for the
Notebook poems, some of which were written some years previously, but it is
not appropriate for *Queen Mab*, which is one long poem and had been composed in the months immediately preceding its publication'. However, as
Cameron himself points out that 'the originally planned volume . . . was to
contain both the Esdaile poems and *Queen Mab*' this argument loses its force. It
is a little more probable that the *Q Mab* version was, by however short an
interval, the earlier written of the two. *Q Mab* was 'finished & transcribed' by
15 February 1813 (*L* i 354), at which time S. still expected his minor poems to
be printed with it, as he added to his publisher: 'You will receive it with the
other poems. I think that the whole should form one volume'. *Q Mab*,
however, was sent independently during March, with the direction: 'Do not
let the title page be printed before the body of the Poem. I have a motto to
introduce from Shakespeare, & a Preface' (*L* i 361). Motto and preface were
never forthcoming; the dedicatory verses, however, were not on the title-page
but immediately before the opening of the poem, so they were probably sent
with it in March; in any case they cannot have been written later than mid-
May. In the arranged part of *Esd* (which was probably once intended to
conclude with 'The Retrospect', No. 79), the latest firmly-dated poem was
written 13 November 1812, but there are late additions to the main collection
in S.'s hand: the sonnets to Ianthe and to Harriet, for instance (Nos. 95 and 96),
were composed in July, after the distribution of *Q Mab*, and were probably
copied into the notebook in September. This poem is added at the front end,
with an interval of one blank page before the heading 'Poems', and is not
recognized in the regular line-counts until its 16 lines are added to the last one
of all–after 'The Wandering Jew's Soliloquy', which itself may be an after-
thought. So 'To Harriet' could have been inserted at any time up to *c.* August
1813; the internal indications are that it was adapted from the *Q Mab* version

13. *from*] alt. *from* to *Esd*.

and prefixed to the *Esd* collection as a personal dedication to Harriet soon after the intention to publish had been abandoned. The phrase 'these early wilding flowers', present in both versions, must refer to the *Esd* poems; but while the *Q Mab* version therefore still anticipates their presence in the printed book ('Then press into thy breast this pledge of love, . . . / Each flowret gathered in my heart / It consecrates to thine'–where 'this pledge' refers to the volume, but 'each flowret' cannot easily apply to *Q Mab* alone), the *Esd* version treats the minor poems as things now put aside ('Then twine the withering wreath-buds round thy brow: / Its bloom may deck their pale and faded prime'), and as more likely to be kept alive by Harriet's possession of them than by publication ('Can they survive without thy love / Their wild and moody birth?'). One *Esd* poem ('Falsehood and Vice', No. 76) had already been introduced into the notes to *Q Mab* as the only way 'that ever will occur of rescuing it from oblivion' (p. 362). Moreover, the *Esd* version alludes in lines 5–6 to *Q Mab* as a worthy achievement of the past ('Whose looks gave grace to the majestic theme, / The sacred, free and fearless theme of truth?').

Dowden noted privately (quoted in *Esd Nbk* 175): 'The form of the stanza ad[a]pted from Southey e.g. 'Ode written on 1st of Jan 1794' (in Poems 1797)'. Southey's ode is in the metre of Collins's influential 'Ode to Evening'; S.'s differs by having an octosyllabic third line in each stanza. In content however S.'s model was either or both of Southey's own dedicatory sonnets to his wife Edith. The first, prefixed to the volume mentioned by Dowden above (*Poems*, Bristol 1797), contains the lines (6–12):

> . . . often pluck'd I, as I pass'd along,
> The wild and simple flowers of poesy;
> And sometimes, unreflecting as a child,
> Entwined the weeds which pleased a random eye.
> Take thou the wreath, BELOVED; it is wild
> And rudely garlanded; yet scorn not thou
> The humble offering . . .

The second, prefixed to *Joan of Arc* (2nd edn 1798), begins:

> EDITH! I brought thee late a humble gift,
> The songs of earlier youth; it was a wreath
> With many an unripe blossom garlanded
> And many a weed, yet mingled with some flowers
> Which will not wither. Dearest! now I bring
> A worthier offering . . .

Text from *Esd* f. 4^r (*Esd* No. 1: quoted by permission of the Carl H. Pforzheimer Library).
Published in *Esd Nbk* 37; *Esd Poems* 1; *SC* iv 924–5 (transcript of *Esd*).

> Whose is the love that gleaming through the world
> Wards off the poisonous arrow of its scorn?
> Whose is the warm and partial praise,
> Virtue's most sweet reward?

5   Whose looks gave grace to the majestic theme,
    The sacred, free and fearless theme of truth?
      Whose form did I gaze fondly on
      And love mankind the more?

    Harriet! on thine–thou wert my purer soul,
10   Thou wert the inspiration to my song,
      Thine are these early wilding flowers,
      Though garlanded by me.

    Then twine the withering wreath-buds round thy brow:
    Its bloom may deck their pale and faded prime;–
15   Can they survive without thy love
      Their wild and moody birth?

98 Stanza, written at Bracknell

Written shortly before 16 March 1814, when S. enclosed the lines (untitled) in a
letter to Hogg. The title is Forman's. S. had been staying about a month at the
house in Bracknell, Berkshire, of Harriet de Boinville, sister of Mrs John Frank
Newton, whose husband had recently died a victim of the retreat from
Moscow (7 February 1813). Her daughter Cornelia, just 19, apparently already
the wife of Godwin's friend Thomas Turner, was also an inmate. S. had
known the Boinvilles since early summer 1813, and Harriet S. was later to
declare 'that last November [1813] he had fallen in love with Mrs Turner,
Madame de Boinville's daughter, and paid her such marked attentions Mr
Turner, the husband, had carried off his wife to Devonshire' (*Dowden Life* i
543). The dates are confused but the facts may be true. As S. recalled his
situation to Hogg on 4 October 1814, this was the crisis of his disintegrating
marriage. 'In the beginning of spring, I spent two months at Mrs Boinville's
without my wife . . . The presence of Mrs Boinville & her daughter afforded a
strange contrast to my former friendless & deplorable condition. I suddenly
perceived that the entire devotion with which I had resigned all prospects of
utility or happiness to the single purpose of cultivating Harriet was a gross &
despicable superstition.–Perhaps every degree of affectionate intimacy with a
female, however slight, partakes of the nature of love . . . It was no longer
possible to practise self-deception: I believed that one revolting duty yet
remained, to continue to deceive my wife' (*L* i 401–2). In the letter enclosing
the poem S. had written: 'They have revived in my heart the expiring flame of
life. I have felt myself translated to a paradise, which has nothing of mortality

¶ 97.5. The phrasing suggests a retrospective allusion to Harriet's beauty at the
opening of *Q Mab* (i 12–44).

but its transitoriness; my heart sickens at the view of that necessity, which will quickly divide me from the delightful tranquillity of this happy home–for it has become my home . . . I have begun to learn Italian again . . . Cornelia assists me in this language. Did I not once tell you that I thought her cold and reserved? She is the reverse of this . . . I have written nothing but one stanza, which has no meaning, and that I have only written in thought: [quotes 'Thy dewy looks' etc.]. This is the vision of a delirious and distempered dream, which passes away at the cold clear light of morning. Its surpassing excellence and exquisite perfections have no more reality than the colour of an autumnal sunset' (*L* i 383–4). Presumably, then, the lines were addressed to Cornelia Boinville. Cameron observes (*SC* iv 616) that Cornelia may well have met S. halfway; and Richard Holmes suggests very plausibly (*Holmes* 227–8) that some erotic Latin written in S.'s hand into Claire Clairmont's journal for 1814 refers to this relationship (text and translation in *Claire Jnl* 61–2). S. also there copied the episode of Paolo and Francesca's first kiss from Dante's *Inferno* v 124–38. S.'s letter of 16 March was not among the *Hogg MSS* acquired by *CHPL*, and its present location is unknown.

Text from *Hogg* ii 516.

Published in *Hogg*. See Appendix 3 for an alternative presentation of this poem.

> Thy dewy looks sink in my breast;
> Thy gentle words stir poison there;
> Thou hast disturbed the only rest
> That was the portion of despair!
> 5 Subdued to Duty's hard control,
> I could have borne my wayward lot:
> The chains that bind this ruined soul
> Had cankered then–but crushed it not.

99 Lines: 'That moment is gone for ever'

The composition-date of this poem is a mystery. It exists only as an untitled rough draft at the 'miscellaneous' end of a notebook apparently used only in late 1821 and early 1822 (*Nbk 22*), between the lyric 'Tell me, Star' (probably late 1821) and many blank pages carrying scribbles (perhaps by Percy Florence S., born November 1819). The ink and handwriting appear more or less homogeneous with those of the lyrics preceding it, though Mrs S. did not publish it with these in *1824*. Garnett, who first published the poem, naturally assigned it to 1822 and it has subsequently always appeared among S.'s last poems, as presumably concerning Jane Williams. Yet it is stylistically very unlike S.'s late lyrics, and very like the lyrics of 1813–15, so that doubts have often been expressed about its dating. Locock, in assigning it to 1822, noticed its striking resemblance to the 'Stanza, written at Bracknell' and to the letter

that accompanied the Stanza, and concluded: 'I infer from this that there may
be a mistake of eight years in the presumed date (1822), and that the Lines may
have been addressed to one of the Bracknell household, probably Cornelia
Turner, in the spring of 1814' (*Locock 1911* ii 530). If so, the Lines must have
been marooned, for nearly eight years, in the middle of an otherwise empty
notebook. Locock's supporting parallel is not a strong one; but the lines to
Mary Godwin 'Mine eyes were dim with tears unshed' (No. 102), an unfinished private poem of the same kind and the same year, were also drafted in
the middle of a blank notebook (*Nbk 11*) and eventually embedded among
poems of much later date. Besides the parallels provided by the printed Lines,
there are many verbal and conceptual parallels between unadopted draft lines
in this poem, S.'s letter of 16 March 1814, and Latin lines in Claire Clairmont's
journal (see headnote to No. 100). Cp. draft lines 8–10: 'The future was darker
still / One moment from birth did borrow / A long life exhausted ill' with 'I
have sunk into a premature old age of exhaustion, which renders me dead to
everything, but the unenviable capacity of indulging the vanity of hope' (*L* i
383); draft lines 11–12: 'O fill high the cup with ruin / Mix delusion & madness
therein' with 'Cur sordidum vene[ris *or* num] vitalis poculi imbibo?' (*Claire Jnl*
61); draft line 16: 'The peace that I knew not till late' with 'the delightful
tranquillity of this happy home' (*L* i 383); draft line 27: 'That your dew was
poison to' with 'Thy dewy looks sink in my breast; / Thy gentle words stir
poison there' ('Stanza, written at Bracknell' 1–2). Cp. also lines 13–14 with *Q
Mab* viii 131–2 (on sexual passion in a rejuvenated world): 'All bitterness is
past; the cup of joy / Unmingled mantles to the goblet's brim'. It would be
remarkable for S. so to have recreated his frame of mind of April 1814 in the
very different emotional and poetic atmosphere of the relationship with Jane
Williams. Possibly, however, the subject of the 'Lines' is dramatic (e.g. the
apocryphal kiss of Tasso and Leonora, or of characters in S.'s 'Unfinished
Drama'). The order of composition of the stanzas is itself hard to determine,
and this may coincide with S.'s intended arrangement. But the traditional
order (Garnett's) cannot be that of composition which seems (revisions apart)
to be one of straightforward progress on consecutive pages (the reverse order
of stanzas is barely possible). The draft has no pointing, except in lines 4, 5, 20,
21, 26, 30–2, where it has been retained.
Text from *Nbk 22* ff. 15ʳ–18ᵛ.
Published in *Relics* 43–4 (stanzas 7, 1, 3, 5 and lines 19–20); *Huntington Nbk* iii
138 (revised); *Peck* ii 258–9 ('from manuscript', but almost identical with
Huntington Nbk).

> That moment is gone for ever,
> Like lightning it flashed and died,
> Like a snowflake upon the river,
> A sunbeam upon the tide—
> 5 Which the dark shadows hide. –

¶ 99. *Stanza 1.* Locock notes (*Locock 1911* ii 530) that in his letter of 16 March

The past was all storm and sorrow,
The future was darker far,
But the present dared to borrow
Light from so fair a star.
10   It is dead, as meteors [are].

That moment from time was singled
As the price of a life of pain,
In the cup of its joy was mingled
Delusion too sweet, though vain,
15   Too sweet to be mine again.

The peace that I knew not till late,
The peace that I must have lost,
The peace that I now seek—that
Methinks were too little cost
20   For a moment so found, so lost!

Sweet lips,—I forswear forever
The sweetness not given to me,
The kisses of mortal fever
Should hallow mine to thee:
25   What I am, will I seem to be.

1814 S. quoted Burns (not quite accurately; cp. 'Tam O'Shanter' (published
1793) 59–62) in connection with his stay at the Boinvilles':

Pleasures are like poppies spread,
You seize the flower—the bloom is fled;
Or like the snow-falls in the river,
A moment white—then lost for ever.

S. there commented: 'I live here like the insect that sports in a transient
sunbeam, which the next cloud shall obscure for ever' (L i 383).
6. storm] Dubious reading.
9. fair] living sweet fixed (uncanc. alternatives).
10. meteors [are]] 'meteors' is canc. and 'are' is not in MS, perhaps because the
rhyme was obvious.
12. pain] Canc. in MS.
16–18. till late . . . now seek] Very dubious readings. S.'s first draft of 16–17 was:
'The peace that I found not before / The peace that I once have lost'.
17. have lost] Canc. in MS.
Stanza 5. It is not clear whether stanza 6 is a sequel or a substitute for stanza 5,
which, however, is uncanc. and so included in the text. Except for lines 23, 25,
the readings are very uncertain.
22. not given to me] Canc. in MS.
24. Possibly this line should read Should hallow deaths lips to thee.
25. Substituted for What I am, should be seen to be: i.e. 'I am not going to hide my
true feelings'.

Sweet lips, could my heart have hidden
That its life was consumed by you
Ye would not have then forbidden
The death which a heart so true
30 Sought in your burning dew. –

We meet not as then we parted–
We feel more than all may see–
My bosom is heavy hearted,
And thine full of doubt for me:
35 One moment has bound the free.

100 Fragments written in Claire Clairmont's Journal

Date of composition unknown; perhaps between 14 and 23 April 1814, though conceivably at various dates before 9 November. The verses are drafted, or copied, on the fourth and fifth pages counting backwards from the back cover of Claire Clairmont's journal for 14 August–9 November 1814 (BL MS Ashley 394), as if S. had used these pages before giving the book to Claire, who turned it upside down and began filling it from the other end. The pages between the back cover and S.'s verses contain the Latin and Italian passages in S.'s hand mentioned in the headnote to No. 99 (see *Claire Jnl* 59–63 for reprint and comment). This suggests that the fragments were in the notebook before S.'s flight to Switzerland with Mary Godwin on 28 July, and belong to the Bracknell period. Fragment (a) could be associated with S.'s despondent retrospect of his situation as described in the letter to Hogg of 16 March (*L* i 383). Fragment (c) could be a description of a fire-balloon (the hiatus in lines 15–16 at the foot of the MS was caused by a burn and a repair), but seems rather to depict aspects of 'the old moon in the new moon's arms' (see especially lines 7–8, suggesting the edge of faint light visible round the gnome's enclosing hand; cp. *PU* IV 206–13), which S. might have seen in the western evening sky at Bracknell on 22 or 23 April. He recalled in his letter to Hogg of 4 October that 'The season was most beautiful. The evenings were so serene & mild' (*L* i 402). At the times the new moons became visible in May, June, and July S. was in London, no longer enjoying the 'delightful tranquillity' of the Boinville home. The only punctuation supplied consists in the commas of lines 4, 5, and 11, in Fragment (c).

Text from BL MS Ashley 394, ff. 105ʳ rev–103ᵛ rev.

Published in *White* i 702–3; *MLR* xlviii (April 1953) 181–4; *Claire Jnl* 62–3.

28. Ye] Addressing the lips.

(a)   The thoughts of my past life
          Rise like the ghosts of an unquiet dream
          Blackening the cheerful morn

(b)   Now the dark boughs of the aeolian pine
          Swing to the sweeping wind, and the light clouds
          And the blue sky beyond so deep and still
          Commingles like a sympathy of sight
   5   With the sweet music!

(c)   How beautiful it sails
          Along the silent and serene expanse
          Blending its sober and aërial tints
          With the pale sky. – Now an extinguished moon,
   5   The frail dim spectre of some quenchèd orb,
          Beamless and broad on the still air upheld
          It hangs in Heaven's deep azure! like a flame
          Sphered by the hand of some belated gnome
          That chides for its delay the pausing blast
  10   Where the red light of evening's solemn smile
          Hangs on the skirts of the exhausted storm,
          Or where the embattled clouds of orient day
          Allow short respite to the waning stars
          Most like a mote that mocks the wandering gaze
  15   When [   ]ary moons
          Troop [   ] feverish dream

(b)

¶ 100.1. On the opposite page of *MS* is an alternative or discarded line, 'Now the eolian chords within yon bower', enclosed by, but spaced apart from, lines 13 and 14 of Fragment (c), into which the editors have incorporated it; this, however, produces evident nonsense. Fragment (b) must have been written out first, and Fragment (c) written round the stray line. *boughs*] bows *White*. *aeolian*] i.e. acting as a wind-harp.

4. Commingles] Singular because the visual scene (clouds and sky united in a single phenomenon) mingles with the music.

(c)

3. sober] silver *MLR*.

6. and broad] and [   ] *MLR*.

9. blast] blush *Claire Jnl*.

11. storm] [?sea] *White*.

12. Or where] As when *White*.

13–14. See note to Fragment (b) line 1, above.

14. mote] [poet?] *White*; moth *MLR, Claire Jnl, Rogers*. *gaze*] fire [?] *Claire Jnl, Rogers*.

15. When] When mill[*Claire Jnl, Rogers*.

101 Stanzas.–April, 1814

According to Claire Clairmont in later life, 'Shelley at Bracknell fell in love with Mrs Turner. Madame de Boinville and Mrs Turner were indignant, and broke off his acquaintance; but Harriet Shelley continued to visit them, and remained at Bracknell, while Shelley took refuge in London. The stanzas dated April, 1814, are addressed to Madame de Boinville and Cornelia Turner' (*Dowden Life* ii 549). Harriet S. in fact went to London with her sister Eliza on 14 April, and S. avoided his own 'desolated hearth' by staying with the Boinvilles. A crisis in their relationship must have alienated Mrs Boinville (the 'friend' of line 6) while Cornelia (the 'lover' of line 7–though 'lover' bears no unequivocally physical implication) would not commit herself to intercede for him. Lines 1–2 suggest a moon in its first quarter, so the poem may well have been composed about 25 April. Mrs Boinville apparently relented so far as to come to nurse S. in London when he took poison early in July (*Dowden Life* ii 544–5).

This self-admonishing poem is in a very unusual (and slightly irregular) metre, which however has affinities with that of Moore's 'The Irish Peasant to his Mistress' (*Irish Melodies* Series iii, 1810).

Text from *1816* 56–8.

Published in *1816*.

> Away! the moor is dark beneath the moon,
>   Rapid clouds have drank the last pale beam of even:
> Away! the gathering winds will call the darkness soon,
>   And profoundest midnight shroud the serene lights of
>   heaven.
> 5 Pause not! The time is past! Every voice cries, Away!
>   Tempt not with one last tear thy friend's ungentle
>   mood:
> Thy lover's eye, so glazed and cold, dares not entreat thy
>   stay:
>   Duty and dereliction guide thee back to solitude.
>
> Away, away! to thy sad and silent home;
> 10   Pour bitter tears on its desolated hearth;
> Watch the dim shades as like ghosts they go and come,
>   And complicate strange webs of melancholy mirth.

¶ *101.1. the moor is dark*] Hogg, who had very recently visited Bracknell, described Ascot Heath at night as 'a land of darkness, of thick, black darkness, of solitude, stillness, and silence' (*Hogg* ii 523–4).

2. drank] A common form of the past participle at this date.

8. Duty and dereliction] i.e. his duty to his wife, and Cornelia's abandonment of him.

The leaves of wasted autumn woods shall float around
    thine head:
The blooms of dewy spring shall gleam beneath thy
    feet:
15 But thy soul or this world must fade in the frost that
    binds the dead,
Ere midnight's frown and morning's smile, ere thou
    and peace may meet.

The cloud shadows of midnight possess their own
                  repose,
For the weary winds are silent, or the moon is in the
                  deep:
Some respite to its turbulence unresting ocean knows;
20   Whatever moves, or toils, or grieves, hath its
                  appointed sleep.
Thou in the grave shalt rest—yet till the phantoms flee
    Which that house and heath and garden made dear to
                  thee erewhile,
Thy remembrance, and repentance, and deep musings
                  are not free
From the music of two voices and the light of one
                  sweet smile.

102 'Mine eyes were dim with tears unshed'

Probably composed just after the first declaration of love between S. and Mary Godwin on 26 June 1814, although mid-July is also possible. The poem exists only as a chaotic pencilled draft in *Nbk 11*, embedded in material of widely differing dates. When after S.'s death his widow worked through his note-books for *1824* she headed her transcription of this poem into Bod. MS Shelley d.9 'To MWG', and dated it 'June. 1814.' (see *Massey* 70–6). Her transcript was presumably Garnett's 'unexpected discovery' that the poem 'hitherto referred to the date of 1821, was in fact written in June, 1814, and addressed to Mary' (*Relics* 161). Copying beyond the first few pages of *Nbk 11*, Mary had evidently lost confidence in her ascription because the accompanying materials all seemed much later in date, cancelled the initials 'MWG' and printed the title

20–1. Whatever moves . . . shalt rest] A recurrent lament of S.'s, deriving ultimately from *Matthew* viii 20: 'The foxes have holes, and the birds of the air have nests; but the Son of man hath not where to lay his head'. Cp. *Mask of Anarchy* 197–208; 'To Edward and Jane Williams' 41–8; 'Tell me, Star', etc.

simply as 'To——' in *1824* (211). In *1839* the non-committal title was retained, and the lyric placed among the 'Poems written in 1821' (iv 115–16), apparently as referring to Emilia Viviani (Mary had found a fragment, six pages earlier in *Nbk 11*, which seemed to begin 'Thy gentle voice Emilia dear'). She would not necessarily have seen a poem written to her in June 1814, because of difficulties which the poem itself explains, and unless S. made a copy he could hardly have expected her to read it. Yet unless dramatic in conception (see notes to lines 10–12, 21–4 below) the poem is, as Rossetti said, unintelligible if it does not address Mary Godwin. On 26 June S. and Mary confessed their love for each other: 'I disguised from myself the true nature of [my] affection. I endeavoured also to conceal it from Mary: but without success. . . No expressions can convey the remotest conception of the *manner* in which she dispelled my delusions. The sublime & rapturous moment when she confessed herself mine, who had so long been her's in secret cannot be painted to mortal imaginations . . . Tho' striktly watched, & regarded with a suspicious eye, opportunities of frequent intercourse were not wanting.–When we meet, I will give you a more explicit detail of the progress of our intercourse: How in opposition to her fathers will, to Harriet's exertions we still continued to meet.–How Godwin's distress induced us to prolong the period of our departure. How the cruelty & injustice with which we were treated, compelled us to disregard, all consideration but that of the happiness of each other' (S. to Hogg, 4 October 1814, *L* i 403). Godwin was told on 6 July, and the elopement took place on the 28th after three weeks of miserable indecision. For accounts of this confused period see *Dowden Life* i 418–38, ii 541–5; *White* i 334–46. The poem describes periods of frustration and pretence (stanzas 1–2, 5–6) before and after an avowal (4–5), and ends with a plea for open sincerity as the only defence of 'sacred friendship' against a corrupting world. See also 'When passion's trance is overpast' and headnote. The draft, obscure in places, was originally in the 2nd person singular; S. then altered most but not all these pronouns to the plural, and any attempt to methodize them is both impractical and destructive. Text from *Nbk 11* ff. 9–11.
Published in *1824* 211–12.

> Mine eyes were dim with tears unshed;
>   Yes, I was firm–they did not flow.
> My baffled looks did seek yet dread
>   To meet your looks . . . I could not know
> 5 How anxiously they sought to shine
>   With soothing pity upon mine.

¶ 102.2. *they did not flow.*] thus did not thou:– *1824*; thus wert not thou;– *1839*, eds.
3. *seek*] Doubtful reading; possibly 'start'; but 'did seek' replaces 'did long' *canc.*
6. *upon*] into *MS alternative in ink.* If the alternative in line 24 is accepted, this must also be.

To sit and curb the soul's mute rage
Which preys upon itself alone–
To curse that life which is the cage
10   Of fettered grief that dares not groan,
Hiding from many a careless eye
The scornèd load of agony,

Whilst you alone then not regarded
The tie which you alone should be,–
15   To spend years thus–and be rewarded
As you, sweet love, requited me
When none were nigh–oh, I did wake
From torture for that moment's sake.

Upon my heart your accents sweet
20   Of peace and pity fell like dew
On flowers half dead, thy lips did meet
Mine tremblingly, thy dark eyes threw
Their soft persuasion on my brain,
Turning to bliss its wayward pain.

10–12 *fettered grief . . . load of agony*] Cp. 'Julian and Maddalo' 300–9.
13–14.   Whilst thou alone, then not regarded,
                  The [   ] thou alone should be, *1824, eds*
              Whilst thou alone then–not regarded,
                  Though hateless–thou alone shouldst be *Rogers*
'Tho hateless' imitates the cryptic scrawl of *MS* but makes no sense, nor could
any imaginable word supplied in the hiatus of *1824* make sense. The text
meaning is: 'You alone disregarded the marriage-tie which you alone have a
right to'. S. had used 'tie' in a similar sense in 'To Mary who died in this
opinion' (No. 40) 9–10: 'Yet is the tie departed / Which bound thy lovely soul
to bliss?'. Thus the characteristic structure of lines 7–18 is: 'To hide my pain
(while you alone were honest about things) for what seemed years, and then to
receive such a reward–oh, that was worth everything'.
22–3. *thy dark eyes . . . on my brain*] Cp. 'Scene for *Tasso*' 37–9: 'Last of the
wingèd children of his brain / Ere yet the soft persuasion of his tongue / Had
coloured it to intellectual sight'.
24. Charming away its dream of *MS alternative in ink* (see note to line 6), *1824,
eds.*

25 We are not happy, sweet, our state
        Is strange, and full of doubt and fear;
    More need for truth, that ills and hate,
        Reserve or censure come not near
    Our sacred friendship, lest there be
30 No solace left for you and me.

    Gentle and good and mild thou art,
        Nor can I live if thou appear
    Aught but thyself–or turn thine heart
        Away from me–or stoop to wear
35 The mask of scorn–although it be
    To hide the love you feel for me.

103 'Dear Home . . .'

These draft lines, themselves cancelled, follow a cancelled opening:

>   Dear Home, thou scene of joys which now are cold
>   And griefs whose gentle memory now reproves

In *Nbk 11* they precede, and appear to pre-date, the draft of 'The Sunset', written at Bishopsgate early in 1816. S. visited his home at Field Place, near Horsham, Sussex, for the last time on 12 January 1815 (*White* i 393–4), to hear the reading of his grandfather's will, but 'His Father would not allow him to enter Field Place; he sits before the door, and reads "Comus" ' (*Mary Jnl* i 60). This seems the likeliest time of composition if 'I visit thee' was literally meant. Text from *Nbk 11* f. 19.
Published in *Relics* 74 (lines 1–3).

27–9.   More need of words that ills abate;–
                    Reserve or censure come not near
                    Our sacred friendship, *1824, eds*

(with 'of' corrected to 'for'). *MS* has no pointing, but the canc. original beginning of line 28, *Or pain or*, shows the construction intended. A facsimile of *MS* appears as frontispiece to *1975*.
27. *truth*] Doubtful reading; perhaps 'trust' or even 'heed'. But see note on line 30. *and hate*] Perhaps originally *or hate*, with the 'o' looped into an ampersand.
30. A secret of such misery *MS canc.*

> Dear Home, thou scene of earliest hopes and joys
> The least of whom wronged Memory ever makes
> Bitterer than all thine unremembered tears –
> I visit thee

104 'On her hind paws the Dormouse stood'

Mary S. quoted 'Shelley's distitch' in a letter to Hogg on 25 April 1815, to describe her reaction to his letters when she was on holiday with S. at Salt Hill near Eton, but the joking lines were no doubt already in circulation among the three of them. 'The Dormouse', 'the Maie', and 'Pecksie' were pet names for Mary S. (she signed this letter 'Your affectionate Dormouse'). It has been suggested that 'Pecksie' derives from one of the nestlings in 'The History of the Robins' in Mrs Trimmer's *Fabulous Histories: Designed for the Instruction of Children* (1786, many edns), where Pecksy could not learn music (ch. ii), was very amiable (ch. iii), and 'knew the value of parental instruction so well, that she should certainly treasure up in her heart every maxim of it' (ch. xxiii), but which, if any, of these characteristics was the operative one is unknown. A 'maie' was a French kneading-trough for bread; but the relevance is even more dubious. Mary S. quoted four more lines in her letter, which may or may not be also S.'s invention:

> For Maië girls are Maië girls
> Wherever they're found
> In air or in water
> Or In the ground

Text from SC 287: quoted by permission of the Carl H. Pforzheimer Library. Published in *Harriet and Mary* (privately printed 1944), reprinted in *New SL* 86; SC iii 466.

On her hind paws the Dormouse stood
In a wild and mingled mood
Of Maiëishness and Pecksietude.

¶ *103.2.* whom] which *Relics*. S. probably embodies his 'hopes and joys' in particular persons.
¶ *104.3. Maiëishness*] The significance of 'Maie' is unknown. It could be just a diminutive of 'Mary'.

105 'What Mary is . . .'

According to Forman, who first printed them, 'These lines . . . are said to have been scratched by Shelley on a window-pane at a house wherein he lodged while staying in London. I have them on the authority of a gentleman whose mother was the proprietress of the house' (*Forman 1876–7* iv 247n.). Corroborative evidence is lacking, but the lines are probably genuine. S. had many London addresses in 1814–15, and the lines could date from almost any time between 14 September 1814 and 3 August 1815; but he was dodging creditors for some weeks at the end of 1814 and is less likely to have marked his presence. A plausible guess is April 1815 at 13 Arabella Road, Pimlico, when Shelley was again reading Italian (*Mary Jnl* i 74–6) and Mary was regaining her spirits after losing her premature baby on 6 March. The lines are translated from Dante's sonnet 'Negli occhi porta la mia donna Amore' 12–14, in *La Vita Nuova*, substituting 'Mary' for the pronoun in the first line:

> Quel ch'ella par, quando un poco sorride,
> Non si può dicer nè tenere a mente,
> Si è nuovo miracolo e gentile.

(Text from *Canzoni e Sonetti di Dante Alighieri*, ed. Romualdo Zotti (London 1809) iv 231–2: 'How she looks when she smiles a little cannot be said or entertained in the mind, it is so new and gracious a miracle'). It is not known when S. first read the *Vita Nuova*; he read Italian poetry (but not Dante) with Hogg in 1813 (*Hogg* ii 376–81), and studied Italian (including Dante) with Cornelia Turner in March 1814.
Text from *Forman 1876–7* iv 247.
Published in *Forman 1876–7*.

> What Mary is when she a little smiles
> I cannot even tell or call to mind,
> It is a miracle so new, so rare.

106 'O! there are spirits of the air'

ΔΑΚΡΥΕΙ ΔΙΟΕΩ ΜΟΤΜΟΝ ΑΜΟΤΜΟΝ

Date of composition unknown; possibly early in 1815. S. ordered 'Coleridge's Poems' (i.e. the 3rd edn of *Poems*, 1803) on 24 December 1812 (*L* i 345), and the book is listed among those read in 1815 (*Mary Jnl* i 90). S. mentions an edition of Euripides on 13 February 1815 (*Mary Jnl* i 64). But he ordered a translation of the *Hippolytus* on 27 September (*L* i 433), so the poem (or just its Greek

heading) may belong to the autumn (see note on line 1). In *1816* the poem
appeared under the Greek heading only; for *1839* (iii 6) Mary S. substituted the
title 'To ✱ ✱ ✱ ✱ .', explaining in her 'Note on the Early Poems': 'The poem
beginning "Oh, there are spirits in the air [*sic*]," was addressed in idea to
Coleridge, whom he never knew; and at whose character he could only guess
imperfectly, through his writings, and accounts he heard of him from some
who knew him well. He regarded his change of opinion as rather an act of will
than conviction, and believed that in his inner heart he would be haunted by
what Shelley considered the better and holier aspirations of his youth.' (iii
15–16). There is no good reason to doubt Mary's long and informed account,
though many have preferred to think the poem addressed to S. himself. If so,
lines 13–16 describe his loss of Harriet Grove, while stanzas 5–6 reflect S.'s
realization of the failure of his marriage to Harriet Westbrook, and the poem
must date from spring 1814. But in writing of one 'whom he never knew' it is
likely, as P. F. Butter has suggested, that S. 'felt, or imagined, an affinity with
Coleridge, and used his own experience in interpreting the other's' (*Butter
(1970)* 246). The poem's picture of its subject is very similar to that of Coleridge in *Peter Bell the Third* (1819) 383–7:

> . . . a man who might have turned
> Hell into Heaven–and so in gladness
> A Heaven unto himself have earned;
> But he in shadows undiscerned
> Trusted, –and damned himself to madness.

S. may have drawn on other supposed experiences too (see note to lines 13–16
below). As Butter also notes, the theme is related to that of *Alastor*. The Greek
title-epigraph is from Euripides, *Hippolytus* 1142–3, slightly truncated: '[For
your sad fate] I shall endure with tears an unfortunate fortune'. The Chorus is
commiserating with Hippolytus, exiled by his father after his mother's false
accusation of rape.
Text from *1816* 53–5.
Published in *1816*.

> O! there are spirits of the air,
>   And genii of the evening breeze,

¶ *106.1. spirits of the air*] Perhaps referring to Alvar's invocation to the spirits
surrounding the earth in Coleridge's *Remorse* (III i 44–5, 53–5). Harriet S. had
ordered two copies of *Remorse* on publication in 1813 (*L* i 351*n*.). Or to 'Lines
on an Autumnal Evening' (1796) 37, 43–4: 'Spirits of Love! / . . . O heed the
spell, and hither wing your way, / Like far-off music, voyaging the breeze'.
2. genii of the evening breeze] A probable reference to Coleridge's 'The Eolian
Harp' (1796). Cp. *Q Mab* i 52–3: '. . . that strange lyre whose strings / The genii
of the breezes sweep'.

And gentle ghosts, with eyes as fair
    As star-beams among twilight trees:—
5   Such lovely ministers to meet
Oft hast thou turned from men thy lonely feet.

With mountain winds, and babbling springs,
    And moonlight seas, that are the voice
Of these inexplicable things
10   Thou didst hold commune, and rejoice
When they did answer thee; but they
Cast, like a worthless boon, thy love away.

And thou hast sought in starry eyes
    Beams that were never meant for thine,
15 Another's wealth:—tame sacrifice
    To a fond faith! still dost thou pine?
Still dost thou hope that greeting hands,
Voice, looks, or lips, may answer thy demands?

Ah! wherefore didst thou build thine hope
20   On the false earth's inconstancy?
Did thine own mind afford no scope
    Of love, or moving thoughts to thee?
That natural scenes or human smiles
Could steal the power to wind thee in their wiles?

25 Yes, all the faithless smiles are fled
    Whose falsehood left thee broken-hearted;

---

3. *gentle ghosts*] One was Chatterton's, from Coleridge's 'Monody on the
Death of Chatterton' (1794) 118–21:

> Here, far from men, amid this pathless grove,
> In solemn thought the Minstrel wont to rove,
> Like star-beam on the slow sequester'd tide
> Lone glittering, through the high tree branching wide.

13–16. *And thou hast sought . . . To a fond faith!*] i.e. 'the eyes you loved were
destined to bestow their favour on another, in acquiescence to Christian
doctrine' ('a fond faith'). Coleridge had been married for five years when in
1799 he met and loved Sara Hutchinson. S. may also remember his own
experience with Harriet Grove, and what he had been told by Southey of the
poet James Montgomery who 'loved an apparently amiable female. He was
about to marry her.—Having some affairs in the West Indies he went to settle
them before his marriage. On his return to Sheffield he actually met the
marriage procession of this woman who had in the meantime chosen another
love. He became melancholy, mad; the horrible events of his life preyed on his
mind . . . the contest between his reason and his faith was destroying. He is
now a methodist . . .' (L i 216).

14. *thine,*] thine *1816*.

The glory of the moon is dead;
   Night's ghosts and dreams have now departed;
Thine own soul still is true to thee,
30   But changed to a foul fiend through misery.

This fiend, whose ghastly presence ever
   Beside thee like thy shadow hangs,
Dream not to chase; – the mad endeavour
   Would scourge thee to severer pangs.
35   Be as thou art. Thy settled fate,
Dark as it is, all change would aggravate.

107 Translated from the Greek of Moschus

ταν ἁλα ταν γλαυκαν ὁταν ὡνεμος ατρεμα βαλλη, κ.τ.λ.

S. is not recorded as having read the 'Works of Theocritus, Moschus, &c' until
1816 (*Mary Jnl* i 97) but *1816* was printed all but one sheet by 6 January (*L* i
438–9), so this sonnet-version of Moschus's Idyll v evidently belongs to 1815
or earlier. The theme of homecoming from a once-seductive sea (and for
'home' in line 7 there is no equivalent in the original) suggests that S. was
drawn to translate it about 1 July 1815 when he and Mary returned from
holiday in Torquay in anticipation of a new home near Windsor. Moschus was
a Greek bucolic poet of the 2nd century B.C.; S. also translated his Idyll vi and
part of Idyll iii, the elegy on Bion that was an important source of *Adonais*. The
Greek subheading is the first line of the poem: 'When the breeze gently stirs the
gray-green sea, etc.'
Text from *1816* 76–7.
Published in *1816*.

When winds that move not its calm surface sweep
The azure sea, I love the land no more;
The smiles of the serene and tranquil deep
Tempt my unquiet mind. – But when the roar
5   Of ocean's grey abyss resounds, and foam
Gathers upon the sea, and vast waves burst,
I turn from the drear aspect to the home
Of earth and its deep woods, where interspersed,
When winds blow loud, pines make sweet melody.
10   Whose house is some lone bark, whose toil the sea,
Whose prey the wandering fish, an evil lot
Has chosen. – But I my languid limbs will fling
Beneath the plane, where the brook's murmuring
Moves the calm spirit, but disturbs it not.

108 Sonnet. From the Italian of Dante Alighieri to Guido Cavalcanti

S.'s translation of this sonnet from the Canzoniere, 'Guido, vorrei, che tu, e Lappo, ed io . . .', was probably suggested by the voyage he himself made up the Thames with Mary S., Peacock, and Charles Clairmont in early September 1815 (see headnote to No. 109). Modern Italian texts differ in some respects from S.'s likely original (see notes to lines 1, 10 below).
Text from *1816* 74–5.
Published in *1816*.

> Guido, I would that Lappo, thou, and I,
> Led by some strong enchantment, might ascend
> A magic ship, whose charmèd sails should fly
> With winds at will where'er our thoughts might wend,
> 5 And that no change, nor any evil chance
> Should mar our joyous voyage; but it might be,
> That even satiety should still enhance
> Between our hearts their strict community:
> And that the bounteous wizard then would place
> 10 Vanna and Bice and my gentle love,
> Companions of our wandering, and would grace
> With passionate talk wherever we might rove
> Our time, and each were as content and free
> As I believe that thou and I should be.

109 A Summer-Evening Churchyard, Lechlade, Gloucestershire

Composed between 4 and 6 September 1815. Relieved financially by his grandfather's death on 5 January and a settlement with his father finalized on 13 May, S. found a house at Bishopsgate adjoining Windsor Park and took several

¶ *108.1.* Guido Cavalcanti and Lapo Gianni (spelt 'Lappo' in earlier Italian texts) were friends of Dante's.
5. And that] So that *1839* (probably Mary S.'s correction for 'Sicchè').
10. Contemporary texts read: 'E Monna Vanna, e Monna Bice poi, / Con quella su il numer della trenta' – 'With her who is named thirtieth on the list [of the most beautiful women in Florence]'. 'Bice' was Beatrice, Dante's own lady, so 'my' could be a misreading of S.'s 'thy'. Modern texts read 'Lagia' for 'Bice'.
¶ *109. Title.* A Summer-Evening Church-yard *1816. Lechlade*] Lechdale *1839.*

brief holidays with Mary, including an excursion by boat to find the source of
the Thames. Peacock and Claire Clairmont's brother Charles also took part
and described the expedition: 'At the end of August 1815 we made an excursion on the Thames to Lechlade, in Gloucestershire, and as much higher as
there was water to float our skiff. It was a dry season, and we did not get much
beyond Inglesham Weir . . . We started from, and returned to, Old Windsor,
and our excursion occupied about ten days . . . We passed two nights in a
comfortable inn at Lechlade, and his lines: *A Summer Evening on the Thames at
Lechlade*, were written then and there' (*Peacock Works* viii 99); see also Clairmont's account in *Dowden Life* i 528–30). Mary S. confusingly assigns the
outing to 'a bright warm July' but in 'autumn' (*1839* iii 16), perhaps because she
had lost her diary. S.'s letters from Bishopsgate on 26 August and 10 September set outside limits for the trip, which must have been approximately 30
August–10 September, and the two nights at Lechlade were probably between
4–6 September and at the New Inn (A. Williams, *Round About the Upper
Thames* (1922) 123–4), the recommended coaching inn which is very near the
church.

   The poem owes much in approach and phrasing to the 'graveyard' poetry of
Gray and Blair, and to Collins.
Text from *1816* 64–6.
Published in *1816*.

　　　The wind has swept from the wide atmosphere
　　　Each vapour that obscured the sunset's ray;
　　　And pallid evening twines its beaming hair
　　　In duskier braids around the languid eyes of day:
　5　Silence and twilight, unbeloved of men,
　　　Creep hand in hand from yon obscurest glen.

　　　They breathe their spells towards the departing day,
　　　Encompassing the earth, air, stars, and sea;
　　　Light, sound, and motion own the potent sway,
　10　Responding to the charm with its own mystery.
　　　The winds are still, or the dry church-tower grass
　　　Knows not their gentle motions as they pass.

　　　Thou too, aërial Pile! whose pinnacles
　　　Point from one shrine like pyramids of fire,

3–4. Cp. Collins, 'Ode to Evening' 5–8: 'O nymph reserved, while now the
bright-haired sun / Sits in yon western tent, whose cloudy skirts, / With brede
ethereal wove . . .'
5. *Silence and twilight*] Perhaps suggested by Young, *The Complaint; or, Night-
Thoughts on Life, Death, and Immortality* (1742–45) i 28–9: 'Silence and darkness! solemn sisters! twins / From ancient Night' etc.
13–14. *Thou too . . . pyramids of fire*] Lechlade Church has a tower with a slender

15   Obeyest in silence their sweet solemn spells,
     Clothing in hues of heaven thy dim and distant spire,
     Around whose lessening and invisible height
     Gather among the stars the clouds of night.

     The dead are sleeping in their sepulchres:
20   And, mouldering as they sleep, a thrilling sound
     Half sense, half thought, among the darkness stirs,
     Breathed from their wormy beds all living things
          around,
     And mingling with the still night and mute sky
     Its awful hush is felt inaudibly.

25   Thus solemnized and softened, death is mild
     And terrorless as this serenest night:
     Here could I hope, like some enquiring child
     Sporting on graves, that death did hide from human sight
     Sweet secrets, or beside its breathless sleep
30   That loveliest dreams perpetual watch did keep.

110   Guido Cavalcanti to Dante Alighieri

Date of composition unknown; possibly late summer 1815. S. seems to have
spent much of this summer writing prose, and the MS (now untraced) com-
prises part of a philosophical work in prose (see *Forman 1880* vi 282, 287–90 for
details). The translation is from Cavalcanti's sonnet 'Io vengo il giorno a te
infinite volte' (*Rime di diversi antichi autori Toscani in dodici libri raccolte* (Venice
1740) 342), and may have been omitted from *1816* because of its obvious
affinity with the sonnet on Wordsworth (No. 111), which it perhaps suggested. There are signs that S. had Wordsworth in mind when translating it:
there is no equivalent in the Italian to '*Changed* thoughts' (line 2), or to 'that

---

central spire and four short spires at the corners. 'Pyramid' was thought to
mean 'flame-shaped' (from the Greek for 'fire'): Satan in *Paradise Lost* (ii 1013)
'Springs upward like a Pyramid of fire'. Perhaps S. remembered Coleridge's
The Friend No. xiv, 23 November 1809 (reprinted 1812): '. . . spire-steeples,
which . . . point as with silent finger to the sky and stars, and sometimes when
they reflect the brazen light of a rich though rainy sun-set, appear like a
pyramid of flame burning heaven-ward'.
15. *their . . . spells*] i.e. those of 'Silence and twilight' (line 5).
20. *mouldering as they sleep*] An inversion: 'as they sleep mouldering'.

sweet mood / When thou wert faithful to thyself and me' (7–8), or to 'In vain / I
seek what once thou wert' (10–11; cp. 'To Wordsworth' 5–6, 13).

Unless Forman's facsimile in *Forman 1876–7* is unreliable his assertion (endorsed by some later editors) that 'The MS is somewhat curiously punctuated'
is inexplicable. The text follows the punctuation of the facsimile, adding a
colon in line 2 and a comma in line 6.
Text from *Forman 1876–7* iv 248 (facsimile).
Published in *Forman 1876–7*.

> Returning from its daily quest, my Spirit
> Changed thoughts and vile in thee doth weep to find:
> It grieves me that thy mild and gentle mind
> Those ample virtues which it did inherit
> 5 Has lost. Once thou didst loathe the multitude
> Of blind and madding men–I then loved thee,
> I loved thy lofty songs and that sweet mood
> When thou wert faithful to thyself and me.
> I dare not now through thy degraded state
> 10 Own the delight thy strains inspire. In vain
> I seek what once thou wert. We cannot meet
> As we were wont. Again and yet again
> Ponder my words: so the false Spirit shall fly
> And leave to thee thy true integrity.

111 To Wordsworth

On 14 September 1814 Mary S. noted: 'Shelley . . . brings home Wordsworth's
"Excursion", of which we read a part, much disappointed. He is a slave' (*Mary
Jnl* i 25). The poem may reflect that initial disillusion with such passages as the
'Poet's Address to the State and Church of England' opening Bk VI. But
paradoxically S.'s interest in Wordsworth's poetry only developed seriously
during the following year; in 1815 he re-read *The Excursion* (*Mary Jnl* i 91), and
procured the *Poems* immediately after their publication (21 April 1815; *Mary Jnl*
i 76). But he never ceased to deplore Wordsworth's change of views, and this
sonnet may well date as late as September–October 1815.
Text from *1816* 67–8.
Published in *1816*.

¶ *110.5–6. the multitude / Of blind and madding men*] A rendering of 'la nojosa
gente' ('the tedious rabble'). Cp. 'To Wordsworth' 9–10: 'Thou hast . . . stood
/ Above the blind and battling multitude'.

Poet of Nature, thou hast wept to know
That things depart which never may return:
Childhood and youth, friendship and love's first glow,
Have fled like sweet dreams, leaving thee to mourn.
5   These common woes I feel. One loss is mine
Which thou too feel'st, yet I alone deplore.
Thou wert as a lone star, whose light did shine
On some frail bark in winter's midnight roar:
Thou hast like to a rock-built refuge stood
10   Above the blind and battling multitude:
In honoured poverty thy voice did weave
Songs consecrate to truth and liberty, –
Deserting these, thou leavest me to grieve,
Thus having been, that thou shouldst cease to be.

112 Feelings of a Republican on the Fall of Bonaparte

The 'fall' of Buonaparte could mean his abdication in April 1814, but the
conclusion of the sonnet, which condemns the deeds and principles of the
Allied victors even more savagely than it does Bonaparte himself, shows that
the lines were written after Waterloo, most likely after the Treaty of the Holy
Alliance (26 September 1815). S. always saw Napoleon as a mighty product of
the French Revolution who, however, had betrayed his great opportunity by
perverting its energies into a new imperialism: he was 'the Anarch of [Free-
dom's] own bewildered powers' ('Ode to Liberty' (1820) 171–80). S. explained in 1819: 'The Revolution in France overthrew the hierarchy, the
aristocracy, and the monarchy, and the whole of that peculiarly insolent and

¶ *111.1–4.* Wordsworth's 'Ode, Intimations of Immortality', 'Elegiac Stanzas
Suggested by a Picture of Peele Castle', 'A Complaint' (all 1807), and 'Surprised by Joy' (1815) are among the poems S. probably had in mind.
7. Thou wert as a lone star] Echoing Wordsworth's own sonnet on Milton,
'London, 1802' 9: 'Thy soul was like a Star and dwelt apart'.
10. blind and battling multitude] 'thoughtless followers of the doctrine of self-
interest' rather than the common people as such.
11. honoured poverty] In 1811 at Keswick S. had heard and believed that
'Wordsworth . . . yet retains the integrity of his independance, but his poverty
is such that he is frequently obliged to beg for a shirt to his back' (*L* i 208–9).
12. Wordsworth had headed one section of his *Poems in Two Volumes* (1807)
'Sonnets Dedicated to Liberty'.

oppressive system on which they were based. But as it only partially extinguished those passions which are the spirit of these forms a reaction took place which has restored in a certain limited degree the old system . . . The usurpation of Bonaparte, and then the Restoration of the Bourbons were the shapes in which this reaction clothed itself, and the heart of every lover of liberty was struck as with a palsy by the succession of these events' ('A Philosophical View of Reform', *Prose* 236).
Text from *1816* 69–70.
Published in *1816*.

> I hated thee, fallen tyrant! I did groan
> To think that a most unambitious slave,
> Like thou, shouldst dance and revel on the grave
> Of Liberty. Thou mightst have built thy throne
> 5 Where it had stood even now: thou didst prefer
> A frail and bloody pomp which time has swept
> In fragments towards oblivion. Massacre,
> For this I prayed, would on thy sleep have crept,
> Treason and Slavery, Rapine, Fear, and Lust,
> 10 And stifled thee, their minister. I know
> Too late, since thou and France are in the dust,
> That virtue owns a more eternal foe
> Than force or fraud: old Custom, legal Crime,
> And bloody Faith the foulest birth of time.

113 Mutability

Date of composition unknown; here assigned to winter 1815–16 mainly on grounds of stylistic maturity. Lines 1–4 suggest a late autumn or winter night, but this could have been equally well a night in 1814. Coleridge's 'Eolian

¶ 112.2. *unambitious*] unaspiring in the true sense, lacking high ideals.
3. *shouldst*] Attracted into the 2nd person by *thou*.
5. *had stood*] would have stood.
7–8 *Massacre, / For this I prayed,*] Massacre, / For this, I prayed, *Rossetti 1870*; Massacre,– / For this I prayed,– *Locock 1911*. The commas of the text function as brackets, making the enclosed phrase a parenthesis.
13. *legal Crime*] The oppressions of the victors after Waterloo. S. wrote to Hogg, in a letter in the Abinger collection postmarked 26 August: 'You will see in the papers the continuance of the same system which the Allies had begun to pursue; and a most spirited remonstrance of the king of France's ministers against the enormities of their troops' (*L* i 430).

Harp', which may have influenced lines 5–8, was read in 1815 (*Mary Jnl* i 90);
and as a meditation on the transience and vulnerability of human life the poem
is likely to be associated with S.'s supposed serious illness in spring 1815 (see
headnote to No. 114). In a letter dated by Jones 4 November 1814 (*L* i 418–19)
S. told Mary: 'I am an harp responsive to every wind. The scented gale of
summer can wake it to sweet melody, but rough cold blasts draw forth
discordances & jarring sounds'; but S.'s letters to Hogg in September 1815
contain reflections on mortality likewise in the mood of the poem. For the
theme of 'mutability' the sources are numerous, and include Ovid's exposition
of the Pythagorean flux, 'cuncta fluunt . . .' (*Metamorphoses* xv 178–355), and
Spenser's 'Two Cantos of Mutabilitie' (*FQ* VII vii 13–56).
Text from *1816* 59–60.
Published in *1816*.

> We are as clouds that veil the midnight moon;
>   How restlessly they speed, and gleam, and quiver,
> Streaking the darkness radiantly!–yet soon
>   Night closes round, and they are lost for ever:
>
> 5   Or like forgotten lyres, whose dissonant strings
>   Give various response to each varying blast,
> To whose frail frame no second motion brings
>   One mood or modulation like the last.
>
> We rest.–A dream has power to poison sleep;
> 10   We rise.–One wandering thought pollutes the day;
> We feel, conceive or reason, laugh or weep;
>   Embrace fond woe, or cast our cares away:
>
> It is the same!–For, be it joy or sorrow,
>   The path of its departure still is free:
> 15 Man's yesterday may ne'er be like his morrow;
>   Nought may endure but Mutability.

¶ *113.5. forgotten lyres*] An Aeolian harp could be left in a window or tree for the
wind to make music. *dissonant*] variously-sounding. Cp. Coleridge's 'Eolian
Harp' (1796) 40–3: '. . . many idle flitting phantasies, / Traverse my indolent
and passive brain, / As wild and various as the random gales / That swell and
flutter on this subject Lute!'
15. *Man's yesterday . . . his morrow*] Cp. Ovid, *Met.* xv 215–16: 'nec quod
fuimusve sumusve, / cras erimus'.
16. *Nought . . . Mutability*] Cp. Spenser, *FQ* VII vii 47, lines 8–9: 'Wherefore,
this lower world who can deny / But to be subject still to *Mutabilitie*?'

114 Alastor; or,
The Spirit of Solitude

Composed at Bishopsgate between 10 September and 14 December 1815 (the
date of the Preface). Mary S. wrote (*1839* i 141) that ' "Alastor" was composed
on his return' from the voyage up the Thames to Lechlade (see headnote to No.
109), for which S.'s letter of 10 September (*L* i 430) provides a terminal date,
and in a letter postmarked 22 September S. told Hogg: 'I have been engaged
lately in the commencement of several literary plans, which if my present
temper of mind endures I shall probably complete in the winter' (*L* i 432). In
sending the poem to Southey in March S. called it 'the product of a few serene
hours of the last beautiful autumn' (*L* i 461). But S. had foreshadowed the
theme of the poem even before his Thames expedition in a letter to Hogg
postmarked 26 August (*L* i 429–30): 'Yet who is there that will not pursue
phantoms, spend his choicest hours in hunting after dreams, and wake only to
perceive his error and regret that death is so near?' By 6 January 1816 the *Alastor*
volume was in print except for the last sheet, and in this state was offered for
publication to Murray (*L* i 438), who declined it. It was eventually announced
as ready for publication 'in a few days' on 6 February by Baldwin, Cradock and
Joy, jointly with Carpenter & Son (*L* i 449), and S.'s father had received a copy
by 27 February (*S in Eng* 463).

The distinction made in the Preface between 'luminaries of the world' and
'meaner spirits' could have been suggested, or reinforced, by Mary Wollstonecraft's *The Wrongs of Woman; or, Maria*, in her *Posthumous Works* (1798),
which S. had read with Mary S. in 1814 (*Mary Jnl* i 86):

> The youths who are satisfied with the ordinary pleasures of life, and do not
> sigh after ideal phantoms of love and friendship, will never arrive at great
> maturity of understanding; but if these reveries are cherished . . . when
> experience ought to have taught them in what human happiness consists,
> they become as useless as they are wretched. (i 69–70)

The Preface's description of those 'pure and tender-hearted individuals', like
the poet-protagonist of the poem, who 'attempt to exist without human
sympathy' and so 'perish through the intensity and passion of their search after
its communities', may also be indebted to Godwin's *Fleetwood* (1805). This
novel, with which S. was familiar from at least 1812 (*L* i 260), characterizes a
'self-centred seclusion' like that of the poet in *Alastor*:

> 'Fleetwood, you are too much alone. I hear people talk of the raptures of
> solitude; and with what tenderness of affection they can love a tree, a rivulet,
> or a mountain . . . still it will not do. There is a principle in the heart of man
> which demands the society of his like. He that has no such society, is in a
> state but one degree removed from insanity. He pines for an ear into which
> he might pour the story of his thoughts, for an eye that shall flash upon him
> with responsive intelligence, for a face the lines of which shall talk to him in

dumb but eloquent discourse, for a heart that shall beat in unison with his own'. (II ch. xv)

Compare also Fleetwood's account of his own wanderings:

'I wanted something, I knew not what. I sought it in solitude and in crowds, in travel and at home, in ambition and in independence . . . I wandered among mountains and rivers, through verdant plains, and over immense precipices; but nature had no beauties'. (II ch. xi)

The issues were probably brought to a sharper intellectual focus for S. by his reading of Sir William Drummond's *Academical Questions* (1805), ordered by S. on 27 September 1815 (*L* i 433), which places the 'interesting situation of the human mind' of S.'s Preface in a context of philosophical scepticism:

We are not satisfied with speaking of the objects of our perception–of what we feel and understand. We seek to attach ideas to mere abstractions, and to give being to pure denominations . . . Is there not one, who perceives his own ideas, and calls them external objects: who thinks he distinguishes the truth, and who sees it not; who grasps at shadows, and who follows phantoms; who passes from the cradle to the tomb, the dupe and often the victim of the illusions, which he himself has created? (Bk II ch. i 166–7)

A further marked influence on both the Preface and the poem itself is from Wordsworth's 'Lines Left upon a Seat in a Yew-tree', first published in *Lyrical Ballads* (1798) but probably read by S. in April 1815 in the two-volume *Poems* published in that year (*Mary Jnl* i 76). This influence extends beyond striking thematic parallels to a general similarity in the handling of blank verse, and to a more particular similarity in some points of detail (e.g. Wordsworth's 'vacancy', 'Lines . . .' 7, cp. *Alastor* 126, 191, 195, 201, 562, 662; 'Lines . . .' 10–12, cp. *Alastor* 431–3). Commentaries have frequently compared the ideas of the Preface and poem with those of S.'s prose fragments 'On Love' and, less decidedly, 'On Life' (*Prose* 169–75), but while these fragments provide valuable glosses on *Alastor* it is almost certain that they are significantly later in date (see *SC* vi 638–9, 971). Much critical discussion has addressed an apparent contradiction between the Preface's judgement of the protagonist in the poem, and the generally more sympathetic attitude of the poem itself; 'the poem tends to romanticize what it was supposed to condemn' (GM). For a convincing account of the relationship between Preface and poem, see Evan K. Gibson, 'Alastor: A Reinterpretation', *PMLA* lxii (1947) 1022–42, which argues that 'what Shelley felt he had presented in the poem when he wrote the Preface' was 'a tragedy of misdirected genius brought to inevitable defeat by the innocent neglect of one of the most necessary elements in the human soul' (1026).

The poem's title is explained in a passage of Peacock's *Memoirs* of S.:

He was at a loss for a title, and I proposed that which he adopted: *Alastor; or, the Spirit of Solitude*. The Greek word Ἀλάστωρ is an evil genius, κακοδαίμων, though the sense of the two words is somewhat different . . . The poem treated the spirit of solitude as a spirit of evil. I mention the true meaning of the word because many have supposed *Alastor* to be the name of the hero of the poem. (*Peacock Works* viii 100)

This account has however led to confusion in its suggestion that the poem's 'Spirit of Solitude' is to be understood as an external supernatural agency, where the poem makes clear (149ff.) that the visionary figure is initially created by the poet-protagonist, and remains imaginary. The Greek ἀλάστωρ can in fact mean either an avenging spirit or, more rarely, the victim of such a spirit, so that S. may after all have intended his title to refer to the poem's protagonist; but the thematic importance of the poet's anonymity (cp. 50–60) makes this unlikely.

Mary S. notes that during the composition of *Alastor* S. 'spent his days under the oak shades of Windsor Great Park; and the magnificent woodland was a fitting study to inspire the various descriptions of forest scenery we find in the poem'. She also points out that S. had 'visited some of the more magnificent scenes of Switzerland, and returned to England from Lucerne, by the Reuss and the Rhine. This river navigation enchanted him. In his favourite poem of "Thalaba", his imagination had been excited by a description of such a voyage' (*1839* i 140–1). The account of these journeys in *1817* suggests interesting similarities to elements of the boat journey in the poem:

> The Reuss is exceedingly rapid, and we descended several falls, one of more than eight feet . . . There is something very delicious in the sensation, when at one moment you are at the top of a fall of water, and before the second has expired you are at the bottom, still rushing on with the impulse which the descent has given . . .
>
> . . . we engaged a small canoe to convey us to Mumph. I give these boats this Indian appellation, as they were of the rudest construction–long, narrow, and flat-bottomed: they consist merely of straight pieces of deal board, unpainted, and nailed together with so little care, that the water constantly poured in at the crevices, and the boat perpetually required emptying. The river was rapid, and sped swiftly, breaking as it passed on innumerable rocks just covered by the water: it was a sight of some dread to see our frail boat winding among the eddies of the rocks, which it was death to touch; and when the slightest inclination on one side would instantly have overset it.
> (*1817* 57–8)

S's poem appears in some respects Southeyan in conception. Editors may however have been mistaken in following Mary S.'s supposition that the idea of an 'underground voyage' derives from Southey's *Thalaba*. Thalaba's boat descends a stream that becomes a river, then crosses the sea (xi 30–xii 8), but the entry into the cavern and all the underground part of his mission is accomplished on foot or in a winged car (xii 8–end). There is an account of a voyage within a magnetic rock in Robert Paltock's *Life and Adventures of Peter Wilkins, a Cornish Man* (1751), which S. had read as a boy (*Medwin (1913)* 24). Cp. for example *Alastor* 369–97 with *Peter Wilkins* ch. x:

> 'I heard a great noise, as of a fall of water . . . the stream insensibly drawing

me on, I soon found myself in an eddy; and the boat drawing forward beyond all my power to resist it, I was quickly sucked under a low arch . . . I could perceive the boat to fall with incredible violence, as I thought, down a precipice, and suddenly whirled round and round with me, the water roaring on all sides, and dashing against the rock with a most amazing noise.'

As Beljame suggested (*Alastor ou Le Génie de la Solitude* (Paris 1895) 95), S. is indebted for details of the poet's overland route described in 140–353 to Alexander the Great's expedition into India of 327 B.C., although S.'s source was not Arrian, whom he apparently did not read before summer 1817, but Quintus Curtius, who provides S.'s place names and other particulars (see notes below). S. ordered a specific edition of Quintus Curtius in December 1815 (*L* i 437–8), and states his preference for Quintus Curtius to Arrian in a letter to Hogg of 6 July 1817 (*L* i 545). The poet's route in the poem is 'through Arabie / And Persia, and the wild Carmanian waste' (i.e. through modern Iran and Afghanistan along the north coast of the Arabian sea) then north over the Indian Caucasus (the Hindu Kush) to the Vale of Cashmire; then (after the vision of 149 ff.) east again, roughly along the Oxus/Amu Darya, through Balk (Balkh in Afghanistan) into Media (south of the Caspian Sea, in Iran). The poet then quits Alexander's route, which was south and back to Babylon, and journeys to the 'lone Chorasmian shore', the eastern coast of the Caspian, finally crossing from there by boat to reach what is now the Soviet Caucasus. For further suggestions about possible literary influences on *Alastor*, see *White* i 700–1.

Alastor represents a dramatic advance in S.'s poetic technique and intellectual range comparable with that made by *Q Mab*. The poem's autobiographical element has been often noticed, and the preoccupation with death and failure doubtless owes something to S.'s ill-health in spring 1815; as Mary S. remarks, at this period 'physical suffering had . . . considerable influence in causing him to turn his eyes inward; inclining him rather to brood over the thoughts and emotions of his own soul than to glance abroad . . . In the Spring of 1815 an eminent physician pronounced that he was dying rapidly of a consumption; abscesses were formed on his lungs, and he suffered acute spasms' (*1839* i 140; see *White* i 405–6. The 'eminent surgeon' was Sir William Lawrence; *L* i 429). But there is a newly controlled detachment in S.'s subordination of personal material to more general thematic concerns, in which hints at the experience of other living poets combine with representations of his own life to enrich a symbolic narrative which is not confined to any one particular biography. For arguments in favour of Wordsworth and Coleridge as possible models for the poet, see Paul Mueschke and Earl L. Griggs, 'Wordsworth as the Prototype of the Poet in Shelley's *Alastor*', *PMLA* xlix (1934) 229–45, and Joseph Raben, 'Coleridge as the Prototype of the Poet in Shelley's *Alastor*', *RES* xvii (1966) 78–92. Short poems critical of Wordsworth and of Coleridge were included in the *Alastor* volume, and S. 'always took care that the minor poems in his collections matched the principal one' (GM). The blank verse of *Alastor* also displays a marked new maturity which, while bearing the mark of S.'s reading in English blank verse, particularly Wordsworth's, is more distinctive of S.'s own manner than obviously derivative. Also distinctive is S.'s use in the poem of landscapes which are 'inseparable from the psychic and emotional states of the Poet passing through them' (GM).

The *Alastor* volume received very scant critical attention on its appearance, most of it hostile and bewildered (see *Unextinguished Hearth* 105–8). A favourable review finally appeared in *Blackwood's Edinburgh Magazine* in November 1819; the review, by John Wilson, was used as the occasion to attack the *Quarterly Review*'s savage attack on S. in its review of *L&C* in April 1819 (see headnotes to *L&C* and *PU*). There are a great many interpretative accounts of *Alastor*: amongst those especially worthy of note are those in *Baker* 41–60; *Cameron* (1974) 219–33; an impressive and searching account in *Wasserman* 15–46; *Holmes* 299–306; Evan K. Gibson, op. cit.; Albert S. Gérard, *English Romantic Poetry* (Los Angeles 1968) 136–62.

Text from *1816*.
Published in *1816*.

Preface.

1   The poem entitled 'ALASTOR' may be considered as allegorical of one of the most interesting situations of the human mind. It represents a youth of uncorrupted feelings and adventurous genius led forth by an imagination inflamed and purified through familiarity with all that is 5   excellent and majestic, to the contemplation of the universe. He drinks deep of the fountains of knowledge, and is still insatiate. The magnificence and beauty of the external world sinks profoundly into the frame of his conceptions, and affords to their modifications a variety not to be exhausted. So long as it is possible for his desires to point 10   towards objects thus infinite and unmeasured, he is joyous, and tranquil, and self-possessed. But the period arrives when these objects cease to suffice. His mind is at length suddenly awakened and thirsts for intercourse with an intelligence similar to itself. He images to himself the Being whom he loves. Conversant with speculations of the sub- 15   limest and most perfect natures, the vision in which he embodies his own imaginations unites all of wonderful, or wise, or beautiful, which the poet, the philosopher, or the lover could depicture. The intellectual faculties, the imagination, the functions of sense, have their respective requisitions on the sympathy of corresponding powers in other human 20   beings. The Poet is represented as uniting these requisitions, and attaching them to a single image. He seeks in vain for a prototype of his

¶ *114. 2–3 Preface. It represents a youth*] The protagonist of the poem is not named; a mark of his failure as a poet. Cp. lines 50–66, 669–71.
19. requisitions] i.e. claims.
21. prototype] ideal embodiment.

conception. Blasted by his disappointment, he descends to an untimely grave.

The picture is not barren of instruction to actual men. The Poet's
25   self-centred seclusion was avenged by the furies of an irresistible passion pursuing him to speedy ruin. But that Power which strikes the
luminaries of the world with sudden darkness and extinction, by
awakening them to too exquisite a perception of its influences, dooms
to a slow and poisonous decay those meaner spirits that dare to abjure
30   its dominion. Their destiny is more abject and inglorious as their
delinquency is more contemptible and pernicious. They who, deluded
by no generous error, instigated by no sacred thirst of doubtful knowledge, duped by no illustrious superstition, loving nothing on this
earth, and cherishing no hopes beyond, yet keep aloof from sympathies
35   with their kind, rejoicing neither in human joy nor mourning with
human grief; these, and such as they, have their apportioned curse.
They languish, because none feel with them their common nature.
They are morally dead. They are neither friends, nor lovers, nor
fathers, nor citizens of the world, nor benefactors of their country.
40   Among those who attempt to exist without human sympathy, the pure
and tender-hearted perish through the intensity and passion of their
search after its communities, when the vacancy of their spirit suddenly
makes itself felt. All else, selfish, blind, and torpid, are those unfore-
seeing multitudes who constitute, together with their own, the lasting
45   misery and loneliness of the world. Those who love not their fellow-
beings, live unfruitful lives, and prepare for their old age a miserable
grave.

'The good die first,
And those whose hearts are dry as summer dust,
Burn to the socket!'·

December 14, 1815.

Nondum amabam, et amare amabam, quaerebam quid
amarem, amans amare.
Confess. St. August.

43. All else] 'utterly different' (*Butter (1970)*).
48–50. '*The good . . . socket!*'] Wordsworth, *Excursion* (1814) i 500–2; S.'s
quotation reads 'those' for 'they', and introduces a comma after 'dust'.
Epigraph. amans amare] amans mare *1816* (a misprint). 'I was not yet in love, and
I loved to be in love, I sought what I might love, loving to be in love' (St
Augustine's *Confessions* III i). S. used this quotation in his 'Advertisement' to
the 'Mary' poems in *Esd* (see headnote to No. 38), and he also copied it into
Claire Clairmont's 1814 journal (BL MS Ashley 394) next to his verse frag-
ments No. 100 (see headnote, and *Claire Jnl* 61–2).

Earth, ocean, air, beloved brotherhood!
If our great Mother has imbued my soul
With aught of natural piety to feel
Your love, and recompense the boon with mine;
5   If dewy morn, and odorous noon, and even,
With sunset and its gorgeous ministers,
And solemn midnight's tingling silentness;
If autumn's hollow sighs in the sere wood,
And winter robing with pure snow and crowns
10   Of starry ice the grey grass and bare boughs;
If spring's voluptuous pantings when she breathes
Her first sweet kisses, have been dear to me;
If no bright bird, insect, or gentle beast
I consciously have injured, but still loved
15   And cherished these my kindred; then forgive

1. *Earth, ocean, air*] 'The three legendary divisions of the world' ('ex fabulis tria regnia divisa'), Cicero, *De Natura Deorum* II xxvi 66. The invocation to the material world was Hymen's at the marriage of Cupid and Psyche in Erasmus Darwin's *Temple of Nature* (ii 243–4): 'Behold, he cries, Earth! Ocean! Air above, / And hail the DEITIES OF SEXUAL LOVE!' Harold Bloom has been followed in his view (*The Visionary Company* (1962) 280) that 'Speaking as the element of fire, the poet addresses earth, ocean, and air as his brothers', but S. is not addressing his own brothers; he is saluting Nature as a brotherhood of elements.

2. *our great Mother*] Cybele, a goddess of the powers of Nature, the 'magna Mater' of the ancients (Lucretius, *De Rerum Natura* ii 589–99; cp. Gray, 'Progress of Poesy' III i 4).

3. *natural piety*] From Wordsworth: 'My heart leaps up' 8–9: 'And I could wish my days to be / Bound each to each by natural piety', and *Excursion* iii 267.

14. *consciously*] i.e. in full moral awareness of the act. According to Medwin S. spent September 1810 in shooting, and once killed three snipe with successive shots (*Medwin (1913)* 68). He was a vegetarian from the age of 19 (*White* i 224; see line 101), and expressed his horror of hunting in *Q Mab* (note to viii 211–12), 'that beings capable of the gentlest and most admirable sympathies should take delight in the death-pangs and last convulsions of dying animals'. The hero of Beattie's *Minstrel* is similarly described: 'His heart, from cruel sport estranged, would bleed / To work the woe of any living thing' (XVIII 3–4).

15. *my kindred*] S. startled Horace Smith in 1817 by referring to 'his animal brethren' (Arthur H. Beavan, *James and Horace Smith* (1899) 171–2). Cp. *Q Mab* viii 225–7: 'Man has lost / His terrible prerogative, and stands / An equal amidst equals'.

This boast, beloved brethren, and withdraw
No portion of your wonted favour now!
Mother of this unfathomable world!
Favour my solemn song, for I have loved
20   Thee ever, and thee only; I have watched
Thy shadow, and the darkness of thy steps,
And my heart ever gazes on the depth
Of thy deep mysteries. I have made my bed
In charnels and on coffins, where black death
25   Keeps record of the trophies won from thee,
Hoping to still these obstinate questionings
Of thee and thine, by forcing some lone ghost
Thy messenger, to render up the tale
Of what we are. In lone and silent hours,
30   When night makes a weird sound of its own stillness,

18. The phrase may be recalled from Holbach (*Système de la Nature* i 59*n.*):
'Platon dit que la matière & la nécessité sont la même chose, & que cette
nécessité est la mère du monde' (see note to *Q Mab* vi 198). H.'s assertion is
presumably based on the *Timaeus* 47e–51c.
21. shadow] image: 'Nature' herself is unseen, apprehended only by her physical
effects.
23–29. I have made my bed . . . what we are] Cp. *Excursion* iii 686–95. As a boy, S.
'was passionately attached to the study of what used to be called the occult
sciences . . . Sometimes he watched the livelong nights for ghosts . . . he even
planned how he might get admission to the vault, or charnel-house, at Warnham Church, and might sit there all night, harrowed by fear, yet trembling
with expectation, to see one of the spiritualised owners of the bones piled
around him' (*Hogg* i 33–4). S. told Hogg on 6 January 1811 'I have been most of
the night pacing a church yard' (*L* i 39). Cp. 'Hymn to Intellectual Beauty'
49–54. The 'visionary boy' of Beattie's *Minstrel* would also 'dream of graves,
and corses pale; / And ghosts that to the charnel-dungeon throng' (I xxxii 5–6).
26. obstinate questionings] From Wordsworth's 'Ode: Intimations of Immortality' 142–3: '. . . those obstinate questionings / Of sense and outward things'.
29–37. In lone and silent hours . . . To render up thy charge] S. noted of himself and
Claire C. on 7 October 1814: 'At one of clock Shelley observes that it is the
witching time of night . . . He inquires soon after whether it is not horrible to
feel the silence of night tingling in our ears . . . We continued to sit by the fire at
intervals engaging in awful conversation relative to the nature of these mysteries' (*Mary Jnl* i 32–3). S. is unlikely, however, to have discussed such things
only with Claire.

Like an inspired and desperate alchemist
Staking his very life on some dark hope,
Have I mixed awful talk and asking looks
With my most innocent love, until strange tears
35   Uniting with those breathless kisses, made
Such magic as compels the charmèd night
To render up thy charge: . . . and, though ne'er yet
Thou hast unveiled thy inmost sanctuary,
Enough from incommunicable dream,
40   And twilight phantasms, and deep noonday thought,
Has shone within me, that serenely now
And moveless, as a long-forgotten lyre
Suspended in the solitary dome
Of some mysterious and deserted fane,
45   I wait thy breath, Great Parent, that my strain
May modulate with murmurs of the air,
And motions of the forests and the sea,
And voice of living beings, and woven hymns
Of night and day, and the deep heart of man.

50   There was a Poet whose untimely tomb
No human hands with pious reverence reared,
But the charmed eddies of autumnal winds
Built o'er his mouldering bones a pyramid
Of mouldering leaves in the waste wilderness:—
55   A lovely youth,—no mourning maiden decked
With weeping flowers, or votive cypress wreath,
The lone couch of his everlasting sleep:—
Gentle, and brave, and generous,—no lorn bard
Breathed o'er his dark fate one melodious sigh:
60   He lived, he died, he sung, in solitude.
Strangers have wept to hear his passionate notes,
And virgins, as unknown he passed, have pined
And wasted for fond love of his wild eyes.

---

38. *sanctuary,*] sanctuary; *1816.*
41–9. serenely now . . . deep heart of man] Eds cite the invocation in Wordsworth's
extract from *The Recluse* as prefaced to *The Excursion*, 83–107, and 'Tintern
Abbey' 94–100; but the symbols are those of Coleridge's 'Eolian Harp' ('Effusion XXXV'), esp. lines 32–6 of the 1803 edn:

> And what if all of animated nature
> Be but organic Harps diversely fram'd,
> That tremble into thought, as o'er them sweeps
> Plastic and vast, one intellectual breeze,
> At once the Soul of each, and God of all?

44. *fane*] temple.

The fire of those soft orbs has ceased to burn,
65 And Silence, too enamoured of that voice,
Locks its mute music in her rugged cell.

By solemn vision, and bright silver dream,
His infancy was nurtured. Every sight
And sound from the vast earth and ambient air,
70 Sent to his heart its choicest impulses.
The fountains of divine philosophy
Fled not his thirsting lips, and all of great,
Or good, or lovely, which the sacred past
In truth or fable consecrates, he felt
75 And knew. When early youth had passed, he left
His cold fireside and alienated home
To seek strange truths in undiscovered lands.
Many a wide waste and tangled wilderness
Has lured his fearless steps; and he has bought
80 With his sweet voice and eyes, from savage men,
His rest and food. Nature's most secret steps
He like her shadow has pursued, where'er
The red volcano overcanopies
Its fields of snow and pinnacles of ice
85 With burning smoke, or where bitumen lakes
On black bare pointed islets ever beat
With sluggish surge, or where the secret caves
Rugged and dark, winding among the springs
Of fire and poison, inaccessible
90 To avarice or pride, their starry domes
Of diamond and of gold expand above
Numberless and immeasurable halls,
Frequent with crystal column, and clear shrines

67–8. *By solemn vision . . . was nurtured*] 'In dreams, in study, and in ardent thought, / Thus was he reared' (*Excursion* i 301–2). Much of the Wanderer's early experience of Nature in Wordsworth's poem (e.g. i 134–62) is paralleled by that of S.'s Poet.

81–9. *Nature's most secret steps . . . fire and poison*] The images; volcanoes, bitumen-lakes, caves, springs, are those in Southey's *Thalaba* V xxi–xxiv and VI ii 5–9, e.g.:

> . . . From where its gushing springs
> Boil their black billows up . . .
> There from a cave, with torrent force,
> And everlasting roar,
> The black bitumen roll'd. (V xxii 4–5, 10–12)

Cp. *Paradise Lost* xii 41–2.

93. *Frequent with*] abundant with (a Latinism; cp. *Paradise Lost* i 797).

Of pearl, and thrones radiant with chrysolite.
95 Nor had that scene of ampler majesty
Than gems or gold, the varying roof of heaven
And the green earth lost in his heart its claims
To love and wonder; he would linger long
In lonesome vales, making the wild his home,
100 Until the doves and squirrels would partake
From his innocuous hand his bloodless food,
Lured by the gentle meaning of his looks,
And the wild antelope, that starts whene'er
The dry leaf rustles in the brake, suspend
105 Her timid steps to gaze upon a form
More graceful than her own.

                                        His wandering step
Obedient to high thoughts, has visited
The awful ruins of the days of old:
Athens, and Tyre, and Balbec, and the waste
110 Where stood Jerusalem, the fallen towers
Of Babylon, the eternal pyramids,
Memphis and Thebes, and whatsoe'er of strange
Sculptured on alabaster obelisk,
Or jasper tomb, or mutilated sphinx,
115 Dark Ethiopia in her desert hills
Conceals. Among the ruined temples there,
Stupendous columns, and wild images
Of more than man, where marble daemons watch
The Zodiac's brazen mystery, and dead men

104. suspend] i.e. would suspend (from line 100).

106–16. His wandering step . . . Conceals.] The Poet's first wanderings take him back through the world's youth (122) towards the birth of time (128). According to Diodorus Siculus (III i–vii) Ethiopia was the most ancient civilization, from which Memphis and Thebes (Luxor) in Egypt had been colonized; while Volney (*Ruins* 19) explains that Jerusalem and Tyre (both at their greatest in Solomon's day) were destroyed by the kings of Nineveh and Babylon. Greek civilization was the latest ruin of time. Geographically the journey is round the eastern Mediterranean and up the Nile: Tyre and Balbec (Baalbek) were in the Lebanon; Babylon was in Iraq south of Baghdad.

109–10. the waste / Where stood Jerusalem] Jerusalem had been finally destroyed by the Emperor Titus in A.D. 70, and still in 1867 had a population of only 16,000.

119. The Zodiac's brazen mystery] In the famous temple of Isis at Dendera in Egypt, Vivant Denon 'had perceived zodiacs, planetary systems, and celestial planispheres' (quoted from *A General Collection of Voyages and Travels . . .* (1813) xxii 222), but these were painted on the ceiling; 'brazen mystery' may have been suggested by Homer's 'οὐράνος χάλκεος' ('brazen firmament').

119–20. dead men . . . mute walls around] Denon later explored an ancient

120 Hang their mute thoughts on the mute walls around,
     He lingered, poring on memorials
     Of the world's youth, through the long burning day
     Gazed on those speechless shapes, nor, when the moon
     Filled the mysterious halls with floating shades
125 Suspended he that task, but ever gazed
     And gazed, till meaning on his vacant mind
     Flashed like strong inspiration, and he saw
     The thrilling secrets of the birth of time.

     Meanwhile an Arab maiden brought his food,
130 Her daily portion, from her father's tent,
     And spread her matting for his couch, and stole
     From duties and repose to tend his steps:—
     Enamoured, yet not daring for deep awe
     To speak her love:—and watched his nightly sleep,
135 Sleepless herself, to gaze upon his lips
     Parted in slumber, whence the regular breath
     Of innocent dreams arose: then, when red morn
     Made paler the pale moon, to her cold home
     Wildered, and wan, and panting, she returned.

140 The Poet wandering on, through Arabie
     And Persia, and the wild Carmanian waste,
     And o'er the aërial mountains which pour down
     Indus and Oxus from their icy caves,
     In joy and exultation held his way;
145 Till in the vale of Kashmir, far within
     Its loneliest dell, where odorous plants entwine
     Beneath the hollow rocks a natural bower,

Egyptian monastery where 'Nothing indicated the remains of the habitation of man but some short sentences written on the walls . . . a vain attempt, which time, that destroys every thing, has entirely frustrated. I presented them to my imagination as dying, and still striving, with fluttering speech, to utter a few words' (loc. cit. 240).

126–7. till meaning . . . strong inspiration] Echoing Wordsworth's 'I wandered lonely as a cloud' (1807) 18–22: 'For oft, when on my couch I lie / In vacant or in pensive mood, / They flash upon that inward eye / Which is the bliss of solitude'.

140–1. The Poet . . . wild Carmanian waste] The Poet passed the Red Sea and crossed Saudi Arabia into the Kerman Desert of Persia (Iran); and over the Hindu Kush mountains (the 'Indian Caucasus' of *PU*), from which the Indus and Oxus (Amu-Darya) flow opposite ways, into the Arabian and into the Aral Sea respectively.

145–9. Till in the vale . . . His languid limbs.] S.'s uses of the Vale of Kashmir in northern India derive mostly from descriptions in an early favourite novel,

Beside a sparkling rivulet he stretched
His languid limbs. A vision on his sleep
150   There came, a dream of hopes that never yet
Had flushed his cheek. He dreamed a veilèd maid
Sate near him, talking in low solemn tones.
Her voice was like the voice of his own soul
Heard in the calm of thought; its music long,
155   Like woven sounds of streams and breezes, held
His inmost sense suspended in its web
Of many-coloured woof and shifting hues.
Knowledge and truth and virtue were her theme,
And lofty hopes of divine liberty,
160   Thoughts the most dear to him, and poesy,
Herself a poet. Soon the solemn mood
Of her pure mind kindled through all her frame
A permeating fire: wild numbers then
She raised, with voice stifled in tremulous sobs
165   Subdued by its own pathos: her fair hands
Were bare alone, sweeping from some strange harp
Strange symphony, and in their branching veins
The eloquent blood told an ineffable tale.
The beating of her heart was heard to fill

Sydney Owenson's *The Missionary: an Indian Tale* (1811): 'He [the Missionary]
rapidly descended the rock, now embossed with odoriferous plants, and
shaded by lofty shrubs . . . countless streams of liquid silver meeting, in natural
basons, under the shade of the seringata . . . offered to his weary frame the most
necessary luxury that he could now enjoy' (i 130–1).
151. a veilèd maid] The Poet's vision parallels Hilarion's meeting in the vale of
Kashmir with Luxima, the veiled heroine of *The Missionary*, of whom S. told
Hogg in June 1811: 'Luxima the Indian is an Angel. What pity that we cannot
incorporate these creations of Fancy; the very thought of them thrills the soul'
(*L* i 107).
153–4. Her voice . . . calm of thought] 'His mind . . . thirsts for intercourse with an
intelligence similar to itself. He images to himself the Being whom he loves'
(S.'s Preface). Cp. 'On Love' (*Prose* 169–71) and *L&C* II xxxi 4–6: 'Hers too
were all my thoughts, ere yet, endowed / With music and with light, their
fountains flowed / In poesy'. The impulse is equalitarian, not narcissistic: cp.
Erasmus: 'It is an especyall swetnes to have one with whom ye may communy-
cate the secrete affectyons of your mynde, with whom ye may speake even as it
were with your owne selfe' (*In Laude and Prayse of Matrymony* Sigs. Cvi–Cvi^v).
154. long] 'for a long time' (adv.).
158–9. Knowledge and truth . . . divine liberty] Her 'theme' resembles Cythna's:
'For with strong speech I tore the veil which hid / Nature, and Truth, and
Liberty, and Love,–' (*L&C* IX vii 1–2).
163. numbers] verse; here a song, with lute accompaniment.

170 The pauses of her music, and her breath
Tumultuously accorded with those fits
Of intermitted song. Sudden she rose,
As if her heart impatiently endured
Its bursting burthen: at the sound he turned,
175 And saw by the warm light of their own life
Her glowing limbs beneath the sinuous veil
Of woven wind, her outspread arms now bare,
Her dark locks floating in the breath of night,
Her beamy bending eyes, her parted lips
180 Outstretched, and pale, and quivering eagerly.
His strong heart sunk and sickened with excess
Of love. He reared his shuddering limbs and quelled
His gasping breath, and spread his arms to meet
Her panting bosom: . . . she drew back a while,
185 Then, yielding to the irresistible joy,
With frantic gesture and short breathless cry
Folded his frame in her dissolving arms.
Now blackness veiled his dizzy eyes, and night
Involved and swallowed up the vision; sleep,
190 Like a dark flood suspended in its course,
Rolled back its impulse on his vacant brain.

Roused by the shock he started from his trance—
The cold white light of morning, the blue moon
Low in the west, the clear and garish hills,
195 The distinct valley and the vacant woods,
Spread round him where he stood. Whither have fled
The hues of heaven that canopied his bower
Of yesternight? The sounds that soothed his sleep,

175–7. *saw by the warm light . . . Of woven wind*] A much-used contemporary image, encouraged by prevailing fashion in women's clothes which approached that reported in antiquity of the women of Cos or Chios (modern Zia) in the Cyclades. S. noted the drapery of a Venus Genetrix in Florence, 'the original of which must have been the "woven wind" of Chios' (*Prose* 346). Cp. the address to Asia in *PU* II v: 'Child of Light! thy limbs are burning / Through the vest which seems to hide them'. The literary source was Petronius, *Satyricon* 55–6: 'Aequum est induere nuptam ventum textilem, / palam prostare nudam in nebula linea' ('Your bride might as well clothe herself in woven wind, as stand forth publicly naked under her mist of muslin').

193. *blue moon*] The moon sheds 'blue blasted light' in Landor's *Gebir* (1798) v 17–18, a favourite poem of S.'s at Oxford (*Hogg* i 201–2). The colour blue often implies sickness or the unearthly (see note to *PU* I 170).

196–8. *Whither have fled . . . Of yesternight?*] A possible echo of Wordsworth's 'Immortality Ode' 56–7; but this type of rhetorical question has numberless antecedents.

The mystery and the majesty of Earth,
200   The joy, the exultation? His wan eyes
Gaze on the empty scene as vacantly
As ocean's moon looks on the moon in heaven.
The spirit of sweet human love has sent
A vision to the sleep of him who spurned
205   Her choicest gifts. He eagerly pursues
Beyond the realms of dream that fleeting shade;
He overleaps the bounds. Alas! alas!
Were limbs, and breath, and being intertwined
Thus treacherously? Lost, lost, for ever lost
210   In the wide pathless desert of dim sleep,
That beautiful shape! Does the dark gate of death
Conduct to thy mysterious paradise,
O Sleep? Does the bright arch of rainbow clouds,
And pendent mountains seen in the calm lake,
215   Lead only to a black and watery depth,
While death's blue vault, with loathliest vapours hung,
Where every shade which the foul grave exhales
Hides its dead eye from the detested day,
Conduct, O Sleep, to thy delightful realms?
220   This doubt with sudden tide flowed on his heart,
The insatiate hope which it awakened, stung
His brain even like despair.

                    While daylight held
The sky, the Poet kept mute conference
With his still soul. At night the passion came,
225   Like the fierce fiend of a distempered dream,
And shook him from his rest, and led him forth
Into the darkness. – As an eagle grasped
In folds of the green serpent, feels her breast

207. *the bounds*] i.e. between illusion and reality, in trying to follow the dream-image into the actual world.

209–11. *Lost . . . That beautiful shape!*] An echo of Aeschylus, *Agamemnon* 420–6: 'In dreams come bitter apparitions bringing empty joy; for vainly, whenever in imagination a man sees delights, the vision slips through his hands and is gone, winging its flight along the paths of sleep'.

219. *Conduct,*] *1816, 1824*; Conducts, *Rossetti 1870*. The verb is treated simply as third item in a series of similar questions: 'Does the dark gate . . . Conduct? Does the bright arch . . . lead? While [does] death's blue vault . . . Conduct?' The Poet asks: Is physical reality merely a beautiful surface concealing nothingness, while death's hideous surface conceals the true beauty we perceive in dreams?

221–2. *The insatiate hope . . . like despair.*] If his speculations in lines 211–19 were justified, the Poet's desire could be satisfied only through death.

228. *green serpent*] Raben (*RES* n.s. xvii (August 1966) 291) compares the 'bright green snake' coiled around the dove in Coleridge's 'Christabel' 548–54.

Burn with the poison, and precipitates
230 Through night and day, tempest, and calm, and cloud,
Frantic with dizzying anguish, her blind flight
O'er the wide aëry wilderness: thus driven
By the bright shadow of that lovely dream,
Beneath the cold glare of the desolate night,
235 Through tangled swamps and deep precipitous dells,
Startling with careless step the moonlight snake,
He fled. Red morning dawned upon his flight,
Shedding the mockery of its vital hues
Upon his cheek of death. He wandered on
240 Till vast Aornos seen from Petra's steep
Hung o'er the low horizon like a cloud;
Through Balk, and where the desolated tombs
Of Parthian kings scatter to every wind
Their wasting dust, wildly he wandered on,
245 Day after day, a weary waste of hours,
Bearing within his life the brooding care
That ever fed on its decaying flame.
And now his limbs were lean; his scattered hair
Sered by the autumn of strange suffering
250 Sung dirges in the wind; his listless hand
Hung like dead bone within its withered skin;
Life, and the lustre that consumed it, shone
As in a furnace burning secretly
From his dark eyes alone. The cottagers,
255 Who ministered with human charity
His human wants, beheld with wondering awe
Their fleeting visitant. The mountaineer,

233. *shadow*] mental image, memory.

240. *vast Aornos seen from Petra's steep*] No place named 'Petra' existed in the area, but Quintius Curtius described the conquest of one steep summit beyond the river Oxus which he called simply 'the rock' ('Una erat petra . . .', *Hist. Alex.* VII xi 1–29). This was the Rock of Soghdiana (at Bukhara in Uzbekistan). Later Alexander stormed the crag of Aornos ('birdless', possibly Pir-Sar) on the Indus (VIII xi 2–19).

242. *Balk*] Now Balkh, in Afghanistan.

242–4. *where the desolated tombs . . . wasting dust*] In A.D. 216 'Antonius [Caracallus] . . . ravaged a large section of the country round Media . . . dug open the royal tombs of the Parthians, and scattered the bones about' (Dion Cassius, *Hist. Rom.* LXXIX i 2). Media and Parthia extended west and east respectively of modern Tehran in Iran.

248–50. *his scattered hair . . . sung dirges in the wind*] The sound of wind in hair was an Ossianic conceit, e.g. 'The winds whistling in my grey hair, shall not waken me' ('Berrathon', in *Fingal, an Ancient Epic Poem* (1762) 269).

Encountering on some dizzy precipice
That spectral form, deemed that the Spirit of wind
260 With lightning eyes, and eager breath, and feet
Disturbing not the drifted snow, had paused
In its career: the infant would conceal
His troubled visage in his mother's robe
In terror at the glare of those wild eyes,
265 To remember their strange light in many a dream
Of after-times; but youthful maidens, taught
By nature, would interpret half the woe
That wasted him, would call him with false names
Brother, and friend, would press his pallid hand
270 At parting, and watch, dim through tears, the path
Of his departure from their father's door.

At length upon the lone Chorasmian shore
He paused, a wide and melancholy waste
Of putrid marshes. A strong impulse urged
275 His steps to the sea-shore. A swan was there,
Beside a sluggish stream among the reeds.
It rose as he approached, and with strong wings
Scaling the upward sky, bent its bright course
High over the immeasurable main.
280 His eyes pursued its flight. – 'Thou hast a home,
Beautiful bird; thou voyagest to thine home,
Where thy sweet mate will twine her downy neck
With thine, and welcome thy return with eyes
Bright in the lustre of their own fond joy.
285 And what am I that I should linger here,
With voice far sweeter than thy dying notes,
Spirit more vast than thine, frame more attuned
To beauty, wasting these surpassing powers
In the deaf air, to the blind earth, and heaven

262. *its*] his *1824, 1839*. An emendation based on supposed personification.
268–9. *would call him . . . / Brother, and friend*] The Arab maiden Oneiza in Southey's *Thalaba* makes the same pretence to her beloved: 'She call'd him Brother; was it sister-love . . .?' (III xxv 1).
272. *the lone Chorasmian shore*] The eastern shore of the Caspian Sea. The Poet has now left the return route followed by Alexander, and turned north instead of south.
275–290. The swan was sacred to Apollo, god of poetry, and sang before death; hence it may symbolize a dying poet. S. had been 'vehemently excited' by Plato's *Phaedo* at Oxford (*Hogg* i 103) and here recalls the parallel Socrates made just before drinking the hemlock:
I believe that the swans, belonging as they do to Apollo, have prophetic powers and sing because they know the good things that await them in the

290 That echoes not my thoughts?' A gloomy smile
  Of desperate hope wrinkled his quivering lips.
  For sleep, he knew, kept most relentlessly
  Its precious charge, and silent death exposed,
  Faithless perhaps as sleep, a shadowy lure,
295 With doubtful smile mocking its own strange charms.

  Startled by his own thoughts he looked around.
  There was no fair fiend near him, not a sight
  Or sound of awe but in his own deep mind.
  A little shallop floating near the shore
300 Caught the impatient wandering of his gaze.
  It had been long abandoned, for its sides
  Gaped wide with many a rift, and its frail joints
  Swayed with the undulations of the tide.
  A restless impulse urged him to embark
305 And meet lone Death on the drear ocean's waste;
  For well he knew that mighty Shadow loves
  The slimy caverns of the populous deep.

  The day was fair and sunny, sea and sky
  Drank its inspiring radiance, and the wind
310 Swept strongly from the shore, blackening the waves.
  Following his eager soul, the wanderer
  Leaped in the boat, he spread his cloak aloft
  On the bare mast, and took his lonely seat,
  And felt the boat speed o'er the tranquil sea
315 Like a torn cloud before the hurricane.

---

unseen world; and they are happier on that day than they have ever been before. Now I consider that I am in the same service as the swans, and dedicated to the same god; and that I am no worse endowed with prophetic powers by my master than they are, and no more disconsolate at leaving this life (84E–85B; Penguin translation).

297. fair fiend] Ostensibly Death, the seductive enigma of lines 294–5; but the ambivalence reflects the Poet's reactions. When Southey's Damsel led Thalaba into extreme danger he questioned her status in similar words: 'And was that lovely Mariner / A fiend as false as fair?' (*Thalaba* XII xvii 12–13).

299. shallop] small dinghy; a new word in Spenser (*FQ* III vii 27) from whom S. probably adopted it. Evan K. Gibson noted that its frailty 'is suggestive of the bodily condition of the poet' (*PMLA* lxii (1947) 1037).

309. the wind] Gibson (loc. cit. 1037–8) interprets this as the wind of Necessity, here 'the necessity of death–the irresistible laws of disintegration in the universe'.

311–13. the wanderer . . . took his lonely seat] Cp. *Thalaba* XI xxxi 2–4: 'A little boat there lay, / Without an oar, without a sail, / One only seat it had, one seat'.

As one that in a silver vision floats
Obedient to the sweep of odorous winds
Upon resplendent clouds, so rapidly
Along the dark and ruffled waters fled
320   The straining boat. – A whirlwind swept it on,
With fierce gusts and precipitating force,
Through the white ridges of the chafèd sea.
The waves arose. Higher and higher still
Their fierce necks writhed beneath the tempest's
          scourge
325   Like serpents struggling in a vulture's grasp.
Calm and rejoicing in the fearful war
Of wave ruining on wave, and blast on blast
Descending, and black flood on whirlpool driven
With dark obliterating course, he sate:
330   As if their genii were the ministers
Appointed to conduct him to the light
Of those beloved eyes, the Poet sate
Holding the steady helm. Evening came on,
The beams of sunset hung their rainbow hues
335   High mid the shifting domes of sheeted spray
That canopied his path o'er the waste deep;
Twilight, ascending slowly from the east,
Entwined in duskier wreaths her braided locks
O'er the fair front and radiant eyes of day;
340   Night followed, clad with stars. On every side
More horribly the multitudinous streams
Of ocean's mountainous waste to mutual war
Rushed in dark tumult thundering, as to mock
The calm and spangled sky. The little boat
345   Still fled before the storm; still fled, like foam
Down the steep cataract of a wintry river;
Now pausing on the edge of the riven wave;
Now leaving far behind the bursting mass
That fell, convulsing ocean. Safely fled –
350   As if that frail and wasted human form
Had been an elemental god.

                              At midnight
The moon arose: and lo! the etherial cliffs

327. *ruining*] *1816*, *1824*; running *1839*, *1840*. An obvious misprint: the word is
from Lat. *ruere*, 'to fall in disorder', and is so used by Milton: 'Heav'n ruining
from Heav'n' (*PL* vi 867–8), and by Wordsworth of a waterfall: 'Ruining from
the cliffs the deafening load / Tumbles' (*Descriptive Sketches* (1793) 204–5).
334. *hung their rainbow hues*] i.e. made sun-bows in the water-vapour.
352. *etherial*] 'reaching into the upper air'.

Of Caucasus, whose icy summits shone
Among the stars like sunlight, and around
355 Whose caverned base the whirlpools and the waves
Bursting and eddying irresistibly
Rage and resound forever. – Who shall save? –
The boat fled on, – the boiling torrent drove, –
The crags closed round with black and jaggèd arms,
360 The shattered mountain overhung the sea,
And faster still, beyond all human speed,
Suspended on the sweep of the smooth wave,
The little boat was driven. A cavern there
Yawned, and amid its slant and winding depths
365 Engulfed the rushing sea. The boat fled on
With unrelaxing speed. – 'Vision and Love!'
The Poet cried aloud, 'I have beheld
The path of thy departure. Sleep and death
Shall not divide us long!'

                The boat pursued
370 The windings of the cavern. Daylight shone
At length upon that gloomy river's flow;
Now, where the fiercest war among the waves
Is calm, on the unfathomable stream
The boat moved slowly. Where the mountain, riven,
375 Exposed those black depths to the azure sky,
Ere yet the flood's enormous volume fell
Even to the base of Caucasus, with sound
That shook the everlasting rocks, the mass
Filled with one whirlpool all that ample chasm;
380 Stair above stair the eddying waters rose,
Circling immeasurably fast, and laved
With alternating dash the gnarlèd roots
Of mighty trees, that stretched their giant arms

353. *Caucasus*] The boat had crossed the Caspian Sea to the mountains of the Caucasus, now in Soviet Georgia, on the western shore.

358–401. What seems on the literal level to happen here is that wind-driven seas pour inland through a cavern, emerging eventually into a whirlpool which spins so fast that at the extreme edge its centrifugal force lifts the boat clear of the rock funnel on to a high plateau; from here a tributary, 'a placid stream', flows downhill in the orthodox way. Gibson (loc. cit. 1038) identifies the cavern (363) as 'the jaws of death'.

376–9. *Ere yet . . . all that ample chasm*] A memory of the escape-route from the garden of bliss in *Thalaba* (VII vi 12–17): 'There adown / The perforated rock / Plunge the whole waters; so precipitous, / So fathomless a fall, / That their earth-shaking roar came deaden'd up / Like subterranean thunders' (see also line 402).

In darkness over it. I' the midst was left,
385   Reflecting, yet distorting every cloud,
A pool of treacherous and tremendous calm.
Seized by the sway of the ascending stream,
With dizzy swiftness, round, and round, and round,
Ridge after ridge the straining boat arose,
390   Till on the verge of the extremest curve,
Where, through an opening of the rocky bank,
The waters overflow, and a smooth spot
Of glassy quiet mid those battling tides
Is left, the boat paused shuddering. – Shall it sink
395   Down the abyss? Shall the reverting stress
Of that resistless gulf embosom it?
Now shall it fall? – A wandering stream of wind,
Breathed from the west, has caught the expanded sail,
And, lo! with gentle motion, between banks
400   Of mossy slope, and on a placid stream,
Beneath a woven grove it sails, and, hark!
The ghastly torrent mingles its far roar
With the breeze murmuring in the musical woods.
Where the embowering trees recede, and leave
405   A little space of green expanse, the cove
Is closed by meeting banks, whose yellow flowers
For ever gaze on their own drooping eyes,
Reflected in the crystal calm. The wave
Of the boat's motion marred their pensive task,
410   Which nought but vagrant bird, or wanton wind,
Or falling spear-grass, or their own decay
Had e'er disturbed before. The Poet longed
To deck with their bright hues his withered hair,
But on his heart its solitude returned,
415   And he forbore. Not the strong impulse hid
In those flushed cheeks, bent eyes, and shadowy frame
Had yet performed its ministry: it hung
Upon his life, as lightning in a cloud
Gleams, hovering ere it vanish, ere the floods
Of night close over it.

406. *yellow flowers*] The narcissus was transformed from a youth whose failure
to respond to the love of others was punished by a passion for his own
reflection (Ovid, *Met.* iii 344–511).
409. *pensive*] S.'s sole use of this adjective.
412–13. *The Poet . . . his withered hair*] A habit of S.'s own: Polly Rose, who
knew him at Marlow, said that sometimes when he returned from the Thames
'on his head would be a wreath of what in Marlow we call "old man's beard"
[wild clematis] and wild flowers intermixed' (*Dowden Life* i 120).

420   The noonday sun
     Now shone upon the forest, one vast mass
     Of mingling shade, whose brown magnificence
     A narrow vale embosoms. There, huge caves,
     Scooped in the dark base of their aëry rocks
425   Mocking its moans, respond and roar for ever.
     The meeting boughs and implicated leaves
     Wove twilight o'er the Poet's path, as led
     By love, or dream, or god, or mightier Death,
     He sought in Nature's dearest haunt, some bank,
430   Her cradle, and his sepulchre. More dark
     And dark the shades accumulate. The oak,
     Expanding its immense and knotty arms,
     Embraces the light beech. The pyramids
     Of the tall cedar overarching, frame
435   Most solemn domes within, and far below,
     Like clouds suspended in an emerald sky,
     The ash and the acacia floating hang
     Tremulous and pale. Like restless serpents, clothed

422. *brown*] dark (a common equivalent of Italian *bruna*).

424. *aëry*] lofty.

425. *Mocking its moans*] echoing the forest's response to the wind. Locock refers *its* to the *torrent* of line 402.

430. *Her cradle*] Butter (*Butter (1970)* 243) notes: 'He is travelling in imagination back to the source of life', and compares *PU* II ii. The Vale of Kashmir in Owenson's *The Missionary* contained a spot 'where an eternal spring seemed to reign, and which looked like the cradle of infant Nature, where she first awoke, in all her primeval bloom of beauty' (i 141). But Granville Penn in 'Remarks on the Eastern Origination of Mankind' summed up evidence and opinion as locating 'the cradle of the present race of mankind . . . near to the borders of those luxuriant regions, which a line drawn from the south-east corner of the Euxine [Black Sea] directly eastward into the Caspian Sea, must necessarily traverse' (*Oriental Collections* II No. i (1797) 73). This line passes through the Russian Caucasus; the adjoining 'luxuriant regions' would be Armenia, Georgia, and Azerbaijan. Luther L. Scales Jr. in 'The Poet as Miltonic Adam in *Alastor*' (*KSJ* xxi–xxii (1972–73) 139–40) relates the physical details of the underground stream bringing the *Alastor* Poet into 'Nature's dearest haunt' (line 429) with those of the underground river that fertilizes Paradise in *PL* iv 223–30.

433–441. *The pyramids . . . The grey trunks*] The terms of the description owe much to those used of the garden of bliss in *Thalaba* (VI xx 12–17): 'fluted cypresses rear'd up / Their living obelisks; / And broad-leav'd plane-trees in long colonnades / O'er-arch'd delightful walks, / Where round their trunks the thousand tendrill'd vine / Wound up and hung the boughs with greener wreaths'.

In rainbow and in fire, the parasites,
440 Starred with ten thousand blossoms, flow around
The grey trunks, and, as gamesome infants' eyes,
With gentle meanings, and most innocent wiles,
Fold their beams round the hearts of those that love,
These twine their tendrils with the wedded boughs
445 Uniting their close union; the woven leaves
Make net-work of the dark blue light of day,
And the night's noontide clearness, mutable
As shapes in the weird clouds. Soft mossy lawns
Beneath these canopies extend their swells,
450 Fragrant with perfumed herbs, and eyed with blooms
Minute yet beautiful. One darkest glen
Sends from its woods of musk-rose, twined with
                                        jasmine,
A soul-dissolving odour, to invite
To some more lovely mystery. Through the dell,
455 Silence and Twilight here, twin-sisters, keep
Their noonday watch, and sail among the shades,
Like vaporous shapes half seen; beyond, a well,
Dark, gleaming, and of most translucent wave,
Images all the woven boughs above,
460 And each depending leaf, and every speck
Of azure sky, darting between their chasms;
Nor aught else in the liquid mirror laves
Its portraiture, but some inconstant star
Between one foliaged lattice twinkling fair,

439. *parasites*] The original Greek compound παρα-σιτος means only 'feeding together', and any climbing plant could be called a parasite-plant without disapprobation. Indeed at this period the word as used of vegetation generally carries the sense of fruitful intimacy rather than of exploitation. See note to *Q Mab* i 43.

444. *wedded boughs*] Butter (*Butter (1970)* 243) notes how the imagery 'has appropriately sexual associations'. The archetype was Milton's Eden (*PL* v 215–17): 'they led the Vine / To wed her Elm; she spous'd about him twines / Her mariageable arms'.

448. *lawns*] grassy clearings (still the usual sense in 1815).

453. *soul-dissolving*] A compound adopted from Thomson's *Castle of Indolence* (1748) I xxxix 6, where 'soul-dissolving airs' are breathed from the Aeolian harp.

455. *Silence and Twilight here, twin-sisters, keep*] Silence and Twilight, here twin-sisters, keep *Locock 1911*. Locock moved the comma because 'without it "here" is tautological with "Through the dell"', but the text implies that it is from here, in 'one darkest glen', that Silence and Twilight supervise the whole cell. See 'A Summer-Evening Churchyard' 5–6 and note.

465   Or painted bird, sleeping beneath the moon,
      Or gorgeous insect floating motionless,
      Unconscious of the day, ere yet his wings
      Have spread their glories to the gaze of noon.
      Hither the Poet came. His eyes beheld
470   Their own wan light through the reflected lines
      Of his thin hair, distinct in the dark depth
      Of that still fountain; as the human heart,
      Gazing in dreams over the gloomy grave,
      Sees its own treacherous likeness there. He heard
475   The motion of the leaves, the grass that sprung
      Startled and glanced and trembled even to feel
      An unaccustomed presence, and the sound
      Of the sweet brook that from the secret springs
      Of that dark fountain rose. A Spirit seemed
480   To stand beside him – clothed in no bright robes
      Of shadowy silver or enshrining light,
      Borrowed from aught the visible world affords
      Of grace, or majesty, or mystery; –
      But, undulating woods, and silent well,
485   And leaping rivulet, and evening gloom
      Now deepening the dark shades, for speech assuming
      Held commune with him, as if he and it
      Were all that was, – only . . . when his regard
      Was raised by intense pensiveness, . . . two eyes,

---

465. Or painted] *1839*; Or, painted *1816, 1824*.

466–8. Or gorgeous insect . . . gaze of noon] i.e. 'or a reflected butterfly, still unaware that outside the forest it is noonday'. Thus the well reflects only leaves and sky by day, only star or bird by night, and perhaps a butterfly that mistakes day for night.

474. Sees its own treacherous likeness there] 'imagines its own dubious survival after death'.

479. A Spirit] Presumably an embodiment of Nature, not visually personified but communicating directly via the landscape. This diverges explicitly from the experiences of the young Wordsworth, for whom the appearances of Nature were 'a feeling and a love / That had no need of a remoter charm, / By thought supplied, nor any interest / Unborrowed from the eye' ('Lines Composed . . . above Tintern Abbey' 80–3). Wasserman sees this Spirit as another realization of the veilèd maid, 'diffused mysteriously throughout nature' (*Wasserman* 32).

484–7. But, undulating woods . . . commune with him] '. . , the Spirit, assuming for speech the undulating woods, silent well [etc.], communed with the Poet' (Forman). Cp. 'Mont Blanc' (Text B) 74–83.

490   Two starry eyes, hung in the gloom of thought,
And seemed with their serene and azure smiles
To beckon him.

               Obedient to the light
That shone within his soul, he went, pursuing
The windings of the dell. – The rivulet
495   Wanton and wild, through many a green ravine
Beneath the forest flowed. Sometimes it fell
Among the moss with hollow harmony
Dark and profound. Now on the polished stones
It danced; like childhood laughing as it went:
500   Then, through the plain in tranquil wanderings crept,
Reflecting every herb and drooping bud
That overhung its quietness. – 'O stream!
Whose source is inaccessibly profound,
Whither do thy mysterious waters tend?
505   Thou imagest my life. Thy darksome stillness,
Thy dazzling waves, thy loud and hollow gulfs,
Thy searchless fountain, and invisible course
Have each their type in me: and the wide sky,
And measureless ocean may declare as soon
510   What oozy cavern or what wandering cloud
Contains thy waters, as the universe
Tell where these living thoughts reside, when stretched
Upon thy flowers my bloodless limbs shall waste
I' the passing wind!'

               Beside the grassy shore
515   Of the small stream he went; he did impress
On the green moss his tremulous step, that caught
Strong shuddering from his burning limbs. As one
Roused by some joyous madness from the couch
Of fever, he did move; yet, not like him,
520   Forgetful of the grave, where, when the flame
Of his frail exultation shall be spent,
He must descend. With rapid steps he went

490. Two starry eyes] The 'beamy bending eyes' of line 179. Butter comments (*Butter (1970)* 243): 'He is beckoned to seek communion beyond that which nature affords, but there is no assurance that the hope of such ideal communion is not an illusion'.

502–14. Eds compare Wordsworth, *Excursion* iii 967–end; but the stream or sea of life is a universally-used metaphor.

519–20. yet, not like him, / Forgetful] i.e. 'yet not resembling the fever-patient in being forgetful . . .' Some editors change the punctuation in various ways to remove the ambiguity, but also change the intended emphasis.

Beneath the shade of trees, beside the flow
Of the wild babbling rivulet; and now
525   The forest's solemn canopies were changed
For the uniform and lightsome evening sky.
Grey rocks did peep from the spare moss, and stemmed
The struggling brook: tall spires of windlestrae
Threw their thin shadows down the rugged slope,
530   And nought but gnarlèd roots of ancient pines
Branchless and blasted, clenched with grasping roots
The unwilling soil. A gradual change was here,
Yet ghastly. For, as fast years flow away,
The smooth brow gathers, and the hair grows thin
535   And white, and where irradiate dewy eyes
Had shone, gleam stony orbs:—so from his steps
Bright flowers departed, and the beautiful shade
Of the green groves, with all their odorous winds
And musical motions. Calm, he still pursued
540   The stream, that with a larger volume now
Rolled through the labyrinthe dell; and there
Fretted a path through its descending curves
With its wintry speed. On every side now rose
Rocks, which, in unimaginable forms,
545   Lifted their black and barren pinnacles
In the light of evening, and its precipice
Obscuring the ravine, disclosed above,
Mid toppling stones, black gulfs and yawning caves,
Whose windings gave ten thousand various tongues
550   To the loud stream. Lo! where the pass expands
Its stony jaws, the abrupt mountain breaks,
And seems, with its accumulated crags,

524. *rivulet;*] rivulet, *1816.*
528. *windlestrae*] A windlestraw is a dry grass-stalk. The Scottish spelling may derive from John Leyden's 'The Elfin-King' 49, in *Tales of Wonder*.
530. *roots*] Perhaps a misprint for *knots*, which would look very similar in S.'s autograph.
546–8. *its precipice . . . yawning caves*] 'the ravine's steep side, obscuring the ravine itself below, revealed at a higher level, amid falling stones, black gulfs' etc. The passage has produced much editorial ingenuity, but the characteristic syntax needs no emendation: the subject of *disclosed* is *its precipice*, which refers proleptically to *the ravine*. The gulfs and caves are not necessarily at the top of the precipice, or they would not echo the noise of the stream, only *above* the ravine-bottom.

To overhang the world: for wide expand
Beneath the wan stars and descending moon
555 Islanded seas, blue mountains, mighty streams,
Dim tracts and vast, robed in the lustrous gloom
Of leaden-coloured even, and fiery hills
Mingling their flames with twilight, on the verge
Of the remote horizon. The near scene,
560 In naked and severe simplicity,
Made contrast with the universe. A pine,
Rock-rooted, stretched athwart the vacancy
Its swinging boughs, to each inconstant blast
Yielding one only response, at each pause
565 In most familiar cadence, with the howl
The thunder and the hiss of homeless streams
Mingling its solemn song, whilst the broad river,
Foaming and hurrying o'er its rugged path,
Fell into that immeasurable void
570 Scattering its waters to the passing winds.

Yet the grey precipice and solemn pine
And torrent, were not all;—one silent nook
Was there. Even on the edge of that vast mountain,
Upheld by knotty roots and fallen rocks,
575 It overlooked in its serenity
The dark earth, and the bending vault of stars.
It was a tranquil spot, that seemed to smile
Even in the lap of horror. Ivy clasped
The fissured stones with its entwining arms,
580 And did embower with leaves for ever green,
And berries dark, the smooth and even space
Of its inviolated floor; and here
The children of the autumnal whirlwind bore,

557. *fiery hills*] Mount Elbruz, highest peak of the Caucasus, has a double
volcanic cone but has not erupted in historical times.
564. *response*] Normally accented on the first syllable at this date.
572. *one silent nook*] Perhaps suggested in some features by the 'hidden nook' in
the mountains described in Wordsworth's *Excursion* iii 50–147.
577–8. *to smile / Even in the lap of horror*] A phrase coined, according to William
Gilpin (*Observations, Relative Chiefly to Picturesque Beauty, made in the Year 1772*
(1786 edn) i 183), by one Mr Avison to describe Derwentwater: 'Here is beauty
indeed–Beauty lying in the lap of Horrour!' The phrase gained currency as an
early Romantic reaction to wild scenery, and S. could have met it in several
sources, including Mrs Radcliffe's *Mysteries of Udolpho* (1794) I ch. v, where an
Alpine landscape presents 'a perfect picture of the lovely and the sublime–of
"beauty sleeping in the lap of horror"'.
583. *children*] i.e. playful gusts of wind.

In wanton sport, those bright leaves, whose decay,
585 Red, yellow, or etherially pale,
Rivals the pride of summer. 'Tis the haunt
Of every gentle wind, whose breath can teach
The wilds to love tranquillity. One step,
One human step alone, has ever broken
590 The stillness of its solitude:–one voice
Alone inspired its echoes;–even that voice
Which hither came, floating among the winds,
And led the loveliest among human forms
To make their wild haunts the depository
595 Of all the grace and beauty that endued
Its motions, render up its majesty,
Scatter its music on the unfeeling storm,
And to the damp leaves and blue cavern mould,
Nurses of rainbow flowers and branching moss,
600 Commit the colours of that varying cheek,
That snowy breast, those dark and drooping eyes.

The dim and hornèd moon hung low, and poured
A sea of lustre on the horizon's verge
That overflowed its mountains. Yellow mist
605 Filled the unbounded atmosphere, and drank
Wan moonlight even to fullness: not a star
Shone, not a sound was heard; the very winds,
Danger's grim playmates, on that precipice
Slept, clasped in his embrace.–O, storm of death!
610 Whose sightless speed divides this sullen night:
And thou, colossal Skeleton, that, still
Guiding its irresistible career
In thy devastating omnipotence,

588–92. *One step . . . among the winds*] The 'one human step alone' is the Poet's, the 'one voice' that of his vision ('like the voice of his own soul'–line 153), or possibly of the stream he has been following (lines 494–515).

598. *blue cavern mould*] Norman Thurston notes (*Studies in Romanticism* xiv (Spring 1975) 126) how the stones are covered with ivy 'for ever green' (580), and how the mould nurses 'rainbow flowers': 'Here death is ambiguous'. Beljame (see headnote) identified the mould as *Aspergillus glaucus*.

602. *The dim and hornèd moon*] The description of the crescent moon may recall a memorable scene near the Swiss frontier on 18 August 1814: 'The evening was most beautiful–the horned moon hung in the light of sunset, that threw a glow of unusual depth of redness above the piny mountains and the dark deep valleys which they included . . . The moon becomes yellow, hangs low–close to the woody horizon' (*Mary Jnl* i 16).

613. *devastating*] Normally accented on the second syllable at this date.

Art king of this frail world, from the red field
615 Of slaughter, from the reeking hospital,
The patriot's sacred couch, the snowy bed
Of innocence, the scaffold and the throne,
A mighty voice invokes thee. Ruin calls
His brother Death. A rare and regal prey
620 He hath prepared, prowling around the world;
Glutted with which thou mayst repose, and men
Go to their graves like flowers or creeping worms,
Nor ever more offer at thy dark shrine
The unheeded tribute of a broken heart.

625   When on the threshold of the green recess
The wanderer's footsteps fell, he knew that death
Was on him. Yet a little, ere it fled,
Did he resign his high and holy soul
To images of the majestic past,
630 That paused within his passive being now,
Like winds that bear sweet music, when they breathe
Through some dim latticed chamber. He did place
His pale lean hand upon the rugged trunk
Of the old pine. Upon an ivied stone
635 Reclined his languid head, his limbs did rest,
Diffused and motionless, on the smooth brink
Of that obscurest chasm;—and thus he lay,
Surrendering to their final impulses
The hovering powers of life. Hope and despair,
640 The torturers, slept; no mortal pain or fear
Marred his repose, the influxes of sense,
And his own being unalloyed by pain,
Yet feebler and more feeble, calmly fed
The stream of thought, till he lay breathing there
645 At peace, and faintly smiling:—his last sight
Was the great moon, which o'er the western line
Of the wide world her mighty horn suspended,

618. *Ruin calls*] Ruin will one day divert Death's undiscriminating attention
from the victims of the world's rulers (lines 614–17) to the rulers themselves.
Then men will die natural deaths, in accordance with their true worth ('like
flowers or creeping worms'). The interpolation parallels the epigram in the
Preface and lines 690–5; the Poet's death is 'a violation of the natural order of
things' (Albert S. Gérard, *English Romantic Poetry* (Berkeley 1968) 158).
629. *images of the majestic past*] As Gibson observes (loc. cit. 1040) S. circum-
vents any impression that the Poet is united with his vision after death, because
'The danger of neglecting love and sympathy with one's fellow-man in *this* life
was to be the theme of the poem', and because 'expecting to find one's ideals
beyond this life is without any certain foundation'.

With whose dun beams inwoven darkness seemed
To mingle. Now upon the jagged hills
650   It rests, and still as the divided frame
Of the vast meteor sunk, the Poet's blood,
That ever beat in mystic sympathy
With nature's ebb and flow, grew feebler still:
And when two lessening points of light alone
655   Gleamed through the darkness, the alternate gasp
Of his faint respiration scarce did stir
The stagnate night:—till the minutest ray
Was quenched, the pulse yet lingered in his heart.
It paused—it fluttered. But when heaven remained
660   Utterly black, the murky shades involved
An image, silent, cold, and motionless,
As their own voiceless earth and vacant air.
Even as a vapour fed with golden beams
That ministered on sunlight, ere the west
665   Eclipses it, was now that wondrous frame—
No sense, no motion, no divinity—
A fragile lute, on whose harmonious strings
The breath of heaven did wander—a bright stream
Once fed with many-voicèd waves—a dream
670   Of youth, which night and time have quenched for
                                              ever,
Still, dark, and dry, and unremembered now.

O, for Medea's wondrous alchemy,
Which wheresoe'er it fell made the earth gleam

651. *meteor*] Any atmospheric phenomenon could be called a 'meteor' at this date, including the moon.

654. *two lessening points of light*] The tips of the setting moon's crescent, of which the middle is already in darkness ('the divided frame'). The two points of light replace the eyes of the dream-maid (lines 179, 489–92) that have hitherto obsessed him.

657. *stagnate*] An earlier form of *stagnant*.

663–5. *Even as a vapour . . . Eclipses it*] 'like a sunlit cloud in attendance on the sun until it sets'.

671. 'It is quite in Shelley's manner . . . to go back to and bring together his illustrations. Here the poet's frame is a lute, a bright stream, a dream of youth. The lute is still, the stream is dark and dry, the dream is unremembered' (Stopford Brooke, *Poems of Shelley* (1880) 324). The illustrations themselves recall lines 41–9 (poet as wind-harp), 149–51 (dream of youth), and 494–514 (stream of life).

672. Medea was the famous sorceress who restored the old father of her lover Jason to youth by replacing his blood by a transfusion of drugs (Ovid, *Met*. vii 279–81): 'at quacumque cavo spumas ejecit aeno / ignis at in terram guttae

With bright flowers, and the wintry boughs exhale
675   From vernal blooms fresh fragrance! O, that God,
Profuse of poisons, would concede the chalice
Which but one living man has drained, who now,
Vessel of deathless wrath, a slave that feels
No proud exemption in the blighting curse
680   He bears, over the world wanders for ever,
Lone as incarnate death! O, that the dream
Of dark magician in his visioned cave,
Raking the cinders of a crucible
For life and power, even when his feeble hand
685   Shakes in its last decay, were the true law
Of this so lovely world! But thou art fled
Like some frail exhalation; which the dawn
Robes in its golden beams, – ah! thou hast fled!
The brave, the gentle, and the beautiful,
690   The child of grace and genius. Heartless things
Are done and said i' the world, and many worms
And beasts and men live on, and mighty Earth
From sea and mountain, city and wilderness,
In vesper low or joyous orison,
695   Lifts still its solemn voice: – but thou art fled –
Thou canst no longer know or love the shapes
Of this phantasmal scene, who have to thee
Been purest ministers, who are, alas!
Now thou art not. Upon those pallid lips

cecidere calentes, / vernat humus, floresque et mollia pabula surgunt' ('And wherever the fire spattered froth from the hollow pot, and hot drops fell to the earth, the soil blossomed and flowers and soft grass sprang up').

676. Profuse of poisons] 'generous with his venomous acts'.

677. one living man] Ahasuerus (see note on Q *Mab* vii 67). The Narrator's wish is that God would confer on mankind as a gift the immortality he inflicted on Ahasuerus as a punishment. Because A. was singled out revengefully in this way he can feel no 'proud exemption' from death, only solitude and misery.

678. Vessel of deathless wrath] From *Romans* ix 22: 'vessels of wrath fitted to destruction', i.e. created beings deserving to be destroyed in anger.

681–2. the dream / Of dark magician] The alchemist's dream of discovering an *elixir vitae* that would overturn the 'true law' of irreversible decay.

691–2. many worms . . . live on] Raben (loc. cit.) notices an echo from *The Ancient Mariner* 236–9; both poets, however, are indebted to *King Lear* V iii 306–7.

696–7. the shapes / Of this phantasmal scene] The 'objects' in this world of appearances. The personal pronoun would for S. apply to the shapes of Nature as well as to human figures.

700　So sweet even in their silence, on those eyes
　　　That image sleep in death, upon that form
　　　Yet safe from the worm's outrage, let no tear
　　　Be shed—not even in thought. Nor, when those hues
　　　Are gone, and those divinest lineaments,
705　Worn by the senseless wind, shall live alone
　　　In the frail pauses of this simple strain,
　　　Let not high verse, mourning the memory
　　　Of that which is no more, or painting's woe
　　　Or sculpture, speak in feeble imagery
710　Their own cold powers. Art and eloquence,
　　　And all the shows o' the world are frail and vain
　　　To weep a loss that turns their lights to shade.
　　　It is a woe too 'deep for tears,' when all
　　　Is reft at once, when some surpassing Spirit,
715　Whose light adorned the world around it, leaves
　　　Those who remain behind, not sobs or groans,
　　　The passionate tumult of a clinging hope;
　　　But pale despair and cold tranquillity,
　　　Nature's vast frame, the web of human things,
720　Birth and the grave, that are not as they were.

115　The Daemon of the World

The *Daemon* (Part I) is the last poem in *1816*. On 6 January 1816 S. sent John
Murray 'a copy of all the sheets but the last of a Vol. of poems which it is my
intention to publish . . . I have written to Mr. Hamilton the printer to send you
the sheet which is deficient, title-page &c' (*L* i 438–9), and Mary S., in her note
on *Q Mab*, states that S. 'never intended to publish Queen Mab as it stands; but

705. senseless] insensate.
713. Quoting from the last line of Wordsworth's 'Ode: Intimations of Immortality'.
720. that are not as they were] Echoing the 'Ode: Intimations of Immortality' 5: 'It
is not now as it hath been of yore'.
¶ *115. Title.* See headnote. The ancients thought of Daemons as mediating
between gods and men. Rogers (*1975* 334–5) identifies this Daemon as Love,
citing Plato's *Symposium* 203A: 'The divine nature cannot immediately communicate with what is human, but all that intercourse and converse which is
conceded by the Gods to men, both whilst they sleep and when they wake,
subsists through the intervention of Love . . .', but S.'s Daemon has also much
in common with the Power embodied in 'Mont Blanc' (cp. i 286–91 with
'Mont Blanc' (Text B) 94–7; ii 248–55 with 'Mont Blanc' (Text B) 1–6,
35–40).

a few years after, when printing Alastor, he extracted a small portion which he entitled "The Daemon of the World"' (*1839* i 103). Part I of this poem, therefore, a revision of Cantos i and ii of Q *Mab*, was probably completed in mid-December 1815 while *Alastor* was actually being printed (see *SC* iv 496–7). Preliminary revisions only were made in a copy of Q *Mab* (SC 296) which is now in the Carl H. Pforzheimer Library, under a heading 'The Queen of the Universe. The Metre Pastor Fido'; the main work must then have been done on loose sheets, which are lost, and the corrections were transcribed for the printer into another copy of Q *Mab* (MS. Ashley 4040) which is now in the British Library. These two copies of Q *Mab* are distinguished below as *Pf.MS* and *Ashley MS*. Besides first-draft revisions of Cantos i and ii, *Pf.MS* also contains speculative changes for Q *Mab* iv 227–36 and v 1–15; the slight modification of vi 72–104 which allowed those lines to be published in *1816* as a separate poem entitled 'Superstition'; and a complete draft revision of Cantos viii and ix, headed 'Second Part'. Cameron, in his study of *Pf.MS* (*SC* iv 487–514), argues that 'The Queen of the Universe' represents a quite distinct poem from 'The Daemon of the World', but this seems unnecessary. Although under the heading 'The Queen of the Universe' (possibly to recall *Paradise Lost* ix 684, where Eve is addressed by Satan as 'Queen of this Universe'), and although 'Queen' is adhered to throughout the early tentative revisions, the revisions of Cantos viii and ix refer to the visiting Power as 'Daemon', of neuter gender (e.g. ii 305: 'The Daemon called its wingèd ministers'); and it is natural to assume that the sub-heading 'Second Part' which announces these later revisions signals a continuation of the section printed as 'The Daemon of the World'. Moreover it has not been noticed that the long final passage of Part I was evidently written so as to link directly with the opening of Part II: neither the submissive homage of Evil's slaves (i 276–9) nor their rage against the Daemon of the World (i 282–7) will persist in the visioned future (ii 15–20; ii 20–23). That the two parts were not, in fact, written-out or published together may have been because the apocalyptic optimism of the 'Second Part' was out of keeping with the other contents of *1816*, or simply because S. could not prepare Part II for the printer in time. Unlike Part I it involved both MS additions and a complex rearrangement of printed passages. S. therefore probably made preliminary changes to Q *Mab* i and ii in *Pf.MS* and a complete sketch of alterations to viii and ix, changing his 'Queen' to 'Daemon' while doing so. He then finished revising i and ii on loose sheets and made a fair copy of Part I into *Ashley MS*, but had no time or eventual wish to make his alterations to viii and ix clearly intelligible for printing; so *Ashley MS* was sent in haste to the printer (unopened from Canto iv onwards) and the drafts in *Pf.MS* were abandoned. 'The Daemon of the World' is no evidence of changed opinions in S. Q *Mab*, though never formally published, had cost him Harriet's two children, and he was unlikely to risk Mary's first child (born 24 January 1816) by the least chance of prosecution; so he revised only the descriptive opening and the ideal end, toning down words and phrases which seemed provocative. The main innovation is the concept of influences from a universal Power, expressed in the wind-harp imagery that appears in other poems of this period, e.g. 'Mutability' 5–8; 'Hymn to Intellectual Beauty' 1–12, 32–4; *Alastor* 37–49.

In the Preface to *Alastor* S. wrote:

> The Fragment, entitled 'THE DAEMON OF THE WORLD', is a detached part of a poem which the author does not intend for publication. The metre in which it is composed is that of Samson Agonistes and the Italian pastoral drama, and may be considered as the natural measure into which poetical conceptions, expressed in harmonious language, necessarily fall.

Since defending the metre of *Q Mab* to Hogg on 7 February 1813 by enlisting 'Miltons Samson Agonistes, the Greek Choruses, & (you will laugh) Southeys Thalaba' (*L* i 352), S. had read Giovanni Battista Guarini's pastoral drama *Il Pastor Fido* ('The Faithful Shepherd' 1589) from 8–15 April 1815 in Italian (*Mary Jnl* i 74), and evidently felt that its versification–a mixture of unrhymed 7- and 11-syllable lines–endorsed his own use of unrhymed trimeters and pentameters. Presumably S. saw the proofs of *1816*, which must therefore be the copy-text for Part I, but there are passages (notably i 108–14, 122–3, 166–7) where the printed pointing gives a different and inferior meaning; here the holograph pointing has been preferred. Two known copies of *1816* contain further minor changes to the text of Part I (see *Julian* i 421 and *SC* iv 592–3), but their status is uncertain and they are not incorporated into the present text, though noted. See *Q Mab* (No. 92), Cantos i, ii, viii, and ix, for notes relevant to both poems.

Text: Part I. *1816* pp. 81–101.

Part II, and Fragment. SC 296: quoted by permission of the Carl H. Pforzheimer Library.

Published: Part I. *1816*.

Part II. *The Daemon of the World* [Parts I and II], ed. H. B. Forman (privately printed) 1876; *Forman 1876–7* iii 367–79; *SC* iv 515–68 (transcript of MS). Fragment. *SC* iv 540–2.

> Nec tantum prodere vati,
> Quantum scire licet. Venit aetas omnis in unam
> Congeriem, miserumque premunt tot saecula pectus.
>
> Lucan, *Phars.* L. v.l. 176

I.

How wonderful is Death,
Death and his brother Sleep!
One pale as yonder wan and hornèd moon,

Epigraph. 'Nor is the prophetess permitted to divulge all she knows. The whole of time comes in one mass, and so many centuries press on her afflicted breast'. S. began reading *Pharsalia* at the end of August 1815 (*L* i 429) and had reached Bk V by 22 September, finding it 'a poem . . . of wonderful genius, & transcending Virgil' (*L* i 432). The first sentence may be a comment on the censorship S. had been forced to exercise on *Q Mab*.

   With lips of lurid blue,
5 The other glowing like the vital morn,
   When throned on ocean's wave
    It breathes over the world:
  Yet both so passing strange and wonderful!

  Hath then the iron-sceptred Skeleton,
10 Whose reign is in the tainted sepulchres,
  To the helldogs that crouch beneath his throne
  Cast that fair prey? Must that divinest form,
  Which love and admiration cannot view
  Without a beating heart, whose azure veins
15 Steal like dark streams along a field of snow,
  Whose outline is as fair as marble clothed
  In light of some sublimest mind, decay?
    Nor putrefaction's breath
  Leave aught of this pure spectacle
20   But loathsomeness and ruin?–
   Spare aught but a dark theme
  On which the lightest heart might moralize?
  Or is it but that downy-wingèd slumbers
  Have charmed their nurse coy Silence, near her lids
25   To watch their own repose?
    Will they, when morning's beam
    Flows through those wells of light,
  Seek far from noise and day some western cave,
  Where woods and streams with soft and pausing winds
30   A lulling murmur weave?–

  Ianthe doth not sleep
  The dreamless sleep of death:
  Nor in her moonlight chamber, silently
  Doth Henry hear her regular pulses throb,

---

i 9. *iron-sceptred*] Ingpen saw a copy of *1816* with 'iron-sceptered Skeleton'
altered to 'gloomy Shadow' in S.'s hand (*Julian* i 421).

i 11. *helldogs that crouch*] Ashley MS, Locock 1911; hell dogs that couch *1816*.

i 16–17. *fair as marble . . . mind*] i.e. fair as work by a great sculptor. Cp. *PU* IV
412–13.

i 21. *theme*] theme, *1816* (*comma canc. in Ashley MS*).

i 24. *Silence,*] Ashley MS; Silence *1816*.

i 26–7. In two copies of *1816* S. changed these lines to read: 'Will they, when
omnipresent morning fills / Those fairest wells of light' (see *SC* iv 592–3).

i 33. *chamber,*] Ashley MS; chamber *1816*. The silence is Henry's, listening to
Ianthe's pulse.

35   Or mark her delicate cheek
With interchange of hues mock the broad moon,
        Outwatching weary night,
        Without assured reward.
        Her dewy eyes are closed;
40   On their translucent lids, whose texture fine
Scarce hides the dark blue orbs that burn below
        With unapparent fire,
        The baby Sleep is pillowed:
        Her golden tresses shade
45   The bosom's stainless pride,
Twining like tendrils of the parasite
        Around a marble column.

        Hark! whence that rushing sound?
'Tis like a wondrous strain, that sweeps
50   Around a lonely ruin
When west winds sigh and evening waves respond
        In whispers from the shore:
        'Tis wilder than the unmeasured notes
Which from the unseen lyres of dells and groves
55   The genii of the breezes sweep.
Floating on waves of music and of light
The chariot of the Daemon of the World
        Descends in silent power:
Its shape reposed within: slight as some cloud
60   That catches but the palest tinge of day
        When evening yields to night,
Bright as that fibrous woof when stars indue
        Its transitory robe.
        Four shapeless shadows bright and beautiful
65   Draw that strange car of glory: reins of light
Check their unearthly speed; they stop and fold
        Their wings of braided air:
The Daemon leaning from the etherial car
        Gazed on the slumbering maid.
70   Human eye hath ne'er beheld
        A shape so wild, so bright, so beautiful,

---

i 49. *strain,*] Ashley *MS*; strain *1816*. The comma was added in MS.
i 54. Line changed in two copies of *1816* to read: 'Which from the unseen lyres of
caves and dells' (*SC* iv 592–3).
i 55. After this line *Pf.MS* has: 'Those lines of rainbow light / Are like such rays
as many coloured streams / Throw on the roof of some impending crag'.
i 62. *indue*] cover, adorn.
i 65. *glory:*] glory, *1816*.

As that which o'er the maiden's charmèd sleep
  Waving a starry wand,
  Hung like a mist of light.
75 Such sounds as breathed around like odorous winds
  Of wakening spring arose,
 Filling the chamber and the moonlight sky.

Maiden, the world's supremest spirit
  Beneath the shadow of her wings
80 Folds all thy memory doth inherit
  From ruin of divinest things,
   Feelings that lure thee to betray,
   And light of thoughts that pass away.

For thou hast earned a mighty boon,
85 The truths which wisest poets see
Dimly, thy mind may make its own,
  Rewarding its own majesty,
   Entranced in some diviner mood
   Of self–oblivious solitude.

90 Custom, and Faith, and Power thou spurnest;
  From hate and awe thy heart is free;
 Ardent and pure as day, thou burnest
  For dark and cold mortality
   A living light, to cheer it long,
95   The watch–fires of the world among.

Therefore from nature's inner shrine,
  Where gods and fiends in worship bend,
Majestic spirit, be it thine
  The flame to seize, the veil to rend
100   Where the vast snake Eternity
   In charmèd sleep doth ever lie.

i 78–83. Ambiguous: 'From ruin' can be taken either with 'Folds' or 'inherit'. Locock (*Locock 1911* i 546) convincingly favours the first alternative, which gives a meaning: 'Guards the divine inheritance of your memory from corruption, such as delusive earthly feelings and fading enlightenment'. The idea is that of Plato's *Phaedrus* 250, mediated through Wordsworth (see next note).
i 85–6. Cp. Wordsworth's 'Ode: Intimations of Immortality' 116–17, of the child fresh from Heaven 'On whom those truths do rest / Which we are toiling all our lives to find'.
i 89. *self-oblivious*] self oblivious *1816, Ashley MS*.
i 92. *day, thou burnest*] *Ashley MS*; day thou burnest, *1816*.
i 99. *rend*] *Ashley MS*; rend, *1816*.

All that inspires thy voice of love,
    Or speaks in thy unclosing eyes,
Or through thy frame doth burn or move,
105   Or think or feel, awake, arise!
      Spirit, leave for mine and me
      Earth's unsubstantial mimicry!

It ceased, and from the mute and moveless frame
    A radiant spirit arose:
110 All beautiful in naked purity
Robed in its human hues it did ascend:
Disparting as it went the silver clouds,
It moved towards the car, and took its seat
    Beside the Daemon shape.

115 Obedient to the sweep of aery song,
    The mighty ministers
Unfurled their prismy wings.
    The magic car moved on;
The night was fair, innumerable stars
120   Studded heaven's dark blue vault;
    The eastern wave grew pale
    With the first smile of morn:—
    The magic car moved on.
From the swift sweep of wings
125 The atmosphere in flaming sparkles flew;
    And where the burning wheels
Eddied above the mountain's loftiest peak
    Was traced a line of lightning.
Now far above a rock the utmost verge
130   Of the wide earth it flew,
The rival of the Andes, whose dark brow
    Frowned o'er the silver sea.

Far, far below the chariot's stormy path,
    Calm as a slumbering babe,
135   Tremendous ocean lay.
Its broad and silent mirror gave to view
    The pale and waning stars,
    The chariot's fiery track,

i *102–3.* i.e. 'all of love that inspires . . . or speaks' (*Locock 1911* i 547).
i *106–7.* i.e. 'Leave Earth's mimicry, and come to me and my realities' (*Locock 1911* i 547).
i *109. arose:*] *Ashley MS*; arose, *1816*.
i *110. purity*] *Ashley MS*; purity. *1816*.
i *111. ascend:*] *Ashley MS*; ascend, *1816*.
i *122. morn:–*] *Ashley MS. 1816* has a stop after 'morn', followed by a space.

And the grey light of morn
140   Tinging those fleecy clouds
That cradled in their folds the infant dawn.
The chariot seemed to fly
Through the abyss of an immense concave,
Radiant with million constellations, tinged
145   With shades of infinite colour,
And semicircled with a belt
Flashing incessant meteors.

As they approached their goal,
The wingèd shadows seemed to gather speed.
150   The sea no longer was distinguished; earth
Appeared a vast and shadowy sphere, suspended
In the black concave of heaven
With the sun's cloudless orb
Whose rays of rapid light
155   Parted around the chariot's swifter course,
And fell like ocean's feathery spray
Dashed from the boiling surge
Before a vessel's prow.

The magic car moved on.
160   Earth's distant orb appeared
The smallest light that twinkles in the heavens,
Whilst round the chariot's way
Innumerable systems widely rolled,
And countless spheres diffused
165   An ever varying glory.
It was a sight of wonder: some were horned
And like the moon's argentine crescent—hung
In the dark dome of heaven; some did shed
A clear mild beam like Hesperus, while the sea
170   Yet glows with fading sunlight; others dashed
Athwart the night with trains of bickering fire,
Like spherèd worlds to death and ruin driven;
Some shone like stars, and as the chariot passed
Bedimmed all other light.

i 153. orb] Ashley MS; orb, 1816 (the comma makes Earth the lightgiver).
i 166. wonder: some were horned] Ashley MS; wonder! Some were horned, 1816.
i 167. And like] Ashley MS; And, like 1816. crescent—hung] Ashley MS; crescent hung 1816.
i 168. heaven; some] Heaven . . . some Ashley MS; heaven, some 1816.
i 170. sunlight;] sunlight, Ashley MS; sun-light; 1816.

175   Spirit of Nature! here
In this interminable wilderness
Of worlds, at whose involved immensity
    Even soaring fancy staggers,
    Here is thy fitting temple.
180   Yet not the lightest leaf
That quivers to the passing breeze
    Is less instinct with thee, –
    Yet not the meanest worm,
That lurks in graves and fattens on the dead
185   Less shares thy eternal breath.
    Spirit of Nature! thou
Imperishable as this glorious scene,
    Here is thy fitting temple.

If solitude hath ever led thy steps
190 To the shore of the immeasurable sea,
    And thou hast lingered there
    Until the sun's broad orb
Seemed resting on the fiery line of ocean,
Thou must have marked the braided webs of gold
195   That without motion hang
    Over the sinking sphere:
Thou must have marked the billowy mountain clouds,
Edged with intolerable radiancy,
    Towering like rocks of jet
200   Above the burning deep:
    And yet there is a moment
    When the sun's highest point
Peers like a star o'er ocean's western edge,
When those far clouds of feathery purple gleam
205 Like fairy lands girt by some heavenly sea:
Then has thy rapt imagination soared
Where in the midst of all existing things
The temple of the mightiest Daemon stands.

    Yet not the golden islands
210 That gleam amid yon flood of purple light,
    Nor the feathery curtains
That canopy the sun's resplendent couch,
    Nor the burnished ocean waves
    Paving that gorgeous dome,
215   So fair, so wonderful a sight
As the eternal temple could afford.
The elements of all that human thought
Can frame of lovely or sublime, did join
To rear the fabric of the fane, nor aught

220 Of earth may image forth its majesty.
Yet likest evening's vault that faëry hall,
As heaven low resting on the wave it spread
  Its floors of flashing light,
  Its vast and azure dome;
225 And on the verge of that obscure abyss
Where crystal battlements o'erhang the gulf
Of the dark world, ten thousand spheres diffuse
Their lustre through its adamantine gates.

  The magic car no longer moved;
230   The Daemon and the Spirit
  Entered the eternal gates.
  Those clouds of aery gold
  That slept in glittering billows
  Beneath the azure canopy,
235 With the etherial footsteps trembled not;
  While slight and odorous mists
Floated to strains of thrilling melody
Through the vast columns and the pearly shrines.

  The Daemon and the Spirit
240 Approached the overhanging battlement.
Below lay stretched the boundless universe!
  There, far as the remotest line
That limits swift imagination's flight,
Unending orbs mingled in mazy motion,
245   Immutably fulfilling
  Eternal Nature's law.
  Above, below, around,
  The circling systems formed
  A wilderness of harmony;
250   Each with undeviating aim
In eloquent silence through the depths of space
  Pursued its wondrous way. –

Awhile the Spirit paused in ecstasy.
Yet soon she saw, as the vast spheres swept by,
255 Strange things within their belted orbs appear.
Like animated frenzies, dimly moved
Shadows, and skeletons, and fiendly shapes,
Thronging round human graves, and o'er the dead
Sculpturing records for each memory
260 In verse, such as malignant gods pronounce,

i 225. *that obscure*] *1816*; the obscure *Ashley MS*. Presumably corrected in proof.
i 249. *harmony;*] harmony, *1816*.

Blasting the hopes of men, when heaven and hell
Confounded burst in ruin o'er the world:
And they did build vast trophies, instruments
Of murder, human bones, barbaric gold,
265 Skins torn from living men, and towers of skulls
With sightless holes gazing on blinder heaven,
Mitres, and crowns, and brazen chariots stained
With blood, and scrolls of mystic wickedness,
The sanguine codes of venerable crime.
270 The likeness of a thronèd king came by,
When these had passed, bearing upon his brow
A threefold crown; his countenance was calm,
His eye severe and cold; but his right hand
Was charged with bloody coin, and he did gnaw
275 By fits, with secret smiles, a human heart
Concealed beneath his robe; and motley shapes,
A multitudinous throng, around him knelt,
With bosoms bare, and bowed heads, and false looks
Of true submission; as the sphere rolled by,
280 Brooking no eye to witness their foul shame,
Which human hearts must feel, while human tongues
Tremble to speak, they did rage horribly,
Breathing in self contempt fierce blasphemies
Against the Daemon of the World, and high
285 Hurling their armèd hands where the pure Spirit,

i 265. Southey's *Madoc* (1805) describes towers of skulls and trophies of human skin in the temples of ancient Mexico, e.g. I vi 181–2 and note: 'on the summit where we stood four Towers / Were piled with human skulls', and note to II xiv 83: 'In some provinces they flayed the captives taken in war, and with their skins covered their drums'.

i 274–6. *he did gnaw . . . his robe*] Possibly suggested by Southey's literal note to *Madoc* I vi 248 concerning the King of Chalco, who 'wore round his neck a chain of human hearts set in gold–the hearts of the bravest men whom he had slain, or taken, and sacrificed'.

i 279. *submission;*] submission, 1816. A heavier stop is needed to mark the transition from kneeling to raging: *Hutchinson* reads 'rolled by. / Brooking' in 279–80; *Locock 1911* reads 'speak; they' in 282.

i 285–8. Paul Turner (*RES* x (August 1959) 269–70) quotes Lucretius, *De Re Nat.* II 7–13: 'nil dulcius est bene quam munita tenere / edita doctrina sapientium templa serena, / despicere unde queas alios passimque videre / errare atque viam palantis quaerere vitae' ('Nothing is sweeter than to occupy high and serene temples, well secured by the teachings of the wise, from which you can look down on others and see them astray everywhere, wandering in search of the path of life'). Cp. 'Mont Blanc' (Text B) 96–7: 'Power dwells apart in its tranquillity, / Remote, serene, and inaccessible'.

Serene and inaccessibly secure,
Stood on an isolated pinnacle;
The flood of ages combating below,
The depth of the unbounded universe
290   Above, and all around
Necessity's unchanging harmony.

II.

O happy Earth! reality of Heaven!
To which those restless powers that ceaselessly
Throng through the human universe, aspire;
Thou consummation of all mortal hope!
5   Thou glorious prize of blindly-working will!
Whose rays, diffused throughout all space and time,
Verge to one point and blend forever there:
Of purest spirits thou pure dwelling-place!
Where care and sorrow, impotence and crime,
10   Languor, disease, and ignorance dare not come:
O happy Earth, reality of Heaven!
Genius has seen thee in her passionate dreams,
And dim forebodings of thy loveliness
Haunting the human heart, have there entwined
15   Those rooted hopes, that the proud Power of Evil
Shall not forever on this fairest world
Shake pestilence and war, or that his slaves
With blasphemy for prayer and human blood
For sacrifice, before his shrine forever
20   In adoration bend, or Erebus
With all its banded fiends shall not uprise

i 287–8. pinnacle; . . . below,] pinnacle, . . . below 1816.
i 291. This passage from line 253, not in Ashley MS or Pf.MS, was evidently composed separately and pinned into Ashley MS for the printer (see SC iv 505–7). However, Pf.MS has a cancelled draft of eight lines added to the end of Q Mab Canto ii:

> None dare relate what fearful mysteries
> The Spirit saw, nor the portentous groan
> Which when the flood was still, the living world
> Sent in complaint to that divinest fane.
> While from the deep a multitudinous throng
> Of motley shapes, the envious Present leads
> Who raging horribly[,] their armed hands
> Hurl high, where inaccessibly serene

ii 1. reality] 'Realisation' (Locock 1911).
ii 15. Power] God canc. Pf.MS.
ii 20–3. or Erebus . . . The dauntless] or that its jaws / Conspiring Hell shall gape

To overwhelm in envy and revenge
The dauntless and the good, who dare to hurl
Defiance at his throne, girt though it be
25 With Death's omnipotence. Thou hast beheld
His empire, o'er the present and the past;
It was a desolate sight—now gaze on mine,
Futurity.

Thou hoary giant Time,
Render thou up thy half-devoured babes,—
30 And from the cradles of eternity,
Where millions lie lulled to their portioned sleep
By the deep murmuring stream of passing things,
Tear thou that gloomy shroud.—Spirit, behold
Thy glorious destiny! The Spirit saw
35 The vast frame of the renovated world
Smile in the lap of Chaos, and the sense
Of hope through her fine texture did suffuse
Such varying glow, as summer evening casts
On undulating clouds and deepening lakes.
40 Like the vague sighings of a wind at even,
That wakes the wavelets of the slumbering sea
And dies on the creation of its breath,
And sinks and rises, fails and swells by fits:
Was the sweet stream of thoughts that with mild
motion
45 Flowed o'er the Spirit's human sympathies.
The mighty tide of thought had paused awhile,
Which from the Daemon now like ocean's stream
Again began to pour.—To me is given
The wonders of the human world to keep—
50 Space, matter, time and mind—let the sight
Renew and strengthen all thy failing hope.

---

to swallow all / The dauntless *canc. Pf.MS.* Erebus, 'Darkness', son of Chaos in
Greek mythology, often signified Hell itself.
ii *28. Time,*] Time *Pf.MS.* S. had cancelled an earlier opening: 'mighty time /
Relentless sire, inexorable King!'
ii *36. Smile in the lap of Chaos*] See *Alastor* 577–8 and note. This modification of
the current phrase supports the view that it was written after *Alastor*.
ii *38. evening casts*] evenings casts *Pf.MS (possibly intending* evenings cast*)*.
ii *39. lakes.*] lakes *Pf.MS.*
ii *45. sympathies.*] sympathies *Pf.MS.*
ii *49. keep—*] keep *Pf.MS.*

All things are recreated, and the flame
Of consentaneous love inspires all life:
The fertile bosom of the earth gives suck
55 To myriads, who still grow beneath her care,
Rewarding her with their pure perfectness:
The balmy breathings of the wind inhale
Her virtues, and diffuse them all abroad:
Health floats amid the gentle atmosphere,
60 Glows in the fruits, and mantles on the stream:
No storms deform the beaming brow of heaven,
Nor scatter in the freshness of its pride
The foliage of the undecaying trees;
But fruits are ever ripe, flowers ever fair,
65 And Autumn proudly bears her matron grace,
Kindling a flush on the fair cheek of spring,
Whose virgin bloom beneath the ruddy fruit
Reflects its tint and blushes into love.

The habitable earth is full of bliss;
70 Those wastes of frozen billows that were hurled
By everlasting snow-storms round the poles,
Where matter dared nor vegetate nor live,
But ceaseless frost round the vast solitude
Bound its broad zone of stillness, are unloosed;
75 And fragrant zephyrs there from spicy isles
Ruffle the placid ocean-deep, that rolls
Its broad, bright surges to the sloping sand,
Whose roar is wakened into echoings sweet
To murmur through the heaven-breathing groves
80 And melodize with man's blessed nature there.
The vast tract of the parched and sandy waste
Now teems, with countless rills and shady woods,
Corn-fields and pastures and white cottages;
And where the startled wilderness did hear
85 A savage conqueror stained in kindred blood,
Hymning his victory, or the milder snake
Crushing the bones of some frail antelope
Within his brazen folds—the dewy lawn,
Offering sweet incense to the sunrise, smiles
90 To see a babe before his mother's door,
Share with the green and golden basilisk
That comes to lick his feet, his morning's meal.
Those trackless deeps, where many a weary sail
Has seen above the illimitable plain,
95 Morning on night, and night on morning rise,
Whilst still no land to greet the wanderer spread
Its shadowy mountains on the sun-bright sea,

Where the loud roarings of the tempest-waves
So long have mingled with the gusty wind
100   In melancholy loneliness, and swept
The desert of those ocean solitudes,
But vocal to the sea-bird's harrowing shriek,
The bellowing monster, and the rushing storm,
Now to the sweet and many-mingling sounds
105   Of kindliest human impulses respond:
Those lonely realms bright garden-isles begem,
With lightsome clouds and shining seas between,
And fertile valleys, resonant with bliss,
Whilst green woods overcanopy the wave,
110   Which like a toil-worn labourer leaps to shore,
To meet the kisses of the flowrets there.

Man chief perceives the change, his being notes
The gradual renovation, and defines
Each movement of its progress on his mind.

115   Man, where the gloom of the long polar night
Lowered o'er the snow-clad rocks and frozen soil,
Where scarce the hardiest herb that braves the frost
Basked in the moonlight's ineffectual glow,
Shrank with the plants, and darkened with the night.
120   Nor where the tropics bound the realms of day
With a broad belt of mingling cloud and flame,
Where blue mists through the unmoving atmosphere
Scattered the seeds of pestilence, and fed
Unnatural vegetation, where the land
125   Teemed with all earthquake, tempest and disease,
Was man a nobler being; slavery
Had crushed him to his country's bloodstained dust.

Even where the milder zone afforded man
A seeming shelter, yet contagion there,
130   Blighting his being with unnumbered ills,
Spread like a quenchless fire; nor truth availed
Till late to arrest its progress, or create
That peace which first in bloodless victory waved
Her snowy standard o'er this favoured clime:
135   There man was long the train-bearer of slaves,
The mimic of surrounding misery,
The jackal of ambition's lion-rage,

ii *104. many-mingling*] many mingling *Pf.MS.*
ii *127–8. Between these lines* S. *inserted but cancelled*: A banquet for the vultures &
the worms, / Beneath that sun, where
ii *132. create*] *canc. Pf.MS* (probably to avoid rhyme; then S. changed the
previous line).

The bloodhound of religion's hungry zeal.
Here now the human being stands adorning
140   This loveliest earth with taintless body and mind;
Blessed from his birth with all bland impulses,
Which gently in his noble bosom wake
All kindly passions and all pure desires.
Him, still from hope to hope the bliss pursuing,
145   Which from the exhaustless lore of human weal
Draws on the virtuous mind, the thoughts that rise
In time-destroying infiniteness, gift
With self-enshrined eternity, that mocks
The unprevailing hoariness of age,
150   And man, once fleeting o'er the transient scene
Swift as an unremembered vision, stands
Immortal upon earth: no longer now
He slays the beast that sports around his dwelling
And horribly devours its mangled flesh,
155   Or drinks its vital blood, which like a stream
Of poison through his fevered veins did flow
Feeding a plague that secretly consumed
His feeble frame, and kindling in his mind
Hatred, despair, and fear and vain belief,
160   The germs of misery, death, disease, and crime.
No longer now the wingèd habitants,
That in the woods their sweet lives sing away,
Flee from the form of man; but gather round,
And prune their sunny feathers on the hands
165   Which little children stretch in friendly sport
Towards these dreadless partners of their play.
All things are void of terror: man has lost
His desolating privilege, and stands
An equal amidst equals: happiness
170   And science dawn though late upon the earth;
Peace cheers the mind, health renovates the frame;
Disease and pleasure cease to mingle here,
Reason and passion cease to combat there;
Whilst mind unfettered o'er the earth extends
175   Their all-subduing energies, and wields
The sceptre of a vast dominion there.

---

ii *142. noble bosom*] *canc. Pf.MS.*
ii *144–8. Him, . . . eternity,*] See Q *Mab* viii 203–7 and note.
ii *173–6. Reason and passion . . . dominion there.*] See Q *Mab* viii 231–4 and note.
S. has changed the construction to mean: 'Unfettered mind extends the energies of reason and passion, and wields . . .'

Mild is the slow necessity of death:
The tranquil spirit fails beneath its grasp,
Without a groan, almost without a fear,
180 Resigned in peace to the necessity,
Calm as a voyager to some distant land,
And full of wonder, full of hope as he.
The deadly germs of languor and disease
Waste in the human frame, and Nature gifts
185 With choicest boons her human worshippers.
How vigorous now the athletic form of age!
How clear its open and unwrinkled brow!
Where neither avarice, cunning, pride, or care,
Has stamped the seal of grey deformity
190 On all the mingling lineaments of time.
How lovely the intrepid front of youth!
How sweet the smiles of taintless infancy.

Within the massy prison's mouldering courts,
Fearless and free the ruddy children play,
195 Weaving gay chaplets for their innocent brows
With the green ivy and the red wall-flower,
That mock the dungeon's unavailing gloom;
The ponderous chains, and gratings of strong iron,
There rust amid the accumulated ruins
200 Now mingling slowly with their native earth:
There the broad beam of day, which feebly once
Lighted the cheek of lean captivity
With a pale and sickly glare, now freely shines
On the pure smiles of infant playfulness:
205 No more the shuddering voice of hoarse despair
Peals through the echoing vaults, but soothing notes
Of ivy-fingered winds and gladsome birds
And merriment are resonant around.

The fanes of Fear and Falsehood hear no more
210 The voice that once waked multitudes to war
Thundering through all their aisles: but now respond
To the death dirge of the melancholy wind:
It were a sight of awfulness to see
The works of faith and slavery, so vast,

ii *180. necessity,*] necessity *Pf.MS.*
ii *185. worshippers.*] worshippers *Pf.MS.*
ii *189. Has*] Had *Pf.MS* (presumably an oversight).
ii *206. Peals*] Pealed *Pf.MS* (an oversight).
ii *208. are*] were *Pf.MS* (an oversight).

215   So sumptuous, yet withal so perishing!
      Even as the corpse that rests beneath their wall.
      A thousand mourners deck the pomp of death
      To-day, the breathing marble glows above
      To decorate its memory, and tongues
220   Are busy of its life: to-morrow, worms
      In silence and in darkness seize their prey.

      These ruins soon leave not a wreck behind:
      Their elements, wide scattered o'er the globe,
      To happier shapes are moulded, and become
225   Ministrant to all blissful impulses:
      Thus human things are perfected, and earth,
      Even as a child beneath its mother's love,
      Is strengthened in all excellence, and grows
      Fairer and nobler with each passing year.
230   Now Time his dusky pennons o'er the scene
      Closes in steadfast darkness, and the past
      Fades from our charmèd sight. My task is done:
      Thy lore is learned. Earth's wonders are thine own,
      With all the fear and all the hope they bring.
235   My spells are past: the present now recurs.
      Ah me! a pathless wilderness remains
      Yet unsubdued by man's reclaiming hand.
      Yet, human Spirit, bravely hold thy course,
      Let virtue teach thee firmly to pursue
240   The gradual paths of an aspiring change:
      For birth and life and death, and that strange state
      Before the naked powers that through the world
      Wander like winds have found a human home,
      All tend to perfect happiness, and urge
245   The restless wheels of being on their way,
      Whose flashing spokes, instinct with infinite life,
      Bicker and burn to gain their destined goal:
      For birth but wakes the universal Mind
      Whose mighty streams might else in silence flow
250   Through the vast world, to individual sense

ii *216. their*] its *Pf.MS.* An oversight, following the change of the 'cathedral' of
Q Mab ix 103 to the more cautious 'fanes of Fear and Falsehood'.

ii *222. These ruins*] i.e. of the 'fanes' of line 209.

ii *231. the past*] the future *Rossetti 1870, Locock 1911, Rogers.* But it is the vision of
the future, not the future itself, which is now past and fading.

ii *242–3. Before the naked powers . . . human home*] These with the new lines
248–50 reverse the simple dualism of S.'s original concept: in *Q Mab* ix 150 the
soul has to seek out an earthly body; here the universal powers find a human
agent in which to embody themselves.

Of outward shows, whose unexperienced shape
New modes of passion to its frame may lend;
Life is its state of action, and the store
Of all events is aggregated there
255 That variegate the eternal universe;
Death is a gate of dreariness and gloom,
That leads to azure isles and beaming skies
And happy regions of eternal hope.
Therefore, O Spirit! fearlessly bear on:
260 Though storms may break the primrose on its stalk,
Though frosts may blight the freshness of its bloom,
Yet spring's awakening breath will woo the earth,
To feel with kindliest dews its favourite flower,
That blooms in mossy banks and darksome glens,
265 Lighting the green wood with its sunny smile.
Fear not then, Spirit, death's disrobing hand,
So welcome when the tyrant is awake,
So welcome when the bigot's hell-torch flares;
'Tis but the voyage of a darksome hour,
270 The transient gulf-dream of a startling sleep.
For, what thou art shall perish utterly,
But what is thine may never cease to be,
Death is no foe to virtue: earth has seen
Love's brightest roses on the scaffold bloom,
275 Mingling with freedom's fadeless laurels there,
And presaging the truth of visioned bliss.
Are there not hopes within thee, which this scene
Of linked and gradual being has confirmed?
Hopes that not vainly thou, and living fires
280 Of mind, as radiant and as pure as thou
Have shone upon the paths of men—return
Surpassing Spirit, to that world, where thou
Art destined an eternal war to wage
With tyranny and falsehood, and uproot
285 The germs of misery from the human heart.
Thine is the hand whose piety would soothe
The thorny pillow of unhappy crime,
Whose impotence an easy pardon gains,

---

ii 270. gulf-dream] 'A dream that one is falling over a precipice' (Locock 1911).
Cp. L&C III xxii 2–6.
ii 279–81. Hopes . . . paths of men] i.e. hopes that you, with others as enlightened,
have not failed to show the way.

Watching its wanderings as a friend's disease:
290   Thine is the brow whose mildness would defy
Its fiercest rage, and brave its sternest will,
When fenced by power and master of the world.
Thou art sincere and good; of resolute mind,
Free from heart-withering custom's cold control,
295   Of passion lofty, pure and unsubdued.
Earth's pride and meanness could not vanquish thee,
And therefore art thou worthy of the boon
Which thou hast now received: virtue shall keep
Thy footsteps in the path that thou hast trod,
300   And many days of beaming hope shall bless
Thy spotless life of sweet and sacred love.
Go, happy one, and give that bosom joy
    Whose sleepless spirit waits to catch
    Light, life and rapture from thy smile.

305   The Daemon called its wingèd ministers.
Speechless with bliss the Spirit mounts the car,
That rolled beside the crystal battlement,
Bending her beamy eyes in thankfulness.
    The burning wheels inflame
310   The steep descent of heaven's untrodden way.
    Fast and far the chariot flew:
    The mighty globes that rolled
Around the gate of the Eternal Fane
Lessened by slow degrees, and soon appeared
315   Such tiny twinklers as the planet orbs
That ministering on the solar power
With borrowed light pursued their narrower way.
    Earth floated then below:
    The chariot paused a moment;
320   The Spirit then descended:
    And from the Earth departing
    The shadows with swift wings
Speeded like thought upon the light of Heaven.
The Body and the Soul united then,
325   A gentle start convulsed Ianthe's frame:
Her veiny eyelids quietly unclosed;
Moveless awhile the dark blue orbs remained:
She looked around in wonder and beheld
Henry, who kneeled in silence by her couch,
330   Watching her sleep with looks of speechless love,
    And the bright beaming stars
    That through the casement shone.

ii 305. *ministers*] messengers *canc. Pf.MS.*

115a. [Fragment revised from *Queen Mab* v 1–15]

Thus do the generations of the earth
Go to the grave, and issue from the womb,
Surviving still the imperishable change
That renovates the world; even as the leaves
5   Which countless autumn storms have scattering heaped
In wild dells of the tangled wilderness
Through many waning years; though long they choke,
Loading with loathsome rottenness the land,
All germs of promise. Yet when the tall trees
10   From which they fell, shorn of their lovely shapes,
Lie level with the earth to moulder there,
They fertilize the land they long deformed,
Till o'er the lawns a forest waves again;
The canker stains more faint, – from each decay
15   Its buds unfold more brightly, till no more
Or frost or shower or change of seasons mar
The lustre in its cup of healing dew
The freshness of its amaranthine leaves.
[   ] decay,
20   The monstrous nurse of loveliness, again
Invests the waste with hues of vital bloom,
Again deep groves wave in the wind, and flowers
Gleam in the dark glens of the tangled woods,
And many a bird and many an insect keeps
25   Its dwelling in the shade, and Man doth bend
His lonely steps to meet my Angels there

116 The Sunset

'The Poem entitled "The Sunset" was written in the spring of the year, while still residing at Bishopsgate' (Mary S.'s 'Note on Poems of 1816', *1839* iii 35).

¶ *115a. Title.* S. may have started preparing these lines for extraction as a separate poem, as he did with 'Superstition' (published with *Alastor*) in the same volume. A transcript of the draft is in *SC* iv 540–2, with a facsimile on pp. 536–7; punctuation has been added to the text above in lines 13, 18, 19, 21, 23, and ampersands have been expanded. It is uncertain whether lines 19–26 were intended as a continuation or as an alternative to lines 14–18.
9. when the tall trees] canc. in *Pf.MS for* again the glens *which is also canc.*
17. lustre in] clearness of canc. in its cup] i.e. cupped in the forest-flowers.
23. Gleam] smile canc. glens] fens transcript.

The S.'s did not officially leave their house at Bishopsgate, Berks., until their journey to the continent on 3 May 1816, but S. was in London on business for much of March and April (*S in Eng* 460–6). February 1816 seems the likeliest time of composition. S.'s own recent reprieve from death largely accounts for the tone of the poem. 'In the spring of 1815, an eminent physician pronounced that he was dying rapidly of a consumption; abscesses were formed on his lungs, and he suffered acute spasms' (Mary S.'s 'Note on *Alastor*', *1839* i 140). The sudden change for the better in his health was not fully assured until the Thames holiday of early September. 'The Sunset' dramatizes the imagined effect of S.'s death on Mary (the cancelled name of the lady in the MS is Maria), and its scenery is that of Windsor Park (cp. the setting of Mary S.'s story 'The Mourner' (1829) in her *Collected Tales and Stories*, ed. Charles E. Robinson (Baltimore 1976) 81–5).

The textual history of this poem and the details of its first appearance have been much confused by editors (see e.g. *1975* 69). The draft is in *Nbk 11*, a long-service notebook containing material of many dates between 1814 and 1821. S. must have made a corrected copy for Ollier–probably one of 'the few scattered poems I left in England [to] be selected by my bookseller' (Advertisement to *1819*)–who published lines 9–20 (under the title "Sunset. From an unpublished Poem") and lines 28–42 (under the title "Grief. A Fragment") in his *Literary Pocket Book for 1821* (published 1820), both over the signature 'Δ'. When after S.'s death Mary S. was preparing *1824* she wrote to Ollier on 15 November 1823 to ask for the holograph from which his selections had been made (*Mary L* i 401–2). As this holograph was not in Ollier's sale-catalogue (Puttick & Simpson 19 July 1877) nor remained among the Shelley papers it was presumably sent as copy for *1824* to the printers, who inadvertently omitted line 37. The missing line was restored in *Forman 1882*. 'The Sunset' was presumably S.'s own title.

Text from *1824* 183–4 (line 37 supplied from *LPB*).

Published in *The Literary Pocket Book; or, Companion for the Lover of Nature and Art for 1821* (1820) 120–1 (lines 9–20, 28–42); *1824* 183–4.

> There late was One within whose subtle being,
> As light and wind within some delicate cloud
> That fades amid the blue noon's burning sky,
> Genius and youth contended. None may know
> 5   The sweetness of the joy which made his breath
> Fail, like the trances of the summer air,

¶ 116.1. *There late was One*] I had a friend *canc. draft.*
4. *Genius and youth*] *1824*, draft; Genius and death *1839*, *eds* (an error; 'youth' must have been the word in the printer's copy). No directly destructive contention is involved, as the simile illustrates: genius struggled to transcend immaturity at the expense of the physical frame.
6. ˙*trances*] suspensions of movement.

When, with the Lady of his love, who then
First knew the unreserve of mingled being,
He walked along the pathway of a field
10 Which to the east a hoar wood shadowed o'er,
But to the west was open to the sky.
There now the sun had sunk, but lines of gold
Hung on the ashen clouds, and on the points
Of the far level grass and nodding flowers
15 And the old dandelion's hoary beard,
And, mingled with the shades of twilight, lay
On the brown massy woods—and in the east
The broad and burning moon lingeringly rose
Between the black trunks of the crowded trees,
20 While the faint stars were gathering overhead. –
'Is it not strange, Isabel,' said the youth,
'I never saw the sun? We will walk here
Tomorrow; thou shalt look on it with me.'

That night the youth and lady mingled lay
25 In love and sleep—but when the morning came
The lady found her lover dead and cold.

Let none believe that God in mercy gave
That stroke. The lady died not, nor grew wild,
But year by year lived on—in truth I think
30 Her gentleness and patience and sad smiles,
And that she did not die, but lived to tend
Her aged father, were a kind of madness,
If madness 'tis to be unlike the world.
For but to see her were to read the tale
35 Woven by some subtlest bard, to make hard hearts

8. *the unreserve of mingled being*] [to] take his soul into her own *canc. draft.*
The word 'mingle' expresses S.'s sense of reciprocity in sexual intercourse,
'mingled being' that of combined sexual and spiritual mutuality.
9. *He*] We *LPB.*
15. *beard*] hair *draft.*
18. *burning*] pallid *draft.*
21. *Isabel*] Maria *canc. draft.* Rosalind *draft.* Rosalind was the name given to
Helen's friend in *R&H*, a poem suggested by Mary S.'s friendship with Isabel
Baxter (see headnote to *R&H*). 'Maria' is the Italian form of 'Mary'.
22. *I never saw the sun*] 'I missed seeing the sunset'.
23–4, 26–7, 44–5. The spaces in *1824* are confirmed by indents in the draft; *1839*
is printed as one continuous passage.
32. *father*] mother *canc. draft.*
33. *the world*] mankind *draft.*

Dissolve away in wisdom-working grief;—
Her eyes were black and lustreless and wan:
Her eyelashes were worn away with tears,
Her lips and cheeks were like things dead—so pale;
40 Her hands were thin, and through their wandering veins
And weak articulations might be seen
Day's ruddy light. The tomb of thy dead self
Which one vexed ghost inhabits, night and day,
Is all, lost child, that now remains of thee!

45 'Inheritor of more than earth can give,
Passionless calm, and silence unreproved,
Whether the dead find, oh, not sleep! but rest,
And are the uncomplaining things they seem,
Or live, a drop in the deep sea of Love;
50 Oh, that like thine, mine epitaph were—Peace!'
This was the only moan she ever made.

117 Verses written on receiving a Celandine in a letter from England

Dated 'Switzerland July–1816' in Mary S.'s hand under her transcript in Harvard MS 258.3–an impossible date for Peacock to have sent *Ranunculus ficaria*, a flower of early spring, but Mary S.'s memory was probably confused by the later reference in S.'s letter to Peacock initially dated 25 July concerning the Alpine plants he proposed to naturalize, 'companions which the celandine, the classic celandine, need not despise;–They are as wild & more daring than he, & will tell him tales of things even as touching & as sublime as the gaze of a vernal poet' (*L* i 501). The flower must have been sent immediately after S.'s arrival at Geneva, probably in response to S.'s first, homesick, letter to Peacock of 15 May: 'So long as man is such as he now is . . . like Wordsworth he will never know what love subsisted between himself & [the country of his birth], until absence shall have made its beauty heartfelt' (*L* i 475). Wordsworth had published three poems on the Lesser Celandine in *Poems in Two*

36–7. *Between these lines:* She was the tomb of her departed joy *canc. draft.*
37. Omitted in *1824. wan*] sickly (*OED* 3).
38. *worn away*] torn away *1839.*
45–9. Mostly canc. in draft.
46. *Passionless calm,*] *draft*; Passionless, calm *1824*; Passionless calm *1839.*
49. *live, a drop*] *draft, 1975*; live, or drop *1824, eds.* The draft makes much better sense, and *or/a* can be almost indistinguishable in S.'s hand.

Volumes (1807), one of which S. quoted to Peacock three years later (*L* ii 100): 'To the Small Celandine' ('Pansies, Lilies, Kingcups, Daisies', i 22), 'To the Same Flower' ('Pleasures newly found are sweet', i 27), and 'The Small Celandine' ('There is a Flower, the Lesser Celandine', ii 47), and S. adopts this evidently favourite flower as a symbol of the Poet himself ('There's a flower that shall be mine, / 'Tis the little Celandine'; 'To the Small Celandine' 7–8). S. rediscovered Wordsworth's poetry on his Swiss visit, and as Byron said 'used to dose me with Wordsworth physic even to nausea' (Medwin, *Conversations of Lord Byron* (1824) 237), but he regarded his later politics with contempt. 'That such a man should be such a poet!' (letter to Peacock, 25 July 1818, *L* ii 26). The transcript, in a notebook that had belonged to Claire Clairmont at Marlow, is the only text and is almost unpunctuated. The draft is in *Nbk 1* with the poem 'The billows on the beach' superimposed.
Text from Harvard MS Eng. 258.3 (Mary S.'s transcript).
Published by W. E. Peck in *The Boston Herald*, 21 December 1925, 12; *Julian* iii 124–6.

I thought of thee, fair Celandine,
    As of a flower aery blue,
Yet small—thy leaves methought were wet
    With the light of morning dew;
5   In the same glen thy star did shine
As the primrose and the violet,
And the wild briar bent over thee
And the woodland brook danced under thee.

    Lovely thou wert in thine own glen
10   Ere thou didst dwell in song or story,
    Ere the moonlight of a Poet's mind
    Had arrayed thee with the glory

¶ *117.1–2*. The apparent sense, 'until now I thought the celandine was blue', must be misleading; it is not credible that S., who according to Mary S. 'knew every plant by its name' (*1824* Preface), did not know that the celandine is yellow. The intended sense is possibly that S. associated the celandine with Wordsworth, just as he associated a blue flower with another writer. Perhaps Rousseau was in S.'s mind; the periwinkle was 'The flower which Rousseau brought into such fashion among the Parisians, by exclaiming one day, "Ah, voilà de la pervenche!"' (Moore's note to *The Fudge Family in Paris* (1818) Letter xii line 72). The incident itself is in R.'s *Confessions* (1781) Bk VI. A less likely possibility is that S.'s reference is to the gentian, and that its association for him was with Coleridge; cp. C.'s note to his 'Hymn before Sun-rise, in the Vale of Chamouni' 56: 'The beautiful *Gentiana major*, or greater gentian, with blossoms of the brightest blue, grows in large companies a few steps from the never-melted ice of the glaciers. I thought it an affecting emblem of the boldness of human hope, venturing near, and, as it were, leaning over the brink of the grave' (*Poetical Register* for 1802 (1803) ii 308).

Whose fountains are the hearts of men—
Many a thing of vital kind
15   Had fed and sheltered under thee,
Had nourished their thoughts near to thee.

Yes, gentle flower, in thy recess
    None might a sweeter aspect wear:
Thy young bud drooped so gracefully,
20   Thou wert so very fair—
Among the fairest ere the stress
Of exile, death and injury
Thus withering and deforming thee
Had made a mournful type of thee;

25   A type of that whence I and thou
    Are thus familiar, Celandine—
A deathless Poet whose young prime
    Was as serene as thine,
But he is changed and withered now,
30   Fallen on a cold and evil time;
His heart is gone—his fame is dim,
And Infamy sits mocking him.

Celandine! Thou art pale and dead,
    Changed from thy fresh and woodland state.
35   Oh! that thy bard were cold, but he
    Has lived too long and late.
Would he were in an honoured grave;
But that, men say, now must not be
Since he for impious gold could sell
40   The love of those who loved him well.

That he, with all hope else of good,
    Should be thus transitory
I marvel not—but that his lays
    Have spared not their own glory,
45   That blood, even the foul god of blood
    With most inexpiable praise,

29. *changed and withered*] One of Wordsworth's Celandines grows grey from age: 'It cannot help itself in its decay; / Stiff in its members, wither'd, changed of hue' ('The Small Celandine' 18–19); Wordsworth's own decay is seen as inward, corrupting the achievement of his prime.

30. Cp. Milton's description of his own situation after the Restoration: 'On evil days though fall'n, and evil tongues' (*PL* vii 26). S. later applied the same phrase to Godwin ('Letter to the Gisbornes' 198).

39. Since meanly he for gold c^{d} sell *draft*.

45. *god of blood*] S. had evidently seen Wordsworth's *Thanksgiving Ode, January*

Freedom and truth left desolate,
He has been bought to celebrate!

They were his hopes which he doth scorn,
50   They were his foes the fight that won;
That sanction and that condemnation
      Are now forever gone.
They need them not! Truth may not mourn
That with a liar's inspiration
55 Her majesty he did disown
Ere he could overlive his own.

They need them not, for Liberty,
      Justice and philosophic truth
From his divine and simple song
60   Shall draw immortal youth
When he and thou shall cease to be,
Or be some other thing, so long
As men may breathe or flowers may blossom
O'er the wide Earth's maternal bosom.

65 The stem whence thou wert disunited
      Since thy poor self was banished hither,
Now by that priest of Nature's care
      Who sent thee forth to wither
His window with its blooms has lighted,
70 And I shall see thy brethren there,
And each like thee will aye betoken
Love sold, hope dead, and honour broken.

---

18 1816, with other short pieces, which contained the notorious 'Ode 1815' 106–9:
'But Thy most dreaded instrument, / In working out a pure intent, / Is
Man–arrayed for mutual slaughter, / Yes, Carnage is thy daughter!'. Other
poems in the collection expressed similar sentiments.
48. bought] Wordsworth had accepted a minor post under Government in 1813.
49–56. 'The hopes he despises were once his own, the reactionary victors of
Europe were once his enemies, his principles are forgotten; but no matter: it is
fitting that he denied the authority of Truth before betraying his own poetic
powers'.
62–3. so long / As men may breathe] Echoing Shakespeare's sonnet 18 13–14: 'So
long as men can breathe or eyes can see, / So long lives this, and this gives life to
thee'.
67. by] 'by the agency of' (a grammatical shorthand).

118 Lines to Leigh Hunt

Written in early summer 1816, after reading Hunt's poem *The Story of Rimini*
(published February). The untitled draft is on two separate leaves torn from
Nbk 1, S.'s Swiss notebook (a full-page sketch of the Lake of Geneva is on the
verso of lines 18–27), which are now foliated in *Box 1*. The verso of the leaf
bearing lines 1–17 carries a diary entry for the thunderstorm of 28 July (actually
29 July), five unadopted lines for 'Mont Blanc', and six draft lines of a poem
evidently addressed to Mary S. for the second anniversary of their elopement
on 28 July 1814, almost indecipherable and with a huge blot in the middle:

> I can not but [   ] there is no bourn
> Where [   ] my thoughts return
> From all my [   ] brief state & we [   ]
> To steep in [   ]–not to mourn
> Aught in ourselves or in the tie
> That makes thee mine unchangeably

Although Mary S.'s journal lists *The Story of Rimini* as read by both S. and
herself in 1816, it is not named in the daily entries through 21 July–31
December, so the book was probably read during the period for which the
journal is lost, 14 May–20 July, most likely from Byron's own copy. The
poem was dedicated to Byron, who had advised Hunt during its composition
and who must have discussed it in Switzerland with S. (see *L* i 518). Leigh
Hunt (1784–1859), later S.'s closest friend, had not as yet had much contact
with him since their first meeting in April 1811, but S. wrote on 8 December
1816: 'I have not in all my intercourse with mankind experienced sympathy &
kindness with which I have been so affected, or which my whole being has so
sprung forward to meet & to return . . . I never knew that you had published
any other [poems] than 'Rimini', with which I was exceedingly delighted.–
The *story* of the poem has an interest of a very uncommon & irresistible
character' (*L* i 516, 518). The story is based on the episode of Paolo and
Francesca in Dante's *Inferno* (v 73–142): the proud and heartless Giovanni
(Gianciotto), son of the Lord of Rimini, allows his brother Paolo to act as his
proxy in wedding Francesca, but forces him to fight a duel when he finds that
Paolo and Francesca have become lovers. Paolo runs on to his brother's sword,
and Francesca dies at the news. There is no evidence that S.'s poem, if
completed, was ever seen by Hunt.

Order of stanzas. Lines 8–17 and 18–27 were published separately (see
below), and A. C. Bradley first proposed their connection and relevance to
The Story of Rimini (*MLR* i (October 1905) 35). Lines 8–17 are headed '3' on f.
72^r, immediately after lines 1–7 which are therefore probably the concluding
lines of stanza 2. Lines 18–27 on f. 71^r are followed by a blank half-page so may

¶ *118. Title*. Lines 18–27 entitled 'Fragment: To a Friend Leaving Prison' in
Forman 1876–7. Lines 8–17 not titled.

represent the final stanza, but they do not follow on from line 17; consequently at least one stanza is missing between the two groups. There is no certainty that the two separate leaves were consecutive in the notebook.

Text from *Box 1* ff. 72, 71.

Published in *1840* 320 (lines 8–17); *Relics* 75–6 (lines 18–end); *1975* 87–8 (whole fragment in a different order).

[Stanza 1 lacking]

. . . . .

Friend, this I hope is true, 'tis thou hast cloven
  The darkest gloom of pride, whose shadow clips
  The Universe in its eclipse,
    With a ray of thy pure feeling –
5   By the light of whose revealing
Men see fair Pleasure smile in peace beside
Majestic Duty, throned as his imperial bride.

  A gentle story of two lovers young
  Who met in innocence, and died in sorrow,
10 And of one selfish heart, whose rancour clung
  Like curses on them: are ye slow to borrow
    The lore of truth from such a tale?
    Or in this world's deserted vale
    Do ye not see a star of gladness
15   Pierce the shadows of its sadness
When ye are told that love is a light sent

1. hope is true, 'tis thou] hope is true tis thou MS (*poss.* truth tis); hope ⟨if it be⟩ thou *1975*.

2. The dark, if love offend, ⟨whose shade has woven⟩ *1975*. A very doubtful line; but the rhyme-scheme does not support Rogers.

5. of whose] of love *1975*.

6. Men see fair Pleasure] Then see, fair Pleasure, *1975*.

7. Duty] Liberty *1975*. Upon the highest step of Duty's awful throne MS *canc.*

11. borrow] Last three letters lacking in MS.

14. Do ye] Dost thou MS. The other singulars in lines 11, 16 were changed to plurals so this was presumably an oversight. *star*] promise theme MS *canc.*

16–17. S. quotes Byron, *The Giaour* (1813) 1131–46: '"Yes, Love indeed is light from heaven / . . . She was my Life's unerring Light: / That quenched– what beam shall break my night?"' Byron's poem, in some ways a harsher parallel to Hunt's, concerns a Moslem concubine, Leila, whose owner drowns her for infidelity with a Venetian Christian; her inconsolable lover then exacts vengeance for her death.

16. ye are told] thou dost hear MS *canc. told that*] cold, that *1840* (Bradley made this correction).

From Heaven, which none should quench, to cheer the
innocent?

[Stanza 4 lacking]

For me, my friend; if not, that tears did tremble
In my faint eyes, and that my heart beat fast
20   With feelings which make rapture pain resemble,
Yet from thy verse that falsehood starts aghast
        I thank thee—let the tyrants keep
        Their chains, and bars; let them weep
        With rage to see thee freshly risen
25   Like strength from slumber, from the prison
In which they vainly hoped the soul to bind
Which on chains must prey that fetter humankind.

119 'A shovel of his ashes'

These untitled lines immediately follow the fair copy of 'Hymn to Intellectual
Beauty' in *Nbk 1*, S.'s Swiss notebook, and as Rogers suggests (*1975* 357) may
originate in the ghost-story competition between Byron, S., Mary S. and
Polidori at the Villa Diodati proposed on 16 June 1816, which eventually
produced *Frankenstein*. '"We will each write a ghost-story," said Lord Byron;
and his proposition was acceded to' (Mary S., Introduction to *Frankenstein*, 3rd
edn 1831). According to Polidori the tales were begun next day, but 'The
illustrious poets . . . annoyed by the platitude of prose, speedily relinquished
their uncongenial task' (ibid.). S. had more ghostly converse with 'Monk'

17. *should*] sh^d MS; shall *1840*, eds.
19. *fast*] fast; MS (the following line originally began *Yet*).
21. *verse*] voice *Relics*.
22–7. *let the tyrants . . . humankind*] Hunt and his brother were each fined £500
and sentenced to two years' imprisonment on 4 February 1813 for libelling the
Prince Regent in *The Examiner*, and (as stated in a note to *The Story of Rimini*
Canto 3 line 4) the 2nd Canto and part of the 3rd were written in prison. Hunt
was released 2 February 1815.
23. *bars; let them*] tears, yea let him *Relics*; bars, yea, let him *1975*. *yea* is editorial;
him is left clear in MS but all other singulars (lines 22, 23, 26) are changed to
plurals.
27. *on chains*] on the chains *Relics*, eds.
¶ *119. Title*. The lines were first headed 'Fragment of a Ghost-Story' in *Forman
1876–7*.

Lewis in August (*Mary Jnl* i 126–9). 'Helen' and 'Henry' are names borrowed
from *R&H*, part of which is drafted in the same notebook.
Text from *Nbk 1* f. 61.
Published in *Relics* 74 (lines 1–2, 5–10); *1975* 87 (complete).

> A shovel of his ashes took
> From the hearth's obscurest nook;
> With a body bowed and bent
>   She tottered forth to the paved courtyard,
> 5 Muttering mysteries as she went. –
> Helen and Henry knew that Granny
> Was as much afraid of ghosts as any,
>   And so they followed hard –
> But Helen clung to her brother's arm
> 10 And her own shadow made her shake.

120 To Laughter

The second poem in S.'s notebook found in 1976 in Byron's friend Scrope
Davies's deposit-box in Barclay's Bank, Pall Mall. (see *The Times* 20 December 1976, 1–2, 5). The notebook had evidently been entrusted to Scrope
Davies, together with MSS of Byron, when he returned from Geneva on about
8 September 1816, but he had failed to execute his commissions. S., who left
Geneva on 29 August, had either mislaid the notebook or left it behind for
Byron to read because his most recent poem, 'Mont Blanc', had only just been
copied into it. The transcript of 'To Laughter' is in Mary S.'s hand. S.'s very
lively sense of fun is well attested: Medwin for instance said he had 'never met
with any one in whom the brilliance of wit and humour was more conspicuous. In this respect he fell little short of Byron' (*Athenaeum* No. 250, 11
August 1832, 523), and Edward Williams described him as 'full of life and fun'
(*Recollections* 12).

But S. regarded undiscriminating mockery as, at best, an evasion of responsibility, and at worst, an instrument of oppression and a bar to human
progress. 'He often talked of "the withering and perverting spirit of comedy"'
(*Peacock Works* viii 81), and to Hogg he once said '"You laugh at everything! I
am convinced that there can be no entire regeneration of mankind until
laughter is put down!"' (*Hogg* ii 304). The occasion of this sharply personal
sonnet is unknown; but it could possibly have originated in the misrepresenta-
tions of Mrs Godwin to her stepdaughter Fanny (Imlay), with whom the S.'s
were corresponding from Switzerland. Fanny wrote on 29 May 1816: 'Mary

10. *shadow*] spasm *Relics*. *1975* prints the start of a new line, 'Henry', but this
word ('Henery' in MS) does not seem a true continuation.

gave a great deal of pain the day I parted from you . . . I love you for *yourselves alone* . . . I understand from Mamma that I am your laughing-stock and the constant beacon of your satire' (quoted *Dowden Life* ii 24). Mary S. who detested and S. who disliked the spiteful Mrs Godwin were probably horrified by this imputation, and S. may here be dissociating himself from Mrs G. and her like. In his next letter to Godwin he added a significant reassurance: 'Remember me kindly to Fanny both for her own & for her sister's sake' (23 June 1816, *L* i 478).

Text from *SDMS* 2.

Published in the *Guardian* 21 December 1976, 11; *RES* xxix (1978) 40–1.

Thy friends were never mine thou heartless fiend:
Silence and solitude and calm and storm,
Hope, before whose veiled shrine all spirits bend
In worship, and the rainbow vested form
5   Of conscience, that within thy hollow heart
Can find no throne–the love of such great powers
Which has requited mine in many hours
Of loneliness, thou ne'er hast felt; depart!
Thou canst not bear the moon's great eye, thou fearest
10 A fair child clothed in smiles–aught that is high
Or good or beautiful. –Thy voice is dearest
To those who mock at Truth and Innocency;
I, now alone, weep without shame to see
How many broken hearts lie bare to thee.

121 'Upon the wandering winds'

The first poem in *SDMS* (see headnote to No. 120), concerned as in 'Mont Blanc' (Text B) 1–48, 139–44 with the relation of thought to the objects of thought, and rehearsing the Aeolian lyre image of 'Hymn to Intellectual Beauty' 32–6. In his letter to Peacock of 12 July 1816 S. wrote that the scenes described in Rousseau's *Julie* 'were created indeed by one mind, but a mind so powerfully bright as to cast a shade of falsehood on the records that are called reality' (*L* i 485); and later (22 July) that the scenery on the approach to Mont Blanc 'was as much our own as if we had been the creators of such impressions in the minds of others, as now occupied our own.–Nature was the poet whose

¶ *120.6. of*] 'conferred by'.

9. the moon's great eye] The moon for S. often symbolized Reason; moon and fair child seem here to stand for the beauty of Truth and of Innocence (line 12). But more personal references are conceivable. There was a full moon on 11 June 1816.

12. Innocency;] Innocency *SDMS*.

harmony held our spirits more breathless than that of the divinest' (*L* i 497). The acknowledgement of 'superior grace in others', however, argues that S. had recently read Byron's descriptions of Switzerland in *Childe Harold's Pilgrimage* III lxii–cix, a poem which he immensely admired (letter to Hogg, 18 July 1816, *L* i 493). Byron had finished Canto III during his tour of Lake Leman with S., while they were detained by rain at Ouchy on 27 June, and Claire Clairmont finished transcribing his fair copy on 4 July (*Byron PW* ii 298). S. read Byron's MS aloud to Mary S. (*Mary Jnl* i 171, under 28 May 1817), so this sonnet was probably written *c*. 1 July or soon after. The transcript is in Mary S.'s hand. Dashes have been added in lines 11 and 12.

Text from *SDMS* 1.

Published in *RES* xxix (1978) 40.

> Upon the wandering winds that through the sky
> Still speed or slumber; on the waves of Ocean,
> The forest depths that when the storm is nigh
> Toss their grey pines with an inconstant motion,
> 5   The breath of evening that awakes no sound
> But sends its spirit into all, the hush
> Which, nurse of thought, old midnight pours around
> A world whose pulse then beats not, o'er the gush
> Of dawn, and whate'er else is musical
> 10 My thoughts have swept until they have resigned
> –Like lutes enforced by the divinest thrall
> Of some sweet lady's voice–that which my mind
> (Did not superior grace in others shown
> Forbid such pride) would dream were all its own.

122 'O that a chariot of cloud were mine'

Date of composition unknown. The lines are written out almost fair in ink in S.'s Swiss notebook, on the verso of a note on Plato's *Symposium* belonging perhaps to summer 1817, and preceding the pencil draft of the Celandine poem

¶ *121.8. gush*] 'outburst' (the objects of Nature are all evoked in terms of sound and motion, in accordance with the lyre image).

10. resigned] 'released', 'given back' (Lat. *resignare*). The difficult sense seems to be: 'My thoughts have played over the objects of Nature until those objects have yielded up a poetic music which (had not greater poets produced better) I would have supposed unique'. *they* invites the same grammatical hesitation (thoughts, or objects of thoughts?) as the pronoun *its* in 'Mont Blanc' 6 (source of thought, or universe of things?).

12. some sweet lady's voice] Claire Clairmont's singing was no doubt in S.'s mind.

(May 1816) over which 'To William Shelley' is drafted in palimpsest (July 1817). They could therefore be a nostalgic fragment of 1817 (Garnett's speculative date in *Relics*) or a jotting of summer 1816; in either case their origin seems to be the Geneva experience. The lines echo Mary Wollstonecraft's 'On Poetry, and our Relish for the Beauties of Nature', *Posthumous Works* (1798) iv 165:

> When a hero [in ancient poetry] is to be transported from one place to another, across pathless wastes, is any vehicle so natural, as one of the fleecy clouds on which the poet has often gazed, scarcely conscious that he wished to make it his chariot?

Text from *Nbk 1* f. 38.
Published in *Relics* 76–7.

O that a chariot of cloud were mine,
Of cloud which the wild tempests weave in air
When the moon over the Ocean's line
Is spreading the locks of her bright grey hair;
5   O that a chariot of cloud were mine–
I would sail on the waves of the billowy wind,
And the mountain peak, and the rocky lake
And the [

123 Hymn to Intellectual Beauty

'"The Hymn to Intellectual Beauty" was conceived during his voyage round the lake [Léman] with Lord Byron' (Mary S.'s 'Note on the Poems of 1816', *1839* iii 35). As Gavin de Beer has now established (*SC* iv 690–701), that expedition took place 22–30 June 1816, so the MS date on *Harvard* (see below), 'Switzerland June–1816', may only be that of the original conception. When S. left Geneva on 29 August a notebook containing this poem in Mary S.'s hand and 'Mont Blanc' in S.'s hand remained with Byron, who entrusted its return to his friend Scrope Davies; the latter, however, never delivered it, and the existence of the notebook (*SDMS*) was revealed only in December 1976 after its discovery in a deposit-box at the Pall Mall branch of Barclay's Bank in London. The poem must therefore have been written between 22 June and 29 August, very possibly on 27–9 June when the lake party was weatherbound at Ouchy, near Lausanne, and Byron used the time to compose *The Prisoner of*

¶ *122.2. the wild tempests weave*] the wild tempest weaves *Relics, eds*; the tempest weaves *1975*.
4. Is spreading] Words run together and imperfect in MS.
7. And the mountain] To the mountain *Relics, eds*.

Chillon (Byron L&J v 82). The absence of a first draft could imply indoor composition, while Mary S. seems uncertain when the actual writing took place. Even so, the poem may not have been completed before August (the last stanza anticipates the end of summer), and could in theory postdate the completion of 'Mont Blanc'. Under the pseudonym 'The Elfin Knight' S. submitted the poem to *The Examiner*, where Hunt acknowledged its receipt on 6 October, but confessed in the issue of 1 December that the MS had been mislaid. S. may already have replaced the loss when he wrote to Hunt on 8 December: 'Next, will I own the Hymn to Intellectual Beauty? I do not care. As you like. And yet the poem was composed under the influence of feelings which agitated me even to tears, so that I think it deserves a better fate than the being linked with so stigmatised & unpopular a name (so far as it is known) as mine' (*L* i 517). Hunt finally published it on 19 January over S.'s own name. The probable sequence is, then, that S.'s fair copy which Mary S. used for her transcription in *SDMS* was the text sent to Hunt and lost, and as *SDMS* itself also seemed to be lost the text Hunt eventually printed derives from a return, in England, to the hasty but clean copy of the poem (missing stanza 4) in S.'s draft notebook, Bod. MS Shelley adds.e.16, ff. 57–61 (*Nbk 1*). The relationship of these versions is discussed in *RES* xxix (1978) 36–49 by Chernaik and Burnett, who reach the same conclusions. The *Examiner* text is certainly closer than *SDMS* to the text in *Nbk 1*. Thus there are two distinct texts of the Hymn, both reproduced below: 'A', the first-completed version from *SDMS*, and 'B', the reworked version printed in *The Examiner*. S. was in Italy when the poem was reprinted in *1819*, and either his publisher Ollier or Peacock was responsible for the changed pointing and other revisions, which have no authority. Mary S.'s pointing in *SDMS* has been respected in Text A except where its absence causes obscurity: commas are added in lines 19, 20, 26, 43, 59, 70, 83, and full stops in lines 36, 48; a colon is added in line 53. Notes that are relevant to both texts will be found under Text B.

The 'Hymn' of the poem's title has the pagan meaning 'song in honour of a god', and its lineage is that of the 18th century odes to abstract qualities, including the 'Hymns' of Revolutionary France. 'Intellectual Beauty', though Platonic in concept, is an expression not used by Plato but widely current in contemporary writing, especially that of Radical intellectuals associated with Godwin, where it means non-sensuous beauty, 'the beauty of the mind and its creations' (*Cameron (1974)* 238). S. probably met it first in Mrs Opie's novel *Adeline Mowbray* (1804; 1805 edn, i 121), which he read in July 1811 (*L* i 122); thereafter in Mary Wollstonecraft's *A Vindication of the Rights of Woman* (1792) ch. iii; in Godwin's *Memoirs of the Author of a Vindication* (1798) ch. xvi (in the 2nd edn he changed 'an intuitive perception of intellectual beauty' to 'an intuitive sense of the pleasures of the imagination'); in Lord Monboddo's *Of the Origin and Progress of Language* i (Edinburgh 1773) 98 (ordered 24 December 1812); in Robert Forsyth's *Principles of Moral Science* (Edinburgh 1805) ch. 16 and i 513–14; and in C. M. Wieland's novel *Agathon* (1766), read early in 1814 in a French translation by F. D. Pernay (*Hogg* ii 531–2) and again the same year with Mary Godwin, perhaps in English. One of the three occurrences of the

phrase in Wieland reveals its usual meaning very clearly in referring to 'a living
instance of this Platonic maxim, that external beauty is the reflection of the
intellectual beauty of the soul' (*History of Agathon*, transl. J. Richardson (1773)
iv 48–9). S.'s title, however, seems closer in meaning to the 'universal beauty'
which he intended by the phrase two years later when translating a passage of
Plato's *Symposium*; here he expanded the original in order to clarify still further
Diotima's distinction between particular beauties and the Beauty that sub-
sumes all beautiful instances:

> contemplating thus the universal beauty, no longer like some servant in love
> with his fellow would he [the lover] unworthily and meanly enslave himself
> to the attractions of one form, nor one subject of discipline or science, but
> would turn towards the wide ocean of intellectual beauty . . .
>
> (*Notopoulos* 449)

Plato has simply 'the wide ocean of beauty' (*Symp*. 210d). S.'s Intellectual
Beauty in the 'Hymn' is not exclusively mental; it is contained or reflected in
forms as well as in thoughts (lines 7, 15, 82), is apprehended during nights
dedicated to 'love's delight' as well as during nights of 'studious zeal' (66), is a
potential agent of social revolution (68–70), and is evoked throughout the
poem in images of conspicuously sensuous appeal. These images of mist,
wind, music, moonlight–all fleeting, insubstantial things–illustrate 'very precisely . . . the hiatus between the lovely, transient effect, as it can be perceived
by the senses, and its stable cause in nature', so providing analogies for the
unseen Power whose reality can be inferred only from its influences (*Chernaik*
38); but the beauty of the analogies offered must itself be interpreted as
evidence in Nature of the Power's visitation. Allusions to this Power, one of
S.'s most persistent intuitions, occur in all later periods of his writing, notably
in *Alastor* (37–49), in the unadopted early stanzas of *L&C* and in 'The Zucca'
(20–40); and Jesus Christ's supposed concept of God, in the prose 'Essay on
Christianity' (1817), is close to S.'s own concept of Intellectual Beauty:

> There is a Power by which we are surrounded, like the atmosphere in which
> some motionless lyre is suspended, which visits with its breath our silent
> chords at will. Our most imperial and stupendous qualities–those on which
> the majesty and the power of humanity is erected–are, relatively to the
> inferior portion of its mechanism, indeed active and imperial; but they are
> the passive slaves of some higher and more omnipotent Power. This Power
> is God . . . But there will come a time when the human mind shall be visited
> exclusively by the influences of the benignant power . . . This is Heaven,
> when pain and evil cease, and when the benignant principle untrammelled
> and uncontrolled visits in the fulness of its power the universal frame of
> things. (*Prose* 202, 205)

Of Diotima's other main precepts in the *Symposium* one, that the lover should
'consider the beauty which is in souls more excellent than that which is in form'
(*Notopoulos* 448; *Symp*. 210b), is disregarded in the 'Hymn', while the other,
that the lover should 'ascend through these transitory objects which are

beautiful, towards that which is beauty itself, proceeding as on steps' (*Noto-poulos* 449; *Symp.* 211c), never appealed to S. Indeed the poem's immediate stimulus was probably not Plato but Rousseau, whose novel *Julie, ou La Nouvelle Héloïse* (1761), set in the locality of Lake Léman, S. was reading obsessively throughout his tour with Byron. The experiences of *Julie's* hero lead him towards the acceptance of a kind of universal love transcending the conventional proprietary sexual love that at first consumes him. For S. the book and the scenery idealized by the book themselves constituted shadows of Intellectual Beauty: he said he found Rousseau's imagination 'so powerfully bright as to cast a shade of falsehood on the records that are called reality', and that Rousseau's 'imperishable creations had left no vacancy in my heart for mortal things' (*L* i 485, 488). The organization of the 'Hymn' was clearly influenced by that of Wordsworth's 'Ode: Intimations of Immortality', but there are wide differences in content: Wordsworth seeks adult consolation for the loss of the child's instinctive harmony with God's creation; while S. reaffirms his early vision that the humanist virtues of 'Love, Hope, and Self-esteem' will eventually redeem a godless and disharmonious world. Extended discussions of the 'Hymn' include those of Notopoulos, who ex-plored its relation to Platonism and Neo-Platonism (*Notopoulos* 196–206); *Chernaik* 32–40; and *Wasserman* 190–7, who postulates that S.'s Intellectual Beauty 'is the governing deity of the '"intellectual philosophy" which iden-tifies existence with mind and rejects all distinction between world and thought' (191).

Text A. From *SDMS* 3–6 (Mary S.'s hand).

Text B. From Harvard MS Eng. 258.3, ff. 22–3, a clipping from *The Examiner* No. 473 corrected in S.'s hand. *Examiner* printing identified as *Ex*, with S.'s corrections as *Harvard Ex*.

Published: A. By Judith Chernaik and Timothy Burnett, *RES* xxix (1978) 43–5.

B. *The Examiner* No. 473 (19 January 1817) 41; *1819*.

A.   [Hymn to Intellectual Beauty]
                              I.
      The lovely shadow of some awful Power
          Walks though unseen amongst us, visiting
          This peopled world with as inconstant wing
      As summer winds that creep from flower to flower,
  5   Like moonbeams that behind some piny mountain
                                          shower
          It visits with a wavering glance
          Each human heart and countenance;–
      Like hues and harmonies of evening–
          Like clouds in starlight widely spread
 10   Like memory of music fled
      Like aught that for its grace might be
      Dear, and yet dearer for its mystery.

2.

Shadow of Beauty!—that doth consecrate
 With thine own hues all thou dost fall upon
15 Of human thought or form, where art thou gone?
Why dost thou pass away and leave our state
A dark deep vale of tears, vacant and desolate?
 Ask why the sunlight not forever
 Weaves rainbows o'er yon mountain river,
20 Ask why aught fades away that once is shown,
  Ask wherefore dream and death and birth
  Cast on the daylight of this earth
Such gloom,—why man has such a scope
For love and joy, despondency and hope.

3.

25 No voice from some sublimer world hath ever
  To wisest poets these responses given,
  Therefore the name of God and Ghosts and Heaven
Remain yet records of their vain Endeavour—
Frail spells, whose uttered charm might not avail to sever
30 From what we feel and what we see
  Doubt, Chance and mutability.
 Thy shade alone like mists o'er mountains driven
  Or music by the night-wind sent
  Through strings of some mute instrument
35 Or moonlight on a forest stream
Gives truth and grace to life's tumultuous dream.

4.

Love, hope and self-esteem like clouds depart—
 And come, for some uncertain moments lent.—
 Man were immortal and omnipotent
40 Didst thou, unknown and awful as thou art
Keep with this glorious train firm state within his heart.
  Thou messenger of sympathies
  That wax and wane in lovers' eyes,

¶ *123* (Text A). *13. Shadow*] Image, (imperfect) copy. Cp. 'Shadow of beauty unbeheld' (*PU* III iii 7).
21. Why, care & pain & death & birth *Nbk 1.*
24. love and joy] love [joy *canc.*] & hate *Nbk 1.* Clearly a mistranscription; as Chernaik & Burnett point out (*RES* xxix (1978) 42) 'The line calls . . . for two opposed terms'.
43. lovers'] lover's *SDMS.*

Thou that to the poet's thought art nourishment
45   As darkness to a dying flame,
        Depart not as thy shadow came!
Depart not!—lest the grave should be
Like life and fear a dark reality.

5.

While yet a boy I sought for ghosts, and sped
50   Through many a lonely chamber, vault and ruin
        And starlight wood, with fearful step pursuing
Hopes of strange converse with the storied dead.
I called on that false name with which our youth is fed:
        He heard me not—I saw them not.—
55   When musing deeply on the lot
Of Life, at that sweet time when winds are wooing
        All vocal things that live to bring
        News of buds and blossoming—
Sudden thy shadow fell on me,
60   I shrieked and clasped my hands in ecstasy.

6.

I vowed that I would dedicate my powers
        To thee and thine—have I not kept the vow?
        With streaming eyes and panting heart even now
I call the spectres of a thousand hours
65   Each from his voiceless grave, who have in visioned
                                                    bowers
        Of studious zeal or love's delight
        Outwatched with me the waning night
To tell that never joy illumed my brow
        Unlinked with hope that thou wouldst free
70   This world from its dark slavery,
That thou, O, awful Loveliness!
Would give whate'er these words cannot express.

7.

The day becomes more solemn and serene
        When noon is past—there is a harmony
75   In Autumn and a lustre in the sky
Which through the summer is not heard or seen
As if it could not be—as if it had not been—

---

44. *poet's*] poets *SDMS.*
52. *the storied dead*] Those whose records are inscribed on their tombs, as on
Gray's 'storied urn' (*Elegy in a Country Church-yard* 41).
53. *that false name*] 'God'.

Thus let thy shade–which like the truth
Of Nature on my passive youth
80   Descended, to my onward life supply
Its hues, to one that worships thee
And every form containing thee
Whom, fleeting power! thy spells did bind
To fear himself and love all human Kind.

B.   Hymn to Intellectual Beauty
                          1.
The awful shadow of some unseen Power
   Floats though unseen amongst us, – visiting
   This various world with as inconstant wing
As summer winds that creep from flower to flower. –
5   Like moonbeams that behind some piny mountain
                                              shower,
         It visits with inconstant glance
         Each human heart and countenance;
Like hues and harmonies of evening, –
         Like clouds in starlight widely spread, –
10   Like memory of music fled, –
         Like aught that for its grace may be
Dear, and yet dearer for its mystery.

                          2.
Spirit of BEAUTY, that doth consecrate
   With thine own hues all thou dost shine upon
15   Of human thought or form, – where art thou gone?
Why dost thou pass away and leave our state,
This dim vast vale of tears, vacant and desolate?
         Ask why the sunlight not forever
         Weaves rainbows o'er yon mountain river,
20   Why aught should fail and fade that once is shown,

¶ 123 (Text B). 1. shadow] image, replica.
6. inconstant glance] See note to lines 18–19, 'inconstant sun'.
7. heart] mind Nbk 1.
9. widely] wildly Nbk 1.
13. doth] dost 1819.
18–19. Perhaps a memory of the waterfall seen at Chède on 21 July 1816: 'in the midst of which hung a multitude of sunbows, which faded or became unspeakably vivid, as the inconstant sun shone through the clouds' (1817 148). Cp. 'Mont Blanc' 25–6.
20. shown] displayed in flower (OED 8a).

Why fear and dream and death and birth
Cast on the daylight of this earth
Such gloom, – why man has such a scope
For love and hate, despondency and hope?

3.

25 No voice from some sublimer world hath ever
    To sage or poet these responses given –
    Therefore the name of God, and ghosts, and Heaven,
    Remain the records of their vain endeavour,
    Frail spells – whose uttered charm might not avail to
                                                sever,
30   From all we hear and all we see,
        Doubt, chance, and mutability.
    Thy light alone – like mist o'er mountains driven,
        Or music by the night wind sent
        Through strings of some still instrument,
35   Or moonlight on a midnight stream,
    Gives grace and truth to life's unquiet dream.

4.

Love, Hope, and Self-esteem, like clouds depart
    And come, for some uncertain moments lent.
    Man were immortal, and omnipotent,
40 Didst thou, unknown and awful as thou art,
    Keep with thy glorious train firm state within his heart.
        Thou messenger of sympathies
        That wax and wane in lovers' eyes –
    Thou – that to human thought art nourishment,
45   Like darkness to a dying flame!

21. *death and birth*] i.e. the condition of mortality. The opposition of 'fear and
dream' corresponds to that of 'despondency and hope' (line 24).
27. *name of God, and ghosts, and Heaven*] names of Demon, Ghost, and Heaven
Ex; names of Ghosts & God & Heaven *Nbk 1*. Corrected by S. in *Harvard Ex*;
the *Ex* text was probably a modification made at Hunt's request (see *Chernaik*
186n.).
33. *sent*] sent, *Ex*.
34. *some still instrument*] An Aeolian harp. *still*] unconscious *Nbk 1*.
35. This image may have had some private association with Mary Godwin; cp.
S.'s letter to Mary of 28 October 1814 (*L* i 414): 'My mind without yours is
dead & cold as the dark midnight river when the moon is down'.
Stanza 4. Omitted in *Nbk 1*.
42. *sympathies*] *SDMS, 1819*; sympathies, *Ex*.
43. *lovers'*] lover's *Ex, 1819*.
44–5. *nourishment, / Like darkness to a dying flame!*] Strong light was believed to

> Depart not as thy shadow came,
> Depart not—lest the grave should be,
> Like life and fear, a dark reality.

5.

> While yet a boy I sought for ghosts, and sped
> 50   Through many a listening chamber, cave and ruin,
>   And starlight wood, with fearful steps pursuing
> Hopes of high talk with the departed dead.
> I called on poisonous names with which our youth is fed,
>   I was not heard—I saw them not—
> 55   When musing deeply on the lot
> Of life, at that sweet time when winds are wooing
>   All vital things that wake to bring
>   News of buds and blossoming,—
>   Sudden, thy shadow fell on me;
> 60   I shrieked, and clasped my hands in ecstasy!

---

stifle a flame, which was therefore literally 'nourished' by darkness (Walker, *A System of Familiar Philosophy* (1799) 412).

Stanzas 5 and 6. Transposed in *Nbk 1*.

49–52. Hogg describes S.'s early experiments in the supernatural: 'Sometimes he watched the livelong nights for ghosts . . . he even planned how he might get admission to the vault, or charnel-house, at Warnham Church, and might sit there all night . . . to see one of the spiritualised owners of the bones piled around him', and at Eton he tried to raise a midnight ghost by means of incantation over a skull (*Hogg* i 33–4). Cp. *Alastor* 23–9; and Wordsworth, *Excursion* iii 686–95.

51. starlight] The normal contemporary form of 'starlit'.

52. 'There studious let me sit, / And hold high converse with the mighty dead' (Thomson, *Seasons*, 'Winter' 431–2).

53. poisonous names] the false name *Nbk 1*. Another possible modification by Hunt.

54. I was not heard—] One of S.'s early correspondents had 'recommended him to try the effect of prayer, and he actually prayed for two months, till finding that tho he observd the prescription as regularly as if it had been to take three table spoonfuls of julep, no effect followed, he gave up the course' (Southey to Danvers, 13 January 1812, *News Letters of Robert Southey*, ed. K. Curry (1965) ii 20).

57–8. Echoing Wordsworth's 'To the Same Flower [Small Celandine]' 17–18: 'Soon as gentle breezes bring / News of winter's vanishing'.

58. buds] birds *Ex* (corrected by S. in *Harvard Ex*), *1819*.

59–72. Webb (*Shelley: A Voice Not Understood* (1977) 34–5) stresses the distinction between autobiographical particularity and the conventional language of religious dedication. But that S. did experience a crisis of self-commitment

6.

I vowed that I would dedicate my powers
     To thee and thine–have I not kept the vow?
     With beating heart and streaming eyes, even now
     I call the phantoms of a thousand hours
65   Each from his voiceless grave: they have in visioned
                                                    bowers
          Of studious zeal or love's delight
          Outwatched with me the envious night–
     They know that never joy illumed my brow
          Unlinked with hope that thou wouldst free
70   This world from its dark slavery,
          That thou–O awful LOVELINESS,
     Wouldst give whate'er these words cannot express.

7.

The day becomes more solemn and serene
     When noon is past–there is a harmony
75   In autumn, and a lustre in its sky,
     Which through the summer is not heard or seen,
     As if it could not be, as if it had not been!
          Thus let thy power, which like the truth
          Of nature on my passive youth
80   Descended, to my onward life supply
          Its calm–to one who worships thee,
          And every form containing thee,
          Whom, SPIRIT fair, thy spells did bind
     To fear himself, and love all human kind.

---

seems evident from many allusions, such as the Dedication to *L&C* 21–42 and
the letter to Hunt of 8 December 1816 which refers both to this Hymn and to
'the task which I had undertaken in early life, of opposing myself, in these evil
times & among these evil tongues, to what I esteem misery & vice' (*L* i 517).
Medwin (for interested reasons) located this event as Syon House Academy
(*Athenaeum* 21 July 1832, 472), which S. left aged eleven; but Eton is more
probable, as Henry Salt argued (*Percy Bysshe Shelley: A Monograph* (1888)
237–40).
66. *love's*] loves *Ex, 1819, Nbk 1.*
73–81. These lines are influenced by Wordsworth's 'Tintern Abbey' 88–102,
and 'Ode: Intimations of Immortality' 176–99, but S. does not distinguish his
recognition of 'the truth of nature' from his maturing receptivity to Intellectual
Beauty as W. separated his early physical response to Nature from his later
compensating awareness of 'a presence' pervading Nature.
83. *SPIRIT fair*] awful Power *Nbk 1.*
84. *Concordance* glosses 'fear' as 'doubt, mistrust'; but it is the only example of

124 Mont Blanc.
Lines Written in the Vale of Chamouni

Mary S. states ('Note on Poems of 1816', *1839* iii 35) that '*Mont Blanc* was inspired by a view of that mountain and its surrounding peaks and valleys, as [S.] lingered on the Bridge of Arve on his way through the Valley of Chamouni'. The poem was almost certainly begun on 22 July 1816, although it is dated 'June 23, 1816' in *1817, 1824*, and *1839*. S., Mary and Claire made their visit to Chamonix, Mont Blanc and environs from Sunday 21 July to Saturday 27 July 1816 (*Mary Jnl* i 112–21; *L* i 494–502). S.'s journal-letter to Peacock of 22 July–2 August 1816 includes for 22 July the following description which (as John Buxton, *Byron and Shelley* (1968) 33, notes) anticipates the poem in a number of ideas and phrases:

> From Servox, three leagues remain to Chamounix. Mont Blanc was before us. The Alps with their innumerable glacie[r]s on high, all round; closing in the complicated windings of the single vale:–forests inexpressibly beautiful–but majestic in their beauty–interwoven beech & pine & oak overshadowed our road or receded whilst lawn of such verdure as I had never seen before, occupied these opening[s], & extending gradually becoming darker into their recesses.–Mont Blanc was before us but was covered with cloud, & its base furrowed with dreadful gaps was seen alone. Pinnacles of snow, intolerably bright, part of the chain connected with Mont Blanc shone thro the clouds at intervals on high. I never knew I never imagined what mountains were before. The immensity of these aerial summits excited, when they suddenly burst upon the sight, a sentiment of extatic wonder, not unallied to madness–And remember this was all one scene. It all pressed home to our regard & to our imagination.–Though it embraced a great number of miles the snowy pyramids which shot into the bright blue sky seemed to overhang our path–the ravine, clothed with gigantic pines and black with its depth below.–so deep that the very roaring of the untameable Arve which rolled through it could not be heard above– was close to our very footsteps. All was as much our own as if we had been the creators of such impressions in the minds of others, as now occupied our own.–Nature was the poet whose harmony held our spirits more breathless than that of the divinest. (*L* i 496–7)

---

this meaning listed, and Elizabeth Nitchie (*PMLA* lxiii (1948) 753) suggests as more likely the meaning 'honour, revere' (*OED* ii 3). *Wasserman* 195n. cites Pythagoras: 'of thy self stand most in fear'. The poem's conclusion would then be a defiant revision of *Ecclesiastes* xii 13: 'Fear God, and keep his commandments: for this is the whole duty of man'.

S.'s draft, in Bod. MS. Shelley adds. e. 16 (*Nbk 1*) ff. 3–13, is headed (after some cancellation; see notes) 'The scene of Pellisier, at the extremity of the vale of Servoz'. It begins as much-cancelled pencil over-written in ink, and suggests that S. may actually have begun 'Mont Blanc' *in situ* at Pont Pellisier on the second day of his journey (the original pencil draft peters out at line 48). S.'s letter to Byron from his hotel in Chamonix, dated 22 July, indicates that he was already himself thinking of a poetic response: 'I shall not attempt to describe to you the scenes through which we have passed. I hope soon to see in poetry the feelings with which they will inspire you' (*L* i 494). Mary's journal records the arrival of the party at Pont Pellisier en route from St Martin to Chamonix on 22 July:

> From Cervaux [*for* Servoz] we continued on a mountainous & rocky path & passed apine [*Mary Jnl (Jones)* 52 reads 'an Alpine'] bridge over the Arve– this is one of the loveliest scenes in the world–the white & foamy river broke proudly through the rocks that opposed its progress–Immense pines covered the bases of the Mountains that closed around it & a rock covered with woods & seemingly detached from the rest stood at the End & closed the ravine– (i 114–15)

S. names this bridge in his account of the return journey to Geneva on Friday 25 July: 'We repassed *Pont Pellisier* a wooden bridge over the Arve & the ravine of the Arve.' (*L* i 501). Pont Pellisier is not actually in the Vale of Chamonix, which extends some twelve miles south-east to north-west from Col-de-Balme to les Houches, but about two miles north-north-west of les Houches, towards Servoz; it seems likely that S.'s topographically exact title in *Nbk 1* was replaced in *1817* by the subtitle 'Lines Written in the Vale of Chamouni' in order to point up the poem's implicit address to Coleridge's 'Hymn: Before Sun-rise, in the Vale of Chamouny' (see below). S. probably worked on 'Mont Blanc' during the wet afternoon and evening of Wednesday 24 July, having spent Tuesday in sight-seeing (*Mary Jnl* i 118), but the poem includes descriptive writing evidently indebted to S.'s experiences of glaciers, including the Mer de Glace, which were not visited until Thursday 25 July (see *Mary Jnl* i 119), and there is evidence to suggest that S. was still working on the poem after his return to Geneva on Sunday 28 July. *Box 1* f. 72 is a leaf torn from *Nbk 1* with part of 'Lines to Leigh Hunt' on the recto (see No. 118 headnote), and on the verso three separate items. At the top there are almost indecipherable lines probably addressed to Mary by S. for the second anniversary of their elopement on 28 July 1814 (these lines are quoted in No. 118 headnote). At the bottom is a description of a thunderstorm dated 'July 28' (really 29 July; see *Mary Jnl* i 121). Between these items, and presumably datable to the same weekend, is a draft of five unused lines for 'Mont Blanc' which reads:

> There is a voice not understood by all
> Sent from these [icy *canc.*] desart caves [this solitude *canc.*]
> [Of ? pines that to the lightest call *canc.*]
> [Of ? ? ? *canc.*] It is the roar

Of the rent ice cliff which the sunbeams call
Plunges into the vale–it is the [blast *canc.* wind *canc.*]
Descending on the pines–[the torrents pour *canc.* it is a rock *canc.*]

By 29 August S. had transcribed a fair copy of 'Mont Blanc' into the notebook
which, for whatever reason, he left with Byron in Geneva when he returned to
England (*SDMS*; see No. 123 headnote); this version of the poem remained
unknown until the discovery of the notebook in 1976. It was first published
together with Nos. 120, 121, and 123A in *RES* xxix (1978) 36–49.

The first published version of 'Mont Blanc' appeared in *1817*. The poem was
transcribed again (S.'s original transcript having apparently been lost) from the
draft in *Nbk 1*, presumably by S. himself at around the same time that Mary
was preparing letters and journal entries for incorporation into *1817* in early
October 1817. It is however conceivable that Mary was responsible for
copying the poem from draft for *1817*; this would account for the striking
number of different readings between *1817* and *Nbk 1*, some of which could be
transcription errors (see notes), and others the result of editorial substitution
and inversion of the kind which characterize Mary's work on other drafts of
comparable difficulty such as 'To Constantia' and 'The Two Spirits'. Mary
seems to have borne sole responsibility for the printing of *1817* (with the
exception of the Preface, attributed in Mary's 'Note on Poems of 1816' to S.).
Mary remained in Marlow while S. was away in London for most of the time
in October 1817; her letters to S. on 28 September, 14 and 16 October mention
transcribing the Geneva letters printed in the volume and sending the completed MS in a parcel to Hookham, the printer, on 15 October (*Mary L* i 47, 54,
56). On Sunday 12 October she noted in her journal:

S. comes down on friday evening–Read & finish miseries of human life [i.e.
James Beresford, *The Miseries of Human Life*: . . . (1806)]–write out letters
from Geneva–S. transcribes his poem on Saturday walk out with him &
Willy. P.[eacock] drinks tea here. S. goes away sunday evening–transcribe.

(*Mary Jnl* i 181)

'S. transcribes his poem' would at this point in the journal most probably refer
to *L&C*, which although finished on 23 September was still being transcribed
for the printer in October (see headnote to *L&C*). Nevertheless, in the absence
of more conclusive evidence the likeliest assumption is that S. did himself
produce a second version of 'Mont Blanc' in the autumn of 1817, sometimes
forgetting choices and substitutions he had made when copying from the draft
in the previous summer, and perhaps at times unable to read his own tangled
draft. Two distinct forms of the poem therefore exist, and are both presented
here; the B text (*1817*) is collated with *Nbk 1* as this makes clear the extent to
which it diverges from the draft relative to the A text (*SDMS*), which is much
closer to *Nbk 1*. Chernaik 288–93 offers a transcription of the draft.

Two primary thematic preoccupations are combined in 'Mont Blanc', with
what many critics have considered uneven success, although more recent
commentaries have argued for the poem's intellectual coherence. S.'s defiantly

atheistical response to the supreme experience of Alpine scenery (see B text 97n.) merges with his epistemological uncertainties concerning the characteristics and mode of existence of a causal power which, not itself knowable, yet determines matter and intelligence. The atheism of 'Mont Blanc' appears to some extent aimed in a specific way at Coleridge, and in particular at his 'Hymn: Before Sun-rise, in the Vale of Chamouny' (1802), which S. probably read in *The Friend* No. 11, 26 October 1809 (the 'Hymn' is in fact closely based on Friederika Brun's 'Chamouny beym Sonneraufgange: Gedichte' (1805); see A. P. Rossiter in the *TLS*, 28 September 1951, 613). For S. and Byron's knowledge of and interest in Coleridge and *The Friend* in 1816, see *Robinson* 32–9, and also Charles E. Robinson, 'The Shelley Circle and Coleridge's *The Friend*', *ELN* viii (1971) 269–74. The tone of Coleridge's poem is well given in the note which accompanied its first publication in the *Morning Post*, 11 September 1802:

> ... the whole vale, its every light, its every sound, must needs impress every mind not utterly callous with the thought–Who *would* be, who *could* be an Atheist in this valley of Wonders!

The poem itself emphatically and–from S.'s point of view–provokingly celebrates the maker of all the components of the scene presented by the valley of the Arve:

> GOD! let the Torrents, like a shout of Nations,
> Answer! And let the Ice plains echo, GOD!
> God! sing, ye meadow streams! with gladsome voice!
> Ye Pine-groves, with your soft and soul-like Sounds!
> And they too have a Voice, yon Piles of Snow,
> And in their perilous Fall shall thunder GOD!
>
> (lines 55–60, *Friend* text)

Coleridge appears to have been on S.'s mind throughout the Swiss journey, perhaps because of Byron's influence; on 17 July S. wrote to Peacock 'Tell me of the political state of England–its literature, of which when I speak Coleridge is in my thoughts' (*L* i 490). 'Mont Blanc' echoes a number of Coleridge's poems in addition to the 'Hymn', including 'Kubla Khan' and 'The Eolian Harp' (see notes). The atheism of 'Mont Blanc' has a further related context–although no mention of it is made by S. or Mary in their journal and letters at the time–in the notorious entries by S. in various visitors' books during his visit to the Vale of Chamonix, mocking the conventional pieties of English tourists' responses to Alpine scenery. At the Hôtel des Londres, for example, S. wrote of himself 'δεμοκρατικὸς φιλανθρωπότατος καὶ αθεος' ('democrat, lover of mankind, and atheist'), and of his destination as 'L'enfer'. Byron rightly guessed that these entries would lead to trouble, as they did when news of them was carried back to England (notably by Southey) and fed the public image of S.'s notoriety in a damaging way (for details of the episode see two articles by Gavin de Beer, 'The Atheist, an incident at Chamonix', in *On Shelley*, ed. Edmund Blunden (1938), and 'An Atheist in the Alps', *KSMB* ix

(1958)). Some thirty months later the memory of these events was revived for
S. when, having read the attack on his atheism and private life in the *Quarterly*'s
review of Leigh Hunt's *Foliage* in May 1818 (see *Unextinguished Hearth* 125), he
composed a passage for *PU* II iii which merges his alpine experiences, and their
representation in 'Mont Blanc', with the impact of the volcanic scenery of
Vesuvius and of the Solfatara region west of Naples (see *PU* headnote and II iii
11–42*nn.*) The descriptive writing and mountain scenery of 'Mont Blanc' also
show the influence of *Childe Harold's Pilgrimage* III, which Byron was working
on during S.'s stay in Geneva (see *Robinson* 31–9) and of other Byron poems
written at Diodati in July 1816, for example 'The Dream' and 'A Fragment'.
There are, too, marked affinities between 'Mont Blanc' and the accounts of
mountain scenery in *Frankenstein* ch. ix, which Mary was writing on the visit
to Chamonix (*Mary Jnl* i 118). The poem also implies S.'s knowledge of
geology and vulcanology in the terms of the speculations prompted by the
mountain and its scenery. S.'s letter to Peacock of 22 July displays this
knowledge in a characteristic conjunction with political and social reflections
that is present in the poem itself:

> Within this last year these glaciers have advanced three hundred feet into the
> valley. Saussure the naturalist says that they have their periods of increase &
> decay—the people of the country hold an opinion entirely different, but, as I
> judge, more probable. It is agreed by all that the snows on the summit of M^t·
> Blanc & the neighboring mountains perpetually augment, & that ice in the
> form of glacier subsists without melting in the valley of Chamounix during
> its transient and variable summer. If the snow which produces the glaciers
> must augment & the heat of the valley is no obstacle to the perpetual
> subsistence of such masses of ice as have already descended into it, the
> consequence is obvious.—The glaciers must augment, & will subsist at least
> until they have overflowed this vale.—I will not pursue Buffons sublime but
> gloomy theory, that this earth which we inhabit will at some future period
> be changed into a mass of frost. Do you who assert the supremacy of
> Ahriman imagine him throned among these desolating snows, among these
> palaces of death & frost, sculptured in this their terrible magnificence by the
> unsparing hand of necessity, & that he casts around him as the first essays of
> his final usurpation avalanches, torrents, rocks & thunders—and above all,
> these deadly glaciers at once the proofs & the symbols of his reign.—Add to
> this the degradation of the human species, who in these regions are half
> deformed or idiotic & all of whom are deprived of anything that can excite
> interest & admiration. This is a part of the subject more mournful & less
> sublime;—but such as neither the poet nor the philosopher should disdain.
>
> (*L* i 499)

As Buxton (*Byron and Shelley* 33) remarks, S. 'was aware of Buffon's theory
that the world would end in a new and universal ice age'. He was also aware of
the Comte de Buffon's proposition in his 'Des Epoques de la Nature!', *Supplé-
ments de l'Histoire Naturelle* (vol. v, Paris 1778) that the earth had at first been at
fluid heat and had cooled slowly and evolved over a great period of time in

seven phases or 'Epoques' corresponding to scriptural days (see below, lines 73–4).

The argument and style of 'Mont Blanc' are difficult, and are made more so by the consequences of its complex textual transmission. S. seeks to engage important questions of the relation between mind and the objects of thought, and between the apparent permanence of nature and an impersonal Power, embodied in the mountain, which compels change over periods of time too great for the imagination to comprehend. S.'s efforts in 'Mont Blanc' to represent this Power anticipate in some respects his conception of Demogorgon in *PU* (see *PU* headnote). The poem represents an important transitional point in S.'s intellectual development, from an early confidence in radical materialism towards the distinctive sceptical idealism of his maturity. *Chernaik* (49) remarks illuminatingly of the poem's form in relation to its argument that in 'Mont Blanc' S. 'seems to make the physical scene contingent upon the generalization it has prompted but which precedes it in the poem'. In its representation of nature as metaphorical of consciousness S.'s poem is comparable with other Romantic poems which dramatize the mind's consciousness of itself such as Wordsworth's 'Lines written a few miles above Tintern Abbey' (1798) and Keats's 'Ode to Psyche' (1819). The style of 'Mont Blanc', broadly Wordsworthian but bleaker and more disturbed, registers a certain intellectual irresolution as well as excitement. S. appears conscious of this in his note on the poem in the Preface to *1817*:

> The poem entitled 'Mont Blanc' . . . was composed under the immediate impressions of the deep and powerful feelings excited by the objects which it attempts to describe; and as an undisciplined overflowing of the soul, rests its claim to approbation on an attempt to imitate the untameable wildness and inaccessible solemnity from which those feelings sprang. (*1817* vi)

For a valuable account of the 'wildly irregular rhyming of ['Mont Blanc'] whereby nearly every line eventually finds its companion, but without any predictable order' (*Wasserman* 234), see William Keach, *Shelley's Style* (1984) 194–200, who follows earlier commentators in noting *Lycidas* as a model for the rhyme scheme. In addition to the discussions by Wasserman, Chernaik, and Keach, cited above, good critical and contextual accounts of the poems include I. J. Kapstein, 'The Meaning of Shelley's *Mont Blanc*', *PMLA* lxii (1947) 1046–60; *Butter (1954)* 118–28; Charles H. Vivian, 'The One "Mont Blanc"', *KSJ* iv (1955) 55–65; Harold Bloom, *Shelley's Mythmaking* (New Haven 1959) 19–35, and *The Visionary Company* (1962) 285–9; and *Reiman (1969)* 42–4.

Text: A. From *SDMS* 7–13. Accents have been added in lines 13, 22, stops in lines 11, 49, and a diaeresis in line 26.

B. From *1817* 175–83.

Published: A. By Judith Chernaik and Timothy Burnett, *RES* xxix (1978) 45–9.

B. *1817*.

Notes relevant to both texts are given for text B.

A.   Scene–Pont Pellisier in the vale of Servox

In day the eternal universe of things
Flows through the mind, and rolls its rapid waves
Now dark, now glittering; now reflecting gloom
Now lending splendour, where, from secret caves
5   The source of human thought its tribute brings
Of waters, with a sound not all its own:
Such as a feeble brook will oft assume
In the wild woods among the mountains lone
Where waterfalls around it leap forever
10 Where winds and woods contend, and a vast river
Over its rocks ceaselessly bursts and raves.

Thus thou Ravine of Arve, dark deep ravine,
Thou many coloured, many voicèd vale!
Over whose rocks and pines and caverns sail
15 Fast cloud shadows and sunbeams–awful scene,
Where Power in likeness of the Arve comes down
From the ice gulfs that gird his secret throne
Bursting through these dark mountains like the flame
Of lightning through the tempest–thou dost lie
20 Thy giant brood of pines around thee clinging
Children of elder time, in whose devotion
The charmèd winds still come, and ever came
To drink their odours, and their mighty swinging
To hear, an old and solemn harmony;
25 Thine earthly rainbows stretched across the sweep
Of the aërial waterfall, whose veil
Robes some unsculptured image; even the sleep
The sudden pause that does inhabit thee
Which when the voices of the desert fail
30 And its hues wane, doth blend them all and steep
Their periods in its own eternity;
Thy caverns echoing to the Arve's commotion
A loud lone sound no other sound can tame:

¶ *124* (Text A). *1. In day*] i.e. during waking consciousness, in contrast to
experience in sleep (50–1).
11–12. There is no break between these lines in *RES*.
27. the sleep] The interval of suspense when the sound is interrupted and the
view obscured by an obstacle. S. described the ravine as in places 'so deep that
the very roaring of the untameable Arve, which rolled through it, could not be
heard above' (*1817* 152; cp. Edward Thomas, 'The Mountain Chapel' 4–5:
'The loss of the brook's voice / Falls like a shadow').
31. Their periods] An ambivalence: 'their times of existence' or 'their times of
cessation'.

       Thou art pervaded with such ceaseless motion
35   Thou art the path of that unresting sound
       Ravine of Arve! and when I gaze on thee
       I seem as in a vision deep and strange
       To muse on my own various fantasy
       My own, my human mind . . . which passively
40   Now renders and receives fast influencings
       Holding an unforeseeing interchange
       With the clear universe of things around:
       A legion of swift thoughts, whose wandering wings
       Now float above thy darkness, and now rest
45   Near the still cave of the witch Poesy
       Seeking among the shadows that pass by,
       Ghosts of the things that are, some form like thee,
       Some spectre, some faint image; till the breast
       From which they fled recalls them–thou art there.

50   Some say that gleams of a remoter world
       Visit the soul in sleep–that death is slumber
       And that its shapes the busy thoughts outnumber
       Of those who wake and live. I look on high:
       Has some unknown omnipotence unfurled
55   The veil of life and death? or do I lie
       In dream, and does the mightier world of sleep
       Spread far around, and inaccessibly
       Its circles?–for the very spirit fails
       Driven like a homeless cloud from steep to steep
60   That vanishes among the viewless gales. –
       Far, far above, piercing the infinite sky
       Mont Blanc appears, still, snowy and serene,
       Its subject mountains their unearthly forms
       Pile round it–ice and rock–broad chasms between
65   Of frozen waves, unfathomable deeps
       Blue as the overhanging Heaven, that spread
       And wind among the accumulated steeps,
       Vast deserts, peopled by the storms alone
       Save when the eagle brings some hunter's bone
70   And the wolf watches her–how hideously
       Its rocks are heaped around, rude, bare and high
       Ghastly and scarred and riven!–is this the scene
       Where the old Earthquake demon taught her young
       Ruin? were these their toys? or did a sea
75   Of fire envelop once this silent snow?
       None can reply–all seems eternal now.

53. high:] high *SDMS, RES.*
71. rude,] rude *SDMS, RES.*

This wilderness has a mysterious tongue
Which teaches awful doubt, or faith so mild
So simple, so serene that man may be
80   In such a faith with Nature reconciled.
Ye have a doctrine, Mountains, to repeal
Large codes of fraud and woe—not understood
By all, but which the wise and great and good
Interpret, or make felt, or deeply feel.

85   The fields, the lakes, the forests and the streams
Ocean, and all the living things that dwell
Within the daedal Earth, lightning and rain,
Earthquake, and lava flood and hurricane—
The torpor of the year, when feeble dreams
90   Visit the hidden buds, or dreamless sleep
Holds every future leaf and flower—the bound
With which from that detested trance they leap;
The works and ways of man, their death and birth
And that of him, and all that his may be,
95   All things that move and breathe with toil and sound
Are born and die, revolve, subside and swell—
Power dwells apart in deep tranquillity,
Remote, sublime, and inaccessible.
And this, the naked countenance of Earth
100 On which I gaze—even these primeval mountains
Teach the adverting mind.—The Glaciers creep
Like snakes that watch their prey, from their far
                                    fountains
Slow rolling on:—there, many a precipice
Frost and the Sun in scorn of human power
105 Have piled: dome, pyramid and pinnacle
A city of death, distinct with many a tower
And wall impregnable of shining ice . . .
A city's phantom . . . but a flood of ruin
Is there that from the boundaries of the sky
110 Rolls its eternal stream . . . vast pines are strewing
Its destined path, or in the mangled soil
Branchless and shattered stand—the rocks drawn down
From yon remotest waste have overthrown
The limits of the dead and living world
115 Never to be reclaimed—the dwelling place

81. *doctrine, Mountains,*] doctrine Mountains *SDMS, RES.*
96. *revolve,*] revolve *SDMS, RES.*
98. *inaccessible.*] inaccessible, *RES.*
101. *mind.—The*] mind.—the *SDMS, RES.*
109. *there*] there, *RES* (*comma canc. in SDMS*).

Of insects, beasts and birds becomes its spoil
Their food and their retreat for ever gone
So much of life and joy is lost—the race
Of man flies far in dread, his work and dwelling
120 Vanish like smoke before the tempest's stream
And their place is not known:—below, vast caves
Shine in the gushing torrents' restless gleam
Which from those secret chasms in tumult welling
Meet in the vale—and one majestic river
125 The breath and blood of distant lands, forever
Rolls its loud waters to the Ocean waves
Breathes its swift vapours to the circling air.

Mont Blanc yet gleams on high—the Power is there
The still and solemn Power of many sights
130 And many sounds, and much of life and death.
In the calm darkness of the moonless nights
Or the lone light of day the snows descend
Upon that Mountain—none beholds them there
Nor when the sunset wraps their flakes in fire
135 Or the starbeams dart through them—winds contend
Silently there, and heap the snows, with breath
Blasting and swift—but silently—its home
The voiceless lightning in these solitudes
Keeps innocently, and like vapour broods
140 Over the snow. The secret strength of things
Which governs thought, and to the infinite dome
Of Heaven is as a column, rests on thee,
And what were thou and Earth and Stars and Sea
If to the human mind's imaginings
145 Silence and solitude were vacancy?

119. *dread, his*] dread. his SDMS.
120. *tempest's*] tempests SDMS.
121. *known:—*] known— RES.
133. *Mountain—*] mountain— RES.
140. *snow. The*] snow. the SDMS.
144. *mind's*] minds SDMS.
145. *vacancy?*] vacancy SDMS.

B.   Mont Blanc.
                   Lines written in the Vale of Chamouni

                                I.

The everlasting universe of things
Flows through the mind, and rolls its rapid waves,
Now dark–now glittering–now reflecting gloom–
Now lending splendour, where from secret springs
5   The source of human thought its tribute brings
Of waters,–with a sound but half its own,
Such as a feeble brook will oft assume
In the wild woods, among the mountains lone,
Where waterfalls around it leap for ever,
10 Where woods and winds contend, and a vast river
Over its rocks ceaselessly bursts and raves.

                                II.

Thus thou, Ravine of Arve–dark, deep Ravine–
Thou many-coloured, many-voicèd vale,
Over whose pines, and crags, and caverns sail
15 Fast cloud shadows and sunbeams: awful scene,

¶ *124* (Text B). *Title.* The scene of [At Pont *canc.*] Pellisier, at the [opening *canc.*]
extremity [of the valley *canc.*] of the vale of Servoz. *draft* (see headnote for S.'s
choice of title in *1817*).
1. In daylight thoughts, bright or obscure *draft canc.* In day the eternal stream of
various thoughts *draft canc.* In day the stream of [?] things *draft.*
2. the mind] The Universal Mind as distinct from the individual mind (lines 5,
37), whose contribution to experience is 'but half its own'. Locock compares
Daemon ii 248–50, but although there are affinities between S.'s Daemon and
the Power embodied in 'Mont Blanc' (see *Daemon*, note to title), the metaphors
here and in *Daemon* ii 248 ff. imply differing conceptions of mind.
4. springs] caves *draft.* 'The interwoven rhymes of [the draft] are more regular
(abcbadcd); Shelley may have been consciously striving in *1817* for the more
irregular rhyme effects of *Lycidas*' (*Chernaik*).
5. source of human thought] fountain of the mind *draft canc. tribute*] Puns on
'tributary' (cp. *PU* III iii 155).
6. but half its own] S.'s formulation suggests Wordsworth's 'Tintern Abbey'
(1798) 107–8. With the ambivalence of *its* (source of thought, or universe of
things?), cp. 'Upon the wandering winds' 10*n*.
9. for ever] forever *Chernaik.*
10. vast] loud *above* vast *canc. draft.*
11. ceaselessly] forever *draft canc.*
14. pines, and crags] rocks and pines *draft.*
15. Fast cloud shadows] And mingling *draft canc.*

Where Power in likeness of the Arve comes down
From the ice gulfs that gird his secret throne,
Bursting through these dark mountains like the flame
Of lightning through the tempest;—thou dost lie,
20   Thy giant brood of pines around thee clinging,
Children of elder time, in whose devotion
The chainless winds still come and ever came
To drink their odours, and their mighty swinging
To hear—an old and solemn harmony;
25   Thine earthly rainbows stretched across the sweep
Of the etherial waterfall, whose veil
Robes some unsculptured image; the strange sleep
Which when the voices of the desert fail

16. *Power*] See note to lines 96–7.
17. *secret*] aerial *draft canc.*
22. *chainless*] charmed *draft canc.*; unchained *draft.*
23. *mighty*] solemn *draft; Chernaik* discerns *mighty* as the original draft reading.
24. *solemn*] awful *draft.*
25–9. These lines are preceded in the draft by a version of lines 30–4 below; there are also two lines in the draft, not used in *1817*, which correspond to the A text lines 28 and 30. S.'s line 29 in the present B text is a conflation of two lines in the draft which read 'And its hues wane, doth blend them all and steep / Their tumult in its own eternity,'. *Chernaik* (following GM) comments that 'the original order of [the draft] is probably clearer than [*1817*]: the "ceaseless motion" and "unresting sound" . . . summarize the coming and going of the winds, the swinging of the pines, and the commotion of the Arve, the "awful harmony" of one and the "loud lone sound" of the other; whereas the "rainbows" stretched across the waterfall and the "sudden pause" are what the poet observes when he gazes on the ravine.' *Rossetti 1870* notes that lines 27–29 have no defined syntactical position; S.'s syntax is in fact resumed at line 30, which returns the reader to the attributes of the Ravine.
25–7. *Thine earthly rainbows . . . unsculptured image*] A conflation of two waterfalls seen from the road to Chamonix: one caused a mist of spray 'in the midst of which hung a multitude of sunbows, which faded or became unspeakably vivid, as the inconstant sun shone through the clouds'; the other 'fell from the overhanging brow of a black precipice on an enormous rock, precisely resembling some colossal Egyptian statue of a female deity. It struck the head of the visionary image, and gracefully dividing there, fell from it in folds of foam more like to cloud than water, imitating a veil of the most exquisite woof.' (*1817* 145–6, 148). *unsculptured*] 'not man-made'.
26. *etherial*] aerial *draft.*
27. *image; the strange sleep*] image—even the sleep *draft.* The phrase 'strange sleep' evokes the eerie silence and stillness of the landscape when its sounds are momentarily inaudible.
28. And when the words and waves [ ] sunbeams *draft canc. voices*] tumult *draft canc.*

Wraps all in its own deep eternity;–
30   Thy caverns echoing to the Arve's commotion,
A loud, lone sound no other sound can tame;
Thou art pervaded with that ceaseless motion,
Thou art the path of that unresting sound–
Dizzy Ravine! and when I gaze on thee
35   I seem as in a trance sublime and strange
To muse on my own separate fantasy,
My own, my human mind, which passively
Now renders and receives fast influencings,
Holding an unremitting interchange
40   With the clear universe of things around;
One legion of wild thoughts, whose wandering wings
Now float above thy darkness, and now rest
Where that or thou art no unbidden guest,
In the still cave of the witch Poesy,
45   Seeking among the shadows that pass by,
Ghosts of all things that are, some shade of thee,
Some phantom, some faint image; till the breast
From which they fled recalls them, thou art there!

32. ceaseless] unceasing *draft canc.*; untameable *draft canc.*
33. that unresting] unreposing *draft canc.*
34. Dizzy Ravine!] Mighty Ravine [of Arve *canc.*] *draft.*
35–40. Cp. *Daemon* ii 248–55. *trance sublime]* vision deep *draft.*
36. I seem to muse on my own phantasy *draft. separate]* separate *draft canc.*
various *draft.*
39. unremitting] unremitted *draft.*
40. clear] vast *draft uncanc. alt.*
41–4. Cp. Lucretius, *De Re. Nat.* iv 26–41.
41. wild] untold *draft canc. wild thoughts* refers back to *influencings,* line 38 above.
42. darkness,] wonders *draft canc.*
43. This line is cancelled in the draft, and omitted in *SDMS. that or thou art]* thou
art surely *draft canc. alt.* The ambiguous reference of the pronouns makes for
real difficulty: the likeliest intended sense is that *thou* refers to the Ravine, and
that to the *legion of wild thoughts* (see *Locock* 1911 490; *Cameron (1974)* 247; *Reiman*
(1977) 90).
44–7. Cp. Byron, *Childe Harold's Pilgrimage* III v; the passage has affinities with
The Earth's speech in *PU* I 191 ff.
44. In the still] Near the wierd *draft. witch]* shade *draft canc.* S.'s cave suggests in
general (but not specific) terms Plato's myth of the Cave, *Republic* 514 ff.
45. by,] by *1817. shadows* is in apposition to *Ghosts* in the following line.
46. all] the *draft.*
47. phantom,] likeness *draft canc. Reiman (1977)* 90 suggests that *the breast* is an
anthropomorphized source for the *Ghosts of all things that are* of line 46.

III.

Some say that gleams of a remoter world
50　Visit the soul in sleep, –that death is slumber,
And that its shapes the busy thoughts outnumber
Of those who wake and live. –I look on high;
Has some unknown omnipotence unfurled
The veil of life and death? or do I lie
55　In dream, and does the mightier world of sleep
Spread far around and inaccessibly
Its circles? For the very spirit fails,
Driven like a homeless cloud from steep to steep
That vanishes among the viewless gales!
60　Far, far above, piercing the infinite sky,
Mont Blanc appears, –still, snowy, and serene–
Its subject mountains their unearthly forms
Pile around it, ice and rock; broad vales between
Of frozen floods, unfathomable deeps,
65　Blue as the overhanging heaven, that spread
And wind among the accumulated steeps;
A desert peopled by the storms alone,
Save when the eagle brings some hunter's bone,
And the wolf tracks her there–how hideously

49–57. Cp. Byron, 'The Dream' 1–26 (dated 'July 1816'), and 'A Fragment' (dated 'Diodati, July 1816'). S.'s phrasing suggests an increasingly characteristic scepticism. *remoter*] *Concordance* glosses as 'future', but the sense is probably 'less accessible to human comprehension'.

52. *on high;*] above *draft canc.*

53–4. Cp. *L&C* XII xv 4581–2. *unfurled*] The gloss in *Locock 1911*, 'drawn aside', appears to offer the best sense in context, but see E. B. Murray, 'Mont Blanc's Unfurled Veil', *KSJ* xviii (1969) 39–48, for a defence of the word in its usual sense. The emendation 'upfurled' in *Rossetti 1870* has been followed by some modern eds, e.g. Harold Bloom (ed.), *English Romantic Poetry* (New York 1963) 163.

56. *Spread*] Speed *1839*.

57. *spirit fails,*] mind is faint / With aspiration. *draft canc.*

58. Cp. 'I visit thee but thou art sadly changed' 13 and note.

59. *That*] Which *draft*.

61. *still, snowy, and serene–*] every pyramid *draft canc.*

63. *around*] round *draft*.

67. *desert peopled*] [lifeless *canc.*] desert *draft*.

68. *when*] where *draft*.

69. *tracks her there–*] *1824*; watches her [afar *canc.*] *draft*; tracts her there–*1817*. *1817* strongly suggests a transcription error; 'watches' in the draft is written with a gap between the c and h. 'A wolf cannot track an eagle, of course, but would in fact watch (hungrily) from a distance' (GM). S.'s journal-letter to Peacock of 22–5 July 1816 gives an account of wolves in the area of Chamonix (*L* i 501–2).

70   Its shapes are heaped around! rude, bare, and high,
     Ghastly, and scarred, and riven. – Is this the scene
     Where the old Earthquake-daemon taught her young
     Ruin? Were these their toys? or did a sea
     Of fire envelop once this silent snow?
75   None can reply – all seems eternal now.
     The wilderness has a mysterious tongue
     Which teaches awful doubt, or faith so mild,
     So solemn, so serene, that man may be
     But for such faith with nature reconciled;
80   Thou hast a voice, great Mountain, to repeal
     Large codes of fraud and woe; not understood
     By all, but which the wise, and great, and good
     Interpret, or make felt, or deeply feel.

70. shapes] rocks *draft*.
71–4. Cp. *Childe Harold's Pilgrimage* III xciii. S. draws in this passage on his
knowledge of the geological theories of Buffon; see headnote. *fire*] fire, *1817*.
76–83. These lines have attracted much critical and textual commentary,
particularly in relation to the phrase in line 79, 'But for such faith'. S.'s basic
intended sense – 'only by such a faith' – is clarified by the reading in *SDMS*, 'In
such a faith' (A text, line 80). S. clearly had difficulty with these lines, which
are much-cancelled and heavily palimpsested in the draft; early and intermediate stages of composition include line 77: *or faith so mild*] faith *above* belief *canc.* a
voice which to the wise *canc.* a voice not understood *canc.* Line 79: *But for such
faith with*] With such faith *canc.* In such a faith *draft*. To such high thoughts of
Nature reconciled *canc.* But for such *canc.* Even with his mother nature *canc.* S.
wrote out the line again completely as 'In such a faith with Nature reconciled–'.
Line 80: Ye have a voice great Mountains–to repeal *draft* Mountains ye have a
voice not understood *canc.* Several critics have offered detailed explication of
S.'s 'But' in line 79, including notably Joan Rees, *RES* n.s. xv (1964) 185–6,
and John Kinnaird, *N&Q* n.s. xv (1968) 332–4. 'But' in the sense of 'only' or
'just only' is not unusual in S.: cp. e.g. *Q Mab* viii 97, *PU* III iv 194–7 and note.
76–83. S.'s experience of the Mountain in its landscape produces a conviction
that institutionalized forms of political and social oppression, and their human
effects (*large codes of fraud and woe*) may be challenged by those who realize they
have no sanction in a Divinity which may be inferred from nature. Nature, and
its magnificent but enigmatic causal Power, may rather be understood either in
a spirit of constructive scepticism (*awful doubt*, glossed as 'reverent open-
mindedness' in *Reiman (1977)*), or of serene confidence (*faith so mild*) in an
unChristian and morally indifferent Power, informing nature, which may be
susceptible of human understanding and control.
80–2. For S.'s earlier draft of these lines, see headnote. *voice* may suggest
Coleridge's influence; cp. the passage from his 'Hymn: Before Sunrise',
quoted in headnote.

IV.

The fields, the lakes, the forests, and the streams,
85   Ocean, and all the living things that dwell
Within the daedal earth; lightning, and rain,
Earthquake, and fiery flood, and hurricane,
The torpor of the year when feeble dreams
Visit the hidden buds, or dreamless sleep
90   Holds every future leaf and flower;–the bound
With which from that detested trance they leap;
The works and ways of man, their death and birth,
And that of him and all that his may be;
All things that move and breathe with toil and sound
95   Are born and die; revolve, subside and swell.
Power dwells apart in its tranquillity
Remote, serene, and inaccessible:
And *this*, the naked countenance of earth,
On which I gaze, even these primeval mountains
100   Teach the adverting mind. The glaciers creep
Like snakes that watch their prey, from their far
                                                  fountains,
Slow rolling on; there, many a precipice,
Frost and the Sun in scorn of mortal power
Have piled: dome, pyramid, and pinnacle,

84. The draft at first read 'The powers that move [*above* rule *canc.*] the world
themselves are still / Remote serene and inaccessible'.
86. daedal] Gk δαίδαλος, 'cunningly wrought'.
87. fiery flood,] flouds of waterspout *draft canc.*
88. The sleep of winter when no human dream *draft canc.* torpor] slumber *draft.*
feeble] deathlike *draft canc.*
94–7. Cp. *Daemon* i 286–91.
94. All things are changed with tumult and with sound / Wave rolling upon
wave with restless swell *draft canc. Locock 1911*, following *Rossetti 1870*, places a
comma after *breathe* so that 'the alteration in sense gives the required contrast
with 96'. But the required contrast is not between sound and silence but
between the verbs of 95 and the serene Power that underlies evolution.
96–7. S.'s conception of the Power embodied in Mont Blanc suggests the
account of Necessity in his note to *Q Mab* vi 198.
97. Mont Blanc is the highest mountain in Western Europe (4810m.). When S.
saw it in 1816 it had been climbed only three times, in 1786 and 1787 (twice).
100. adverting] 'heedful, attentive' (*Concordance*). *Cameron (1974)* 250 cites
Godwin, *Political Justice* Bk IV ch. ix, i 404: 'Consciousness is a sort of
supplementary reflection, by which the mind not only has the thought,
but adverts to its own situation, and observes that it has it. Consciousness
therefore, however nice the distinction, seems to be a second thought.'
103. Frost] [Which *canc.*] frost *draft.*

105 A city of death, distinct with many a tower
    And wall impregnable of beaming ice.
    Yet not a city, but a flood of ruin
    Is there, that from the boundaries of the sky
    Rolls its perpetual stream; vast pines are strewing
110 Its destined path, or in the mangled soil
    Branchless and shattered stand; the rocks, drawn down
    From yon remotest waste, have overthrown
    The limits of the dead and living world,
    Never to be reclaimed. The dwelling-place
115 Of insects, beasts, and birds, becomes its spoil;
    Their food and their retreat for ever gone,
    So much of life and joy is lost. The race
    Of man flies far in dread; his work and dwelling
    Vanish, like smoke before the tempest's stream,
120 And their place is not known. Below, vast caves
    Shine in the rushing torrents' restless gleam, .
    Which from those secret chasms in tumult welling
    Meet in the vale, and one majestic River,
    The breath and blood of distant lands, for ever
125 Rolls its loud waters to the ocean waves,
    Breathes its swift vapours to the circling air.

105. *distinct*] 'decorated, adorned' (a latinism; cp. *PU* III iii 162).
107. *flood*] stream *draft canc.*
108. *boundaries*] silence *draft canc.*; desarts *draft canc.* *sky*] air *draft canc.*
109. *perpetual*] eternal *draft canc.*
110. *mangled*] ruined *draft canc.*
116–17. An absolute construction: 'Their food being gone, the world is so much the poorer by losing the insects, beasts and birds'. *is lost.*] has fled *draft canc.*
118. *man*] man, *1817.*
119. *like*] as *draft.*
120. *And their place is not known*] Cp. *Psalms* ciii 15–16, and *Nahum* iii 17 (a more specific echo, perhaps suggested by a recollection of *Nahum* i 5–6 in connection with the poem's volcanic imagery).
121. *rushing*] gushing *draft.* *torrents'*] torrent's *1817.*
122. An unmistakable echo of Coleridge's 'Kubla Khan'. Although S. did not receive his copy of Coleridge's *Christabel* volume until 26 August 1816, too late to influence 'Mont Blanc', he may well have known the poem already in MS, or through Byron or even Southey; see *Robinson* 36–7.
123–4. *one majestic River . . . distant lands*] The Arve flows into Lake Geneva, from which the Rhône flows out through France to the Mediterranean.
123. *the*] one *draft.*
124. *for ever*] forever *Chernaik.*
125. *Rolls*] Bears *draft.*
126. *swift*] *Chernaik* reads 'soft' in the draft.

V.

Mont Blanc yet gleams on high:—the power is there,
The still and solemn power of many sights
And many sounds, and much of life and death.
130 In the calm darkness of the moonless nights,
In the lone glare of day, the snows descend
Upon that Mountain; none beholds them there,
Nor when the flakes burn in the sinking sun,
Or the star-beams dart through them:—Winds contend
135 Silently there, and heap the snow with breath
Rapid and strong, but silently! Its home
The voiceless lightning in these solitudes
Keeps innocently, and like vapour broods
Over the snow. The secret strength of things
140 Which governs thought, and to the infinite dome
Of heaven is as a law, inhabits thee!
And what were thou, and earth, and stars, and sea,
If to the human mind's imaginings
Silence and solitude were vacancy?

125 'My thoughts arise and fade in solitude'

These lines are written vertically on a page of *Nbk 1*, superimposed over a
Swiss journal entry for 22 July 1816. Mary S. quoted the lines later in her own
journal on 18 October 1820. In *1839* she assigned them to 1817, which may be
correct, but the situation and mood fit the nine-day period from 9 September
1816 when S. was alone in London or Marlow, describing himself to Byron on

128. *sights*] sights, *1817*.
129. *life and death.*] good and ill *draft canc.*
131. *In the lone glare*] Or in the starlight *draft canc.*; Or the lone light *draft. descend*]
flakes fall *draft canc.*
132. *there,*] then *draft.*
133. Nor when the sunlight wraps their flakes in flame *draft canc.*
139. The draft reads 'Over the snow—The unpolluted dome / Of Heaven is not
more silent.—'
140. *to the infinite*] rules the starry *draft canc.*
142. *And what were thou*] A characteristic construction in Coleridge, e.g. 'The
Eolian Harp' 44; 'The Destiny of Nations' 60.
142–4. 'What would your effect be if the mind did not detect (infer) the
existence of this strength in your silent solitudes?' (GM).

the 11th as 'at my antient lodgings, dreadfully vacant and lonely', and regretting 'the time that I must inevitably waste in this peopled desert' (a cancelled first line of the fragment reads: 'Why waste I in my solitude'). There was a full moon on 7 September 1816.
Text from *Nbk 1* f. 66.
Published in *1839* iii 70 (notes).

> My thoughts arise and fade in solitude—
> The verse that would invest them melts away
> Like moonlight in the beam of spreading day—
> How beautiful they were—how firm they stood
> 5   Freckling the starry sky like woven pearl!—

126 'Her voice did quiver as we parted'

These fragments are on a detached sheet in *Box 1*, lines 1–13 in the centre of the page, lines 14–23 tucked into the top right-hand corner as if added later. The cancelled words 'No (or 'In') sympathy' above the lines do not seem to have been intended as a title. Reasons for regarding both fragments, though probably composed at a year's interval, as a single lament for the death of Fanny Godwin are given fully in *The Evidence of the Imagination*, ed. D. H. Reiman, M. C. Jaye, and Betty T. Bennett (New York 1978) 254–60. Briefly: Mary S. printed the two fragments in separate volumes of *1839*, entitling the first 'On F.G.' (dated 1817) and the second 'To William Shelley' (undated), and hitherto this identification has been followed without question. But she had evidently not seen these fragments before finding them after S.'s death, and in her initial transcription she had noted beside the first: 'I think on F G. written before Italy' and beside the second: 'before Italy', including both under the same transcript number (Bod. MS Shelley adds.d.7, f. 82). 'Before Italy' would have ruled out the association with William S. who died in Rome on 7 June 1819, so Mary must have forgotten this note when preparing the poems for *1839*. Rossetti (*Rossetti 1870* ii 321) first gave 'Thy little footsteps' the date 1819, although line 17 makes this impossible. However, the reverse side of S.'s MS bears a drawing (reproduced in the frontispiece of the present volume, and in Claire Tomalin, *Shelley and His World* (1980) 67) which appears to show a flight of steps in a formal garden—possibly steps leading down to a vault—with a

¶ *125.1.* Why waste I in my solitude *draft canc.*
2. *melts away*] is so frail *draft canc.*
3. Like moonlight clouds before the dawning day *draft canc.* beam] heaven *1839*
5. *Freckling*] Flecking *1839*.

flowerpot at the foot of the page on which S. has written: 'I drew this flower pot in October 1816 and now it is 1817'. Fanny Godwin committed suicide in Swansea on 9 October 1816, as S. learned three days later, and a reasonable assumption is therefore that he wrote lines 1–13 soon after this event, when he drew the flowerpot, and added lines 14–23 in 1817, perhaps on or near the anniversary of Fanny's death. Other scraps on the page include the lines: 'These cannot be forgotten–years / May flow', written vertically on the left of the page; to the right, 'Breaking thine indissoluble sleep', with the word 'miserable' below; and lower down: 'It is not my fault–it is not to be attributed to me–', with 'when said I so?' in different ink just above.

The notes which follow establish the connection between lines 14–23 and Fanny Godwin. But what was the 'secret grief' implied in S.'s draft lines as the cause of her suicide? Frances, always called Godwin, was really the daughter of Gilbert Imlay, but it can hardly have been the revelation of this fact as Kegan Paul and others have suggested (*William Godwin: His Friends and Contemporaries* (1876) ii 243–4); at 22 she was the eldest of a circle of girls thoroughly familiar with Godwin's long-published *Memoirs* and *Posthumous Works* of Mary Wollstonecraft, whose memory they all idolized. On 9 July 1820 Maria Gisborne was told by Godwin 'that the three girls were all equally in love with [Shelley] and that the eldest put an end to her existence owing to the preference given to her younger sister' (*Gisborne Jnl* 39), and in later life Claire Clairmont gave some support to this story (*L about S* 43). Perhaps the emotional Fanny had more feeling for S. than she allowed to appear; but in any case the elopement had left her isolated in the Godwin household, and in the autumn of 1816 she was in despair over S.'s recent failure to pay Godwin £300 on which the latter had staked his own solvency. S. had met Fanny several times in London in September, and at their final meeting, probably on 24 September (Dowden *Life* ii 55n.), Fanny thought S. had purposely deceived her by the encouraging message he had caused her to take to Godwin. On October 3, Fanny wrote to Mary S. 'I cannot help thinking that he [S.] had arranged everything with Longdill [his solicitor] before I parted from him in Piccadilly the other day, and for these reasons he chose not to be frank with me' (*Dowden Life* ii 55). To believe herself to be made the vehicle of false messages from a man she admired to a stepfather whose welfare depended on their reliability must have been an intolerable situation for her. She may also have been disappointed in her hopes of escaping her troubles by joining her Aunt Everina in Ireland. She could not have paid for her passage, but did not call on S. in Bath on her way to Wales, so the probability is that she chose Swansea in order to destroy herself at the furthest distance from London, and so (as her suicide note affirmed) 'put an end to the existence of a being whose birth was unfortunate, and whose life has only been a series of pain to those persons who have hurt their health in endeavouring to promote her welfare' (*White* i 470).

Text from *Box 1* f. 68.

Published in *1839* iii 64 (lines 1–6), iv 182 (lines 14–19); *V&P* 73–4 (complete); *Massey* 282–3 (complete transcript).

Her voice did quiver as we parted—
   Yet knew I not the heart was broken
From which it came—and I departed
   Heeding not the words then spoken—
5 Misery—oh misery
   This world is all too wide for thee!

Some secret woes had been mine own—
   And they had taught me that the good
The free [

                             ]
10 And that for those who are lone and weary
   The road of life is long and dreary.

Some hopes were buried in my heart
   Whose spectres haunted me with sadness

        ★   ★   ★   ★   ★

Thy little footsteps on the sands
15   Of a remote and lonely shore—
   The twinkling of thine infant hands

¶ 126. 1–2. Friend had I known thy secret grief / Should we have parted so MS canc.

7. woes] griefs MS canc.

9. free] pure 1839, Massey, 1975 (perhaps correct, or perhaps true).

10. those] MS canc.

14–15. On her journey to Tönsberg in Norway for Gilbert Imlay in 1795, Mary Wollstonecraft had left their year-old child in care of a nursemaid at Gothenberg in Sweden. Stranded one night on the Norwegian coast, Mary W. had dreamed of Fanny:

Light slumbers produced dreams, where Paradise was before me. My little cherub was again hiding her face in my bosom. I heard her sweet cooing beat on my heart from the cliffs, and saw her tiny footsteps on the sands. (*Letters Written during a Short Residence in Sweden, Norway and Denmark* (1796; 1802 edn) Letter x, 127)

15. a remote] some remote MS canc. shore] sea MS canc.

16–17. Transferred from Mary Wollstonecraft's semi-autobiographical fiction *The Wrongs of Woman; or, Maria*, in which an imprisoned mother is separated from her baby:

Her infant's image was continually floating on Maria's sight, and the first smile of intelligence remembered, as none but a mother, an unhappy mother, can conceive. She heard her half speaking half cooing, and felt the little twinkling fingers on her burning bosom—a bosom bursting with the nutriment for which this cherished child might now be pining in vain. (*Posthumous Works of the Author of A Vindication of the Rights of Woman*, ed. W. Godwin (1798) i 2–3)

Where now the worm will feed no more,
Thy look of mingled love and glee
When *one* returned to gaze on thee–

20   These footsteps on the sands are fled,
Thine eyes are dark–thy hands are cold,
And she is dead–and thou art dead–
And the [

127/128 To [   ]
Nov. 5 1815
Nov. 5 1817

Despite their headings, the composition dates of both these poems are uncertain. The texts, fair copies with minor corrections, occur together written in the same ink in *Nbk 11*, which contains material dating from 1814 to 1821; they interrupt the draft of *PU* II, so the only certainty is that both poems were composed before spring 1819. 5 Nov. 1815 cannot be the night described in the poem, as there had been a new moon three days earlier and the weather in the London area was mild (*GM* December 1815, 478). It has generally been assumed since Medwin's first suggestion in about 1869 (*Medwin (1913)* 181) that '1815' was a slip, or a deliberate substitution, for '1816', and that this poem concerns Harriet S.'s suicide. The name or phrase after the dedication 'To' (which may originally have been 'For') has been carefully obliterated, but it contained no descenders, so cannot have involved 'Mary' or 'Fanny' unless by initials. 'Harriet' or 'Ianthe' is not impossible. The dedication may have been

17. *Where*] Upon thy *MS canc.* Mary W. had been buried in St Pancras churchyard since 15 September 1797.

18. *of mingled love and glee*] of love, thy laugh of glee *MS canc.*

19. *When* one *returned*] On her way back to Gothenberg, Mary W. reflected: 'I was returning to my babe, who may never experience a father's care or tenderness' (*Letters Written during a Short Residence* Letter xvi, 188). Imlay never did rejoin his family.

21. *cold*] still *MS uncanc. alternative.*

22. For her own suicide Fanny chose the eve of her mother's suicide attempt in 1795 (see Margaret Tims, *Mary Wollstonecraft: A Social Pioneer* (1976) 273).

23. And we remain to know how old *MS. canc., blotted, and dubious.*

¶ 127. *Title. In Nbk 11* what follows 'To' is indecipherably cancelled. In *Box 1,* the title is 'November–1815' without either day or dedication.

applicable to both poems. There was a full moon on 5 November 1816, but the weather was again exceptionally mild and also wet, though a cold spell followed from 6–11 November (*GM* November 1816, 386). Harriet S. left her lodgings in Elizabeth St (Hans Road) only on 9 November, did not die in the Serpentine until 7 December, and was not known to have died until 10 December (see *SC* iv 769–802). Water is only mentioned in the poem once, and then as a simile for 'deep dark' eyes; and the girl is not dead, but exposed to cold wind and darkness. Fanny Godwin, whose death (so S. told Byron soon after both events) 'affected me far more deeply' (17 January 1817, *L* i 530), had committed suicide on 9 October 1816, but by poison in the Mackworth Arms, Swansea. In fact the associations of moonlit stream and exposure were with Mary S. rather than with Harriet or Fanny, e.g. in S.'s letter of 28 October 1814 (*L* i 414): 'My mind without yours is dead and cold as the dark midnight river when the moon is down'. The love-encounter in *L&C* VI shares several features with this first poem, e.g. 'the wind that flows / Through night' (xx 3–4); 'her dark hair was dispread / Like the pine's locks upon the lingering blast; / Over mine eyes its shadowy strings it spread / Fitfully' (xxi 5–8); and especially:

> Cythna's sweet lips seemed lurid in the moon,
> Her fairest limbs with the night wind were chill,
> And her dark tresses were all loosely strewn
> O'er her pale bosom: (xxxviii 1–4)

–which closely parallels lines 19–23 of the poem. ('Raven hair' in the version for publication (line 20) was a gothic property, fitting neither Harriet's light brown nor Mary's fair hair. Mary S. rejected 'raven' for 'tangled' when printing the later version.) It seems clear that if the poem does derive from any particular death or deaths its relationship to those events is much more complicated than one of direct lament. Another fair copy of 'The cold Earth' is in *Box 1*. It was one of four poems (with 'Invocation to Misery', 'Stanzas in Dejection', and 'On a Faded Violet') apparently sent to Ollier on 10 November 1820 ('all my saddest verses raked up into one heap', *L* ii 246) for inclusion in the *Julian and Maddalo* volume that was never published. Ollier printed it later in the *Literary Pocket Book for 1823* (1822), identified below as *LPB*, and it was the principal source-text for *1824*. Although it reverts to several readings cancelled in *Nbk 11* it is thus a later text; but *Nbk 11* has been preferred here because of its close relationship with 'That time is dead'.

To preserve the same relationship 'That time is dead' is printed here although presumably written in 1817 at about the anniversary time of the two deaths. In the same metre and evidently a sequel, it is more plausibly concerned with death by drowning than 'The cold Earth' yet increases the latter's ambiguity of subject ('The stream we gazed on then, rolled by'). Again the heading date has no identifiable significance in S.'s life. But many other poems were published bearing the date '5 Nov. 1817', lamenting the death of the Princess Charlotte (who in fact died in the early hours of the following morning) and containing such lines as those in *Blackwoods* (ii 400) addressed to the Realm:

'The Waters are around thee. Weep– / But struggle not–thy doom is cast'. It is possible that S. adopted this date, of public mourning, as a convenient cover, attaching a deliberately approximate 'anniversary' date to the earlier poem when copying them both into *Nbk 11*. There is no need to assume with the *Julian* editors that both poems were composed in 1817 because they were copied out together in that year: in No. 126 S. added lines in 1817 to a poem written in 1816. No drafts of either poem are known.

'The cold Earth': Text from *Nbk 11* ff. 29–30.
Published in *The Literary Pocket Book for 1823* (1822) 114 ('November, 1815'); *1824* 202–3 ('Lines'); *SC* iv 799–800 (transcript of *Nbk 11* MS).

'That time is dead': Text from *Nbk 11* ff. 30–1.
Published in *1824* 216 ('Lines').

To [   ]
Nov. 5 1815

 The cold Earth slept below,
  Above the cold sky shone;
   And all around
   With a chilling sound
5 From caves of ice and fields of snow
 The wind of night like death did flow
  Under the sinking moon.

 The wintry hedge was black–
  The brown grass was not seen–
10   The birds did rest
   In the dark thorn's breast
 Whose roots beside the pathway track
 Bound its hard edge, and many a crack
  The black frost made between.

15 Thine eyes glowed in the gleam
  Of the departing light;

1. *Earth*] earth *Box 1, LPB, 1824.*
3–4. These lines are combined into one in each stanza in *Box 1* and *LPB.*
6. *wind*] breath *Box 1, LPB, Nbk 11 canc.*
7. *Under*] Beneath *Box 1, LPB.*
9. *brown*] green *Box 1, LPB, Nbk 11 canc.*
11. *in the dark*] on the bare *Box 1, LPB.*
13. *Bound its hard edge, and*] Had bound their folds o'er *Box 1, LPB*; Had bound the hard sedge, and *SC*; Had bound the hard soil, and *Nbk 11 canc.*
14. *The black frost made*] Which the frost had made *Box 1, LPB.*
15–21.   Thine eyes glowed in the glare
       Of the moon's dying light;

As a starry beam
On a deep dark stream
Shines dimly—so the moon shone there
20 And it shone through the strings of thy tangled hair
Which shook in the blast of night.

The moon made thy lips pale, beloved—
The wind made thy bosom chill;
The air did shed
25   On thy dear head
Its frozen dew, and thou didst lie
Where the bitter breath of the naked sky
Might visit thee at will.

Nov. 5 1817

That time is dead forever, child,
Drowned, frozen, dead forever;
We look on the past
And stare aghast
5 At the spectres wailing, pale and wild,
Of hopes which thou and I beguiled
To death in life's dark river.

The stream we gazed on then, rolled by,
Its waves are unreturning;
10   But we yet stand
In a lone land
Like tombs to mark the memory
Of hopes and fears which fade and flee
From bleak life's brief morning.

As a fenfire's beam on a sluggish stream
Gleams dimly, so the moon shone there,
And it yellowed the strings of thy raven hair,
That shook in the wind of night. *Box 1, LPB*

20. *shone through*] yellowed *1824*.

24. *air*] night *Box 1, LPB.*

¶ *128.1. That time*] Those hours *Nbk 11 canc.*

5. *and wild,*] and ghast, *1824.*

7. *in*] on *1824.*

11. A word which looks like 'disested' is written beside this line in *Nbk 11.*

14. In the light of life's dim morning. *1824;* In the light of *Nbk 11 canc. brief*] breif *Nbk 11.*

129 'They die–the dead return not'

Lines 1–12 are drafted on ff. 47–46 of *Nbk 1*, and copied out on f. 46 with two additional lines and a cancellation. There is no authority in the MS for a repetition of lines 7–8 in the second stanza, which Mary S. evidently introduced in *1824* in order to complete the fragment. Under the title 'Death' Mary S. included the lines in *1839* among the poems of 1817; they are probably motivated by the suicides in October and December 1816 of Fanny Godwin and Harriet S. The 'parent, friend, and lover' of line 4 could apply to Mary Wollstonecraft, Fanny Godwin, and Harriet S. (the unadopted draft line 6 had a cancelled beginning: 'Parent & sister'), but the fragment resists direct biographical interpretation.
Text from *Nbk 1* f. 46.
Published in *1824* 189 ('Death').

They die–the dead return not–Misery
Sits near an open grave and calls them over,
A youth with hoary hair and haggard eye–
They are the names of parent, friend, and lover
5 Which he so feebly calls–they all are gone,
Fond wretch–all dead–those vacant names alone,
  This most familiar scene–thy pain–
  These tombs alone remain. –

Misery, my sweetest friend–oh, weep no more–
10 Thou wilt not be consoled–I wonder not!
For I have seen thee from thy dwelling's door
Watch the calm sunset with them–and thy lot
Was even so bright and calm–but transitory,
And now thy hopes are gone–thy hair is hoary
15 [Thou sittest in the cold and w
  Thou lookest on this life with]

¶ *129.3–9.* A youth with hoary hair & sunken eye–
  [Muttering like Madness]–yes, they are all gone
  Fond wretch, & thou mayst count their names alone
  Their graves reminding thee of parent, lover
  And friend, thy heart's companions–thou dost groan–
  I wonder not–for when the shadows come,
  And evening falls upon thy lonely home– *draft*
4. parent] kindred *uncanc. above* parent *fair copy, 1824.*
9. Dear friend, Sweet Misery, peace! *draft.*
12–13. this spot / Has seen thee with a pencil or a brush *fair copy canc.;*
yon spot / Of lawn among the pines may be forgot *draft canc.*
15–16. Probably alternatives, not two separate lines; both are canc. in *fair copy.*

130 A Hate-Song
(improvised)

W. M. Rossetti, who first printed this quatrain, explained: 'Mr Browning has favoured me with this amusing absurdity, retailed to him by Leigh Hunt. It seems that Hunt and Shelley were talking one day (probably in or about 1817) concerning Love-Songs; and Shelley said he didn't see why Hate-Songs also should not be written, and that he could do them; and on the spot he improvised these lines of doggerel' (*Rossetti 1870* ii 602). If, consciously or unconsciously, the woman of line 4 was Eliza Westbrook, as is suggested by 'ditch' (the Serpentine?) and by the implied rhyme avoided in 'brute', the date of the improvisation may well have been January 1817.

Text from *Rossetti 1870* ii 532.

Published *Rossetti 1870*.

> A hater he came and sat by a ditch,
>   And he took out an old cracked lute;
> And he sang a song which was more of a screech
>   'Gainst a woman that was a brute.

131 To the [Lord Chancellor]

Composed soon after 27 March 1817, the date of Lord Eldon's formal decree 'that the Defendant Percy Bysshe Shelley and his Agents be restrained from taking possession of the persons of the Plaintiffs Eliza Ianthe Shelley and Charles Bysshe Shelley the Infants or intermeddling with the said Infants until the further order of this Court', and that Chancery should authorize 'a proper plan for the maintenance and education of the said . . . Infants and also . . . enquire with whom and under whose care the said Infants should remain during their minority' (*Medwin (1913)* 474–7).

The decree followed the judgment that S.'s principles would lead him 'to recommend, to those whose opinions and habits he may take upon himself to form, that conduct . . . as moral and virtuous which the law calls upon me to consider as immoral and vicious' (quoted in *Dowden Life* ii 90). 'No words can express the anguish he felt', Mary S. wrote of S. in her notes to his poems of 1819, 'when his elder children were torn from him. In his first resentment against the Chancellor, on the passing of the decree, he had written a curse, in which there breathes, besides haughty indignation, all the tenderness of a

¶ *130.2. took out an*] took an *Forman 1876–7, Woodberry 1893, Hutchinson, 1975.*
¶ *131. Title.* To the [Lord Chancellor] *Harvard Nbk;* [To L★★d E★★★n] To ——— *Houghton MS.*

father's love, which could imagine and fondly dwell upon its loss and the consequences' (*1839* iii 207–8). 'He was pre-eminently an affectionate father', as Peacock records (*Peacock Works* viii 70), and he never gave up the hope of recovering his children (see letters of 23–4 January 1819 and 17 February 1821, *L* ii 75, 264–5). John Scott, Earl of Eldon, Lord Chancellor from 1801, was one of S.'s chief aversions. According to Peacock S. used to recall his early ordeals at Eton 'with feelings of abhorrence which I never heard him express in equal degree in relation to any other subject, except when he spoke of Lord Chancellor Eldon' (*Peacock Works* viii 52).

The poem is drafted in the middle of *Nbk 15*, which must otherwise have remained empty for three years, as its other contents all date 1820–21. However, other more private poems are found similarly embedded in later material (e.g. Nos. 127–8). The number of transcripts in Mary S.'s hand is less confusing than at first appears (though at least one remains untraced). It can be proved that the text in S.'s hand in the *Harvard Nbk* is a revision derived immediately from his own draft; consequently all Mary S.'s copies, including that from which the present text is taken, must depend, directly or indirectly, on the *Harvard Nbk*, her variants from it being either inadvertencies or misreadings or both, and they are generally ignored in the notes below. S. must have found his almost finished 1817 draft when he began to use *Nbk 15* again in summer 1820, and revised it then into the *Harvard Nbk*, from which Mary S. made the transcript which S. corrected for the press and sent to be published on 10 November (*L* ii 246). This finding of the draft after three years may be why Mary S. added, in her note quoted above, that this poem and 'To William Shelley' 'were not written to exhibit the pangs of distress to the public' but 'spontaneous outbursts' of one compelled to express his feelings in art. In his letter to Ollier S. speaks only of enclosing one poem for adding to the second edition of *The Cenci* ('I . . . have marked the Poem I mean by a cross'), but two poems are on the sheet so marked, and 'Corpses are cold in the tomb' was probably the one intended. The texts printed by Mary S. in *1839* and *1840* are from her transcript in Bod. MS Shelley adds.d.9, which in turn is closely related to that in the Brotherton Library, Leeds University (a further transcript is now in the Berg Collection of the New York Public Library, OYD MS 740); but her only transcript to have authority is the one amended for publication by S. himself.

Text from Houghton f. MS Eng 822 (1).
Published in *1839* iii 208–9 (lines 17–36, 49–52, 57–60); *1840* 252 (complete incl. deleted stanza); *Massey* 231–7 (transcript of draft).

> Thy country's curse is on thee, darkest Crest
> Of that foul, knotted, many-headed worm
> Which rends our mother's bosom!–Priestly Pest!
> Masked Resurrection of a buried form!

2. *worm*] Hydra Snake *draft canc.*

4. *buried form*] Identified by Mary S. in a note in *1840* as 'The Star Chamber', which before 1640 could impose sentences outside the courts of law; but Carl

5   Thy country's curse is on thee—Justice sold,
     Truth trampled, Nature's landmarks overthrown,
     And heaps of fraud-accumulated gold
     Plead, loud as thunder, at destruction's throne.

     And whilst that sure, slow Fate which ever stands
10   Watching the beck of Mutability
     Delays to execute her high commands
     And, though a nation weeps, spares thine and thee—

     O let a father's curse be on thy soul
     And let a daughter's hope be on thy tomb,
15   Be both, on thy grey head, a leaden cowl
     To weigh thee down to thine approaching doom.

     I curse thee! By a parent's outraged love, —
     By hopes long cherished and too lately lost, —
     By gentle feelings thou couldst never prove,
20   By griefs which thy stern nature never crossed;

     By those infantine smiles of happy light
     Which were a fire within a stranger's hearth
     Quenched even when kindled, in untimely night
     Hiding the promise of a lovely birth—

25   By those unpractised accents of young speech
     Which he who is a father thought to frame

Woodring, noting S.'s 'Priestly Pest', sees a reference to a 'threatened resurrection specifically of the ecclesiastical High Commission of Elizabeth's reign'
(*Politics in English Romantic Poetry* (Cambridge, Mass. 1970) 253).
6. Youth blasted, Age dishonoured, Faith *draft canc.*
7. *fraud-accumulated gold*] At his death in 1838 Lord Eldon left a fortune of over
half a million pounds].
9. *Fate which ever*] Angel which aye *Harvard Nbk canc.*
9–11. Recalling *Lycidas* 130–1: 'But that two-handed engine at the door, /
Stands ready to smite once, and smite no more'. Between stanzas 3–4, *draft* has:
              Thy countrys curse is on thee . . . Freedom store
              Thy mitre & the bloody cross away
              That decent dust yet hide thy path of gore
              Through the delusions of this later day
14. *a daughter's*] Eliza Ianthe S. was nearly four years old. S. had not known
Charles, born after the separation.
18. *too lately*] untimely *Harvard Nbk canc.*; *draft.*
19. *prove*] experience.
21–4. First canc. then marked 'Insert this!' in *Houghton MS.*
22. *a stranger's hearth*] Since the separation, care of S.'s children had been
deputed to the Rev. John Kelsall at Warwick, who was not known to S.
25–8.   By those pure accents, which at my command
              Should have been framed to love & lore divine—

To gentlest lore, such as the wisest teach—
   Thou strike the lyre of mind!—oh, grief and shame!

   By all the happy see in children's growth,
30   That undeveloped flower of budding years—
   Sweetness and sadness interwoven both,
     Source of the sweetest hopes, the saddest fears—

   By all the days under a hireling's care
     Of dull constraint and bitter heaviness—
35   Oh, wretched ye, if any ever were—
     Sadder than orphans—why not fatherless?

   By the false cant which on their innocent lips
     Must hang like poison on an opening bloom,
   By the dark creeds which cover with eclipse
40   Their pathway from the cradle to the tomb—

   By thy complicity with lust and hate:
     Thy thirst for tears—thy hunger after gold—

     Now like a lute fretted by some rude hand,
     Uttering harsh discords—they must echo thine
                     Harvard Nbk canc.

After line 28, *draft* has:
     By thy smooth slaves who will be thy successors
     And by thy fellow [   ] who would be thee
     [A senate of impostors & oppressors]
     Whose words are serpents tangled cunningly

35. if any ever] Houghton MS, *Draft*; if ever any *other transcripts.* Perhaps an unnoticed slip.

36. why not fatherless?] yet not fatherless *draft and other transcripts; changed by S. in Houghton MS.* The change adds another twist to the irony: 'since they are to lose their father, why not execute him?'

37–40.   By thy dark creed of thee & of thy crew
     With which thou dost infect the infant mind
     A tender flower fed upon poison dew
     That scatters stench, not fragrance, on the wind *draft canc.*

Between lines 40–1 *Houghton MS* (also in other transcripts) has an additional stanza, struck through by S. and marked 'dele' (= delete):
     By thy most impious Hell, and all its terror
     By all the grief, the madness, & the guilt
     Which (*for* Of] thine impostures, which must be their error
     That sand on which thy crumbling Power is built

41. complicity with lust] S. implies that if he had taken Mary Godwin as his mistress while keeping Harriet as his wife the law would not have penalized him.

42. thirst for tears] i.e. sadistic judgements.

The ready frauds which ever on thee wait—
The servile arts in which thou hast grown old—
45 By thy most killing sneer, and by thy smile—
By all the snares and nets of thy black den;
And—(for thou canst outweep the crocodile)—
By thy false tears—those millstones braining men—

By all the hate which checks a father's love,
50 By all the scorn which kills a father's care,
By those most impious hands which dared remove
Nature's high bounds—by thee—and by despair—

Yes—the despair which bids a father groan
And cry—'My children are no longer mine—
55 'The blood within their veins may be mine own
'But, Tyrant, their polluted souls are thine;—'

I curse thee, though I hate thee not.—O, slave!
If thou couldst quench that earth-consuming Hell
Of which thou art a daemon, on thy grave
60 This curse should be a blessing—Fare thee well!

132 'Maiden / Thy delightful eyne'

The difficult draft interrupts *L&C* II in *Nbk 2* ff. 50–1, and is therefore datable to April 1817 (see headnote to *L&C*). The lines are mainly in pencil with some corrections in ink, and are mostly cancelled, although possibly S. intended to revise them (cp. the heavy cancellations in the 'Mont Blanc' draft). The lines begin in what seems a clear pattern of indentation, and the first line may represent an undecided form 'My . . . Maiden'; but no firm conclusions about the intended stanza form are possible because of the confusion and illegibility

46. And by the jackalls of thy deadly den *draft*.
47–8. Eldon was notorious for weeping in court (see *Mask of Anarchy* 1/ -17).
millstones] A combination of *Matthew* xviii 6: 'whoso shall offend one of these little ones which believe in me, it were better for him. 'ot a millstone were hanged about his neck', and *Troilus and Cressida* I ii 143–5: 'Pa.. · But there was such laughing! Queen Hecuba laughed, that her eyes ran o'er. *Cressida*. With millstones'.
51. When Christians with their impious hands remove *draft*.
52. Nature's high bounds] Nature's laws, such as parenthood.
56. souls are] Houghton MS, *1840*; soul is *all other transcripts and draft*.
58–9. Changed to the present reading in *Harvard Nbk* from: 'If thou couldst quench that ever-blazing Hell / Within thee, ere thou crawlest to thy grave'.

of S.'s draft and corrections (the pencil has grown very faint). The poem (if not dramatic) is presumably biographical in its reference, about either Fanny Godwin or Harriet S.; the theme appears actually to be death. No anniversaries were near at the time of composition, except Claire's birthday; the poem is conceivably a dramatic conception, as from Byron to Claire (S. wrote to Byron on 23 April; *L* i 539–40).

Text from *Nbk 2* ff. 50–1.

Published in *1975* 367–8.

> My   Maiden
> Thy delightful eyne
> That their spirit snow-laden
> Might repose on thine
> 5 The simoon to the tulip tree
> Is that which I have been to thee
> Heavily oh heavily
>
> Why is the weight not on me now
> Which thou hast not foreborne to share
> 10 Alas, I found too late the griefs
> Oh! that there had been no morrow
> To one sweet even
> Doubles not divides our sorrow
> Thou must have seen it was ruin
> 15 Thou must have known that well

¶ *132.1.* S. may have left the middle of the line blank, intending to return to it; but *my* may on the other hand be meant as an alternative to *thy* in line 2. *Maiden* is written higher on the page.

2. eyne] anguish *uncanc. draft alt.*; *1975* prints both words. The archaic plural is Spenserian.

3. snow-laden] *conj.*, possibly sorrow-laden; over-laden *1975*.

5. simoon] simoom *draft*. 'A hot, dry, suffocating sand-wind which sweeps across the African and Asiatic deserts at intervals during the spring and summer' (*OED*). The word occurs in 'A Retrospect of Times of Old' (No. 86) 25 (see also 8n.); cp. Coleridge, 'Religious Musings' (1796) 269 (the word also occurs in Byron, though not before this date). *tulip tree*] *Liriodendron tulipifera*, related to the Magnolia, and introduced into Britain in the seventeenth century. It blossoms in June and July.

8. conj.; *1975* reads two lines: [weight not on me now] / [Why is the same]. ('same' is written below 'not'.)

9. Which] To Which *draft. share*] *conj.*; *1975* reads 'show', which may be correct.

10. found too] found the too *draft. late*] Into *1975*. The line perhaps suggests a reference to Fanny Godwin.

12. even] eve *1975*.

13–14. No space may be intended, but S. starts a new page with line 14.

14. ruin] *conj.*; ?ruined *1975*.

15. that] *conj.*; it not *1975*.

> Yet thou didst sit and sing and smile
> Lifting those sweetest eyes the while
>
> The simoon to the almond blossom
> The lightning to the mountain pine
> 20 Nay worse a child that mocks the bosom
> Which feeds it, have I been to thee
> When human hopes are ever quiet
> Death, and the everlasting tomb
> Is that which I have been to thee

133 'In the yellow western sky'

This fragment is written upside-down (and cancelled) in *Nbk 2* f. 76, below a draft of *L&C* II xxxvi–xxxvii and next to a list in faint pencil reading 'Baxter Godwin Hunt Lackington Groves'. It presumably dates from around the time at which S. reached that point in *L&C*, i.e. April 1817 (see *L&C* headnote). The evocation of a waxing moon in its first quarter indicates 18–23 April; there was a new moon 17 April 1817.
Text from *Nbk 2* f. 76.
Not previously published.

> In the yellow western sky
> The horned moon is high
> The gentle south

15–16. S.'s draft indicates a definite space between these lines.
17–18. No space may be intended; the draft is interrupted by a sideways sketch of a tree.
17. sweetest] sweet *1975*.
18. almond] Written in pencil above 'desart flower', which is *canc.*; *1975* reads '[ches[t]nut flower]'. The almond tree blossoms exceptionally early, and has attracted symbolic connotations of blighted early hope; cp. *PU* II i 135 and note.
20. The line (written in pencil, and lightly *canc.* in pencil) at first read 'A child that mocks its mothers bosom'; 'its mothers' is *canc.* in ink and 'the' written above, and 'Nay worse' is written in ink above and slightly to the left of 'A child'. *1975* reads 'Nay worse / [A child that mocks the mothers bosom]'.
22. quiet] guilt *1975* (a possible reading).
23. tomb] the *draft* has two alternatives here, both *canc.*: 'grave' and 'tomb'. *1975* prints both.
¶ *133.3. gentle south*] evening *canc. draft alt.*

134 To Wilson S——th

The two holograph versions of this fragment are in *Nbk 2*, where it is embedded in the *L&C* draft of Canto I (*c.* April 1817), and in *Nbk 11*, where it is apparently an abridged copy, untitled and undatable. In *Nbk 2* S. stopped composing at Canto I stanza 25 (27 by S.'s revised numbering), postponing treatment of the Temple of the Spirit until it could be co-ordinated with that to come in Canto XII (see headnote to *L&C*), and resumed several pages later with what was then intended as the beginning of Canto II. The present fragment is pencilled on the third of the intervening pages. In theory, therefore, it could have been inserted at almost any date; but *Nbk 2* is devoted to the initial stages of composition of *L&C* and everything in it probably belongs to April–May 1817: these lines may even have been in the notebook before the draft of the major poem reached them. Except for one rhyme they are themselves in the metre of *L&C*.

In *Nbk 2*'s uncancelled title, 'Wilson' and the first letter of his presumed surname are clear; the other more elaborate sign could be Th, Tt, T, or possibly H or, as Rogers deciphered it (*1975* 366), F. S. read *The City of the Plague* (1816) by John Wilson ('Christopher North') in 1817, probably in April or May (Mary S. read it on 27 May: *Mary Jnl* i 99, 171), in preparation for the plague scenes in Canto X of *L&C*, but otherwise he had no known contact, personal or reading, with Wilson. Rogers's own dating (*1975* 366) rules out the *Blackwoods* attack on Hunt or on Keats, which did not appear until October 1817 or 1 September 1818; both attacks in any case were anonymous, and S. could not have called 'Z' a 'Fair Spirit'. Dowden's proposal of Wordsworth (*Dowden Life* ii 218n.) and White's reminder of S.'s own 'mysterious grief of 1818' (*White* ii 554) depend on the mistaken dating in *Rossetti 1870* derived from Garnett. Charles E. Robinson's advocacy of Byron (*Robinson* 263–4) also relies on too late a date as well as a faulty text, though Byron is a more plausible suggestion. The addressee must be eminent, and greatly admired, but a source of acute personal distress in the spring of 1817: cold and blind as well as 'clear'. The alternatives are either a figure hitherto unknown, or a known figure addressed under a disguised name–an expedient likely to be adopted only if the real name might be noticed, even in a private notebook, by someone to whom it would give offence or pain. Any proposed name must be conjectural, but William Godwin's fits the conditions. A letter from Godwin on 7 March 1816 had caused feelings in S. 'so bitter & so excruciating' that in future he would have to avoid the issues that aroused them (*L* i 460). Relations improved following S.'s remarriage on 30 December 1816, but remained tense, and some further dispute while Godwin was his guest at Marlow from 2–6 April 1817 might have driven S. out into the garden to cool off. Both Godwin and S. used pseudonyms: Godwin published in the Juvenile Library as 'Edward Baldwin', and returned one cheque to S. (in 1816?) with the words: 'You may make it payable to Joseph Hume or James Martin, or any other name in the whole directory' (*Dowden Life* i 538). S. called himself 'Jones' in 1820 (*L* ii 179). The advantage of a formula such as 'Wilson S——th' is that it would seem to be protecting some real person while not applying to any real acquaintance. The title 'City of the Plague' is inscribed inside the front cover of *Nbk 2*, and the author's surname (or possibly of Falkland's physician in Godwin's *Caleb Williams*) may have seemed convenient to borrow.

The *Nbk 11* version is almost certainly the later, but the earlier has been preferred below for its fuller text and its title. Punctuation at the line-endings, and after *miscreeds* and *clear*, has been added.

Text from *Nbk 2* f. 36.

Published in *Rossetti 1870* 312–13 (from *Nbk 11* f. 24 via Garnett, dated 1818); *1975* 319 (from *Nbk 11*), 366 (from *Nbk 2*).

> My head is wild with weeping for a grief
> Which is the shadow of a gentle mind –
> I walk into the air, yet no relief
> I seek, or haply if I sought should find:
> 5 It comes uncalled – the woes of humankind,
> Their actual miscreeds, their false belief –
> Fair Spirit, thou art cold as clear and blind
> As beautiful

135 Otho

In her notes to the Poems of 1817 Mary S. wrote: 'He had this year also projected a poem on the subject of Otho, inspired by the pages of Tacitus' (*1839* iii 70). However it is not impossible that the 'Otho' draft, which interrupts that of *R&H* between lines 239 and 240, was written in 1816, as *R&H* 40–73 (see headnote) and 'Mont Blanc' were. But it is more likely that the writing of *R&H* was resumed from line 73 in September 1817 after the completion of *L&C*, and S. had to skip the draft of 'Otho', which could have been abandoned just as serious work began on *L&C*. The stanzas appear in the draft in the order 4, 5, 1 (with title), 2, 3, 6, 7; if the order assumed below is correct, S. must have turned back beyond stanza 1 of 'Otho' on f. 25 in order to add stanzas 4 and 5 on f. 24, and *R&H* 239–40 could not have then existed. 'Otho' then probably

¶ *134.3. yet*] but *Nbk 11*.
4–7. To seek, or haply if I sought to find –
It comes unsought . . . for wonder that a chief
Like thee, mid spirits, should be cold & blind
And *Nbk 11*

dates from early summer 1817 (there is a detailed sketch of a may-fly on f. 26). Otho's story is in Tacitus, *Histories* I xxi–II l, Suetonius, *On the Lives of the Caesars* VII, and Plutarch's *Lives*. After Nero's assassination in A.D. 68, his successor Servius Galba was quickly eliminated on the orders of Marcus Otho, but the latter's rule was contested by Aulus Vitellius, and the Roman people lamented 'that two men, the worst in the world for their shamelessness, indolence, and profligacy, had been apparently chosen by fate to ruin the empire' (Tacitus, *Hist.* I l). But after many atrocities and a military setback at the Battle of Bedriacum, although Otho could still have triumphed in the end, he stabbed himself in order to avoid any more civil bloodshed, declaring: 'Others may cling to the imperial power longer, no one shall relinquish it more bravely. Do you want me to allow so much Roman youth, such fine armies, to be struck down and torn from the community?' (*Hist.* II xlvii). S. saw a parallel here with his own oppressive times (lines 21–4), and a faint hope that England's rulers might themselves find the magnanimity to surrender power in order to spare their people the horrors of revolution. The ink draft is very difficult, except for the two last stanzas, and some readings are doubtful. All five pages of draft are cancelled by vertical strokes.

Text from *Nbk 1* ff. 24–8 (cancelled).

Published in *1839* iii 70–1 (lines 38–53); *Relics* 75 (lines 17–24), 76 (lines 9–10); *1975* 315–16 (complete except for lines 25–9, 54).

> The mistress and the monitress of Earth
> Had fallen—her throne was vacant, and upon
> Its paltry footstool, in unnatural mirth,
> Robed royally, a sceptred skeleton
> 5 Smiled at its praise.—The voice whose mastery
> Was empire, virtue, greatness, now was gone—
> Numbered among what things sad Memory
> Once having noted cannot cease to be.
>
> Dark is the realm of grief—but human things
> 10 Those may not know who cannot weep for them.
> Sadness is joy's sweet mother, for she brings
> Such gentle looks as render vain, and stem
> Power's hard and heartless triumph—we retrieve
> The good that is gone by while we condemn

¶ 135.2. *her throne was vacant*] 'Progenies Caesarum in Nerone defecit': 'The race of Caesars ended with Nero' (Suetonius, *De Vita Caesarum* VII i).
3. paltry] painted *1975*.
4. a sceptred skeleton] Servius Galba, proclaimed emperor at the age of 72, was liquidated by Otho within a year.
5. its] i.e. the skeleton's. The *draft* reads: 'Grinned from beneath its crown'. *The voice*] Of Rome at its greatest. *mastery*] mystery *1975*.
7. sad] our *1975*.

15 Ourselves in frail humanity, and grieve
    That much is past which it did once achieve.

    Those whom nor power, nor lying faith, nor toil,
    Nor custom–queen of many slaves–makes blind
    Have ever grieved that man should be the spoil
20 Of his own weakness, and with earnest mind
    Fed hopes of his redemption–these recur
    Chastened by doubtful victory now, and find
    Foundations in this foulest age, that stir
    Me whom they cheer to be their minister. –
    [
                                              ]
25 The peaceful funeral pile–the mighty sound
    Of hymns to faith and freedom–racks that tell
    Degraded woman's greatness, the dread bound
    Of life and death passed fearlessly and well,
    And what may else be irresistible.

30 Such thoughts, befitting well a parent's bier,
    Are mine of Rome, when although desolate
    Its genius yet delayed to disappear–
    Even while each palace, fane and trophied gate
    Showed like its tomb. – What still inhabited
35 Fallen greatness–even the record of its state, –
    Looks like some image wandering from the dead
    To say that [   ]

18. *custom–queen of many slaves–*] Pindar, Fragm. 169: 'νόμος ὁ πάντων
βασιλεὺς / θνατῶν τε καὶ ἀθανάτων': 'Custom, king of all things, of mortals
and immortals'. But S. probably took his version from Montaigne, whose
Essays he had finished reading 'to his great sorrow' on 10 November 1816
(*Mary Jnl* i 145): '. . . there is nothing that custom will not or cannot do; and
with reason Pindar calls her . . . the queen and empress of the world' (*Essays* I,
23).

22. *Chastened by doubtful victory now*] 'Today these hopes seem unlikely of
fulfilment'.

23. *this foulest age*] Otho's, described by Tacitus as 'ipsa etiam pace saevum',
'savage even in peace' (*Hist.* I ii).

25. About three lines are torn from the top of the MS page. Some or all of this
stanza was incorporated into *L&C* VII xxxvi.

26–7. *racks that tell . . . greatness*] Perhaps suggested by the 'glorious example' of
a Ligurian woman who, tortured to death by Otho's soldiers, steadfastly
refused to disclose her son's hiding-place (*Hist.* II xiii).

36. *Looks*] Seems 1975. A doubtful word in MS, resembling 'Soothes'.

Thou wert not, Cassius, and thou couldst not be
Last of the Romans! though thy memory claim
40 From Brutus his own glory and on thee
Rest the full splendour of his sacred fame—
Nor he who dared make the foul tyrant quail
Amid his cowering senate with thy name,
Though thou and he were great—it will avail
45 To thine own fame that Otho's should not fail.

I wrong thee not—thou wouldst if thou couldst feel
Abjure such envious fame—great Otho died
Like thee—he sanctified his country's steel,
At once the tyrant and tyrannicide,
50 In his own blood—a deed it was to bring
Tears from all men—though full of gentle pride,
Such pride as from impetuous love may spring
That will not be refused its offering. —

How Otho died, I tell.

136 'Mighty Eagle, thou that soarest'

This fragment first occurs (with later forged signatures) on the address cover of a letter from Godwin dated 29 April 1817, now in the Carl H. Pforzheimer collection ('*Pf.MS*'), and was written out again with brief continuations in *Nbk 10* (*c.* May–September 1819), and in *Nbk 17* (*c.* December 1820–March 1821) from which the concept and phrasing of lines 5–6 were used for *Hellas* 76–93. Presumably the lines were composed *c.* May 1817, but the latest version is preferred below as being also the fullest. Forman, who from *Pf.MS* first printed these lines, entitled them 'Lines to William Godwin' because of the letter they were drafted on (*Forman 1882* ii 162); Locock was told by W. M. Rossetti that the lines dated from 1819, apparently from their occurrence in

38. *Cassius*] Conspirator with his friend Brutus in attempting to save the Roman Republic by the murder of Julius Caesar. After Cassius's suicide at Philippi Brutus said that he deserved to be called the last of the Romans.
42. *he who dared*] Cremutius Cordus, who defied Tiberius and a subservient Senate when on trial for his life for praising Brutus and calling Cassius the last of the Romans in his *History* (Tacitus, *Annals* IV 3).
46. Above this stanza on f. 27 is a jotting: 'Vitellius visits the field of Battle', evidently for treatment in the poem. Vitellius was delighted by viewing the hideous relics of Bedriacum, at which he had not himself been present (*Hist.* II lxx).

Nbk 10, and identified the Eagle as Byron (Locock 1911 ii 496), followed more recently by Charles E. Robinson (Robinson 68, 259–60); Rogers identified the Eagle as Plato, on the strength of S.'s translation 'Eagle! why soarest thou above that tomb' (1975 ii 304, 381). But as Reiman concluded after discussing the eagle images in S.'s poetry (SC v 205–14) 'there is no need to suppose that "Mighty Eagle" was addressed to any particular person'. In Hellas 76–93 the Eagle is Freedom, recalling Milton's vision of a free England in Areopagitica: 'Methinks I see her as an Eagle [renewing] her mighty youth, and kindling her undazzled eyes at the full mid-day beam'; in 'Ode to Liberty' 6–11 the Eagle is the Imagination, and this fragment as well as the Ode may have been influenced by Goethe's lyric 'Harzreise im Winter' (1777), a translation of which (possibly by John Gisborne, or even by Shelley) Claire Clairmont wrote into her journal under the headings May–June 1818 (SC v 455–7): 'Like the vulture on the massy clouds of Morning, resting on his soft pinions & looking down for his prey, hover thou my Song . . . With the many coloured morning thou sweetly clearest [thy poet's] bosom–thou raisest him aloft in the drifting tempest [Mit dem beizenden Sturm]. In his song torrents rush from the rocks; & the fearful verge of the snow crowned Summit which superstitious nations encircled with Spectres, to him becomes an altar of the purest devotion . . .' (1–5, 71–81). S.'s lines may also have defiant reference to Obadiah 3–4: '. . . thou that dwellest in the clefts of the rock, whose habitation is high; that saith in his heart, who shall bring me down to the ground? Though thou exalt thyself as the eagle, and though thou set thy nest among the stars, thence will I bring thee down, saith the Lord.'
Text from Nbk 17 f. 139 rev.
Published in Forman 1882 ii 162 (from Pf.MS); SC v 206 (facs. 210); Huntington Nbk ii 16 (from Nbk 10).

Mighty Eagle, thou that soarest
O'er the misty mountain forest
And amid the shades of morning
Like a cloud of glory liest,
5   And when night descends, the warning
Of the embattled storm defiest:
Mighty Eagle, thou whose dwelling
Is among the precipices
And the [

¶ 136.3. shades] light Pf.MS (subst. for clouds); blaze Nbk 10.
4. liest] hiest eds.
5–6. And when night descends defiest / The embattled tempests warning Pf.MS. Nbk 10.
6. Pf.MS ends with line 6.
7–8. Leaves thy [   ] habitation / On the verge of desolation Nbk 10.

137 'I visit thee but thou art sadly changed'

These scribbled lines are distributed over four pages of *Nbk 3*, which contains material belonging to summer 1817, interrupting the draft of *L&C* at IX xxxi 5. S. told Hunt on 3 August (*L* i 551) that he had arrived at the 380th stanza of his poem; by his numbering in the notebook this was Canto X xxix. If composition averaged three stanzas a day, the interruption came at about 24 July 1817, which is a possible date. All visitors had finally left Albion House, and S. went alone to Virginia Water and to Egham between 23 and 31 July (*Mary Jnl* i 177). Both were very near Bishopsgate, where he had lived with Mary in 1815, and not far from Bracknell, where he had lived with Harriet and with the Boinvilles. On f. 130, following the verse, is a draft advertisement for a house-exchange: 'Wanted to purchase by exchange for an equivalent secured on a large property in England, a villa in the neighbourhood of Naples'. S. first mentioned a possible move to Italy in a letter to Byron of 9 July (*L* i 547). However, the lines may have been embedded in the notebook before the *L&C* draft reached them. Between the two fragments, which are three pages apart, are these scrawled jottings (which are difficult to decipher, but seem to read):

> The pine is here
> The sky where the moon was
> The grass the hawthorn
>   blooming now

*   *   *   *   *

> The last scene too with her
> there Colerigdes &c

> And each dreadful remorse
> afterwards–telling a
>   truer & more sorrowful
> truth.

If this is reminiscence and not a projected poem, 'the hawthorn blooming now' would rule out July but suggests 26–9 May 1817 when S. returned alone to Marlow from London by boat (*Mary L* i 36), passing Egham within easy reach of Bishopsgate on the edge of Windsor Forest (line 9). S. who had rented the Bishopsgate house until 3 August 1816 had thought of re-renting it after his summer in Switzerland, but was told it had been sold for demolition and enlargement (*L* i 490, 493). Apparently it was not demolished, but stood empty for a long time; and either the state of the house or the finding of S.'s lines in *Nbk 3* could have suggested Mary S.'s later description of 'Perdita's' former home on the same spot in *The Last Man* (1824):

> A slight circumstance induced me . . . to return home by Egham and Bishopsgate. I alighted at Perdita's ancient abode, her cottage . . . This spot,

dedicated to sweetest recollections, the deserted house and neglected garden were well adapted to nurse my melancholy . . . It was now in ruin . . . The sky was blue above . . . The trees moved overhead . . . but the melancholy appearance of the choaked paths, and weed-grown flower beds, dimmed even this gay summer scene. The time when in proud and happy security we assembled at this cottage, was gone–

(ch. vii; ed. H. J. Luke (Lincoln Nebraska 1965) 186)

The two passages could be unconnected, though they are in the same pencilled scrawl. The MS punctuation has been followed unaltered.

Text from *Nbk 3* ff. 126–7, 129a.

Published in *1975* 371–2.

I visit thee but thou art sadly changed
Thy former home is now made desolate
It has become the path of homeless winds
The moon and stars and sun find entrance there
5 For their tired beams where once this busy heart
From many beatings, and in many thoughts
After its wanderings found a brief years [   ]
And I am changed, and many things are changed
The Earth the Forests and the Sky remain
10 These things remain
And unforgiving memories linger there
Which heap forth sorrow

    ★   ★   ★   ★   ★

One was a homeless cloud–the other rested
Upon a pinnacle of mountain snow
15 So pure and beautiful, that time who hasted
With his swift footstep
Passed over it and left no ruin there
But cold–too cold

¶ *137.1. I visit thee*] The same words end the fragment 'Dear Home', but this cannot be a continuation because of line 7.

2. Thy] The pronouns in line 1 seem addressed to the home, this to its occupant.

3. homeless winds] Coleridge called Freedom 'the guide of homeless winds' in 'France: an Ode' (1798), one of S.'s favourite poems.

7. a brief years] S. may have intended an adjective before *brief* or a noun after *year's*. S. had rented the Bishopsgate house for one year from 3 August 1815, but quitted it finally in May 1816.

13. One] *Canc. in MS, perhaps for* Thou (?Thine). Possibly the two clouds refer to Claire Clairmont and Mary S. (cp. *L&C* II xxiii).

15. So pure and beautiful] S. wrote later of Mrs Boinville 'Nothing earthly appeared to me more perfect than her character and manners', but he thought

138 Marianne's Dream

Mary S.'s transcript of this poem (Harvard MS 258.3, identified below as *Harvard*) is dated 'Marlow May–1817', and the poem presumably describes a real dream of Marianne Hunt's while she and her husband Leigh Hunt were staying with S. at Albion House between 10 April and 25 June 1817. As it is uncertain how much S. invented, interpretation is not feasible, but certain dream-materials can be recognized. 'He used to sit in a study adorned with casts, as large as life, of the Vatican Apollo and the celestial Venus', Hunt wrote of S. at this time (*Hunt Autobiography* ch. xv), and at the end of her stay Marianne scraped and scrubbed these plaster statues (*Mary Jnl* i 175) so as to restore them to a 'milky whiteness' (*Mary L* i 38). The poem contains echoes of Spenser's *Faerie Queene* Bk II which S. had been reading aloud during May, including the word *sheen* (line 10), S.'s only use of this adjective. Nonnus, *Dionysiaca* vi 206–388, describes how Zeus first burns, then drowns, the earth. S. ordered this poem only on 7 December 1817, and again (not having obtained it) on 23 December (*L* i 585), but Peacock may already have interested the Marlow circle in it.

The descent of the texts is hard to determine; but *Harvard* was possibly Mary S.'s transcript of S.'s (lost) draft, which would explain the lack of line-ending punctuation. The poem was not intended for publication. The MS given to Marianne Hunt was copied from this copy, again by Mary S. to judge from the printer's error at line 62; but S. must have overseen it (lines 80, 109). Eighteen months later, in a letter of 12 November 1818, Leigh Hunt wrote to S. in Italy: 'I have been writing a *Pocket-Book* . . . It . . . contains original poetry, among which I have taken the liberty ("Hunt is too ceremonious sometimes") of putting Marianne's *Dream* to the great delight of said Marianne, not to mention its various MS. readers' (*Hunt Correspondence* i 125). S. replied: 'As to my little poem, I can only lament that it is not more worthy of the lady whose name it bears' (*L* ii 65). It appeared in Hunt's *Literary Pocket-Book; or, Companion for the Lover of Nature and Art for 1819* (1818) 218–22 (identified below as *LPB*) over the signature 'Δ'. The MS probably served as printer's copy and is lost, and the printed accidentals are largely editorial, so punctuation has been revised from *Harvard*, which also may preserve correct readings in lines 62, 72, 91. The *1824* text was printed from *LPB* and is ignored in the collation.

Text from *LPB for 1819* 218–22.

Published in *LPB for 1819* 218–22; *1824* 123–8.

---

her too subtle-minded 'to be quite sincere and constant' (to Peacock, 6 April 1819, *L* ii 92).

15–17. time who hasted . . . no ruin there] S. called Mrs Boinville 'Maimuna, from Southey's *Thalaba*: "Her face was as a damsel's face / And yet her hair was grey." She was a young-looking woman for her age, and her hair was as white as snow' (*Peacock Works* viii 74).

A pale dream came to a Lady fair,
   And said, A boon, a boon, I pray—
I know the secrets of the air,
   And things are lost in the glare of day
5 Which I can make the sleeping see
   If they will put their trust in me.

And thou shalt know of things unknown
   If thou wilt let me rest between
The veiny lids whose fringe is thrown
10   Over thine eyes so dark and sheen:
And half in hope and half in fright
The Lady closed her eyes so bright.

At first all deadly shapes were driven
   Tumultuously across her sleep,
15 And o'er the vast cope of bending heaven
   All ghastly-visaged clouds did sweep;
And the Lady ever looked to spy
If the golden sun shone forth on high.

And as towards the east she turned
20   She saw aloft in the morning air
Which now with hues of sunrise burned
   A great black anchor rising there;
And wherever the Lady turned her eyes
It hung before her in the skies.

25 The sky was as blue as the summer sea,
   The depths were cloudless overhead,
The air was calm as it could be,
   There was no sight or sound of dread
But that black anchor floating still
30 Over the piny eastern hill.

The Lady grew sick with a weight of fear
   To see that anchor ever hanging,
And veiled her eyes; she then did hear
   The sound as of a dim low clanging,
35 And looked abroad if she might know
Was it aught else, or but the flow
Of the blood in her own veins to and fro.

There was a mist in the sunless air
   Which shook as it were with an earthquake's shock,

¶ *138.10. sheen*] shining.
25. *was as blue*] was blue *1824* (a misprint), *eds.*

40 But the very weeds that blossomed there
    Were moveless, and each mighty rock
Stood on its basis steadfastly;
    The anchor was seen no more on high.

But piled around, with summits hid
45   In lines of cloud at intervals,
Stood many a mountain pyramid
    Among whose everlasting walls
Two mighty cities shone, and ever
Through the red mist their domes did quiver.

50 On two dread mountains, from whose crest
    Might seem the eagle for her brood
Would ne'er have hung her dizzy nest,
    Those tower-encircled cities stood.
A vision strange, such towers to see
55 Sculptured and wrought so gorgeously
    Where human art could never be.

And columns framed of marble white,
    And giant fanes dome over dome
Piled, and triumphant gates, all bright
60   With workmanship which could not come
From touch of mortal instrument,
Shot o'er the vales a lustre lent
From its own shapes magnificent.

But still the Lady heard that clang
65   Filling the wide air far away;
And still the mist whose light did hang
    Among the mountains shook alway,
So that the Lady's heart beat fast
As half in joy, and half aghast
70 On those high domes her look she cast.

Sudden, from out that city sprung
    A light which made the earth grow red;
Two flames, that each with quivering tongue
    Licked its high domes and overhead

57–63. *And columns . . . magnificent*] i.e. the columns, fanes, and gates radiated a lustre deriving from workmanship that cannot have been human.
62. *vales a lustre*] *Harvard*; vales, or lustre *LPB*, eds (an evident misreading of Mary S.'s indefinite article).
63. *its*] the workmanship's.
71. *that city*] i.e. the city at which she was looking.
72. *light which*] *Harvard*; light that *LPB*, eds (probably an error induced by *that* in both previous and following lines).

75   Among those mighty towers and fanes
      Dropped fire, as a volcano rains
      Its sulphurous ruin on the plains.

      And hark! a rush, as if the deep
          Had burst its bonds; she looked behind
80   And saw over the western steep
          A raging flood descend and wind
      Through that wide vale; she felt no fear
      But said within herself, 'Tis clear
          These towers are Nature's own, and she
85   To save them has sent forth the sea.

      And now those raging billows came
          Where that fair Lady sate, and she
      Was borne towards the showering flame
          By the wild waves heaped tumultuously,
90   And on a little plank, the flow
      Of the whirlpools bore her to and fro.

      The flames were fiercely vomited
          From every tower and every dome,
      And dreary light did widely shed
95   O'er that vast flood's suspended foam
      Beneath the smoke which hung its night
      On the stained cope of heaven's light.

      The plank whereon that Lady sate
          Was driven through the chasms about and about
100   Between the peaks so desolate
          Of the drowning mountains in and out,
      As the thistle beard on a whirlwind sails,
      While the flood was filling those hollow vales.

      At last her plank an eddy crossed
105   And bore her to the city's wall

80. *western*] *LPB*, eastern *Harvard; 1975*. The *LPB* reading must represent a
correction of *Harvard*, as the Lady has been facing east (line 19) and now looks
behind her.
91. *whirlpools*] *Harvard*; whirlpool *LPB, eds*. The plural ending was more likely
lost than added accidentally; also 'to and fro' suggests several conflicting
currents.
92. *flames*] waves *LPB, Harvard*. Although both texts read 'the waves', 'Nothing . . . can well be clearer than that we should here read "the flames" . . .
Even if the general context did not dictate this emendation, the necessity of
finding some adequate nominative for the clause "did shed light" would
demand it' (*Rossetti 1870* ii 559). The water does not reach the cities until lines
105–6.

Which now the flood had reached almost;
  It might the stoutest heart appal
To hear the fire roar and hiss
  Through the domes of those mighty palaces.

110 The eddy whirled her round and round
  Before a gorgeous gate, which stood
Piercing the clouds of smoke, which bound
  Its aery arch with light like blood;
She looked on that gate of marble clear
115 With wonder that extinguished fear.

For it was filled with sculptures rarest
  Of forms most beautiful and strange,
Like nothing human, but the fairest
  Of winged shapes, whose legions range
120 Throughout the sleep of those that are,
Like this same Lady, good and fair.

And as she looked, still lovelier grew
  Those marble forms;–the sculptor sure
Was a strong spirit, and the hue
125 Of his own mind did there endure
After the touch whose power had braided
Such grace was in some sad change faded.

She looked, the flames were dim, the flood
  Grew tranquil as a woodland river
130 Winding through hills in solitude;
  Those marble shapes then seemed to quiver
And their fair limbs to float in motion
Like weeds unfolding in the ocean.

And their lips moved;–one seemed to speak,
135 When suddenly the mountains cracked
And through the chasm the flood did break
  With an earth-uplifting cataract:
The statues gave a joyous scream
And on its wings the pale thin dream
140 Lifted the Lady from the stream.

The dizzy flight of that phantom pale
  Waked the fair Lady from her sleep

109. domes] rifts Harvard uncanc. alternative. mighty] rifted Harvard uncanc.
alternative.
124–7. the hue . . . change faded] i.e. the impress of the sculptor's genius outlasted
the physical powers that had shaped the marble. Cp. 'Ozymandias' 4–8.
138. gave] Omitted Harvard.

And she arose, while from the veil
Of her dark eyes the dream did creep,
145   And she walked about as one who knew
That sleep has sights as clear and true
As any waking eyes can view.

139   'The billows on the beach are leaping around it'

Mary S. printed parts of this poem, without title, in her notes to S.'s poems of 1819 in *1839* and *1840*, explaining how

> At one time, while the question was still pending, the Chancellor had said some words that seemed to intimate that Shelley should not be permitted the care of any of his children, and for a moment he feared that our infant son would be torn from us. He did not hesitate to resolve, if such were menaced, to abandon country, fortune, everything, and to escape with his child; and I found some unfinished stanzas addressed to this son . . . written under the idea that we might suddenly be forced to cross the sea, so to preserve him.
>
> (*1839* iii 209)

There were no developments in the Chancery case between Lord Eldon's judgment and decree (see headnote to No. 131) and the report of the Master (1 August) recommending that the children should stay with the Rev. Kendall, the Westbrooks' nominee, so the words that came to alarm S. must have been in the initial judgment—possibly in Eldon's expressed concern to protect 'those whose opinions and habits [S.] may take upon himself to form', words that could be understood to include any children S. might have, such as the 'several illegitimate children' the formal decree attributed to him. In a letter of 23 April (*L* i 539–40) S. told Byron he was living at Marlow with his 'accustomed tranquillity and happiness', but by 9 July he had taken fright: '. . . it may become necessary that I should quit the country. It is possible that the interference exercised by Chancery in the instance of my two other children might be attempted to be extended to William' (*L* i 547). Perhaps Mary's pregnancy with Clara (lines 18–19) had made him unduly nervous. It is likely, therefore, that the poem was written in July 1817. It is a draft only, superimposed on the pencil draft of the 'Verses . . . on . . . a Celandine' (No. 117), but it does not seem unfinished. All known transcripts and texts derive from this draft in *Nbk 1*, one detached page of which (from between ff. 62–3 of the notebook) is now in *Box 1*. The familiar title 'To William Shelley' was conferred by Rossetti (*Rossetti 1870*); neither S. nor Mary S. ever gave it a title. Some punctuation has been supplied.

Text from *Nbk 1* ff. 39–42, 63–4 (lines 1–52); and *Box 1* f. 63ʳ (lines 53–62). Published in *1839* iii 209–10 (lines 1–8, 33–52); *1840* 253 (lines 1–52); *Relics* 77 (lines 53–8, with addn. lines for 55–8); *1975* 311 (with alt. addn. lines for 55–9); *Massey* 298–303 (full transcript of draft).

The billows on the beach are leaping around it,
The bark is weak and frail. –
The sea looks black and the clouds that bound it
Darkly strew the gale–
5 Come with me, delightful child!
Come with me though the wave is wild
And the winds are loud–we must not stay
Or the slaves of law may rend thee away.

They have taken thy brother and sister–dear,
10 They have made them unfit for thee:
They have withered the smile, and dried the tear
Which should have been sacred to me;
To a blighting faith, and a cause of crime
They have bound them slaves in a youthly time,
15 And they will curse my name and thee
Because we fearless are and free.

Come thou, beloved as thou art. –
Another sleepeth still
Near thy sweet mother's anxious heart
20 Which thou with joy wilt fill,
With fairest smiles of wonder thrown
On that which is indeed our own
And which in distant lands will be
The dearest playmate unto thee.

25 Fear not the tyrants will rule for ever
Or the priests of the evil faith,
They stand on the brink of that raging river
Whose waves they have tainted with death;
It is fed from the depths of a thousand dells,
30 Around them it foams and roars and swells–
And their swords and their sceptres I floating see
Like wrecks on the surge of eternity.

¶ *139.3. sea . . . bound it*] MS *canc.*
7. loud] loose *1839, 1840, eds.*
9. sister–dear,] sister–dear *MS*; sister dear, *1840.* S.'s dash seems meant to detach
the adjective from William's brother and sister.
11. dried] MS *canc.*
13. a cause of crime] i.e. the opposite of 'a good cause'.
14. in a youthly] in an youthly *MS*; in youthly *1840, eds.*
17. Come thou,] Come, thou *MS.*
18. Another] Clara S., born 2 September 181⁷.
21. fairest] MS *canc.*
25–32. These lines, slightly modified, were used in *R&H* 894–901.

Rest, rest, shriek not, thou gentle child,
The rocking of the boat thou fearest
35 And the cold spray and the clamour wild—
There sit between us two, thou dearest,
Me and thy mother; well we know
The storm at which thou tremblest so,
With all its dark and hungry graves,
40 Less cruel than the savage slaves
Who hunt thee o'er these sheltering waves.

Sometime this hour will live in thee
A dream of days forgotten long;
We soon shall dwell by the azure sea
45 Of serene and golden Italy,
Or Greece the mother of the free,
And I will teach thine infant tongue
To call upon those heroes old
In their own language—and will mould
50 Thy growing spirit in the flame
Of Grecian lore, that by such name
A patriot's birthright thou mayst claim.

Mild thoughts of man's ungentle race
Shall our contented exile reap—
55 For who, that in some happy place
His own free thoughts can freely chase
By words and waves, can clothe his face

41. thee] us *Massey*.
48. those] their *Massey*.
51. by such name] i.e. by invoking the 'heroes old'.
54. For our beloved country soon *MS uncanc. alt.*
55. Beginning at this line S. twice attempted a revised ending:

(a) The cynic starts from Pride's embrace
And smiles in Miserys withered face
But thou and I sweet Child will weep
The woes we share not—that mad war
[Whose waves we then shall hear afar
Which the world wages]

(b) The world is now our dwellingplace—
Where'er the earth one fading trace
Of what was great & free, doth keep
That is our home—[& waves] & wood
[And bright sea sands & rocks & caves
And sculptured ruins vast] & grey
And our [own thoughts shall make us two]

In cynic smiles? Child! we shall weep–
'Twill be the balm of soothing tears
60 Like memories of delightful years
When, mourning for the world's strange war,
We feel how meek and calm we are.

140 Translated from an Epigram of Plato, cited in the *Apologia* of Apuleius

This epigram, which was incorporated into *L&C* (IX xxxvi 5–8), is found in S.'s draft for that passage (*Nbk 3* f. 134), and in a transcript by Mary S. (Harvard MS Eng.258.3) to which she gave the present title. She never printed her transcript, which was in a notebook given to Claire Clairmont, and it remained unpublished until 1925. Although S. identified the source of his pencil draft, in ink, as 'Apuleius', perhaps intending a footnote reference in *L&C*, the epigram is excluded from modern editions of Apuleius's *Apologia* X 24. S. probably read it in a copy of Apuleius's *Works* after finishing the same author's *Metamorphoses* (*The Golden Ass*) in May 1817 (*Mary Jnl* i 169–70). On 3 August S. told Hunt: 'I have arrived at the 380th stanza of my Poem' (*L* i 551): by his numbering in *Nbk 3* this was stanza xxix of Canto X, so assuming an overall composition-rate of 3 stanzas per day, the place of the epigram could have been reached about the last week in July. Edward A. Silsbee, who acquired the notebook from Claire Clairmont in Florence, noted below the transcript: 'Shelley came in from his study & showed them this. They were delighted–C[laire] remembers it–'. This may have happened at any time from mid-May. The Hunts were at Albion House until 25 June, and Hogg was in Marlow 26–31 July; otherwise 'they' must simply mean Mary S. and Claire herself. The metrical irregularity in the *L&C* text clearly derives from the draft in *Nbk 3* (see note below), while the corrections made to the draft suggest that the Harvard transcript preserves S.'s final version. In both *L&C* and *Harvard* S. much elaborated the original Greek (see Webb, *The Violet in the Crucible* (Oxford 1976) 133):

ἀστέρας εἰσαθρεῖς Ἀστὴρ ἐμός; εἴθε γενοίμην
οὐρανός, ὡς πολλοῖς ὄμμασιν εἰς σὲ βλέπω

(*Anth. Pal.* VII No. 669; Diogenes Laertius, *Lives of Eminent Philosophers* III sect. 29). ('You gaze at the stars, my Aster: would I were the sky, to gaze at you with many eyes'). The pun on 'Aster', a boy's name also meaning 'star', is not

60. *memories of delightful*] *MS canc.*
61. *world's strange*] *MS canc.*
62. *meek*] *MS canc.*

used by S.; the lines in *L&C* ('Fair star of life and love') are addressed to
Cythna, and here the sex of 'Sweet Child' is ambiguous.
Text from Harvard MS Eng.258.3 (facs. in *Notopoulos* 568).
Published in W. E. Peck, *The Boston Herald*, 21 December 1925, 12.

> Sweet Child, thou star of love and beauty bright,
>   Alone thou lookest on the midnight skies;
> Oh! that my spirit were yon Heaven of light
>   To gaze upon thee with a thousand eyes.

141 'Shapes about my steps assemble'

These pencilled lines are scrawled, with the page reversed, after the end of the
draft of *L&C* in *Nbk 3*, just below a comment: 'We all act a false part in the
world–'. Their despondency may reflect the illness of body and mind that S.
suffered in the late summer and autumn of 1817; and as there are verbal links
with the conclusion of *L&C* (XII xxix 8: '. . . slowly shall its memory ever
burning,' etc., and XII xxvi 2–3: 'I saw the black and half-extinguished pyre /
In its own grey and shrunken ashes lying'), this seems the likeliest time of
composition.
Text from *Nbk 3* f. 217^r.
Published in *1975* 374.

> Shapes about my steps assemble,
>   Ghosts of hope which unreturning
> And unreturned, has ceased to tremble
>   In my heart forever burning
> 5   Like a firebrand slowly dying

¶ *140.1–4.*   I cried
                  Fair star of life & love my souls delight
                  Why [gazest] lookest thou on the crystalline skies
                  O that my spirit were [that] yon Heaven of Night
                  Which gazes on thee with [its] a thousand eyes– *draft*
¶ *141.2. Ghosts of hope*] Hopes of youth *uncanc. alternative.*
3. has ceased] like spirits *canc.*
5. Like a firebrand] Recalling Shakespeare's Sonnet 73, 9–12:
                  In me thou seest the glowing of such fire,
                  That on the ashes of his youth doth lie,
                  As the death bed, whereon it must expire,
                  Consumed with that which it was nourished by.

Among its own dead ashes lying.

The winds are soft the skies are blue
  And the

8. One probably unconnected line below the fragment seems to read: *As the ivy
binds the roots of her*

Appendix A: The Order of the Poems in the Esdaile Notebook

For a somewhat different proposed chronological ordering, see *MYR* i 195–7.

Appendix B: The Order of the Poems in Shelley's Collections, 1810–1816

(i) *Original Poetry by Victor and Cazire* (1810)	*Number in this Edition*
Letter	[by Elizabeth Shelley]
Letter	[by Elizabeth Shelley]
Song. ('Cold, cold is the blast')	20. [version from *Esd*]
Song. ('Come ——! sweet is the hour,')	15.
Song. Despair	19.
Song: Sorrow	23.
Song. Hope	24.
Song. Translated from the Italian	21.
Song. Translated from the German	5.
The Irishman's Song	6.
Song ('Fierce roars the midnight storm')	9.
Song. To —— ('Ah! sweet is the moonbeam')	25.
Song. To —— ('Stern, stern is the voice')	26.
Saint Edmond's Eve	[by Elizabeth Shelley]
Revenge	8.
Ghasta; or the Avenging Demon!!!	10.
Fragment, or the Triumph of Conscience	22.

(ii) *Posthumous Fragments of Margaret Nicholson* (1810)	
Ambition, power, and avarice, now have hurled	32.
Fragment. Supposed to be an Epithalamium	33.
Despair	34.
Fragment ('Yes! all is past')	35.
The Spectral Horseman	36.
Melody to a Scene of Former Times	37.

(iii) *Alastor . . . and Other Poems* (1816)	
Alastor; or, the Spirit of Solitude	114.
'O! there are spirits of the air'	106.
Stanzas. — April, 1814	101.
Mutability	113.
'The pale, the cold, and the moony smile'	93.
A Summer-Evening Churchyard . . .	109.
To Wordsworth	111.
Feelings of a Republican . . .	112.
Superstition	[see *Q Mab* vi 72–102]
Sonnet. From the Italian of Dante	108.
Translated from the Greek of Moschus	107.
The Daemon of the World	115.

Appendix C: 'Thy dewy looks sink in my breast' and 'Thy gentle face, Priscilla dear'

GM conjectured a connection between these two stanzas, which are from quite separate sources. S. quoted 'Thy dewy looks' in his letter to Hogg of 16 March 1814 (see poem no. 98, 'Stanza written at Bracknell', pages 435–6). 'Thy gentle face' was first printed in *V&P* 5, from *Nbk 11*, where it is untitled and undated; the editorial heading 'To Emilia Viviani' and the date 1821 were added because the name in line 1 was misread as 'Emilia' and because *Nbk 11* does contain material for *Epipsychidion* (from f. 38). However *Nbk 11* also contains material from 1814 (at f. 9). Reasons for connecting the two stanzas can be summarized as follows:

(a) They are the only two stanzas in all S's works with this rhyme-scheme and in this metre; and on external evidence they could both belong to 1814.

(b) When Hogg printed 'Thy dewy looks' he indented alternate lines (S.'s original is lost); the lines of 'Thy gentle face' are correspondingly indented in MS.

(c) S. told Hogg that 'Thy dewy looks' was 'only written in thought', yet it was also written in his letter; his insistence, therefore, that he had 'written but one stanza' raises a suspicion that he had really written more, perhaps too revealing to communicate. S's comments after his quotation of 'Thy dewy looks' then virtually paraphrase 'Thy gentle face'.

(d) S. was learning Italian with Cornelia T., and he attempted an Italian translation of 'Thy gentle face' on f. 1 of *Nbk 11*. That the stanza was first written in English is indicated by the fact that *face* (line 1) was originally *voice* (as *V&P* prints it), while the Italian begins *Il tuo viso*. It is true that one Italian letter of S. to Emilia Viviani, cancelled in draft, resembles this stanza in content (*L* ii 449), but the name in line 1 of 'Thy gentle face' is not Emilia but *Priscilla* or *Prisilla*. (In the Italian version the name is unclear, but it rhymes with *brilla*). There seems nothing to connect Teresa Emilia Viviani with this name. *Priscilla*, which is not an Italian name, is presumably a diminutive of Lat. *Prisca*, 'woman of an elder generation'. S. told Hogg in his letter with 'Thy dewy looks' that Cornelia Turner 'shared all the divinity of her mother'; her mother he had nicknamed 'Maimuna' because 'Her face was as a damsel's face,/ And yet her hair was grey' (Southey, *Thalaba* VIII xxiii 7–8).

(e) Internally, the poetic entities itemized in 'Thy gentle face' are resumed, in order, in 'Thy dewy looks': *face/looks*; *voice/words*; *peace/rest*; *being/soul*. This is a characteristic structural procedure in S.'s lyrics (Stopford Brooke, *Studies in Poetry* (1907; 1920 edn.) 161–70). Moreover *Thy gentle words* in stanza 2 here repeat the poet's first thoughts in stanza 1, *Thy gentle face*; and the notion of disturbed rest (when waking) reverses the *dream of peace* (when sleeping). Both stanzas may be associated with S.'s obscure Latin jottings in Claire Clairmont's journal for 1814:

She pressed kisses on my lips! Suddenly everything earthly is clothed in the colours of the eternal sky. Still I live . . . still I behold the sad light! I have looked on love like an unhappy captive, content with terrible solitude. I am still to live! I was awakening from slumbers, unaware of delicious desire . . .

(*Claire Jnl* 61; the suggested translation differs from that printed).

Text for 'Thy gentle face' from *Nbk 11* f. 3. Punctuation has been added in lines 1, 2, 4, 5, and 8.
Published in *V&P* 5.

Thy gentle face, Priscilla dear,
　　At night seems hanging over mine;
I feel thy trembling lips – I hear
　　The murmurs of thy voice divine.
5　O God, why comes the morning blank
　　To quench in day this dream of peace
From which the joys my being drank
　　Yet quiver through my burning face?

Thy dewy looks sink in my breast;
10　Thy gentle words stir poison there;
Thou hast disturbed the only rest
　　That was the portion of despair!
Subdued to Duty's hard control,
　　I could have borne my wayward lot:
15　The chains that bind this ruined soul
　　Had cankered then – but crushed it not.

Index of Titles

Index of First Lines